Global Monitoring Report 2015/2016

Development Goals in an Era of Demographic Change

A joint publication of the World Bank Group and the International Monetary Fund

1 2 3 4 18 17 16 15

ISBN (paper): 978-1-4648-0669-8
ISBN (electronic): 978-1-4648-0670-4
DOI: 10.1596/978-1-4648-0669-8

Cover image: The image on the cover is a segment of a painting by Sue Hoppe, an artist based in South Africa. Titled "Conflict Resolution," the painting explores the idea that people who seem irreversibly divided and with little in common can unite if they focus on what they have in common instead of what divides them. Hoppe's work examines war, conflict, and the plight of children and women in Africa, but is also inspired by nature and architecture. To learn more about Sue Hoppe and her work, visit www.southafricanartists.com/home/SueHoppe. Used with permission; further permission required for reuse.

Cover design: Original design by Debra Naylor of Naylor Design. This edition designed by Bill Pragluski of Critical Stages.

Global Monitoring Report 2015/2016

Development Goals in an Era of Demographic Change

Contents

Foreword

This is a pivotal year for global development. The Millennium Development Goals (MDGs) have guided countries and partners over the last 15 years in improving the living conditions of the poor. We are now transitioning to the Sustainable Development Goals (SDGs), a new set of global targets that embrace economic, social, and environmental priorities through 2030.

As we reflect on the hard-fought progress since the launch of the MDGs, we have an opportunity to make important changes in how we approach development. We can celebrate that the MDGs mobilized the world behind an ambitious agenda, that many countries have reduced poverty and illness, and that more children today are in school than ever before.

Our mission, however, is far from complete. During the last quarter-century, more than 1 billion people have lifted themselves out of extreme poverty. Yet, about one tenth of the global population still lives on less than $1.90 a day—the updated international poverty line.

Looking ahead, three critical challenges remain:

- A large percentage of the remaining poor are deeply poor, with income levels far below the poverty line. Policy action and programs need to focus more directly on the men, women, and children that live in deep poverty. This year's *Global Monitoring Report* presents new and more intuitive measures of poverty that allow us to measure depth and help contribute to the policy dialogue and action agenda in this urgent area.
- We have seen progress in achieving shared prosperity, with a majority of countries registering solid income growth in the poorest 40 percent of their income distributions. But in many countries, the incomes of the bottom 40 percent declined, including in half of the high-income countries. Ensuring that income is shared more equitably should be a priority for all countries.
- Poverty reduction and shared prosperity are held back by unequal progress on the non-income dimensions of development, like access to essential services. We must urgently address the widespread inequalities of opportunity in education, health, and other sectors.

The thematic section of this report shows that advancing these critical challenges will take place against the background of major demographic changes. The global population is growing much slower in 2015 than at the beginning of the MDG period in 2000. It is also aging at record speed.

There is significant cross-country heterogeneity because while some countries still maintain young and growing populations, particularly those where global poverty is concentrated, others are aging, especially the high- and middle-income countries. Projections for global growth over the SDG period trend down in line with the decrease in population growth, but demographic change can also be a contributor to growth and development if the right policies are adopted.

To advance development amid demographic change, we must place our policies and financing behind three strategic priorities: ***grow*** economies in ways that are sustainable and create jobs; ***invest*** in people's social and economic potential; and ***insure*** against ever-changing risks, which tend to disproportionately impact the poor. These policies will be tailored to each country's demographic profile.

Moreover, the recent European refugee crisis only further highlights the importance of making the best out of demographic change. Whether people migrate for more opportunities in life or just a safer life, migration—together with fertility and mortality—is a critical driver of demographic change. Along with capital flows and trade, it is also a key channel through which mutual benefits can be realized in response to diverse demographic trends across countries. Challenges must be managed, but international cooperation is key.

With the right policies in place, demographic change can contribute to the movement to end extreme poverty, boost shared prosperity, and achieve the SDGs. This year's *Global Monitoring Report* will help all countries—rich and poor alike—to navigate the challenges and to take advantage of demographic change and advance on global development goals that will improve living standards around the world.

Jim Yong Kim
President of the
World Bank Group

Christine Lagarde
Managing Director of the
International Monetary Fund

Acknowledgments

This report was prepared jointly by the staffs of the World Bank Group and the International Monetary Fund (IMF), with contributions from the following partner institutions: the African Development Bank (AfDB), the Asian Development Bank (ADB), the European Bank for Reconstruction and Development (EBRD), the Inter-American Development Bank (IADB), and the Organisation for Economic Co-operation and Development (OECD). Beyond these institutions, many academics and consultants also helped make this report possible. The contributions of all are gratefully acknowledged.

Philip Schellekens was lead author and manager of the report, under the guidance of Kaushik Basu (Senior Vice President and World Bank Chief Economist), Indermit Gill (Director of Development Policy), and Ayhan Kose (Director of Development Economics Prospects Group). The main authors and contributors from the World Bank Group were: Syud Amer Ahmed, Vandana Chandra, Marcio Cruz, Allen Dennis, Christian Eigen-Zucchi, Michele Gragnolati, Hans Lofgren, Maryla Maliszewska, Bryce Quillin, and Kenneth Simler. Key analytical and data support was provided by Pinyi Chen, Huade Huo, Jin Ho Kim, Csilla Lakatos, Fabian Mendez Ramos, Eugenia Moran-Suarez, Israel Osorio-Rodarte, and Kevin Kamto Sonke. Mark Felsenthal, Graeme Littler, Bruce Ross-Larson and Dana Vorisek provided editorial support. Rosalie Singson Dinglasan managed the desktop production of the report and handled administrative aspects, with additional support from Maria Hazel Macadangdang.

The lead author in the IMF was Lynge Nielsen, under the guidance of Tam Bayoumi, Rupa Duttagupta, and Sean Nolan. The core contributors from the IMF were: Sibabrata Das, Davide Furceri, Carla Intal, Vimal Thakoor, John Wakeman-Linn, and Peichu Xie.

The report benefited from the following principal external contributors. The report's external advisors were James Foster (George Washington University), Homi Kharas (Brookings Institution), Ronald Lee (University of California, Berkeley), Andrew Mason (University of Hawaii), and Warwick McKibbin (Australian National University). Key contributions from partner institutions were made by: Debra Kertzman, Marie Christine Montoya, and Manju Senapaty (ADB); Patricia N. Laverley, Luigi de Pierris, and Adeleke Salami (AfDB); Mandeep Bains and Jasmine Lief (EBRD); Erin Bautista, Tracy Betts, and Amy Marie Lewis (IADB) and Romina Boarini, Hervé Boulhol, Jean-Christophe Dumont, Lamia Kamal-Chaoui, Fabrice Murtin, Ana Llena Nozal and Shaun Reidy (OECD), who provided boxes on pensions reforms and migration and an update on the OECD's multi-dimensional living standard measure.

Additional contributions to boxes are furthermore acknowledged from the following people (all World Bank, except where mentioned): Lucilla Bruni, Carmen de Paz, Andrew Mason (University of Hawaii), Susan McAdams, Emmanuel Milet (University of Geneva), Marco Scuriatti, Sara Troiano, and Quentin Wodon. The Global Poverty Working Group provided data and analytical input on extreme poverty and shared prosperity, with special thanks to: Raul Andres Castaneda Aguilar, Aziz Atamanov, Shaohua Chen, Minh Cong Nguyen, Andrew Dabalen, Reno Dewina, Carolina Diaz-Bonilla, Francisco H. G. Ferreira, Roy Katayama, Nandini Krishnan, Leonardo Ramiro Lucchetti, Jose Montes, Rose Mungai, David Locke Newhouse, Monica Yanez Pagans, Ana L. Revenga, Prem Sangraula, Liliana D. Sousa, Hiroki Uematsu, João Pedro Wagner De Azevedo, Christina Wieser, and Nobuo Yoshida. Data support on the Maquette for Millennium Development Goal Simulations (MAMS) for Brazil and Japan was provided by Martin Cicowiez (CEDLAS-Universidad Nacional de La Plata). Dennis Botman (IMF), Sebastien Dessus, Cornelius Fleischhaker, Edith Kikoni, Lars Moller, Antonio Nucifora, Sergei I. Shatalov, and Quentin Wodon also provided data and feedback for the MAMS work, while Saniya Ansar, Leora Klapper, David Reher (Universidad Complutense de Madrid), and Robert Schmidt (University of Richmond) contributed data and feedback on other analytical aspects and simulations. The MDG report card and other related contributions were prepared by Mahyar Eshragh-Tabary, Neil Fantom, Juan Feng, Masako Hiraga, Haruna Kashiwase, Buyant Khaltarkhuu, Hiroko Maeda, Umar Serajuddin, Rubena Sukaj, Emi Suzuki and Dereje Wolde.

Guidance from the Executive Directors of the World Bank and the IMF and their staff during discussions of the draft report is gratefully acknowledged. The report also benefited from many useful comments and suggestions from World Bank and IMF management and staff in the course of preparation and review.

Specific thanks in this respect go to: Ahmad Ahsan, Jorge A. de Thompson R. Araujo, Elena Bardasi, Antonella Bassani, Kathleen Beegle, Benu Bidani, Moussa Blimpo, Erik A. Bloom, Zeljko Bogetic, Carter J. Brandon, Bénédicte de la Brière, Javier Bronfman Horovitz, Maurizio Bussolo, César Calderón, Shubham Chaudhuri, Luc Christiaensen, Fionna Douglas, Roberto Echandi, Sidney J. Edelmann, David Evans, Tim Evans, Cornelius Fleischhaker, Alan Fuchs, Emanuela Galasso, Franck O. Gbaguidi, Frederico Gil Sander, Caren Grown, Stephane Guimbert, Lucia Hanmer, Phillip J. Hay, Yumeka Hirano, Monika Huppi, Elena Ianchovichina, Malathi S. Jayawickrama, Dean M. Jolliffe, Andy Kotikula, Nicole Klingen, Aart C. Kraay, Megumi Kubota, Thomas Laursen, Kihoon Lee, Xue Li, Peter Kusek, Samira Lindner, Audrey Liounis, Gladys Lopez-Acevedo, Luis-Felipe Lopez-Calva, Leonardo Lucchetti, Mattia Makovec, Bill Maloney, Eliana R. Matulevich, Cristina Mejía, Steisianasari Mileiva, Rinku Murgai, Raj Nallari, Ambar Narayan, Mario Negre, Antonio Nucifora, Philip O'Keefe, Eko Pambudi, Samuel Pienknagura, Alberto Portugal, Sonia Plaza, Espen B. Prydz, Martin Rama, Dilip Ratha, Michele Ruta, Imam Setiawan, Sudhir Shetty, Joana Silva, Carlos Silva-Jauregui, Hoon S. Soh, Sebastian Stolorz, Lynne Sherburne-Benz, Xiaolun Sun, Marvin Taylor-Dormond, Hans Timmer, Augusto de la Torre, Matthew Wai Poi, Jan Walliser, Bagus A. Wirapati, Liang Yu, Qinghua Zhao.

The World Bank's Publishing and Knowledge Unit managed editorial services, design, production, and printing of the report, with Susan Graham and Kia Penso as the production editing team. Others who assisted with the report's publication included Denise Bergeron, Aziz Gökdemir, Patricia Katayama, Nancy Lammers, and Stephen McGroarty. Marta Gottron copy-edited the report. The report's dissemination and outreach were coordinated by Phillip J. Hay, working with Mark Felsenthal, Vamsee K. Kanchi, and Mikael E. Reventar. Graeme Littler and Katherine Rollins provided web support.

Abbreviations and Acronyms

ADB	Asian Development Bank
AEs	advanced economies
AfDB	African Development Bank
AIDS	acquired immune deficiency syndrome
B10	bottom 10 percent
B20	bottom 20 percent
B40	bottom 40 percent
CIS	Commonwealth of Independent States
CO_2	carbon dioxide
CPR	contraceptive prevalence rate
DAC	Development Assistance Committee
EM	emerging market
EMDCs	emerging market and developing countries
EU	European Union
FCS	fragile and conflict-affected states
FDI	foreign direct investment
G20	Group of 20
GDP	gross domestic product
GMR	*Global Monitoring Report*
HIV	human immunodeficiency virus
IDA	International Development Association
IDP	internally displaced persons
IMF	International Monetary Fund
LIDCs	low-income developing countries
MDGs	Millennium Development Goals
MFN	most favored nation
MMR	maternal mortality rate
NTA	National Transfer Accounts project
ODA	official development assistance
OECD	Organisation for Economic Co-operation and Development
PISA	Programme for International Student Assessment
PPP	purchasing power parity
SDGs	Sustainable Development Goals
T10	top 10 percent
T20	top 20 percent
T60	top 60 percent
TDR	total dependency ratio
TFP	total factor productivity
TFR	total fertility rate
UN	United Nations
UNAIDS	Joint United Nations Programme on HIV/AIDS
UNCTAD	United Nations Conference on Trade and Development
UNDP	United Nations Development Programme
UNESCO	United Nations Educational, Scientific and Cultural Organization
UNFCC	United Nations Framework Convention on Climate Change
UNICEF	United Nations Children's Fund
UNPD	United Nations Population Division
WEO	*World Economic Outlook*
WHO	World Health Organization
WTO	World Trade Organization

All dollar amounts are U.S. dollars unless otherwise indicated.

Executive Summary

With 2015 marking the transition from the Millennium to the Sustainable Development Goals, the international community can celebrate many development successes since 2000. Despite the global financial crisis, economic growth was generally strong and robust. About 1 billion people rose out of extreme poverty. Most developing countries saw solid income growth for the bottom 40 percent of their income distribution. Millions of children who were unlikely to survive their fifth birthday passed beyond these critical years and went on to school in ever greater numbers. The incidence of preventable diseases such as AIDS, malaria, and tuberculosis is falling. The share of those with access to clean water and better sanitation has risen. Overall, the Millennium Development Goals played an important role in galvanizing the global development community, and that experience will help drive progress toward achievement of the Sustainable Development Goals by 2030.

Despite solid development gains, progress has been uneven, and significant work remains. With an estimated 900 million people in 2012 living on less than $1.90 a day—the updated international poverty line—and a projected 700 million in 2015, extreme poverty remains unacceptably high. It has also become more concentrated in Sub-Saharan Africa and South Asia. Addressing moderate poverty and mitigating the vulnerability of falling back into poverty have become more pressing issues in many countries, including in those where the bottom 40 percent saw their incomes decline. Even in a world of single-digit extreme poverty, non-income disparities, such as limited access to quality education and health services, pose a bottleneck to sustained poverty reduction and shared prosperity. Wider environmental sustainability concerns are a major challenge throughout the world, in regard to climate change and its impact on the natural resources upon which many of the poorest depend, such as water. In sum, while development progress was impressive, it has been uneven and a large unfinished agenda remains.

Three key challenges stand out: the depth of remaining poverty, the unevenness in shared prosperity, and the persistent disparities in non-income dimensions of development. First, the policy discourse needs to focus more directly on the poorest among the poor. While pockets of ultra-poverty exist around the world, Sub-Saharan Africa is home to most of the deeply poor. To make depth a more central element in policy formulation, easy-to-communicate measures are needed—and this report attempts a step in this direction with person-equivalent measures of poverty. Second, the eradication of poverty in all of its forms requires steady growth of the incomes of the bottom 40 percent. Yet, economic growth—a key driver of shared prosperity—

may not be as buoyant as it was before the global financial crisis. Third, unequal progress in non-income dimensions of development requires addressing widespread inequality of opportunity, which transmits poverty across generations and erodes the pace and sustainability of progress for the bottom 40. To meet these challenges, three ingredients are core to the policy agenda: sustaining broad-based growth, investing in human development, and insuring the poor and vulnerable against emerging risks.

In view of these challenges, the Sustainable Development Goals aim to scale up impact in a changing world through a more integrated approach to development. Recognizing the interconnections between development objectives, the SDGs embrace an ambitious and holistic vision to foster inclusive and sustainable development with scaled-up impact. Shared by all countries, they recognize that collective action is required. Global challenges—resilient financial systems, common resources, climate change—require internationally coordinated solutions. Meeting SDG investment needs will depend on shifting from "billions" in official development assistance to "trillions" in investments of all kinds, unlocking, leveraging, and catalyzing public and private resources. The SDGs will need to be pursued in a changing world, with new opportunities and challenges brought by evolving megatrends, including climate change, continued globalization, rapid urbanization, and, as discussed in the special theme of this report, demographic change.

Profound changes in global demography have the potential to alter the trajectory of global development over the SDG period. Global demography is at a turning point: the world's population is growing more slowly and is aging at an unprecedented rate. These trends reflect past development successes—women's empowerment, improved education, better child, maternal and reproductive health, and increased longevity. The working-age share of the population peaked in 2012 and is now on the decline. Aging means that population increases are reflected in larger numbers of older people. The global count of children is stabilizing at a plateau of 2 billion. Yet, underneath these global trends lies considerable diversity in the direction and pace of demographic change. Regional and subregional patterns vary across and within countries. To frame the impact of diverse demographic trends on development across countries, this report lays out a new typology of demographic change, applied to the latest 2015 UN population statistics.

The diversity of demographic change at the country level presents unique opportunities and challenges to the world's centers of global poverty and engines of global growth. More than 90 percent of poverty is concentrated in pre- and early-dividend countries with swelling working-age populations that lag in key human development indicators and continue to register rapid population growth. In these countries, the demographic transition to lower fertility creates a golden opportunity to raise living standards. Over 85 percent of global economic activity and 78 percent of global growth over the last 15 years can be attributed to late- and post-dividend countries, which have much-lower fertility rates and some of the highest shares of the elderly in the world. In these countries, population aging may weaken growth prospects. To be sure, demographic change is not inherently good or bad and presents opportunities and challenges everywhere. In each case, policies can make a critical difference in how demographic change affects progress toward the development goals.

Navigating the dynamic implications of demographic change will require sound policies informed by a long-run perspective and tailored to a nation's demographic context. To eradicate persistent poverty, the centers of global poverty need to accelerate their demographic transition, invest in their young and still-growing populations, and lay the foundations for sustained growth. Among other policy initiatives, these goals require better education and health services, as well as greater empowerment of women. Facing weakening economic dynamism, the lower-fertility, richer countries that make up the current engines of global growth need to address headwinds arising from shrinking labor forces. They also need to adapt their policies and institutions to foster healthy and productive aging. Selected policy priorities include mobilizing savings for productive investment in human and physical capital, as well as strengthening welfare systems—pensions, health care, and long-term care—while ensuring fiscal sustainability and protection for the elderly and vulnerable.

Policy opportunities also exist to arbitrage demographic diversity across countries. The extent of demographic diversity across countries is starker than ever, with large and inevitable impacts on the global economy. Returns on capital and labor are affected. Comparative advantages in trade are altered. Given these implications, flows of capital, labor and goods and services will be affected and, together, they can help respond to growing demographic imbalances globally. Mutual benefits can be realized: capital can flow to rising consumer markets; older countries can benefit from legal immigration; younger countries can produce labor-intensive products. But challenges need to be managed and international cooperation is key.

With effective policies, this era of intense demographic change may herald a period of sustained development progress. Global demography is changing and has the potential to alter the trajectory of global development profoundly. To speed up progress, countries need to step up efforts to sustain broad-based growth, invest in people, and insure the poor and vulnerable against ever-changing risks. However, they must undertake these measures by taking into account demographic change. Where possible, this requires capturing and harnessing demographic dividends. Elsewhere, it requires adaptation. Everywhere, it calls for turning demographic change into one of the most consequential development opportunities of our times.

MONITORING GLOBAL DEVELOPMENT PROGRESS: A SNAPSHOT

Projections show that the global poverty rate may have fallen to single digits in 2015. Yet, the number of poor remains high.

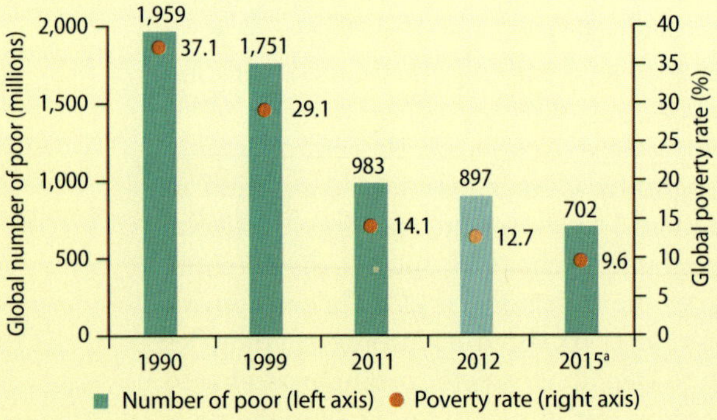

Note: Based on the $1.90 poverty line and 2011 PPP.
a. Forecast.

While income poverty fell rapidly during the MDG-era, a large unfinished agenda remains for the SDGs with respect to non-income goals.

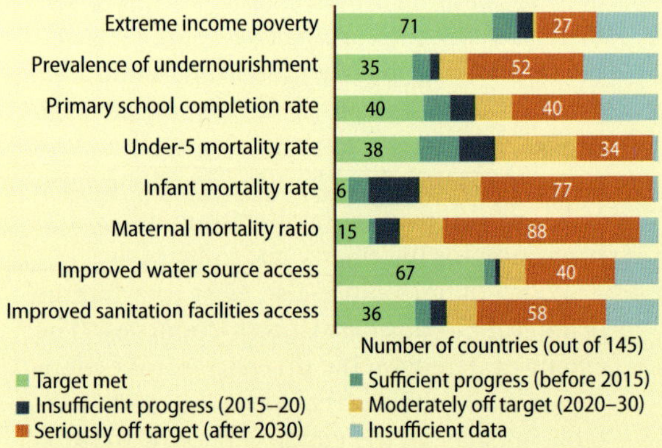

With extreme poverty concentrating in Sub-Saharan Africa, more focus is needed on the poorest among the poor.

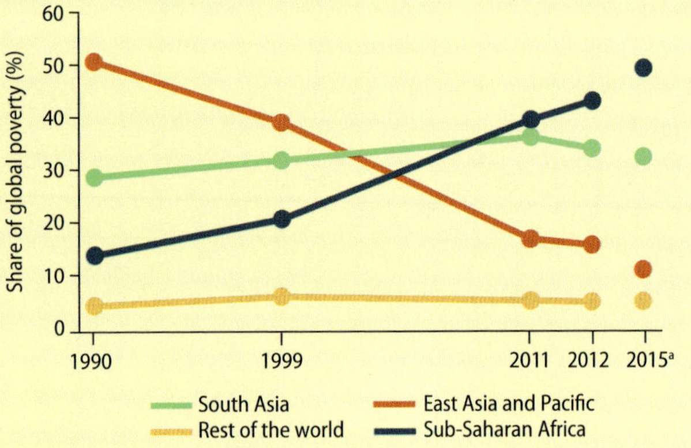

Note: Based on the $1.90 poverty line and 2011 PPP.
a. Forecast.

Prosperity needs to be better shared with the bottom 40 percent of the income distribution, especially in high-income countries.

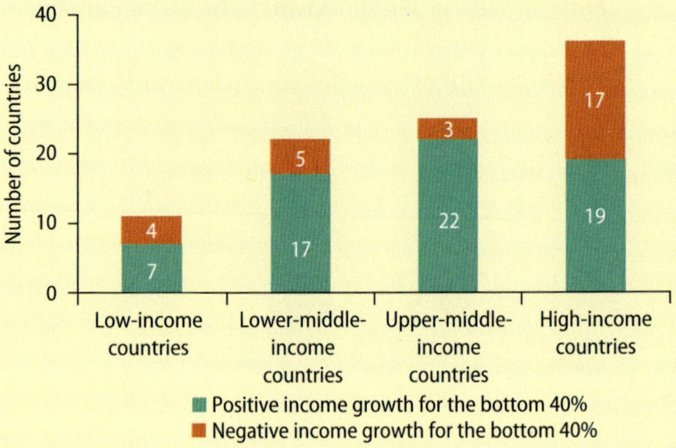

With less buoyant growth expected at the start of the SDG period, increased effort is needed to sustain broad-based growth.

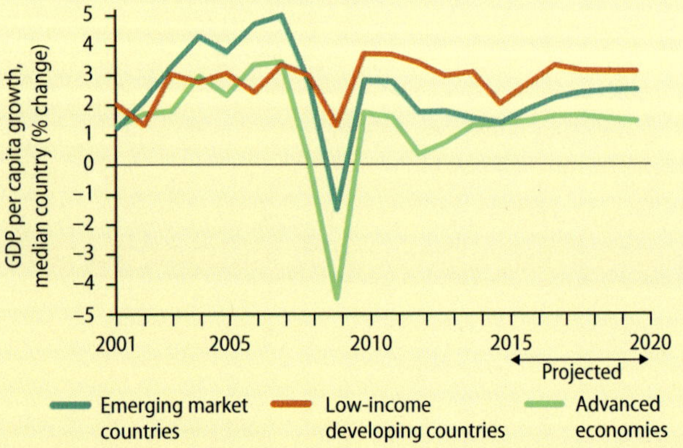

We need to invest in people and protect them from risk with adequate human development policies and social protection.

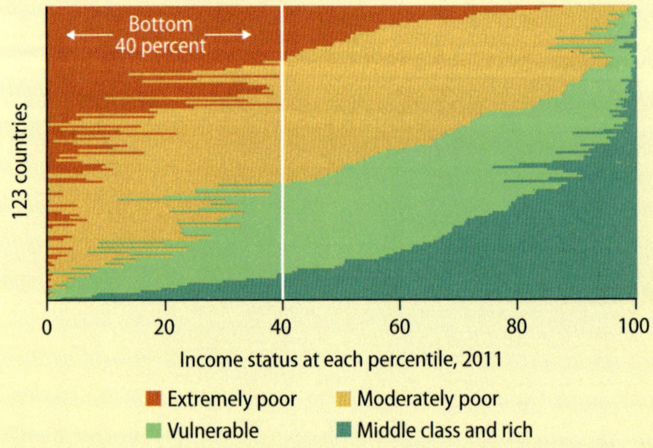

Note: Based on the $1.25 poverty line and 2005 PPP. Extreme poverty (< $1.25 a day), moderate poverty ($1.25–$4), vulnerability ($4–$10), middle class and rich (> $10).

Sources: PovcalNet (2015), World Bank Global Database for Shared Prosperity, World Economic Outlook.

DEVELOPMENT IN AN ERA OF DEMOGRAPHIC CHANGE: A SNAPSHOT

Global demographic change is intense: the working-age share peaked, the population grows much slower and ages at record speed.

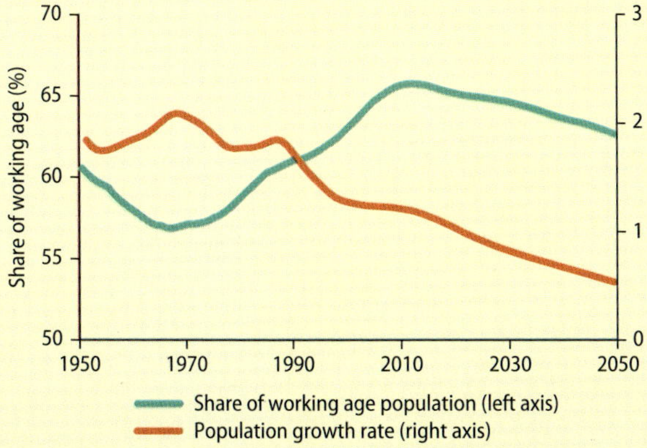

Underneath global trends lies stark diversity, with countries facing different opportunities to capture demographic dividends.

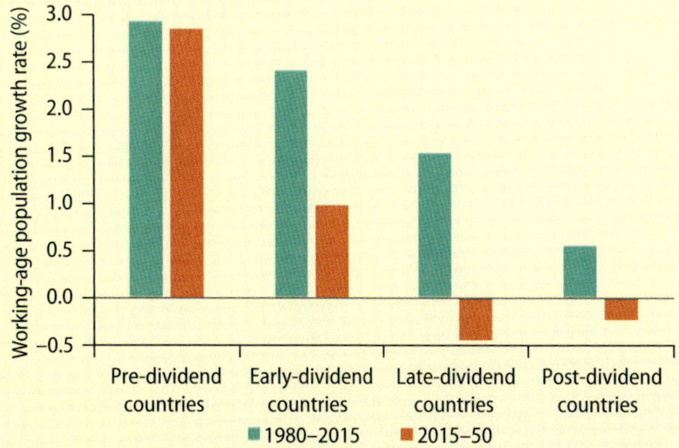

Pre- and early-dividend countries need to spark demographic transition, invest in human development and create jobs for the youth bulge.

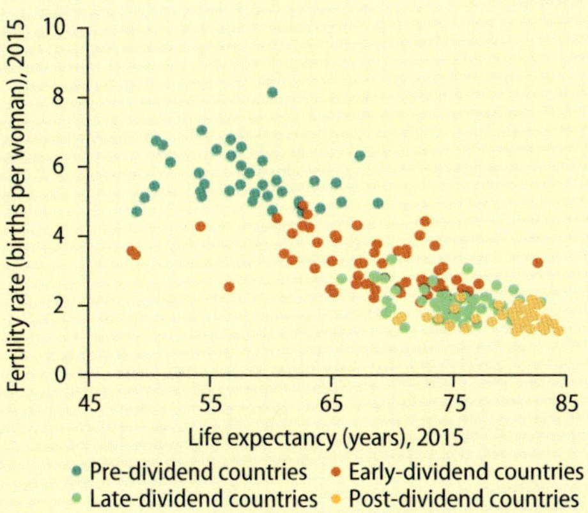

Late- and post-dividend countries need to sustain productivity growth amidst demographic headwinds, and adapt institutions and policies to rapid population aging.

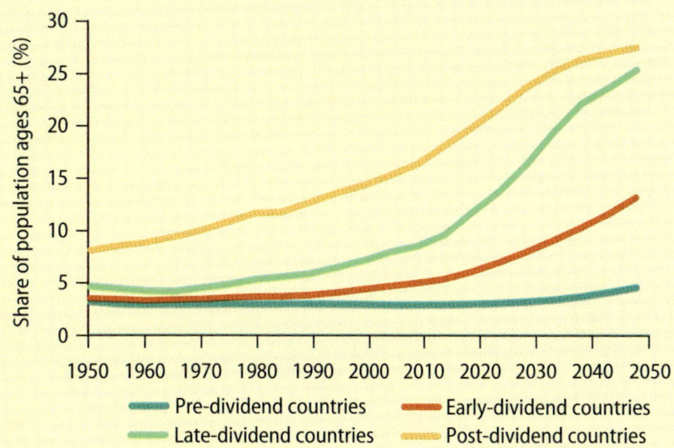

Demographic fault lines separate *centers of global poverty* needing further development and *engines of global growth* facing rapid aging.

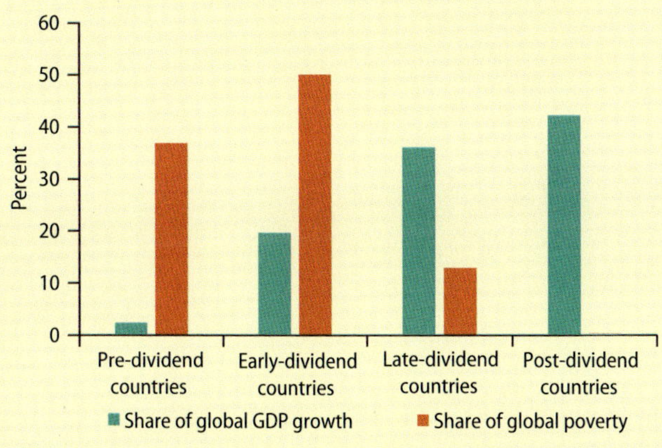

Freer flows of capital, trade and, especially, people present an increasingly compelling global opportunity to arbitrage demographic diversity across countries.

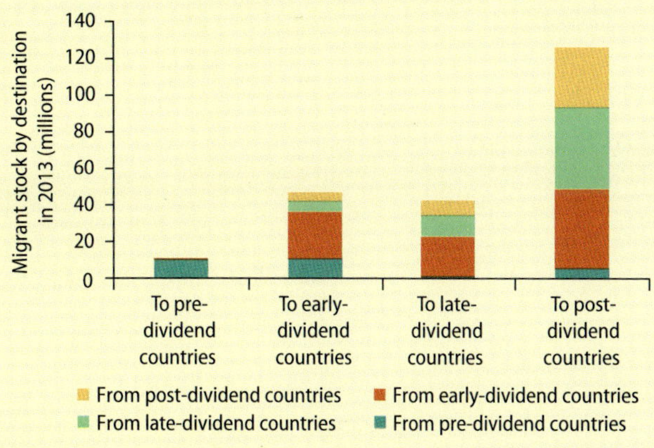

Sources: UN (2015), PovalNet (2015), World Development Indicators (2015).

Overview

The world is at a global development crossroads, as 2015 marks the end of the 15-year window for achieving the Millennium Development Goals (MDGs) and the beginning of the Sustainable Development Goals (SDGs). The world met the MDG target of halving the global poverty rate in 2010, five years ahead of schedule. The latest data suggest that extreme poverty has continued its decades-long descent. Still, poverty remains unacceptably high, with an estimated 900 million people in 2012 living on less than $1.90 a day—the new international poverty line; the projected number for 2015 under the new line is 700 million people. Poverty also is becoming increasingly concentrated in Sub-Saharan Africa, where its depth and breadth remain an overriding challenge. The MDGs were successful in reducing income poverty, but they were less successful in ameliorating non-income deprivations, such as access to quality education or to basic health services. Few countries have combined growth with reducing the level of environmental externalities and carbon emissions. Yet, increasing land degradation, overfishing, deforestation, extreme weather events, and urban air pollution endanger recent progress. Looking forward, three challenges stand out: the depth of remaining poverty, the unevenness in shared prosperity, and the persistent disparities in non-income dimensions of development. The MDGs were helpful in galvanizing global development progress—an experience that will help drive the achievement of the SDGs by 2030.

The world is also at a crossroads for global demographic trends. Global population growth is slowing: the share of the working-age population (15–64 years) peaked in 2012 at 66 percent and is now falling, while the total number of children (ages below 15 years) will remain at a plateau of around 2 billion into the next decades. These trends reflect past successes in development—women's empowerment, improved education, better reproductive health services, and increased longevity. But the direction and pace of demographic change vary starkly across countries, with sizable disparities between the centers of global poverty (marked by high fertility) and the engines of global growth (marked by rapid aging). The latter comprise almost all high-income and most middle-income economies. In many cases, they have completely eliminated extreme income poverty, but they continue to face challenges in sharing the benefits of increased prosperity, particularly if aging weakens their economic dynamism. The former include lower-income countries in earlier stages of demographic transition to lower fertility levels and longer life expectancy, making them the focus of the continuing battle against global poverty.

Demographic change brings unique opportunities and challenges to further the post-2015 development goals. But countries have very different starting lines and face stark differences in demographic characteristics and projected trends. The way forward, as underpinned by the SDGs, is a more synergistic approach between the various dimensions of development. Three ingredients will frame the policy agenda: sustainable broad-based growth, investment in human development, and measures that insure the poor and vulnerable against evolving risks. These strategies must be sensitive to demographics. The centers of global poverty need to accelerate their demographic transition, invest in their young and growing populations, and lay the foundations for sustained growth to capture demographic dividends. The engines of global growth need to address headwinds arising from shrinking labor forces and adapt their policies and institutions to foster healthy and productive aging. In addition, to eradicate poverty and invigorate economic dynamism, all countries must also grasp the opportunities and manage the challenges that arise from demographic imbalances at the global level—through capital flows, migration, and trade. With the right set of policies, this era of intense demographic change can be turned into one of sustained development progress.

Global Monitoring Report 2015/2016 investigates these issues in two parts:

Part I—the global monitoring part—examines global development progress, the unfinished agenda, and the policy opportunities looking ahead. Chapter 1 examines the progress made on sustainable poverty reduction and shared prosperity, as well as the policies that are needed to make further progress. With 2015 being a watershed year for global development goals, Chapter 2 reviews the development successes during the MDG period and examines the unfinished agenda left for the SDGs. Chapter 3 assesses the macroeconomic performance over the MDG period, provides the near- and medium-term outlook, and examines what the world might be like in 2030.

Part II—the thematic part—examines how demographic change can be tilted in favor of the development goals. Chapter 4 characterizes demographic change at the global, regional, and country level. It also examines the drivers of demographic change that have shaped the diversity of demographic patterns and trends. Chapter 5 examines how demography affects development. It develops a new global typology that ties demographic change to development potential and analyzes the various pathways through which demographic change affects the prosperity of nations. Chapter 6 analyzes how policies can leverage demographic change in support of the development goals. It examines policy opportunities at both the country and the global level.

Part I: Monitoring global development progress

Development progress over the MDG period has been impressive

In many ways, development has advanced more rapidly over the 15-year MDG era than at any other time in human history. Since the launch of the MDGs, economic growth has been rapid, aided by strong commodity prices and generally improved macroeconomic policies. Poverty reduction also has been rapid, particularly in East Asia and the Pacific. Millions of children who were unlikely to survive to their fifth birthday have passed beyond these critical years and gone on to school in ever greater numbers, including many more girls than was the case 15 years ago. The incidence of preventable diseases such as acquired immunodeficiency syndrome (AIDS), malaria, and tuberculosis is falling, and the share of people with access to clean water and better sanitation has risen markedly. The MDGs helped frame the broader goals of development and build a coalition of partners to work toward common goals.

One of the most remarkable achievements during the MDG era was the significant decline in the share of the extremely poor in the global population. The first MDG target—cutting the extreme poverty rate to half its 1990 level by 2015—was met five years ahead of schedule. Poverty was on the decline before the MDG period, but progress was fastest in the 2000s (figures O.1a, O.1b). Particularly notable are the substantial reductions in poverty in East Asia and the Pacific and South Asia, where the rapid growth and development of China and India helped lift millions of people out of poverty (figures O.1c and O.1d). As the number of poor declined, the average shortfall of income below the poverty line improved as well from 13.1 percent in 1990 to 3.7 by 2012.

Based on the updated poverty line of $1.90 a day, the *estimate* for 2012 puts the number of extremely poor people at about 900 million, or 12.7 percent of global population (table O.1). Global poverty estimates have been updated to reflect a re-estimated international poverty line of $1.90 a day, new 2011-based purchasing power parity (PPP)

FIGURE O.1 Global poverty declined, but Sub-Saharan Africa lagged

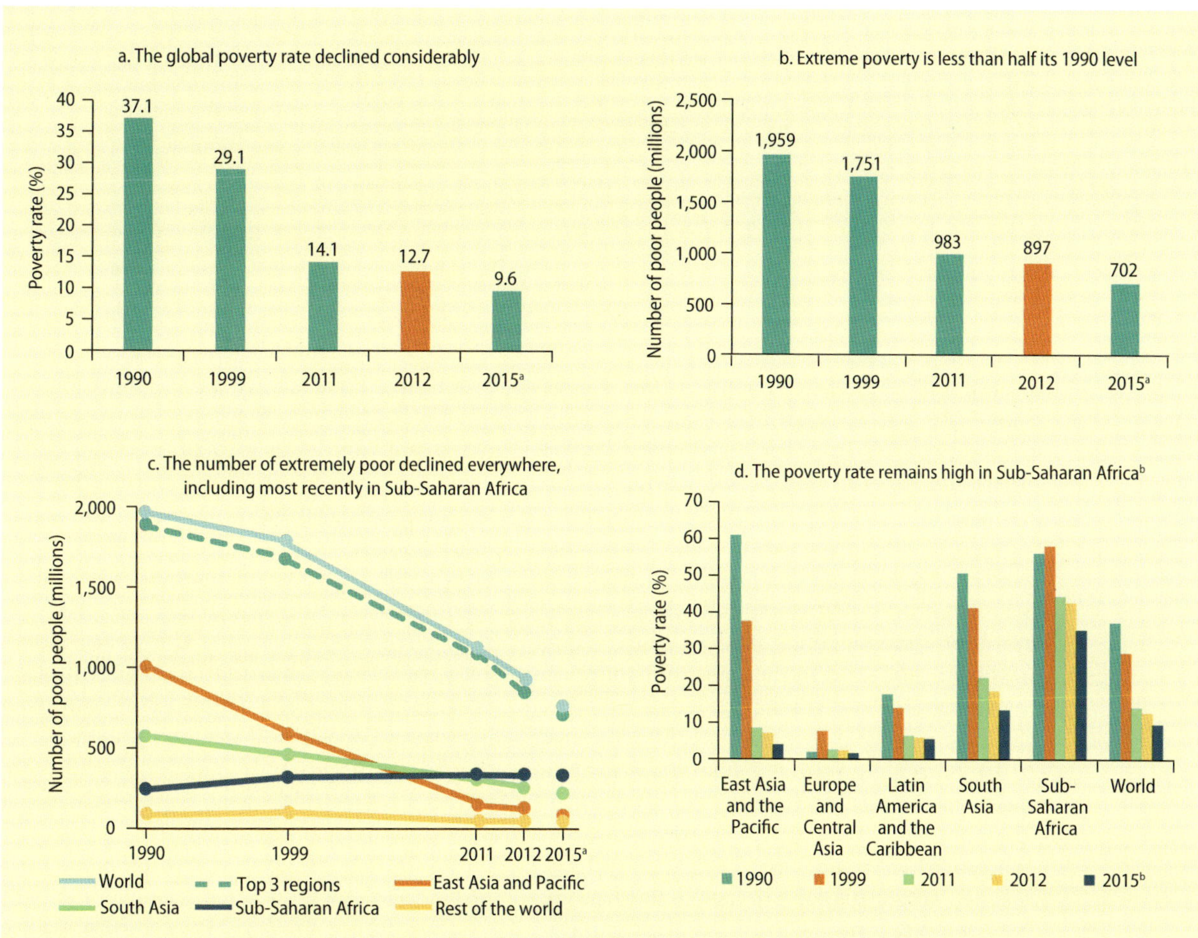

Source: PovcalNet 2015.

Note: Estimates based on the $1.90 poverty line and 2011 PPP prices.

a. Given the production lags for household surveys, 2012 is the latest year for which the World Bank is able to produce regional and global poverty estimates. All numbers for 2015 and beyond are statistical projections based on growth scenarios and distributional assumptions, and should be treated with considerable circumspection.

b. Regional aggregates for the Middle East and North Africa are omitted because of lack of sufficient observations.

TABLE O.1 Global poverty is assessed with the re-estimated poverty line

	Historical			Headline	Projection
Region	**1990**	**1999**	**2011**	**2012**	**2015[a]**
Share of population below $1.90 a day (2011 PPP) (%)					
East Asia and Pacific	60.6	37.5	8.5	7.2	4.1
Europe and Central Asia	1.9	7.8	2.4	2.1	1.7
Latin America and the Caribbean	17.8	13.9	5.9	5.6	5.6
Middle East and North Africa[b]	—	—	—	—	—
South Asia	50.6	41.8	22.2	18.8	13.5
Sub-Saharan Africa	56.8	58.0	44.4	42.7	35.2
Developing world	44.4	34.3	16.5	14.9	11.9
World	37.1	29.1	14.1	12.7	9.6
Millions of people below $1.90 a day (2011 PPP)					
East Asia and Pacific	995.5	689.4	173.1	147.2	82.6
Europe and Central Asia	8.8	36.8	11.4	10.1	4.4
Latin America and the Caribbean	78.2	71.1	35.3	33.7	29.7
Middle East and North Africa[b]	—	—	—	—	—
South Asia	574.6	568.0	361.7	309.2	231.3
Sub-Saharan Africa	287.6	374.6	393.6	388.8	347.1
World	1,958.6	1,751.5	983.3	896.7	702.1

Source: PovcalNet 2015.

Note: Poverty estimates based on the $1.90 poverty line and 2011 purchasing power parity (PPP) prices. Box O.1 explains how the global poverty estimates were calculated. Regional aggregates for the Middle East and North Africa are omitted because of lack of sufficient observations.

a. Given the production lags for household surveys, 2012 is the latest year for which the World Bank is able to produce regional and global poverty estimates. All numbers for 2015 and beyond are statistical projections based on growth scenarios and distributional assumptions, and should be treated with considerable circumspection.

b. Even though five countries in the Middle East and North Africa region are omitted from the database of country-level poverty estimates, poverty estimates for these countries are calculated for the purposes of global poverty estimation (see box O.1). The 2011 and 2012 poverty estimates for this region implied by these global estimates are 2.5 and 2.3 percent, respectively.

prices, and revisions to complementary data (box O.1). The 2012 estimate represents continued progress in poverty reduction as the revised headcount in 2011 was 983 million people (14.1 percent of global population). Comparison between 2011 and 2012 reveals a modest decline in the number of poor in Sub-Saharan Africa, potentially heralding an era of poverty reduction not just in the share of the poor but also in their absolute number.

Although the estimate for 2012 remains the most reliable recent estimate, World Bank *projections* suggest that global poverty may have reached 700 million, or 9.6 percent of global population, in 2015. For the first time, the global extreme poverty rate may have reached single digits. The projected decline between 2012 and 2015 is 200 million people (some 80 million in South Asia, about 65 million in East Asia and the Pacific, and close to 40 million in Sub-Saharan Africa). This projection is extrapolated from 2012 based on growth scenarios and distributional assumptions. Given that the collection and processing of nationally representative household surveys—on which actual poverty estimates are based—usually takes two to three years, the 2012 number remains the most reliable recent estimate.

Turning to broader segments of the population, the Bottom 40 percent (B40) of the income distribution in many countries has seen rising incomes over the past decade, yet progress was unequal. Considering five-year periods starting around 2007 and ending around 2012, B40 incomes grew in 65 of the 94 countries with adequate and comparable household data. Among them, 47 countries registered a "shared prosperity premium," meaning that B40 incomes grew faster than the incomes of the average population (figure O.2). This premium ranged from less than 1 percentage point to well above 3 points, suggesting that growth in many countries has been considerably pro-poor. Progress on shared prosperity was especially significant in middle-income countries, where some 85 percent of countries

BOX O.1 Drawing global poverty lines

Global Monitoring Report 2015/2016 unveils poverty data based on a new $1.90 international poverty line, using 2011 purchasing power parity (PPP). To be comparable, the global poverty estimates are based on a common poverty line across all countries. As with the previous line of $1.25 a day, in 2005 prices, the new line is calculated by averaging the national poverty lines of the 15 poorest developing countries. It represents a very low threshold standard of living which is believed to correspond to the minimum costs of basic needs. Changes in this value over time thus reflect the increasing cost of obtaining these basic needs.

A key driver behind the raising of the international poverty line to $1.90 is the release of the 2011 PPP index. Cross-country comparisons of poverty rates require PPP indexes, produced by the International Comparison Program. New rounds of PPP indexes estimate the cost of living across countries and provide price data for countries not covered by previous rounds. Introducing new PPPs typically require the re-estimation of the international poverty line and can involve, in some cases, significant changes in our understanding of poverty levels in some countries or the relative ranking of poverty across countries.

Including this year's revision, there have been four major changes to the World Bank Group's estimate of the international poverty line, reflecting different methodologies and PPP indexes. The revisions to PPP indexes in 1985, 1993, and 2005 corresponded to poverty lines of $1.01, $1.08, and $1.25, respectively. Different methods have been followed to estimate these lines. Beginning with the $1.25 line, the poverty line was calculated by taking the average of the 15 poorest countries (Chad, Ethiopia, The Gambia, Ghana, Guinea-Bissau, Malawi, Mali, Mozambique, Nepal, Niger, Rwanda, Sierra Leone, Tajikistan, Tanzania, and Uganda).[a] This same practice was followed for the $1.90 revision.

a. The list of the 15 poorest countries used to estimate the $1.25 poverty line based on the 2005 PPP, as described in Ravallion, Chen, and Sangraula (2009), does not necessarily represent the current 15 poorest countries in the world. Some of the countries originally included in this list may have made significant progress.

in the sample registered an increase in B40 incomes. Among developing regions, Latin America and the Caribbean performed remarkably well.

The evidence suggests that most of the variation in B40 income growth can be explained by *growth in average incomes* for the entire population. Over long periods of time (several decades), B40 income growth closely tracks average income growth. Historical data for 151 high-income and developing countries shows that average income growth was the primary explanation for cross-country and over-time variations in B40 income growth. Yet, average income growth does not provide the only explanation. Changes in the *income share* of the B40 played an increased role especially during the 2000s, a period of particularly fast income growth for the B40. It also appears that for lower-income countries, as well as for the lower deciles of the income distribution in any country, average income growth offers diminished explanatory power.

Despite solid development gains, significant work remains

A first key challenge is the depth of poverty, especially in Sub-Saharan Africa. The decline in poverty rates has been impressive. Yet, poverty still remains unacceptably high—around 900 million extremely poor people in 2012 and a projected 700 million people in 2015. It is also becoming increasingly concentrated in Sub-Saharan Africa. Over the last decades, the vast majority (about 95 percent) of global poverty has been concentrated in three regions: East Asia and the Pacific, South Asia, and Sub-Saharan Africa (figure O.1c). Over time, the composition of global poverty across these three regions has shifted dramatically. East Asia and the Pacific registered a spectacular decline. South Asia saw an initial increase and a later decline, with rates remaining high. Sub-Saharan Africa saw a steady increase in its share and was home to 43 percent of the global poor in 2012. The growing global

FIGURE O.2 Experiences on shared prosperity differ: While the majority of countries have seen solid growth in B40 incomes, many countries have not

Annualized B40 income growth (bars with no black outline) and average population income growth (shown with a black outline) for a five-year period, circa 2007–12 (%)

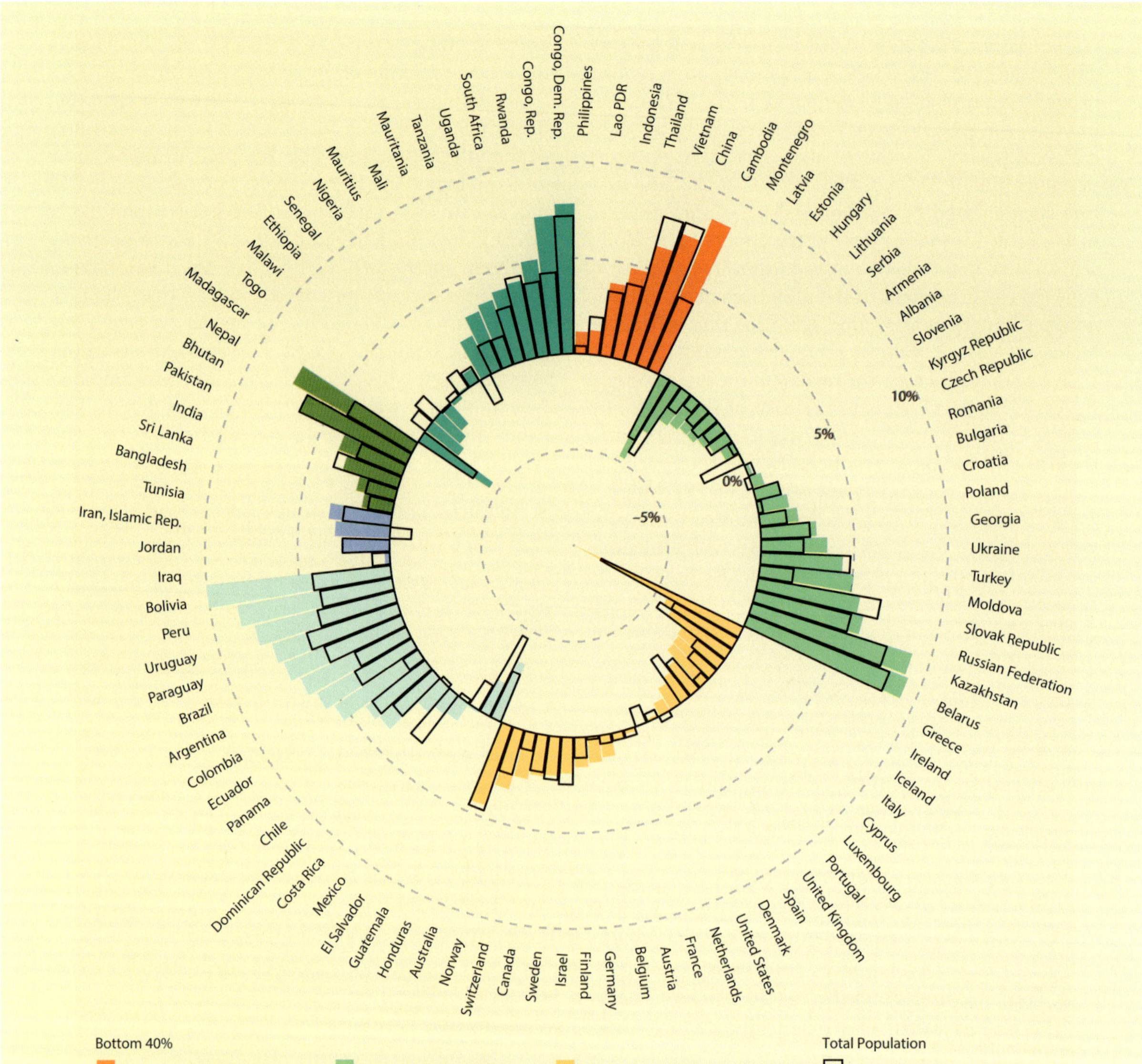

Source: World Bank Global Database for Shared Prosperity.

Note: Data availability varies across countries. Shared prosperity estimates are provided only for comparable survey years. In Sub-Saharan Africa, only 16 of the 48 countries have shared prosperity numbers even though more survey years exist. Starting points are about 2007 and end points are about 2012. B40 = Bottom 40 percent.

share of Sub-Saharan Africa reflects slower poverty reduction there amid rapid population growth: in 2012 the region's poverty rate stood at 42.7 percent, which is only 14.1 points lower than in 1990 (figure O.1d).

The policy discourse needs to focus more fully on the poorest among the poor. Poverty headcount statistics present distorted views of the spatial distribution of poverty and the pace of progress over time. Two countries could record the same poverty headcount rate, where in one country poverty is shallow and in the other it is very deep. Similarly, a country may be successful in lifting its poorest citizens—the poorest of the poor—from abject poverty to a level just below the poverty line. Such improvement would not show up in a poverty headcount measure. Measures that account for depth, such as the "poverty gap" (shortfall from the poverty line), are not as simple to grasp as headcount measures. To make "depth" a more central element of policy formulation, easy-to-communicate measures are needed—and this report attempts a step in this direction with the new "person-equivalent" approach. It finds that, in person-equivalent terms (a benchmark poor person with a typical income shortfall), the poverty headcount ratio in Sub-Saharan Africa for 2012 rises from 42.7 to 46.7 percent, whereas that for South Asia falls from 18.8 to 10.6 percent.

With extreme poverty on the decline globally, a second key challenge is the unevenness in shared prosperity for the B40. The B40 may include many possible populations. Among developing regions, the income of the richest person among the B40 makes that person either extremely or moderately poor, particularly in Sub-Saharan Africa and parts of East Asia, or vulnerable, primarily in Latin America and the Caribbean and parts of Europe and Central Asia (Map O.1). In countries where reducing poverty and vulnerability is key, the shared prosperity focus on the B40 thus enhances that focus. Among richer countries, the B40 may encompass the relatively poor. Promoting healthy B40 income growth represents an ongoing challenge, as well as an opportunity to make the development process more inclusive and socially sustainable.

In many countries, stepped-up effort is needed to sustainably build shared prosperity. The latest comparable household data

MAP O.1 The income of the richest person in the bottom 40 percent differs greatly across countries

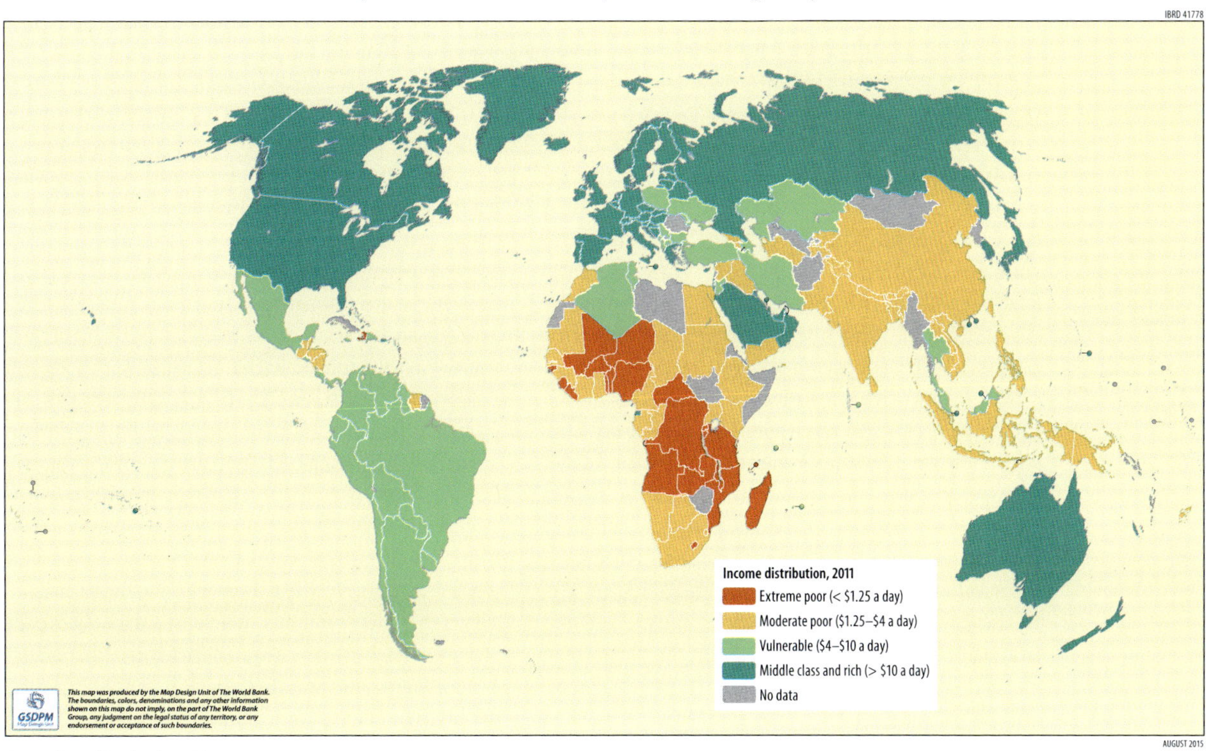

Source: PovcalNet database 2015.
Note: Based on the $1.25 poverty line and 2005 purchasing power parity (PPP) prices, as full distributional data using 2011 PPP pricees was not yet available.

points to a decline in the growth of B40 incomes over the period circa 2007–12. Half of the high-income countries and more than a third of low-income countries saw an actual outright decline in B40 incomes. The United States saw a decline in B40 incomes during the 2000s, perpetuating a trend of rising inequality between B40 and the rest of the population—a trend observed in several other high-income countries and exacerbated by the global financial crisis. Indeed, compared with the earlier period circa 2006–11—as reported in *Global Monitoring Report 2014/2015*—the latest shared prosperity data suggest a significant deterioration. For countries with consistent time series, average B40 income growth slowed from 4.6 to 2.9 percent, whereas average income growth for the entire population declined from 3.0 to 1.7 percent.

A third key challenge relates to the persistent disparities in the non-income dimensions of development. Compared with the MDG goal on income poverty, non-income goals saw more mixed success. Progress fell particularly short for targets related to health (maternal and infant mortality), nutrition (undernourishment and hunger), and sanitation (Kenny and Dykstra 2013). Close to one-fifth of all children under five remain undernourished, and some 860 million people continue to live in slums. Access to primary school education and literacy rates have improved, yet the quality of education remains a concern. Moreover, while the tide has turned on the incidence of major deadly diseases, a high number of preventable deaths persist. With the development of new medicines, human immunodeficiency virus (HIV) patients receiving treatment have nearly the same life expectancy as those without HIV. However, three-fifths of those people living with HIV, mostly in developing countries, lack access to antiretroviral drugs. Tuberculosis killed 1.5 million people in 2013, many in the prime of their productive lives. An estimated 198 million cases of malaria were registered in 2013, claiming the lives of about 453,000 children.

In addition, little progress has been made in improving the long-term environmental sustainability of development. Although some countries have successfully "delinked" trends in environmental degradation from growth, most have not. The cost of environmental degradation—externalities associated with outdoor and indoor air pollution, water pollution, deforestation, carbon emissions, and other environmental hazards—rose 50 percent during 1990–2010. Furthermore, in 2013, over 5 billion people in developing countries were breathing polluted air with concentrations of PM2.5 in excess of the guideline levels recommended by the World Health Organization, up 42 percent since 1990 (Brauer et al. 2015). In 2010, between 11 and 21 percent of all deaths in developing countries were the result of pollution and other environmental risk factors. Only about 25 percent of the countries in the world, primarily high-income countries, have managed to grow economically while simultaneously decreasing their environmental externalities. Even fewer have managed to delink carbon emissions from growth, challenging the world's ability to contain the impacts of future climate change to agreed-upon levels of acceptability.

To sustainably end extreme poverty and promote shared prosperity, more attention is needed to the non-income dimensions of development. First, to "end poverty in all of its forms everywhere," it must be recognized that poverty is multidimensional. Income poverty is typically accompanied by inadequate access to education, health, housing, employment, and personal security—areas where improvements would increase the chances for escaping poverty. Second, the B40 consistently underperform in non-income dimensions. Children from B40 households are more likely to die before age five than children in the top 60 percent (T60) households and are also more likely to be underweight. Access to improved water sources (piped water) and technology (the Internet) is uneven, too. Despite rising enrollment rates in poorer countries, access to primary education remains inequitably low. Third, greater efforts are needed to monitor the sustainability of development progress in its economic, environmental, and social aspects. Environmental sustainability concerns, particularly regarding natural resources, environmental health, and ecosystem sustainability, need to enter more fully into economic decision making.

Amid an uncertain outlook, stronger effort is needed to grow, invest, and insure

Sustained economic growth has been the key building block of poverty reduction and shared prosperity during the MDG era. After the launch of the MDGs in 2000 until the global financial crisis in 2009, developing economies grew on average by 6.6 percent a year, compared with just over 2 percent a year in advanced economies. Even during the depth of the financial crisis and its immediate aftermath, developing economies grew by 5.5 percent, while advanced economies stalled. Moreover, this strong economic expansion was accompanied by greater income convergence. The global Gini coefficient—a measure of inequality in income distribution—declined. The global per capita distribution of income exhibited greater global income convergence during 2000–15, in part thanks to rapid income growth in major economies like China and India.

Economic growth is expected to be less buoyant in the period ahead. Global growth is expected to trend down somewhat in 2016–30 relative to the MDG period. This slowing may reflect weaker levels of investment and the gradually diminishing growth dividends from information and communication technology. Moreover, demographic trends in major advanced and emerging markets could be a drag on economy-wide growth—even if they also present significant opportunities to raise living standards. Lower growth prospects threaten the income convergence of developing and high-income economies. Developing economies require strong growth to support the hard-won gains of the MDG era. Looking ahead, a number of risks remain as geopolitical tensions, the tightening of financial conditions, and lower commodity prices present sources of uncertainty.

Economic growth may not transmit into poverty reduction as easily as in the past. First, with global poverty at 37.1 percent in 1990, many poor people were just below the poverty line, leading to a large percentage point reduction in poverty for a given (distribution-neutral) increase in household income growth. Now that the headline rate is 12.7 percent (latest most reliable estimate for 2012), the same distribution-neutral increase in GDP is unlikely to produce as much poverty reduction since comparatively more people will be situated in the lower end of the income distribution. Second, the deepest pockets of poverty may be less readily reached through growth as many of the remaining poor live in narrowly diversified natural-resource-based economies and fragile and conflict-affected states. Poverty is less responsive to growth in such economies because the availability of jobs—the main channel through which growth uplifts the poor—is more limited. Capital-intensive, natural-resource sectors may generate growth but are likely to have weaker linkages to job creation.

Given the unfinished agenda and the uncertain outlook, additional efforts are needed to promote broad-based growth, investment in people, and insurance against risks. These three priorities require a strategy that promotes competitive economies and stable business environments, thus ensuring broad-based growth and income-earning opportunities to benefit the poor and the B40. Investment in human development is needed to tackle non-income deprivations and inequalities of opportunity so that these same groups can gain the capacity to benefit from and contribute to economic growth and prosperity (Fryer and Levitt 2004; Paxson and Schady 2007). And robust insurance mechanisms are required so that people—although not necessarily jobs, firms, or industries—are protected against evolving risks for individuals, nations, and the world, all in the spirit of nurturing a competitive economy and fostering an inclusive society.

An environment that fosters sustainable growth—the first big priority—is complex. Among economies that have sustained growth

FIGURE O.3 Five characteristics have been key among countries that sustained rapid growth

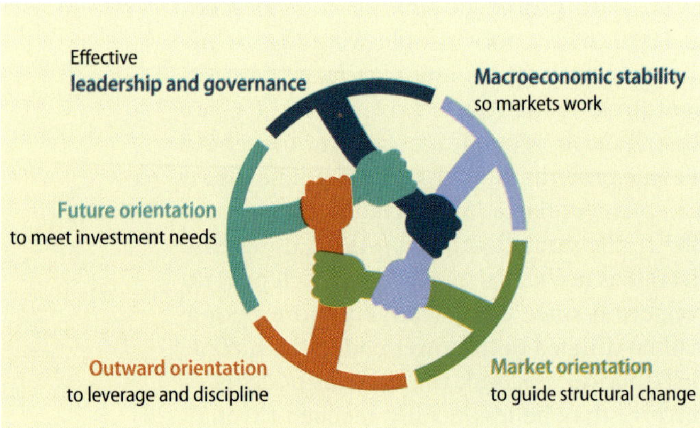

Source: GMR team adaptation from *Commission on Growth and Development* 2008.

for extended periods, five characteristics are key (figure O.3): effective leadership and governance; macroeconomic stability so markets work; a market orientation to guide structural change; an outward orientation to achieve scale and impose discipline; and a future orientation to boost savings and meet investment needs (Commission on Growth and Development 2008). Sustained growth can bite deep into poverty and contribute to shared prosperity, but for that to happen it must create jobs (Gill and Revenga forthcoming). Growth is most effective in reaching low-income people when it leads to productive employment. Policy makers must be mindful of the impacts of job creation and income growth on the extreme poor and the B40. That will require attention not only to the pace of economic growth but also to its pattern.

To leverage human resources to their fullest potential—the second priority—focused investment is needed in human development. The capacity of households to promote their well-being depends on the assets they control, the returns on these assets, and how intensively the assets can be used. Human capital assets have both intrinsic value (contributing to a person's well-being) and instrumental value (raising a person's capability to earn income). The unequal distribution of assets may prevent poorer households from borrowing to accumulate human capital, thus perpetuating poverty and inequality. Policies that reduce inequalities of opportunity are crucial for enabling poorer households to invest in their human potential. As technological change increasingly affects the structure of economies, worker skills must evolve.

Robust insurance mechanisms—the third priority—are needed to protect the extremely poor from destitution and the vulnerable against evolving risks, including climate change. These mechanisms can help families avoid irreversible losses and prevent them from having to make decisions with costly long-run implications. Noncontributory social assistance programs for the chronic or extremely poor protect them from destitution and promote investments in their children's human capital. Social insurance programs prevent people from falling back into poverty, whether from individual illness, temporary unemployment, or localized droughts. Generally, the poor in developing countries are disproportionally affected by shocks. One reason is that the poor have lower access to resources and savings to absorb the impact of shocks, whether they come from climate change or political, economic, or financial instability. Climate change may have a greater impact on the poor relative to other types of shocks because the poor tend to be more dependent on agriculture and have more perilous access to water. Insurance mechanisms are needed to help countries cope with systemic shocks.

Evolving circumstances demand a new approach—enter the SDGs

Several "megatrends" are playing a critical role in framing what will be feasible through 2030. These include the unprecedented increase in global connectedness, including the cross-border movements of trade, services, capital, and people; the shift of the global economic center of gravity toward the East; the pace of technological change and adoption; the move toward urbanization; the evolution of demographic trends; the general failure of countries to secure long-term environmental sustainability; and the impact of human activity on climate change. Trade, finance, communications, and migration are

FIGURE O.4 Communication and trade are increasing global economic integration

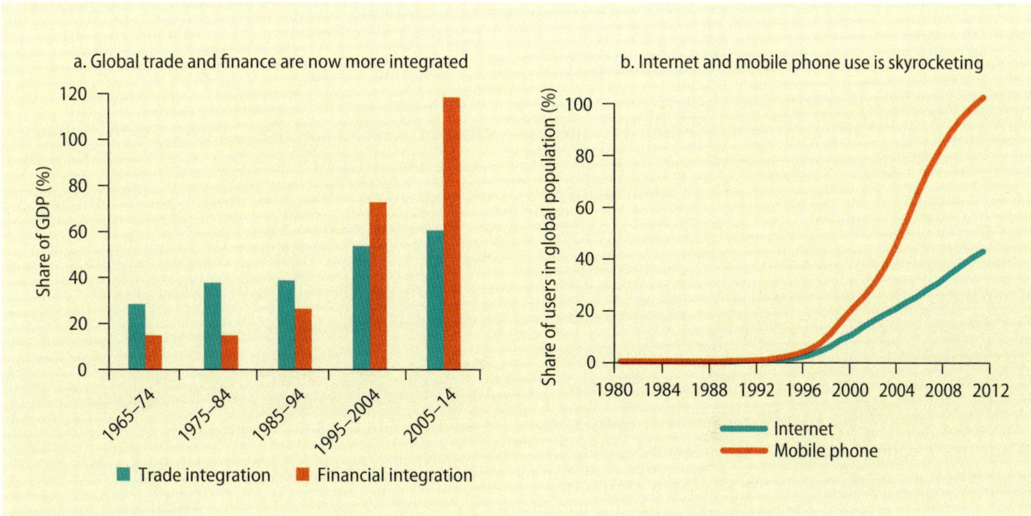

Source: Kose and Ozturk 2014.
Note: Trade integration reflects ratio of total imports and exports to global GDP. Financial integration is the ratio of total financial in-flows and out-flows (including bank loans, direct investment, bonds, and equities) to global GDP.

Source: World Development Indicators, World Bank.

all expanding rapidly, bringing the world closer together and increasing economic integration (figure O.4).

These megatrends may help or hinder efforts to reach the development goals. On the positive side, the shift in the global economic center of gravity to developing countries creates opportunities. The deepening of global trade and investment connections could help reverse slipping potential growth in some countries, and technological change is also proving to be a driver of productivity growth. On the other hand, increased connectedness permits the rapid spreading of economic crises in one country to the rest of the world. Urbanization is associated with economic growth, but it can also give rise to urban slums and environmental damage. Lower fertility rates reflect improved health and labor market opportunities for women, yet falling shares of the working-age population can produce headwinds to growth and put the fiscal sustainability of many public services at risk.

Cognizant of these trends, the SDGs represent a greater level of ambition and a more holistic vision of sustainable development. By shifting focus to quality, the SDGs seek to address the unfinished agenda and scale up impact. The SDGs recognize that collective action is needed to address global challenges such as the need for more resilient international financial systems, the sharing of transboundary resources, and, most urgently, slowing and coping with climate change. Meeting the SDG investment needs requires a shift from "billions" in official development assistance to "trillions" in investments to unlock, leverage, and catalyze domestic public resources and private capital flows. The SDGs need to be pursued in a changing world, with new opportunities and challenges brought by evolving global megatrends that shape development prospects. A central challenge in this respect is demographic change.

The SDGs recognize the interconnections between development objectives. There are important interactions between development goals, and they cannot be effectively pursued separately from each other. For example, progress on health goals depends on investments in infrastructure that provides access to safe water and improved sanitation. Similarly, limiting carbon monoxide (CO_2) emissions to slow global warming requires the modernization of energy supplies. Hence, the SDGs explicitly articulate goals that are "integrated and indivisible and balance the three dimensions of sustainable development: the economic, social, and environmental" (UN 2015). The breadth of the SDGs has raised questions about whether the scale of the agenda will dilute focus, especially when some development exigencies are likely to be more pressing than others at the country level. Still, the SDGs are not simply a menu of development objectives, and policy makers and other stakeholders are called upon to pursue the goals as an integrated whole.

The World Bank Group (WBG) supports the 2030 agenda for sustainable development. In 2013, the WBG established clear goals to guide its own work: to end extreme poverty globally by 2030, promote shared prosperity in every country, and to do so in ways that sustainably secure the future of the planet and its resources, promote social inclusion, and limit the economic burdens that future generations inherit. These goals, conceptually and in practice, are fully aligned with the SDGs: end poverty, promote prosperity, and improve people's well-being while protecting the environment. The WBG is committed to partnering closely with its client governments and its development partners to further the 2030 agenda. Building on and learning from the experience of the MDGs, the WBG will help to secure financing; help to deliver development solutions at the country, regional, and global levels; and work with partners to help convene, connect, and coordinate.

The International Monetary Fund (IMF) actively participated in the debate on the new global development agenda and it is strongly committed, within the scope of its mandate, to support the SDGs. The IMF will help member countries achieve the SDGs by providing advice on strengthening macroeconomic policies, technical assistance on building capacity, and resources to boost economic resilience against adverse shocks. New IMF initiatives in support of member countries' development efforts include enhancing support for countries building domestic capacity in tax policy and administration; expanding assistance, through a package of tools, for countries seeking to address large infrastructure gaps without imperiling public debt sustainability; increasing access to IMF concessional resources to provide countries with a wider safety net should they encounter balance of payments pressures; and strengthening the effectiveness of the Fund's engagement with countries in post-conflict and fragile situations. The IMF is also deepening its focus on aspects of economic, social, and gender inclusion and environmental protection, which are core SDG objectives.

Part II: Development in an era of demographic change

Global demography is at a turning point

The world population is growing more slowly and aging at unprecedented speed. While the global population has tripled since the postwar "baby boom" era (figure O.5a), population growth is now slowing markedly (figure O.5b). After increasing for five decades, the proportion of people ages 15 to 64—the typical working-age population—reached a peak in 2012 and is now starting to fall (figure O.5c). The rise in the share of dependents is driven mainly by an increase in the share of elderly (figure O.5d). These global trends—slower population growth and population aging—have been shaped by a steady decline in fertility rates and a rapid improvement in life expectancy. In the 1950s total fertility rates were more than 5 births per woman, but since then they have steadily declined to 2.45 births per woman in 2015. A further decline is projected through 2050. In parallel, average life expectancy at birth has risen from 47 years in 1950 to 72 years in 2015, while infant mortality has declined. The coming decades are expected to see further improvements in life expectancy, although at a slower pace than in the past.

Global population dynamics are driven mainly by the demographic transition in developing countries. Falling mortality rates and still-high fertility led to a "child bulge" in developing countries in the 1960s and 1970s, while population growth slowed in high-income countries. In most developing

FIGURE O.5 Global demography is at a turning point: Slower growth, unprecedented aging

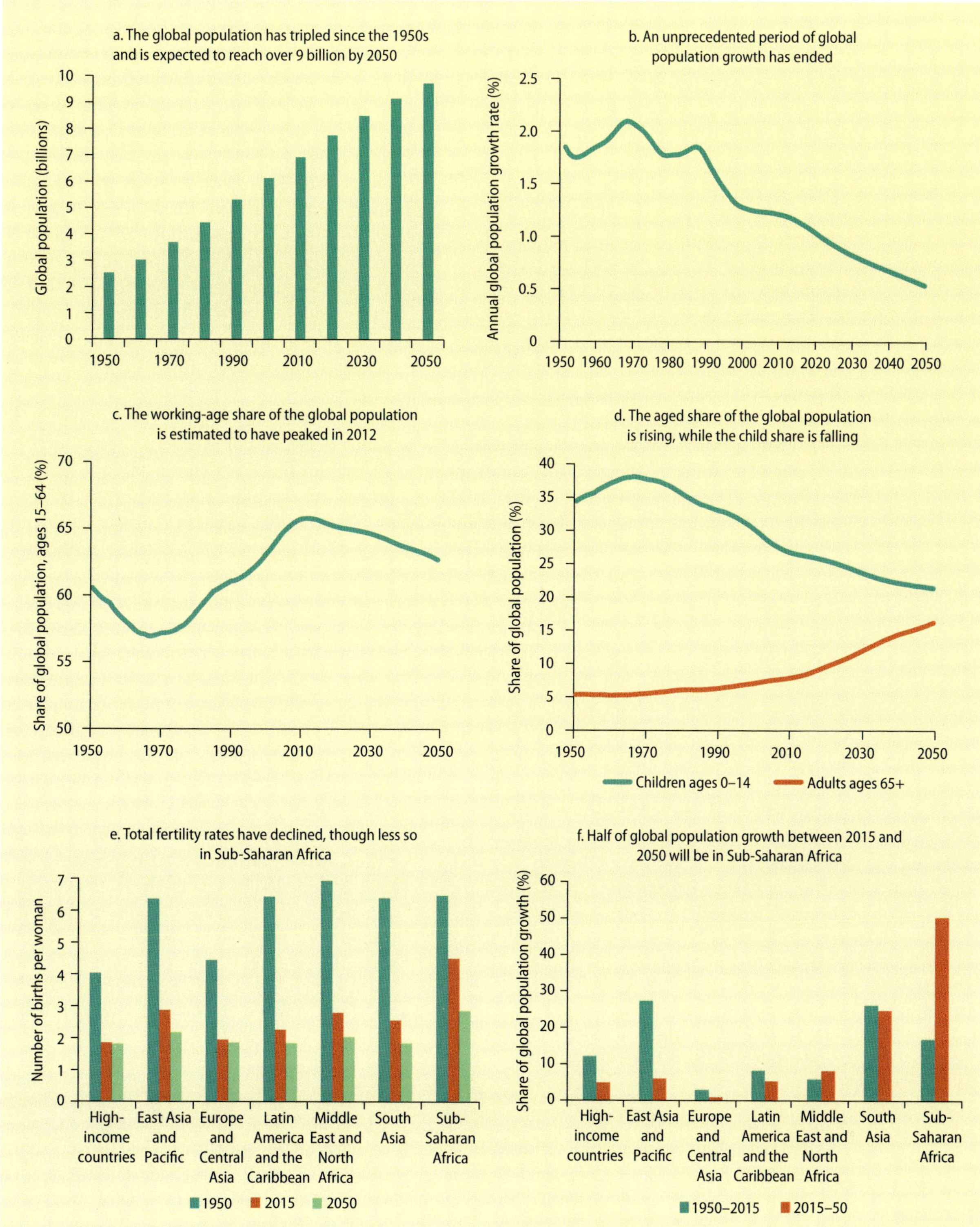

Source: World Bank calculations, based on data from UN 2015.

countries (outside lower-fertility Europe and Central Asia), population growth picked up and age structures shifted, with the share of children rising. Population growth later slowed as fertility fell (figure O.5e). The working-age share rose and populations started to age rapidly, partly thanks to improved life expectancy, especially in East Asia and the Pacific. By then, fertility rates had fallen dramatically in many developing regions, in some cases to levels below replacement fertility. Slower global population growth ensued, with populations in several countries now expected to contract. Sub-Saharan Africa is the exception among developing regions, with still high fertility and mortality rates, low life expectancies, and HIV/AIDS slowing progress.

Demographic change has a profound impact on the share of the global population that lives in developing countries. In 1950, 32 percent of the global population lived in high-income countries. Developing East Asia and the Pacific—the region with some of the most rapid fertility declines and life expectancy improvements in recent years—accounted for 29 percent of the population, while Sub-Saharan Africa—the region with the most modest improvements—accounted for only 7 percent. By 2015, this distribution had shifted substantially: high-income countries accounted for just 17 percent of the global population and Sub-Saharan Africa for 14 percent; the share of developing East Asia and Pacific remained about the same. Looking further ahead, Sub-Saharan Africa is expected to account for almost a quarter of the global population and half of the world's population growth during 2015–50 (figure O.5f).

Demographic change may alter the trajectory of global development

As fertility rates decline, countries are presented with the opportunity for two types of "demographic dividend" (Lee and Mason 2006). Child dependency ratios fall both within households and within a population, while the share of the working-age population rises and remains high for a few generations. A first demographic dividend is possible as the growing labor force supports fewer children. As changes in the age structure expand production and resources, a second demographic dividend may arise as savings build up and greater investment is possible in human and physical capital. The bonus provided by the first dividend is transitory, while the second dividend produces lasting benefits in the form of greater productivity growth and enhanced sustainable development. Yet, these outcomes are not automatic—they depend on effective policies. The two demographic dividends thus represent an opportunity—and not a guarantee—of greater prosperity and improved living standards.

A new typology is presented that distinguishes between countries in their ability to capture and harness demographic dividends. Underneath the global and regional averages lies considerable diversity in the direction and pace of demographic change across and even within countries. As a result, a country's demographic characteristics and trends may in principle have more in common with countries in another continent than with its regional neighbor. Despite the diversity, there is considerable commonality across countries in their ability to capture the first and second demographic dividends. These common factors are captured in a new global typology that ties demographic change to development potential and is based on the latest revision of the United Nations (UN) population statistics of July 2015.

Based on this typology, the world can be divided into four types of countries (figure O.6 and map O.2).

- *Pre-dividend countries* are mostly low-income countries, lagging in key human development indicators and with current fertility levels above four births per woman. They face very rapid population growth. Their high dependency ratios, however, are expected to decline as more and more children reach working age. These countries need to lay the foundations for realizing the first demographic dividend.

FIGURE O.6 Most of the global population lives in early- and late-dividend countries

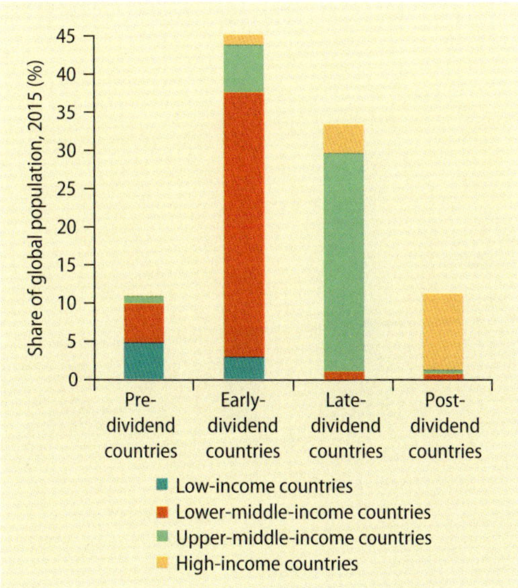

Source: World Bank calculations, based on data from UN 2015.
Note: Classifications are based on World Bank Group classifications.

- ***Early-dividend countries*** are mostly lower-middle-income countries further along the fertility transition. Fertility rates have fallen below four births per woman and the working-age share of the population is likely rising considerably. These countries need to focus on capturing the first demographic dividend and laying the foundations for realizing the second demographic dividend.
- ***Late-dividend countries*** are mostly upper-middle-income countries where fertility rates are typically above replacement levels of 2.1 births per woman, but fertility continues to decline. Even though they have shrinking working-age shares, their overall age structures are still favorable for the first demographic dividend. However, they are experiencing very rapid aging, so reaping the second demographic dividend is crucial.
- ***Post-dividend countries*** are mostly high-income countries where fertility has

MAP O.2 The world through the lens of demography

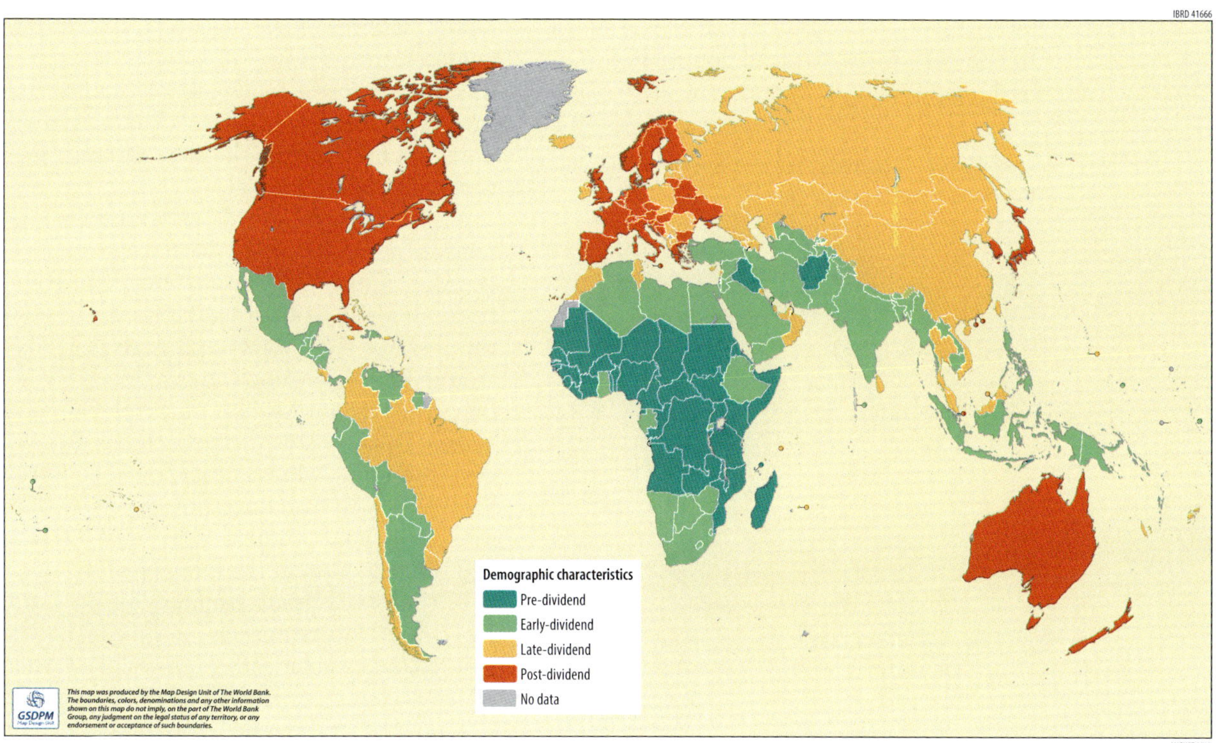

Source: World Bank calculations, based on data from UN 2015.

transitioned below replacement levels. These countries continue to see shrinking working-age shares and have some of the highest shares of elderly in the world. While they are past the point of additional benefits from the first demographic dividend, they can still reap the second dividend from rising savings and investments.

The development characteristics among these demographic types vary considerably, particularly among the pre- and early-dividend countries. Development successes are found mostly in countries with falling population growth, rising life expectancy, and declining infant mortality and fertility rates (figure O.7). Unfortunately, fewer than one-fifth of pre-dividend countries and only a quarter of early-dividend countries were able to reduce under-five child mortality rates by three-fourths in 1990–2011. Urbanization, which can play a role in reducing poverty, has been slow in pre-dividend countries and has not necessarily provided improved access to services. In these countries, less than one-fourth of the population lives in urban areas, more than two-thirds of which live in slums. In contrast, early-dividend countries urbanized rapidly, almost doubling the urban share to half over the period, with roughly one-third living in urban slums. Education is another factor. Whereas lower secondary education completion rates are 72 percent for early-dividend countries, they are just half of that in pre-dividend countries. This disparity poses a challenge in the face of continued rapid population growth.

FIGURE O.7 Countries are at different stages in the demographic transition

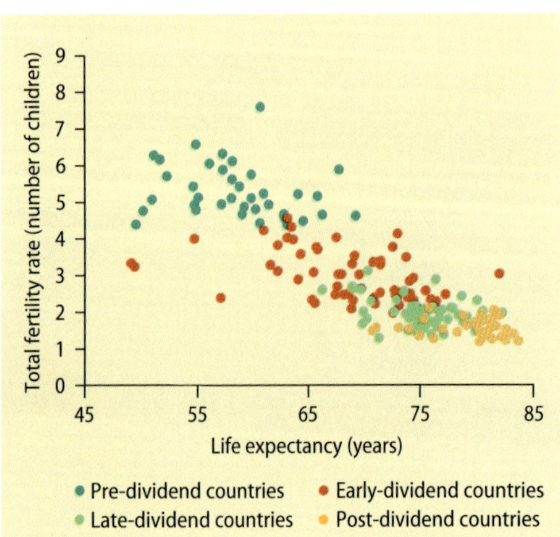

Source: World Bank calculations based on data from UN 2015.
Note: The total fertility rate is the average number of births a woman in a given country has, assuming she lives to the end of her reproductive life.

FIGURE O.8 Pre-dividend and early-dividend countries account for most of global poverty

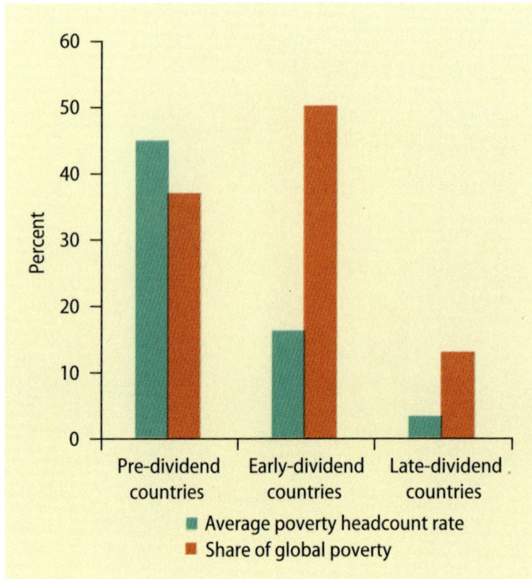

Source: World Bank staff.
Note: Data are for 2012 and are based on a poverty line of $1.90 a day and 2011 purchasing power prices. The average poverty headcount rate is the unweighted average across countries in a given group.

Pre- and early-dividend countries currently account for about 90 percent of global poverty (figure O.8). In pre-dividend countries, almost half the population lives below the poverty line. Although early-dividend countries have a much lower poverty rate, they still account for half of the global poor, largely because this group includes Bangladesh and India. Many pre-dividend countries have managed to reduce poverty headcount rates, but rapid population growth has limited the reduction in the number of the poor. While poverty is dominated by pre- and early-dividend countries, it should not be ignored in late-dividend countries like China, which accounts for a tenth of global poverty.

Late-dividend countries are experiencing demographic change at a much faster pace than many post-dividend countries, potentially resulting in headwinds to economic growth. In the 1950s, late-dividend countries had double the fertility rates of post-dividend countries, and life expectancies were shorter by nine years. Since then, late-dividend countries have made substantial improvements in these metrics, with extremely rapid improvements in life expectancy. As a result, late-dividend countries will have the same age structure as post-dividend countries by 2050. These trends are likely to present challenges to growth. The ongoing demographic changes are likely to further dampen the growth engine in these economies, particularly in the absence of policy adjustments.

Post-dividend countries' contributions to global growth have also been slowing, with potential spillovers for other countries. These countries accounted for 42 percent of global GDP growth between 2000 and 2014, and 60 percent of global economic activity in 2014 (figure O.9). Post-dividend economies are also the major export destinations for early- and pre-dividend countries and account for two-thirds of global import demand. If growth in post-dividend countries slows, early- and pre-dividend countries will need to find alternative export markets. Also, as post-dividend economies age, their national savings rate is expected to fall, leading to a possible slowdown in capital flows to the rest of the world.

FIGURE O.9 Aging countries accounted for most of global growth during 2000–14

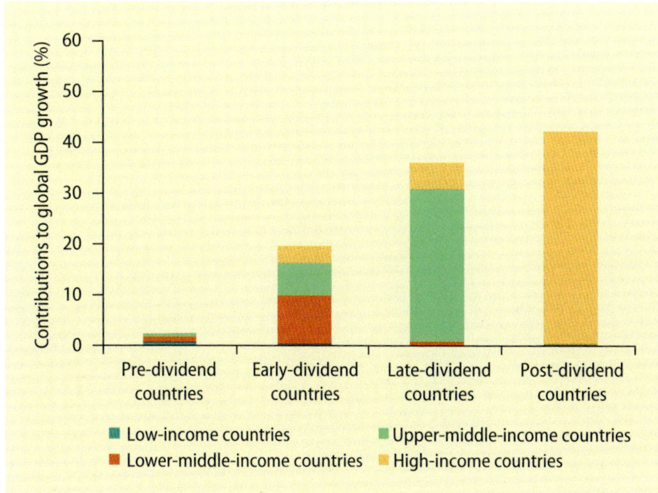

Source: World Bank staff based on UN 2015 and World Bank World Development Indicators.

Effective policies can leverage demographic change within countries

Demographic dynamics can support development if governments implement demography-informed policies (table O.2). Countries moving from high to low fertility can benefit from a growing working-age population share. These countries have the potential to realize the first and second demographic dividends, which are beneficial to poverty reduction and shared prosperity as well as to overall growth and development. Half of the world's population—and most of the world's poor—live in countries where the working-age population share is rising. Whether a rising working-age share is beneficial depends on the extent to which governments ensure that policies and institutions take advantage of these trends. The other half of the world's population lives in countries where populations are aging and working-age shares are dwindling. In these countries, policies will need to be adapted to demographic change. Demographically informed policies can cover a wide range of areas, including human, private sector, and financial development, as well as improved governance. To be sure, demographic change is neither universally good nor bad, and presents opportunities as well as challenges everywhere. Policies can make a critical difference in tilting the impact of demographic change in favor of the development goals.

Navigating these dynamics requires sound policies that are tailored to a country's demographic context. In pre-dividend countries, policies need to *spark demographic transition* by addressing human development challenges and speeding up the decline in fertility needed to raise the working-age population share and boost economic growth. In early-dividend countries, the priority is to *accelerate job creation* by investing in human capital and ensuring an enabling environment for private sector development to help realize

TABLE O.2 Policy priorities that leverage demographic change at the country level

Country type	Policy priorities	Recommendations
Pre-dividend	*Sparking demographic transition* Improving human development outcomes to reduce fertility rates	Improve maternal and child health by strengthening provision of basic health care services. Expand education without letting girls fall behind. Empower women and give them access to comprehensive family planning services.
Early-dividend	*Accelerating job creation* Creating productive jobs for the growing share of the population in working age to reap the first demographic dividend	Invest in human capital, including vocational and technical training. Enhance labor market mobility. Reduce barriers to female labor force participation. Strengthen conditions conducive to savings and job creation (public services underpinning private sector activity, contract enforcement; financial inclusion; protection of labor rights).
Late-dividend	*Sustaining productivity growth* Creating conditions necessary to reap the second demographic dividend and beginning to prepare for aging	Continue mobilization of savings for productive investment. Ensure that public policies encourage labor force participation of both sexes. Design cost-effective and sustainable systems for welfare and human development that address current needs (including health, child care, education, and support to the vulnerable elderly) and that can be adapted to meet the needs that emerge as aging proceeds.
Post-dividend	*Adapting to aging* Maintaining and improving welfare in the context of a declining working-age share and a growing old-age share	Complete reforms of welfare systems—including pensions, health care, and long-term care—that ensure fiscal sustainability and, as part of integrated approaches, protection of the vulnerable, elderly and others, and encouragement of work among those who are able. Raise labor force participation and productivity (including incentives for participation targeted at women and older cohort; and lifelong learning for all). Pursue policies that encourage higher birth rates by making it easier for men and women to combine child rearing and participation in the labor market.

Source: GMR team elaboration.

the first demographic dividend and lay the groundwork for the second dividend. In late-dividend countries, where fertility rates are low and the working-age population share is high (but shrinking), the key challenge is to *sustain productivity growth* by mobilizing savings for productive investment, while also preparing for aging. Finally, in post-dividend countries the overriding policy priority is to *adapt to aging* through efforts to maintain welfare and accommodate changing demands for services while at the same time encouraging a rise in fertility rates toward the replacement level.

Policy action focused on human development may help pre-dividend countries progress to the next stage in the demographic transition. These policies include improving maternal and child health; expanding education, particularly for girls; and empowering women in the household, in the labor force, and in the economy more generally (Bloom et al. 2009; Soares and Falcão 2008; World Bank 2015a). Given their potential to reduce total fertility rates and reduce child mortality, these three policy areas can be considered "interactive accelerators" that spark demographic transition, in addition to being important development goals in their own right. Concluding the unfinished MDG agenda related to these policies should be considered one of the priorities for pre-dividend countries.

To maximize demographic dividends, early-dividend countries need to focus on interventions that help absorb new workers into productive jobs. The first demographic dividend arises only to the extent an economy is able to create productive jobs for the growing working-age population. In addition, early-dividend countries need to lay the foundation for the second demographic dividend. There is a need to accelerate job creation, by ensuring that both the supply side (particularly human capital development) and the demand side (job-intensive economic growth) of job creation are sufficient to absorb the labor force across income levels (Fox and Sohnesen 2012; Lee and Mason 2006; Troiano 2015; World Bank 2013b). These policies would also include the removal of barriers to female labor force participation, given persistent gender gaps in the labor market.

Late-dividend countries face the challenge of sustaining the first demographic dividend into the more durable second demographic dividend. How much of the second dividend these countries can realize will depend on the accumulation of physical and human capital. Capital accumulation is, in turn, affected by policies. For example, late-dividend countries need to implement sound financial sector policies to help mobilize private savings in support of investments. Given projected declines in the share of the population that is of working age, a more capital-intensive development path is often needed to support growth. Policies that encourage the geographic expansion of the financial sector and broaden access to banks and other intermediating institutions may help channel savings to investments in small and medium enterprises, as well as underserved regions.

In post-dividend countries, the challenge is to maintain and improve living standards in the face of shrinking labor supply and rising proportions of the elderly. The decline in the working-age population share could be partly offset by family-friendly measures that facilitate a rebound in fertility rates to near replacement levels. Raising the labor force participation and employment prospects of older people will become increasingly pressing as population aging progresses. A more inclusive labor market requires adequate incentives to sustain human capital investment through the life cycle, more flexible work arrangements, lifelong learning programs, and improved incentives in the social protection systems to continue working in old age (Bussolo, Koettl, and Sinnott 2015).

In addition, adjustments to fiscal and social protection systems will generally be necessary to address the challenges posed by demographic changes in aging countries (particularly those in the late- and post-dividend stages). Given the growing need for spending on the aged, tax increases may not be a viable option, in view of likely price distortions and disincentives. Governments should strive to enhance the efficiency and cost-effectiveness of overall and aging-related spending. Pension reforms need to ensure a minimum level of protection for the vulnerable elderly. Lowering coverage and adequacy of pension systems may raise vulnerability among current and future elderly generations, whose private savings are limited. Pension systems, health care, and long-term care will have to be put on fiscally sustainable paths without neglecting the social safety nets that all those services represent (Bussolo, Koettl, and Sinnott 2015; World Bank 2015b). In particular, population aging will naturally bring about an increase in pension and health expenditure.

Opportunities exist to arbitrage demographic diversity across countries

In pursuing their domestic agendas, countries can also arbitrage and in the process leverage demographic change at the global level through cross-border capital flows, international migration, and global trade. Differences in the demographic dynamics at the country level are producing important spillovers across countries, contributing to changes in comparative advantages underpinning trade, and in the returns earned by labor and capital. These changes require the implementation of policies to support enhanced trade in goods and services as well as greater factor mobility. This would encourage labor-intensive production to shift from aging countries to younger societies or migration from countries with growing working-age populations to countries where the number of workers is falling,

TABLE O.3 Policy priorities that leverage the differences in demographic change across countries

Area of focus	Policy priorities	Recommendations
International trade	Promoting foreign provision of education services to boost educational opportunities in countries with a high share of youths, or to facilitate lifelong learning for aging countries	Ease visa requirements for the free flow of international students and academics; address qualification recognition issues; reduce limits on foreign ownership; and increase transparency of government education regulations
	Using foreign providers to meet demand for health services in aging countries	Address restrictions affecting the physical presence of foreign suppliers, foreign equity ceilings, or barriers on the movement of health care professionals across borders
	Supporting comparative advantage in producing labor-intensive products in labor-abundant countries	Streamline customs, border and transit procedures; improve logistics and transport services and extend physical infrastructure; tackle remaining tariff and nontariff barriers on goods trade
Migration	Promoting legal migration flows to counteract the decline in working-age populations in aging countries and to mitigate labor market pressures in labor-abundant countries	Formulate clear migration policies; enforce minimum wage laws; provide adequate information to migrants about their rights and obligations; facilitate their contribution to and benefits from social protection schemes and public services; sanction potential abuses by firms.
	Reducing the burden of brain drain in sending countries	Develop comprehensive and targeted policies to retain, attract talent; encourage return migration.
International finance	Attracting international capital flows to young, labor-abundant countries	Create favorable investment climate; strengthen macroeconomic stability, the financial sector, and governance.
	Addressing challenges posed by large and volatile capital flows to developing countries	Undertake measures to relax investment barriers at the domestic, regional, and global level.
	Supporting opportunities for capital-abundant countries to increase returns and diversify investment portfolios	Introduce macroeconomic policies to address risks from volatile capital inflows, supervision, regulation, strong institutions.
		Provide investment guarantees or technical assistance.

Source: GMR team elaboration.

FIGURE O.10 Early-dividend countries are more specialized in labor-intensive exports

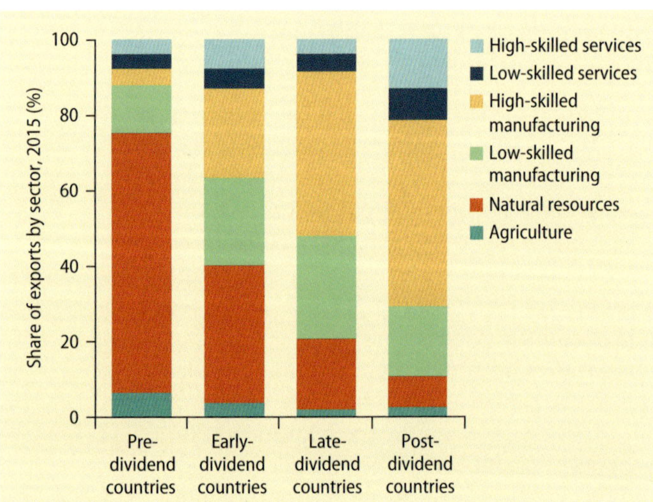

Source: World Bank calculations.

thereby delivering non-tradable services such as elderly care (table O.3). International cooperation—in addition to domestic measures—is needed on trade facilitation, legal migration, and capital flows to ensure smooth adjustment to demographic change.

In coming decades, global trade flows are projected to continue shifting toward countries earlier in their demographic transition, possibly yielding substantial benefits for poorer countries. Differences in demographic change may lead to comparative advantages that influence trade patterns. Countries with slower population growth tend to become more capital-abundant over time, while countries with faster population growth become more labor-abundant (figure O.10). Trade can reduce poverty through faster growth, more economic diversification, and greater macroeconomic stability. It can also facilitate through knowledge embodied in goods and services production, boosting productivity and growth. Knowledge transfers from trade in health and education products and services, for instance, have contributed significantly to development, while medical imports are associated with lower mortality rates.

Trade policy measures can be powerful tools in enabling countries to adapt to the opportunities and challenges in demographic change. Agricultural trade is still distorted by high tariffs, export subsidies, and domestic support. Although average tariffs on manufactured goods have been declining over the years, substantial tariff and nontariff barriers still affect the free flow of goods between countries (UNCTAD 2013; WTO 2012). Reductions in those barriers, coupled with improving trade facilitation, could encourage firms to relocate production to relatively more labor-abundant countries and allow developing countries to take full advantage of their growing labor forces. In pre- and early-dividend countries, additional trade facilitation measures may add to their comparative advantage in labor-intensive products and help create jobs. Trade can also help meet the demand for health services in aging countries and the demand for education services in young countries. Both health care and education are traded only lightly across borders due to high barriers, so liberalizing trade in those areas could potentially yield substantial benefits.

Migration can help countries' adjustment to uneven demographic change. Given the generally high level of restrictions on the movement of people across borders, the potential gains from expanding legal and safe migration are large (Borgy et al. 2010; Tyers and Shi 2007; Walmsley, Winters, and Ahmed 2011; World Bank 2006). Demographic disparities can amplify those gains. While South–South migration flows have grown rapidly, substantial migration also takes place from younger developing countries to aging high-income countries (figure O.11). International migration flows can mitigate the decline in working-age population shares in aging countries. Younger immigrants can help ease the pressures of aging populations in late- and post-dividend countries, improve the growth prospects, and ensure the sustainability of public finances in destination countries. But the impact of migration on both origin and destination countries depends on the skills of migrants, and socio-political challenges must be managed.

FIGURE O.11 Post-dividend countries tend to receive the most migrants

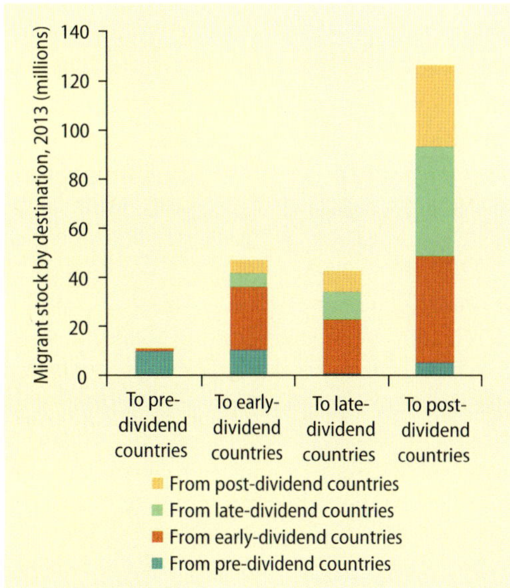

Source: World Bank calculations, based on UN 2013.

A wide range of policies could potentially foster legal migration, with benefits to both sending and receiving countries. In the past 10 years, many countries revised their migration laws in response to changes in demography, labor market conditions, and political contexts (OECD 2013). Pre-departure orientation and training, protecting the rights and preventing the abuse of migrants, lowering remittance costs, and removing regulatory and bureaucratic barriers to return migration are all actions that can enhance the net development benefits. Migration not only benefits sending countries through remittances but also presents challenges (such as brain drains or "Dutch disease" effects), but these can be actively managed. Tackling the underlying push and pull factors of migration and targeting interventions to retain, attract, or reattract talent are essential.

Different trajectories of demographic change have important implications for capital flows. Countries early in their demographic transition need to boost investment, and those later in their transition must seek higher returns than may be available domestically. So demography can augment the impetus for international capital flows. Facilitation of such flows would allow young, labor-abundant countries to attract much-needed capital. In the initial stages of the demographic transition, investment demand exceeds savings, stimulating current account deficits. The opposite tends to be true for countries in later stages of demographic transition. Capital flows could generate an increase in labor productivity and wages, contributing to faster growth in young, labor-abundant countries. For sending countries, increasing investment in young economies can provide opportunities to raise capital returns and diversify investment portfolios, especially if labor-abundant countries create favorable investment climates, ensure macroeconomic stability, deepen their financial sectors, and strengthen governance (World Bank 2013a).

Improving institutional quality and developing the financial sector will attract capital flows to pre- and early-dividend countries. Countries early in their demographic transition can promote foreign direct investment by reducing the economic, political, and legal risks facing investors. Host countries can relax investment barriers, such as caps on foreign ownership and requirements for joint ventures. Home countries can facilitate outflows through investment guarantees and technical assistance. At the global level, reforms are needed to allow countries to take full advantage of international investment agreements, including by reforming investment dispute settlements. Macroeconomic policies need to address risks from volatile capital inflows in tandem with sound financial supervision and regulation. Minimum levels of financial and institutional development are needed to reduce the riskiness of financial liberalization (Sahay et al. 2015). International regulatory coordination can bring bilateral and multilateral benefits, including by strengthening and institutionalizing swap lines that provide liquidity for non-key currencies.

* * *

Strategies to sustainably end poverty and build shared prosperity need to keep demography in mind as countries pursue broad-based growth, invest in human development, and insure against evolving risks. Each country's demographic context matters greatly in setting priorities in these three areas, defining the opportunities and challenges for ending poverty and sharing prosperity. The centers of global poverty need to spark the transition to lower fertility and accelerate development by taking advantage of demographic shifts and absorbing youth bulges in the labor market. The engines of global growth need to address headwinds to growth and adapt institutions and policies to aging populations. Because the centers of global poverty continue to face significant poverty reduction challenges and the engines of global growth are weakening, all countries must grasp the opportunities stemming from cross-border capital flows, international migration, and global trade. With such strategies in place, the world stands a better chance of successfully ending extreme poverty by 2030 and lifting the well-being of lower-income people throughout the world.

References

Borgy, V., X. Chojnicki, G. Le Garrec, and C. Schwellnus. 2010. "Macroeconomic Consequences of Global Endogenous Migration: A General Equilibrium Analysis." *Annals of Economics and Statistics* 97/98: 13–39.

Bloom, D. E., D. Canning, G. Fink, and J. E. Finlay. 2009. "Fertility, Female Labor Force Participation, and the Demographic Dividend." *Journal of Economic Growth* 14 (2): 79–101.

Brauer M., G. Freedman, J. Frostad, A. van Donkelaar, R. V. Martin, F. Dentener, R. van Dingenen, K. Estep, H. Amini, J. S. Apte, K. Balakrishnan, L. Barregard, D. Broday, V. Feigin, S. Ghosh, P. K. Hopke, L. Knibbs, Y. Kokubo, Y. Liu, S. Ma, L. Morawska, J. S. Texcalac Sangrador, G. Shaddick, R. T. Burnett, H. R. Anderson, T. Vos, M. H. Forouzanfar, A. Cohen. 2015. "Ambient Air Pollution Exposure Estimation for the Global Burden of Disease 2013." Paper submitted for publication, Institute for Health Metrics and Evaluation, University of Washington, Seattle.

Bussolo, M., J. Koettl, and E. Sinnott. 2015. *Golden Aging: Prospects for Healthy, Active, and Prosperous Aging in Europe and Central Asia*. Washington, DC: World Bank.

Commission on Growth and Development. 2008. *The Growth Report. Strategies for Sustained Growth and Inclusive Development*. Washington, DC: World Bank.

Fox, L., and T. P. Sohnesen. 2012. "Household Enterprises in Sub-Saharan Africa: Why They Matter for Growth, Jobs, and Livelihoods." Policy Research Working Paper 6184. World Bank, Washington, DC.

Fryer R. G., and S. D. Levitt. 2004. "Understanding the Black-White Test Score Gap in the First Two Years of School." *Review of Economics and Statistics* 86 (2): 447–64.

Gill, I., and A. Revenga. Forthcoming. *Grow, Invest, Insure—A Plan to End Poverty*. Washington, DC: World Bank.

Kenny, C., and S. Dykstra. 2013. "The Global Partnership for Development: A Review of MDG 8 and Proposals for the Post-2015 Development Agenda." Policy Paper 026, Center for Global Development, Washington (July).

Kose, A. M., and E. O. Ozturk. 2014. "A World of Change: Taking Stock of the Past Half Century." *Finance and Development* 51(3):6–11.

Lee, R., and A. Mason. 2006. "What Is the Demographic Dividend?" *Finance and Development* 43 (3).

OECD (Organisation for Economic Co-operation and Development). 2013. *International Migration Outlook 2013*. Paris: OECD Publishing.

Paxson C., and N. Schady. 2007. "Cognitive Development among Young Children in Ecuador: The Roles of Wealth, Health, and Parenting." *Journal of Human Resources* 42 (1): 49–84.

Sahay, R., M. Čihák, P. N'Diaye, A. Barajas, S. Mitra, A. Kyobe, Y. N. Mooi, and S. Reza Yousefi. 2015. "Financial Inclusion: Can It Meet Multiple Macroeconomic Goals?" IMF Staff Discussion Note, International Monetary Fund, Washington, DC.

Soares, Rodrigo R., and B. L. S. Falcão. 2008. "The Demographic Transition and the Sexual Division of Labor." *Journal of Political Economy* 116 (6): 1058–104.

Troiano, S. 2015. "Population Dynamics and the Implications for Economic Growth, Poverty and Inequality—What Is Relevant for Southern Africa." World Bank, Washington, DC.

Tyers R., and Q. Shi. 2007. "Demographic Change and Policy Responses: Implications for the Global Economy." *World Economy* 30 (4): 537–66.

UN (United Nations). 2013. "Trends in International Migrant Stock: Migrants by Destination and Origin." United Nations database, POP/DB/MIG/Stock/Rev.2013, Department of Economic and Social Affairs.

———. 2015. "Transforming our World: The 2030 Agenda for Sustainable Development." United Nations, New York.

UNCTAD (United Nations Conference on Trade and Development). 2015. *World Investment Report 2015: Reforming International Investment Governance*. Geneva: United Nations.

Walmsley, T. L., A. Winters, and S. A. Ahmed. 2011. "The Impact of the Movement of Labour: Results from a Model of Bilateral Migration Flows." *Global Economy Journal* 11 (4).

World Bank. 2006. *Global Economic Prospects 2006: Economic Implications of Remittances and Migration*. Washington, DC: World Bank.

———. 2013a. *Capital for the Future: Saving and Investment in an Interdependent World*. Global Development Horizons. Washington, DC: World Bank.

———. 2013b. *World Development Report: Jobs*. Washington, DC: World Bank.

———. 2015a. *From Potential to Reality: What Will It Take to Harness a Demographic Dividend in Africa?* Washington, DC: World Bank.

———. 2015b. *Live Long and Prosper: Aging in East Asia and the Pacific*. Washington, DC: World Bank.

WTO (World Trade Organization). 2012. *World Trade Report 2012: Trade and Public Policies: A Closer Look at Non-Tariff Measures in the 21st Century*. Geneva: World Trade Organization.

Part I

Monitoring Global Development Progress

Development progress over the past 15 years has been impressive. Most developing countries grew at a sustained strong pace during the Millennium Development Goal (MDG) monitoring period, notwithstanding the negative impact from the 2009 global financial crisis. Together with strong per capita growth, income differences between countries were reduced, and about 1 billion people exited extreme poverty. The latest available data suggest that extreme poverty continued its descent and a majority of countries saw solid income growth for the bottom 40 percent of the income distribution. Progress was also observed in other dimensions. Millions of children who were unlikely to survive to their fifth birthday have passed beyond these critical years and gone on to school in ever greater proportions. The incidence of preventable diseases such as HIV/AIDS, malaria, and tuberculosis is falling, and the share of people with access to clean water and better sanitation has risen markedly. A few countries have succeeded in growing while simultaneously reducing the level of environmental externalities and carbon emissions—a virtuous state of green growth.

Despite such development gains, significant work remains. MDG outcomes have been marked by significant heterogeneity in dimensions, across regions, and between urban and rural areas, resulting in unevenness in poverty reduction and shared prosperity. Extreme poverty remains unacceptably high and geographically concentrated in areas where both the depth and breadth of poverty are grave. Many countries—especially high-income ones—saw bottom 40 incomes decline in recent years, likely due to the recent crisis, while the bottom 40 persistently lag in their access to quality social services, such as education and health, due to inequality of opportunity. Sustainability concerns have risen, endangering recent progress. For example, in most countries, land degradation, overfishing, deforestation, and extreme weather events are increasingly impacting rural livelihoods and spurring migration, while urban air pollution has emerged as a leading cause of ill health in developing countries.

At the same time, new opportunities and challenges are emerging in connection with changing prospects for growth and evolving global megatrends. For many countries, the near-to-medium-term outlook suggests weakened economic dynamism. Moreover, global demographic trends—explored in part II—could weigh down on longer-term growth prospects. In rural areas where resource dependence is high and opportunities for economic diversification are limited, burgeoning cities offer both opportunities and create accelerating economic, social, and environmental challenges. Further globalization can bring new opportunities to connect with global centers of dynamism, as can the ever-quickening pace of technological innovation and adoption. But a more connected world also means that crises can transmit more easily to poorer countries, while fragility and insecurity can be passed to richer countries. Climate change is bringing warmer and more extreme weather, requiring urgent mitigation and adaptation efforts. A rising frequency of humanitarian crises stemming from pandemics, natural disasters, war, conflict, and rising extremism may reverse development gains.

Building on the MDGs, the Sustainable Development Goals (SDGs) will scale up impact to address the unfinished development agenda in a changing world. The SDGs represent a greater level of ambition and a more holistic vision of sustainable development in a number of ways. They incorporate a greater focus on quality rather than quantity and more explicitly recognize the inter-connectedness of development challenges and hence the need for integrated multisectoral approaches. They emphasize the need to protect the planet and leave no one behind. They are meant to be shared by all countries, rich and poor, recognizing the collective action needed to address global challenges, such as more resilient international financial systems, shared transboundary resources, and most urgently, the central challenge facing the world today—climate change. Meeting the investment needs of the SDGs, the global community will need to move the discussion from "billions" in official development assistance to "trillions" in investments of all kinds and unlock, leverage, and catalyze both domestic public resources and private capital flows.

Part I of this report explores these themes in the following sequence:

- Chapter 1 examines the progress made on sustainable poverty reduction and shared prosperity, as well as the policies that are needed to make further progress.
- Chapter 2 reviews the development successes during the MDG period and examines the unfinished agenda left for the SDGs.
- Chapter 3 assesses the macroeconomic performance over the MDG period, provides the near- and medium-term outlook, and looks into the future toward 2030.

1

Ending Extreme Poverty and Sharing Prosperity: Progress and Policies

The world faces urgent and complex challenges to sustainably end extreme poverty and share prosperity. The latest data suggest that extreme poverty is continuing its three-decade-long descent. Yet it remains unacceptably high, deep, and concentrated in some regions, with the poor experiencing not only income shortfalls but also deprivations in multiple non-income dimensions. Many countries have seen solid progress in shared prosperity over the past decade as measured by income growth in the bottom 40 percent of the income distribution. This progress has been uneven, however, with pronounced disparities in non-income indicators between the bottom 40 and the top 60 percent. Only a few countries have succeeded in growing while simultaneously reducing the level of environmental externalities in their economies, and environmental trends in the majority of countries are not sustainable. To sustainably end extreme poverty and share prosperity, additional policy efforts will be needed to cope with uncertainties about the pace of economic growth and its incidence, as well as contextual factors such as the difficulties of reaching the remaining poor. Key priorities will be to deliver sustainable broad-based economic growth, invest in the human development potential of people, and insure the poor and vulnerable against evolving risks.

To guide its work toward a "world free of poverty," the World Bank Group in 2013 established two clear goals: end extreme poverty by 2030, and promote shared prosperity. Along with the requirement to pursue these goals sustainably—economically, environmentally, and socially—the two goals are comprehensive in nature. They are fully aligned to support the Sustainable Development Goals (SDGs) set by the United Nations to replace the Millennium Development Goals (see chapter 2). To evaluate progress, the two goals are measured by two overall indicators: a reduction in the global headcount ratio of extreme poverty (the share of the population whose income is below the international poverty line) to 3 percent by 2030, and the promotion of income growth in the bottom 40 (B40) percent of the income distribution in each country.[1]

This chapter updates the assessment of progress toward these two goals in a sustainable manner. The poverty goal is examined through three lenses: the evolution of income poverty based on the new international poverty line that has been re-estimated at $1.90

a day; an assessment of person-equivalent income poverty, a new intuitive indicator that combines the incidence with the depth of poverty; and a review of the breadth of poverty, recognizing that income shortfalls often coexist with multiple non-income deprivations. The shared prosperity goal is examined on the basis of the latest comparison of (comparable) household data on B40 income growth. As part of its analysis of the two goals, the chapter also comments on the status of defining and monitoring sustainability in its economic, environmental, and social aspects.[2]

When measured in all of its dimensions, progress in poverty reduction and shared prosperity has been significant but uneven. The latest data suggest that global poverty continued its three-decade descent, but it remains unacceptably high and geographically concentrated. Pockets of very deep and multidimensional poverty continue to persist, leading to conflicting views about the extent and pace of progress over time and across space. As for shared prosperity, solid income growth was observed among the B40 in many countries—at least until recently and subject to data caveats—but, again, experiences differed. A large share of countries—including half of high-income countries and a third of low-income countries in the sample—saw B40 incomes fall. Beyond income, the B40 lag persistently behind the national top 60 percent (T60) in various non-income indicators.

Contextual factors and uncertainties pose a challenge to the economic and social sustainability of recent trends. The structural characteristics of the poorest countries make it harder to reach the remaining poor. Moreover, average income growth, which has been a key driver of shared prosperity, may not be as buoyant as it was before the global financial crisis, in part owing to demographics—discussed in part 2 of this Report. In addition, factors that underpinned the recent rise in B40 income shares may turn out to be transitory or unsustainable. Continued high levels of inequality in both outcomes and opportunity in both income and non-income dimensions pose additional sustainability risks.

Less progress has been made in improving the long-term environmental sustainability of development. Even though some countries have successfully "delinked" trends in environmental degradation from growth, most have not. The annual cost of environmental degradation—resulting from externalities due to outdoor and indoor air pollution, water pollution, deforestation, carbon emissions, and other environmental hazards—has gone up 50 percent from 1990 to 2010, in constant dollars. Only about 25 percent of the countries in the world, primarily high-income countries, have managed to grow economically while simultaneously decreasing their environmental externalities.[3] Even fewer have managed to delink carbon emissions from growth—a record that challenges the world's ability to contain the impacts of future climate change to agreed-upon levels of acceptability. Therefore, while experience shows that sustainable economic development is possible, the goal remains difficult to achieve.

This chapter also examines the policy actions and institutional interventions needed to accelerate progress on reducing poverty and sharing prosperity. While the two goals hold general relevance in promoting "growth with equity," their immediate focus is on populations who are extremely poor and those who constitute the B40—two groups who may in some countries overlap significantly and in others be distinct. Interventions required to spur sustainable progress toward both goals interact in multiple ways. Although details and emphasis vary across countries, three common ingredients are key to an integrated strategy: sustaining broad-based growth, investing in human development, and insuring the poor and vulnerable against evolving risks. In designing integrated strategies, natural capital, environmental health, and ecosystem sustainability need to be fully incorporated into economic decision making.

Extreme poverty: Updated numbers and remaining challenges

Ending extreme poverty by 2030 is the first of the World Bank Group's goals. Ending extreme poverty is defined as reducing the share of the global population living below the international poverty line to below 3 percent, with an interim target of 9 percent by 2020. The goal requires a reduction of almost 10 percentage points from the 2012 level of 12.7 percent. Despite significant progress toward this goal, the updated global poverty statistics show that poverty levels remain high and that "business as usual" policies are unlikely to be sufficient to reach the goal.

This section provides a textured understanding of extreme poverty, the progress that is being made in reducing it, and the remaining challenges that lie ahead. First, it analyzes the incidence of poverty—the share of the poor in the total population—and provides data based on updated 2011 purchasing power parity (PPP) prices and the reestimated international poverty line. Second, it offers complementary perspectives by analyzing the depth and breadth of poverty, taking into consideration how far a population is from the poverty threshold and in what aspects a population is disadvantaged other than in ways indicated by income. Third, it assesses the challenges in reaching the ambitious poverty target by 2030.

Assessing the incidence of poverty

Global poverty estimates have been updated to reflect the re-estimated international poverty line at $1.90 a day, new 2011-based PPP prices, and revisions to complementary data. Ensuring maximum comparability, the new poverty line is based on the 15 national poverty lines of the same countries that previously defined the $1.25 line. Because currency exchange rates fail to provide for a conversion that maintains equivalent costs of living across countries, PPP prices provide a unifying standard. Poverty updates also reflect revisions to complementary data, including population, inflation, and national income accounts. Box 1.1 discusses the

BOX 1.1 Global poverty estimates based on 2011 PPP data: Methods and challenges

World Bank estimates of global extreme poverty rely on many different data sources—among them are the price data that measure differences in the cost of purchasing a bundle of goods across countries. This measure of purchasing power parity (PPP) is used to ensure that the global poverty line reflects the same real standard of living across countries. In 2014 the International Comparison Program released PPP data from 2011, the first global update since the 2005 round. New PPP data have implications for both the value of the global poverty line and the estimated number of people below this line in each country. The poverty estimates released in this Report are based on the new 2011 PPP data following an approach that emphasizes comparability with previous global poverty estimates.

The first issue faced in using the 2011 PPP data is that the global extreme poverty line needs to be expressed in 2011 PPP values rather than in 2005 PPP values. World Bank (2015c) describes the various approaches that have been used in the past to estimate a value for the global poverty line, and, in all cases, the aim has been to estimate a value that reflects how the poorest countries in the world define minimum, basic needs. The earlier approach that resulted in the $1.25 global poverty line was based on taking the average value of national poverty lines from 15 of the poorest economies in the world (Chad, Ethiopia, The Gambia, Ghana, Guinea-Bissau, Malawi, Mali, Mozambique, Nepal, Niger, Rwanda, Sierra Leone, Tajikistan, Tanzania, and Uganda).[a] These 15 national poverty lines come from a sample of 74 national

(box continues next page)

BOX 1.1 Global poverty estimates based on 2011 PPP data: Methods and challenges (continued)

poverty lines, and the lines were converted into 2005 PPP dollars. The new \$1.90 poverty line is based on the same 15 national poverty lines previously used, except these lines are now converted from local currency into U.S. dollars using the new 2011 PPP data. The average value of these lines in 2011 rounds to \$1.90, which is the new extreme poverty line for global counts.[b]

Although no new PPP data were collected for developing countries between 2005 and 2011, many global indicators have nonetheless been reported annually in PPP terms throughout this period. One method for handling the interim years, used by the World Development Indicators, is to estimate extrapolated PPP conversion factors by the relative rates of inflation between the United States and the local country. Global poverty estimates do not directly use the extrapolated PPP estimates but follow an approach that is conceptually equivalent to using the extrapolations. Specifically, the current value of consumption in local currency is brought back or forward to the relevant PPP benchmark year (such as 2005 or 2011) by the national consumer price index (CPI), and then the benchmark year PPP conversion factor is applied to obtain the PPP U.S. dollar value of consumption. The poor are then identified as those whose consumption (or income for some countries) in PPP U.S. dollars is less than the global extreme poverty line (\$1.90 in 2011 PPP U.S. dollars).

An implication of the extrapolation approach is that one can estimate poverty based on either new PPP data or the extrapolated old PPP data for any given year. For example, when the 2005 PPP data were released, Chen and Ravallion (2010) used the new 2005 data to reestimate the global poverty line and headcount and observed significant changes in the poverty line and average value of consumption (relative to expectations based on the extrapolated PPP adjustment factors from the 1993 PPPs). Because of changes in the poverty line and the new PPP data, Chen and Ravallion's analysis indicated that past estimates of global poverty needed to be adjusted upward by 500 million persons. With the latest release of the global poverty estimates, an explicit rule was imposed to reduce the scope for large differences between the new poverty estimates based on the 2011 PPP data and the expected poverty estimates based on the extrapolated 2005 PPP data. This rule was based on comparing the rate of change in PPP factors ($\Delta PPP = PPP_{2011} / PPP_{2005}$) relative to the rate of change in domestic consumer price indexes ($\Delta CPI = CPI_{2011} / CPI_{2005}$) for each country. If these two ratios deviate significantly for a particular country, the 2011 PPP poverty estimates will likely differ significantly from the extrapolated 2005 PPP estimate for 2011.

Because further investigation is needed for some countries, the poverty update for these countries will continue to be based on extrapolations of 2005 PPP data. When examining all countries that participated in both the 2005 and 2011 International Comparison Program, the standard deviation of the ratio $\Delta CPI/\Delta PPP$ is 0.3 and its simple average is 1.47. This average indicates that the change in price levels used for measuring inflation was typically greater than the change in PPP prices, which is also linked to the relatively large increase in the global poverty line. The set of countries in PovcalNet for which this ratio is more than two standard deviations from the mean was examined.[c] For the purposes of global poverty estimation, large deviations in this ratio are interpreted as evidence that the price data (both CPI and PPP) require further investigation before the estimates are updated. Therefore, for these countries (Bangladesh, Cabo Verde, the Arab Republic of Egypt, Iraq, Jordan, and the Republic of Yemen), the 2012 global poverty estimates are based not on the 2011 PPP data, but rather on the \$1.25 poverty line and the extrapolated 2005 PPP data. Countries where the ratio is more than one standard deviation from the mean were subsequently examined on a case-by-case basis. For two of them (Cambodia and the Lao People's Democratic Republic), the exploratory analysis indicated that the poverty estimates based on 2005 PPPs are more consistent with regional patterns than those suggested by the 2011 PPPs. Therefore, the 2012 poverty estimates for Bangladesh, Cabo Verde, Cambodia, Jordan, and Lao PDR are based on the extrapolated 2005 PPP data and not the new 2011 PPP data.

A further complicating issue concerns estimating poverty for the Middle East and North Africa region. In particular, Iraq, the Syrian Arab Republic, and the Republic of Yemen are countries in protracted conflict whose poverty estimates will unlikely reflect the true current state of poverty in these countries.

(box continues next page)

BOX 1.1 Global poverty estimates based on 2011 PPP data: Methods and challenges (continued)

The measure of well-being in Egypt is expected to be substantially revised in the near future in a way that will affect the poverty estimate, and it was decided to wait until release of the revised measure to report on poverty there. Algeria's latest available household survey data (1995) are too old to produce reliable poverty estimates. Therefore, country-level poverty estimates for Algeria, Egypt, Iraq, Syria, and the Republic of Yemen are omitted. Consequently, for this region, poverty estimates are reported only for Djibouti, the Islamic Republic of Iran, Jordan, Morocco, Tunisia, and West Bank and Gaza. Given that these six account for only a small share of the region's population, and that poorer countries in the region are not included, regional poverty estimates for the Middle East and North Africa are not reported in table 1.1.[d]

While PPPs are used to adjust for price differences between countries in the International Comparison Program base years, spatial price adjustments are used within some countries. Specifically, for China, India, and Indonesia, adjustments are made to reflect cost-of-living differences between rural and urban areas. For these three countries, the global poverty line is converted to local currency units and then unpacked into implicit urban and rural poverty lines that are derived to be consistent with the urban-rural differential in the national poverty lines and the sectoral split of the International Comparison Program sample. In the case of India, an Expert Group constituted by the Government of India (2009) to examine India's poverty lines retained the prior official poverty line for urban areas but recommended a higher rural poverty line based on corrections for biases in past price deflators. These new poverty lines imply nearly half the cost-of-living difference (22 percent in 2011) between urban and rural areas, as compared with the old poverty lines. Estimates for India in this Report have been updated to reflect the lower urban-rural gap implicit in the new lines.

a. The list of the 15 poorest countries used to estimate the $1.25 poverty line based on the 2005 PPP, as described in Ravallion, Chen, and Sangraula (2009), does not necessarily represent the current 15 poorest countries in the world. Some of the countries originally included in this list may have made significant progress.

b. See Ravallion, Chen, and Sangraula (2009) for details on the sample of 74 countries and how the 15 were selected. See Jolliffe and Prydz (2015) for more discussion on methodology for updating the global poverty line. Their line differs somewhat from $1.90 because of recent revisions to CPI data, but the methodology is the same.

c. See PovcalNet (iresearch.worldbank.org/povcalnet), the World Bank's online tool for global poverty estimation.

d. Despite being excluded from country-level estimation, these countries are included for the purpose of global poverty rate estimation. In this case, poverty estimates are calculated using 2005 PPP data and the $1.25 poverty line for the Arab Republic of Egypt, Iraq, and the Republic of Yemen and using the 2011 PPPs and $1.90 poverty line for Algeria and the Syrian Arab Republic.

methodology and challenges relating to the transition from 2005 to 2011 PPPs.

Global poverty continued its decades-long descent

The latest headline estimate for 2012 based on the new data suggests that close to 900 million people (12.7 percent of global population) lived in extreme poverty (table 1.1; figures 1.1a and 1.1b). Compared with 2011—the year when PPPs were updated—this number represents continued poverty reduction, because the headcount estimate for 2011, using 2011 PPP data, was 983.3 million people (14.1 percent of global population). While broadly similar to the old estimate for 2011 based on 2005 PPP data, this estimate is some 28 million people lower. Comparison of the 2011 and 2012 data reveals a (modest) decline in the number of poor in Sub-Saharan Africa, potentially heralding an era of continued reduction not just in the share of the poor but also in their absolute number.

The recent decline of global poverty occurs against a backdrop of a decades-long descent. Comparisons with the data available for 1990 and 1999 confirm that the world has made rapid strides in poverty reduction since 1990 (see table 1.1). The proportion of global population living on less than $1.90

TABLE 1.1 Global poverty is assessed with the re-estimated poverty line

	Historical			Headline	Projection
Region	1990	1999	2011	2012	2015[a]
Share of population below $1.90 a day (2011 PPP) (%)					
East Asia and Pacific	60.6	37.5	8.5	7.2	4.1
Europe and Central Asia	1.9	7.8	2.4	2.1	1.7
Latin America and the Caribbean	17.8	13.9	5.9	5.6	5.6
Middle East and North Africa[b]	—	—	—	—	—
South Asia	50.6	41.8	22.2	18.8	13.5
Sub-Saharan Africa	56.8	58.0	44.4	42.7	35.2
Developing world	44.4	34.3	16.5	14.9	11.9
World	37.1	29.1	14.1	12.7	9.6
Millions of people below $1.90 a day (2011 PPP)					
East Asia and Pacific	995.5	689.4	173.1	147.2	82.6
Europe and Central Asia	8.8	36.8	11.4	10.1	4.4
Latin America and the Caribbean	78.2	71.1	35.3	33.7	29.7
Middle East and North Africa[b]	—	—	—	—	—
South Asia	574.6	568.0	361.7	309.2	231.3
Sub-Saharan Africa	287.6	374.6	393.6	388.8	347.1
World	1,958.6	1,751.5	983.3	896.7	702.1

Source: PovcalNet 2015.
Note: Poverty estimates based on $1.90 poverty line and 2011 PPP prices. Box 1.1 explains how the global poverty estimates were calculated. Regional aggregates for the Middle East and North Africa are omitted because of lack of sufficient observations.
a. Given the production lags for household surveys, 2012 is the latest year for which the World Bank is able to produce regional and global poverty estimates. All numbers for 2015 and beyond are statistical projections based on growth scenarios and distributional assumptions, and should be treated with considerable circumspection.
b. Even though five countries in the Middle East and North Africa region are omitted from the database of country-level poverty estimates, poverty estimates for these countries are calculated for the purposes of global poverty estimation (see box 1.1). The 2011 and 2012 poverty estimates for this region implied by these global estimates are 2.5 and 2.3 percent, respectively.

a day in 2012 was about a third of what it was in 1990.[4] This finding confirms that the first Millennium Development Goal target—cutting the extreme poverty rate to half of its 1990 level—was met well before its 2015 target date. From a broader historical perspective, the global poverty rate has fallen by approximately 1 percentage point a year since 1990, with rapid poverty reduction in China and India playing a central role in this outcome.

Tentative projections for global poverty in 2015 suggest that the global headcount may have reached 700 million, leading to a poverty rate of 9.6 percent. Compared with the headline estimate of 2012, poverty may thus have declined by close to 200 million people (some 80 million of whom were in South Asia, about 65 million in East Asia and Pacific, and more than 40 million in Sub-Saharan Africa). The projections extrapolate poverty estimates based on growth scenarios and distributional assumptions. Given that the data collection and processing for a nationally representative household survey, on which poverty estimates are based, usually take two to three years, the 2012 number remains the most reliable recent headline poverty estimate.

Global poverty remains high and concentrated

Poverty levels remain unacceptably high and are particularly concentrated in Sub-Saharan Africa and South Asia. For several decades, three regions have accounted for some 95 percent of global poverty: East Asia and Pacific, South Asia, and Sub-Saharan Africa. The latest 2012 estimates confirm this high degree of concentration (figure 1.1c, 1.1d). Yet the composition of global poverty across these three regions has shifted over the years. The share of Sub-Saharan Africa in global poverty has risen to 43 percent alongside a slower pace of poverty reduction in this region amid rapid population growth. The poverty rate fell only

FIGURE 1.1 Global poverty declined, but Sub-Saharan Africa lagged

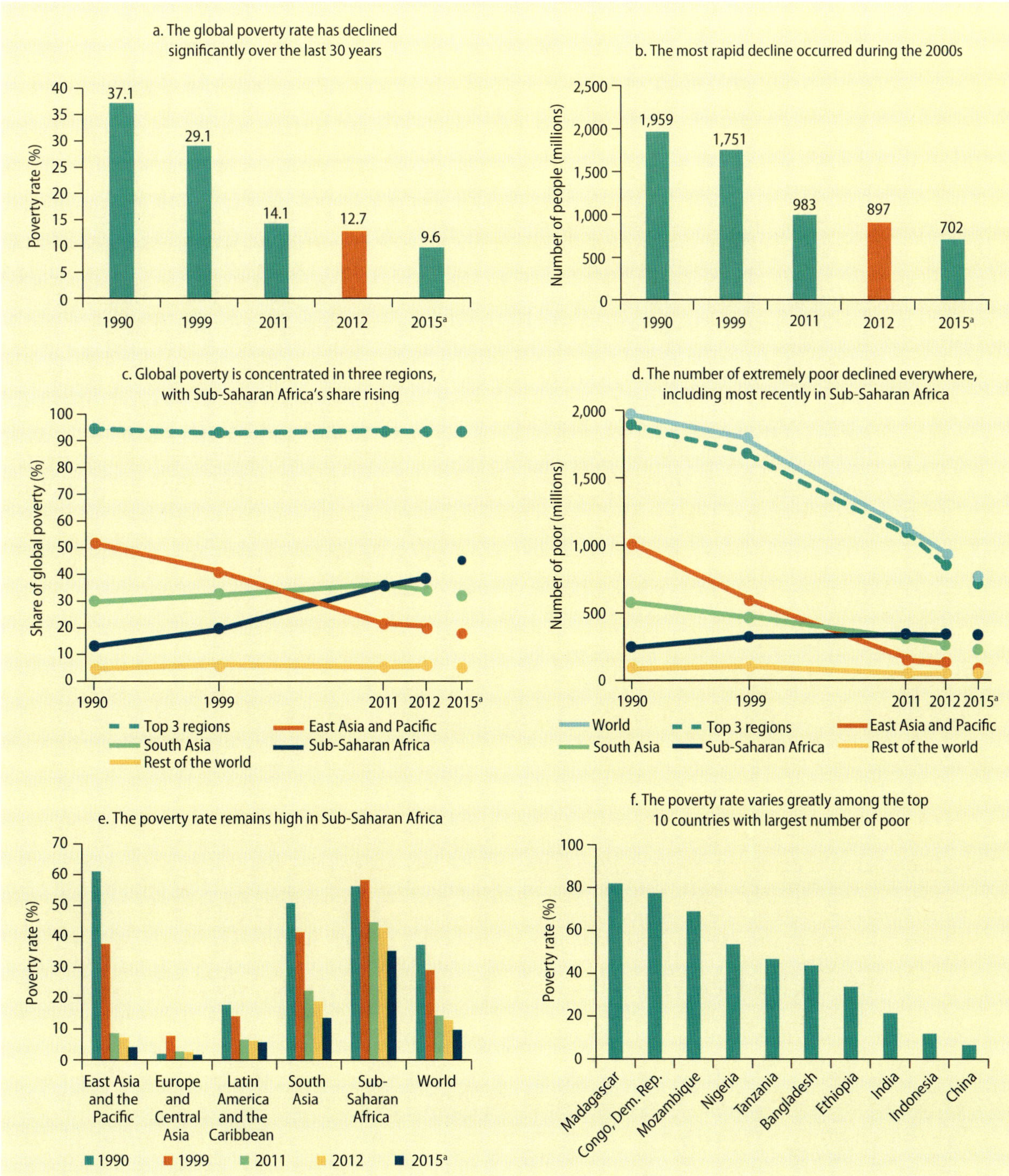

Source: PovcalNet 2015.

Note: Estimates based on the $1.90 poverty line and 2011 PPP prices. Panel f lists poverty rate as of the latest survey year, in parentheses: Bangladesh (2010); China (2012); Congo, Dem. Rep. (2012.4); Ethiopia (2010.5); India (2011/12); Indonesia (2012); Madagascar (2010); Mozambique (2008/09); Nigeria (2009.8); and Tanzania (2011.8). (The decimal points in parentheses refer to the proportion of the survey conducted in the following year.) Estimates for Bangladesh are based on the $1.25 poverty line and 2005 PPP prices.

a. Given the production lags for household surveys, 2012 is the latest year for which the World Bank is able to produce regional and global poverty estimates. All numbers for 2015 and beyond are statistical projections based on growth scenarios and distributional assumptions, and should be treated with considerable circumspection.

from 56.8 to 42.7 percent between 1990 and 2012 (figure 1.1e). South Asia achieved more rapid poverty reduction over the past 30 years, even though it is still home to about a third of the world's poor.

Despite significant geographic concentration, the poverty rate varies widely across the 10 countries with the greatest number of poor people. The estimates for 2012 indicate that these 10 countries account for almost 70 percent of global poverty. Yet their poverty rates (as of the latest household survey, that is, not necessarily 2012) vary from 6.5 percent in China to 81.8 percent in Madagascar (figure 1.1f). India was home to the largest number of poor in 2012, but its poverty rate is one of the lowest among those countries with the largest number of poor. A new methodology applied to household surveys in India suggests that its poverty rate could be even lower (box 1.2).

Even though the rate of extreme poverty is much higher in low-income countries, most of the global poor live in lower-middle-income countries. The poverty rate in low-income countries averaged 43 percent in 2012, compared with 19 percent in lower-middle-income countries. Yet lower-middle-income countries are home to about half of the global poor; another third live in low-income countries (figure 1.2a). Part of the reason is that four countries with the largest populations were once classified as low-income but have moved into the lower-middle-income category: China (reclassified in 1999), India (in 2007), and Indonesia and Nigeria (in 2011).[5]

The combined share of the world's poor living in natural resource–based (NRB) and fragile and conflict-affected countries in 2011 was about 50 percent. About 37 percent of the global poor lived in NRB economies, defined as countries where the share of

BOX 1.2 Why poverty in India could be even lower

Poverty measures for India are based on the household expenditure surveys done as part of the National Sample Surveys (NSS). Since the survey began in the 1950s, it has used 30-day recall for consumption of both food and nonfood items to measure expenditures. These so-called "uniform reference period" (URP) consumption aggregates collected in every consumption survey (except 1999/2000) provide the longest consistent series for measuring poverty in India. Historically, these have been the basis of the World Bank's poverty estimates for India at the international poverty line.

Since 2015 is the target year for the Millennium Development Goals, the assessment of changes in poverty over time is best based on the URP method, which was used to set the baseline poverty rates for India in 1990. As reported in this *Global Monitoring Report,* for 2011/12, India's poverty rate using URP-based consumption was 21.2 percent.

The National Sample Survey Organization introduced a new consumption series based on a "modified mixed reference period" (MMRP) in the 2009/10 survey. The MMRP series (which modified the 30-day recall to a 7-day recall for some food items and to a 1-year recall for low-frequency nonfood consumption items) was recommended as a more accurate reflection of consumption expenditures, following experimental rounds to examine nonsampling errors.[a] As a result of the shorter recall period for food items, MMRP-based consumption expenditures in both rural and urban areas are 10–12 percent larger than URP-based aggregates. These higher expenditures, combined with a high population density around the poverty line, translate to a significantly lower poverty rate of 12.4 percent for 2011/12.

The MMRP, which is available from 2009/10 onward, is expected to be the consumption aggregate of choice for monitoring poverty in the future. This year's MMRP-based estimate of 12.4 percent will set the baseline for future India and global poverty estimates, one consequence of which will be a break in the global series.

a. MMRP is a modified version of the mixed reference period, which has used two recall periods, 30 days for some items and 365 days for others; the NSS consumption surveys have used these two recall periods since the early 1990s.

FIGURE 1.2 Global poverty is concentrated in lower-middle-income countries and countries dependent on natural resources as well as fragile and conflict-affected states (FCS)

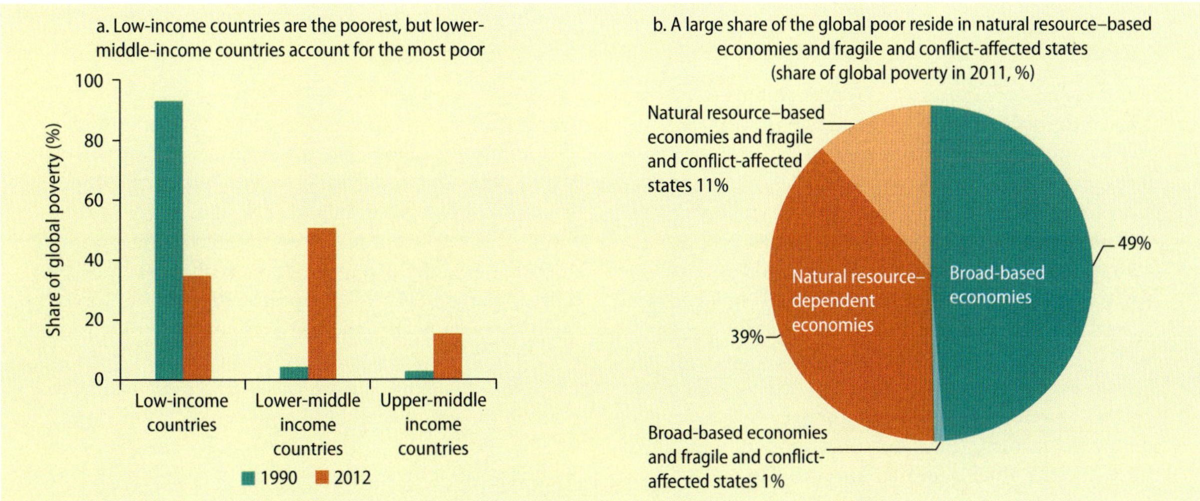

Sources: PovcalNet 2015; WITS 2014; and World Bank 2014 classification of fragile and conflict-affected states.
Note: Panel a is based on the World Bank income classification for the respective years using only countries for which household surveys are available. Panel b is based on the World Bank 2014 classification of fragile and conflict-affected states. In natural-resource-based economies, natural-resource exports account for more than 30 percent of total merchandise exports in 2011 (those with less than 30 percent are termed broad-based economies).

NRB exports such as coffee, wood, copper, and petroleum products was 30 percent or higher, and at least 12 percent of the global poor lived in countries classified by the World Bank as fragile and conflict-affected states.[6] Almost all fragile and conflict-affected countries were also NRB economies.

Accounting for poverty's depth and breadth

Are all extremely poor populations the same? No, conditions can vary significantly across extremely poor populations. The poor do not experience poverty as an "either-or" concept but as a continuum of intensities ranging from bad to far worse. This section captures these different intensities of poverty by looking into its depth and breadth.

Controlling for depth offers new perspectives

A new variety of poverty measures—person-equivalent headcounts—tallies the number of poor while controlling for depth (box 1.3). The new measures are closely related to poverty gap measures, but their numerical values have intuitive meanings as headcounts that control for the conditions of the poor. Traditional headcounts can mislead when conditions of the poor change significantly. Person-equivalent headcounts benchmark the initial conditions of the poor; this benchmark is then used as a measuring rod to count the number of standardized poor or person-equivalents (Castleman, Foster, and Smith 2015). A person who is twice as deeply poor as the standardized poor person is counted as two person-equivalents. Conversely, a person who is half as deeply poor would be counted as half a person-equivalent. The poverty headcount is then simply the sum of all person-equivalents.

As did the traditional poverty rate, the person-equivalent poverty rate fell significantly between 1990 and 2012, and much of this decline occurred during the 2000s (figure 1.3a). Benchmarked against the global average depth of poverty in 1990, the person-equivalent headcount declined by more than the traditional poverty headcount as the average depth of poverty also fell over this period (figure 1.3b). While the global numbers are

BOX 1.3 Person-equivalent poverty: An intuitive headcount measure that controls for depth

The traditional poverty headcount ratio is insensitive to the large variation in living standards among those living below the poverty line (Sen 1976). The headcount ratio can present distorted views of the spatial distribution of poverty and the extent of progress on reducing poverty. Two countries could record the same poverty headcount rate, where in one country poverty is shallow and in the other it is very deep, well below the poverty line. Similarly, a country may be successful in lifting its poorest citizens—the poorest of the poor—from abject poverty to a level just below the poverty line. Such improvement would not show up in a poverty headcount measure.

Accounting for depth of poverty ensures that poverty reduction efforts are targeted to those most deprived. With the global population around 9 billion by 2030, achievement of the global poverty target of 3 percent would leave an estimated 270 million people impoverished—including some of the most deeply deprived and difficult to reach. Just as worrying, relying solely on headcount measures may encourage policy makers to ignore the poorest of the poor and concentrate efforts on the richest of the poor to meet poverty targets (Bourguignon and Fields 1990). A focus is therefore needed not only on helping people to lift themselves out of poverty but also on the depth of deprivation of those left behind.

The poverty gap ratio is a widely available measure that captures depth. The ratio measures the extent to which individuals fall below the poverty line as a proportion of the poverty line. Aside from being regularly provided and updated, this ratio has desirable properties, such as focus (poverty is independent of the incomes of the nonpoor), monotonicity (other things equal, a decrease in a poor person's income increases the overall poverty level), and decomposability (overall poverty is linked to subgroup poverty levels).

However, for many, the poverty gap measure lacks the simplicity of a headcount and as a result is often dismissed from the policy discourse as too "unintuitive" to have traction. The traditional headcount ratio is easy to understand but is insensitive to the depth of poverty. The poverty gap ratio is sensitive to the depth of poverty but is more difficult to understand. Accordingly, the poverty gap ratio has not been a central element of poverty policy formulation, even though measures of the depth of poverty have quite clearly helped shape policies in especially rich countries (the U.S. food stamp program being one such example, where the benefit level is linked to income).

The person-equivalent approach remedies this problem, while retaining all the desirable features of the poverty gap measures. The person-equivalent approach has the core simplicity of a headcount and yet accounts for the varying conditions of the poor. The approach developed by Castleman, Foster, and Smith (2015) can be compared to measuring full-time equivalent jobs relative to the standard of the 40-hour workweek: those working 20 hours are counted as 0.5 of a full-time equivalent, whereas those working 60 hours would count as 1.5 full-time equivalents. Thus, if in the benchmark year the average depth of poverty is 40 cents, then a person with a shortfall of 20 cents relative to the poverty line is considered half a person-equivalent; conversely, a poor person with a gap of 60 cents is one-and-a-half person-equivalents. The person-equivalent headcount measure is obtained by adding all the person-equivalents across a population.

An appealing feature of the person-equivalent headcount is that it attributes higher weights to the deeply poor and thus redistributes poverty toward areas where poverty is at its deepest. If a deeply poor person were to escape poverty, the impact on the person-equivalent headcount would be larger than if a marginally poor person did. The same change would likewise have a bigger impact on the poverty gap index (also known as P1 or FGT1) than it would on the conventional poverty headcount ratio (or P0 in the FGT class).

by design the same in the benchmark year, by 2012 there were 743 million person-equivalent headcounts, some 17.1 percent less than the traditional headcount of 896.7 million. The same pattern holds for the poverty rate—the headcount as a ratio of total population. By 2012, the global person-equivalent poverty rate was 10.5 percent, some 2.2 percentage points lower than the traditional poverty rate.

As indicated by the "depth elasticity," the world registered different degrees of progress

FIGURE 1.3 Person-equivalent poverty headcount measures offer supplementary perspectives on the patterns and trends of global poverty across countries

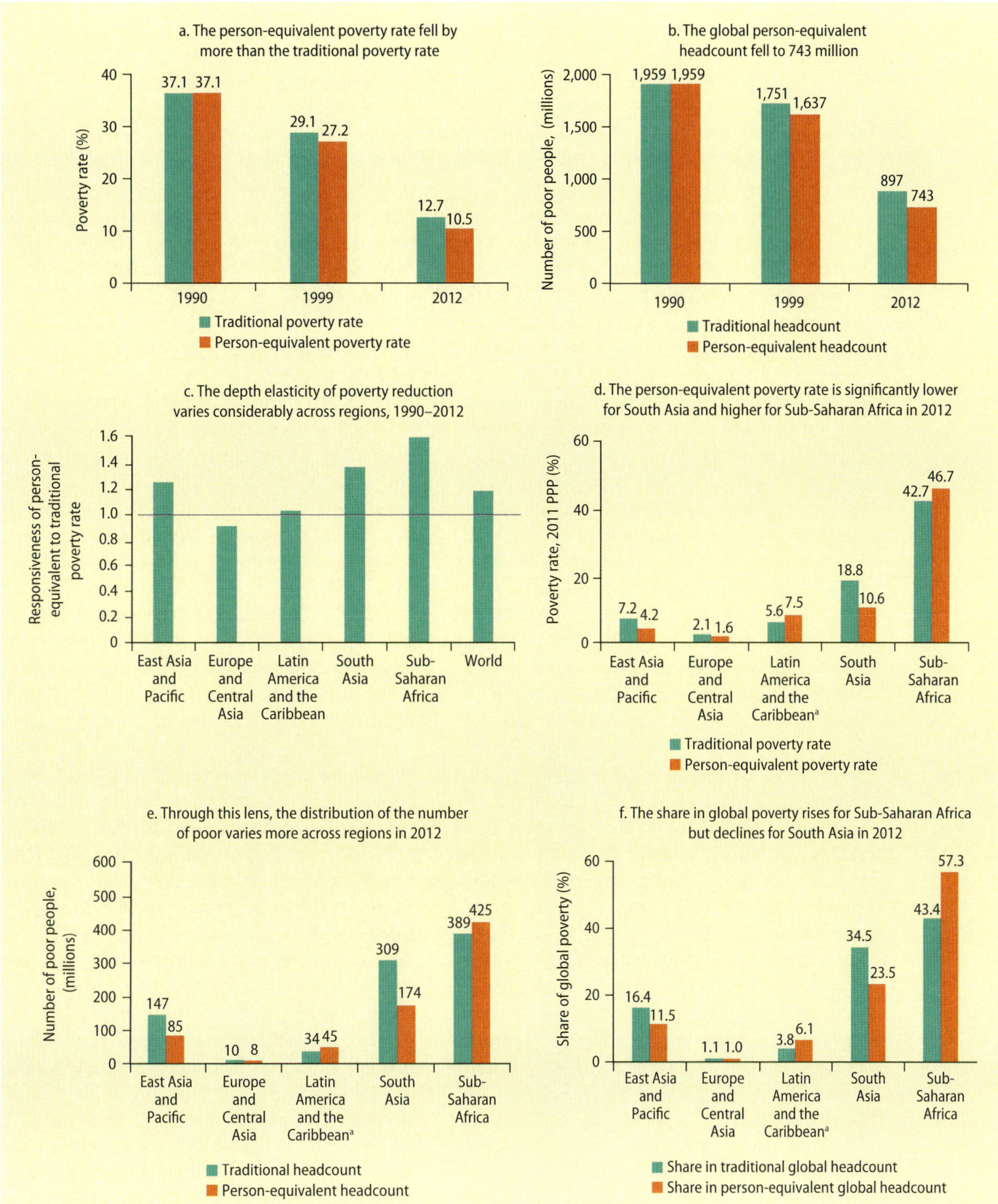

Sources: World Bank calculations and PovcalNet 2015.

Note: Estimates based on the $1.90 poverty line and 2011 PPP prices.

a. The increase in Latin America and the Caribbean reflects the sensitivity of the person-equivalent measure to the use of income-based (as opposed to consumption-based) poverty measures, which are prevalent within the region. See box 1.4 for more details.

in translating traditional poverty reduction into person-equivalent poverty reduction (figure 1.3c).[7] The depth elasticity measures the percentage point reduction in the person-equivalent headcount ratio as the result of a 1 percentage point reduction in the traditional headcount ratio. Globally, the depth elasticity between 1990 and 2012 was 1.2, suggesting that the reductions in traditional poverty rates were accompanied by even larger reductions in person-equivalent terms. The regional depth elasticities confirm that poverty reduction, especially in Sub-Saharan Africa, South Asia, and East Asia and Pacific, was accompanied by a much larger reduction in person-equivalent terms over this period. These findings reflect the good progress made over this longer period of time in reducing not only the number of poor but also the depth of poverty.

The person-equivalent lens sheds a different light on the geographical distribution of poverty as of 2012 (figure 1.3d, 1.3e, 1.3f). First, it suggests that, when accounting for depth, the person-equivalent poverty rate is much higher in Sub-Saharan Africa than the traditional poverty rate because the depth of poverty is large compared with other regions. South Asia's person-equivalent poverty rate is lower than its traditional poverty rate, suggesting that the depth of poverty is smaller relative to other parts of the world. The person-equivalent ratio in Latin American and the Caribbean is larger than the traditional headcount ratio, which is partially due to the prevalence of income-based household survey data in that region (box 1.4). Second, expressed as a share of global poverty, the geographical concentration of global poverty shifts further to Sub-Saharan Africa under the person-equivalent measure, with the region accounting for some 57.3 percent of global poverty, whereas the relative importance of both South Asia and East Asia and Pacific declines.

While these results provide insightful perspectives, they need to be interpreted with caution and complemented with additional analysis of observed patterns and trends. For example, greater poverty depth—and lower depth elasticity—may be linked to whether poverty is measured using income or consumption data (again, see box 1.4). The estimates for Latin America and the Caribbean, for example, are generally based on income data (see figure 1.3). Yet in the countries of the region where both income and consumption data are available, the incidence, depth, and severity of poverty are greater for income than for consumption expenditure. Income data are more susceptible to measurement error and temporary fluctuation. Moreover, poor households have an incentive to employ some form of saving mechanism to smooth income shocks.

Multidimensional assessments are complementary

Poverty is a multifaceted phenomenon. Central to this phenomenon are income deprivations that restrict an individual's ability to consume certain basic goods. Yet, poverty goes beyond income and is often accompanied by lack of access to education, health, housing, employment, personal security, and more (UNDP 1997; World Bank 2001). The association between the components of poverty when measured in all of its dimensions is generally strong given that the poor tend to be simultaneously deprived in multiple dimensions (Ferreira and Lugo 2013). However, the strength of association varies across space and time. As a result, a person may be considered nonpoor according to the traditional income-based measure despite being subject to multiple deprivations in other dimensions. If this person does not have access to the basic services or personal security that are an integral part of living without deprivations in basic human needs, can this person be considered to be free of poverty (Bourguignon et al. 2010)?

The goal of "ending poverty in all of its forms everywhere" is likely to lead to growing interest in the multidimensional measurement of global poverty. The SDG1.2 incorporates an explicitly multidimensional focus: "By 2030, reduce at least by half the proportion of men, women and children of all ages living in poverty in all its dimensions according to national definitions." The universal nature of the SDGs suggests that

BOX 1.4 Poverty in Latin America: Income-based versus consumption-based estimates

Poverty incidence and depth measured by income data are susceptible to upward bias compared with consumption data. First, income differs from consumption at a conceptual level, since income can be saved and consumption can be financed by borrowing. Second, income surveys often exclude household production, and households are sometimes reluctant to disclose income information to survey enumerators. Third, in developing countries, formal employment tends to be less common than in high-income countries, with households facing multiple and changing source of income (O'Donnell et al. 2008; Ravallion 2003; Székely et al. 2000).

Given the reliance in Latin America on income surveys, poverty numbers in this region are likely to be biased upward compared with the consumption alternative, as the case of Mexico confirms. To examine this discrepancy in consumption- and income-based poverty measures, Mexico's case is useful because the same survey collects both types of data. As figure B1.4.1a suggests, the use of income data raises the headcount ratio and the poverty gap and results in a more persistent pattern of poverty.

While the issue also affects traditional headcount ratios, the person-equivalent headcount ratios may be especially affected. Because they rely on the same primary data, person-equivalent incidence measures tend to be lower when based on consumption data—just like traditional incidence measures. However, because person-equivalent indicators take into account the depth of poverty, and poverty is typically deeper when using income-based measures, person-equivalent incidence measures may well amplify the difference. The example of Mexico is again instructive (figure B1.4.1b). If Mexico's person-equivalent rate were calculated based on income, it would be well above the traditional headcount ratio because the average gap among the poor is higher than the global average benchmark gap. However, if consumption data were used, Mexico's person-equivalent headcount ratio would be much lower than the traditional headcount ratio given that the average gap is much lower than the global benchmark gap.

FIGURE B1.4.1 Poverty measures can be sensitive to the source of data collection

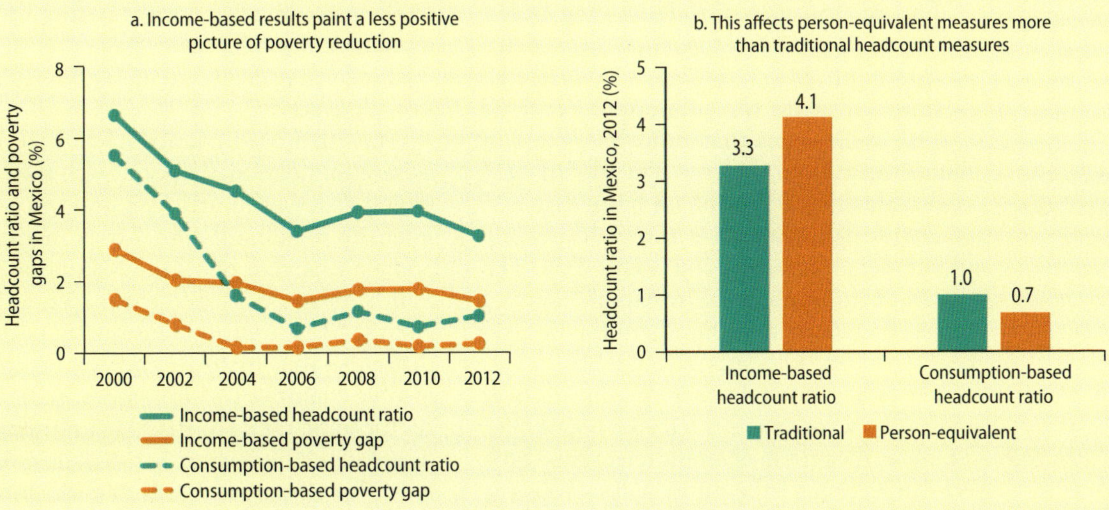

Sources: World Bank calculations and PovcalNet 2015.
Note: Estimates are based on the $1.25 poverty line and 2005 PPP prices.

as the post-2015 process unfolds, demand for harmonized multidimensional poverty assessments at the country and global levels is likely to rise. Several countries have already implemented variants of multidimensional poverty measures, including Bhutan, Chile, Colombia, Mexico, and the Philippines.

BOX 1.5 Multidimensional poverty measurement: *E pluribus unum*?

While poverty is widely accepted as a multidimensional phenomenon, there is no universal consensus on whether and how to aggregate multiple dimensions of poverty into a single welfare measure. A simple way to categorize the various approaches is by aggregating multiple measures into a single, scalar index or by laying out individual measures of each dimension to obtain a "dashboard" of separate vectors. The dashboard approach provides detailed information on the magnitudes of the constituent indicators and can readily draw on different data sources and different types of data. To the extent that dashboards avoid aggregation, they also avoid the difficult question of whether aggregation is best done in the space of "attainments" weighted by prices, or "deprivations" based on weights set by an analyst (Ravallion 2010, 2011; World Bank 2015a).[a] Yet dashboards are unable to establish hierarchies among various dimensions of poverty. Nor can dashboards reflect the joint distribution of various deprivations and thus measure the prevalence of individuals affected by deprivations in multiple dimensions at the same time. Dashboards also lack an identifiable poor population and a single headline figure that can be easily communicated and compared with income-based measures (Alkire and Foster 2011; Stiglitz, Sen, and Fitoussi 2009).

The salient feature of multidimensional poverty is the interdependence between dimensions. The dashboard approach tends to overlook this interdependence by examining deprivations separately. Other methodological approaches that capture interdependency—such as the simple Venn of overlap of deprivations across dimensions, multivariate stochastic dominance analysis, and the analysis of copula functions—may therefore complement the dashboard approach. Scalar multidimensional indexes allow for a complete ordering, with the ability to rank two years, countries, or regions, but need to deal with the increased complexity at the identification and aggregation steps.

Note: E pluribus unum is Latin for "out of many, one."

a. Establishing weights is fundamentally difficult; for related discussions, see Alkire, Foster, et al. 2015.

The Multidimensional Poverty Index (MPI) is one possible implementation of this approach (boxes 1.5 and 1.6).[8] MPI decompositions identify the subnational regions and the dimensions that contribute most to multidimensional poverty. The global MPI is available for 101 countries but is also calculated for 884 subnational regions, mostly in Sub-Saharan Africa and South Asia. The decomposition analysis reveals pockets of poverty that national numbers might conceal. Country and subnational MPI levels can be broken down further into dimensional indicators whose profiles vary by region. For example, the profile of multidimensional poverty in Salamat—the poorest region in the world in southeast Chad—is different from that of Moyen Chari, a neighboring region; in particular, educational deprivations are much larger in Salamat than in Moyen Chari. Other regions that have lower MPIs than Salamat have higher individual components in their profile. Breaking down poverty by dimension provides policy makers with localized information for reducing multidimensional poverty.

The 2015 MPI counts 1.6 billion people as multidimensionally poor, with the largest global share in South Asia and the highest intensity in Sub-Saharan Africa (figure 1.4). Some 54 percent of all the MPI poor live in South Asia and 31 percent in Sub-Saharan Africa. Most multidimensionally poor—70 percent—live in low- and lower-middle-income countries (Alkire, Jindra, et al. 2015). As for monetary poverty, MPI poverty incidence is the highest in Sub-Saharan Africa. It is also the most intense as measured by the multiplicity of deprivations. South Asia follows second. While the MPI headcount is much lower in other regions, the breadth of deprivation among the multidimensionally poor is only slightly lower than that found in those two regions. Multidimensional poverty

BOX 1.6 The Multidimensional Poverty Index: An example

The Multidimensional Poverty Index (MPI) is an adjusted headcount indicator that measures the incidence and breadth of those who are deprived in multiple dimensions (table B1.6). The approach begins with a specification of the dimensions and indicators upon which poverty will be based. The MPI identifies 3 dimensions: health, education, and standard of living. These dimensions are measured using 10 indicators: child mortality and nutrition (for health); years of schooling and school attendance (for education); and cooking fuel, toilet, water, electricity, floor, and assets (for living standards). Each dimension and each indicator within a dimension is equally weighted. For each of the indicators a deprivation cutoff is set: For example, for years of schooling, deprivation amounts to no household member having completed five years of schooling, whereas for electricity, deprivation means having no access to electricity. A person is considered poor if he or she is deprived in at least a third of the weighted indicators. The multidimensional headcount ratio measures the incidence of multidimensional poverty by comparing the number of all those that are multidimensionally poor to the total population. The intensity of poverty denotes the proportion of indicators in which they are deprived. The adjusted headcount ratio is obtained by the product of the multidimensional headcount ratio and the average intensity of poverty.

The metric provides a complement to poverty measures based on income and traditional dashboards in monitoring and directing policies toward the poor. It directly measures the nature and magnitude of overlapping deprivations in health, education, and living standards at the household level. With the adjusted headcount ratio, overall poverty is directly linked to the poverty levels of population subgroups, a decomposition property it shares with traditional monetary poverty indexes. This permits the construction of poverty profiles and can help in locating the poor. The multidimensional poverty measure can also be broken down into a dashboard of indicators, one for each dimension, to reveal the components of poverty and help guide policy priorities. In this way, the adjusted headcount ratio and its dimensional indicators form a coordinated dashboard for policy analysis with a headline number for monitoring and communication purposes and dimensional indicators for deeper analysis (Alkire, Foster, et al. 2015).

TABLE B1.6 Illustration of MPI calculation across three persons

Dimension	Indicator	Weight	Person A (%)	Person B (%)	Person C (%)
Education	Years of schooling less than five?	1/6	0	0	0
	Not attending school up to class 8?	1/6	0	0	0
Health	Any child has died in the family?	1/6	100	100	0
	Anyone malnourished?	1/6	0	100	0
Living standards	No electricity?	1/18	0	100	0
	Sanitation facility not improved? Improved but shared with others?	1/18	0	100	0
	No or difficult access to safe drinking water?	1/18	0	0	100
	Dirt, sand or dung floor?	1/18	100	100	100
	Cooking with dung, wood or charcoal?	1/18	100	0	100
	Own no more than one of the following assets—radio, TV, phone, bike, motorcycle or fridge—and does not own a car or truck?	1/18	100	0	100
Weighted deprivation score			33	50	22
Status: Poor if intensity ≥ 33%			Poor	Poor	Not poor
Headcount ratio of MPI poor (H)		2/3 = 66%			
Average intensity among the poor (A)		(33% + 50%) / 2 = 41%			
MPI index (H x A)		66% x 41% = 27%			

Source: GMR team elaboration.

FIGURE 1.4 The Multidimensional Poverty Index (MPI) provides a complementary perspective to the poverty headcount

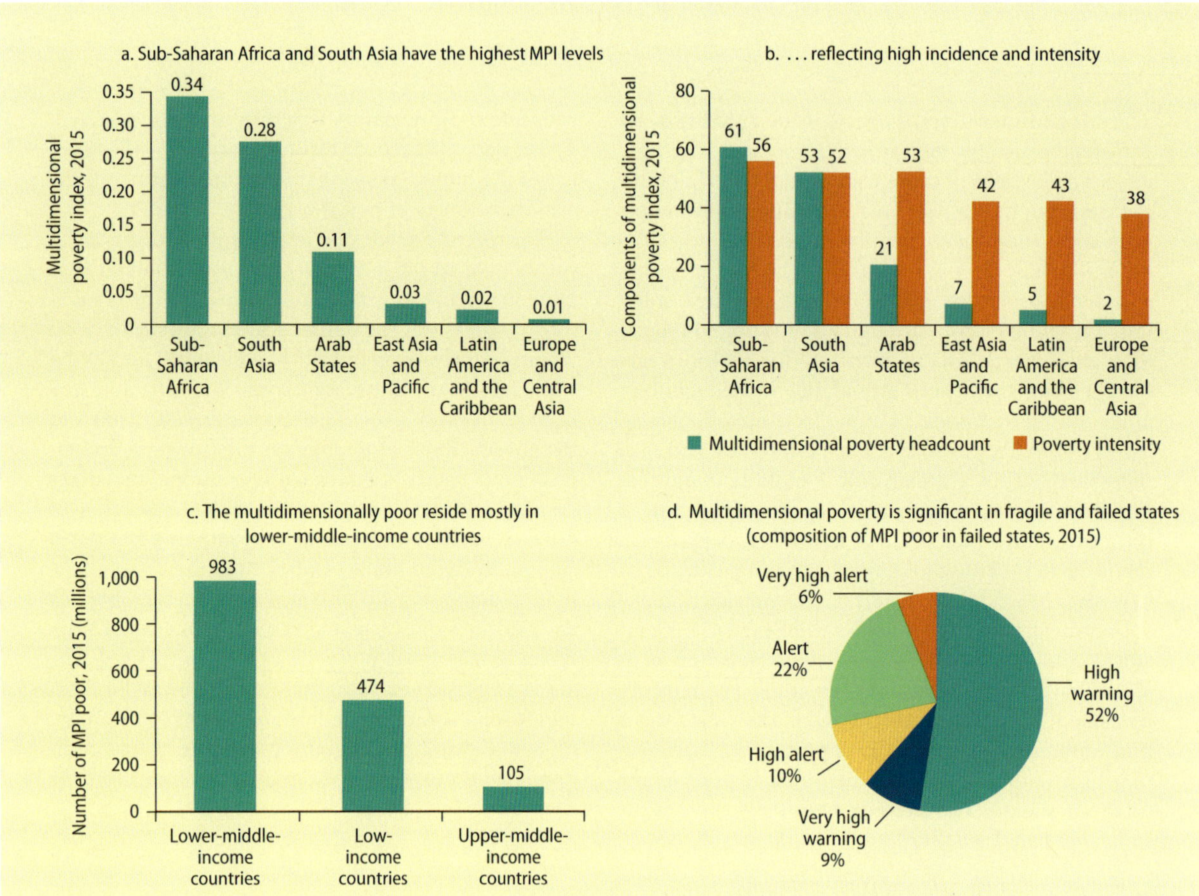

Source: Alkire, Jindra, et al. 2015.
Note: Panel d is based on the Failed States Index (FSI) provided by the Fund for Peace. The index uses several social economic and political indicators to classify countries from "Very High Alert" (most-fragile states) to "sustainable" (less-fragile states). The less-fragile countries in this figure are classified as "high warning."

is significant among those living in fragile states. Just as in the case of income poverty, multidimensional poverty is most intense in fragile and conflict-affected states, with the extent of poverty varying with the intensity of fragility and conflict. The vast majority of these countries are located in Sub-Saharan Africa and South Asia.

At the individual country level, the country with the highest rate of multidimensional poverty is Niger. Niger also has very high fertility levels, as discussed in part 2. The country-level patterns of monetary and multidimensional poverty may deviate significantly from each other. For example, in Zambia, the multidimensional poverty rate as measured by the MPI was 57 percent in 2013–14, whereas the income-based poverty rate was 74 percent in 2010. For Pakistan the opposite was true, with the multidimensional poverty rate in 2013–14 of 44 percent, while the income-based poverty rate in 2010 was 13 percent. Both comparisons indicate significant differences in the poor populations identified by the two methods. Turning from international measures to national measures, Chile has two official poverty measures: an income-based measure and a

FIGURE 1.5 A multidimensional lens suggests slower poverty reduction progress in India

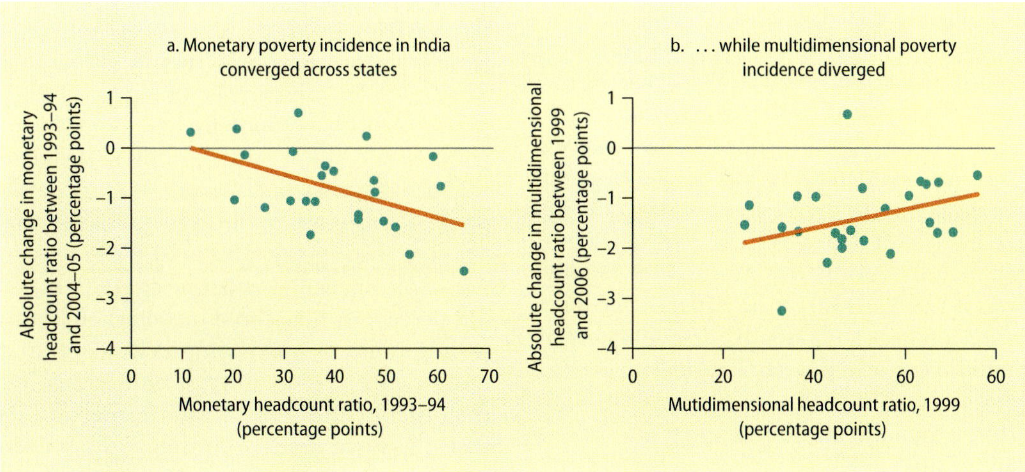

Source: Alkire and Seth 2013.

multidimensional measure. The poverty rates associated with the two in 2013 were 14.4 percent (income) and 20.4 percent (multidimensional); however, the share of the entire population that is poor under both definitions is just 5.5 percent.

Decomposition of the MPI into the subnational level and its component indicators may shed light on patterns of intense deprivation. As noted, the poorest subnational region in the world is Salamat in southeast Chad. Nearly 98 percent of its 354,000 inhabitants are MPI poor, and, on average, they are deprived in nearly 75 percent of the MPI dimensions, ensuring that Salamat also is the region with the greatest breadth of poverty. Three of the five poorest subnational regions in the world are in Chad while two are in Burkina Faso. The profile of multidimensional poverty may also reveal intense poverty in certain dimensions. Of the 884 regions, the region with the highest dimensional indicator for nutrition is Affar in Ethiopia; for child mortality it is Nord-Ouest in Côte d'Ivoire; and for sanitation, electricity, and assets it is Warap in South Sudan. Yet Salamat, which has high rates of deprivation in many dimensions at the same time, is the poorest by the MPI.

Multidimensional poverty measures may provide useful complementary perspectives on the dynamics of poverty over time. India, for example, exhibits a marked difference across its various states between the behaviors of the income-based and multidimensional poverty rates through time. Figures 1.5a and 1.5b plot the annualized absolute change in the poverty rate over a period of time against the initial value, for a multidimensional poverty measure and an income-based approach. The line in each graph is the linear regression of the annualized absolute change on the starting level. Clearly, the income poverty rates across states in India exhibit a classical converging pattern, where the reduction in the income-based poverty rate is higher in the states with the higher initial poverty values. For multidimensional poverty, the opposite is true: the states with low multidimensional poverty are making greater progress, whereas those with the highest poverty rates are lagging behind. These examples suggest a need to monitor multidimensional poverty directly.

Aspiring to end poverty by 2030

In light of the progress made and the challenges remaining, what does the future of poverty reduction look like? As argued below, the 2030 target is aspirational, and attaining it will require fortuitous circumstances. Moreover, contextual factors arising from the changing nature of the poverty that remains are likely to make poverty reduction more challenging than it was in the past. Finally, even if the 2030 target of 3 percent poverty is met on average globally, deep pockets of multidimensional poverty are likely to persist.

While attainable, the 2030 target is aspirational

Although most regions continue to reduce poverty, meeting the global poverty target by 2030 remains aspirational in all but the most optimistic of scenarios. Poverty scenarios depend on the assumptions on the pace and incidence of per capita household income (or consumption) growth over the next 15 years (World Bank 2015c). For example, one could assume that income growth will follow that of the 2000s, which was an extraordinary period of income growth for developing countries. If one adopts the optimistic scenario that per capita income growth in every developing country meets the developing-country average during the 2000s (4.4 percent in per capita national account aggregates, or 3.9 percent in household incomes), and also assumes that the distribution of income and cross-country inequality remain constant, then the 3 percent headcount target can be met (the third scenario in figure 1.6). Even so, poverty in Sub-Saharan Africa would still remain at 14.4 percent.

FIGURE 1.6 World poverty scenarios suggest that the poverty target is aspirational but attainable

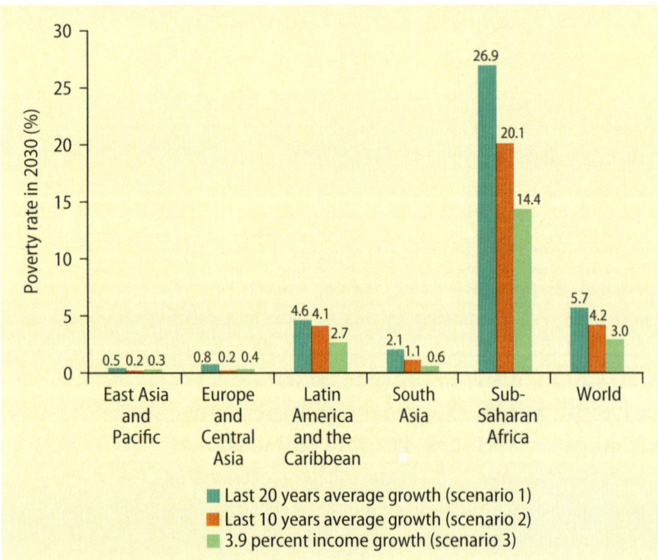

Source: World Bank calculations.
Note: Based on $1.90 poverty line (2011 PPP prices). The first scenario assumes that each country grows at the country-specific average growth rate observed over 1994–2013. The second scenario assumes that each country grows at the country-specific average growth rate observed over 2004–13. The third scenario assumes that each country grows at 4.4 percent a year (national accounts) or 3.9 percent (household incomes). That is a scenario under which the 3 percent target for the Bank's poverty reduction goal would be reached by 2030. Since per capita private consumption is missing for many countries, especially in Africa, per capita GDP growth rates are used for all countries instead. As in all previous cases, the within-country distribution neutrality assumption is used.

More pessimistic scenarios suggest that global poverty will continue to be a challenge in 2030, both globally and in specific countries. One cannot take for granted that the rapid growth rates of the 2000s will be repeated for the next decade and a half for all countries simultaneously. If developing countries realize the same country-specific per capita growth rates as observed during the 10-year period 2004–13, the global 3 percent poverty target would be missed, and poverty in Sub-Saharan Africa would remain high at 20.1 percent (the second scenario in figure 1.6). Moreover, if incomes were to rise at the average growth rate observed at the country level over the 20-year period 1994–2013, the incidence of global poverty in 2030 would be 5.7 percent (the first scenario in figure 1.6). South Asia would reduce its poverty rate to 2.1 percent, but Sub-Saharan Africa's would still stand at 26.9 percent.

The pursuit of shared prosperity can increase the chance of meeting the 3 percent poverty goal. This point is developed later in the chapter, but for now it suffices to highlight that the simulations shown in figure 1.6 assume distributionally neutral growth. If, however, the poor, or the B40 including the poor, were to experience income growth that was systematically higher than the mean income growth for the total population, then the poverty target would be more easily achieved. Simulations by Lakner, Negre, and Prydz (2014) show that if average economic growth rates are extrapolated from the early 2000s, the extreme poverty target would not be met unless the growth rate among the B40 is at least 2 percentage points higher than the mean.

Poverty reduction will meet new challenges

A further challenge is the possibility that future growth may not reach the poor as readily as in the past. As noted, global poverty fell by about 1 percentage point a year in response to the average annual GDP growth rate of 4 percent. Even if the growth rate still averaged 4 percent from now to 2030, would poverty continue to fall by 1 percentage point a year? The distributional pattern of household income and consumption puts a relatively high proportion of the population near the median income or consumption value, with small proportions at extremely high or low values (Battistin, Blundell, and Lewbel 2009). Thus, when the global poverty rate was 37.1 percent in 1990, at the start of the Millennium Development Goals, many poor people were just below the poverty line, leading to a large percentage point reduction in poverty for a given distribution-neutral increase in GDP. With global poverty incidence at 12.7 percent in 2012, the same distribution-neutral increase in GDP will lead to less poverty reduction. Poverty's responsiveness to distribution-neutral growth will continue to decline as the 3 percent target is approached (World Bank 2015c). In short, as the 3 percent target gets nearer, higher rates of income growth will be needed, and the distribution of that growth will need to be more favorable to those with the lowest incomes.

Ending poverty is also complicated by the structural characteristics of the most impoverished nations, particularly those in Sub-Saharan Africa. Taking into account their demographic dynamics, by 2030 a larger share of the world's impoverished will reside in NRB economies and fragile and conflict-affected states, primarily in Sub-Saharan Africa. Poverty is less responsive to growth in such economies because the availability of jobs—the main channel through which growth uplifts the poor—is limited (IMF 2014b; Inchauste and Saavedra-Chanduvi 2014; Inchauste et al. 2014; Loayza and Raddatz 2010; World Bank 1990). Capital-intensive, natural-resource sectors may generate growth but are likely to have weak backward and forward links with the rest of the economy, even during commodity boom periods. In the fragile and conflict-affected states (which include several NRB countries), the poverty problem is even more complex. Conflicts, whether they arise because of contested natural resource wealth or are politically motivated, inevitably disrupt or even reverse growth. The impact of conflict is often felt long after peace is restored.

Continued poverty reduction will require incorporating natural resources and natural capital in economic decision making. Land degradation and poverty are often deeply intertwined, with an estimated 42 percent of the world's poorest living on land that is classified as degraded (Nachtergaele et al. 2010). About 1.3 billion people are reliant on forests, and the majority of these are extremely poor. Their level of dependence on forests is surprisingly large and often equal in magnitude to income obtained from agriculture (Angelsen et al. 2014; Shepherd, Kazoora, and Müller 2013). In addition, 1 billion people in developing countries depend upon fish as their primary source of affordable protein. The rural poor often endure a litany of environmental health risks too. Illness, disability, and early death from environmental risks, such as household air pollution from wood burning in primitive stoves, remain a major cause of child mortality in the developing world, followed by inadequate sanitation.

Climate change may become another important drag on poverty reduction in many countries (Field 2014; Hertel and Rosch 2010; Leichenko and Silva 2014; Skoufias, Rabassa, and Olivieri 2012). Global estimates suggest that climate change could account for 10.1 million additional poor by mid-century in the absence of comprehensive and successful greenhouse gas emissions abatement. The size and incidence of the impact of climate change on a given country depends on country-specific factors related to its exposure to climate shocks and the country's ability to adapt (Füssel and Klein 2006; Yohe and Tol 2009). Generally, the poor in developing countries are disproportionally affected. One reason is that the poor have less access to resources and savings to absorb the impact of shocks, whether they come from climate change or from political, economic, or financial instability. Climate change may have a greater impact on the poor relative to other types of shocks because the poor tend to be more dependent on agriculture and have more perilous access to water (World Bank 2012).

Deep pockets of dimensionally broad poverty will likely remain

Even if the aggregate 3 percent poverty target is reached, the distribution of poverty reduction within countries will be uneven, and deep pockets of impoverishment will remain. Just as poverty reduction occurs at vastly different rates across countries and global regions, poverty reduction within countries is normally a spatially uneven process. Deep pockets of poverty can persist even in countries that, at the aggregate level, are experiencing rapid poverty reduction. Country-level poverty assessments regularly identify specific areas or groups of people with particular characteristics experiencing higher-than-average probabilities of being poor. They may be locked in poverty traps or other low-level equilibriums in which aggregate economic growth does not translate into employment income or transfers for them. These groups may be defined by education, ethnicity, or region of residence. In particular, there is evidence that pockets of poverty cluster geographically in rural areas that are poorly connected to urban centers of growth, where the poor may become trapped in low-productivity jobs (Kraay and McKenzie 2014). For example, although China's rate of poverty reduction has been rapid, poverty is higher in rural areas where the productivity of farmers' investments is lower (Jalan and Ravallion 2001).

Shared prosperity: Conceptual issues and recent trends

The second of the World Bank Group goals articulates the commitment to promote "shared prosperity," defined as seeking to sustainably raise the well-being of the poorer segments of society. The goal reflects a practical compromise between the single-minded pursuit of prosperity in the aggregate and an equity concern about the ability of the less well-off in society to improve their well-being by participating in a country's prosperity. The goal thus gives more explicit attention to inclusive development and growth than has been the case in the past and paves the way for a focus on inequality. The goal is measured by the pace of real income or consumption growth at the household level, on average and over time, for the B40 of the income distribution in each country.[9]

This section sheds further light on the concept of shared prosperity and examines its recent trends. It explores in some depth conceptual questions relating to the goal and indicator of shared prosperity. Specifically, it examines the connections between shared prosperity and non-income dimensions of well-being, links with equity ("justness"), and connections to equality ("the state of being equal"). Second, it analyzes recent trends in shared prosperity, underlying drivers, and continuing disparities, and assesses whether recent trends can be sustained.

Revisiting the concept of shared prosperity

What is shared prosperity? While the shared prosperity concept is not new, the effort to promote it through the B40 indicator has raised interest in how the goal of shared prosperity should be interpreted.[10] The concept of shared prosperity, with its focus on the B40, has been around at least as long as the early use of the term by the economist Simon Kuznets in discussions on growth and inequality (Kuznets 1955) and its invocation by World Bank president Robert S. McNamara in 1972 (box 1.7).[11] However, the approach of seeking to raise the average

BOX 1.7 Back to "Basics": McNamara's prescient 1972 speech on shared prosperity

At the Annual Meetings in Nairobi in September 1972, World Bank President Robert S. McNamara addressed the Board of Governors with a speech that linked the growth imperative to social justice. The speech demarcated the so-called basic needs approach. It contained various references—some of them little-known at the time—to the concept of "shared prosperity" that the World Bank Group would institute as one of its corporate objectives some four decades later. The interpretations that he offered remain pertinent today and offer apt perspectives on how shared prosperity relates to social equity, social sustainability, inequality, and multidimensionality.

- *Social equity and social sustainability.* "We know, in effect, that there is no rational alternative to moving toward policies of greater social equity. When the highly privileged are few and the desperately poor are many—and when the gap between them is worsening rather than improving—it is only a question of time before a decisive choice must be made between the political costs of reform and the political risks of rebellion. That is why policies specifically designed to reduce the deprivation among the poorest 40 percent in developing countries are prescriptions not only of principle but of prudence. Social justice is not merely a moral imperative. It is a political imperative as well."
- *Income inequality.* "The first step should be to establish specific targets, within the development plans of individual countries, for income growth among the poorest 40 percent of the population. I suggest that our goal should be to increase the income of the poorest sections of society in the short run—in five years—at least as fast as the national average. In the longer run—ten years—the goal should be to increase this growth significantly faster than the national average."
- *Multidimensionality.* "The task, then, for the governments of the developing countries is to reorient their development policies in order to attack directly the personal poverty of the most deprived 40 percent of their populations. This the governments can do without abandoning their goals of vigorous overall economic growth. But they must be prepared to give greater priority to establishing growth targets in terms of essential human needs: in terms of nutrition, housing, health, literacy, and employment—even if it be at the cost of some reduction in the pace of advance in certain narrow and highly privileged sectors whose benefits accrue to the few."

income growth of the B40 in *absolute terms* has raised interest in the role of non-income dimensions and the connections of the concept with equity and equality.

Shared prosperity means multidimensional development

The shared prosperity goal recognizes that the pursuit of well-being among the most vulnerable in a society is a key development objective. Thus, while the average income growth among the B40 has become the agreed-upon indicator of shared prosperity, the goal itself is much broader in that it aspires to sustainably elevate the well-being of the poorer segments of society. Embedded in the goal, therefore, are both intertemporal and multidimensional objectives: shared prosperity requires well-being to be shared across individuals over time. This multidimensional aspect of the goal points to the need for a focus on non-income dimensions of prosperity such as education, health, nutrition, and access to essential infrastructure, as well as on enhancing the voice and participation of all segments of society in the economic, social, and political spheres (World Bank 2013b).

The broad focus of the shared prosperity goal is in keeping with the call for development goals that go beyond access to or ownership of material goods. Amartya Sen (1983, 1985, 1999)—a key proponent—has called for income to be viewed not as the sole end to development but rather as a gauge of what a person is able to do (capability) and manages to do (functioning). This broader perspective of development has been influential in the literature on broad-based growth and has led first to efforts to measure the non-income dimensions of development and then to work on inclusive growth that examines how growth trickles down to the poor. That work, in turn, has led, through the introduction of multidimensionality, to the notion of "inclusive development."[12]

While the chosen indicator of shared prosperity is an income-based metric, the non-income dimensions of the shared prosperity goal are important (Narayan, Saavedra-Chanduvi, and Tiwari 2013). The use of a relatively simple indicator—growth in the real value of income or consumption (depending on the methodology of the household surveys on which the concept is based) for the B40—does not mean that non-income aspects of well-being should be disregarded.[13] The B40 income-based indicator is a first step toward making a critical point: growth in an economy should not be assumed to mean that development progress is automatically occurring. It is also necessary for this growth to reach the less well-off in society. Beyond that, however, development progress should be assessed in all of its dimensions. The second step, therefore, is to consider explicitly how, given their synergies, the income and non-income aspects of shared prosperity feed into each other and together can produce greater well-being for the poorer segments of society.[14]

Equality of opportunity underpins shared prosperity

Equity is a fundamental building block of shared prosperity. As Mahatma Gandhi famously noted, "A nation's greatness is measured by how it treats its weakest members." Yet, as societal preferences have evolved and moral philosophies have changed, concerns about the less well-off have varied. For example, Bentham's utilitarian preference for the "greatest happiness for the greatest number," first published in the 1780s, is devoid of any distributional concern, while Rawls's principle of maximizing opportunity for the "least privileged," published nearly 200 years later, takes a radically opposite view (Bentham [1789] 2000; Rawls 1971). The World Bank Group's institutional objective of promoting shared prosperity targets the B40 as an anonymous group irrespective of the identity of its members.[15] This strong focus on the less privileged places equity at the very heart of the goal and the indicator of shared prosperity.[16]

Underpinned by equity, the shared prosperity concept is intricately related to the inequality of opportunity. World Bank (2013b) highlights that even though the shared prosperity indicator is focused on outcomes, the requirement to pursue shared prosperity in a socially sustainable fashion ties the concept to the promotion of equality of opportunity. This focus is also present in modern theories of social equity, which, like Rawls's, build on Harsanyi's (1955) "veil of ignorance argument": an equitable resource allocation should reflect what all prospective members of society would agree on before they knew which position they would occupy in that society. Accordingly, while modern theories of equity remain concerned that individuals be spared from extreme deprivation in *outcomes*, they emphasize the importance of ensuring equal *opportunities* for individuals to pursue a life of their choosing.[17] The outcome of a person's life, in its many dimensions, should reflect efforts and talents, and not predetermined circumstances—such as family origins, race, gender, or place of birth—or the social groups a person is born into.

In and of itself, however, the shared prosperity goal is not aimed at reducing the inequality of outcome. Considerable heterogeneity exists in the opinions of individuals about whether inequality is good or bad and should be reduced or not. The most recent wave of the World Value Survey illustrates the degree of polarization in views around the world and also how the preference for inequality gradually rises across the income distribution, with large differences across regions (figure 1.7). Reflecting these differences of views, the shared prosperity concept does not directly link to outcome inequality. Positive B40 income growth may, for example, be avoided with rising inequality,

FIGURE 1.7 Views of income inequality vary across regions and income deciles

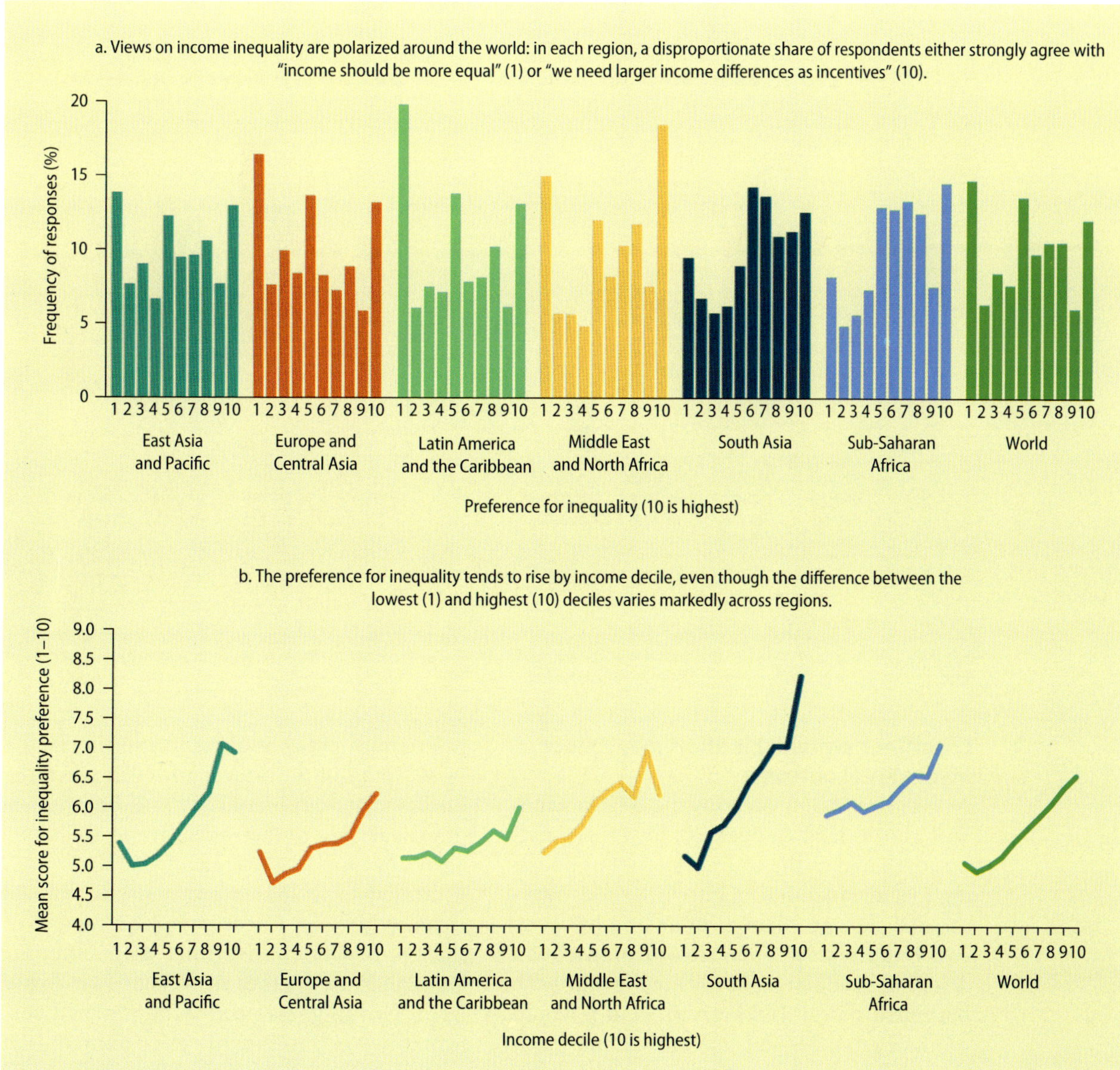

Source: World Bank calculations, based on World Value Survey.
Note: Calculations are based on data for the 2010–14 "wave." Preference for inequality ranges from agreement with (1), "Income should be more equal," to agreement with (10), "We need larger income differences as incentives." The survey question, "whether income should be made more equal or we need larger income differences as incentives for individual effort," was asked to surveyors from 60 countries.

both within the B40 and between groups. First, inequality may rise within the B40 by virtue of the mean indicator, in which positive growth may occur at the expense of the poorest.[18] Second, absolute income growth of the B40 is neither necessary nor sufficient for lower inequality between the B40 and other income groups. Negative B40 income growth could lower inequality if T60 growth does even worse, but positive B40 income growth might not prevent a rise in inequality if T60 growth does even better.

FIGURE 1.8 While inequality may still rise, a consistent focus on B40 income growth will always (weakly) lower inequality relative to the counterfactual of focusing on average income growth

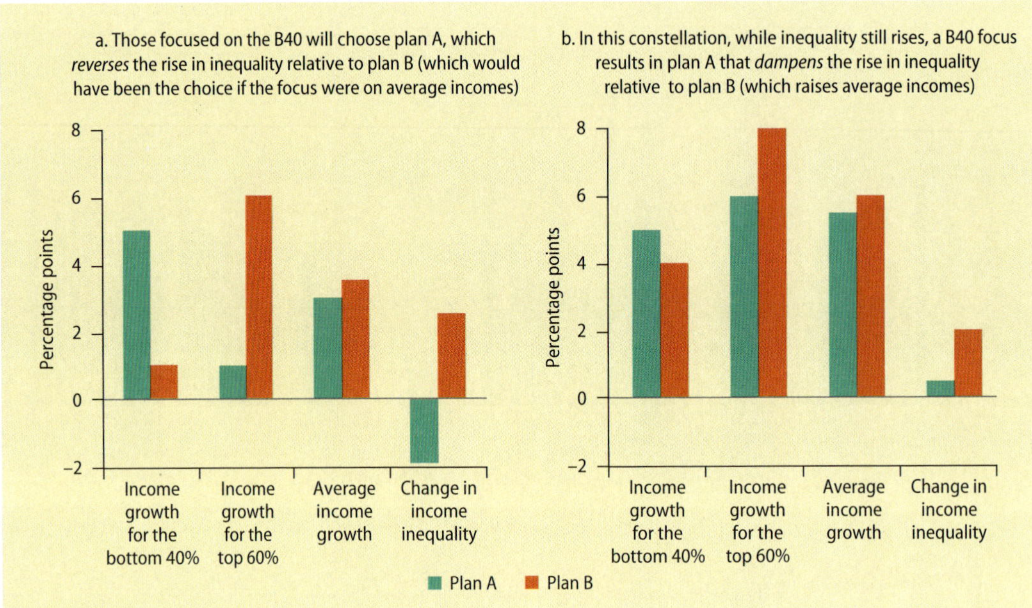

Source: GMR team elaboration.
Note: The example illustrates the choice between two illustrative "plans" of alternative growth rates for the B40 and T60 (the first two indicators). Derived from these are the average income growth rate (third indicator) and the difference between average and B40 income growth (fourth indicator), which is the opposite of the shared prosperity premium, and a measure of inequality.

Consistent, sustainable effort may reduce inequality of outcome

A *consistent* focus on boosting B40 incomes will always lead to (weakly) lower inequality compared to the counterfactual of boosting average incomes. Figure 1.8a illustrates the decision problem of choosing between two hypothetical scenarios or plans. Plan A would produce rapid B40 income growth but much slower T60 growth. Plan B would produce rapid T60 income growth but much slower B40 growth. A policy maker who maximizes B40 incomes between these two choices will choose plan A,[19] whereas a policy maker focused on maximizing average income growth will choose plan B. Clearly, a B40 focus in this case helps *reverse* the rise in inequality relative to the counterfactual of maximizing average income growth. Figure 1.8b illustrates a similar decision problem with different parameter values, showing that a B40 focus helps *dampen* the rise in inequality relative to the counterfactual. Other examples can be construed that do not entail a growth-inequality trade-off and where both policy makers would choose the same. In all of the above, however, when the B40 is targeted, inequality will be lower—or at least not higher—relative to the alternative of pursuing average growth.

Moreover, if shared prosperity is pursued sustainably—an underlying requirement of the goal—the connections with outcome inequality are further tightened. The World Bank Group goals need to be pursued sustainably—economically, environmentally, and socially—over time and across generations. The sustainability requirement imposes additional feasibility constraints on the socioeconomic strategies that policy makers may select as they pursue shared prosperity. Economically, strategies that lead to the sustained underperformance of the B40 may eventually stifle the economy-wide growth process (Berg, Ostry, and Zettelmeyer 2012; Easterly 2007). No country has transitioned beyond middle-income status while maintaining high levels of inequality (World Bank 2013b). Environmentally, if the B40 bears a disproportionate share of the cost of environmental degradation and pollution, a more environmentally sustainable growth model may strengthen the group's capacity to participate in society's prosperity. Socially, a continued rise in the gap between rich and poor may be socially unsustainable and incompatible with social equity in the longer term. All of these additional constraints impinge on the choice of optimal socioeconomic policies, which may result in outcomes of lower inequality.

Assessing trends in shared prosperity

What are the recent trends in shared prosperity? While overall trends in B40 income growth appear generally positive, the heterogeneity and sustainability of these trends are a concern. Data availability and quality remain key challenges. However, the data consistently available and comparable through 2012 suggest that the B40 has in many parts of the world enjoyed a prolonged spell of solid income growth. Even so, significant variation exists across regions and countries. In addition, the B40, both within and across countries, continues to lag significantly in non-income dimensions that are crucial to individual well-being and income-generating capacity. In light of generally healthy income growth but lagging non-income indicators, the sustainability of recent progress may be in question.

Growth has become more pro-poor over the past decade

Rising incomes over the past decade have helped the B40 in many countries (figures 1.9 and 1.10). Considering five-year periods starting about 2007 and ending around 2012, B40 incomes grew in 65 of the 94 countries with adequate and comparable data. Among them, 47 countries registered a "shared prosperity premium," with B40 incomes growing faster than the incomes of the average population, thus reducing income inequality between these groups. For these countries, the premium ranged from less than 1 percentage point to well above 3 points, suggesting that growth in many countries has been considerably propoor. Indeed, the average shared prosperity premium stood at 1.7 percent.

As with poverty reduction, not all countries made equal progress on shared prosperity. Incomes for the B40 grew in 65 countries but declined in 29. For 20 of the latter, the shared prosperity premium was negative: not only did the incomes of the B40 decline, inequality also rose. For these countries, the premium ranged from zero to –3.1 percentage points, with an average around –1.2. Interestingly, whereas 72 percent of the countries that registered positive B40 income growth registered a decline in inequality between the B40 and T60 groups, about 70 percent of those where B40 incomes declined saw an increase in inequality between these groups.

Interesting patterns stand out across regions and country groupings, with low- and especially high-income countries registering more mixed experiences. B40 incomes declined in half of the high-income countries and more than a third of the low-income ones. This pattern stands in stark contrast to middle-income countries, where some 85 percent registered an increase in B40 incomes. Interestingly, all low-income countries that registered positive B40 income growth also registered a positive shared prosperity premium, whereas more than a third of high-income countries with positive B40 growth saw a negative premium. Among developing regions, B40 income growth exceeded 5 percent in eight countries of Latin America and the Caribbean, reducing income inequality between the B40 and the rest of the population in all of them. Other regions saw a more mixed performance.

The more mixed performance on shared prosperity reported here is the result of a fundamental deterioration of B40 growth and a changing composition of the sample compared with the last year's *Global Monitoring Report*. First, new comparable household data were available for 36 of the 66 countries that were included in both updates.[20] Among these 36 countries, average B40 income growth (across sample periods) decelerated from 4.6 percent in last year's Report to 2.9 percent in this Report. Average income

FIGURE 1.9 Experiences on shared prosperity differed: While the majority of countries saw solid growth in B40 incomes, many countries did not

Annualized B40 income growth (bars with no black outline) and average population income growth (shown with a black outline) for a five-year period, circa 2007–12 (%)

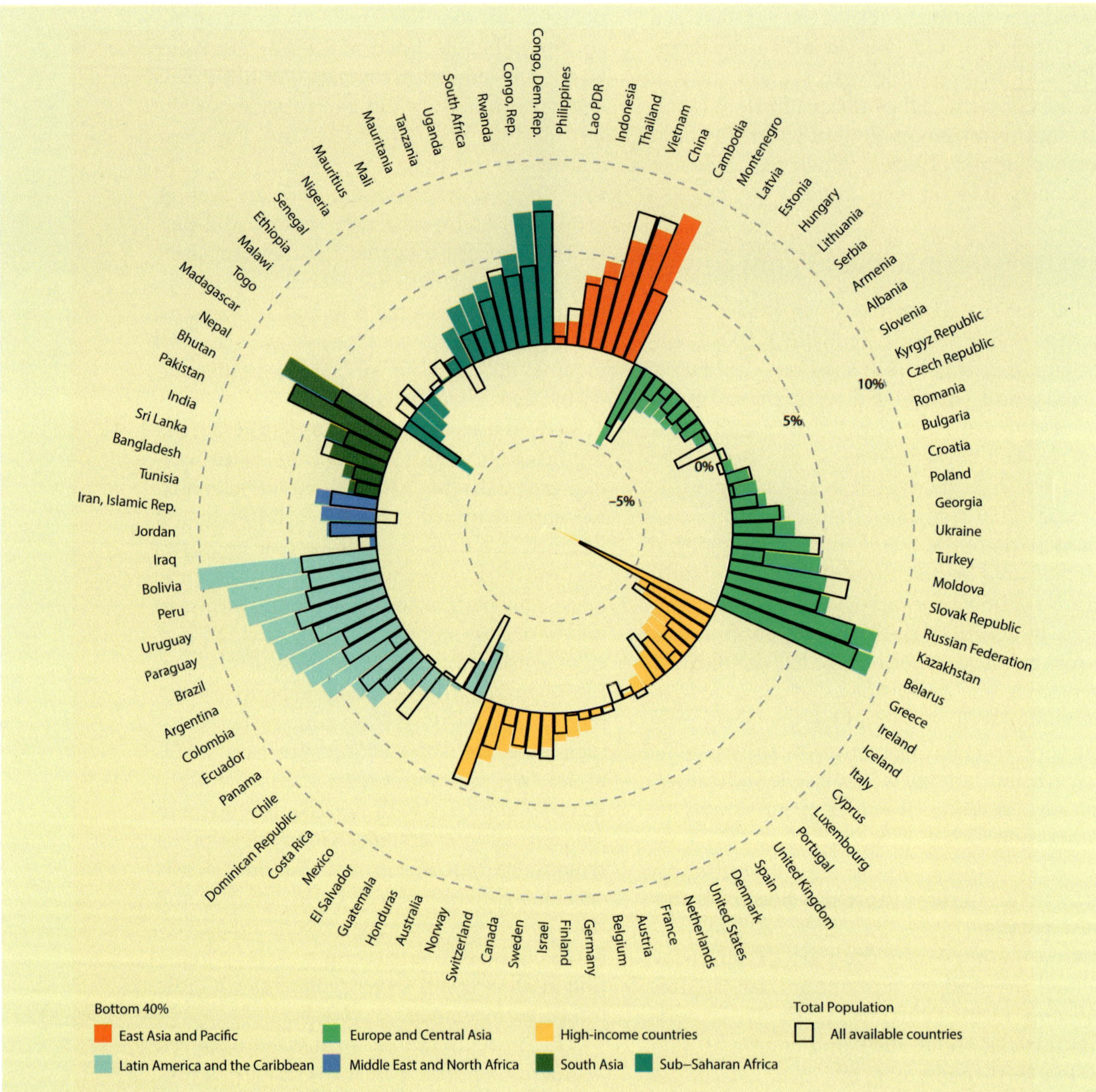

Source: World Bank Global Database for Shared Prosperity.

Note: Data availability varies across countries. Shared prosperity estimates are provided only for comparable survey years. In Sub-Saharan Africa, only 16 of the 48 countries have shared prosperity numbers even though more survey years exist. Starting points are about 2007 and end points are about 2012. See appendix C for precise periods by country.

growth of the population decelerated from 3.0 to 1.7 percent. As a result, the average shared prosperity premium declined from 1.6 to 1.2 percent. Second, compared with last year's Report, 28 new countries were added, of which 5 developing countries had solid growth in B40 incomes, on average, and 23 high-income countries had a decline in B40 incomes, on average. Third, 6 observations were dropped in 2015–16 on the time

FIGURE 1.10 Many but not all countries registered a shared prosperity premium

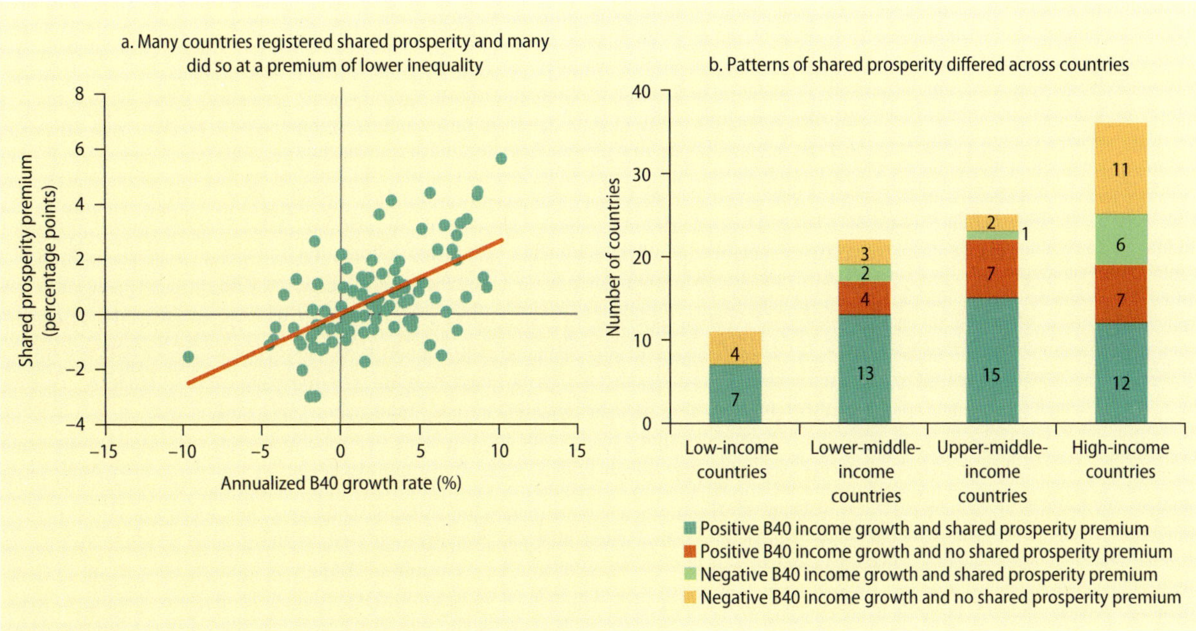

Source: World Bank Global Database for Shared Prosperity.
Note: See the classification of economies for the definition of income designations.

FIGURE 1.11 Countries have registered varied patterns of shared prosperity, with different implications for inequality

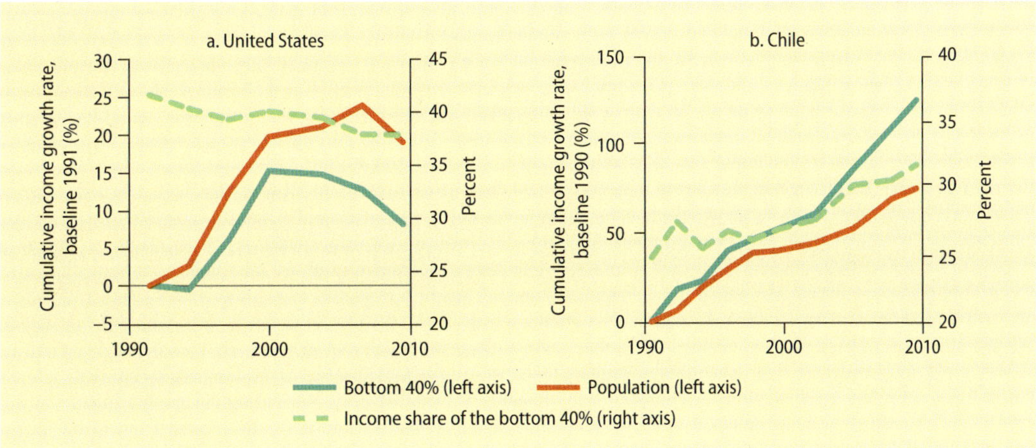

Source: World Bank PovcalNet database.
Note: Cumulative growth of household consumption expenditure or income per capita in constant 2005 PPP prices. Historical series based on 2011 PPP prices are not yet fully available.

periods for which data were available no longer matched the common reference period. In 2014–15 these 6 countries had registered solid income growth.[21]

The evolution of shared prosperity trends highlights further heterogeneity across countries, as illustrated by Chile and the United States (figure 1.11). In the United States, B40 incomes declined during the 2000s, perpetuating a trend of rising inequality (as measured by the B40 income share)—a trend also observed in several other high-income countries.[22] Chile, on the other hand, experienced exactly the opposite.

Recent progress reflects changing drivers of shared prosperity

What explains the variation in shared prosperity across countries and over time: average income growth or changes in the income share of the B40?[23] Shared prosperity, or growth in average incomes of the B40, consists of growth in average incomes plus growth in the income share of the B40. The variation of growth in average incomes of the B40 across countries and over time can be decomposed into the variation due to growth in average incomes, and the variation due to growth in the income share of the B40. Empirical analysis of the relative contribution of mean incomes and B40 shares provides a simple way to distinguish the underlying drivers of B40 income growth.

The evidence suggests that most of the variation in B40 growth is due to variation in growth in average incomes. Over the recent period of 2007–12, average income growth tracked B40 income growth rather closely (figure 1.12a). Dollar, Kleineberg, and Kraay (2013, 2015) confirmed that this finding also held over the past four decades.[24] Figure 1.12b shows that average income growth over this long time period was, in the average country and over the average five-year sample period, positive and larger than the change in the B40 income share, which was close to zero. It also shows that the variation of changes in B40 income shares across the sample of growth spells was much lower than that in average growth rates. These findings, taken together, show that average income growth clearly dominates in the explanation of B40 income growth.[25]

Yet, average income growth is not the only driver of B40 income growth, as illustrated by subsamples of low-income countries for the most recent decade. A good illustration is the relationship in figure 1.12a, which shows significant variation from the trend for 2005–12 that can be explained by changes in the B40 income share. Interestingly, the statistical properties of changes in the B40 income share (figure 1.12b) differ markedly when the four-decade sample is split into subsamples according to income level or decennial period. For example, the B40 changes are on average more positive and more variable across the sample of growth spells in low-income countries than in higher-income countries (figure 1.12c). This pattern is also observed when comparing the 2000s with the 1980s (figure 1.12d).

The explanatory power of average income growth is further diminished when examining the poorest income deciles, such as the B10 and the B20. Regardless of income classification, B20 and especially B10 incomes are much less responsive to average income growth than B40 incomes.[26] In low-income countries, for example, average income growth explains less than a third of the total variation. But even for low- and middle-income countries, the explanatory power remains well under half. Across decades, the explanatory power of average income growth diminishes significantly across all indicators, but the decline is most pronounced for the B10. All of this suggests that changes in the B40 income share have played a nontrivial role in explaining increases in B40 income growth (figures 1.12e, 1.12f).

Given the increased importance of the rise in the income shares of the lower quintiles, it comes as no surprise that income inequality in many countries has declined since the 2000s. Figure 1.13 shows that more countries experienced declining inequality than increasing inequality. Latin America has generally seen significant declines in inequality in virtually every country, which is consistent with the good shared prosperity performance in that region over that decade. Conversely, many high-income countries appeared to have registered an increase in inequality.

Significant disparities remain in non-income dimensions

To evaluate their well-being comprehensively, it is important to examine how the B40 fared in non-income dimensions of well-being. Doing so presents similar challenges as making a multidimensional assessment of poverty over time and space. As of now, few systematic attempts have been made to analyze how the B40 have performed in various

FIGURE 1.12 The drivers of B40 income growth appear to have changed somewhat

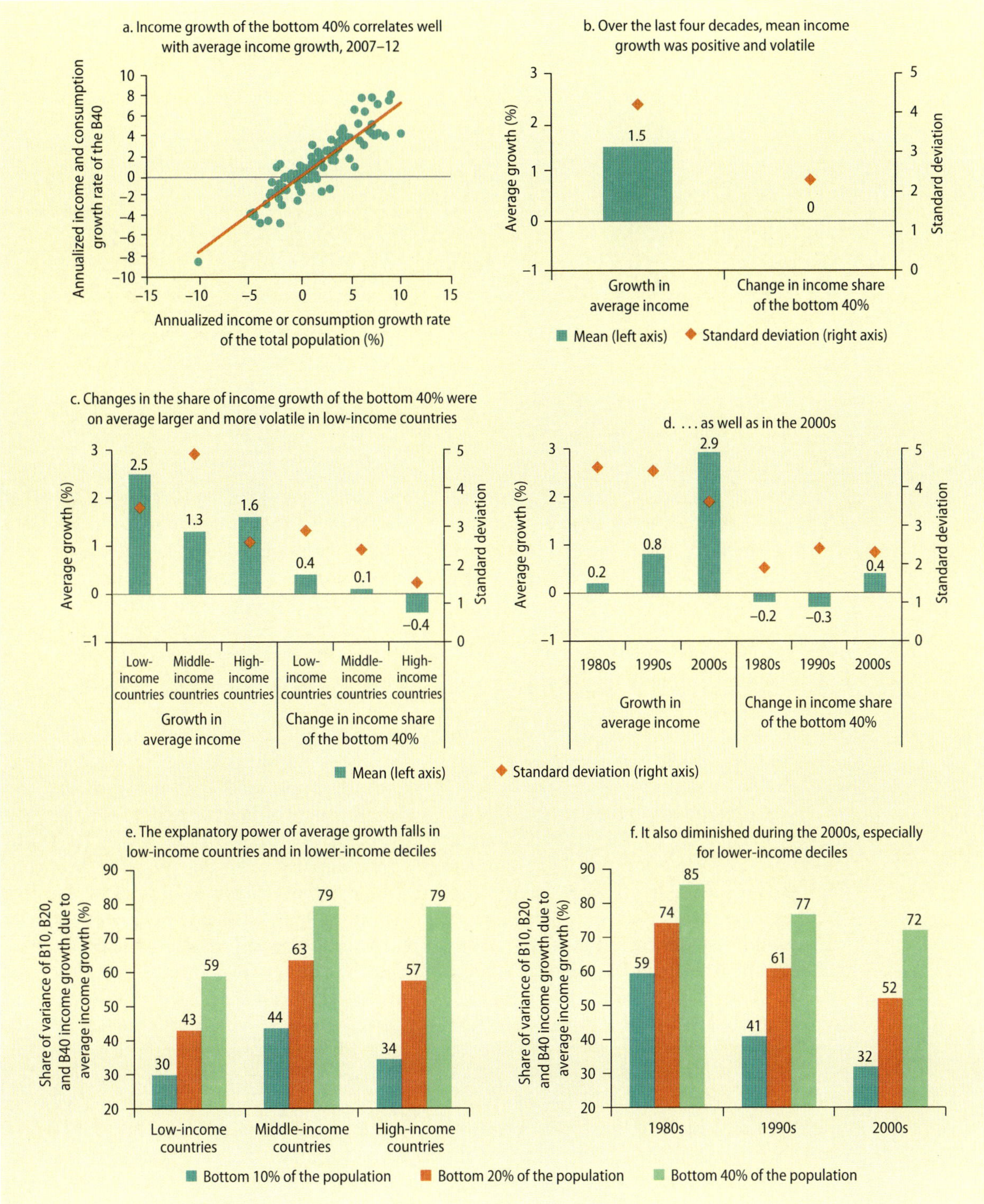

Sources: World Bank Global Database for Shared Prosperity, around 2007–12 (panel a); Dollar, Kleineberg, and Kraay 2013, 2015 (panels b–f).
Note: In panels b–f, mean and standard deviations are reported for the distribution of minimum five-year spells of average income growth and change in the share of B10, B20, or B40 in total income, distinguished by income level or decade. Unless period is specified, sample includes 1980s–2000s.

FIGURE 1.13 Income inequality declined over the 2000s in a small majority of countries

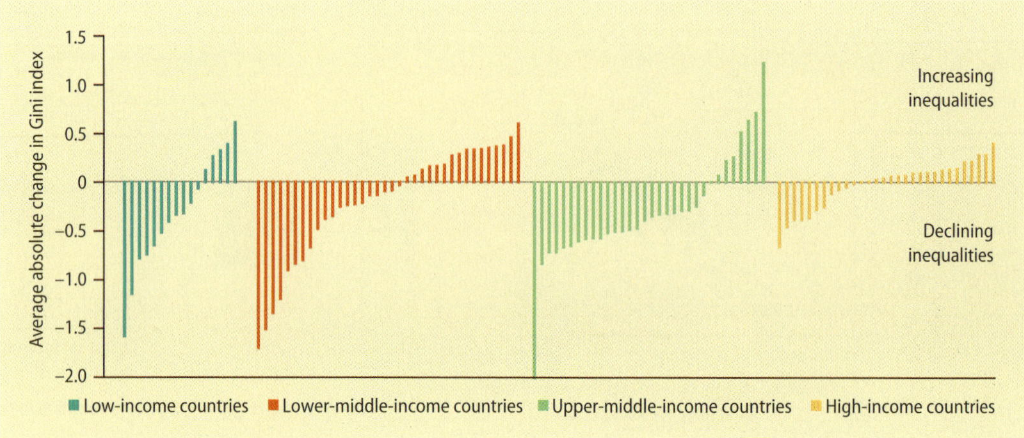

Source: World Bank calculations, based on World Development Indicators, Gini index.
Note: The time period varies depending on the availability of data. Typically, it is from late 1990s and early 2000s to later 2000s and early 2010s. The following outliers are not shown for visualization purposes: Central African Republic (2.55), Niger (−2.52), and Seychelles (3.29). A Gini index of 0 represents perfect equality, whereas an index of 100 implies perfect inequality.

non-income indicators. A key question is whether such analysis is best undertaken with a dashboard (analyzing the dimensions separately) or an aggregate indicator (which requires identifying weights for the various dimensions). Other questions relate to whether multidimensional shared prosperity is analyzed over time (dynamically), across the income distribution (statically, comparing B40 and other segments), or both. Examples of various approaches are presented in the following discussion.

The evolution of living standards in countries belonging to the Organisation for Economic Co-operation and Development (OECD) has seen marked cross-country differences over the past two decades. The OECD multidimensional living standards metric is one example of an aggregate measure that can be compared over time and across the income distribution. Figure 1.14 shows the implementation of the measure for the B40 target group, where average household income growth and B40 inequality are considered together with aggregate measures for jobs (unemployment) and health (life expectancy).[27] The measure suggests positive developments in many of the 18 countries: reduced B40 inequality (14 countries), supportive employment conditions (11 countries), and rising life expectancy (all countries). At the same time, significant diversity is observed when the various dimensions are considered jointly, with Finland and Australia registering living standard improvements at an annualized rate over the past two decades of 4.3 and 4.1 percent, respectively, and the United States and Japan registering much smaller improvements at 1.5 and 1.1 percent, respectively.

Despite robust income growth in developing countries, large disparities linger in the access of the B40 to education, health, and other non-income dimensions. Among developing countries, women in the B40 group face more difficult access to health care compared with the T60, and their children are more likely to die before age five (figures 1.15a, 1.15b). Many people around the world, especially those in the B40, report that they do not always have enough money to feed themselves or their families (figure 1.15c). Unsurprisingly, their children are more likely to be underweight (figure 1.15d). Primary enrollment may have increased in many developing countries, but access to primary education remains unequal (World Bank 2014a, 2015c).[28] Among lower-income countries, a larger share of children in B40 families are out of school (figure 1.15e). These inequalities transmit to outcomes, as international test scores in math suggest (figure 1.15f, with the same results for science).

FIGURE 1.14 OECD countries have seen diverse developments in multidimensional living standards over the past two decades

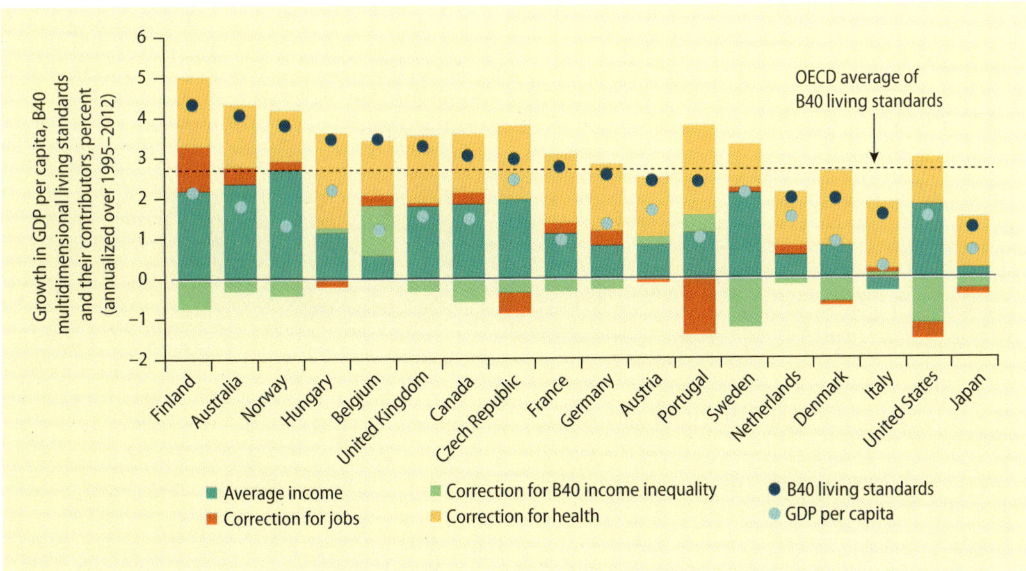

Sources: OECD; Boarini, Murtin, and Schreyer forthcoming.
Note: The stacked bars show contributions of average income growth, (adjusted for the bottom 40 percent income inequality), aggregate unemployment (jobs), and aggregate life expectancy (health) to the OECD's multidimensional living standard measure for the bottom 40 percent (the dot within the stacked bars, which is compared with GDP per capita shown as another dot). The adjustments are implemented as *y**(1-*d_U*-*d_T*)*[1-*I(tau)*; where *y* is average household income, *d_U* is the correction for aggregate unemployment, *d_T* the correction for life expectancy, and *I(tau)* the correction for income inequality that depends on a given aversion to inequality parameter tau. When the target group is the bottom 40 percent, tau is set so that the inequality penalty equals the difference between average and the bottom 40 percent income. The World Bank Group's bottom 40 percent income indicator corresponds to *y**{1-*I*[*tau*(B40)]}. The correction for inequality depends on the target group (in this case the B40) but is independent from the other components capturing health and jobs, which apply to the aggregate population.

The B40 appear to be disadvantaged in areas other than health and education. Examples from Latin America suggest unequal access to the Internet and to basic services such as piped water (figure 1.15g, 1.15 h).

Intergenerational transmission of inequality of opportunity explains part of the persistence of these disparities among the B40. Although the definition of "opportunities" is still being debated, most societies define them as a set of basic goods and services in the early life of an individual that improve the probability of success in life, and in most cases are considered basic economic and social rights (Barros et al. 2009). The "accident of birth" into a B40 household that does not enjoy equal opportunity in these important basic goods and services is likely to be transmitted to the next generation. Indeed, the higher the inequality of opportunity, the greater the persistence in income inequality from one generation to the next (Brunori, Ferreira, and Peragine 2013).[29]

These persistent socioeconomic disparities across the income distribution affect the income-generating capacity of the B40. Few of the B40 own capital assets, and, with the exception of transfers, most depend primarily on labor earnings and income from self-employment (World Bank 2014c). Most of them work in less skill-intensive sectors (such as agriculture, construction, or retail trade). A job in a dynamic, high-wage sector would be the B40's passport to steady and rapid income growth, but the human capital levels of the B40 often limit such prospects. Those who are self-employed among the B40 also may have unequal access to financial capital or essential public inputs such as good-quality infrastructure and efficient institutions that connect workers, farms, and firms to markets. If they are to prosper and pass on this prosperity to the next generation, the B40 needs to be able to learn and compete alongside the T60 for the same jobs.

FIGURE 1.15 Disparities in health, education, and nutrition are noteworthy

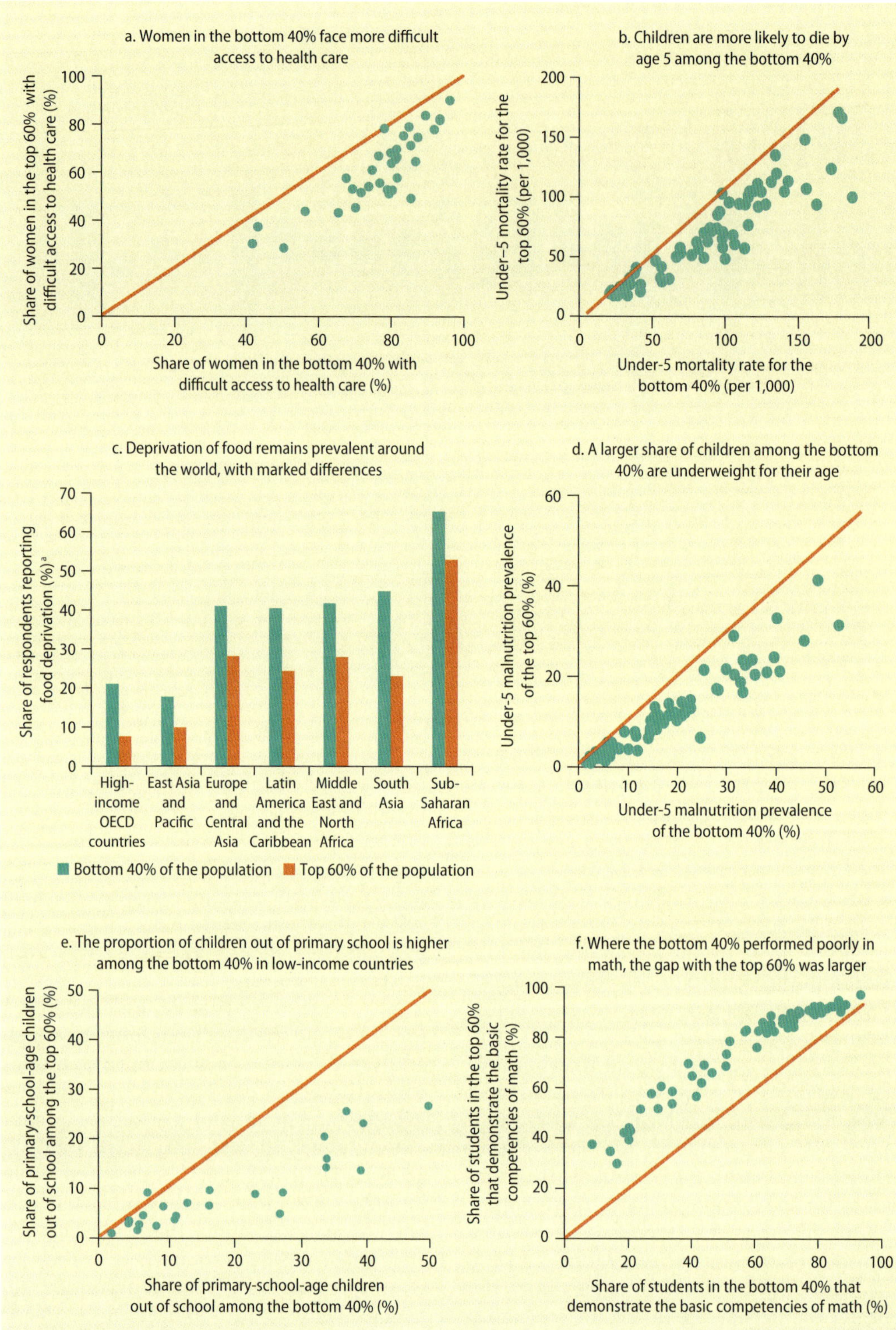

(figure continues next page)

FIGURE 1.15 Disparities in health, education, and nutrition are noteworthy (continued)

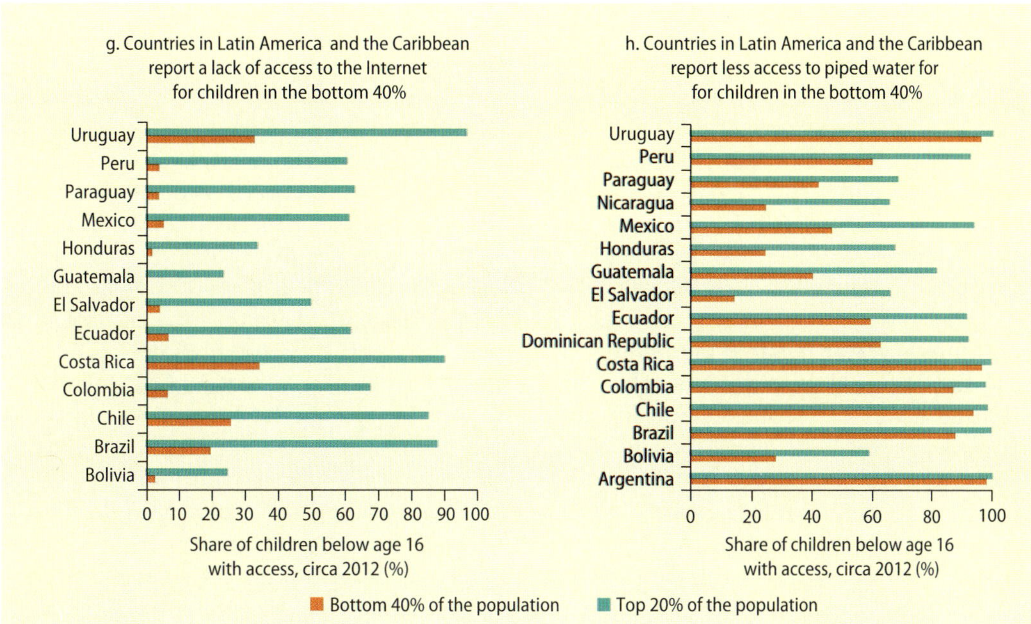

Source: Health Nutrition and Population Statistics by Wealth Quintile Database (panels a, b, and d); World Gallup Database (panel c, 2014); DHS Surveys (panel e); OECD Program for International Student Assessment (PISA) (panel f); World Bank (panels g and h).
Note: In panel d, the under-5 malnutrition prevalence reflects two standard deviations of being underweight by age. In panel e, most countries displayed are low-income countries, with data after 2010.
a. Share of respondents that answered "yes" in 2014 to the question "Have there been times in the past 12 months when you did not have enough money to buy food that you or your family needs?"

Past trends may not be sustainable

Average income growth—one key driver of shared prosperity—may not be as buoyant as it was before the global financial crisis. As chapter 3 elaborates, the medium-term outlook is projecting weaker potential growth in many middle- and high-income economies compared with the precrisis period. Emerging markets face a structural slowdown, and potential growth in high-income economies is likely to recover to slightly lower levels than before. Demographic pressures in many countries dampen potential growth, whereas the sluggish recovery of investment since the crisis in some countries and the declining prospects for rapid productivity improvement in other countries pose further constraints. Barring policy adjustments, jobs and incomes are expected to be affected in these countries.

The other factor that underpinned rising B40 incomes—the increase in the income share of the B40—may, likewise, not be as appropriate as before. The 2000s saw a rise in the B40 income share unlike previous decades. Whether there is a reversal to more muted historical patterns remains to be seen. Surveys suggest that improvements in living standards are perceived as unequal and linked to perceptions about poverty reduction efforts (figure 1.16). The factors that supported the

FIGURE 1.16 Perceptions of improvements in living standards and poverty efforts are related

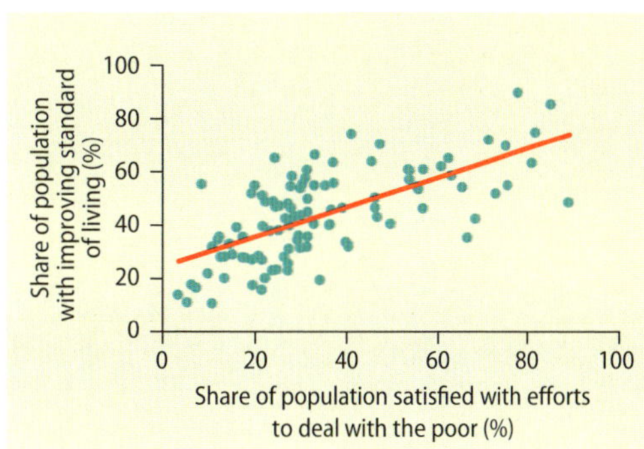

Source: World Bank calculations, based on Gallup World Poll 2014.
Note: These results refer to the following questions: "In this country, are you satisfied or dissatisfied with efforts to deal with the poor?" (horizontal axis); "Right now, do you feel your standard of living is getting better or getting worse?" (vertical axis).

rise in the income share may turn out to have been transitory or unsustainable. For example, if high commodity prices lifted wages in the labor-intensive services sector, the onset of a period of lower commodity prices may remove some of that impetus. Some countries have seen generous minimum wage developments that have lifted the incomes of the B40. To the extent that such policies produce negative fiscal implications or mounting unit labor costs, their sustainability is at risk.

Continued elevated levels of inequality pose an additional sustainability risk

Elevated levels of income inequality may not be compatible with a sustained improvement in shared prosperity if they damage the growth process. Indirect evidence for this statement is illustrated in figure 1.17, which shows that no country has moved beyond middle-income status while maintaining high levels of inequality (Ferreira and Ravallion 2011; World Bank 2013b). Too much inequality (whether vertically in income levels, horizontally across groups, or dimensionally in aspects other than income) is bound to affect social sustainability. Too much inequality may also slow growth, as recent literature suggests. That in turn affects the ability of countries to sustainably climb the income ladder (Banerjee and Duflo 2003; Forbes 2000; Li and Zou 1998; Marrero and Rodriguez 2012, 2013; van der Weide and Milanovic 2014; Voitchovsky 2005).

FIGURE 1.17 Income inequality in richer countries tends to be lower

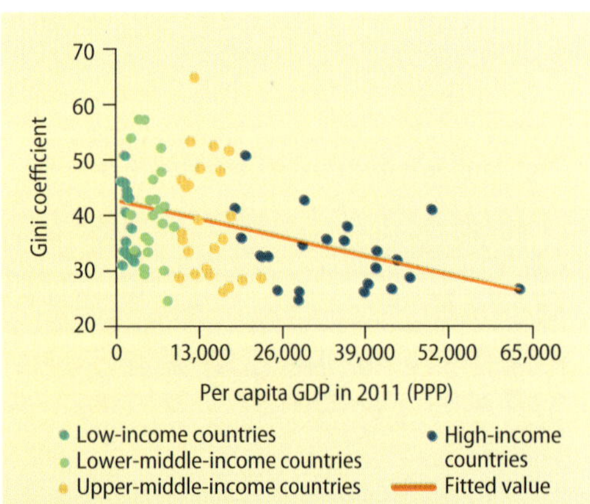

Sources: World Bank calculations and World Development Indicators.
Note: Each point refers to a pair of the Gini and GDP per capita for the same year for one country. The chart includes the most recent information available for all countries over the 2010–12 period and is based on the World Bank income classification (using the Atlas method). Because the latest income classification for 2015 is used, it is possible that the income levels shown for 2010–12 deviate slightly from the income groupings.

Persistent inequality of opportunity in non-income dimensions may eventually dampen the dynamism of B40 income growth. The B40 continues to exhibit large disparities with the rest of the population in its access to basic goods and services of good quality, reflecting in large part inequality of opportunity. The B40—and among them, especially women—is thus limited in making the best of their most important asset, labor, and in earning higher incomes reflective of their marginal productivity. To be sustainable, longer-term wage developments need to be underpinned by productivity.

Moreover, environmental aspects of recent development patterns are not sustainable. Trends for indicators showing the sustainable use of natural resources (land, water, forestry, fisheries, biodiversity), pollution (air, water, toxics, solid waste), and carbon emissions are all going the wrong way.[30] Conservatively measured, the combined value of the associated environmental damages rose by 50 percent between 1990 and 2010, mainly in developing countries. A broader indicator of growth sustainability is the "change in total wealth per capita."[31] This measure subtracts from a country's gross national savings all forms of capital depreciation, including the loss of natural capital (that is, mineral depletion and natural resources degradation). The results for 1990–2011 show that low- and lower-middle-income countries have fared the worst in terms of depleting per capita wealth (figure 1.18). Natural capital depletion in the low-income countries has averaged about 6 percent of gross national income per capita since 1990. A regional breakdown shows that 84 percent of Sub-Saharan countries are depleting their capital, followed by 42 percent in the Middle East and North Africa and 40 percent in Latin America and the Caribbean (figure 1.19).

The rise in pollution is of particular concern, especially in cities where much of the global population resides. Urban poverty, particularly in poor countries, typically starts as rural deprivation with migrants being driven by the lack of opportunity in rural areas. The irresistible pull of cities has done much to provide employment and propel growth, which is essential for alleviating poverty, but urbanization has also brought new problems. Urban air pollution has emerged as a leading cause of ill health in developing countries—with more than triple the impact of malaria, HIV, and tuberculosis combined. The population exposed to ambient levels of unhealthy air pollution rose by more than a third in developing countries between 1990 and 2013 (figure 1.20); the increase was around 40 percent in middle-income countries, and 98 percent in low-income countries. Virtually all developing countries thus face a double burden of environmental health risks: the impact of disease associated with underdevelopment, such as inadequate sanitation, and the impact of health risks derived from growth, such as ambient pollution and waste. While trends in "traditional" water and sanitation problems show great improvement over the past 25 years, trends in "modern" problems of environmental management and sustainability point to the reverse.

FIGURE 1.18 Low- and lower-middle-income countries have fared the worst in depleting per capita wealth

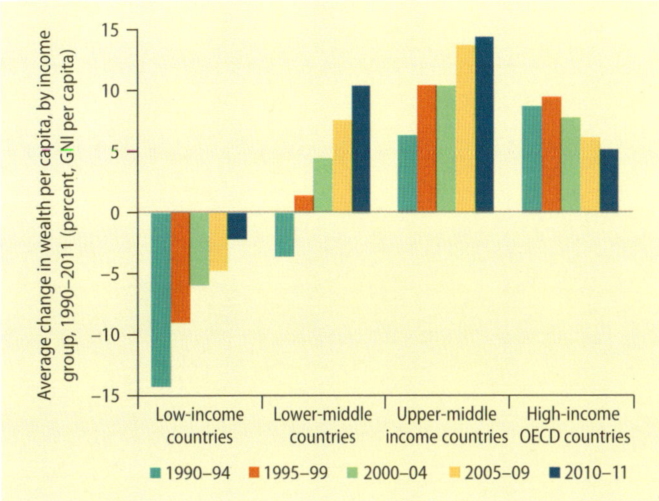

Sources: World Bank Development Indicators and forthcoming update of World Bank 2011a.

Ending extreme poverty and sharing prosperity: Policy agenda

Putting an end to extreme poverty and promoting shared prosperity are ongoing challenges. Country circumstances and contexts differ, and so policy priorities will also vary across countries. For example, some countries have eradicated extreme poverty already and therefore the second goal on shared prosperity is more relevant for them. In addition, significant overlap exists in the types of policies needed to end poverty or share prosperity, and these common ingredients hold relevance for a broad set of countries.

This section delineates the policy agenda and articulates key priorities that are of common interest to a wide range of countries. First, it examines the rationale for policy intervention, looks at the possible synergies between goals of ending extreme poverty and sharing prosperity, and explores how efficiency and equity interact. Second, it spells out a three-component strategy that centers on growth, investment, and insurance.

Delineating policy approaches

In light of country specifics, is there common ground among policy approaches that purport to end poverty and share prosperity? The answer is yes, but the policy mix needs to be sensitive to the complementarities and trade-offs between the two goals.

Growth with equity is essential for meeting the two goals

The policy agenda underpinning the World Bank Group's goals is "growth with equity." Growth has played a key role in reducing extreme poverty and promoting shared prosperity and is critical to sustaining progress. Yet, aggregate growth by itself is not enough; it needs to be pursued with equity, complemented by policies that enable the poorest

FIGURE 1.19 The share of countries with evidence of unsustainable economies rose between 1995 and 2010

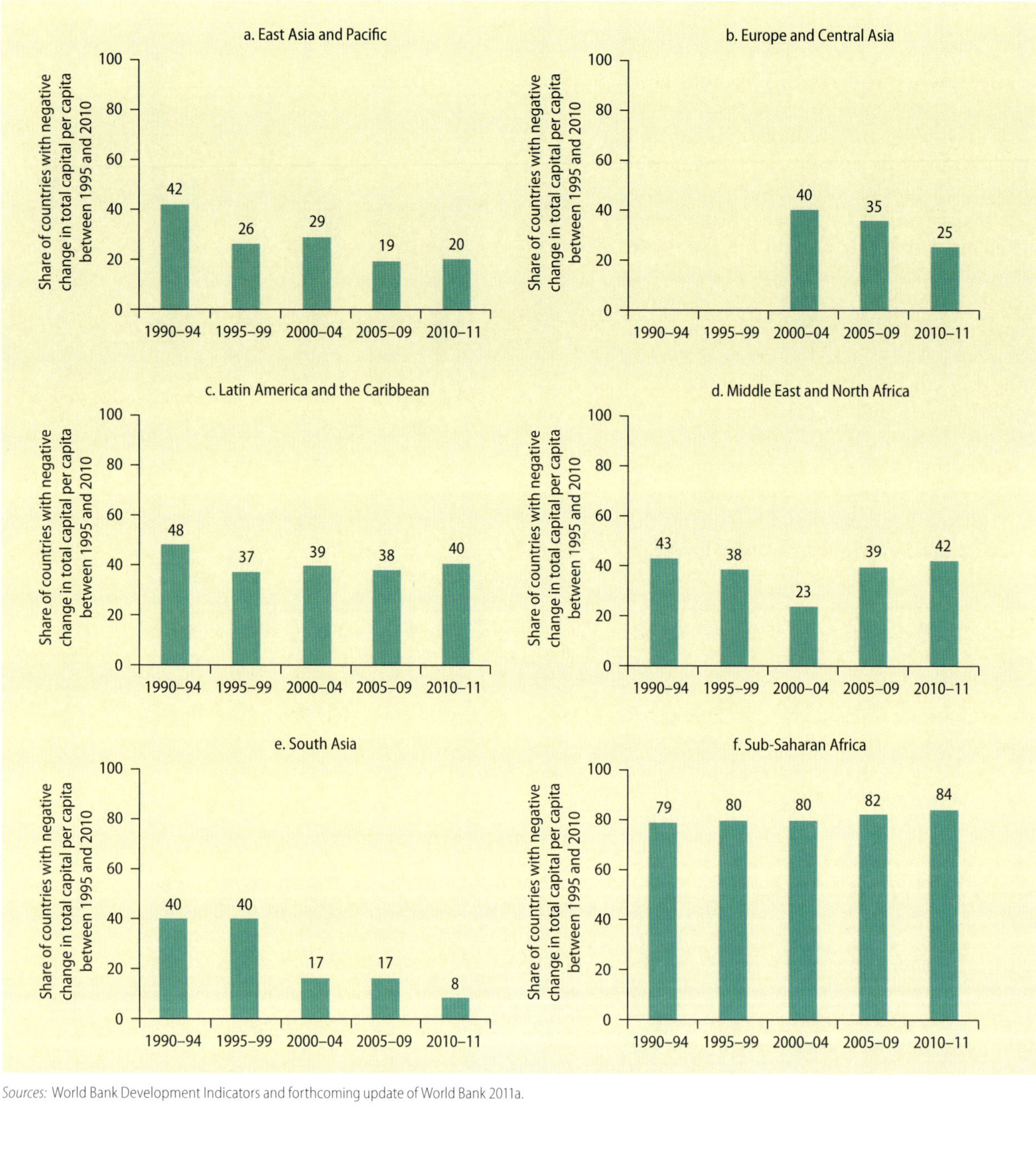

Sources: World Bank Development Indicators and forthcoming update of World Bank 2011a.

and the B40 to fully participate in and benefit from the growth process. To pursue growth without equity would be socially destabilizing and to pursue equity without growth would tend to "redistribute economic stagnation," as Robert McNamara stated in 1980.[32]

The two aspects of equity that delineate the policy agenda are *avoidance of absolute deprivation* and *equality of opportunity*. The quest to end extreme poverty builds on the societal preference to avoid absolute deprivation and protect the livelihoods of its poorest members regardless of whether the equal opportunity principle has been upheld. The quest to promote shared prosperity reflects the principle of equal opportunity, whereby the outcomes of a person's life, in its many dimensions, should mostly reflect his or her efforts and talents, not his or her background. The notion of pursuing the World Bank Group's goals in an economically, environmentally, and socially sustainable manner in turn serves equity and equality of opportunity intertemporally, reaching future generations who too can then live lives without deprivation and full of opportunity.

The poverty and shared prosperity goals are mutually reinforcing

Country circumstances will determine the relative importance of the extreme poverty and shared prosperity goals, as the B40 may comprise many possible populations (box 1.8). In countries where extreme poverty rates are around 40 percent, the two goals almost completely overlap: increasing the income growth of the B40 accelerates the reduction of poverty and promotes shared prosperity. In countries where extreme poverty rates are significantly greater than 40 percent (mostly in Sub-Saharan Africa), the shared prosperity goal implies a focus on the poorest of the poor and therefore has a narrower scope than the poverty eradication goal. In other countries, where extreme poverty exists but at rates well below 40 percent, the shared prosperity objective is broader than the poverty goal because it includes a potentially much larger group of those who are, in absolute terms, moderately poor or vulnerable to falling into poverty. Finally, in countries where extreme poverty is no longer an issue, the shared prosperity objective focuses a lens on those who are relatively poor, a concept intrinsically connected to inequality.

In countries where poverty reduction is a key priority, the shared prosperity lens enhances that effort. In some countries, shared prosperity may complement national poverty lines and strengthen the focus on the poor. In others, it may help broaden the focus of international poverty lines to whomever

FIGURE 1.20 Exposure to urban pollution is on the rise

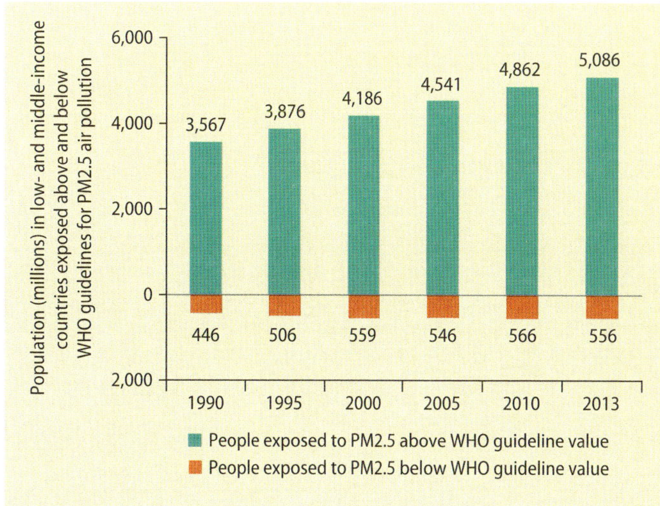

Source: Ambient PM2.5 exposure data from Brauer et al. forthcoming; both urban and rural areas are included.
Note: PM 2.5 refers to fine particulate matter.

national authorities consider to be deprived based on the standards of their societies. In all of these circumstances, shared prosperity is doubly good for the poor: First, effective shared prosperity strategies that expand the opportunities of the B40 through greater participation in the development process will affect poverty reduction directly if indeed many of the B40 are poor. Second, to the extent that shared prosperity reduces inequality, the poverty reduction power of future economic growth is likely to be enhanced, leading to a greater growth elasticity of poverty reduction.[33]

This reinforced focus on poverty reduction is essential if the world is to reach the ambitious goal of 3 percent global poverty by 2030. As is argued in World Bank (2015c), meeting the poverty goal by 2030 requires both strong aggregate economic growth and an increase in the income share of the extremely poor. Reductions in inequality arising from higher income growth among the B40 can make the difference. One estimate suggests that a shared prosperity premium of 2 percentage points, which requires B40 incomes to grow significantly faster than mean incomes, is necessary to achieve the poverty goal (Lakner, Negre, and Prydz

BOX 1.8 Who is in the B40?

To assess trends in shared prosperity and calibrate policies, it is essential to understand the composition of the bottom 40 percent (B40). Just like the poor, the B40 is not a static subgroup of the population. Some people move in and out of the B40, whereas others are chronically at the lower end of the income distribution. Yet, it is possible to characterize the B40 as a group. As shown below, the composition of the B40 is very different across countries. These differences need to be taken into account when identifying strategies to boost shared prosperity, which in some countries will overlap strongly with the struggle against extreme poverty, whereas in others the connections with reducing inequality will be stronger.

The profile of the richest B40 person varies considerably across countries. Map B1.8.1 illustrates the geographical distribution of the characteristics of the 40th percentile, identifying whether the richest person belonging to the B40 is extremely poor as defined by the international poverty line, moderately poor, vulnerable, or none of these but rather a member of the "middle class" or even rich.

Most of the countries in which the richest among the B40 are still extremely poor are in Sub-Saharan Africa. In some places in Sub-Saharan Africa, most of East Asia and Pacific, and all of South Asia, the richest of the B40 are moderately poor. The B40 in these countries thus consists entirely of populations that are either extremely poor or moderately poor. In most of Latin America and the Caribbean, the richest among the B40 are vulnerable. Following impressive gains in shared prosperity that lifted many out of poverty, the richest B40 person in that region remains susceptible to falling back into poverty.

Overall, the B40 group as a whole encompasses many different combinations of extreme poverty,

MAP B.1.8.1 The income of the richest B40 person differs greatly across countries

Income status of the B40 of the income distribution in 2011

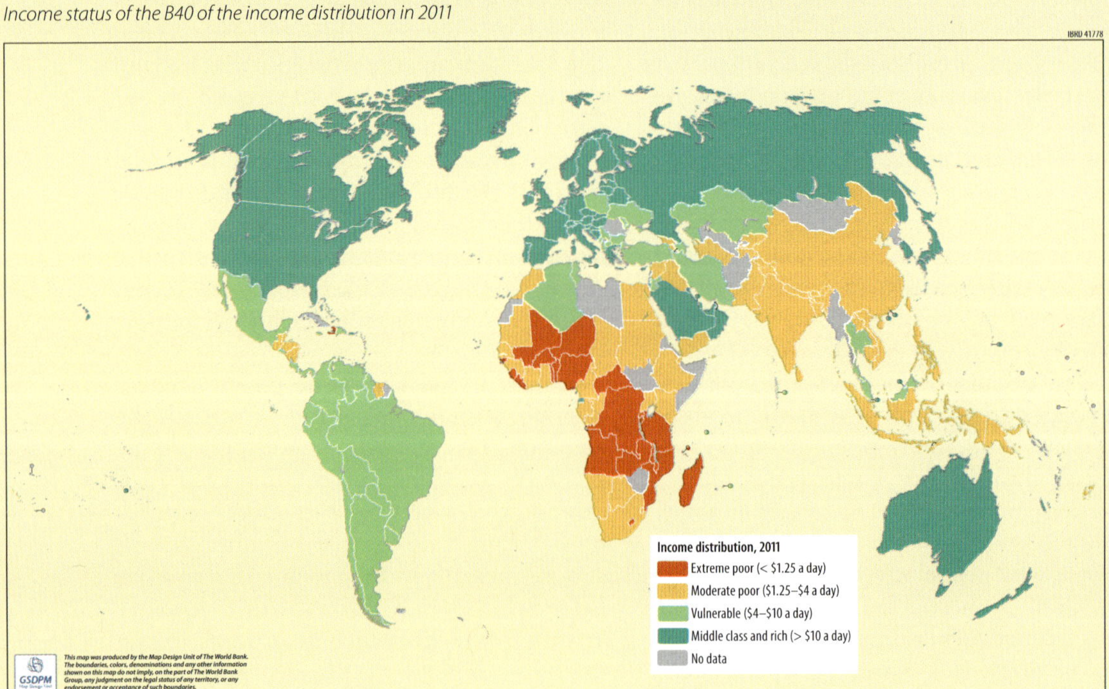

Source: PovcalNet database 2015.
Note: Estimates based on the $1.25 poverty line and 2005 purchasing power parity prices. The full distributional data using 2011 prices are still being developed.

(box continues next page)

BOX 1.8 Who is in the B40? (continued)

FIGURE B1.8.1 Whether viewed through the lens of absolute or relative deprivation, the B40 encompasses diverse populations that vary significantly across countries

The bottom 40% includes the absolutely poor and ulnerable, to differing degrees (selected countries)

b. The bottom 40% also includes a significant share of those considered to be relatively deprived (selected countries)

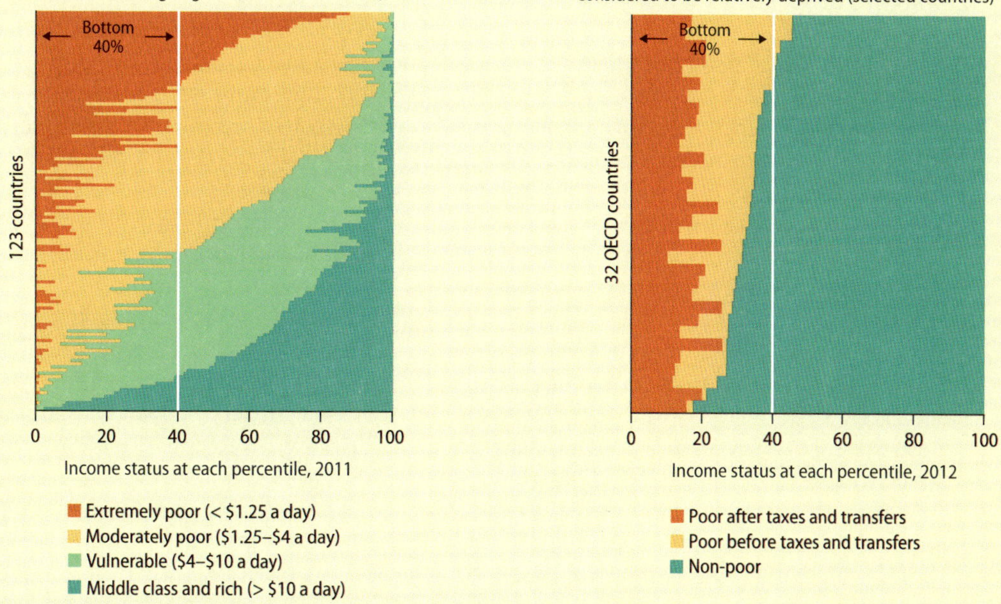

Sources: PovcalNet (panel a) and OECD Income Distribution Database (panel b).
Note: Panel a is based on the $1.25 poverty line and 2005 purchasing power parity prices. It includes 123 countries, most of them developing countries, for which data are available at PovcalNet. Panel a is ranked lexicographically according to the category of the 40th percentile; that is, first, all extremely poor countries at the 40th percentile are sorted by the share of this group in the total population. Then the same procedure is followed for the moderately poor, the vulnerable, and the middle class and rich. Panel b is based on the OECD definition of relative poverty and includes 32 OECD countries.

moderate poverty, and vulnerability. At the top of figure B1.8.1a are countries where extreme poverty rates exceed 40 percent, suggesting that a B40 focus in those countries would emphasize the poorest among the extremely poor and potentially overlook others in extreme poverty above the B40 cutoff but below the extreme proverty line. Directly below are countries where moderate poverty is becoming an increasing concern, since poverty rarely ends when a poor person climbs over the extreme poverty line. The lower half of the figure shows countries where extreme poverty has been mostly eradicated, but many people remain moderately poor and a significant share may be characterized as vulnerable to falling back into poverty. At the bottom of the figure are richer countries, where most of the B40 have become middle class and have low risk of falling into extreme poverty.

Among richer countries, where absolute poverty is of lesser concern, the B40 may encompass many of those who are considered to be relatively poor. Figure B1.8.1b shows that in OECD countries many of the less well-off are considered to be living in relative poverty, even after taking transfers into account. They are seen to be unable to enjoy an acceptable standard of living relative to that of the majority of the population. Given that the relative poverty measure is based on a poverty line set at 60 percent of median national income, the notion is more closely related to within-country inequality. Yet, it does show that the focus on the B40 allows for flexibility in focusing on what societies care most about.

2014). This focus on raising the income share of the poor will be all the more necessary given the ambitiousness of the poverty target, the elevated poverty rates that are expected to persist in much of Sub-Saharan Africa, and the large number of people in Sub-Saharan Africa and South Asia who are expected to continue experiencing multiple deprivations beyond income poverty.

"More equitable" need not mean "less efficient"

The equity-efficiency trade-off has for a long time animated the discussion on the feasibility and desirability of redistributive policies. Arthur Okun (1975) hypothesized that redistributive policies intended to reduce inequality imply a "big trade-off," where lower inequality can be achieved only at a great efficiency cost (the "leaky buckets" hypothesis).[34] The trade-off rests on the premise that markets work perfectly and that redistribution produces administrative costs, disincentive effects, and productivity distortions. In the presence of market failures, however, the equity-efficiency trade-off need not always hold, a fact that gives rise to the possibility of redistributive policies that also enhance efficiency (World Bank 2005).[35] While complementarities exist between equity and efficiency, this is not to say that the trade-off does not exist anymore. In the presence of resource constraints, many investment and policy choices will likely need to contend with a trade-off of some sort (where the time horizon plays a key role in assessing the trade-off). How the trade-off is resolved lies at the heart of how growth with equity is operationalized in the real world.

Given that such a trade-off need not always hold, policies may be able to simultaneously improve growth and equity. Growth and its incidence across the income distribution are determined jointly and therefore policies that affect one will also affect the other. An equity component need not be embedded in each policy. It suffices that the overall package is consistent with growth and equity and that the underlying process is fair (World Bank 2005). Moreover, there is a substantial reform agenda that comprises policies that can simultaneously raise growth and equity. Such synergistic, win-win policies address equality of opportunity and help broaden participation in the process of growth; examples are policies that improve access to markets, level the playing field for firms large and small, build human capabilities, and remove barriers to job creation (Qureshi 2015).

Growth gives governments the fiscal space to implement redistributive policies that raise the incomes and welfare of the poor and the B40. In the presence of significant failures in credit, insurance, labor, or land markets, where market outcomes may not be efficient, there is scope for efficient and equitable redistributive policies. Policies that redistribute wealth can help poorer people overcome credit constraints to invest in human capital or can effectively insure them against transient shocks; targeted safety nets have dynamic efficiency effects that ultimately support growth and enhance its sustainability.

More sustainable development does not imply lower growth

The promise of sustainable development requires greater commitment to green growth policies. Such policies typically have the broad objectives of protecting and ensuring the sustainable use of natural capital, improving environmental quality, and advancing lower carbon and more resilient growth in the face of a changing climate. Green growth policies not only reduce large welfare costs and environmental externalities. They can contribute directly to economic growth and the well-being of the poor in several ways, including by promoting efficiency gains that are cost-effective, reduce energy and materials use, and increase private sector profits; reducing future costs of natural resources, such as water, through improved management; improving the health and productivity of the workforce and lowering health expenses in the state budget; promoting the expansion of new industries and technologies that offset losses in sunset industries; Responding to changes in consumer preferences through expansion of less-polluting and energy-intensive service industries (often including realizing opportunities that would otherwise be lost, such as tourism); and proactively adapting to disaster risks in ways that reduce the impact of those risks, reduce costs, and improve knowledge.

Identifying key policy ingredients

To sustainably end extreme poverty and boost shared prosperity, three policy ingredients are needed in any strategy.[36]

- *Sustaining broad-based growth.* Economic growth has been the main building block of poverty reduction and shared prosperity over the past several decades. Among economies that have managed to sustain rapid growth for extended periods, five characteristics are common: effective leadership and governance, macroeconomic stability, a market orientation to guide structural change, an outward orientation for domestic and external discipline, and a future orientation to boost savings and meet investment needs. Growth is not an end in itself, however. It is a means for increasing the incomes and well-being of people, and it is most effective in reaching low-income people when it increases their labor incomes by supporting productive employment. Policy makers must keep in mind the effects of interventions on job creation and income growth for the extremely poor and the B40.
- *Investing in human development.* Human development is essential to remedying the multidimensional deprivations of the poor and the B40, and a requirement for broad-based economic growth. Vital human development investments include education, health and population programs, safe water, and sanitation. These services are especially important for children, whose opportunities early in life determine their future lives as adults. The quality of services is also important. It is not enough to get children to school: teachers need to show up, textbooks need to arrive, and children need to be taught in ways that enable them to learn. Health clinics need to be staffed with trained personnel, stocked, and able to provide adequate services. Effective service delivery, in turn, requires effective, accountable, and transparent mechanisms and institutions.
- *Insuring against risks.* Social policies can protect the extremely poor from destitution and protect the vulnerable against risks. They can help families avoid irreversible losses and prevent them from having to make decisions with costly long-run implications. Good social programs support growth and human development and come in three kinds. Noncontributory social assistance programs for the chronic or extremely poor protect them from destitution and promote investments in their children's human capital. Social insurance programs prevent people falling back into poverty, whether caused by individual illness, temporary unemployment, or localized droughts. And global insurance mechanisms help countries cope with massive natural disasters or pandemics. To design such programs, a dynamic understanding of poverty and vulnerability is essential.

In all of the above, it is essential that natural capital, environmental health, and ecosystem sustainability concerns are integrated into economic decision making. In both rural and urban areas, poverty alleviation strategies need to give greater attention to the environmental and resource dimensions of poverty because the number of people involved is large and the consequences of neglect significant. Where resource dependence is high and opportunities for economic diversification are limited, it is unlikely that policies can eliminate poverty without acknowledging the critical role of natural resources in supporting the poor. Natural resources are often the only significant assets that the poor have access to, and if managed efficiently they could provide a sustainable foundation for economic viability. If not, however, the loss of natural capital through weaknesses in property rights, poor local knowledge, price distortions, or poor infrastructure means that eradicating poverty over the longer term will be unachievable.

Broad-based growth must be sustained over time

Continued progress in poverty reduction and shared prosperity requires economic dynamism to generate income-earning opportunities for broad segments of society. As part of this endeavor, economic growth—both its pace and pattern—is critical. In very poor countries, it is arithmetically impossible to reduce poverty significantly without growth because the pool to redistribute from is very small. In richer countries, growth again is key because it explains most of the variation in income among the B40. In addition to the pace of growth, its pattern also matters. Some kinds of growth benefit the poor or the B40 more effectively than other kinds. The expansion of smallholder farming or labor-intensive manufacturing, for example, may convey greater benefits to the poor than the expansion of capital-intensive mining does. Moreover, for growth to have a lasting impact, it must be sustained over a long period of time. Sustained growth results in mass job creation, making labor more scarce and valuable and thereby lifting incomes. Growth can thereby bite deeply into poverty and contribute to prosperity by being shared within and between generations.

Fast growth in labor-intensive sectors will help reduce poverty and share prosperity, especially when coupled with efforts to increase labor force participation. Two distinct, but not mutually exclusive, pathways for boosting labor incomes exist: fuller employment and higher returns to employment. Growth in labor incomes was the foundation of the rapid reduction in poverty in East Asia during the 1970s and 1980s, as well as in the developing countries that were most successful at reducing poverty in the 1990s and 2000s. Much of the recovery since the 2008 economic crisis has been in the form of jobless growth, which has dampened the benefits of growth for lower-income groups.

The Commission on Growth and Development (2008) has highlighted five characteristics as key to rapid and sustained growth (figure 1.21). The Commission identified 13 economies that since 1950 have grown at an average rate of 7 percent or more for 25 years or longer.[37] Despite the differences between them, these economies all exhibited the following: They had committed, credible, and capable governments; they maintained macroeconomic stability; they let markets allocate resources; they fully "exploited" the world economy; and they mustered high rates of saving and investment.

FIGURE 1.21 Five characteristics have been key among countries that sustained rapid growth

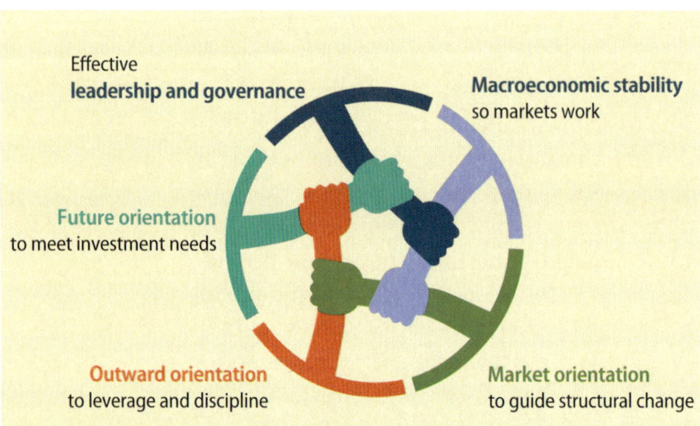

Source: GMR team adaptation from Commission on Growth and Development 2008.

Effective leadership and governance

Sustained growth requires committed, credible, and capable governments. Growth does not "just happen." It requires a decades-long commitment to the credible implementation of enabling policies that are designed by capable governments. The effectiveness of governments depends in the first place on the talent of their workforce, the incentives they foster, the vigor of their debates, and the organizational structure they impose (Commission on Growth and Development 2008). Governments are not only policy makers but also service providers, investors, arbitrators, and employers, requiring good governance in all of these roles. Good governance also requires strong accountability measures between policy makers and people, to raise the voices of the ultimate beneficiaries of government policy, especially the marginalized and the poor, and between policy makers and providers, so as to raise the quality of service delivery (World Bank 2003).

Macroeconomic stability so markets work
Macroeconomic stability is a key prerequisite for growth to flourish. Instability in price levels, interest rates, the exchange rate, or the tax burden deters private investment. Sound macroeconomic policies reduce distortions in relative prices and returns to assets and encourage investments in productive sectors. Macroeconomic stability also ensures that fiscal resources are productively used to finance critical expenditures, including in education, health, and infrastructure, rather than merely servicing the debt (Commission on Growth and Development 2008). The recent financial crisis has brought to the fore the damaging consequences of macroeconomic instability on economic growth and living standards, contributing to job losses, rising poverty levels, and thereby endangering progress toward poverty reduction and shared prosperity.

Market orientation to guide structural change
Microeconomic dynamism is a necessary feature of an adaptive economy and, guided by the market mechanism, a key driver of structural change. Growth entails structural transformation within and across sectors.[38] Within sectors, opportunities arise to deepen comparative advantages and boost productivity by operating more efficiently and moving up the value chain. As comparative advantages evolve, structural shifts occur between sectors, from agriculture to industry and services, from rural to urban areas, and from informal to formal activities. Well-functioning markets are essential to guide these processes. Their price signals ration scarce resources to their most productive uses. This rationing is accomplished through competition, buttressed by contestability in product markets and mobility in capital and labor markets.[39] The negative impact of inefficient resource allocation may not be immediately visible, but it will slowly accrue over time. Recent evidence from Latin America suggests, for example, that 80 percent of the efficiency gap between the region and the United States is explained by misallocation of resources, where the efficiency gap itself explains about half of the income gap (Araujo et al. 2015). Key priorities are the following:

- *Accelerating productivity growth in agriculture.* Increased agricultural productivity growth is important because the majority of the poor continue to live in rural areas where agriculture is central to their livelihoods. Special consideration is needed for women, who make up over 43 percent of the global agricultural labor force, yet continue to face major constraints reducing their productivity (O'Sullivan et al. 2014). Experience in all regions has shown that improving the living conditions of the extremely and moderately poor hinges on the creation of a dynamic agricultural sector. Despite some inroads into productivity-enhancing agricultural technology, agricultural success stories in Africa are few compared with the experiences in Asia and Latin America, and yields per hectare in Africa are about the same as they were in 1970. Better output prices through more open trade (as seen in Cambodia, Ethiopia, and Rwanda, among others) provide necessary incentives to adopt fertilizer and improved seed varieties, especially when reinforced by complementary policies to reduce the cost of inputs, such as improved infrastructure and access to finance and insurance. Institutional measures such as land reform, market infrastructure, and more effective producers' organizations can catalyze investment in agriculture (Gill and Revenga forthcoming).
- *Widening the economic footprint of natural resources.* Many countries have opportunities to enhance the economywide potential of the natural resource sector. Depending on the location, suitable policies may include improved rural-to-urban connectivity, stronger value-chains, rural finance, protection of community and indigenous property rights, and environmental regulation. The potential pitfalls of NRB growth are well understood, both at

the microeconomic level (resource degradation) and macroeconomic level (possible real exchange rate appreciation that may render the manufacturing sector uncompetitive, and heightened volatility due to commodity prices). At the micro-level, the appropriate response to these potential negative effects is very location specific but often has to do with property rights, access, and fostering alternatives to traditional practices. At the macro-level, appropriate policies include not limiting commodity exports or erecting costly import barriers to protect domestic industries. Instead, policies should alleviate demand and supply constraints on productivity activity by improving infrastructure, creating a conducive investment climate, and facilitating private sector access to capital, skills, technology, and markets (Chandra, Lin, and Wang 2012; De Cavalcanti, Mohaddes, and Raissi 2012; IMF 2011).

- *Sustaining competitiveness in manufacturing.* In other countries, structural transformation of the manufacturing sector will be a key priority. Competitive pressure has transformed the landscape of manufacturing industries worldwide, placing a high premium on maintaining a competitive edge in line with a country's comparative advantage. For poorer countries, where the fields are still so oversupplied with labor that the marginal productivity of agricultural labor is low, the objective will be to efficiently produce low-cost, high-volume, labor-intensive manufacturing goods, helping absorb low-skilled labor in higher-value-added activities. For others, the objective is to move up the value chain into more skill-intensive and innovation-driven manufacturing, and in the process to develop new competitive niches, generating jobs and lifting incomes along the way. In both cases, exposure to internal and external competition is key so that market forces can help firms explore and develop their comparative advantages (World Bank 2010a, 2014c).
- *Raising the efficiency and quality of services.* Many countries grapple with inefficiencies in segments of their services sectors, producing a loss in productivity. Large segments of the services sector remain informal, expensive, of low quality, or inefficient. Services play a key role in economic growth and job creation. Improvements in the productivity, quality, and range of services contribute to economic growth directly but also indirectly, given the role of services as inputs into all other sectors. Services are typically labor intensive, and they may be skill intensive too. Increased job creation in services can contribute to poverty alleviation and B40 income growth. Enhanced service delivery in the areas of education and health can also promote human capital development to the benefit of longer-term growth prospects. A more dynamic services sector also allows countries to insert themselves more fully into the production of tradable services—a rapidly growing dimension of global trade (World Bank 2010b, 2014b).

Outward orientation to leverage and discipline

Outward orientation—openness to the global economy—plays a distinct role in fostering structural change and can contribute to growth in multiple ways. By leveraging the global economy, domestic firms are offered deep, elastic markets for exports, which may support job creation and income growth. Trade may also raise real incomes by lowering the prices of products. For example, imports of lower-priced consumption goods from China have helped expand Brazil's "consumption frontier" (World Bank 2014b). Trade openness provides an economy the freedom to specialize in whatever it is best at producing, while also imposing discipline to use resources efficiently. Labor mobility across borders may contribute to remittances and beneficial return migration. Capital flows can complement domestic savings, alleviate credit constraints, and impose discipline on macroeconomic policies. Knowledge flows contribute to ideas, technologies, and know-how that are all shared and augmented across borders.

However, the capacity of the poor and the B40 to benefit from a greater outward orientation is not guaranteed, suggesting a role for complementary and compensatory policies. It is generally accepted that relatively open economies fare better in the aggregate than closed ones and that relatively open policies contribute considerably to development. Yet, openness may lead to greater uncertainty, and greater openness may not always be positive for the poorest in the short run; even in the longer run, some people may be left behind in poverty (World Bank and WTO 2015). Various challenges may be present, such as market barriers in agriculture, fragility and conflict, informality, and gender biases. Complementary policies may help the poor to extract maximum benefit. For example, trade facilitation can be strengthened and connectivity can be improved to reduce remoteness from markets at the subnational level, broadening access for poor and small traders. Moreover, since trade liberalization can produce adjustment costs that raise poverty, compensatory policies can be considered to mitigate this impact (Winters, McCulloch, and McKay 2004).

Future orientation to meet investment needs

An orientation toward the future—the willingness to postpone current consumption in return for higher consumption later—is essential to generate the savings needed to finance investment. The speed of growth, especially in early stages of development, is limited mainly by the pace of investment—both public and private—which reflects the availability of both domestic and foreign savings. Future-oriented economies are characterized by their ability to raise funds and invest them productively, generating lasting growth in the process. Investment needs are broad and cover infrastructure as well as education and health. Public infrastructure investment (in roads, ports, airports, and power) helps attract private investment and paves the way for diversification and structural transformation. Sufficient fiscal space is needed to finance infrastructure needs, but governments can also team up with the private sector in public-private partnerships that share financial benefits and burdens while clearly delineating risks.

Access to infrastructure has potentially important effects on the ability of the poor to generate income. Connective infrastructure is a crucial means of linking the farms and firms where the poor live and work to markets. Electrification of poor areas in South Africa has resulted in a 9 percentage point increase in female labor force participation, consumption, and earnings by allowing reallocation of time use within the household thanks to time-saving electric appliances (Dinkelman 2011). Along the same lines, rural electrification in India has caused changes in consumption and earnings, with increases in the labor supply of both men and women, and it has promoted girls' schooling by reallocating their time to tasks more conducive to school attendance. Investment in integration and connectedness through railroads in India has helped to reduce the exposure of agricultural prices and real income to rainfall shocks, and to diminish the famine and mortality risks associated with recurrent weather shocks (Burgess and Donaldson 2010).

Investment in human development is key

Achieving the ambitious World Bank Group goals will require leveraging human resources to their fullest potential. The capacity of households to contribute to overall growth and their own well-being depends on the assets they control, the returns to these assets, and how intensively the assets can be used (World Bank 2014c). The assets come in many forms, including human capital (education, health, nutrition), financial capital, physical capital (land, machinery), and social capital. Many of these assets—especially human and social capital—have both intrinsic and instrumental value. They are goods in their own right and contribute to well-being, and they also increase a person's income-generating capabilities. The focus on inequality of opportunities rather than inequality of outcomes is motivated by the need to provide incentives to accumulate human and physical capital. However, the same inequality of outcomes may prevent poorer households from borrowing to accumulate human and physical capital, which perpetuates poverty and inequality. Policies that enable poorer households to accumulate assets by reducing inequalities of opportunity are therefore crucial.

Equitable access to quality social services is key. To upgrade the human capital of lower-income groups, investments need to be made to ensure equality of access for critical basic social services, such as education, health, water, and sanitation. These investments often take place over multiple periods, with critical windows and sensitive periods depending on the type of investment. For example, in low- and middle-income countries, policies targeted at promoting infant and child survival and those focused on investments in nutrition and stimulation during the first years of life have the highest potential returns. Addressing deprivations during the prenatal period is critical. Providing access to prenatal care and ensuring that births are managed by skilled professionals will reduce the odds of maternal and child mortality (Campbell and Graham 2006). Beyond birth and survival, early environments have a powerful influence on shaping long-term outcomes. Socioeconomic gaps in child development emerge early in life, before school begins; persist through childhood; and are strongly predictive of adult outcomes, shaping social and economic inequalities in the long run (Fryer and Levitt 2004; Paxson and Schady 2007).

Access to quality education for all

Investments to increase access to education and vocational training and to improve educational quality are needed to equip poor people to take advantage of opportunities. Despite impressive gains in school enrollment over the past 25 years, 55 million primary-school-age children do not attend school, especially in Sub-Saharan Africa. In some cases no school is nearby, but more often other obstacles prevent children from attending school. School fees may be prohibitively expensive for parents. Even schools that are nominally free may be unaffordable because of ancillary costs such as books, supplies, uniforms, or miscellaneous fees. The opportunity cost of attending school may be too high for children who are needed to attend to household chores such as collecting water or firewood, cooking, caring for younger children, or helping with the family farm. Parents may consider the financial and opportunity costs too high if they are unaware of the potential returns to investing in their children's education, or they may rightly calculate that the returns are low because absentee teachers or lack of supplies deliver a low-quality education.

In middle- and high-income countries, where the quantity of education has been more impressive than its results, it is a priority to ensure quality of education. Access to primary and secondary education is widespread or universal in richer countries, where indicators of enrollment and years of schooling are generally good (see box 1.9 for the example of Chile). But important differences persist in the terms of access and outcomes (figure 1.22). Students from poorer families often receive inferior-quality education, worsening their learning outcomes. For example, in countries such as Argentina, Brazil, Bulgaria, Indonesia, and Tunisia, the share of B40 students who demonstrate basic math competencies in the Programme for International Student Assessment test is less than half that of top 20 percent students (World Bank 2015e). In South Asia, inequalities in educational outcomes appear to be increasingly driven by differences in school quality rather than by access to schools (World Bank 2015a). This situation is especially apparent in settings where higher-income households can turn to private schools when public schools are failing.

Improvements in educational quality require that schools and teachers be held accountable for student performance. Building schools, training teachers, and procuring supplies are only the first steps. In addition to adequate resources, school systems and teachers need to be accountable for using resources to deliver results according to established metrics. Not only must teachers show up but they also must be given the right incentives, as well as the complementary inputs and support, to teach effectively. Evidence from Kenya shows

BOX 1.9 Chile's growth-with-equity approach

Chile's growth-with-equity approach has produced substantial development progress. Infant mortality declined between 1990 and 2011 from 16 deaths per 1,000 births to 7—the second-lowest level in Latin America. As measured by the Gini index, income inequality declined from 57.3 to 50.8 between 1990 and 2011, and the income share held by the bottom 40 percent (B40) rose from 9.9 to 12.7. Since 1990, gross domestic product (GDP) per capita growth has averaged 3.9 percent a year. This progress can be associated with policies that aligned growth with equity. The economy was opened to international trade and disciplined by fiscal prudence. Government expenditures were directed toward programs that prioritized families' investments in health and human capital to reduce the inequality of opportunity. Overall Chileans are healthier and better educated than they were in 1990, and they enjoy higher standards of living.

The policies Chile undertook resulted in broad benefits for the B40. For instance, figure B1.9.1 shows increasing secondary completion rates for workers in the B40 across all sectors in the economy. As a result, the education gap between the B40 and the T60, shown in figure B1.9.2, decreased steadily as Chile progressed toward universal secondary education. Alongside these developments, national labor productivity increased from $12 to $28 for an hour of work.[a]

More work, however, remains to be done. Chile's level of inequality remains high compared with the region and Organisation for Co-operation and Development (OECD) countries. Chile's inequality is also reflected in low intergenerational social mobility, which is largely caused by unequal access to quality education (Núñez and Miranda 2011). Social public spending has risen significantly over the last two decades, especially on health and education, but still lags regional and OECD averages. The Chilean tax-transfer system is characterized by low progressivity and has been less effective in reducing poverty and income inequality compared with the experience in the OECD (IMF 2014a).

FIGURE B1.9.1 Across all sectors, Chilean B40 workers are now better educated

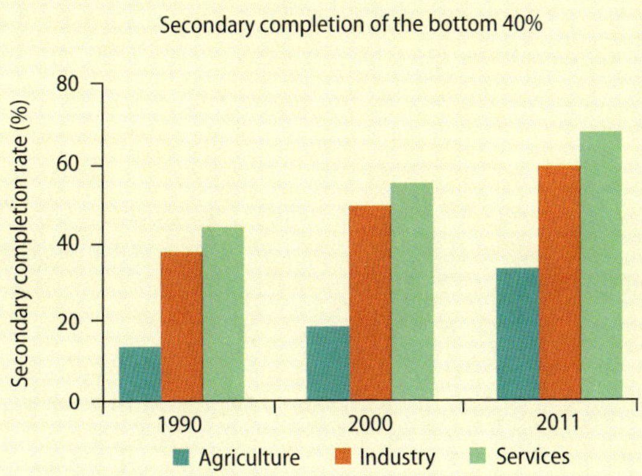

FIGURE B1.9.2 Educational catch-up of the B40 went hand-in-hand with rising productivity

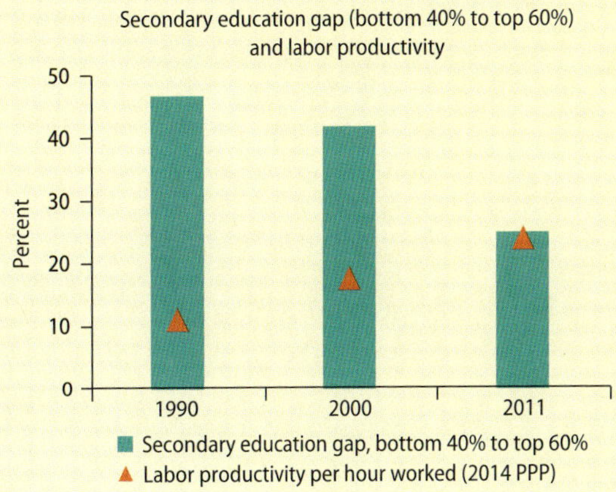

Source: World Bank calculations, based on CASEN and data from the Conference Board.
Note: For productivity: Total Economy Database; share of workers by sector and level of skill from the B40 was calculated using household surveys (Encuesta de Caracterización Socioeconómica Nacional) from Chile for the respective years. PPP = purchasing power parity.

a. The Conference Board's Total Economy Database. http://www.conference-board.org/data.

how greater parental and parent-teacher association involvement in teacher selection and school governance can improve the quality of education and student performance (Duflo, Dupas, and Kremer 2015). Greater exposure to the quality of services available elsewhere may also help parents and teachers demand better educational quality. Despite

FIGURE 1.22 Socioeconomic gaps are observed related to education

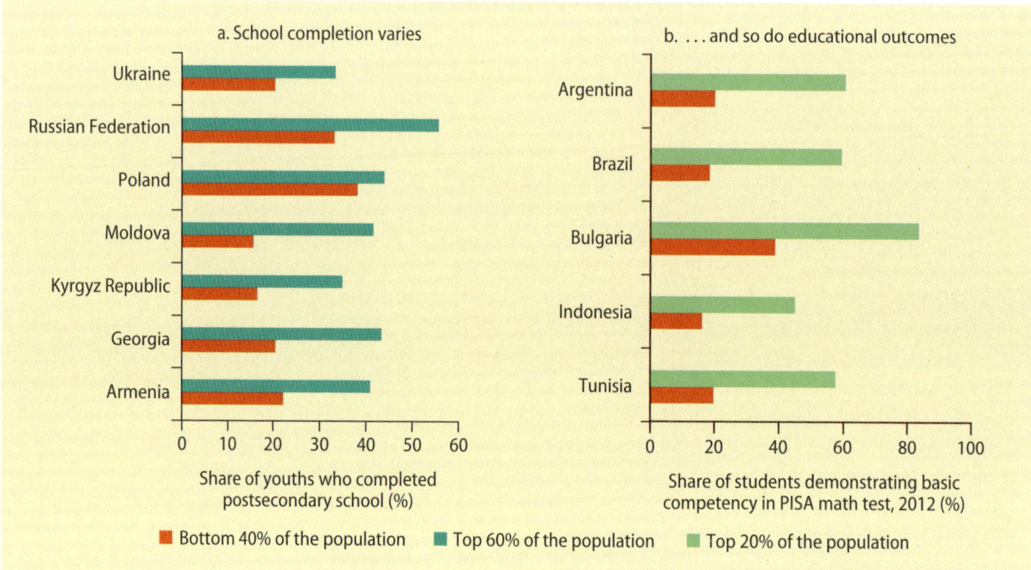

Sources: For panel a, ECAPOV 2015; for panel b, World Bank calculations, based on OECD 2012.
Note: For panel a, the age cohort for the estimates refers to youth ages 22–25 years for Georgia, the Kyrgyz Republic, Moldova, and the Russian Federation; ages 21–24 for Armenia and Ukraine; and ages 24–27 for Poland. All data are from 2012. For panel b, the PISA test score is for the share of students above level 2 in math.

the pronounced gaps in educational performance, people in the B40 express as much or more satisfaction with public education services than do those in the T20 in most regions; the main exceptions are South Asia and, to a lesser extent, Sub-Saharan Africa (figure 1.23).

Health care to meet evolving needs

In the health sector, investments are needed to strengthen the physical infrastructure, especially the systems that deliver health care. The quality of health care delivery needs to be upgraded, particularly in key areas such as primary care and maternal and child health. At the same time, health care services need to be extended to areas that are currently underserved, possibly through partnerships with the private sector and greater use of community-level providers. As in education, increasing the accountability of the health system is crucial and can be achieved by better linking spending to results, as community-level monitoring has done in Uganda (Gill and Revenga forthcoming). Reducing the costs of health care for low-income individuals is also needed, including better control of both official out-of-pocket payments and unofficial fees that are sometimes paid to speed delivery of services.

Richer countries, especially those whose populations are aging rapidly, need health systems that are equipped to meet the growing burden of chronic noncommunicable diseases. Treatment of cardiovascular diseases, chronic respiratory diseases, cancer, and diabetes claims a rapidly growing share of national health care budgets. For low-income households without adequate health insurance, these diseases also have a major impact on household budgets. The incidence of noncommunicable disease can be curbed by prevention-oriented policies such as dietary education, food price policies that do not effectively subsidize unhealthy foods, public funding for smoking-cessation programs, and programs to encourage more physically active lifestyles. Policies that contain the out-of-pocket costs for low-income patients are also needed.

Water and sanitation for healthy environments

Creating an environment conducive to good public health is just as important as improving the health care system. Improving health and physical well-being begins with prevention. Lack of access to clean water and sanitation leaves poor people susceptible to infectious disease both in the rural countryside and in congested urban slums. Provision of piped water and latrines has been shown to reduce disease and child mortality. A healthy environment has an intrinsic positive impact on the quality of life and an instrumental impact on productivity in the workplace and on full participation in society. Beyond the initial investment to install adequate water supply, sanitation, and drainage facilities, it is critical that the systems be maintained regularly.

The poor and vulnerable need robust insurance

Robust mechanisms are needed to assist both those left behind in the development process and those whose well-being can be severely negatively affected by various shocks. Contrary to the general perception of social protection as a narrowly defined cash transfer program, a range of public interventions can protect the poor and vulnerable while promoting competitiveness and growth. Social assistance and insurance schemes are key components of a social protection system. They combine with labor market policies and regulations to form the broader social protection system. A well-functioning social protection system also enhances people's capacity to manage risks, cushions the impact of crises or economic adjustments, and enables people to take greater advantage of economic opportunities. As cross-country experiences illustrate, social protection institutions are essential to address adversity and foster long-term prosperity (World Bank 2010b).

Social assistance to address poverty

Effective social assistance programs can provide the poor with a floor that keeps them from destitution, as well as a ladder to help escape poverty. Noncontributory social transfers ensure that those who are not able to take advantage of opportunities in the labor market can still meet their basic needs. These transfers may also give poor households the financial breathing room to pursue investment opportunities, such as schooling for their children, which might otherwise be unaffordable. They also provide an element of protection from transient shocks. Fiscally efficient transfers are those that are both well targeted to the poor population (low errors of inclusion) and have good coverage (low errors of exclusion). The design of social assistance

FIGURE 1.23 In several regions, satisfaction with access to public services for health care and education is low

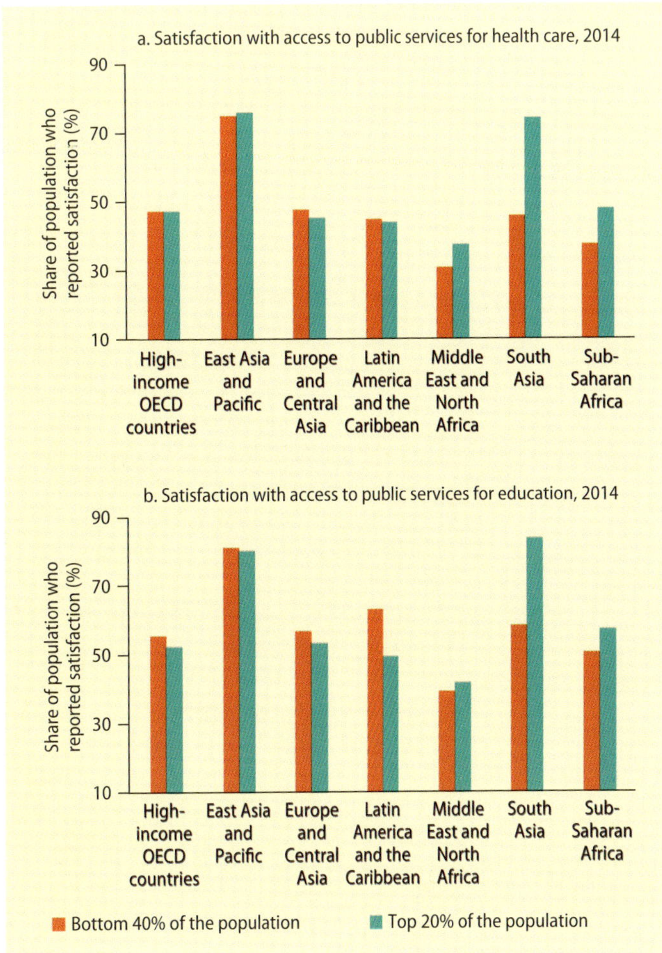

Source: World Bank calculations, based on Gallup World Poll.
Note: Population groups are defined based on income or consumption per capita. Views on satisfaction with access to public services are assessed on a scale from 1 (dissatisfied) to 10 (satisfied).

policies is an important determinant of their effectiveness; avoiding disincentives to work, such as sharp reductions in benefits for relatively small increases in earned income, is particularly important.

Conditional cash transfers provide benefits to alleviate current poverty while simultaneously promoting behavior that is likely to provide a pathway out of poverty. Pioneered in Latin America and now in place around the globe, such programs provide cash or noncash benefits to families on the condition that they make investments in human capital, such as taking their children for vaccinations or other preventive health services or sending their children to school. The cash transfers received by households not only ease their poverty but also allow them to look beyond their immediate subsistence needs to invest in their children's futures.

Social insurance to deal with vulnerability

Individuals—especially those among the already poor and the B40—face a variety of risks that can have serious consequences for their well-being. External shocks, such as localized droughts or floods, and repeated shocks can drive households into (deeper) poverty. Commodity price volatility may depress income from agriculture and may hurt the vulnerable the most. Events specific to individuals, such as illness or poor health of the head of household, can have the same effect. In these cases it is not joblessness per se that pushes families into poverty but rather the destruction of personal and household assets. Even taking these shocks into account, however, job losses remain a critical factor sending people deeper into poverty. More generally, as countries pursue market-oriented structural change and expose their economies to greater forces of competition, adjustment costs may arise in the near term even if over the longer term net positive benefits may accrue. However, a competitive economy can coexist with an inclusive society if minimum levels of protection are provided against the risks of economic restructuring.

Social insurance policies are an important mechanism for providing protection against such risks. Social insurance policies are not only designed to help families through idiosyncratic shocks but are also geared to keep people out of poverty from predictable events; contributory old-age pensions to provide income during retirement are one example. The choice of policy instrument depends upon the nature of the risk being considered and the affordability of the intervention. Precautionary policies can cushion the vulnerable against shocks to a limited extent. In developing countries, where farming and self-employment are more prevalent and income support mechanisms more limited, macroeconomic instability caused by price shocks has less impact on open unemployment and more on earnings from work (World Bank 2013b). Governments can adopt active social protection policies to mitigate the impact of shocks on the poor. Many countries have public unemployment insurance systems to help mitigate the risk of job loss. Many also have disability insurance to cover situations where illness or injury affects employment opportunities.

Global insurance to absorb systemic shocks

Beyond assisting the destitute and insuring against individual risks, protection also needs to extend to large systemic shocks. Natural disasters or global pandemics are examples of systemic shocks that can set progress back for years. Natural and climate-related shocks appear to be growing in importance, with the poor in low-income countries the least prepared for managing such risks. To better equip them to cope with these risks, a range of options exists that transcends borders. One option is to ensure that funding for disaster preparedness and disaster response is already available before such events occur. In this context, the World Bank Group has worked with donors and the private sector to develop a Disaster Risk Financing and Insurance facility that does exactly this. A similar initiative, the Pandemic Emergency Facility, is being developed to quickly disburse substantial funding in response to objective epidemiological criteria. An additional goal of such initiatives is to stimulate greater country investments in preparedness. These include early-warning systems, response planning, training of frontline professionals, and preparedness equipment and logistics, as well as investments in health systems (Gill and Revenga forthcoming; World Bank 2013c.)

Conclusion

Every country in the world—low-, middle-, and high-income—continues to grapple with poverty. In developing countries, extreme poverty remains a concern. As indicated by the new global poverty estimates, based on the 2011 PPP indexes, developing countries have made a great deal of progress in reducing extreme poverty. Yet the challenges remain vast. Reaching the World Bank's target of reducing extreme poverty to 3 percent of the world's population by 2030 is ambitious, particularly for NRB and conflicted-affected countries in Sub-Saharan Africa. The latest poverty estimates and projections show that, to meet the global target, policies must go beyond targeting rates of aggregate economic growth, because growth alone will not be sufficient to achieve the goal. Economic growth has helped reduce poverty by about 1 percentage point a year since the 1980s. Yet, in the absence of targeted and effective policies, it is likely that this rate will not be sustainable, particularly as the 3 percent target is approached. Unless extra efforts are made to ensure economic, environmental, and social sustainability, the pace of poverty decline associated with a given rate of economic growth can be expected, at some point, to diminish markedly and possibly even reverse.

Just as critically, ending global poverty requires more than reducing the number of people living below the extreme poverty line. Even if the 3 percent target were reached in the aggregate, many countries would still have high levels of poverty. Similarly, within countries deep pockets of poverty would remain, often in rural areas, where broader economic growth as a poverty eliminator may still not reach the poor. The deepening impact of climate change will contribute to such spatial concentrations of poverty by endangering agricultural output through different channels, including through negative effects on access to fresh water. Moreover, poverty is not just about income: the levels and trends in income-based poverty are imperfectly correlated with other basic variables such as under-five mortality, primary education, and undernourishment. It is possible that even if the first goal of eradicating extreme poverty were achieved in income-based terms, acute multidimensional poverty could still be prevalent.

Many countries—including high-income countries—have seen robust income growth among the poorer segments of the population, but progress has been uneven and challenges remain. Persistent inequalities in opportunities continue, constraining not only the well-being of those affected but also their income-generating capacity and thereby the prospects for broad-based economic growth that benefits everyone. New challenges are also appearing. In a range of countries, growth—a key driver of shared prosperity—may be less buoyant than it was before the global financial crisis. Further constraints may arise if the underlying factors that led to an increase in the B40 income share in many countries turn out to be transitory or unsustainable. In light of these factors, further policy efforts will be needed not only to advance the agenda where progress has remained incomplete or uneven but also to preserve the gains of the past.

The policy approaches for sustainably ending global poverty and boosting shared prosperity are similar in spirit. Complementary policies are needed to foster economic growth while also lifting the incomes of those on the bottom rungs of the economic ladder. Good identification methods are needed to assess poverty in all its dimensions. Efforts can be targeted geographically to regions (particularly Sub-Saharan Africa), to individual countries, and to locations within countries. Countries also would do well to pursue a comprehensive strategy focused on generating broad-based growth, investing in human development, and providing robust social protection mechanisms. Throughout, such strategy needs to be mindful of sustainability—economic, social, and environmental. With such strategies in place, the world stands a better chance of ending extreme poverty by 2030 and lifting the well-being of lower-income people in every country of the world.

Notes

1. Monetary poverty measures are based on household surveys that measure deprivation on the basis of either income or consumption data. To simplify, this Report refers to "income" poverty for both cases. In a similar vein, most references to poverty, unless explicitly stated otherwise, mean "extreme" poverty.
2. The availability and the quality of data remain a concern in the assessment of both goals, and the robustness of underlying methodologies will require continued scrutiny. Increasing the availability and quality of data is a key priority to strengthen analysis, policy formulation, and policy implementation (World Bank 2015d).
3. Forthcoming update of World Bank 2011a. Furthermore, 7.0 million deaths in developing countries in 2010, or 18 percent of total deaths, were due to pollution (IHME 2010).
4. Based on the international poverty line of \$1.90 a day (2011 PPP). A similar trend is observed when comparing 1990 with 2011 using a poverty line of \$1.25 a day (2005 PPP).
5. China became an upper-middle-income country in 2010.
6. Because poverty data for several fragile and conflict-affected states are unavailable, the actual numbers of poor living in these countries could be much higher.
7. To evaluate the inclusiveness of growth, it is useful to examine how the rate of average income growth transmits into changes in poverty alleviation. The depth elasticity compares the growth elasticities of the person-equivalent and traditional headcount ratios. It also indicates how well changes in the traditional headcount predict changes in the person-equivalent measure (Castleman, Foster, and Smith 2015).
8. The MPI is calculated and reported yearly by the Oxford Poverty and Human Development Initiative and the United Nations Development Programme (Alkire and Foster 2011; Alkire and Santos 2013).
9. While household surveys may track consumption or income, reference is made just to income for convenience.
10. The second of the World Bank Group's goals has been extensively discussed in World Bank (2013b, 2015c). The discussion in this Report builds on these publications, focusing selectively on only two aspects: links to equity and inequality, and the non-income dimension.
11. See also the influential book on redistribution with growth (Chenery et al. 1974) and the broad-based growth discussion in World Bank (1990).
12. Rauniyar and Kanbur (2010) provide an example of the latter, which closely connects to examining how shared prosperity, when measured in all of its dimensions, benefits the less well-off.
13. In some respects, the indicator is itself a multidimensional amalgamation because it summarizes the ability to obtain goods and services critical for welfare through market transactions.
14. Basu (2001, 2006) noted that income indicators focusing on the poorer income deciles may correlate more strongly than average incomes with non-income indicators of well-being, such as greater life expectancy and higher literacy.
15. If the shared prosperity objective were illustrated by a social welfare function, it would attach positive weights through the 40th percentile but zero weight thereafter. A singular focus on the B40, however, would conflict with the poverty goal (given that in many countries extreme poverty incidence is well above 40 percent); it would also be inconsistent with the requirement of social sustainability (which requires that the interest of the B40 cannot be considered with total disregard to or independently of the rest of the income distribution).
16. Derived from "prosperitas" ("doing well" in Latin), *prosperity* can be defined as a state, the optimal distribution of which over a

given population inevitably involves normative questions about social equity. Therefore, shared prosperity—or "prosperitas vulgaris" (that is, prosperity shared by all)—intrinsically reflects a societal value judgment about the equitable distribution of resources as articulated through a process of social choice.

17. World Bank (2005) refers to the theories by John Rawls (1971), Amartya Sen (1985), Ronald Dworkin (1981a, 1981b), and John Roemer (1998).
18. Indicators based on mean income growth tend to penalize the less well-off. Since average income weights the incomes of everyone equally, it assigns a greater weight to those in richer percentiles of the income distribution, since richer percentiles have higher incomes (World Bank 2015b).
19. Such a strategy is indicated in World Bank (2013b, 19), where the shared prosperity objective is articulated "to *achieve the maximum possible increase* in living standards of the less well-off." Other references, however, such as World Bank (2015c, 1) suggest that the objective merely entails "*increasing* the average incomes of the bottom 40 percent of the population in each country."
20. The 2014–15 GMR assesses the shared prosperity performance of countries around 2006–11, whereas the 2015–16 Report examines the period around 2007–12.
21. Botswana, Mozambique, Namibia, Nicaragua, Tajikistan, and West Bank and Gaza.
22. Today, the richest 10 percent of the population in Organisation for Economic Co-operation and Development countries earns 9.5 times the income of the poorest 10 percent; in the 1980s this ratio stood at 7:1, and it has been rising ever since (Cingano 2014).
23. The previous section examined B40 income growth and its implications for the B40 percent income share, a measure of inequality of independent interest, with a view to *illustrate* different patterns across countries. In this section, the B40 income growth is *explained* by the constituent components that are thought to drive the explanatory variable: average income growth and its elasticity with respect to the B40 (the change in the B40 income share), where the latter measure of inequality is treated as an instrument rather than an end in itself.
24. The authors examine the relationship through the lens of the social welfare function that corresponds to the shared prosperity concept, which coincides with the average income of the B40 group.
25. The observation also appears to hold within countries. Skoufias, Tiwari, and Shidiq (2014) find a strong positive correlation between overall consumption growth and B40 growth across provinces in Thailand.
26. The role of growth in accounting for changes in social welfare appears to be smaller for bottom-sensitive social welfare functions, mainly because the growth rate of the income shares of the poorest deciles exhibits the highest volatility between spells. This volatility is amplified by social welfare functions that place a high weight on the poor. Dollar, Kleineberg, and Kraay (2013) argue that part of this variation may be due to sampling variation.
27. Efforts are under way to incorporate inequality in longevity and unemployment across educational groups.
28. Primary completion rates in low-income countries are 20–30 percent for the B40 (70–100 percent for the T20). Even in middle-income countries, such as Albania, Lesotho, Nicaragua, and Nigeria, the gaps are significant.
29. For example, among 41 countries, the index of the inequality of opportunity is 2 percent in Norway compared with 34 percent in Guatemala.
30. World Development Indicators, World Bank, July 2015.
31. The concept of change in total wealth per capita rests upon the premise of three forms of capital—natural, human, and physical. Transformation of one form of capital into another is possible. Thus, education expenditures are added to gross natural savings and partly offset the depletion of natural capital (World Bank 2014a, 124–29).
32. Specifically, McNamara said: "The two goals are intrinsically related, though governments are often tempted to pursue one without adequate attention to the other. But from a development point of view that approach always

fails in the end. For the pursuit of growth without a reasonable concern for equity is ultimately socially destabilizing, and often violently so. And the pursuit of equity without a reasonable concern for growth merely tends to redistribute economic stagnation. Neither pursuit, taken by itself, can lead to sustained, successful development." (McNamara 1980).

33. World Bank (2005) finds that this elasticity is close to zero in countries with high income inequality.
34. The year 2015 marks the 40th anniversary of publication of Arthur M. Okun's famous book, *Equality and Efficiency: The Big Trade-Off*. One of the original supply-side economists, Okun introduced the metaphor of the leaky bucket, which has become famous among economists: "The money must be carried from the rich to the poor in a leaky bucket. Some of it will simply disappear in transit, so the poor will not receive all the money that is taken from the rich" (Okun 1975, 91).
35. Some financial inclusion policies, such as broadening credit access (in government's efforts toward achieving equitable opportunities), could entail a trade-off with macroeconomic stability even if they achieve higher growth (Sahay et al. 2015).
36. This section builds on Gill and Revenga (forthcoming) and World Bank (2010b, 2010c, 2014c).
37. These economies were Botswana; Brazil; China; Hong Kong SAR, China; Indonesia; Japan; the Republic of Korea; Malaysia; Malta; Oman; Singapore; Taiwan, China; and Thailand.
38. Commission on Growth and Development (2008) notes: "The growth of GDP may be measured up in the macroeconomic treetops, but all the action is in the microeconomic undergrowth, where new limbs sprout, and dead wood is cleared away."
39. Howitt 2009. Aghion, Harris, and Howitt (2001) find, however, that greater competition does not automatically lead to faster productivity growth, because preconditions need to be satisfied so that firms are sufficiently enabled to innovate. For competition to effectively spur innovation, elementary risk mitigation and coping mechanisms need to be in place to protect individuals—though not necessarily industries, firms, or jobs—from the downside risks of failure.

References

Aghion, P., C. Harris, and P. Howitt. 2001. "Competition, Imitation and Growth with Step-by-Step Innovation." *Review of Economic Studies* 68 (3): 467–92.

Alkire, S., and J. Foster. 2011. "Understandings and Misunderstandings of Multidimensional Poverty Measurement." *Journal of Economic Inequality* 9: 476–87.

Alkire, S., J. Foster, and M. E. Santos. 2011. "Where Did Identification Go?" *Journal of Economic Inequality* 9: 501–05.

Alkire, S., J. Foster, S. Seth, M. E. Santos, J. M. Roche, and P. Ballon. 2015. *Multidimensional Poverty Measurement and Analysis*. Oxford, U.K.: Oxford University Press.

Alkire, S., C. Jindra, G. R. Aguilar, S. Seth, and A. Vaz. 2015. *Global Multidimensional Poverty Index 2015*. Oxford, U.K.: Oxford Poverty and Human Development Initiative.

Alkire, S., and M. E. Santos. 2013. "Measuring Acute Poverty in the Developing World: Robustness and Scope of the Multidimensional Poverty Index." Working Paper 59, Oxford Poverty and Human Development Initiative, Oxford, U.K.

Alkire, S., and S. Seth. 2013. "Multidimensional Poverty Reduction in India between 1999 and 2006: Where and How?" Working Paper 60, Oxford Poverty and Human Development Initiative, Oxford, U.K.

Angelsen, A., P. Jagger, R. Babigumira, B. Belcher, N. J. Hogarth, S. Bauch, and S. Wunder. 2014. "Environmental Income and Rural Livelihoods: A Global-Comparative Analysis." *World Development 64 (Supplement 1):* S12–S28.

Araujo, J. A. de T. R., E. Vostroknutova, K. M. Wacker, and M. Clavijo. 2015. *Understanding Latin America and the Caribbean's Income Gap*. Washington, DC: World Bank Group.

Atkinson, A. B. 2014. "After Piketty?" *British Journal of Sociology* 65: 619–38.

Atkinson, A. B., T. Piketty, and E. Saez. 2011. "Top Incomes in the Long Run of History." *Journal of Economic Literature* 49 (1): 3–71.

Banerjee, A. V., and E. Duflo. 2003. "Inequality and Growth: What Can the Data Say?" *Journal of Economic Growth* 8 (3): 267–99.

Basu, K. 2001. "On the Goals of Development." In *Frontiers of Development Economics: The Future in Perspective*, edited by G. M. Meier and J. E. Stiglitz, 61–86. New York: Oxford University Press.

———. 2006. "Globalization, Poverty, and Inequality: What Is the Relationship? What Can Be Done?" *World Development* 34 (8): 1361–73.

Battistin, E., R. Blundell, and A. Lewbel. 2009. "Why Is Consumption More Log Normal than Income? Gibrat's Law Revisited." *Journal of Political Economy* 117: 1140–54.

Bentham, J. 2000. (Published in 1789.) *The Principles of Morals and Legislation*. Kitchener, Ontario: Batoche Books.

Berg, A., J. D. Ostry, and J. Zettelmeyer. 2012. "What Makes Growth Sustained?" *Journal of Development Economics* 98 (2): 149–66.

Boarini R., F. Murtin, and P. Schreyer. Forthcoming. "Inclusive Growth: The OECD Measurement Framework." OECD Statistics Directorate Working Paper, Organisation for Economic Co-operation and Development, Paris.

Bourguignon, F., and G. Fields. 1990. "Poverty Measures and Anti-Poverty Policy." *Recherches Economique de Louvain* 56 (3–4): 409–27.

Bourguignon, F., and L. Pereira da Silva, eds. 2003. *The Impact of Economic Policies on Poverty and Income Distribution: Evaluation Techniques and Tools*. New York: Oxford University Press for the World Bank.

Bourguignon, F., et al. 2010. "The Millennium Development Goals at Midpoint: An Assessment." In *Equity and Growth in a Globalizing World*, edited by R. Kanbur and A. M. Spence, 17–39. Washington, DC: Commission for Growth and Development.

Brauer, M., et al. Forthcoming. "Ambient Air Pollution Exposure Estimation for the Global Burden of Disease 2013." Institute for Health Metrics and Evaluation, University of Washington, Seattle.

Brunori, P., F. H. G. Ferreira, and V. Peragine. 2013. "Inequality of Opportunity, Income Inequality and Economic Mobility: Some International Comparisons." Policy Research Working Paper 6304, World Bank, Washington, DC.

Burgess R., and D. Donaldson. 2010. "Can Openness Mitigate the Effects of Weather Shocks? Evidence from India's Famine Era." *American Economic Review* 100 (2): 449–53.

Bussolo, M., R. De Hoyos, D. Medvedev, and D. van der Mensbrugghe. 2008. "Global Growth and Distribution: Are China and India Reshaping the World?" Working Paper RP2008/29, United Nations University World Institute for Development Economic Research, Helsinki.

Campbell, O., and W. Graham. 2006. "Strategies for Reducing Maternal Mortality: Getting On with What Works." *Lancet* 368 (7): 1284–99.

Castleman, T., J. Foster, and S. C. Smith. 2015. "Person-Equivalent Headcount Measures of Poverty." Institute for International Economic Policy Working Paper Series 2015-10, Elliot School of International Affairs, George Washington University, Washington, DC.

Chandra, V., J. Y. Lin, and Y. Wang. 2012. "Leading Dragons Phenomenon: New Opportunities for Catch-Up in Low-Income Countries." Policy Research Working Paper 6000, World Bank, Washington, DC.

Chen, S., and M. Ravallion. 2003. "Household Welfare Impacts of China's Accession to the World Trade Organization." Policy Research Working Paper 3040, World Bank, Washington, DC.

———. 2010. "The Developing World Is Poorer than We Thought, but No Less Successful in the Fight against Poverty." *Quarterly Journal of Economics* 125 (4): 1577–625.

———. 2013. "More Relatively Poor People in a Less Absolutely Poor World." *Review of Income and Wealth* 59 (1): 1–28.

Chenery, H., C. Bell, J. Duloy, and R. Duloy. 1974. *Redistribution with Growth*. Oxford, U.K.: Oxford University Press.

Cingano, F. 2014. "Trends in Income Inequality and its Impact on Economic Growth." OECD Social, Employment and Migration Working Paper 163, Organization for Economic Co-operation and Development, Paris.

Commission on Growth and Development. 2008. *The Growth Report: Strategies for Sustained Growth and Inclusive Development*. Washington, DC: World Bank.

De Cavalcanti, T., K. Mohaddes, and M. Raissi. 2012. "Commodity Price Volatility and the Sources of Growth." IMF Working Paper 12/12, International Monetary Fund, Washington, DC.

Dinkelman, T. 2011. "The Effects of Rural Electrification on Employment: New Evidence from South Africa." *American Economic Review* 101 (7): 3078–108.

Dollar, D., T. Kleineberg, and A. Kraay. 2013. "Growth Still Is Good for the Poor." Policy Research Working Paper 6568, World Bank, Washington, DC.

———. 2015. "Growth, Inequality, and Social Welfare: Cross-Country Evidence." *Economic Policy* 30 (82): 335–77.

Dollar, D., and A. Kraay. 2002. "Growth Is Good for the Poor." *Journal of Economic Growth* 7: 195–225.

Dreze, J., and A. Sen. 2011. "Putting Growth in its Place." *Outlook*, November 14.

Duflo, E., P. Dupas, and M. Kremer. 2015. "School Governance, Teacher Incentives, and Pupil-Teacher Ratios: Experimental Evidence from Kenyan Primary Schools." *Journal of Public Economics* 123: 92–110.

Dworkin, R. 1981a. "What Is Equality? Part 1: Equality of Welfare." *Philosophy and Public Affairs 10* (3): 185–246.

———. 1981b. "What Is Equality? Part 2: Equality of Resources." *Philosophy and Public Affairs* 10 (3): 283–345.

Easterly, W. 2007. "Inequality Does Cause Underdevelopment: Insights from a New Instrument." *Journal of Development Economics* 84 (2): 755–76.

ECAPOV. 2015. Database Harmonization as of June 2015. Europe and Central Asia Team for Statistical Development, World Bank, Washington, DC.

Ferreira, F. H. G., and M. A. Lugo. 2013. "Multidimensional Poverty Analysis: Looking for a Middle Ground." *World Bank Research Observer* 28 (2): 220–35.

Ferreira, F. H. G. and M. Ravallion. 2011. "Poverty and Inequality: the Global Context." In *The Oxford Handbook of Economic Inequality*, edited by B. Nolan, W. Salverda, and T. M. Smeeding. Oxford, U.K.: Oxford University Press.

Field, C. B., ed. 2014. *Climate Change 2014: Impacts, Adaptation, and Vulnerability. Vol. 1.* Geneva: Intergovernmental Panel on Climate Change (IPCC).

Forbes, K. J. 2000. "A Reassessment of the Relationship between Inequality and Growth." *American Economic Review* 90(4): 869–87.

Foster, J. 2015. "A Framework for Measuring Inclusive Growth." Unpublished paper, Institute for International Economic Policy, George Washington University, Washington, DC.

Foster, J., and S. Smith. 2014. "Measuring Ultrapoverty: A New Class of Indices and an Application to Rural Ethiopia Panel Data." Unpublished paper, Institute for International Economic Policy, George Washington University, Washington, DC.

Fryer R. G., and S. D. Levitt. 2004. "Understanding the Black-White Test Score Gap in the First Two Years of School." *Review of Economics and Statistics* 86 (2): 447–64.

Füssel, H.-M., and R. J. T. Klein. 2006. "Climate Change Vulnerability Assessments: An Evolution of Conceptual Thinking." *Climatic Change* 75: 301–29.

Gill, I., and H. Kharas. 2007. *An East Asian Renaissance. Ideas for Economic Growth.* Washington, DC: World Bank.

Gill, I., and A. Revenga. Forthcoming. *Grow, Invest, Insure—A Plan to End Poverty.* Washington, DC: World Bank.

Government of India, Planning Commission. 2009. *Report of the Expert Group to Review the Methodology for Estimation of Poverty.*

Harsanyi, J. C. 1955. "Cardinal Welfare, Individualistic Ethics, and Interpersonal Comparisons of Utility." *Journal of Political Economy* 63 (4): 309–21.

Hertel, T. W., and S. D. Rosch. 2010. "Climate Change, Agriculture, and Poverty." *Applied Economic Perspectives and Policy* 32 (3): 355–85.

Howitt, P. 2009. "Competition, Innovation and Growth: Theory, Evidence and Policy Challenges." In *Innovation and Growth: Chasing a Moving Frontier*, edited by Chandra, V., and D. Erocal. Paris: Organisation for Economic Co-operation and Development.

IHME (Institute for Health Metrics and Evaluation). Global Burden of Disease 2010 Study (database). IHME, University of Washington, Seattle (accessed August 2015).

IMF (International Monetary Fund). 2011. *New Growth Drivers for Low-Income Countries: The Role of BRICS*. Washington, DC: IMF.

———. 2013. *Regional Economic Outlook, Sub-Saharan Africa: Keeping the Pace*. https://www.imf.org/external/pubs/ft/reo/2013/afr/eng/sreo1013.htm.

———. 2014a. "Chile: Selected Issues." IMF Country Report 14/219. http://www.imf.org/external/pubs/ft/scr/2014/cr14219.pdf.

———. 2014b. *Regional Economic Outlook, Sub-Saharan Africa: Staying the Course*. https://www.imf.org/external/pubs/ft/reo/2014/afr/eng/sreo1014.pdf.

Inchauste, G., and J. Saavedra-Chanduvi. 2014. "Opportunity Knocks: Deepening Our Understanding of Poverty Reduction." In *Understanding Changes in Poverty*, 1–13. Washington, DC: World Bank.

Inchauste, G., J. P. Azevedo, B. Essama-Nssah, S. Olivieri, T. Van Nguyen, J. Saavedra-Chanduvi, and H. Winkler. 2014. *Understanding Changes in Poverty. Directions in Development: Poverty*. Washington, DC: World Bank.

Jalan, J., and M. Ravallion. 2001. "Household Income Dynamics in Rural China." Policy Research Working Paper 2706, World Bank, Washington, DC.

Jolliffe, D., and E. B. Prydz. 2015. "Global Poverty Goals and Prices: How Purchasing Power Parity Matters." Policy Research Working Paper 7256, World Bank, Washington, DC.

Kraay, A., and D. McKenzie. 2014. "Do Poverty Traps Exist?" Policy Research Working Paper 6835, World Bank, Washington, DC.

Kuznets, S. 1955. "Economic Growth and Income Inequality." *American Economic Review* 45 (1): 1–28.

Lakner, C., and B. Milanovic. 2013. "Global Income Distribution: From the Fall of the Berlin Wall to the Great Recession." Policy Research Working Paper 6719, World Bank, Washington, DC.

Lakner, C., M. Negre, and E. B. Prydz. 2014. "Twinning the Goals: How Can Promoting Shared Prosperity Help to Reduce Global Poverty?" Policy Research Working Paper 7106, World Bank, Washington, DC.

Leichenko, R., and J. A. Silva. 2014. "Climate Change and Poverty: Vulnerability, Impacts, and Alleviation Strategies." *Wiley Interdisciplinary Reviews: Climate Change* 5 (4): 539–56.

Li, H., and H.-F. Zou. 1998. "Income Inequality Is Not Harmful for Growth: Theory and Evidence." *Review of Development Economics* 2 (3): 318–34.

Loayza, N., and C. Raddatz. 2010. "The Composition of Growth Matters for Poverty Alleviation." *Journal of Development Economics* 93: 137–51.

Marrero, G., and J.-G. Rodriguez. 2012. "Inequality of Opportunity in Europe." *Review of Income and Wealth* 58 (4): 597–621.

———. 2013. "Inequality of Opportunity and Growth." *Journal of Development Economics* 104 (C): 107–22.

McNamara, R. S. 1972. "Address to the Board of Governors by Robert S. McNamara." World Bank, Washington, DC. http://documents.worldbank.org/curated/en/1972/09/15535489/address-board-governors-robert-s-mcnamara.

———. 1980. "Remarks to the Foreign Relations Association and Economic Society of the Canton of Berne, November 28, 1980." World Bank, Washington, DC. https://archivesholdings.worldbank.org/remarks-to-foreign-relations-association-and-economic-society-of-canton-of-berne-nov-28-1980-correspondence-01.

Messner, J. J., N. Hakenn, P. Taft, H. Blyth, K. Lawrence, S. Pavlou Graham, and F. Umaña. 2015. *Fragile States Index 2015: The Book*. Washington, DC: The Fund for Peace.

Milanovic, B. 2015. *All the Ginis Database*. Washington, DC: World Bank.

Nachtergaele, F., M. Petri, R. Biancalani, G. Van Lynden, and H. van Velthuizen. 2010. *Global Land Degradation Information System (GLADIS), Beta Version, An Information Database for Land Degradation Assessment at Global Level: Land Degradation Assessment in Drylands*. Technical Report 17. Rome: United Nations Food and Agriculture Organization.

Narayan, A., J. Saavedra-Chanduvi, and S. Tiwari. 2013. "Shared Prosperity: Links to

Growth, Inequality and Inequality of Opportunity." Policy Research Working Paper 6649, World Bank, Washington, DC.

Núñez, J., and L. Miranda. 2011. "Intergenerational Income and Educational Mobility in Urban Chile." *Estudios de Economia* 38 (1): 195–221.

O'Donnell, O., E. van Doorslaer, A. Wagstaff, and M. Lindelow. 2008. "Measurement of Living Standards." In *Analyzing Health Equity Using Household Survey Data: A Guide to Techniques and their Implementation*. Washington, DC: World Bank Institute.

OECD (Organisation for Economic Co-operation and Development). 2012. Results of the Programme for International Student Assessment (PISA). http://www1.worldbank.org/poverty/visualizeinequality/Overview/overview.

Okun, A. M. 1975. *Equality and Efficiency: The Big Tradeoff*. Washington, DC: Brookings Institution.

O'Sullivan, M., A. Rao, R. Banerjee, K. Gulati, and M. Vinez. 2014. *Levelling the Field: Improving Opportunities for Women Farmers in Africa*. Washington, DC: World Bank.

Paes de Barros, R., F. H. G. Ferreira, J. R. Molinas Vega, and J. Saavedra-Chanduvi. 2009. *Measuring Inequality of Opportunities in Latin America and the Caribbean*. Washington, DC: World Bank; London: Palgrave Macmillan.

Palma, J. G. 2011. "Homogeneous Middles vs. Heterogeneous Tails, and the End of the 'Inverted-U': It's All about the Share of the Rich." *Development and Change* 42 (1): 87–153.

Paxson C., and N. Schady. 2007. "Cognitive Development among Young Children in Ecuador: The Roles of Wealth, Health, and Parenting." *Journal of Human Resources* 42 (1): 49–84.

Piketty, T. 2014. *Capital in the Twenty-First Century*. Translated by A. Goldhammer. Cambridge, MA: Harvard University Press/Belknap Press.

PovcalNet. 2015. World Bank PovcalNet Database. http://iresearch.worldbank.org/PovcalNet.

Qureshi, Z. 2015. "Addressing Rising Inequality in G20 Economies." *Let's Talk Development* (blog). June 16. http://blogs.worldbank.org/developmenttalk/addressing-rising-inequality-g20-economies.

Rauniyar, G., and R. Kanbur. 2010. "Inclusive Development: Two Papers on Conceptualization, and the ADB Perspective, Working Paper 57036. Department of Applied Economics and Management, Cornell University, Ithaca.

Ravallion, M. 2003. "Measuring Aggregate Welfare in Developing Countries: How Well Do National Accounts and Surveys Agree?" *Review of Economics and Statistics* 85 (3): 645–52.

———. 2010. "Mashup Indices of Development." Policy Research Working Paper 5432, World Bank, Washington DC.

———. 2011. "On Multidimensional Indices of Poverty." *Journal of Economic Inequality* 9 (2): 235–48.

———. 2012. "Why Don't We See Poverty Convergence?" *American Economic Review* 102 (1): 504–23.

———. 2013. "How Long Will It Take to Lift One Billion People Out of Poverty?" *World Bank Research Observer* 28 (2): 139–58.

Ravallion, M., S. Chen, and Prem Sangraula. 2009. "Dollar a Day Revisited." *World Bank Economic Review* 23: 163–84.

Rawls, J. 1971. *A Theory of Justice*. Cambridge, MA: Harvard University Press.

Roemer, J. E. 1998. *Equality of Opportunity*. Cambridge, MA: Harvard University Press.

Sahay, R., M. Čihák, P. N'Diaye, A. Barajas, S. Mitra, A. Kyobe, Y. N. Mooi, and S. Reza Yousefi. Forthcoming. "Financial Inclusion: Can It Meet Multiple Macroeconomic Goals?" IMF Staff Discussion Note, International Monetary Fund, Washington, DC.

Sen, A. 1976. *Poverty: An Ordinal Approach to Measurement*. *Econometrica* 44 (2): 219–31.

———. 1983. "Poor, Relatively Speaking." *Oxford Economic Papers* 35 (2): 153–69.

———. 1985. *Commodities and Capabilities*. Amsterdam: North-Holland.

———. 1999. *Development as Freedom*. Oxford, U.K.: Oxford University Press.

Shepherd, G., C. Kazoora, and D. Müller. 2013. "Forests, Livelihoods and Poverty Alleviation: The Case of Uganda." Forestry Policy and Institutions Working Paper 32, United Nations Food and Agriculture Organization, Rome.

Skoufias, E, M. Rabassa, and S. Olivieri. 2012. "The Forecast for Poverty: A Review of the Evidence." In *The Poverty and Welfare Impacts of Climate Change: Quantifying the Effects, Identifying the Adaptation Strategies*, edited by E. Skouafias. Washington, DC: World Bank.

Skoufias, E., S. Tiwari, and A. R. Shidiq. 2014. "Sharing Prosperity: The Poverty, Growth and Equity Nexus in Thailand." Policy Research Working Paper, World Bank, Washington, DC.

Stiglitz, J. E., A. Sen, and J.-P. Fitoussi. 2009. *Report by the Commission on the Measurement of Economic Performance and Social Progress*. The Commission on the Measurement of Economic Performance and Social Progress. http://ec.europa.eu/eurostat/documents/118025/118123/Fitoussi+Commission+report.

Székely, M., and M. Hilgert. 2000. "What Drives Differences in Inequality across Countries?" IDB Working Paper 369, Inter-American Development Bank, Washington, DC.

Székely, M., N. Lustig, M. Cumpa, and J. A. Mejía. 2000. "Do We Know How Much Poverty There Is?" IDB Working Paper 437, Inter-American Development Bank, Washington, DC.

UNDP (United Nations Development Program). 1997. *Human Development Report*. New York: UNDP.

van der Weide, R., and B. Milanovic. 2014. "Inequality Is Bad for Growth of the Poor (But Not for That of the Rich." Policy Research Working Paper 6963, World Bank, Washington, DC.

Voitchovsky, S. 2005. "Does the Profile of Income Inequality Matter for Economic Growth?" *Journal of Economic Growth* 10: 273–96.

Winters, L. A, N. McCulloch, and A. McKay. 2004. "Trade Liberalization and Poverty: The Evidence So Far." *Journal of Economic Literature* 42 (1): 72–115.

WITS (World Integrated Trade Solution) Database. 2014. http://wits.worldbank.org.

World Bank. 1990. *World Development Report 1990: Poverty*. New York: Oxford University Press.

———. 2001. *World Development Report 2000/2001: Attacking Poverty*. Washington, DC: World Bank.

———. 2003. *World Development Report 2003/2004: Making Services Work for Poor People*. Washington, DC: World Bank.

———. 2005. *World Development Report 2005/2006: Equity and Development*. Washington, DC: World Bank.

———. 2010a. *Malaysia Economic Monitor: Growth through Innovation*. Washington, DC: World Bank.

———. 2010b. *Malaysia Economic Monitor: Inclusive Growth*. Washington, DC: World Bank.

———. 2010c. *World Development Report: Development and Climate Change*. Washington DC: World Bank.

———. 2011a. *The Changing Wealth of Nations: Measuring Sustainable Development in the New Millennium*. Washington, DC: World Bank.

———. 2011b. *World Development Report: Conflict, Security, and Development*. Washington, DC: World Bank.

———. 2012. *Inclusive Green Growth: The Pathway to Sustainable Development*. Washington, DC: World Bank.

———. 2013a. *Economic Mobility and the Rise of the Latin American Middle Class*. Washington, DC: World Bank.

———. 2013b. *The World Bank Group Goals: End Extreme Poverty and Promote Shared Prosperity*. Washington, DC: World Bank

———. 2013c. *World Development Report: Risk and Opportunity: Managing Risk for Development*. Washington, DC: World Bank.

———. 2014a. *Global Monitoring Report 2014/2015: Ending Poverty and Sharing Prosperity*. Washington, DC: World Bank.

———. 2014b. *Implications of a Changing China for Brazil: A New Window of Opportunity?* Washington, DC: World Bank.

———. 2014c. *Shared Prosperity Paving the Way in Europe and Central Asia*. Washington, DC: World Bank.

———. 2015a. *Addressing Inequality in South Asia*. Washington, DC: World Bank.

———. 2015b. *Global Economic Prospects: Having Fiscal Space and Using It*. January, Washington, DC: World Bank.

———. 2015c. *A Measured Approach to Ending Poverty and Boosting Shared Prosperity:*

Concepts, Data, and the Twin Goals. Washington, DC: World Bank.

———. 2015d. *The Poverty Focus of Country Programs: Lessons from World Bank Experience*. Independent Evaluation Group. Washington, DC: World Bank.

———. 2015e. *Visualize Inequality: PISA, the Bottom 40%*. Washington, DC: World Bank.

———. 2015f. World Development Indicators 2015 (database). Washington, DC. http://data.worldbank.org/products/wdi.

———. Forthcoming. *Poverty in Africa: Revisiting the Facts*. Washington, DC: World Bank.

World Bank and WTO (World Trade Organization). 2015. *The Role of Trade in Ending Poverty*. Unpublished report, World Bank, Washington, DC.

Yohe, G., and R. S. J. Tol. 2009. "Indicators for Social and Economic Coping Capacity—Moving Towards a Working Definition of Adaptive Capacity." *Global Environmental Change* 12: 25–40.

Yoshida, N., H. Uematsu, and C. E. Sobrado. 2014. "Is Extreme Poverty Going to End? An Analytical Framework to Evaluate Progress in Ending Extreme Poverty." Policy Research Working Paper 6740, Washington, DC: World Bank.

2

Scaling Up Impact: Transitioning from Millennium to Sustainable Development Goals

With 2015 marking a watershed between the MDGs and the SDGs, the world can celebrate the many development achievements since 2000. Still, outcomes vary substantially between regions, across the rural-urban divide, and by demographic characteristics. Even where good progress has been made, deprivations persist, leaving a substantial unfinished agenda. In a context of megatrends that are reshaping challenges and opportunities, the SDGs forge a global compact for transformational human progress while safeguarding the environment. The MDG experience highlights the importance of inclusiveness and country ownership, effective monitoring, and strong implementation, supported by enhanced financing for development.

Building on the Millennium Development Goals (MDGs) experience, the transition to the Sustainable Development Goals (SDGs) framework in 2015 reflects a welcome move into a more comprehensive, multidimensional approach to development. During this watershed year, with the MDGs expiring and the SDGs being adopted, it is worth reflecting on what has been accomplished during the past 15 years, and how the SDGs can best carry the development agenda forward over the coming 15 years.

Substantial progress has been made in recent decades, although there is much heterogeneity among regions, between rural and urban areas, and in demographic features. In many ways, development has advanced more rapidly over the past 15 years than at any other time in human history. Millions of people have realized major improvements in well-being. Still, the wide variation in outcomes translates into a substantial unfinished development agenda. With over 900 million people still living in poverty in 2012 (defined as living on less than $1.90 a day, 2011 purchasing power parity), persistent and increasingly concentrated deprivations urgently need to be addressed (chapter 1). At the same time, the importance of environmental sustainability has moved to the fore, and new patterns of eco-friendly production and consumption are necessary to ensure continued development progress.

The MDGs played an important role in galvanizing global efforts for development. Given the complexity of development, the gains of recent decades cannot be attributed to any single factor or process. Nonetheless, the MDGs helped frame the broader goals of development and build a coalition of partners—international agencies, national entities, philanthropic and civil society organizations, academic institutions, and private sector representatives—to work toward common goals.

In sync with the megatrends reshaping the world, the SDGs represent a new, more comprehensive approach for scaled-up impact. These megatrends—rising global connectedness, the importance of the dynamic economies in the East, the increasing pace of technological change and adoption, accelerating urbanization, changing global demographic trends, and the growing impact of human activity on environmental degradation and climate change—have all emerged over the past two decades and are having profound effects on the evolution of development outcomes. Whereas the MDGs of the Millennium Declaration were conceived as a framework committing nations to reduce extreme poverty through enhanced assistance to developing countries, the SDGs represent a global compact that is applicable to all countries, so that all may benefit more from global interconnections while safeguarding the environment and the global commons.

The SDGs seek to accelerate progress with a strong focus on implementation. The SDGs reflect learning from the MDG experience. Better implementation, based on strengthened policies and institutions, as well as resource mobilization, will be essential to accelerate progress between now and 2030.

The Millennium Development Goals: Current status

Development progress over the past 15 years has been impressive. Millions of children who were unlikely to survive to their fifth birthday have passed beyond these critical years and gone on to school in ever greater proportions, including many more girls than was the case 15 years ago. The incidence of preventable diseases such as AIDS (acquired immune deficiency syndrome), malaria, and tuberculosis is falling, and the share of people with access to clean water and better sanitation has risen markedly (see figure 2.1 and the MDG Report Card in appendix A for details). Overall, the MDGs played an important role in helping to galvanize the development community (McArthur 2013), and that experience will serve the achievement of the newly endorsed SDGs well.

The MDG period saw substantial development progress

The proportion of people facing extreme poverty has declined sharply (detailed in chapter 1). The world met the global MDG 1 target of halving the proportion of the population living in extreme poverty five years ahead of the 2015 deadline (World Bank 2014). China contributed the bulk of this decline. Even excluding China, progress in reducing extreme poverty has been good, and more than two-thirds of countries have reached, or are close to achieving, the target of halving extreme poverty. With the incomes of households in the lowest quintiles (at the national level) rising together with average incomes, the accelerated growth of developing countries in recent decades relative to previous ones made an important contribution to the reduction in extreme poverty (Dollar and Kraay 2002, 2013).

Developing countries have made impressive strides in reducing hunger and malnutrition, although the target of halving the number of people living in hunger is unlikely to be reached by 2015. The prevalence of malnutrition among children under age five dropped from 28 percent in 1990 to 17 percent in 2013. Several international nutrition initiatives, such as the "Nutrition for Growth" project and the "Zero Hunger Challenge," as well as country-led efforts, have contributed to the improvement. Brazil remains a remarkable success story. In 1990–92, it was home to some 22 million undernourished people, yet over the past decade it has reduced hunger by some 80 percent. Poverty reduction efforts, support for family farmers, school feeding programs, social safety nets, and food access schemes were instrumental in reducing hunger in Brazil. Nonetheless, at the global level, one in eight people in the world

FIGURE 2.1 Stark variations exist in achievement of MDGs

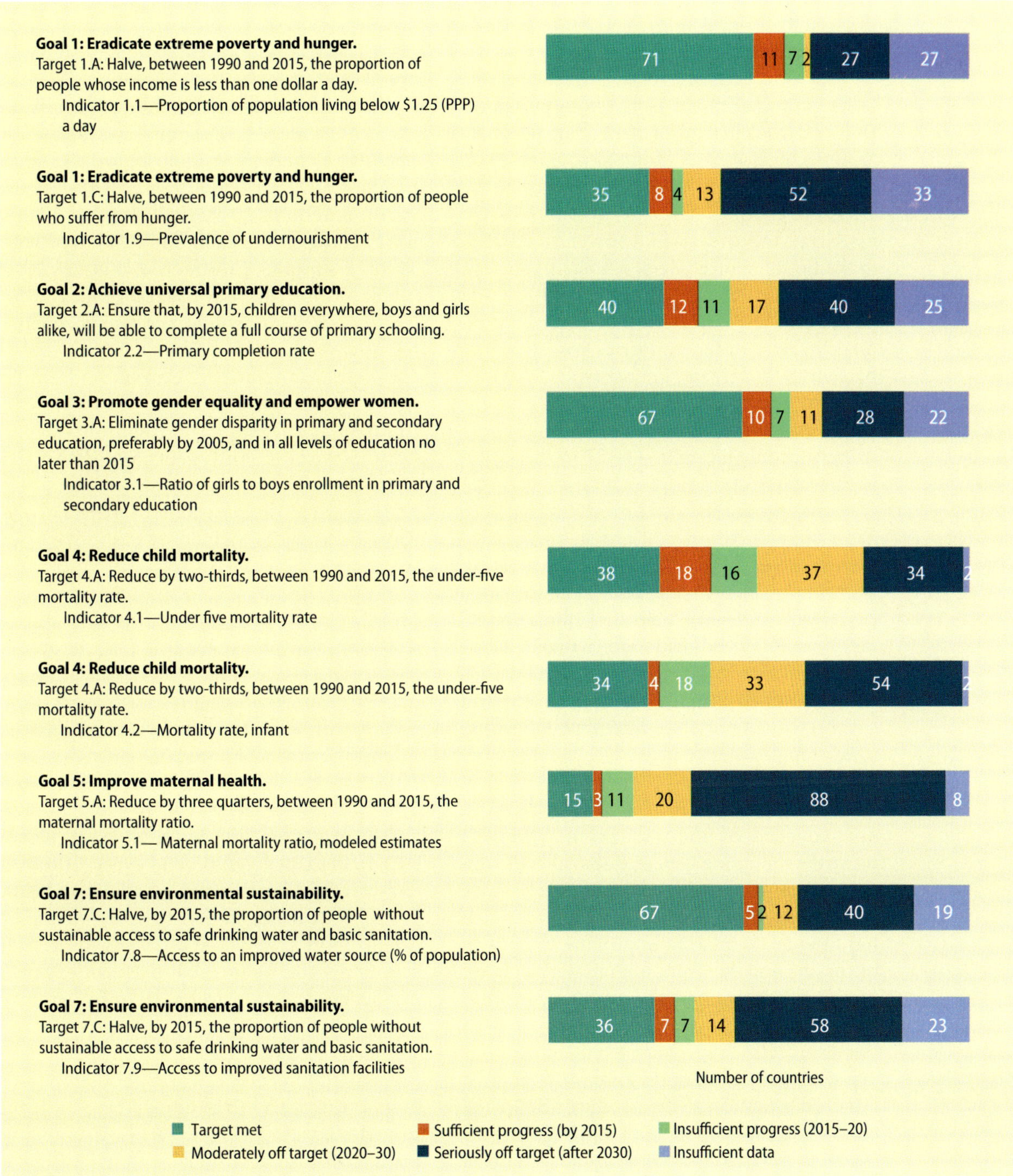

Sources: World Development Indicators and Global Monitoring Report team estimates.
Note: Progress is based on extrapolation of latest five-year annual growth rates for each country, except for MDG 5.0, which uses the latest three years. "Sufficient progress" indicates that an extrapolation of the last observed data point with the growth rate over the last observable five-year period shows that the MDG can be attained. "Insufficient progress" is defined as being able to meet the MDG between 2016 and 2020. "Moderately off target" indicates that the MDG can be met between 2020 and 2030. "Seriously off target" indicates that the MDG will not even be met by 2030. "Insufficient data" means that not enough data points are available to estimate progress or that the MDG's starting value is missing (except for MDG 2 and MDG 3). In the poverty target, 11 of the 66 countries that have met the target have less than 2 percent of people living below $1.25 a day.

continues to go hungry because of interrelated factors such as low agricultural productivity and unemployment (Sanchez and Swaminathan 2005).

Access to primary school education and literacy rates are increasing strongly. Education is a goal in and of itself, but it is also a powerful driver of progress toward other MDGs. Education builds what Amartya Sen (1999) refers to as "human capabilities—the essential and individual power to reflect, make better choices, seek a voice in society, and enjoy a better life." Between 2000 and 2012, the increase in primary school enrollment in developing countries rose from 83 percent to 90 percent, almost twice as fast as over the preceding 12 years. Consequently, the number of children not attending school dropped from 102 million to 57 million, notwithstanding continued population growth. National programs that lowered barriers to accessing education and global initiatives, like the Global Partnership for Education (previously known as the Education for All—Fast Track Initiative), helped to ramp up primary school enrollments rates (Bruns, Mingat, and Rakotomalala 2003; Riddell 2003). In addition to ongoing efforts to expand coverage to all children, attention is turning toward improving quality.

The promotion of gender equality and empowerment of women is moving forward, as evidenced by the remarkable progress toward eliminating gender disparities in education. Almost two-thirds of countries have reached the target. Greater education for girls has long-term impacts: improving the health of infants and children, immunization rates, family nutrition, and the next generation's schooling attainment (World Bank 2001). For every 100 boys who attended secondary school in 2000, there were only 90 girls. Focused attention to girls' education at the country level, supported by global partnerships (such as the Girls Education Initiative), is helping promote gender parity in primary and secondary enrollment. Despite progress in school attendance, questions remain on the quality of education, and less progress is evident at the tertiary (postsecondary) level.[1] In addition, closing gender gaps is necessary but not sufficient for achieving the broader goal of gender equality and women's empowerment (UN 2005). Wide gender disparities persist, acting as major hindrances to development progress.

Many developing countries are achieving major reductions in child mortality. The number of children who die before their fifth birthday fell from 13 million in 1990 to just over 6 million in 2013, implying that 17,000 fewer children die each day compared with 1990. Examples of effective country-level interventions that have saved thousands of lives come from around the world, including 10 low- and middle-income "fast-track" countries: Bangladesh, Cambodia, China, the Arab Republic of Egypt, Ethiopia, the Lao People's Democratic Republic, Nepal, Peru, Rwanda, and Vietnam (PMNCH et al. 2014). Contributing to the success were an increase in the provision of maternal and neonatal services (helped by cash incentives to use them), an expansion of immunization programs, greater use of mobile phones to promote health (including information on nutrition and breast-feeding), wider access to sanitation and safe water, and stronger data systems to inform policy (Roberts, Carnahan, and Gakidou 2013). Yet, at current trends, the target of reducing under-five mortality rate by two-thirds between 1990 and 2015 will not be met.

Maternal mortality has declined by nearly two-fifths since 2000. For every 100,000 live births, 370 mothers perished in 2000. By 2013, this had fallen to 230—a rate of decline more than twice as fast as in the preceding decade. Progress hinged on expanding access to both prenatal and postnatal care (such as increasing the share of births attended by skilled practitioners), strengthening patient referral networks, boosting family planning, and expanding the education of girls (PMNCH et al. 2014). Enhancing the educational attainment of girls has been found to be especially effective—the risk of maternal death is 2.7 times higher among women with no education than among those who have completed 12 years of school, and 2 times higher for women with 1 to 6 years of education (Karlsen et al. 2011). Despite the progress over the past decade, the target of reducing maternal mortality rates by three-quarters will not be achieved.

The incidence of AIDS, malaria, and tuberculosis has fallen sharply in recent decades. Since 2001, the number of people newly infected with HIV (human immunodeficiency virus, the virus that causes AIDS) has declined by about 33 percent. In addition, access to antiretroviral medicines has increased to a record 9.7 million people. In Sub-Saharan Africa, only 10,000 people had access in 2000. Likewise, the incidence of tuberculosis fell at an average rate of 1.5 percent a year between 2000 and 2013, and deaths from malaria fell by some 26 percent. It is estimated that since 2000, about 1.1 million deaths from malaria have been averted. Complementing national plans, global initiatives such as the Global Fund to Fight AIDS, Tuberculosis and Malaria; the U.S. President's Emergency Plan for AIDS Relief initiative; the World Health Organization's (WHO's) "3 by 5" initiative; the MDG Health Alliance; and the "Malaria No More" campaign helped accelerate progress. Lower burdens of AIDS and noncommunicable diseases have been associated with much greater progress toward reducing child mortality (Stuckler, Basu, and McKee 2010).

The MDG targets on access to safe drinking water and sanitation, and reducing the number of slum dwellers, have been reached. Between 1990 and 2011, about 1.9 billion people gained access to improved sanitation facilities, helping curb the incidence of illness associated with open defecation. The most progress occurred in East Asia and Pacific. Between 2000 and 2010, more than 200 million slum dwellers gained access to improved water and sanitary conditions, well above the MDG target of 100 million. Yet with increased urbanization and rapid population growth in some regions, the overall number of slum dwellers increased from 650 million in 1990 to 863 million in 2012. More work needs to be done to reduce the absolute number of slum dwellers, despite the attainment of the MDG goals.

The MDG process helped strengthen global partnerships. In 2013, Development Assistance Committee members of the Organisation for Economic Co-operation and Development (OECD) increased development aid disbursements to $134.7 billion, compared with about $80.0 billion in the mid-1990s. However, at 0.3 percent of GDP, official development assistance (ODA) remains well below the target of 0.7 percent of GDP. On the goal of access to Internet and communication technologies, there has been much progress. Spearheaded by private sector investments, mobile/cellular subscriptions have risen dramatically in developing countries since 2000, enabling a range of services such as cellphone banking and information sharing on market prices of agricultural produce. Nonetheless, broadband Internet access remains out of reach for many.

Synergies across the MDGs have helped progress

While progress on each of the MDGs is often considered separately, they are mutually reinforcing and interrelated. Income and non-income dimensions of poverty are closely intertwined, with several studies showing that households in the lowest income quintiles also face deprivation on other dimensions of development (as elaborated in chapter 1). There are also strong correlations among non-income MDGs, such as female literacy and under-five mortality (figure 2.2). In some instances, these correlations are the result of common drivers, such as the quality of public institutions, the capacity to deliver social services, the extent of urbanization, and demographic trends. Nonetheless, strong causal relationships exist among various MDGs, such as between maternal health and school enrollment, gender gaps in education and infant mortality, and access to sanitation and stunting among children, highlighting areas that are mutually reinforcing.

The MDGs related to health are especially important in providing mutual reinforcement. Improving maternal health has been critical for both neonatal and under-five mortality, helping to reduce complications during pregnancy and at birth (King, Klasen, and Porter 2009). Interventions to expand immunization

FIGURE 2.2 Synergies across MDGs have helped progress

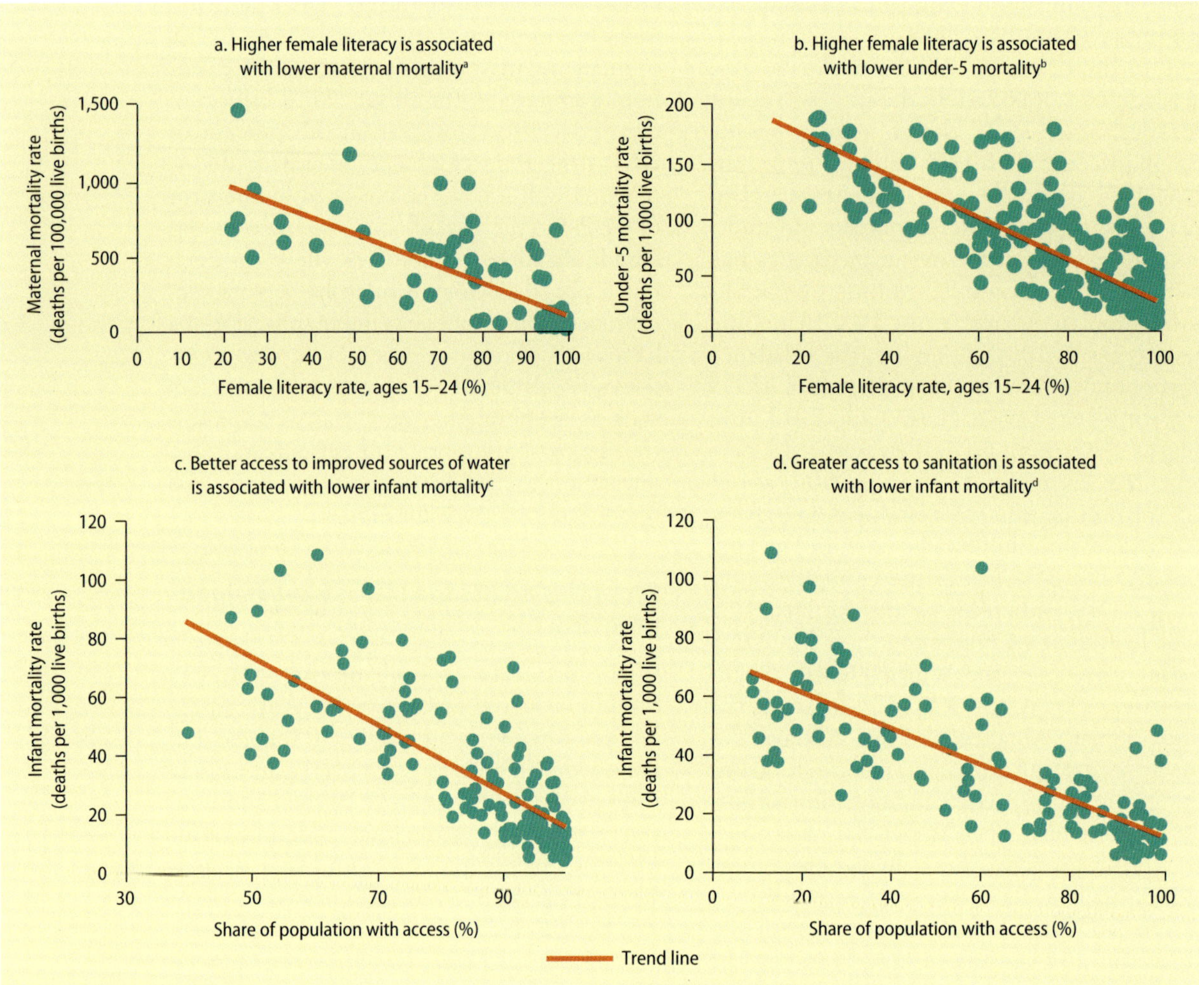

Source: World Bank calculations.

Note: The scatter plots use data on all available developing economies over the 2000–13 period. All the pairwise correlation coefficients are significant at the 5 percent level. Robustness checks with alternate conditional correlations were computed using the residuals from a regression equation conditioned on per capita income. The results remained similar.

a. Pairwise correlation = −0.77. See Karlsen et al. 2011 for similar analyses and conclusions.

b. Pairwise correlation = −0.83. See Klasen 2005 for similar analyses and conclusions.

c. Pairwise correlation = −0.8. See Prüss et al. 2002 and Fay et al. 2005 for similar analyses and conclusions.

d. Pairwise correlation = −0.79. See Andres et al. 2014 and Kumar and Vollmer 2013 for similar analyses and conclusions.

and nutrition programs contributed to the fall in under-five mortality rates in several countries (Lay 2010). The increased rollout of antiretroviral drugs over the past decade contributed to a reduction in maternal mortality in regions where HIV prevalence was high (WHO et al. 2014). In addition, health-related MDGs matter for other MDGs. Fewer maternal deaths boosts school enrollment, since children whose mothers are absent are more likely to drop out of school.

Likewise, improvements in MDGs related to gender equality influence both income and non-income goals. Closing the gender gap in education is essential to boosting women's voice and agency and appears to be the single most important driver for reducing poverty and child mortality, as well as for boosting the overall education of children (Klasen 2005; Klugman et al. 2014). Education of girls can reduce infant and maternal mortality, because educated mothers are more likely to use available health services. The odds of children in Sub-Saharan Africa receiving the tuberculosis vaccine is 50 percent higher among children of mothers with primary school education relative to those without (Lay and Robilliard 2009). While the availability of piped water reduced the overall incidence of child deaths in rural India, the effect was weaker among poorly educated mothers. Better education leads to higher earnings for women, which contributes to lower child mortality as mothers are able to spend more on children's health. As noted above, education for girls remains key to reducing maternal mortality through its effect on lowering adolescent pregnancies and enhancing health-seeking behaviors. Education for girls and boys is also a strong preventive weapon against HIV/AIDS, and it contributes to better natural resource management, including the conservation of the tropical rain forest (Godoy and Contreras 2001; World Bank 2003).

Expanding access to sanitation is essential to reducing stunting among children. Open defecation has a significant impact on the incidence of diarrhea and stunting among children (Hammer and Spears 2013; Spears 2013). For example, after controlling for factors such as socioeconomic status, maternal education, and calorie availability, differences in open defecation still explain 35–55 percent of the statistical differences in rates of childhood stunting across different districts in India (Spears, Ghosh, and Cumming 2013). Sanitation still remains a major challenge in India, where more than half the population defecates in the open. In Cambodia, five-year-old children were found to be 2.0–3.6 centimeters shorter in communities where all households defecate openly than in communities where no one does (World Bank 2013b). Access to safe water, sanitation, women's education, gender equality, and the quantity and quality of food available are key drivers of past reductions in stunting, with income growth and governance playing essential facilitating roles (Smith and Haddad 2015).

Strong institutions and economic growth enhance the synergies among the MDGs. Theoretical and empirical evidence demonstrate how MDGs reinforce one another, but the effects vary. For example, in some instances there is little correlation between poverty reduction and non-income goals, such as under-five mortality or primary school completion rates (Bourguignon et al. 2008a). Among pairs of non-income MDGs, such as gender parity and child mortality, performance varies significantly across developing countries (Klasen and Lo Bue 2013). Positive spillovers between MDGs are hampered by low-quality public services and weak political commitment, as well as by violence and inequality. In contrast, countries exhibiting high rates of economic growth, strong institutions, and good governance tend to show stronger synergistic relationships among the MDGs, because these determinants mutually reinforce each other over time (Lo Bue 2013, 2015; Klasen and Lo Bue 2013).

Progress toward the MDGs varied greatly

Despite the solid development gains in many areas, significant work remains, particularly regarding the non-income goals. The tide has turned on the incidence of major deadly diseases, but a high number of preventable deaths persist. With the development of new medicines, HIV patients receiving treatment have nearly the same life expectancy as those without HIV. However, about 63 percent of people living with HIV, mostly in developing countries, lack access to antiretroviral drugs. Tuberculosis killed 1.5 million people in 2013, many in the prime of their productive lives. An estimated 198 million cases of malaria were registered in 2013, claiming the lives of about 453,000 children a year and robbing Sub-Saharan economies of an estimated $12 billion in lost economic activity. As noted, the global partnerships needed to help address these challenges are not reaching their potential, with ODA averaging well below the target set by the MDGs (Kenny and Dykstra 2013). The heterogeneity of outcomes manifests across regions, between urban and rural areas, and by demographic features.

Variation across regions

While more than two-thirds of countries achieved the MDG target on halving extreme poverty—the highest success rate of all the MDGs—the decline in poverty across regions has been uneven.[2] East Asia and Pacific realized an unprecedented fall of extreme poverty, led by China. In 1990, extreme poverty in the region was on par with Sub-Saharan Africa, and about a third higher than the average for all developing countries. China was a major driving force in the decline of the poverty rate of East Asia and Pacific. Buoyed by strong growth in India, poverty in South Asia fell rapidly during 1990–2012 reaching the MDG target.

Sub-Saharan Africa is the only region not on target to halve extreme poverty. There is substantial variation across Sub-Saharan Africa: 16 countries are expected to meet MDG 1 (based on the $1.25 income threshold) by the end of 2015, but 21 countries are not expected to reach the target even by 2030. Given that Sub-Saharan Africa started off the MDG period with the lowest average per capita income and exhibits a comparatively lower sensitivity of poverty to changes in growth (growth elasticity of poverty), the framing of the MDG benchmarks may place a greater onus on the region to achieve the goals (Clemens and Moss 2005; Easterly 2007). Compared with the two preceding decades, where extreme poverty either rose or remained flat, trends in the post-2000 period exhibited an acceleration of progress, with the $1.25 a day poverty head count ratio falling from about 60.0 percent in 2000 to 46.8 percent in 2011. That is a meaningful achievement, but concern is growing in the development community that poverty will become increasingly concentrated in natural-resource-based economies and fragile and conflict states, many in Sub-Saharan Africa (as discussed in chapter 1).

The three regions with better initial conditions also made progress. Compared with other developing regions, Europe and Central Asia, Latin America and the Caribbean, and the Middle East and North Africa started off with relatively low levels of poverty and managed to lower poverty further over the 1990 to 2012 period. Nonetheless, wide disparities in poverty levels exist across and within countries in these regions.

Wide disparities in the non-income MDGs persist across and within regions. For example, the primary school completion rate in developing countries as a whole rose from about 79 percent in 1990 to 91 percent in 2012, but only two regions, East Asia and Pacific and Europe and Central Asia, have achieved or are close to the goal of 100 percent. Consider MDG 4, which aims to reduce the under-five mortality rate by two-thirds between 1990 and 2015. Only East Asia and Pacific and Latin America and the Caribbean have met the target, while 17 countries in Sub-Saharan Africa and three countries in the Middle East and North Africa are seriously off track. Regarding HIV/AIDS, the number of people globally who are newly infected is falling, down 38 percent since 2000. Still, the epidemic remains centered in Sub-Saharan Africa, home to about 70 percent of the world's adults living with HIV, with prevalence rates of 4.5 percent of the population in 2013, compared with below 1 percent elsewhere. Non-income MDG performed unevenly across countries and regions, reflecting initial conditions, economic growth, macro- and microeconomic policy, population dynamics, and effectiveness of government service delivery (Bourguignon, Diaz-Bonilla, and Lofgren 2008b).

Variation between urban and rural areas

Within countries, there are large disparities in development outcomes between better performing urban centers and lagging rural areas. More than three-quarters of the world's extremely poor live in rural areas in developing countries. While overall poverty and the gap between rural and urban areas has been falling, poverty rates in rural areas remain substantially higher than in urban areas, as more high-paying and productive jobs are created in urban centers. Households in rural communities in East Asia and Pacific and Latin America and the Caribbean are more than four times as likely to be living in extreme poverty as those in urban areas (World Bank 2013a). Sub-Saharan Africa has the largest gap in absolute terms, with poverty rates in rural areas of 29.4 percent in 2008, compared with 11.6 percent in urban areas—a gap of 17.8 percentage points.

Similar rural-urban differences are observed for the non-income indicators, largely because of the higher unit cost of delivering services in rural areas. For example, gaps in access to safe water and sanitation are substantial between rural and urban areas (figure 2.3). In East Asia and Pacific, while 98 percent of people living in urban areas have access to improved water sources and 80 percent have access to improved sanitation facilities, the corresponding figures for rural communities are 85 percent and 59 percent, respectively. The divergence is even wider in Sub-Saharan Africa, where the difference in access to improved water sources between urban and rural dwellers is more than 30 percentage points. Such disparities are also evident in other non-income dimensions. For example, in Senegal, 83 percent of children in urban areas complete primary school, but in rural areas only 57 percent of children reach this critical stepping stone.

Urbanization varies substantially across regions and is associated with large differences in development progress. The three regions with the highest rates of urbanization in 1990—Europe and Central Asia (74 percent), Latin America and the Caribbean (71 percent), and the Middle East and North Africa (55 percent)—also performed relatively better on both the income and non-income dimensions of poverty. Indeed, only a few countries have transitioned from poverty to prosperity without urbanizing (Ciccone and Hall 1996; Glaeser and Joshi-Ghani 2013; Glaeser and Maré 2001). Productivity and urban scale tend to go together (Melo, Graham, and Noland 2009; Puga 2010; Rosenthal and Strange 2004, 2010). However, urbanization stood at only 32.2 percent in South Asia and 36.7 percent in Sub-Saharan Africa in 2013. This disparity suggests substantial scope to reap development benefits from urbanization in terms of higher productivity from agglomeration economies and lower unit costs of service provision. Still, urbanization needs to be managed to

FIGURE 2.3 Large disparities exist between urban and rural areas

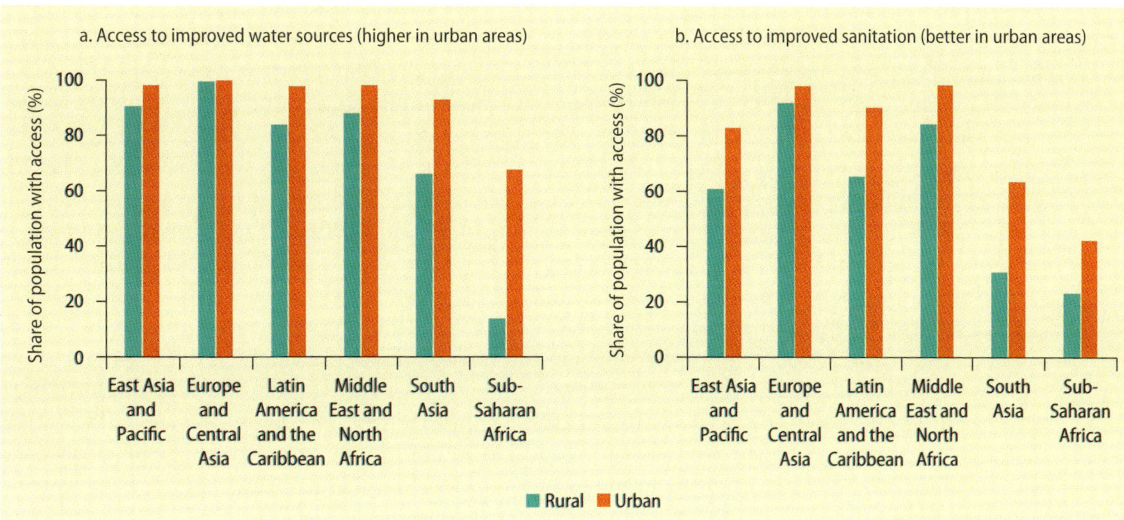

Source: World Bank calculations.

ensure adequate service provision. As noted, although the MDG of improving the lives of 100 million slum dwellers was met, increased urbanization and population growth in some regions raised the overall number by one-third between 1990 and 2012.

Variation across demographic patterns

Finally, progress on the MDGs differs markedly depending on key demographic features. Of the countries deemed to be far from achieving the extreme poverty reduction target, 92 percent are in a demographic phase characterized by high fertility rates exceeding four children per woman, high ratios of dependents to people of working age, and rapid population growth. Countries in this demographic phase are also far from achieving most non-income MDG targets, including those on undernourishment (74 percent), under-five mortality (77 percent), maternal mortality (74 percent), sanitation (82 percent), and access to safe water (74 percent). In other key areas, such as gender equality as reflected in the share of women in secondary education or in wage employment outside the agricultural sector, there are major data gaps and indications of large disparities (UNESCO 2015). Almost all countries still in this demographic phase are in Sub-Saharan Africa (97 percent). (See part 2 of this report for a detailed discussion of demographic dynamics and development).

Rapid population growth can make development progress more difficult, and the MDG monitoring framework tends to magnify the impact of population growth. Not only can rapid population growth complicate efforts to expand coverage of public services, many MDG targets are expressed relative to population (Hermann 2015). For instance, Sub-Saharan Africa's school-age population increased by 70 percent during the MDG period, and while the overall numbers of out-of-school children fell, the region is still lagging behind the MDG targets on universal school enrollment, given the large increase in the absolute number of children attending school. In another example from Sub-Saharan Africa, the under-five malnutrition rate fell from 29.2 percent in 1992 to 21.0 percent in 2013, but the number of malnourished children increased by 4.8 million, because of a 70 percent increase in the under-five population over this period.

Age structures also matter for the attainment of development goals. Savings and investment tend to be lower in countries with higher total dependency ratios than in countries where more of the population is of working age and the economy is benefiting from the so-called "demographic dividend."[3] Hence, countries with higher dependency ratios (often due to high fertility rates) generally have fewer domestic resources per capita to invest in social services, unless they are able to access international capital markets or receive substantial aid flows.

A large unfinished agenda remains

Taken together, disparities in MDG outcomes mean that much remains to be done. None of the MDGs has been achieved by all developing countries. The largest gaps in MDG progress are increasingly concentrated in countries characterized by high fertility and rapid population growth, many of which are natural-resource-based economies and struggling with fragility and conflict situations. However, even for developing countries that have made good progress toward the MDGs, an unfinished agenda remains internally across spatial dimensions, particularly along the urban-rural divide. Further, for most developing countries, some of the greatest challenges lie in meeting the non-income MDGs, in particular those related to health (maternal and infant mortality), nutrition (undernourishment and hunger), and environmental sustainability, including forest cover, fish stocks and ecosystem protection, as well as limiting carbon emissions.[4] Nevertheless, the unprecedented development gains made over the past decade and a half, in part supported by the MDG process (box 2.1), provide ample evidence that the trajectory of development progress can be bent toward accelerated achievement on this unfinished agenda, while also tackling the emerging challenges in a changing world.

BOX 2.1 The MDG process has played a generally positive role in supporting development

Did the process of setting development goals make a discernable difference? What might have happened in the absence of the MDGs? Several empirical approaches have been adopted to address these questions. One method of trying to evaluate the impact of the partnership and monitoring framework on development progress centers on estimating counterfactuals, and then comparing how various indicators actually evolved (McArthur 2014). Another related approach is to analyze the trend of MDG indicators before and after the adoption of the MDGs and apply statistical tests aimed at discerning changes in their trajectories.

The evidence available shows that the MDG process had major impacts in some indicators but little direct effect in others. Under-five mortality (MDG 4), for example, has fallen dramatically in the poorest countries since the MDGs were agreed (McArthur 2014). Controlling for various factors, statistical methods applied to 19 MDG indicators checking for an interruption in the time series between 1992 and 2008 found an acceleration (in progress on an indicator like the primary enrollment ratio going up) or deceleration (in progress on an indicator like maternal mortality going down) in the trajectories after 2001 in five indicators (Friedman 2013). For instance, the incidence of tuberculosis (Target 6C) began falling sharply in 2000, for HIV (Target 6A) the turning point is identified as 1996–97, and for the adolescent child birth rate (Target 5B) the marked fall began in 2004. As for the proportion of children under age one immunized against measles (Target 4A), there was no statistically discernable change in the trajectory during the time period under review. It is also worth noting that these analyses abstract from what else could have been undertaken with the resources, if they had not been applied to achieving the MDGs.

Variations in how underlying trends of individual MDGs changed at the regional level are also notable (figure B2.1.1). For example, using pre-MDG data to generate linear counterfactual trends on the education enrollment ratio for females and males, the post-MDG enrollment rates were higher than what would have been expected in both South Asia and Sub-Saharan Africa. In South Asia, the statistically determined structural break occurred in 2003, a few years after the launch of the MDGs. In contrast, in Sub-Saharan Africa it occurred in 1997, before the commencement of the MDGs, suggesting that even though enrollment accelerated during the MDG period, some positive underlying factors providing support were already in place. Similar accelerations are observable for Europe and Central Asia and Latin America and the Caribbean. In East Asia and Pacific, however, where female-to-male enrollment ratios were already at very high levels, there has been no dis-

FIGURE B2.1.1 Sample of actual progress compared with counterfactuals based on pre-MDG trends

Gender parity in primary school enrollment improved more quickly than before

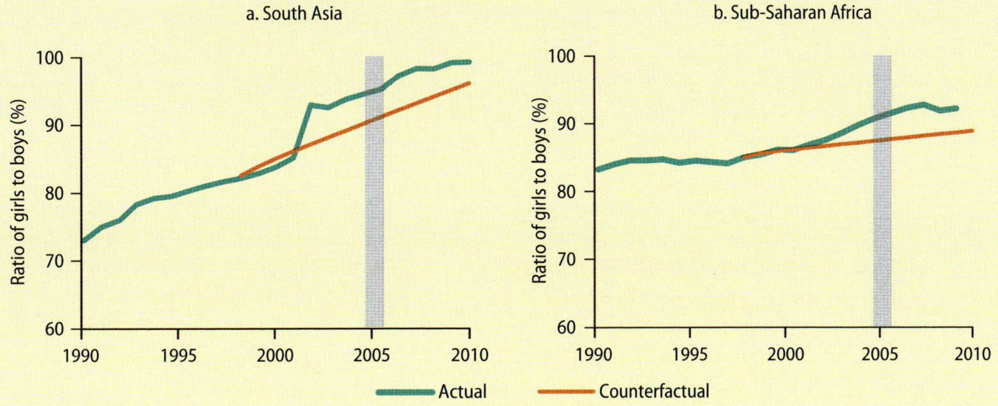

(box continues next page)

BOX 2.1 The MDG process has played a generally positive role in supporting development (continued)

FIGURE B2.1.1 Sample of actual progress compared with counterfactuals based on pre-MDG trends (continued)

Incidence of tuberculosis fell sharply compared to pre-MDG trends

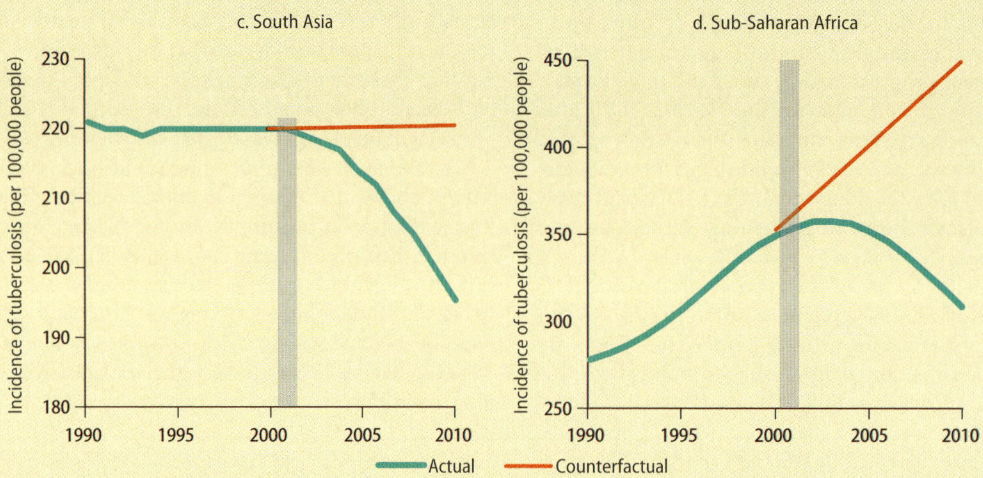

Source: World Bank calculations.
Note: The gray columns represent the year 2000, referencing the baseline situation before the adoption of the MDGs. The counterfactuals, represented by the orange lines, extend the 1990–2000 (pre-MDG) trends into the 2001–13 period, based on a regression including a trend and autoregressive terms. An alternate approach using the Hodrick-Prescott filter to extend the pre-MDG trends into the MDG period was also used, generating similar results. The Bai-Perron methodology was used to test for the presence of structural breaks. For gender parity, the results confirmed the presence of a structural break for South Asia and Sub-Saharan Africa in 2003 and 1997, respectively. For tuberculosis, the test results confirmed the presence of a structural break for South Asia and Sub-Saharan Africa in 2004 and 2002, respectively. Structural breaks were observed for other MDG indicators including primary school enrollment and child mortality rates.

cernable acceleration. In the Middle East and North Africa, actuals were lower than pre-MDG trends, possibly because of conflict.

The overall impact of the MDGs depends on factors unique to each MDG, some of which are country specific. Each MDG has its own history, such as the establishment of implementation arrangements (including the timing and size of targeted global funds, like the Education for All—Fast Track Initiative that was established in 2002), or of technical breakthroughs (like the development of antiretroviral drugs to combat AIDS). Even where the impact at the time of the Millennium Declaration in 2000 is not statistically discernable in outcomes, the MDG process has provided a valuable platform to galvanize coalitions of stakeholders seeking to address some of the world's toughest development problems.

The sustainable development goals: A new approach

Scaling up impact to address the unfinished development agenda depends on adopting new approaches that reflect ongoing megatrends, as well as on learning from the MDGs. The post-2015 development framework of the SDGs aims to seize the extraordinary opportunity offered by these megatrends to make transformational development progress. The framework is based on a more integrated partnership that emphasizes universality, responsibility, and accountability. So that all will benefit more from global interconnections, the SDGs apply universally to all countries as a global compact, based on shared responsibility (especially for the global commons) and on improved accountability frameworks to monitor contributions and progress (Kharas and Zhang 2014). The SDGs are also able to build on the MDG experience, reflecting valuable learning on what worked and what was less effective in promoting development progress. The World Bank Group supports the SDGs, aligning its strategy for engagement through the goals of ending poverty and promoting shared prosperity in a sustainable manner (box 2.2).

BOX 2.2 What is the relationship between the World Bank Group's goals and the Sustainable Development Goals?

The World Bank Group's goals anchor its overarching mission of a world free of poverty to two high-level objectives of ending extreme poverty and promoting shared prosperity, and doing so sustainably. They were established to bring focus and greater accountability to the organization's own work. As the authors of the report setting out the goals (World Bank 2013d, 9) point out: "The goals we have articulated are not solely for the World Bank Group to achieve but rather are goals that we hope are consistent with those of our 188 member countries." The SDGs follow in the tradition of the Millennium Development Goals and are endorsed by the General Assembly of the United Nations and speak to the breadth of the development challenge (UN 2015f).

The World Bank Group's goals are embedded in the SDGs, with some minor differences in goals, targets and indicators. The poverty goal (TG1), for example, calls for ending extreme poverty, which is defined as reducing the share of those living on less than $1.25 poverty a day (in 2005 constant dollars) to 3 percent by 2030. The corresponding SDG goal is stronger in that it aspires to end poverty everywhere and in all of its forms, a goal that amounts to reducing the same indicator to zero by 2030 (SDG1.1). The shared prosperity goal (TG2) sets out to increase the well-being of the poorer segments of society, as measured by income growth of the bottom 40 percent of the population in each country, without specifying a target ("fostering" and "promoting" income growth). The corresponding SDG goal is somewhat different; it aspires to reduce inequality within and among countries, defined as the extent to which, by 2030, countries progressively achieve and sustain income growth in the bottom 40 percent in excess of the national average (SDG 10.1) without stipulating a specific target on the extent of this excess. The SDG goal is focused relatively more on inequality than the World Bank Group's goal.

A broader perspective that recognizes the multidimensionality of the World Bank Group's goals and the underlying sustainability requirement would, however, suggest that these goals and the SDGs are aligned. The World Bank Group's goals need to be pursued in a manner that is economically, socially, and environmentally sustainable. The goals themselves are also inherently multidimensional, as elaborated in chapter 1, even if their monetary indicators manifest themselves more narrowly. Yet, "ending poverty and promoting shared prosperity are unequivocally also about progress in non-monetary dimensions of welfare including education, health, nutrition, and access to essential infrastructure, as well as about enhancing voice and participation of all segments of society in economic, social, and political spheres." (World Bank 2013d, 8). Furthermore, the additional requirement that the World Bank Group's goals be achieved in a sustainable manner raises the need for additional analysis, monitoring, and dialogue. Hence, the two sets of goals can be seen as very similar, even if they remain different with respect to their original intent and the level of aggregation at which they are presented.

Recognizing that accelerating development is a shared endeavor, the World Bank Group fully supports the SDGs. The World Bank Group has worked closely with the United Nations on various aspects of the post-2015 agenda, among them financing for development and data issues, and is expected to continue to work with the UN on implementation. Realizing the extraordinary opportunity of ending extreme poverty in a generation and promoting shared prosperity more widely is feasible only through collective efforts of all stakeholders, most importantly through national initiative, supported by international entities. The global compact applies universally, to high- and low-income countries alike, and to national and international implementing agencies and financiers alike. The World Bank Group will benchmark its activities with a view to help accelerate progress on the post-2015 agenda.

The highly inclusive and open SDG process augurs well for sustaining the buy-in needed to accelerate progress. The SDGs emerged from wide-ranging stakeholder engagements, reflecting views from 193 governments and more than 7 million respondents to an online survey conducted by the United Nations (UN) (Bhattacharya and Kharas 2015; United Nations 2015e). They also benefited from the insights of a UN High Level Panel of Eminent Persons (from government, civil society, and the private sector), the Open Working Group of the UN General Assembly on Sustainable Development Goals (drawing on extensive thematic consultations), and the Intergovernmental Committee of Experts on Sustainable Development Financing. The work of these and other key bodies reach important milestones in 2015 with the Financing for Development Conference in Addis Ababa in July, the UN General Assembly meeting endorsing the SDGs in September, and the United Nations Framework Convention on Climate Change (UNFCC) Conference of the Parties meeting in Paris in December. These are building critical momentum for action going forward.

Changed circumstances demand a new approach

Grounded in a global compact for human development and preservation of the planet, the SDGs represent a qualitative departure from previous frameworks (UN 2015f). With their emphasis on universality, responsibility, and accountability, the SDGs are more holistic in approach than the MDGS were, and in their very nature reflect and respond to several megatrends that are having a profound impact on the trajectory of economic, social, and environmental progress around the world. Given the extensive progress to date, and the growing power of humanity to affect change, there is an extraordinary opportunity to end poverty in all of its forms, while safeguarding the environment and pursuing other development goals. Sustained advancement, however, will require concerted effort, including through the fuller participation of business and civil society.

Evolving context of development

Several megatrends are playing a critical role in framing what will be feasible over the SDG period to 2030. These include the unprecedented increase in global connectedness, the pace of technological change and adoption, the move toward urbanization, the evolution of demographic trends, and the impact of human activity on environmental degradation and climate change (Dobbs, Manyika, and Woetzel 2015; Singh 2012). Effective implementation of the SDGs will need to be mindful of these trends and their wide-ranging implications in order to mitigate risks and accelerate transformational development progress.

Extraordinary and intensifying connectedness is changing the world. Trade, finance, communications, and migration are all expanding rapidly, bringing the world closer together. Between 1990 and 2015, global merchandise trade grew 1.4 to 2.4 times as fast as the world economy, rising to the equivalent of around 60 percent of world GDP (figure 2.4a).[5] Over the same period, financial flows—including foreign direct investment (FDI), official development aid, and private capital—rose from about $87 billion to $1.3 trillion. The composition of financial flows has also undergone a major shift: in 1990 FDI was $21 billion, less than half of ODA at $53 billion; by 2014, FDI reached $735 billion and was more than five times larger than ODA flows of $135 billion. Global communications have skyrocketed: for example, mobile subscriptions rose from 5 per million in 1980 to more than 90 for every 100 people today (figure 2.4b) (Kose and Ozturk 2014). People are also on the move, with 1 billion international tourists in 2013, and 232 million international migrants (compared with 154 million in 1990) (UN 2013b). Another 750 million people have migrated internally. In seeking a global compact to address many of the world's most difficult challenges, the

FIGURE 2.4 Global connectedness has increased through intensified trade and communications

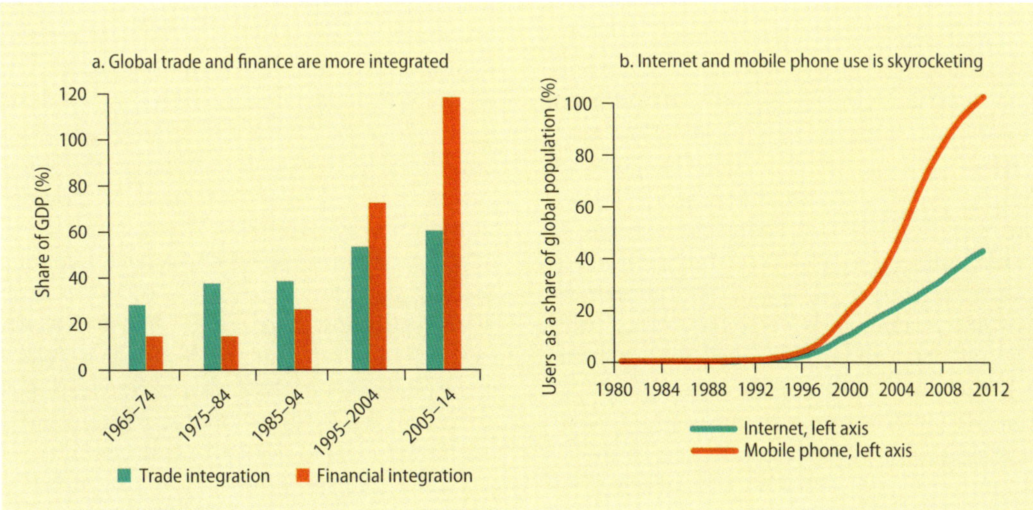

Source: Kose and Ozturk 2014.
Note: Trade integration reflects ratio of total imports and exports to global GDP. Financial integration is the ratio of total financial in-flows and out-flows (including bank loans, direct investment, bonds, and equities) to global GDP.

Source: World Development Indicators, World Bank.

SDGs reflect the unprecedented connectedness of the present age.

The global center of economic growth is rapidly moving toward emerging markets, but their comparatively faster growth needs to be supported by expanded investment. For almost 2000 years, the center of global growth moved slowly from a point between China and India, the world's two most populous nations, toward industrializing Europe and North America (Dobbs, Manyika, and Woetzel 2015, 19). The process has reversed and is accelerating dramatically—from a position just north of Europe in 2000, the center of global economic growth could return to its origin in Asia in just 25 years. This trend is generally welcome, as more populous and poorer countries in the emerging South sustain high rates of growth and "catch up" with advanced countries. Realizing the potential for faster growth, however, depends on scaling up high-return investment in the emerging South, both public and private. The SDGs reflect this imperative in their call for sustainable industrialization, greater infrastructure investment, and accelerated per capita income growth in low-income countries.

Deepening global trade and investment connections could also help reverse slipping potential growth in high-income countries. Concerns about weakening growth prospects in high-income economies are reflected in the "secular stagnation" hypothesis, which highlights a chronic excess of savings over investment because interest rates are unable to adjust to equate savings with investment at full employment (Summers 2015). Low productivity growth and an aging population in high-income countries may also be limiting investment opportunities and contributing to the excess of savings. In such circumstances, greater public investment in high-income countries is likely to lower the debt-to-GDP ratios. They also provide substantial scope for a debt-financed infrastructure push in emerging markets, both to increase high-return public capital stock and to spur private investment (Arslanalp, Bornhorst, and Gupta 2011; IMF 2014). Through expanded trade and investment links, greater public investment in emerging market economies can also help generate opportunities for exports and boost growth in high-income countries.

Progress is being supported by a quickening of technological innovation and adoption, enabling more sustainable and efficient practices. Humankind will generate more data in the next five years than in the previous 5,000. The digital and data revolutions are driving technical change in a range of fields, and are expected to underpin accelerating technical change in next-generation genomics, materials science, energy storage and renewables, advanced robotics, and information technologies, among others.[6] The adoption of new technologies is also accelerating (although developing countries sometimes have difficulty in using them effectively), largely because of the nature of offerings at almost zero cost, as well as the increased communications and greater connectedness of the world. These trends and efforts to broaden access to technology are a central part of numerous SDGs, including boosting agricultural productivity, promoting the empowerment of women, expanding access to clean energy, diversifying industry and breaking the link between carbon emissions and economic growth.

The urbanization megatrend brings great scope for accelerating development progress if key challenges can be met. The population of cities in emerging economies is projected to double from 2 billion in 2000 to 4 billion by 2030, and the footprint of urban areas is expected to triple from 200,000 to 600,000 square kilometers (World Bank 2013c). About 80 percent of the world's GDP is generated in cities, attracting rapid inflows of people. While the economies of scale of urban agglomeration and lower unit costs of service provision generate prosperity and improved well-being, the rapid pace of urbanization raises numerous challenges (also for rural areas losing people) that need to be addressed with effective planning, connecting, and financing, to ensure resilient and sustainable development (World Bank 2013c). The SDGs give due emphasis to the critical role of the impulse toward urbanization in development.

Demographic change is exerting a powerful influence on development trajectories. As discussed in more detail in part 2, several demographic changes, including the rise of the total dependency ratio at the global level for the first time since the 1960s, the cessation in the growth of the global youth population (ages 0–15), and the aging of populations in many countries, are giving rise to new opportunities and challenges over the coming decades. In addition to promoting women's empowerment and universal access to sexual and reproductive health as development objectives in their own right, the SDGs are motivated by demographic pressures and the urgent need to prioritize sustainability.

Global consumption is growing rapidly, especially in emerging market economies, and it will be essential to promote patterns that are environmentally sustainable. The global consuming class, defined as people with disposable income above $10 a day, is expected to exceed 4.2 billion by 2025, compared with 1.2 billion in 1990, with most purchasing power garnered in emerging market economies (Dobbs, Manyika, and Woetzel 2015). On top of existing ecological challenges, the current trajectory of resource and energy intensity of production scaled to this future level of demand show impacts that are unsustainable in terms of water, forests, fish, pollution, and climate. The consuming class is benefiting greatly from new technologies, with information, applications, and online services that are increasingly available at extremely low or no cost. However, as emphasized in the SDGs, it will be paramount that emerging production and consumption patterns be increasingly environmentally and socially sustainable. The World Bank Group, among others, is promoting a conceptualization of development progress that goes beyond traditional measures of GDP to reflect changes in physical, human, and natural capital, which helps countries better estimate whether their growth is sustainable (World Bank 2011).

Finally, climate change is bringing a warming world with more extreme weather events, and urgent mitigation as well as adaptation is required if development gains are to be preserved (World Bank 2014). The science on global warming caused by human activity is unequivocal, and the signs are clear. Of the 15 hottest years since record keeping began 130 years ago, 14 occurred between 2000 and 2015. The world may already be locked in to a warming of 1.5°C by midcentury, and if a sharp course correction is not undertaken, 4°C by the end of the century. The focus of the SDGs on environmental sustainability recognizes that ending extreme poverty, securing broader development gains, and lowering the risk of fragility and conflict will be very difficult in a +2°C world, and may not be possible at all in a +4°C world (Burke, Hsiang, and Miguel 2015).

A new approach

Mindful of these megatrends, the SDGs explicitly adopt a more universal approach spanning all countries, while recognizing that many key actions and policies are undertaken at the national level. The SDG framework applies to all countries and centers on the key elements needed to improve the future of the planet (UN 2015a, 10). Every country shares responsibility to contribute toward the transformational change that is within reach. The SDGs' enhanced monitoring framework also responds to the need for enhanced accountability, aimed at ensuring that all are doing their part both to keep their own houses in order and to contribute to the global commons (Kharas 2015).

The framing of the SDGs emphasizes the interconnections between development objectives in setting out an integrated development agenda. There are important interactions between development goals, and they cannot be effectively pursued separately from each other (UN 2015c, 21). For example, progress on health goals depends on investments in infrastructure that gives everyone access to safe water and improved sanitation. Similarly, limiting carbon dioxide emissions to slow global warming requires the modernization of energy supplies. Hence, the SDGs explicitly articulate goals that are "integrated and indivisible and balance the three dimensions of sustainable development: the economic, social and environmental" (UN2015f, 3). The breadth of the SDGs has raised questions about whether the scale of the agenda will dilute focus, especially when some development exigencies are likely to be more pressing than others at the country level. Still, the SDGs are not simply a menu of development objectives, and policy makers and other stakeholders are called upon to pursue the goals as an integrated whole.

A more comprehensive agenda

The SDG agenda goes beyond the MDGs in scope, expanding into wider objectives for peaceful, well-governed, and inclusive societies.[7] The commitment to the SDGs extends from the experience with the MDGs, and similarly aims to mobilize the international community toward common purpose on core elements of well-being by identifying compelling goals, specifying targets with set timeframes, and rendering them more concrete with indicators for monitoring (table 2.1). While similarities with the MDGs are apparent, the transition from the MDGs with 8 goals, 21 targets, and 60 indicators, to the SDGs with 17 goals, 169 targets, and 304 indicators (at the time of writing), reflects a fuller recognition of the multidimensional nature of development.

The commitment to ending extreme poverty is the overarching goal and the first pillar of the MDGs, the World Bank Group's goals, and the SDGs. The MDG goal to "eradicate extreme poverty and hunger" has evolved into the SDG goal to "end poverty in all of its forms everywhere." The recognition of the broad nature of deprivation is reflected in the associated targets of SDG1, covering both absolute poverty (as measured by the global poverty line of $1.25 a day) and national definitions, as well as in the call for provision of adequate social protection, access to basic services and economic resources, and mitigation of vulnerability to economic, social, and environmental shocks. The World Bank Group's goal of reducing extreme poverty to less than 3 percent by 2030 at the global level is in the same vein.

TABLE 2.1 The SDG agenda is centered on seventeen goals

SDG 1.	End poverty in all its forms everywhere.
SDG 2.	End hunger, achieve food security and improved nutrition and promote sustainable agriculture.
SDG 3.	Ensure healthy lives and promote well-being for all at all ages.
SDG 4.	Ensure inclusive and equitable quality education and promote lifelong learning opportunities for all.
SDG 5.	Achieve gender equality and empower all women and girls.
SDG 6.	Ensure availability and sustainable management of water and sanitation for all.
SDG 7.	Ensure access to affordable, reliable, sustainable and modern energy for all.
SDG 8.	Promote sustained, inclusive and sustainable economic growth, full and productive employment and decent work for all.
SDG 9.	Build resilient infrastructure, promote inclusive and sustainable industrialization and foster innovation.
SDG 10.	Reduce inequality within and among countries.
SDG 11.	Make cities and human settlements inclusive, safe, resilient and sustainable.
SDG 12.	Ensure sustainable consumption and production patterns.
SDG 13.	Take urgent action to combat climate change and its impacts.[a]
SDG 14.	Conserve and sustainably use the oceans, seas and marine resources for sustainable development.
SDG 15.	Protect, restore and promote sustainable use of terrestrial ecosystems, sustainably manage forests, combat desertification, and halt and reverse land degradation and halt biodiversity loss.
SDG 16.	Promote peaceful and inclusive societies for sustainable development, provide access to justice for all and build effective, accountable and inclusive institutions at all levels.
SDG 17.	Strengthen the means of implementation and revitalize the global partnership for sustainable development.

Source: UN 2015f.
a. Acknowledging that the United Nations Framework Convention on Climate Change is the primary international, intergovernmental forum for negotiating the global response to climate change.

The hunger component of MDG 1 has been captured in a separate SDG 2. Reflecting the complexity of food issues, SDG 2 aims to "end hunger, achieve food security and improved nutrition, and promote sustainable agriculture." Associated targets encompass not only hunger and nutrition but also efforts to boost agricultural productivity, ensure sustainable practices, remove distortionary trade restrictions in world food markets, and enhance the functioning of food commodity markets with better market information to help reduce volatility.

SDG 3 on health pulls together several related MDGs but is expanded to cover additional dimensions of healthy living. It seeks to "ensure healthy lives and promote well-being for all at all ages," addressing MDGs 4, 5, and 6 on maternal and child health, as well as the key communicable diseases of malaria, tuberculosis, and HIV/AIDS. Both the MDGs and the SDGs include targets on universal access to reproductive health, which plays a key role in shaping demographic trajectories. The expansions center on efforts to seek more investment in neglected tropical diseases, address the increasingly important issue of non-communicable diseases, ensure universal health coverage, reduce the number of deaths and illnesses from environmental contamination, and lower global deaths and injuries from road traffic accidents.

The SDGs on education and gender equality are broadened from the corresponding MDGs. SDG 4 builds on MDG 2's focus on the achievement of universal primary education and includes early childhood development; equal access for women and men to technical, vocational, and tertiary education; literacy among adults; and learning about sustainable development and lifestyles. SDG 5 aims to "achieve gender equality and empower all women and girls" by emphasizing additional dimensions of inequality in the treatment of females, including ending violence against all women and girls everywhere, eliminating harmful practices such as child, early, and forced marriage, and ending female genital mutilation. Ensuring universal access to sexual and reproductive health and rights is another component. Significantly, the SDGs recognize that reproductive health is also a critical rights issue.

A major shift in the evolution of the commitment to development goals centers on the heightened focus of the SDGs on environmental issues. MDG 7 on ensuring environmental sustainability has been expanded into five dedicated SDGs, including SDG 6 on water and sanitation; SDG 12 on ensuring sustainable consumption and production patterns; SDG 13 on the need to "take urgent action to combat climate change and its impacts"; SDG 14 on the oceans, seas, and marine resources; and SDG 15 on terrestrial ecosystems, including forests, deserts, and biodiversity. Environmental issues also feature prominently in several additional SDGs. These include SDG 2 on agriculture; SDG 7 on energy (seeking to increase the share of renewable energy); SDG 8 on economic growth (referring to the need to "decouple economic growth from environmental degradation"); SDG 9 on industrialization (emphasizing "increased resource-use efficiency and greater adoption of clean and environmentally sound technologies"); and SDG 11 on human settlements (aiming to "reduce the adverse per capita environmental impact of cities" and implement "holistic disaster risk management"). These expansions reflect growing concern about environmental sustainability and the recognition that even the primary SDG 1 on poverty will not be reachable if the present trends of rural resource degradation and climate change continue.

The new monitoring framework places greater focus on income distribution, which is also reflected in the World Bank Group's goal on shared prosperity. While MDG 1 noted the "share of poorest quintile in national consumption" as an indicator of the poverty target, it did not receive much attention in the development discourse during the MDG period. In contrast, distributional issues have been elevated to a separate goal, with SDG 10 aiming to "reduce inequality within and among countries." This goal includes a tractable target of sustaining the "income growth of the bottom 40 percent of the population at a rate higher than the national average." As detailed in chapter 1, the second of the World Bank Group's goals is on shared prosperity, which emphasizes the income growth of the bottom 40 percent of the income distribution in each country, but it does not specify that it should be higher than the national average. Goals on inequality and shared prosperity are evidently universal, applying to all countries.

The SDG framework includes several other new components, including SDG 7 on energy, and SDG 16 on promoting peaceful and inclusive societies. SDG 7 on ensuring universal access to affordable, reliable, and modern energy services is central to development and underpins many other SDG goals. Similarly, SDG 16 recognizes that development is thwarted or highly vulnerable in fragile and conflict situations, as well as in contexts where governance is weak. Years of development progress can rapidly be undone by the outbreak of conflict. And, poverty and deprivation are increasingly concentrated in countries characterized by fragility, violence, and limited institutional progress. SDG 16 calls for promoting the rule of law and access to justice, reducing illicit arms flows, and lessening corruption and bribery in an effort to address the drivers of conflict.

Finally, SDG 17 focuses squarely on the key elements needed to ensure effective implementation. This goal focuses on arranging and facilitating sufficient financing, cooperating on technology, enhancing capacity-building efforts, and promoting an open and equitable multilateral trading system. SDG 17 also notes the need for greater policy and institutional coherence; multi-stakeholder partnerships; and enhanced data, monitoring, and accountability.

To accelerate progress, the SDGs can learn from the MDGs

To maximize the odds of success on the unfinished development agenda, it is important to learn from the MDGs. Numerous lessons emerge from the MDG process (including challenges faced; see Fehling, Nelson, and Venkatapuram 2013), some of which have already contributed to the framing of the SDGs and others that can help underpin development efforts between now and 2030 (Kanie et al. 2014; UN 2012). These center on ensuring inclusiveness and ownership at the country level; building on synergies between goals; specifying targets that can be monitored with good data and that are time bound; and supporting strong implementation, including ensuring adequate financing and effective use of resources.

Inclusiveness and ownership

A key lesson is to adopt highly consultative goal-setting processes. Given that most of the critical actions required to make progress on the MDGs had to be implemented at the country level, inclusiveness and ownership were essential, extending to policy makers, representatives from the private sector and civil society, and other stakeholders. The SDG process has sought to reflect this lesson, and the proposals are built upon extensive consultations, facilitating adoption in country development programs.

Synergies between development goals

Progress toward the MDGs was helped by synergies, and the effectiveness of SDG efforts will also depend on leveraging gains in one goal for advances in others. The links between MDGs on infant mortality and access to sanitation and safe water are well documented. The SDGs reflect this experience in their more integrated approach, and will benefit from synergies across numerous SDGs. For example, progress toward SDG 5 on achieving gender equality would have a major impact on the prospects for lowering infant mortality, eliminating hunger, and raising school attendance. SDG 16 on promoting peaceful and inclusive societies has targets on reducing all forms of violence and corruption, both of which are key impediments to progress on all other SDGs. The scope for synergies is also an important consideration when prioritizing efforts on the SDGs at the country level.

Sound monitoring

Like the MDGs, the SDGs require sound monitoring, which in turn hinges on more and better data. Much of the success of the MDGs in moving the development agenda forward has been attributed to the specificity of targets that were time bound. Progress was weaker on goals that were less specific and harder to monitor, and where good data were lacking. Building strong data systems is essential in this regard (box 2.3). With 304 proposed indicators, some of which are difficult to monitor or have very little data coverage and availability, monitoring the SDGs will be challenging, and will entail large costs. Substantial work is needed to strengthen statistical systems at the national level and improve methodologies. About $1 billion a year may be needed in 77 low-income countries to strengthen statistical systems to support and track the SDGs consistently (SDSN 2015). Scaled-up data and monitoring will require enhancing global mechanisms and support.

Strong implementation

Success or failure will hinge on implementation. Moving from goal setting to implementation requires analysis and tailoring of the targets to the country level. It also calls for enhanced accountability for financing and other key steps among development partners and the wider international community. In the case of several MDGs, implementation arrangements were effectively not in place until five to seven years after the Millennium Declaration, leading to significant delays. Building on MDG structures, the implementation of the SDGs is better placed, despite the added areas of focus.

Still, several structural factors pose challenges that need to be confronted if the goals are to be met. As highlighted in chapter 1, the evolution of poverty points to an increasing concentration of poverty in hard-to-reach places, such as in fragile and conflict situations, where governance is weak. In addition, the growth elasticity of poverty is falling, suggesting that the remaining pockets of poverty are less responsive to economic growth. Finally, the prospects for growth over the coming years are somewhat dampened compared with the MDG period, when strong growth supported progress, as is discussed in chapter 3.

BOX 2.3 What gets measured gets done: The importance of data

Data availability has improved under the MDG framework. While setting goals remains a key step to solving development challenges, without critical data inputs measuring initial conditions and monitoring progress, effective policy making is hampered. One beneficial outcome of the MDG process has been the push for better data (Manning 2009) and its contribution to the ongoing data revolution (UN 2014b). In 2003, only four developing countries had two or more data points for at least 16 of the 22 MDG indicators. By 2013, 129 countries met this metric of data availability. The improvement in data was greatly facilitated by the expansion of household surveys, a key data source for monitoring the MDGs. For instance, the average number of surveys produced each year in both Ethiopia and Ghana has almost doubled since 2000. Behind the increased availability of data lies enhanced national statistical capacity building, with data often collected in collaboration with international experts.

Much more needs to be done to fill data gaps. Ongoing improvements in data notwithstanding, significant gaps remain for key MDG indicators. For instance, on the goal of maternal mortality, only 11 percent of developing countries have available data. In part, that is because civil registration systems on births and deaths are incomplete, with coverage ranging from 50 percent in Latin America to 25 percent in South Asia, and a mere 6 percent in Sub-Saharan Africa (Boerma and Stansfield 2007; Devarajan 2013; Murray, 2007). Another challenge is the lack of disaggregation by gender, income quintile, or disabilities, which complicates targeted policy formulation. Even when data are available, they often come with significant lags, and there are concerns about consistency and reliability. For instance, less than 60 percent of developing countries report data with less than a two-year lag on the MDGs related to health and education (including gender parity in education, maternal mortality, and the prevalence of undernourishment), and in many cases broad assumptions were made in order to arrive at existing estimates (Sachs 2012).

Several factors account for the data challenges in the MDG process. The effort to generate the data needed to monitor the MDGs has often been driven by external actors, rather than being embedded in the priorities of national statistical offices. For instance, on the maternal mortality indicator, while some trend analysis can be carried out for about 80 percent of developing countries, this share drops to about 10 percent when data collected from international organizations are excluded. In some cases, national statistical offices perceived the approach of international actors as top-down and undermining their own efforts, especially when estimates differed from national ones. Finally, some of the MDGs were not readily quantifiable (such as "achieve full and productive employment and decent work," or "universal access to reproductive health"), making it difficult to generate relevant monitoring indicators.

Governments and other stakeholders should invest more in statistical capacity building and a "smart data revolution." Given the increased number of goals, targets, and indicators under the SDGs, the associated data challenges are even more onerous than those of the MDGs. It is important to invest in statistical capacity and build on existing mechanisms and systems to gather the micro-level data needed for monitoring the SDGs. Monitoring efforts, however, will benefit from the ongoing smart data revolution, which is filtering through all aspects of modern society, such as elections managed with biometrics, forests monitored by satellite imagery, banking undertaken on smart phones, and medical x-rays sent for examination halfway around the world. The associated data revolution has the potential to reduce long lags and dramatically improve the quality of data. Between household survey years, national statistical offices could leverage the expertise of telecommunication companies and software developers to carry out real-time surveys on mortality rates and even poverty data. By one estimate this could reduce the cost of surveys by about 60 percent.

As with the MDGs, demographic patterns may also pose significant challenges to achieving the SDGs. The demographic trends projected over the coming decades will have a major impact on the trajectory of development (see part 2 of this report). For example, more than 2 billion babies will be born worldwide between now and 2030 (UN 2015b). When comparing the coming 15 years with the past 15 years, relatively more births are expected in low-income countries in Africa, where health systems are weak, coverage is incomplete, and maternal and infant mortality rates are high. Making progress on related SDG indicators and expanding the coverage of health services when the underlying demand continues to increase is a major challenge. The same is true for the 2 billion children that are projected to reach school age over the next 15 years. Africa may see a 34 percent increase in school-age children (five-year-olds), making it even harder to expand coverage and increase the quality of schooling. More targeted approaches will be needed in these contexts.

The challenges associated with the sheer scale and breadth of the SDGs require concerted effort and scaled-up financing. Ultimately, the SDGs are the product of a deep political process. Sustaining support among political constituencies, especially when difficult and unpopular actions are required, hinges on leadership and continuing engagement on core SDG issues. Building on the investment in implementation arrangements of the MDGs, the SDGs are better placed for scaled-up action. Still, more needs to be done to boost implementation capacity, including by mobilizing adequate financing (box 2.4). Some prioritization of SDG-related activities at both the global and the country levels will need to be reflected in spending plans (Lomborg et al. 2014). The

BOX 2.4 Mobilizing financing for development

Mobilizing adequate resources and ensuring their effective use is essential to making progress on the unfinished development agenda.[a] The renewed commitment to development in 2015 is an important opportunity to strengthen enabling policies and institutions, as well as to mobilize needed resources. Experience shows that these elements are closely related, especially in a rapidly changing global context, where more low- and middle-income countries are able to access international capital markets (more than 70 emerging market countries have bond ratings), and foreign direct investment in 2013 was more than five times larger than official development assistance (ODA). The 2002 Monterrey Consensus on the MDGs highlighted the importance of global development cooperation to mobilize and increase the effective use of financial resources. The post-2015 financing framework will build on the lessons learned during the MDG era, emphasizing the need to mobilize domestic resources and ensure sound management of public expenditures, encourage private sector resources oriented toward development goals, and boost international public finance. More detailed financing plans need to be prepared at the country level (Kharas and McArthur 2014, 2015).

Domestic resources will continue to make up the bulk of public spending aimed directly at key development priorities. Only about half of developing countries are able to collect 15 percent of GDP or more in taxes (this figure is even lower in fragile and conflict states), a modest level given wide-ranging needs (IMF 2011). Improving the tax structure for domestic resource mobilization also remains a challenge. For example, policy makers are urged to avoid creating economic distortions through tax holidays, or discouraging trade openness with various tax measures. Increasing the quality and efficiency of public spending will help generate needed resources to meet key development goals. Around 8 percent of government spending around the world, equivalent to $1.9 trillion, is spent on subsidies in one form or another, with energy subsidies alone costing the public purse

(box continues next page)

BOX 2.4 Mobilizing financing for development (continued)

about $300 billion (IMF 2014). The recent fall in oil prices presents a golden opportunity to eliminate or dramatically reduce such subsidies. Expanding the evidence base on the incidence of such subsidies may encourage positive change. Strengthening public expenditure management systems, including enhanced independent oversight, multiyear budgeting, and fiscal responsibility laws, can also contribute meaningfully.

Private resources play a central role, and efforts should focus on incentivizing flows. Private sources, including foreign direct investment, bank loans, capital markets, private transfers (such as workers' remittances), and philanthropy, account for the bulk of external resource flows to emerging market economies. Given that much of these flows are motivated by risk/reward considerations, public policy needs to help lower and manage risk or increase the rewards associated with private investment. Development partners, such as the multilateral development banks and the International Monetary Fund, seek to serve as "leveraging machines," catalyzing private sector flows (through both advice and policy-based lending), and by helping to underpin strong macroeconomic conditions and investment climates (World Bank 2015b). Their agenda also includes the promotion of local capital markets for more effective resource intermediation.

ODA is the foundation and catalyst for leveraging greatly expanded public and private sector capital flows for development. ODA remains the largest source of external resources to low-income and fragile and conflicted countries, where private investment and access to international capital markets is limited. However, current levels of ODA, which reached about $135 billion in 2013, will be insufficient to meet the SDGs. Indeed, ODA flows to Africa have fallen in real terms over the past few years. ODA would have to more than double to meet the 0.7 percent of gross national income target set by the Development Assistance Committee of the Organisation for Economic Co-operation and Development. ODA needs to be used more intelligently to channel additional sources of financing towards development goals, leveraging "billions for trillions." Issues of aid quality and effectiveness, including predictability, alignment, harmonization, and coherence with the World Bank's goals and the SDG agenda, remain salient. A diverse group of countries has gained prominence in the aid landscape, including the BRICS (Brazil, the Russian Federation, India, China, and South Africa), the Republic of Korea, Saudi Arabia, and Turkey.

Climate finance is a relatively new and growing source of funding available to developing countries for climate change mitigation and adaptation projects and programs. The term has been used in a narrower sense to refer to transfers of public resources from developed to developing countries in light of UN Climate Convention obligations to provide "new and additional financial resources," and in a wider sense to refer to all financial flows relating to climate mitigation and adaptation. Developed country governments currently provide between $10 billion to $20 billion per year of such funds, and at the 2009 UN climate change conference in Copenhagen, they committed to providing a collective $100 billion per year by 2020. While the focus of climate finance is clearly on climate mitigation and adaptation, many mitigation actions (investments in energy and resource efficiency), adaptation actions (public transit and sustainable cities), capacity building, and research and development also have national and local "co-benefits."

The multilateral development banks play a fundamental role not only as financial intermediaries leveraging shareholder contributions but also in supporting debt restructuring initiatives, strengthening public expenditure management, and crowding in private sector financing. The multilateral development banks and the IMF are committed to delivering financing solutions that will help countries achieve the SDGs, and they are exploring ways to increase available financial resources, expand policy guidance and technical assistance, promote and catalyze private investment, support international action on regional and global development issues, and improve coordination and alignment (World Bank 2015a, 23). Toward these ends, the World Bank Group and other multilateral development banks have made commitments of over $400 billion for the three-year period 2016–18. Ongoing efforts emphasize additionality, efficiency, and effectiveness. The IMF has also increased access norms and limits across concessional facilities by 50 percent for all eligible countries.

a. The discussion in this section is based on World Bank 2015a.

Outcome Document from the Third International Financing for Development Conference in Addis Ababa emphasizes seven key areas (UN 2015e):

- *Delivering social protection and essential public services,* with a social compact for ensuring adequate service provision, supported by appropriate spending at the national level and augmented with international resources.
- *Scaling up efforts to end hunger and malnutrition,* including by investing in sustainable agriculture and fisheries, especially the productivity of smallholder farmers.
- *Establishing a new forum to bridge the infrastructure gap,* increasing sustainable and inclusive infrastructure investment in developing countries, with additional finance, better technology, and elevated technical assistance.
- *Promoting inclusive and sustainable industrialization,* which is essential for growth, economic diversification, innovation, and high-value-addition jobs.
- *Generating full and productive employment and decent work for all, promoting micro-, small, and medium enterprises,* including credit and other financial services, and creating an environment where the business sector plays a central role in generating employment and growth.
- *Protecting our ecosystems for all,* through coherent policy, financing, trade, and technology that will be essential to mitigating and avoiding harmful activities.
- *Promoting peaceful and inclusive societies* as the foundation of socially, economically, and environmentally sustainable development.

Conclusion

As the world transitions from the MDGs to the SDGs, the opportunities presented by rapid global change hold great promise for transforming development while safeguarding the environment. The MDGs shaped the development agenda since the turn of the century, with wide-ranging and impressive achievements. The SDGs are the next step in the global efforts to transform development: much broader in nature, with clear targets for monitoring and a sharpened focus on safeguarding the world's fragile ecosystems. The lessons learned from the MDGs improve the likelihood of success of the more sweeping SDGs. Realizing the potential of the so-called "megatrends"—such as global connectedness and the shift of the global economic center of gravity toward dynamic economies in the East—can help facilitate progress toward reaching the SDGs. To achieve its promise, however, the SDGs require major commitments regarding policy and institutional reform and mobilization of adequate financing. Achievement of the SDGs also requires meeting emerging economic challenges over the medium term, the subject of the next chapter.

Notes

1. Empirical evidence suggests that what counts for economic growth is what students actually learn, not how many years of schooling they complete. While nearly all education systems are expanding quantitatively, many are failing in this fundamental purpose (Hanushek and Woessmann 2007). For instance, in 2006, even though Brazil and Mexico were on track to meet the MDG target, a large share of Brazilian (78 percent) and Mexican youth (50 percent) lacked minimally adequate competencies in mathematics, and over 90 percent did not reach a reasonable global standard (Filmer, Hasan, and Pritchett 2006; Pritchett, Banerji, and Kenny 2013). Similarly, another study focusing on East Africa found that while primary enrollment rates have risen significantly over the past 15 years, children remain functionally illiterate or innumerate, despite completing multiple years of schooling (Jones et al. 2014).
2. See the MDG Report Card in appendix A for more detailed regional comparisons of each MDG and associated targets.
3. The "total dependency ratio" is the sum of people ages 0–14 and 65 and over, divided by the number of people ages 15–64, multiplied by 100.

4. In addition to improved water, sanitation, and slums, MDG 7 (on ensuring environmental sustainability) included indicators on the proportion of land area covered by forest, the proportion of fish stocks within safe biological limits, the proportion of total water resources used, the proportion of terrestrial and marine areas protected, the proportion of species threatened with extinction, the level of CO_2 emissions per capita and per $1 GDP (PPP), and the consumption of ozone-depleting substances.
5. Trade growth has slowed in the postcrisis years—in 2012 and 2013, trade grew more slowly than the world economy for the first time in four decades. This slowdown has sparked a debate about "peak trade": while there may be scope for further growth in trade, structural changes in U.S. and Chinese supply chains, together with the end of the big push from the fragmentation of production networks, may signal that trade growth has peaked (Constantinescu, Mattoo, and Ruta 2014).
6. Dobbs, Manyika, and Woetzel 2015. See Gordon 2014 for a skeptical view about "techno-optimism."
7. U.N. Secretary General Ban Ki-moon indicated that "the SDGs break new ground with goals on inequalities, economic growth, decent jobs, cities and human settlements, industrialization, energy, climate change, sustainable consumption and production, peace, justice, and institutions. The environmental dimension of the agenda is articulated across the whole agenda. The SDGs are underpinned with a goal on global partnerships for the means of implementation" (UN 2014a).

References

Andres, L., B. Briceño, C. Chase, and J. A. Echenique. 2014. "Sanitation and Externalities: Evidence from Early Childhood Health in Rural India." Policy Research Working Paper 6737, World Bank, Washington, DC.

Arslanalp, S., F. Bornhorst, and S. Gupta. 2011. "Investing in Growth: Revisiting the Debate over Whether Public Investment in Infrastructure Is Productive." *Finance and Development*. International Monetary Fund, Washington, DC (March).

Bhattacharya, A., and H. Kharas. 2015. "Worthy of Support." *The Economist*, April 8.

Boerma, J. T., and S. K. Stansfield. 2007. "Health statistics: Are we making the right investments?" *Lancet* 369: 779–86.

Bourguignon, F., A. Bénassy-Quéré, S. Dercon, A. Estache, J. W. Gunning, R. Kanbur, S. Klasen, S. Maxwell, J-P Platteau, and A. Spadaro. 2008a. *Millenium Development Goals at Midpoint: Where Do We Stand and Where Do We Need to Go?* European Report on Development.

Bourguignon, F., C. Diaz-Bonilla, and H. Lofgren. 2008b. "Aid, Service Delivery, and the Millennium Development Goals in an Economy-wide Framework." Policy Research Working Paper 4683, World Bank, Washington, DC.

Bruns, B., A. Mingat, and R. Rakotomalala. 2003. *Achieving Universal Primary Education by 2015: A Chance for Every Child*. Washington, DC: World Bank.

Burke, M., S. M. Hsiang, and E. Miguel. 2015. "Climate and Conflict." *Annual Review of Economics* (forthcoming).

Ciccone, A., and R. E. Hall. 1996. "Productivity and the Density of Economic Activity." *American Economic Review* 86 (1): 54–70.

Clemens, M., and T. Moss. 2005. "What's Wrong with the Millennium Development Goals?" *CGD Brief*, Center for Global Development, Washington, DC (September).

Constantinescu, C., A. Mattoo, and M. Ruta. 2014. "Slow Trade: Part of the Global Trade Slowdown since the Crisis Has Been Driven by Structural, Not Cyclical, Factors." *Finance and Development*. International Monetary Fund, Washington, DC (December).

Devarajan, S. 2013. "Africa's Statistical Tragedy." *Review of Income and Wealth*, International Association for Research in Income and Wealth, Ottawa.

Dobbs, R., J. Manyika, and J. Woetzel. 2015. *No Ordinary Disruption—The Four Global Forces Breaking All the Trends*. New York: McKinsey and Company, Public Affairs.

Dollar, D., and A. Kraay. 2002. "Growth Is Good for the Poor," *Journal of Economic Growth* (7): 195–225.

———. 2013. "Growth Is Still Good for the Poor." Policy Research Working Paper 6568, World Bank, Washington, DC.

Easterly, W. 2007. "How the Millennium Development Goals Are Unfair to Africa." Brookings Global Economy and Development Working Paper 14, Brookings Institution, Washington, DC (November).

Fay, M., D. Leipziger, Q. Wodon, and T. Yepes. 2005. "Achieving Child-Health-Related Millennium Development Goals: The Role of Infrastructure." *World Development* 33: 1267–84.

Fehling, M., B. D. Nelson, and S. Venkatapuram. 2013. "Limitations of the Millennium Development Goals: A Literature Review." *Global Public Health* 8 (10): 1109–22.

Filmer, D., A. Hasan, and L. Pritchett. 2006. "A Millennium Learning Goal: Measuring Real Progress in Education." Working Paper 97, Center for Global Development, Washington, DC.

Friedman, H. S. 2013. "Causal Inference and the Millennium Development Goals (MDGs): Assessing Whether There Was an Acceleration in MDG Development Indicators Following the MDG Declaration." MPRA Paper 48793, August. http://mpra.ub.uni-muenchen.de/48793/.

Glaeser, E. L., and A. Joshi-Ghani. 2013. "Rethinking Cities: Toward Shared Prosperity." *Economic Premise* 126, World Bank, Washington, DC.

Glaeser, E. L., and D. Maré. 2001. "Cities and Skills." *Journal of Labor Economics* 19 (2): 316–42.

Godoy, R., and M. Contreras. 2001. "A Comparative Study of Education and Tropical Deforestation among Lowland Bolivian Amerindians: Forest Values, Environmental Externality, and School Subsidies." *Economic Development and Cultural Change* 49 (3): 555–74.

Gordon, R. J. 2014. "The demise of U.S. economic growth: Restatement, rebuttal, and reflection." NBER Working Paper 19895, February.

Hammer J., and D. Spears. 2013. "Village Sanitation and Children's Human Capital: Evidence from a Randomized Experiment by the Maharashtra Government." Policy Research Working Paper 6580, World Bank, Washington, DC.

Hanushek, E. A., and L. Woessmann. 2007. "The Role of Education Quality for Economic Growth." Policy Research Working Paper 4122, World Bank, Washington, DC.

Hermann, M., ed. 2015. *Consequential Omissions: How Demography Shapes Development Lessons from the MDGs for the SDGs.* Berlin Institute for Population and Development, and the United Nations Population Fund.

IMF (International Monetary Fund). 2015. "Financing For Development—Revisiting the Monterrey Consensus." International Monetary Fund, Washington, DC.

———. 2014. *World Economic Outlook.* Washington, DC: International Monetary Fund.

Jones, S., Y. Schipper, S. Ruto, and R. Rajani. 2014. "Can Your Child Read and Count? Measuring Learning Outcomes in East Africa." *Journal of African Economies* 23 (5): 643–72.

Kanie, N., N. Abe, M. Iguchi, J. Yang, N. Kabiri, Y. Kitamura, S. Mangagi, et al. 2014. "Integration and Diffusion in Sustainable Development Goals: Learning from the Past, Looking into the Future." *Sustainability* 6 (4): 1761–75.

Karlsen, S., L. Say, J.-P. Souza, C. J. Hogue, D. L. Calles, A. M. Gülmezoglu, and R. Raine. 2011. "The Relationship between Maternal Education and Mortality among Women Giving Birth in Health Care Institutions: Analysis of the Cross-Sectional WHO Global Survey on Maternal and Perinatal Health." *BMC Public Health* 11 (606).

Kenny, C., and S. Dykstra. 2013. "The Global Partnership for Development: A Review of MDG 8 and Proposals for the Post-2015 Development Agenda." Policy Paper 026, Center for Global Development, Washington, DC (July).

Kharas, H. 2015. "The Post-2015 Agenda: A Road Map for a Developing World." Future Development Blog, Brookings Institution, Washington, DC, February 10.

Kharas, H. and J. W. McArthur. 2014. "Three Breakthrough Agreements Will Underpin the Post-2015 Global Agenda." Upfront Blog, Brookings Institution, Washington, DC, December 9.

———. 2015. "Nine Priority Commitments to be Made at the UN's July 2015 Financing for Development Conference in Addis Ababa, Ethiopia." *Global Views* 50, Brookings Institution, Washington, DC (February).

Kharas, H. and C. Zhang. 2014. "New Agenda, New Narrative: What Happens after 2015?" *SAIS Review of International Affairs* 34 (2).

King, E. M., S. Klasen, and M. Porter. 2009. "Women and Development." In *Global Crises, Global Solutions,* edited by B. Lomborg, 2nd ed. Cambridge, UK: Cambridge University Press.

Klasen, S. 2005. "Bridging the Gender Gap to Promote Economic and Social Development." *Journal of International Affairs* 58 (2): 245–56.

Klasen, S. and M. C. Lo Bue. 2013. "Identifying Synergies and Complementarities between MDGs: Results from Cluster Analysis." *Social Indicators Research* 113 (2): 647–70.

Klugman, J., L. Hanmer, S. Twigg, T. Hasan, J. McCleary-Sills, and J. Santamaria. 2014. *Voice and Agency: Empowering Women and Girls for Shared Prosperity.* Washington, DC: World Bank Group.

Kose, A. M. and E. O. Ozturk. 2014. "A World of Change: Taking Stock of the Past Half Century." *Finance and Development,* International Monetary Fund, Washington, DC (September).

Kumar, S., and S. Vollmer. 2013. "Does Access to Improved Sanitation Reduce Childhood Diarrhea in Rural India?" *Health Economics* 22: 410–27.

Lay, J. 2010. "MDG Achievements, Determinants, and Resource Needs: What Has Been Learnt?" Policy Research Working Paper 5320, World Bank, Washington, DC.

Lay, J., and A. S. Robilliard. 2009. "The Complementarity of MDG Achievements. The Case of Child Mortality in Sub-Saharan Africa." Policy Research Working Paper 5062, World Bank, Washington, DC.

Lo Bue, M. C. 2013. "Are There Synergies between MDGs?" Development in Brief 3, KFW-Development Research.

———. 2015. The Complementarities of Child Health Achievements in Developing Countries. Ph.D thesis, University of Gottingen, Germany.

Lomborg, B., et al. 2014. "Preliminary Benefit-Cost Assessment of the Final OWG Outcome." Copenhagen Consensus Center, Copenhagen (August).

Manning, R. 2009. "Using Indicators to Encourage Development: Lessons from the Millennium Development Goals." Report 2009:1, Danish Institute for International Studies, Copenhagen.

McArthur, J. W. 2013. "Own the Goals: What the Millennium Development Goals Have Accomplished." *Foreign Affairs* 92 (2): 152–62.

———. 2014. "Seven Million Lives Saved: Under-5 Mortality since the Launch of the Millennium Development Goals." Global Economy and Development Working Paper 78, Brookings Institution, Washington, DC (September).

Melo, P. C., D. J. Graham, and R. B. Noland. 2009. "A Meta-Analysis of Estimates of Urban Agglomeration Economies." *Regional Science and Urban Economics* 39 (3): 332–42.

Murray, C. J. 2007. "Towards Good Practice for Health Statistics: Lessons from the Millennium Development Goal Health Indicators." *The Lancet* 369: 862–73.

PMNCH (Partnership for Maternal, Newborn and Child Health), WHO (World Health Organization), World Bank, and AHPSR (Alliance for Health Policy and Systems Research). 2014. *Success Factors for Women's and Children's Health: Policy and Programme Highlights from 10 Fast-Track Countries.* Geneva: World Health Organization.

Pritchett, L., R. Banerji, and C. Kenny. 2013. "Schooling Is Not Education! Using Assessment to Change the Politics of Non-Learning." Report of the Center for Global Development Study Group on Measuring Learning Outcomes, Washington, DC.

Prüss, A., D. Kay, L. Fewtrell, and J. Bartram. 2002. "Estimating the Burden of Disease from Water, Sanitation, and Hygiene at a Global Level." *Environmental Health Perspectives* 110: 537–42.

Puga, D. 2010. "The Magnitude and Causes of Agglomeration Economies." *Journal of Regional Science* 50 (1): 203–19.

Riddell, A. 2003. "The Introduction of Free Primary Education in Sub-Saharan Africa." Background Paper commissioned for *Global Monitoring Report 2003/4—Education for All,* World Bank, Washington, DC.

Roberts, T., E. Carnahan, and E. Gakidou. 2013. "Burden Attributable to Suboptimal Breastfeeding: A Cross-Country Analysis of Country-Specific Trends and Their Relation to

Child Health Inequalities." *The Lancet* 381: S126.

Rosenthal, S. S., and W. C. Strange. 2004. "Evidence on the Nature and Sources of Agglomeration Economies." In *Handbook of Regional and Urban Economics*, vol. 4, edited by J. V. Henderson and J.-F. Thisse. Amsterdam: North-Holland.

———. 2010. "Small Establishments/Big Effects: Agglomeration, Industrial Organization and Entrepreneurship." In *The Economics of Agglomeration*, edited by E. L. Glaeser. Cambridge, MA: National Bureau of Economic Research.

Sachs, J. D. 2012. "From Millennium Development Goals to Sustainable Development Goals." *The Lancet* 379 (June): 2206–11.

Sanchez, Pedro, and M. S. Swaminathan. 2005. "Cutting World Hunger in Half." *Science* 307 (January).

SDSN (Sustainable Development Solutions Network). 2015. "Data for Development: A Needs Assessment for SDG Monitoring and Statistical Capacity Development." April.

Sen, Amartya. 1999. *Development as Freedom*. New York: Oxford University Press.

Singh, Sarwant. 2012. *New Mega Trends*. London: Palgrave Macmillan.

Smith, L., and L. Haddad. 2015. "Reducing Child Undernutrition: Past Drivers and Priorities for the Post-MDG Era." *World Development* 68 (April): 180–204.

Spears, D. 2013. "How Much International Variation in Child Height Can Open Defecation Explain?" Policy Research Working Paper 6351, World Bank, Washington, DC.

Spears D., A. Ghosh, and O. Cumming. 2013. "Open Defecation and Childhood Stunting in India: An Ecological Analysis of New Data from 112 Districts." *PLoS ONE* 8 (9): e73784.

Stuckler, D., S. Basu, and M. McKee. 2010. "Drivers of Inequality in Millennium Development Goal Progress: A Statistical Analysis." *PLoS Med* 7(3): e1000241.

Summers, L. 2015. "On Secular Stagnation: A Response to Bernanke." Blog.

UN (United Nations). 2005. *Taking Action: Achieving Gender Equality and Empowering Women*. United Nations Development Programme, New York.

———. 2012. "Review of the Contributions of the MDG Agenda to Foster Development: Lessons for the Post-2015 UN Development Agenda." UN System Task Team on the Post-2015 UN Development Agenda, New York (March).

———. 2013a. "Lessons Learned from MDG Monitoring From A Statistical Perspective." Report of the Task Team on Lessons Learned from MDG Monitoring of the IAEG-MDG, March. United Nations, New York.

———. 2013b. Trends in International Migrant Stock: Migrants by Destination and Origin United Nations database, POP/DB/MIG /Stock/Rev.2013.

———. 2014a. "The Road to Dignity by 2030: Ending Poverty, Transforming All Lives and Protecting the Planet." Synthesis Report of the Secretary-General on the Post-2015 Sustainable Development Agenda, United Nations, New York (December).

———. 2014b. "A World that Counts: Mobilizing the Data Revolution for Sustainable Development." United Nations, New York (November).

———. 2015a. *Global Sustainable Development Report*. Advance unedited edition. New York: United Nations Department of Economic and Social Affairs, Division for Sustainable Development.

———. 2015b. "Integrating Population Issues into Sustainable Development, Including in the post-2015 Development Agenda." Report of the Secretary General, Economic and Social Council, Commission on Population and Development, United Nations, New York.

———. 2015c. *The Millennium Development Goals Report 2015*. New York: United Nations.

———. 2015d. "My World: The United Nations Global Survey for a Better World." United Nations, http://vote.myworld2015.org/.

———. 2015e. "Outcome Document of the Third Financing for Development Conference Addis Ababa Action Agenda." United Nations, New York (July 15).

———. 2015f. "Transforming our World: The 2030 Agenda for Sustainable Development." United Nations, New York (August).

UNESCO (United Nations Educational, Scientific and Cultural Organization). 2015. *Education for All 2000–2015: Achievements and Challenges*. Paris: UNESCO Publishing.

WHO (World Health Organization), United Nations Children's Fund, United Nations Population Fund, World Bank, and United Nations Population Division. 2014. *Trends in Maternal Mortality: 1990 to 2013*. Geneva: World Health Organization.

World Bank. 2001. *Engendering Development: Through Gender Equality in Rights, Resources, and Voice*. Policy Research Report 21776. New York: Oxford University Press.

———. 2003. *Achieving Universal Primary Education by 2015: A Chance for Every Child*. Washington, DC: World Bank.

———. 2011. *The Changing Wealth of Nations: Measuring Sustainable Development in the New Millennium*. Washington, DC: World Bank.

———. 2013a. *Global Monitoring Report 2013: Rural-Urban Dynamics and the Millennium Development Goals*. Washington, DC: World Bank.

———. 2013b. "Investing in the Next Generation: Growing Tall and Smart with Toilets—Stopping Open Defecation Improves Children's Height in Cambodia." Water and Sanitation Program: Research Brief, World Bank, Washington, DC (November).

———. 2013c. *Planning, Connecting & Financing Cities—Now*. Washington, DC: World Bank.

———. 2013d. *The World Bank Group Goals—End Extreme Poverty and Promote Shared Prosperity*. Washington, DC: World Bank.

———. 2014. *Turn Down the Heat: Confronting the New Climate Normal*. Washington, DC: World Bank.

———. 2015a. "From Billions to Trillions: Transforming Development Finance." Development Committee Paper, DC2015-0002, World Bank, Washington, DC.

———. 2015b. "Information Note: Post-2015 Financing for Development in the World Bank Group." World Bank, Washington, DC.

3

Global Macroeconomic Performance and Outlook: Prospects for Growth

This chapter includes an overview of recent macroeconomic developments, a short-term global economic outlook, and the risks facing the outlook, which draw on the International Monetary Fund's (IMF's) *World Economic Outlook* (WEO).[1] It also assesses the appropriateness of macroeconomic policies in advanced, emerging market, and low-income developing countries. With the year marking a shift in the objectives of the global development agenda—with the Sustainable Development Goals (SDGs) replacing the Millennium Development Goals (MDGs) of the past 15 years—the chapter discusses the global economic performance in a longer-term perspective, by also drawing on the key demographic trends that influence economic prospects of different groups of economies. The main messages are the following:

- Overall, global growth in 2015 is projected to be lower than in 2014, with prospects across major countries and regions uneven. Domestic inflation is expected to remain subdued, in large part due to the significant weakening in global commodity prices, although inflation is projected to rise in some emerging market countries (EMs) that have suffered from sizable exchange rate depreciations. Downside risks to the outlook have risen: They include risks from China's growth transition, excessive financial market volatility and tightening of financial conditions, the impact of a sizable appreciation of the U.S. dollar on balance sheet exposures, even lower commodity prices, rising geopolitical risks, and lower potential growth.
- Growth in advanced economies (AEs) is expected to continue to recover into 2015–16, and accommodative monetary policy is appropriate to support this recovery. Fiscal policy needs to be supportive where conditions allow, while many AEs need to establish credible medium-term fiscal frameworks and consolidation plans. Strengthening of regulation and supervision of rapidly expanding nonbank financial activities is also needed. Overall, given the weakened near- and medium-term growth outlook for many AEs, raising actual and potential growth is a key economic policy priority.
- The 2015–16 growth outlook for EMs is uneven and has weakened overall for many with the end of the commodity prices supercycle. Geopolitical tensions, tightening of financial conditions, and lower commodity prices weigh on the outlook for many countries. Overall, demand support

needs to be carefully weighed against the need to manage vulnerabilities. Those with policy flexibility should use it to the extent possible; for others, the priority should be growth friendly fiscal rebalancing; financial buffers, where available, should be used to smooth the impact of lower commodity export prices. Lower commodity prices also call for a timely reform of energy subsidies. As in AEs, raising potential growth over the medium term is a priority.

- Low-income developing countries (LIDCs) are projected to see growth slow in 2015 as growth in oil-exporting LIDCs drops off sharply before recovering in 2016. Where warranted, policies should remain focused on rebuilding fiscal and external buffers and achieving medium-term development priorities. In many emerging market and developing countries, allowing for exchange rate flexibility will help adjust to external shocks.
- During the MDG-monitoring period, most emerging market and developing countries (EMDCs) grew at a sustained strong pace, notwithstanding the negative impact from the 2009 global financial crisis. Together with strong growth, per capita income differences among countries were reduced, and absolute poverty was halved over this period.
- For the SDG-monitoring period, prospects are for global growth to trend down, mostly because of a decrease in global population growth. Developing countries would need to address disparate demographic evolutions with an appropriate set of macroeconomic and structural policies to enable further reductions in absolute poverty levels and to narrow income differences relative to more advanced economies.

Recent developments and short- and medium-term prospects

In 2014, global growth was 3.4 percent, broadly in line with the projections made in the *Global Monitoring Report* (GMR) 2014/15, and reflecting growth of 1.8 percent in AEs and 4.6 percent in EMDCs (table 3.1). Growth in AEs picked up as the euro area pulled out of recession. In contrast, growth in EMDCs slowed down further with the continued adjustment in many countries to lower potential growth prospects. Among EMs, the slowdown in 2014 was driven to a large extent by subdued growth in Latin America and the Caribbean and in the Commonwealth of Independent States (CIS). Growth in LIDCs was maintained at a robust 6.0 percent, even though several countries in Africa were severely affected by the Ebola epidemic.

In 2015, global growth is projected at 3.1 percent—some 0.7 percentage point lower than the forecast made in GMR 2014/15—with growth in AEs projected to average 2.0 percent and in EMDCs 4.0 percent. Growth in AEs is projected to pick up relative to 2014 on further strengthening of the recovery in the euro area and the return to positive growth in Japan, supported by declining oil prices. In contrast, growth in EMDCs is expected to decline again—the fifth year in a row and the lowest since the 2009 global financial crisis. This reflects lower growth in both EMs and LIDCs, held back in many by lower commodity prices, tighter external financial conditions (especially in Latin America and the Caribbean), and distress related to geopolitical factors (in the CIS and in the Middle East and North Africa).

Economic conditions in the CIS remain very weak. Growth in Russia and Ukraine is projected to be negative with adverse spillovers to the rest of the region. The deep recessions in both countries reflect the persistent effects of the sharp decline in oil prices combined with international sanctions in Russia and, for Ukraine, the continuing conflict in the eastern part of the country.

Growth in emerging and developing Asia is expected to continue its downward trend in 2015 largely due to lower growth in China. Growth in India will benefit from policy reforms, a pick-up in investment, and lower commodity prices. Average growth in other countries in the region is projected to remain about unchanged.

In emerging and developing Europe, growth is expected to remain broadly unchanged from 2014. The economic contraction in the CIS weighs on growth, but low oil prices and continued recovery in the

TABLE 3.1 The global growth rebound has been pushed back to 2016

Global output, annual percent change

	Actual				Projections		
	2001–08	2009–12	2013	2014	2015	2016	2017–20
World	**4.2**	**3.3**	**3.3**	**3.4**	**3.1**	**3.6**	**3.9**
Advanced economies	2.2	0.6	1.1	1.8	2.0	2.2	2.1
Emerging market and developing countries	6.5	5.5	5.0	4.6	4.0	4.5	5.1
Commonwealth of Independent States	7.2	1.7	2.2	1.0	−2.7	0.5	2.4
Emerging and developing Asia	8.4	8.0	7.0	6.8	6.5	6.4	6.4
Emerging and developing Europe	4.6	2.1	2.9	2.8	3.0	3.0	3.3
Middle East, North Africa, Afghanistan, and Pakistan	5.4	4.1	2.3	2.7	2.5	3.9	4.3
Latin America and the Caribbean	3.6	3.2	2.9	1.3	-0.3	0.8	2.6
Sub-Saharan Africa	6.1	5.0	5.2	5.0	3.8	4.3	5.0
Low-Income developing countries	6.4	5.9	6.1	6.0	4.8	5.8	6.0
Emerging market countries	6.5	5.5	4.9	4.5	3.9	4.4	5.1
Fragile States	5.0	6.6	4.9	1.3	1.4	6.3	6.8
Small States	5.5	2.4	1.6	2.3	1.4	2.8	3.1

Source: IMF *World Economic Outlook*.
Note: Country groupings are defined in appendix table C5.2.

Euro Area provide an offset. High corporate debt levels and subdued domestic demand will weigh on growth in Turkey.

Growth across the Middle East, North Africa, Afghanistan, and Pakistan is expected to remain modest, in line with growth in 2014. Growth is expected to be negatively affected by low oil prices, regional conflicts, and social tensions.

Growth in Latin America and the Caribbean is expected to turn negative in 2015. In Brazil, the economy is expected to contract with a sharp drop in private sector confidence, the needed tightening of the macroeconomic policy stance to contain inflation, along with weaker in commodity prices, with negative spillovers for the rest of the region. Venezuela is expected to enter into a deep recession as the oil price decline has exacerbated macroeconomic imbalances. Growth in many other countries in the region is negatively affected by low metal, oil, and other commodity prices.

Growth in Sub-Saharan African countries is expected to slow down on lower growth in oil-exporting countries, particularly Nigeria. Growth is also expected to be negatively affected by slowing growth in China and, for some, a tightening of global financial conditions and a retreat in other commodity prices besides oil.

Despite a small recovery relative to 2014, growth in fragile states is projected to remain low in 2015. This reflects continuing civil strife and conflict in some countries (for example, South Sudan and Yemen), and the continued effects of the Ebola epidemic for some economies in West Africa (Liberia and Sierra Leone).

The downward revision of the global growth forecast for 2015 is largely driven by a significant lowering of growth prospects in EMs (from 4.8 percent in the 2014/15 GMR to 3.9 percent). Indeed, some of the key downside risks identified in GMR 2014/15 have materialized—such as tighter external financial conditions and geopolitical tensions—working on top of the sharp, unanticipated retreat in oil and other commodity prices. But growth in AEs has also been revised down slightly relative to GMR 2014/15, on lower growth in the United States and, in LIDCs, on account of lower growth in commodity exporters, including Nigeria.

Per capita growth in the median LIDC has been drifting lower since the strong rebound from the 2009 global crisis, but it remains above growth in the median AE country and median EM country (figure 3.1). With the concurrent slowdown in EMs and recovery in AEs, per capita growth in the median AE country and median EM country is expected

FIGURE 3.1 Steady income gains for a typical LIDC continue to be maintained

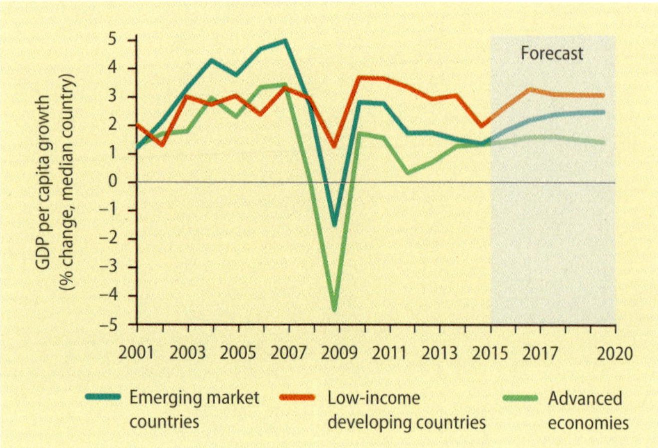

Source: IMF *World Economic Outlook*.
Note: Country groupings are defined in appendix table C5.2.

to converge in 2015—at about 1.5 percent—for the first time since the early 2000s.

Global growth is expected to increase to 3.6 percent in 2016, reflecting a growth pick-up in all three main country groups. The continued recovery in AEs, averaging 2.2 percent, is projected to be led by a rebound in the United States that is expected to be supported by lower energy prices, reduced fiscal drag, strengthened balance sheets, and an improving housing market. The pick-up in growth in EMs to 4.4 percent is predicated on an expected turnaround in growth in several distressed economies in the CIS, Middle East and North Africa, as well as a recovery in Latin America and the Caribbean, on a partial normalization of economic growth in Brazil and spillovers from stronger growth in the United States. Growth in LIDCs is projected to return to about 6 percent growth as growth in oil-exporting LIDCs recovers.

Medium-term global growth is expected to be somewhat higher than the level projected for 2016 on higher growth in EMDCs. Higher growth in EMDCs is predicated on a return to normalcy for several countries that have been growing at below potential (due to an easing of geopolitical tensions in the CIS, the Middle East and North Africa, and on a recovery of investment confidence and growth in Latin America and the Caribbean). Growth in AEs will trend down as output gaps are closed.

Global inflation is expected to be subdued, with consumer price inflation in most countries remaining in the low single digits, partly driven by declining international commodity prices (figure 3.2). In twenty-some countries—mainly European AEs and EMs—deflation took hold in 2014. With the exception of Switzerland, the countries with deflation in 2014 are expected to return to low inflation in 2016. In about one dozen countries, however—all EMs or LIDCs—inflation is in the double digits, and for some—including Belarus, Iran, and Venezuela—inflation is projected to remain high in 2016, in part reflecting the effects of exchange rate depreciation.

Commodity prices—which were on a roller coaster during 2008–11—trended lower during 2012–15 against the background of increased supplies but also subdued economic growth. Oil prices have fallen on large supply increases in the United States, Iraq, and, at times, Libya, while at the same time oil demand slowed, including because of weaker global activity. Prices of agricultural commodities eased on record or near-record harvests of major crops. With the sharp correction in 2015, real commodity prices have, to a large extent, reverted back to their levels of the early 2000s. The WEO projections suggest a gradually increasing or broadly stable

FIGURE 3.2 The commodity price supercycle is coming to an end

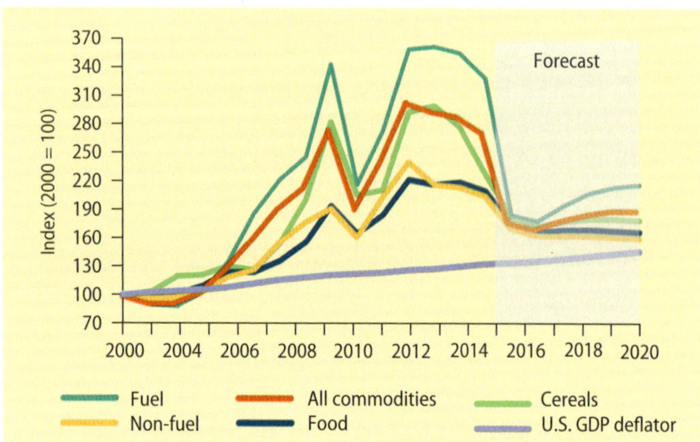

Source: IMF *World Economic Outlook*.
Note: Indexes are in U.S. dollars.

FIGURE 3.3 The commodity price shock in 2015 is broadly of the same magnitude as in 2009

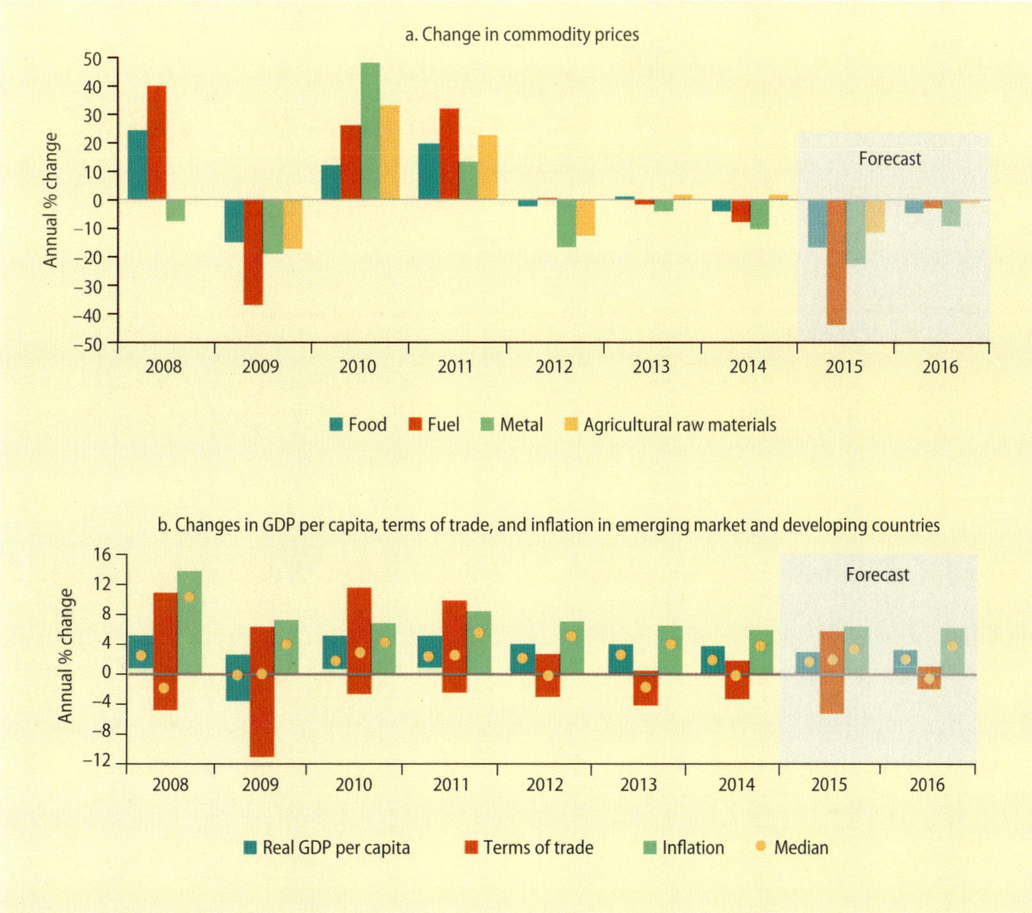

Source: IMF *World Economic Outlook.*
Note: In panel a, commodity price indices are in U.S. dollars. In panel b, bars represent the range between the 25th and 75th percentiles. Country groupings are defined in appendix table C5.2.

path for oil and other commodity prices, respectively, through 2020.

Many developing countries are dependent on the exports or imports of a few commodities, and as the prices of such export or import commodities change, so do these countries' terms of trade and domestic inflation (figure 3.3). Higher commodity prices in 2010 and 2011 were associated with terms-of-trade gains for the majority of EMDCs. As commodity prices weakened in 2012–15, these terms-of-trade gains were eroded. While the commodity price decline in 2015 is of about the same magnitude as in 2009, the expected dispersion of growth, inflation, and terms-of-trade changes across EMDCs are projected to be significantly lower this year than in 2009. This suggests that both supply and demand shifts lie behind the 2015 price correction, in contrast to 2009 where the price correction was mostly driven by lower demand.

Downside risks have risen, particularly for EMDCs, given the interaction of external and domestic headwinds, as well as risks from China's growth transition. Risks for AEs include disruptive asset price shifts and financial market turmoil, with adverse spillovers for EMDCs. In the context of weak demand and low inflation, the risk of secular stagnation and hysteresis for AEs remains, particularly given constraints posed by monetary policy at the zero lower bound and high debt levels.

Risks for EMDCs have increased in the context of slowing growth. Although

FIGURE 3.4 Global imbalances are projected to continue to trend down, but at a more gradual pace

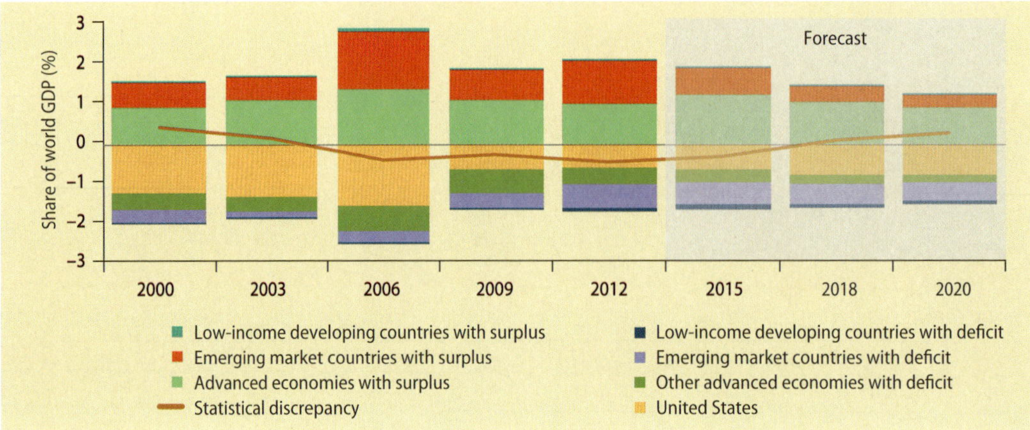

Source: IMF *World Economic Outlook.*
Note: Country groupings are defined in appendix table C5.2.

commodity prices have fallen significantly, as discussed above, there are risks that they could fall further, straining balance sheets and growth prospects for commodity-exporting EMDCs. Also, adjustments in commodity markets can be slow and price volatility in the interim high. A further dollar appreciation against the backdrop of asynchronous monetary policy stances in major economies could lead to an unbalanced global recovery and associated capital flow reversal from EMDCs, and exacerbate balance sheet exposures. China's ongoing growth transition is creating spillovers, and an abrupt growth slowdown in China could have major repercussions for growth in other economies, both directly and through the impact on commodity prices. Moreover, further increases in geopolitical tensions (stemming from ongoing events in Russia, Ukraine, the Middle East, and parts of Africa) could generate regional and global spillovers and disrupt global trade and financial activity.

For the third year in a row, world trade was subdued in 2014, reflecting in part, low economic growth. Even though AEs' trade performance is expected to remain resilient, world trade is expected to pick up only marginally in 2015 as trade growth slows further in EMs (particularly in Asian EMs, such as China). Against the background of broadly stable prices of traded goods and services, a further modest uptick in world trade is expected for 2016 and beyond.

The sharp widening in global current account imbalances in the run up to the 2009 financial crisis has reversed since, but recent progress in further lowering the imbalances has been slow. Global current account imbalances peaked at 3 percent of global GDP in 2006, narrowing sharply post-crisis as the current account deficits in the United States and some smaller AEs narrowed, together with the surpluses in emerging market capital exporting countries (figure 3.4). However, current account balances are expected to remain broadly stable in 2015, with the contraction in the surpluses in oil-exporting economies offset by surpluses in oil importers. Moreover, there has been a rotation of imbalances with a widening of imbalances for several EMDCs. The downward trend in imbalances from 2012 to 2015 is projected to continue at a gradual pace through 2020.

Current account imbalances in LIDCs remain wider than before the global financial crisis (figure 3.5). The current account deficit (defined here as net of foreign direct investments to focus attention on the residual deficit) for the median LIDC has increased from around 2 percent of GDP in 2009–11 to about 3–4 percent in recent years, peaking at

FIGURE 3.5 A typical LIDC has a higher current account deficit now than before the 2009 global crisis

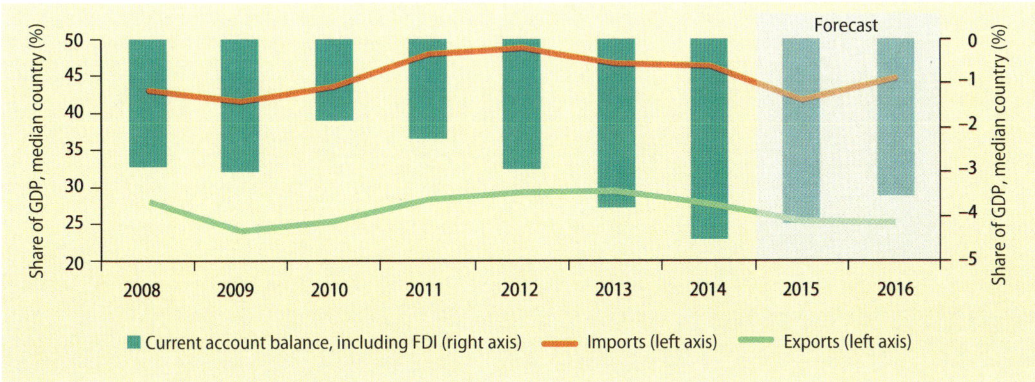

Source: IMF *World Economic Outlook.*
Note: Country groupings are defined in appendix table C5.2. FDI = Foreign direct investment.

above 4 percent in 2014. The current account deficit is expected to narrow somewhat in 2016, but still remains higher than precrisis averages.

Net capital inflows to LIDCs (defined here to include current transfers to focus attention on the net available external resources) have remained fairly constant in recent years at 10–11 percent of LIDCs' GDP (table 3.2). These inflows are mostly in the form of transfers. Net capital inflows (relative to GDP) to EMs are significantly lower than those to LIDCs. Net inflows to EMs dropped off sharply in 2014 and are projected to become a net outflow in 2015 in part because of a further expected tightening in external financial conditions. This turnaround in net capital inflows is being offset by an equivalent change in official reserve accumulation. For 2016 and beyond, a partial reversal is projected.

Official reserves in months of imports are expected to remain relatively stable in 2015 and decrease slightly in 2016 (figure 3.6). The typical emerging market country holds somewhat larger reserves than the typical LIDC. The share of LIDCs that hold reserves of less than 3 months of imports is steadily increasing from about one-quarter in 2012 to almost one-half in 2016. These countries are more vulnerable if they are hit by an external shock.

Update on recent macroeconomic policies

In AEs, policy makers strive for a macroeconomic policy stance that can support growth, while at the same time buttressing private sector confidence and containing risks in the financial sector and to medium-term fiscal sustainability. Following sustained fiscal consolidation in 2014, the average fiscal deficit in AEs dropped to about 3½ percent of GDP, down from a deficit of 9 percent in the 2009 crisis year. A further narrowing of deficits is projected to bring the average fiscal deficit down to around 2½ percent by 2016. Monetary policy easing has been maintained against the background of well-anchored inflation expectations and continued low inflation.

Fiscal deficits in 2014 in both the median EM and the median LIDC widened (figure 3.7). Thus, further progress toward rebuilding the fiscal buffers that were used during the 2009 crisis has stalled. Domestic revenue mobilization in EMDCs has remained relatively constant in recent years, and little change is expected for the period ahead (table 3.3), with fiscal revenues in the median LIDC about 8 percentage points of GDP lower than those in the median EM.

About 40 percent of all EMDCs—with similar shares among EMs and LIDCs—saw

TABLE 3.2 LIDC net capital inflows stay flat while EM net capital flows turn negative in 2015

Net capital inflows, weighted averages, percent of GDP

	Actual				Projections		
	2001–08	2009–12	2013	2014	2015	2016	2017–20
Emerging market countries	2.6	2.7	2.1	0.7	−1.6	0.4	1.0
Transfers, net	1.1	0.7	0.4	0.3	0.4	0.4	0.4
Financial flows, net	1.4	2.0	1.7	0.4	−2.0	0.0	0.5
Direct investment, net	2.2	1.7	1.6	1.4	1.1	1.1	0.6
Portfolio investment, net	−0.4	0.8	0.5	0.4	0.2	0.4	0.3
Other investment, net	−0.4	−0.5	−0.4	−1.5	−3.3	−1.5	−0.3
Memorandum item:							
Change in reserve assets (–, accumulation)	−3.9	−2.9	−2.1	−0.4	1.7	−0.2	−0.3
Low-Income developing countries	6.9	10.3	10.8	10.2	10.7	11.0	10.5
Transfers, net	6.4	6.9	6.0	5.8	6.0	5.9	5.5
Financial flows, net	0.5	3.4	4.8	4.3	4.7	5.0	5.0
Direct investment, net	2.7	3.5	3.1	2.6	2.8	3.2	3.5
Portfolio investment, net	0.1	0.4	0.9	0.6	0.5	0.4	0.5
Other investment, net	−2.4	−0.5	0.8	1.1	1.4	1.4	1.1
Memorandum item:							
Change in reserve assets (–, accumulation)	−2.1	−0.6	−0.3	−0.5	0.1	−0.2	−0.9
Fragile states	8.6	6.4	5.7	7.7	7.2	8.5	9.5
Transfers, net	6.2	4.6	3.4	4.4	5.0	3.9	4.4
Financial flows, net	2.4	1.7	2.4	3.3	2.2	4.6	5.1
Direct investment, net	2.7	2.7	2.4	2.2	2.3	2.7	3.5
Portfolio investment, net	−0.5	−1.0	−0.1	0.1	0.1	0.1	0.4
Other investment, net	0.2	0.1	0.1	1.0	−0.2	1.7	1.2
Memorandum item:							
Change in reserve assets (–, accumulation)	−6.7	−3.4	0.9	4.5	6.4	2.8	−1.3
Small states	2.4	1.5	0.5	2.7	3.3	3.8	2.7
Transfers, net	0.5	0.7	−0.1	−0.2	−0.4	−0.6	−0.6
Financial flows, net	1.9	0.7	0.6	3.0	3.7	4.4	3.3
Direct investment, net	3.8	6.7	2.7	3.4	4.2	4.7	4.4
Portfolio investment, net	−2.8	3.2	0.7	−18.1	3.7	3.7	3.8
Other investment, net	0.8	−9.2	−2.8	17.7	−4.2	−3.9	−4.9
Memorandum item:							
Change in reserve assets (–, accumulation)	−2.2	−1.7	−1.2	−1.0	1.2	0.9	0.0

Source: IMF *World Economic Outlook.*
Note: Country groupings are defined in appendix table C5.2.

FIGURE 3.6 Share of LIDCs with reserve coverage of less than three months is expected to increase

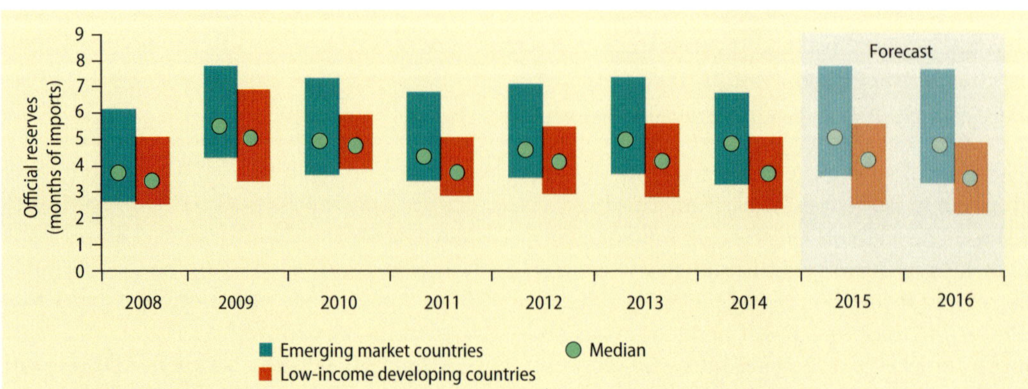

Source: IMF *World Economic Outlook.*
Note: Bars represent the range between the 25th and 75th percentiles. Country groupings are defined in appendix table C5.2.

a loosening of monetary conditions in 2014 (figure 3.8). In LIDCs, there was relatively less reliance on monetary policy loosening in the form of a lowering of short-term interest rates rather than allowing for a depreciation of the exchange rate, but the difference between EMs and LIDCs in that respect was not large.

Against the background of these policy measures, monetary aggregates continued to grow faster than nominal GDP in EMs until 2014 (figure 3.9). These monetary trends have taken place in the context of low to moderate inflation in the vast majority of countries.

Against the background of slower growth and broadly stable inflation in 2014, less than

FIGURE 3.7 Fiscal deficits are higher now than before the 2009 global crisis

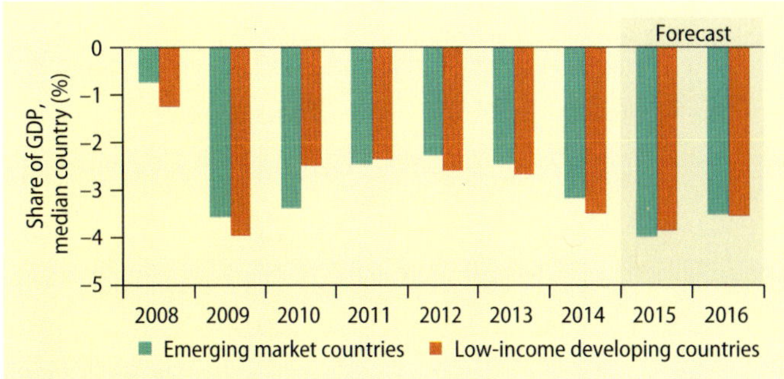

Source: IMF *World Economic Outlook.*
Note: General government balance (net lending/net borrowing) as defined in *IMF Government Finance Statistics Manual 2001.* Country groupings are defined in appendix table C5.2.

TABLE 3.3 Government revenue performance remains about constant
General government revenue excluding grants, median country, percent of GDP

	Actual							Projections	
	2008	2009	2010	2011	2012	2013	2014	2015	2016
Emerging market and developing countries	**24**	**23**	**23**	**24**	**24**	**24**	**24**	**23**	**23**
Commonwealth of Independent States	34	32	32	32	34	33	33	30	30
Emerging and developing Asia	22	22	21	22	23	24	24	22	22
Emerging and developing Europe	35	34	34	35	35	37	36	36	36
Latin America and the Caribbean	25	24	23	25	24	24	24	24	24
Middle East, North Africa, Afghanistan, and Pakistan	28	26	25	25	26	25	25	23	24
Sub-Saharan Africa	18	16	18	18	18	18	18	19	19
Low-income developing countries	18	16	18	18	18	18	19	19	19
Emerging market countries	27	27	26	27	27	27	28	27	26
Fragile states	19	17	19	19	19	18	19	18	19
Small states	26	25	26	25	26	27	27	26	26

Source: IMF *World Economic Outlook.*
Note: Country groupings are defined in appendix table C5.2.

FIGURE 3.8 The share of emerging market countries as well as low-income developing countries that experienced loosening monetary conditions fell somewhat in 2014

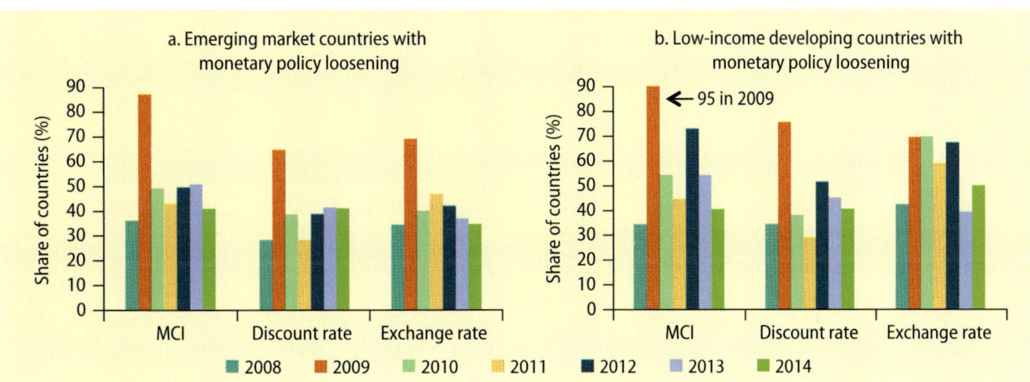

Source: IMF International Financial Statistics.
Note: Monetary policy loosening is based on Monetary Conditions Index (MCI) calculations. MCI is a linear combination of nominal short-term interest rates and the nominal effective exchange rate (with a one-third weight for the latter). Country groupings are defined in appendix table C5.2.

FIGURE 3.9 The growth in monetary aggregates is trending down in 2014 and early 2015

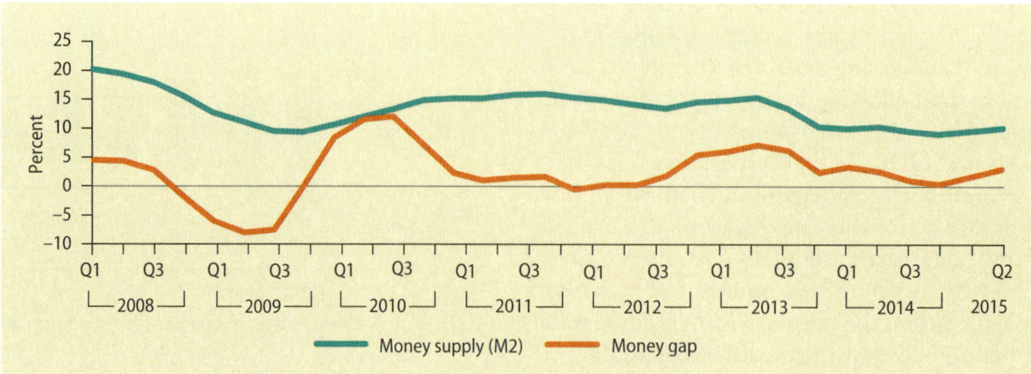

Source: IMF International Financial Statistics.
Note: The money gap is the difference between year-on-year growth rates of M2 and nominal GDP. The sample includes emerging market countries that have data on both for the whole sample period shown. Country groupings are defined in appendix table C5.2.

FIGURE 3.10 The share of emerging market countries as well as low-income developing countries that loosened both monetary and fiscal policies fell sharply in 2014

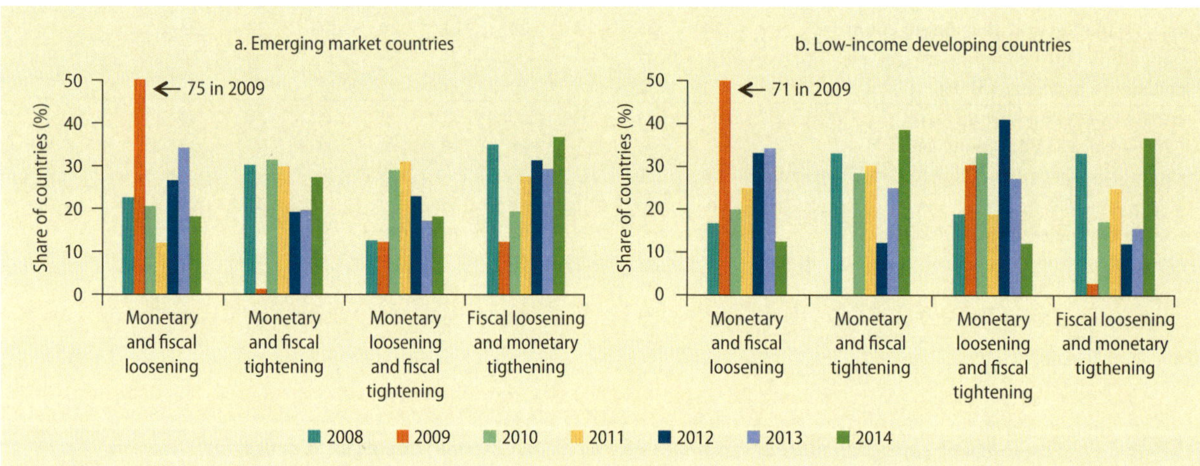

Source: IMF International Financial Statistics.
Note: Fiscal conditions are defined based on annual change in government balance (net lending/net borrowing) as a percent of GDP in 2008, 2009, 2010, 2011, 2012, 2013 and 2014. Monetary conditions are based on the change in the MCI; changes are calculated Q4 over Q4. MCI is a linear combination of nominal short-term interest rates and the nominal effective exchange rate (with a one-third weight for the latter). Country groupings are defined in appendix table C5.2.

20 percent of EMDCs loosened both fiscal and monetary policies (figure 3.10). A significantly larger number of countries—about 30 percent—tightened macroeconomic policies. Among countries that neither tightened nor loosened policies, but changed the mix of policies, more countries loosened fiscal policies and tightened monetary policies rather than the other way around.

Quality of macroeconomic policies in low-income countries

To gain a better perspective on the quality of macroeconomic policies in low-income countries, IMF country desks in these countries have been surveyed annually since 2003 about their assessment of the quality of countries' economic policies.[2] In the period leading up to the 2009 global financial crisis, the assessments became more positive, with particularly positive assessments of macroeconomic policies in the crisis year. While the perceived quality of macroeconomic policies has since deteriorated somewhat, it is generally still higher now than in the early part of the MDG-monitoring period (figure 3.11). Selected macroeconomic indicators—the background against which IMF country teams have assessed policies—are shown in figure 3.12.

In 2014, the perceived consistency of macroeconomic policy slipped, with the number of countries with unsatisfactory performance increasing sharply. The assessments of monetary policy continue to be somewhat more positive than those of fiscal policy, with assessments of both types of policies becoming less positive in 2014.

To further gauge the geographical differences in perceived quality of policies, one can also consider the breakdown in answers across geographical areas (table 3.4). These differences are minor over time.

Long-term convergence and growth trends

With the completion of the MDG-monitoring period and the launching of the SDGs, it is an opportune moment to provide a longer-term perspective on growth and income convergence. How did outcomes during 2000–15 compare with historical trends? And what are the prospects for the SDG-monitoring period of 2016–30?

An impressive global economic expansion took place in the half century leading up to the adoption of the Millennium Declaration in 2000, although with diverging income levels across countries. Total GDP expanded sevenfold and GDP per capita tripled (in constant U.S. dollars at market exchange rates). However, as the Lorenz curve, which provides a comprehensive representation of global per capita income distribution (figure 3.13) shows, the associated Gini coefficients increased from 67 percent in 1950 to 75 percent in 2000. Indeed, Burkina Faso and China were the two poorest countries in 1950 with income levels one-tenth of the global average; by 2000 one-fourth of all countries had relative incomes lower than that.

In contrast, the strong economic expansion during the MDG-monitoring period was accompanied by greater income convergence. The global Gini declined from 75 percent in 2000 to 62 percent in 2015.[3] And as intercountry income differences diminished over the MDG-monitoring period, per capita GDP growth at 2.1 percent remained about in line with the historical trend of 2.3 percent annually (figure 3.14).

Notwithstanding this narrowing of global income differences, the share of poor countries has remained high. One-seventh of all countries still have GDP per capita below one-tenth the mean global income level, and the countries where the poorest 40 percent of the world's population live account for just 6 percent of global income (figure 3.15). Excluding China and India, per capita GDP in these countries increased sharply over the past 15 years, but their income level relative to mean global income is no larger now than in 1950.

An alternative measure of progress during the MDG-monitoring period is the number of countries that graduated into high-income status. About one-fourth of all countries are now high-income countries, as compared with one-fifth in 2000 (figure 3.16). The pace at which countries graduate from middle-income to high-income status has picked up, but it trails the pace at which countries graduate from low-income to middle-income status. Although the number of high-income countries increased significantly from 2000 to 2015, the share of the world's population living in high-income countries remained about constant over this period because of relatively lower population growth in the richer countries.

Looking ahead, prospects for growth and income convergence over the SDG-monitoring period would be influenced by demographic trends. The average annual global population increase is projected to fall to 1 percent during 2015–30 from 1¼ percent during 2000–15. But population growth will

FIGURE 3.11 The quality of macroeconomic policies is lower now than during the 2009 global crisis

Quality of macroeconomic policies in low-income countries, 2003–14[a,b]

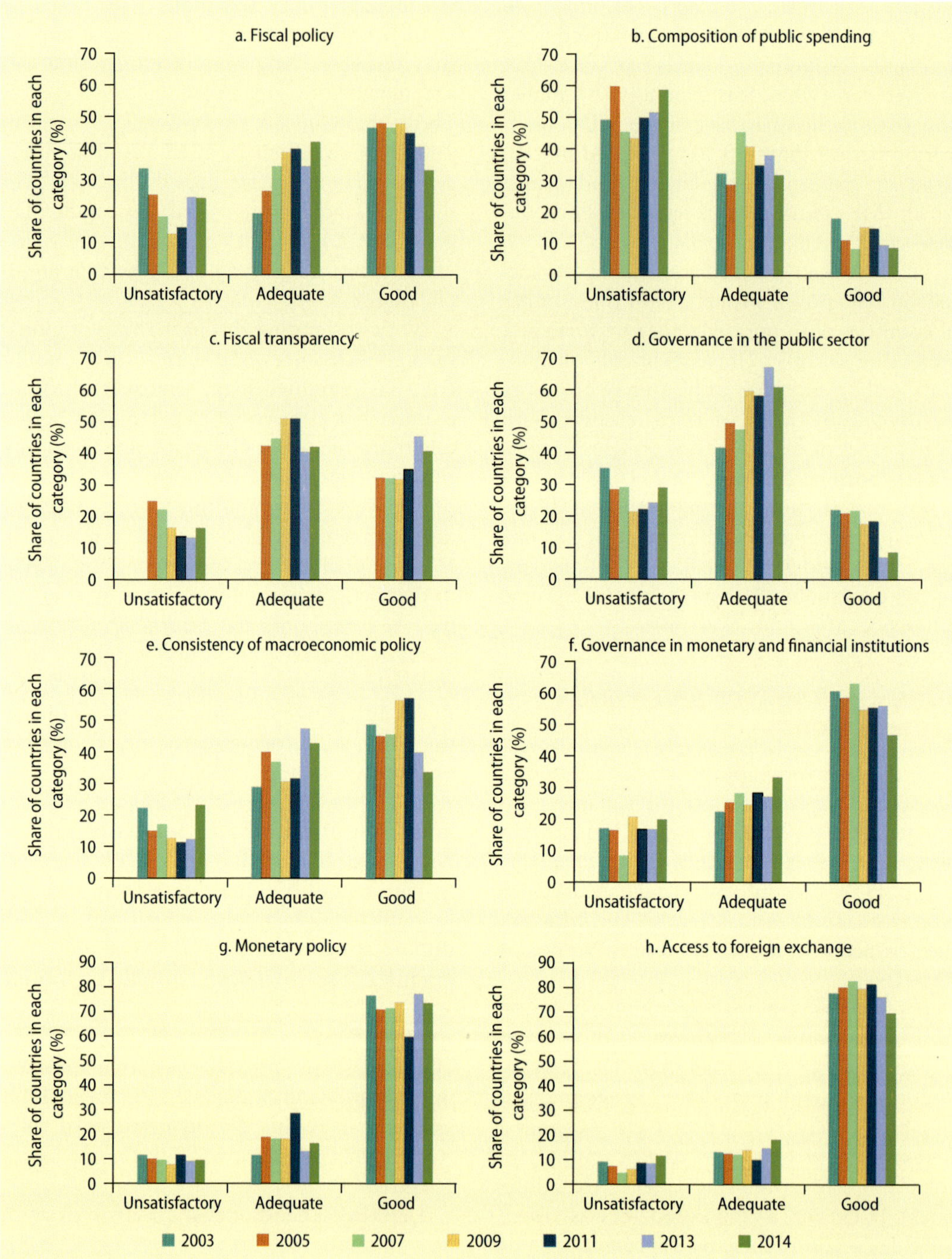

Source: IMF staff estimates.

a. IDA-eligible countries.

b. IMF staff have assessed each low-income country according to a common set of criteria. Policies are assessed as unsatisfactory, adequate, and good for this purpose. For example, a country with an unsustainable level of public debt and a large fiscal deficit would be judged to have an unsatisfactory fiscal policy.

c. Fiscal transparency data are available from 2005.

FIGURE 3.12 Selected macroeconomic indicators for low-income countries,[a] 2000–15

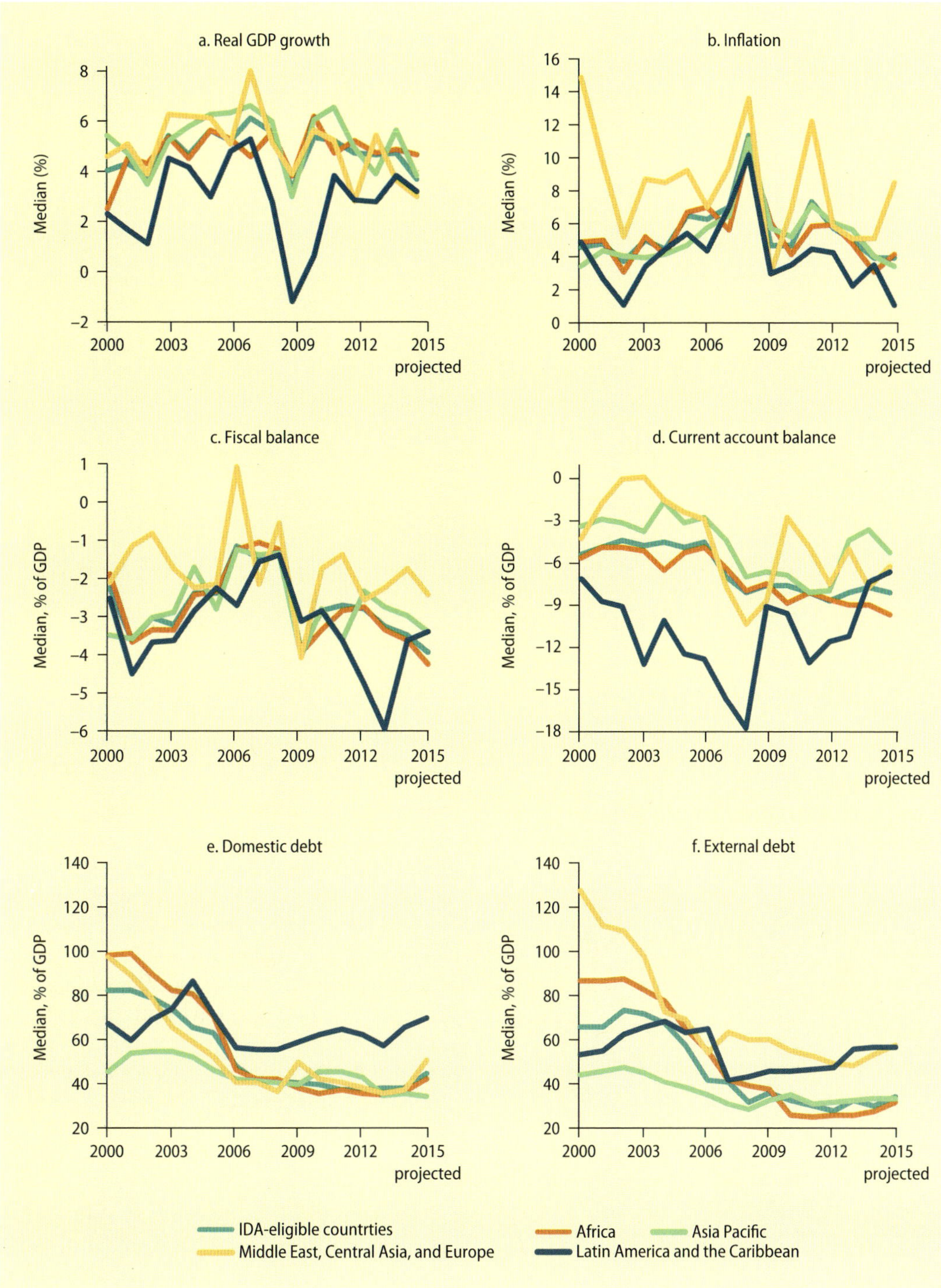

Source: IMF *World Economic Outlook.*
a. IDA-eligible countries.

TABLE 3.4 Macroeconomic policies in low-income countries, 2005–14

Percent of countries in each category, with adequate and good policy ratings

Macroeconomic policy	Years	All countries	Africa	Asia Pacific	Middle East, Central Asia and Europe	Western Hemisphere
Fiscal policy	2005	75	66	79	92	78
	2013	75	74	76	83	67
	2014	76	69	76	89	89
Composition of public spending	2005	40	39	26	57	44
	2013	48	49	57	33	44
	2014	41	36	48	33	56
Monetary policy	2005	90	92	84	86	100
	2013	91	97	76	82	100
	2014	90	92	88	75	100
Consistency of macro policies	2005	85	79	89	86	100
	2013	88	90	90	91	67
	2014	77	77	71	88	78
Access to foreign exchange	2005	93	89	95	93	100
	2013	91	92	90	83	100
	2014	88	89	90	67	100
Governance in the public sector	2005	71	74	68	71	67
	2013	75	67	81	75	100
	2014	71	64	71	67	100
Fiscal transparency	2005	75	68	79	71	100
	2013	86	82	81	100	100
	2014	83	74	90	100	89
Governance in monetary, financial institutions	2005	84	79	78	93	100
	2013	83	85	76	100	67
	2014	80	82	83	78	67

Source: IMF staff estimates.
Note: IDA-eligible countries.

FIGURE 3.13 There is a steady income convergence among countries from 2000 onward

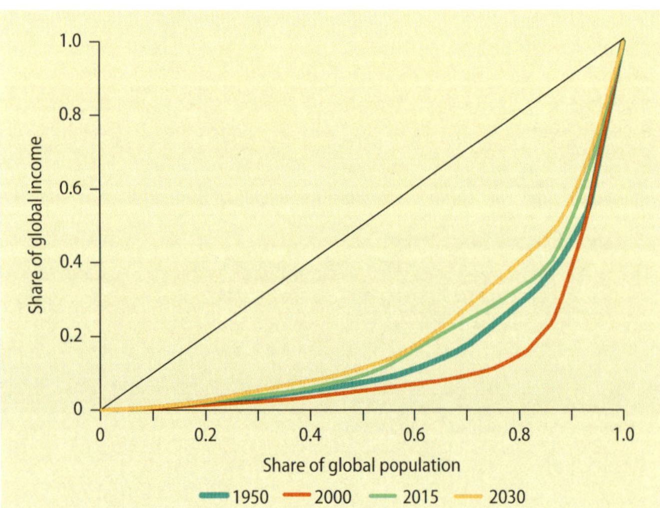

Sources: UN statistical yearbooks and publications; IMF International Financial Statistics, IMF *World Economic Outlook*; and IMF staff estimates.
Note: At market exchange rates.

differ sharply across different country groupings. Average annual population growth from 2015 to 2030 in AEs, EMs, and LIDCs is projected to be 0.4 percent, 0.7 percent, and 2.0 percent respectively. Looking only at growth in the working-age population (15 to 64 years), the differences across country groupings are even starker: in AEs the working-age population will decline by 0.1 percent annually, compared with increases of 0.6 and 2.4 percent annually in EMs and LIDCs.[4] In consequence, there is a marked relative shift in population structures in the three groups of countries, as discussed further in part 2 of this report.

Against the background of this demographic outlook and the medium-term economic WEO outlook, global growth is expected to trend down in 2016–30 relative to 2000–15. In particular, demographic trends in major advanced and emerging markets will be a drag on their potential growth (see box 3.1 and chapter 5). Other reasons for why one can expect a slowing of growth include weaknesses in investments, slower pace of human capital accumulation, and gradually diminishing growth dividends from information and communication technology.

Thus, increasing potential output will be a key policy priority in major advanced and emerging economies. Priorities vary across countries, but they include reforms to boost labor supply, addressing energy infrastructure bottlenecks, and improving business conditions. Also, open markets for goods, services, and capital, under appropriate safeguards, should be maintained so that countries can maximize inter- and intra-temporal gains from trade. In countries where dependency ratios are expected to rise, fiscal policy space should be right-sized in anticipation of increased demand for public social services.

The demographic trends in LIDCs could, in contrast, induce a growth dividend, if met with the right set of policies, and help in driving further income convergence. To harness this demographic dividend while maintaining macroeconomic stability is of the utmost importance; it also requires pursuing a broad, interlinked structural policy agenda. Policies need to focus on enhancing human capital, furthering financial sector development, and building infrastructure that lowers costs and better connects domestic and global markets. Promoting economic diversification will also be essential. The implementation of these policies will likely require fiscal space to reprioritize government spending toward social and infrastructure spending, and still maintain debt sustainability. Flexible and deep labor markets are essential to ensure that workers are matched with available jobs efficiently, while compensation remains aligned with productivity. These policy issues are discussed further in subsequent chapters.

FIGURE 3.14 The global per capita income growth in 2015–30 is projected to be slightly lower than in 2000–15

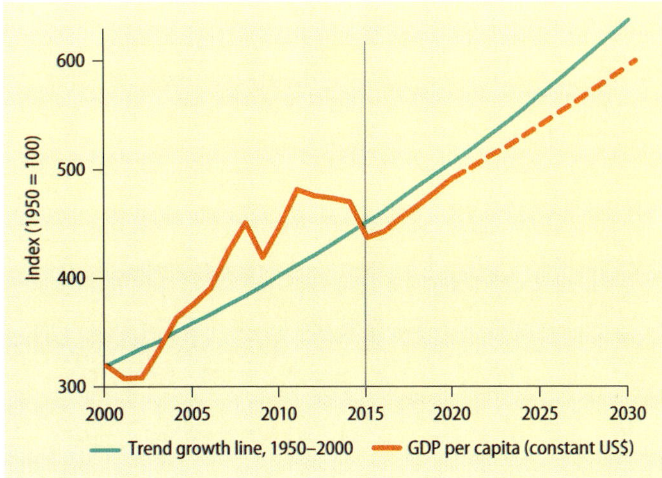

Sources: UN statistical yearbooks and publications, IMF International Financial Statistics, IMF *World Economic Outlook*; and IMF staff estimates.
Note: At market exchange rates.

FIGURE 3.15 The income convergence in the world's poorest countries is ongoing, but income differences between poor and rich countries remain very large

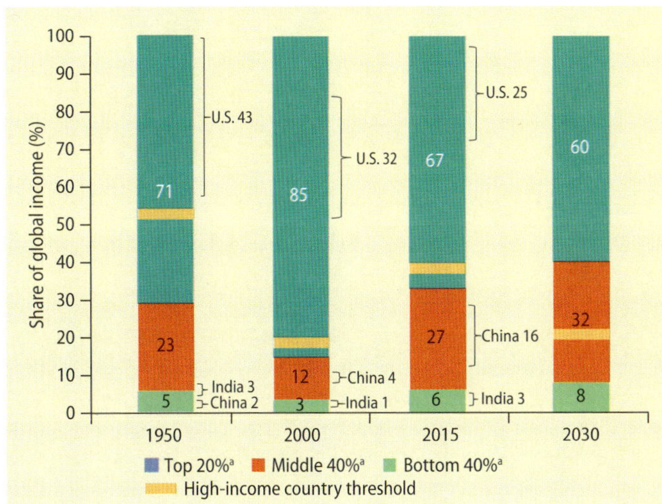

Sources: UN statistical yearbooks and publications, IMF International Financial Statistics, IMF *World Economic Outlook*; and IMF staff estimates.
Note: At market exchange rates. The high-income country threshold indicates the division of the world's income pie between the high-income countries on the one hand and middle-income and low-income countries on the other hand.
a. Of the world's population.

Conclusion

Global growth remains moderate, with growth in 2015 expected to be lower than in 2014, with stronger growth in AEs offset by overall weaker growth in many EMs with the end of the commodity prices supercycle. Growth in 2016 in AEs is expected to continue to recover, and pick up as well in EMs. Geopolitical tensions, tightening of

FIGURE 3.16 The share of high-income countries is expected to increase from one-fifth in 2000 to one-third in 2030

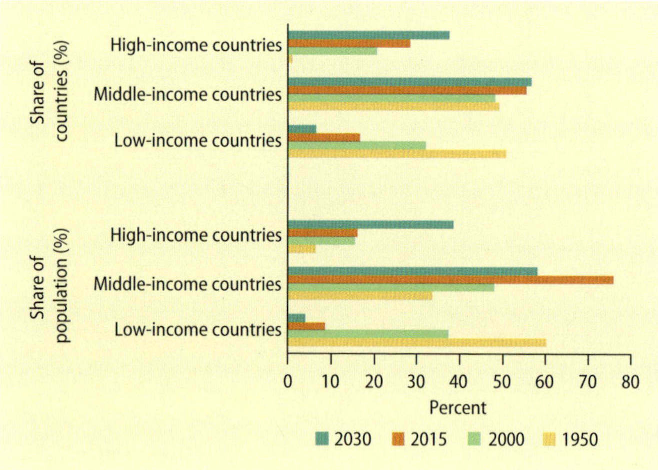

Sources: UN statistical yearbooks and publications; International Financial Statistics, IMF *World Economic Outlook*, and IMF staff estimates.
Note: Using the World Bank's LIC/MIC and MIC/HIC income thresholds of $1,045 and $12,735 respectively (in 2014 prices and exchange rates).

financial conditions, and lower commodity prices weigh on the outlook. While growth in LIDCs should slow down in 2015 on lower growth in oil-exporting LIDCs, it is expected to recover in 2016.

Downside risks have increased for EMDCs in the context of slowing growth, including from increased financial market volatility, a further dollar appreciation and its impact on balance sheet exposures, even lower commodity prices, an abrupt growth slowdown in China, and heightened geopolitical tensions in Russia, Ukraine, the Middle East, and parts of Africa. Risks for AEs include disruptive asset price shifts and financial market turmoil.

During the MDG-monitoring period (2000–15), most EMDCs grew at a sustained strong pace. Together with strong growth, per capita income differences among countries were reduced and absolute poverty was halved over this period.

For the SDG-monitoring period (2015–30), prospects are for global growth to trend down, mostly because of a decrease in global population growth. Poorer countries would need to address disparate demographic evolutions with an appropriate set of macroeconomic and structural policies to enable further reductions in absolute poverty levels and to further narrow income differences relative to richer countries. Richer countries' support for a global economic system with open markets for goods, services, and capital, under appropriate safeguards, remains essential.

BOX 3.1 The effects of demographic factors on potential output

This box—drawing on the April 2015 *World Economic Outlook: Uneven Growth—Short- and Long-term Factors*—assesses the effects of demographic factors on potential output for 10 advanced economies (Australia, Canada, France, Germany, Italy, Japan, the Republic of Korea, Spain, the United Kingdom, and the United States) and 6 major emerging market economies (Brazil, China, India, Mexico, Russia, and Turkey).

Demographic factors can influence potential output by affecting working-age population and trend labor force participation rates. The former is a function of the same variables as population growth more broadly. For example, declines in fertility rates slow future working-age population growth. The second demographic dimension is the age composition of the working-age population, which affects the aggregate participation rate, since the propensity to participate in the labor force starts declining steeply beyond a particular age threshold, typically in the early 50s. An increased share of older people in the population therefore lowers the average participation rate and thereby potential employment.

Figure B3.1.1 presents the evolution of potential growth and the effects of demographic factors over the period 2001–20. In the aftermath of the crisis,

(box continues next page)

BOX 3.1 The effects of demographic factors on potential output (continued)

FIGURE B3.1.1 Effect of demographics on potential growth

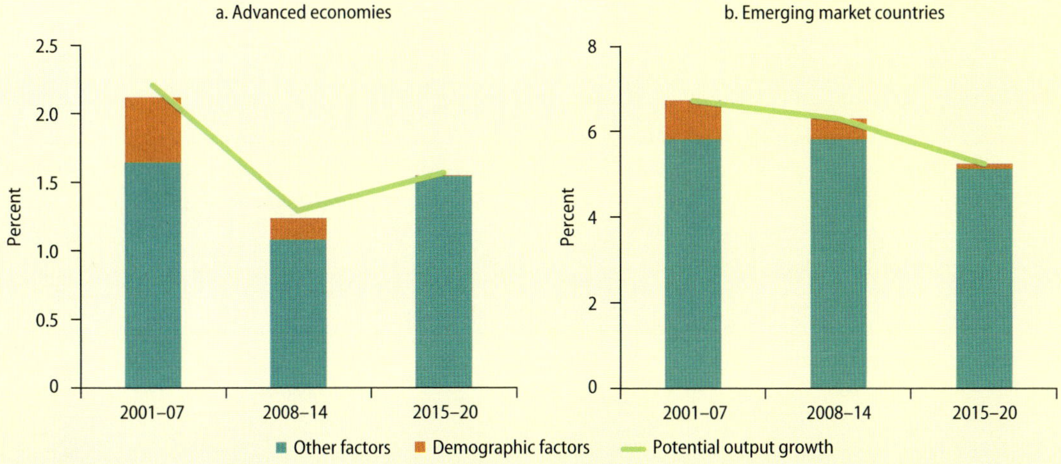

Source: Chapter 3 of the IMF's *World Economic Outlook: Uneven Growth—Short- and Long-term Factors*. April, 2015. Washington, D.C.

potential growth declined in both advanced and emerging market economies. While the largest part of this decline is associated with the scars of the crisis (in particular in advanced economies), demographic factors have also played an important role. In particular, demographic factors contributed to lower potential growth in advanced and emerging market economies by about 0.3 and 0.4 percentage point during 2008–14, respectively.

Looking forward, demographic factors are expected to be an increasing drag on potential growth. In advanced economies, demographic factors are projected to reduce potential growth by about 0.2 percentage point in the medium term (figure B3.1.1a). Working-age population growth is likely to decline significantly in most advanced economies, particularly Germany and Japan, where it will reach about –0.2 percent a year by 2020. At the same time, rapid aging is expected to further decrease the average trend labor force participation rates.

In emerging market economies, demographic factors are expected to reduce potential growth by about 0.4 percentage point by 2020 (figure B3.1.1b). Working-age population growth is likely to slow faster, most sharply in China, and to remain negative in Russia. Aging is expected to accelerate, lowering trend labor force participation rates. Again, this effect is expected to be strongest in China.

Notes

1. Unless otherwise noted, the analysis in this chapter is confined to the 188 member countries of the IMF and the World Bank. These countries constitute 99 percent of the world's population and economic activity. This chapter draws on the October 2015 WEO. The classification of countries follows the one used therein. Emerging market and developing countries are those countries that are not designated as advanced. Low-income developing countries are countries eligible for IMF's concessional financial assistance with a per capita gross national income (measured according to the World Bank's *Atlas* method) in 2011 of below twice the International Development Association's effective operational cutoff level, and Zimbabwe. Other emerging market and developing countries are considered emerging

market countries. Small states are emerging market and developing countries with a population of less than 1.5 million. Fragile states are countries included in the World Bank's list of fragile and conflict-affected states as of July 2015. Appendix table C5.2 includes the list of all countries and the groupings to which they belong. In line with standard WEO practice, growth for country aggregates is calculated using purchasing power parity weights.

2. Each low-income country has been assessed according to a common set of criteria. For example, a country's quality of fiscal policy is assessed by considering its fiscal deficit and the sustainability of its public debt (a country with a large fiscal deficit and an unsustainable level of public debt would be judged to have an unsatisfactory fiscal policy).
3. These coefficients are calculated weighting countries' GDP per capita with their populations; thus they anchor the calculations to the mean global income level but abstract from inequality within countries (see chapter 5 for a discussion of income inequality within countries). The weighted averages are naturally influenced by developments in the larger economies (for example, China, India, and the United States account for 41 percent of global population and 43 percent of global output in 2015). On an equally weighted basis (treating each country as a single data point), the Gini coefficient increased from 53 in 1950 to 69 in 2000 and then fell to 63 percent in 2015.
4. These estimates are based on the medium fertility scenario in the United Nations' *World Population Prospects: The 2015 Revision*.

Part II

Development in an Era of Demographic Change

Profound changes in global demography are expected to affect the development outlook and policy agenda. The world population is growing more slowly and aging at unprecedented speed. These trends reflect past development successes—women's empowerment; improved education; better child, maternal, and reproductive health; and increased longevity. The working-age share peaked in 2012 and is now on the decline. Aging means that population increases are reflected in larger numbers of older people. The global count of children is already stabilizing at a plateau of 2 billion. Yet, underneath these global demographic trends lies significant diversity in the direction and pace of demographic change. Regional and subregional patterns vary significantly across and within countries.

Demographic change brings unique opportunities and challenges to centers of global poverty (marked by high fertility) and engines of global growth (marked by rapid aging). More than 90 percent of poverty is concentrated in pre- and early-dividend countries with young populations that lag in key human development indicators, register rapid population growth, and are seeing their working-age populations swell. In these countries, the demographic transition to lower fertility creates a golden opportunity to raise living standards. Over 85 percent of global economic activity and 78 percent of global growth arises in late- and post-dividend countries with much lower fertility rates and some of the highest shares of the elderly in the world. In these countries, population aging may weaken growth prospects. Neither all good nor all bad, demographic change presents opportunities and challenges everywhere. In each case, policies will make a critical difference in how countries manage their demographic change.

Policies must recognize and respond to demographic change at the country level. To eradicate persistent poverty, the centers of global poverty need to accelerate their demographic transition, invest in the young in their still-growing populations, and lay the foundations for sustained growth. Among other policy initiatives, better education and health services are required, as well as more women empowerment. Facing weakening economic dynamism, the lower-fertility, richer countries that make up the current engines of global growth need to address headwinds arising from shrinking labor forces. They also need to adapt their policies and institutions to foster healthy and productive aging. Selected policy priorities include mobilizing savings for productive investment in human and physical capital and designing welfare systems—pensions, health care, and long-term care—while ensuring fiscal sustainability and protection for the elderly and vulnerable.

Freer capital flows, migration, and trade can help respond to growing demographic imbalances globally. The extent of demographic diversity across countries is starker than before and has a large and inevitable impact on the global economy. Returns on capital and labor are affected. Comparative advantages in trade are altered. Given these implications, flows of capital, labor, and goods and services will be affected. Mutual benefits can be realized: capital can flow to rising consumer markets; older countries can benefit from legal immigration; younger countries can produce labor-intensive products. But challenges need to be managed, and international cooperation is key.

With the right set of policies, this era of intense demographic change can be turned into one of sustained development progress. Global demography is changing and has the potential to profoundly alter the trajectory of global development. To accelerate progress, countries need to elevate efforts to sustain broad-based growth, invest in people, and insure the poor and vulnerable against evolving risks. But they must do so by taking into account demographic change. Where possible, they must capture demographic dividends. Elsewhere, adaptation is required. Everywhere, demographic change must be turned into opportunities for development and improved well-being.

Part II of this report explores the connections between development and demography in the following sequence:

- Chapter 4 characterizes demographic change at the global, regional, and country levels. It also examines the drivers of demographic change that have shaped the diversity of demographic patterns and trends.
- Chapter 5 examines how demography affects development. It develops a new global typology that ties demographic change to development potential and analyzes the various pathways through which demographic change affects the prosperity of nations.
- Chapter 6 analyzes how policies can leverage demographic change in support of the development goals. It examines policy opportunities at both the country and the global level.

4

Demographic Change: Disparities, Divergences, and Drivers

Global demographic trends are at a turning point: population growth is slowing markedly, and after increasing for five decades, the proportion of people ages 15 to 64—the typical working-age population—peaked in 2012 and is now starting to fall again. The rise in the number of dependents per person of working age is driven mainly by an increase in the elderly as a share of the population. Beneath these global dynamics lie major differences in demographic characteristics and trends at the country level. Some countries continue to experience high levels of fertility and population growth, while in others fertility rates have fallen below replacement levels, and rapid aging and gradual population contractions are expected in the coming decades. Demography and development affect each other. Key dimensions of development are drivers of demography, accounting for much of the variation in demographic features across countries, and are highlighted in this chapter. The role of demography in shaping development trajectories is then the focus of chapter 5.

Global demographics are on the cusp of significant change, with the unprecedented population growth of past decades slowing sharply and the global age structure shifting dramatically. Since the 1950s, the world as a whole has experienced substantial improvements in life expectancy, accompanied by a rapid decline in fertility rates and a steady fall in the share of children in the global population. These shifts led to continual increases in the share of the working-age population (lowering the number of dependents per worker) until it peaked in 2012.[1] With the stabilization of the share of the population that is under 15, the fall in the share of working-age population over the coming decades will be driven by rapid aging, with people over 64 accounting for an ever greater proportion of the global population. Most of these trends are "locked in" with a high degree of certainty, with the pace of declines in fertility in countries with persistent high fertility rates the main source of uncertainty (box 4.1).[2]

Global trends mask wide differences at the country level both in their current demographic profiles and in the direction and pace of future change. Many of today's high-income countries have had decades of low fertility rates and high life expectancies.[3] In contrast, many developing countries have seen declines in their fertility rates only more recently, with some of the poorest countries still experiencing persistently high fertility.

BOX 4.1 Accuracy and uncertainty in population projections

Several different national and multilateral institutions estimate historical population data and make projections. Since 1951 the United Nations Population Division (UNPD) has been publishing population estimates, vital statistics and projections for all countries, currently running from 1950 to 2100. The World Bank Group (WBG) also prepares population projections, which draw upon the UNPD figures but include differences in some countries that are well identified and discussed with the UNPD. Several research institutions also have demography programs, such as the Wittgenstein Center, affiliated with the International Institute for Applied Systems Analysis (IIASA).

A wide range of methodologies are applied to project future populations. The dominant methodology for making projections has been deterministic models using "cohort components" based on the age structure of the population and components of change: births, deaths, and migration. The uncertainty of the future is conveyed using alternative assumptions on these key variables to develop different scenarios (Cohen 2001; Lutz, Sanderson, and Scherbov 2001). The United Nations' World Population Projections 2015 Revision covers different scenarios, with varying assumptions on fertility, mortality, and migration (figure B4.1.1). With fertility variants labeled high (+ half child), medium, and low (- half child), the medium variant typically receives the most attention, with the other two conveying a sense of uncertainty about the projections, especially in the outer years. Uncertainty regarding population projections in this deterministic approach is related to the assumptions on fertility, mortality, and migration.

The United Nations projections are also advancing methodologically by using parametric functions to model demographic change (Wilmoth 2015). Currently, total fertility rates (TFR) and life expectancy for a given country are modeled using a Bayesian Hierarchical Model that draws on information from other countries to estimate parameters distributed around the world average. This method yields estimates for TFR, for example, where uncertainty grows over time, and is higher for countries with higher initial fertility. The UNPD is now using probabilistic approaches together with the presentation of alternative scenarios, to illustrate uncertainty about future trends.

FIGURE B4.1.1 Different assumptions about future fertility rates can lead to vastly different population projections in the long run

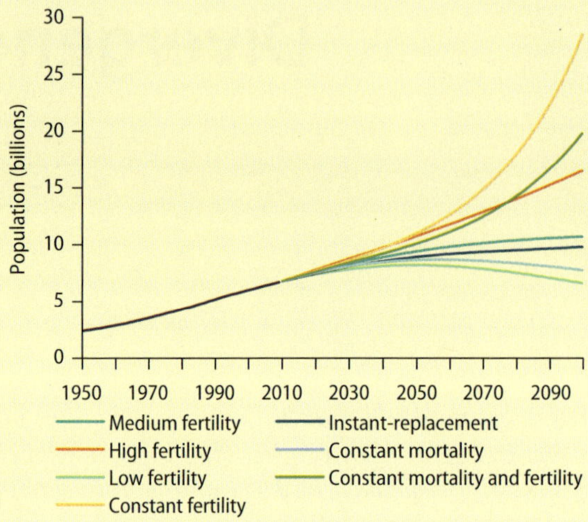

Source: World Bank calculations, based on UN 2015.

Other projections, such as those from IIASA, take a more structural approach by explicitly considering the effect of education on fertility rate. So, as populations in high-fertility countries become better educated, their fertility rates tend to fall. That is one reason why long-term IIASA projections tend to differ substantially from UN projections. In the former, global population growth has a high probability to reach a peak by the end of this century, while in the latter, global population will keep growing beyond 2100 (Gerland et al. 2014; Lutz et al. 2007). The key source of this difference is associated with projections for Asia and Africa, where several countries have high fertility rates and low levels of education.

Global population projections do not differ much until after 2030 because of the current age structure and population size (figure B4.1.2). Even if fertility rates everywhere were to fall immediately to "replacement level" (about 2.1), the global population would keep rising to 11 billion by the end of the century (population would not stabilize this century). This "population momentum" occurs because older cohorts differ in absolute size from those cohorts

(box continues next page)

BOX 4.1 Accuracy and uncertainty in population projections (continued)

FIGURE B4.1.2 World population projections from different sources are relatively similar for the 2015–30 time frame

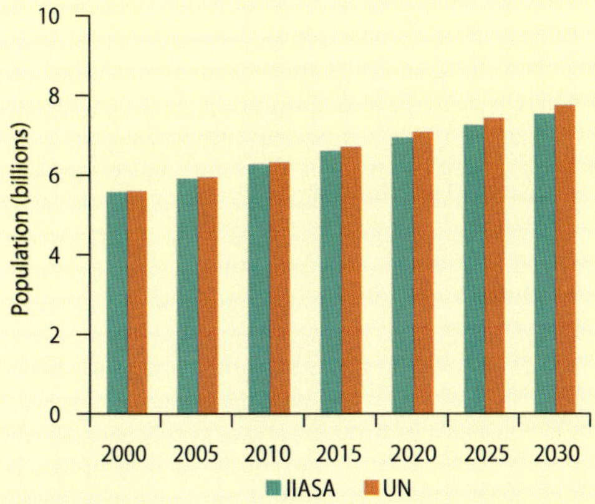

Source: World Bank calculations, based on UN 2015 and Lutz and KC 2010.
Note: The figure reports only on countries for which both projections are available, and it refers to the population above 15 years old. The UN 2015 projections are made for different scenarios with different assumptions regarding fertility and mortality.

currently bearing children, affecting the immediate fertility and mortality rates that together with migration determine population growth. In high-fertility countries, the population momentum suggests continued rapid growth, with more uncertainty regarding the projections than in low-fertility countries, where population size tends to be more stable.

At the global level, population projections have been relatively accurate and stable over time, despite differences between methodologies. For example, in 1973 the United Nations projected a world population of 6.400 billion in 2000 (Coale 1974). In 1984, the WBG projected that the world population would reach 6.082 billion in 2000 (World Bank 1994). Projections have in many instances also remained quite stable over various forecasts. In 1994, the WBG projected a global population of 9.758 billion in 2050. Twenty years later, in 2014 the WBG projected a global population in 2050 of 9.478 billion, a difference of –2.87 percent.

As a result, half of the world's population will be in countries that will experience slowdowns in population growth with rising shares of the elderly over the coming decades (albeit at different paces). The other half will live in countries with relatively young populations, whose high fertility is driving global population growth.

These differences in demographic patterns and trends across countries closely reflect development progress. Population size and age structure are determined by three fundamental demographic factors—fertility, mortality, and migration. These factors are driven in large part by income and non-income development outcomes, such as improvements in health, education, and gender equality. Generally, countries that have made solid progress in these dimensions experience falling rates of infant mortality and fertility and rising life expectancy much sooner than countries that were—or are—lagging developmentally.

Characteristics of demographic change

This section reviews the evolution of key demographic features since 1950 and analyzes how the demographic landscape is likely to change through 2050. It describes the wide diversity of trends across regions and groups of countries with similar levels of economic development, illustrating how changes in fertility, mortality, life expectancy, and migration explain past and future trends at the global level and how they are changing the population centers of the world.

Global trends are at a turning point

Global demographic trends are going through unprecedented shifts, with the rapid growth observed in the global population over the past decades slowing dramatically. The global population grew by 174 percent between 1950 and 2015, from 2.5 billion to 6.9 billion, and is almost 7.3 billion today (figure 4.1a). Population growth was the fastest from the mid-1950s through the mid-1970s, causing development policy discussions to be marked by concerns about unfettered population growth and a perceived need to control the so-called "population bomb" (World Bank 1984). Then, in the 1990s, population growth started to fall: by 2022 the average annual growth rate is expected to fall below 1 percent, down from more than 2 percent in the late 1960s (figure 4.1b). This shift in the pace of population growth has also shifted the policy discussion on the links between development and demography.

In parallel with the slowdown in population growth, the global age structure is shifting. After rising steadily since the 1960s,

FIGURE 4.1 Global demographic trends are at an inflection point

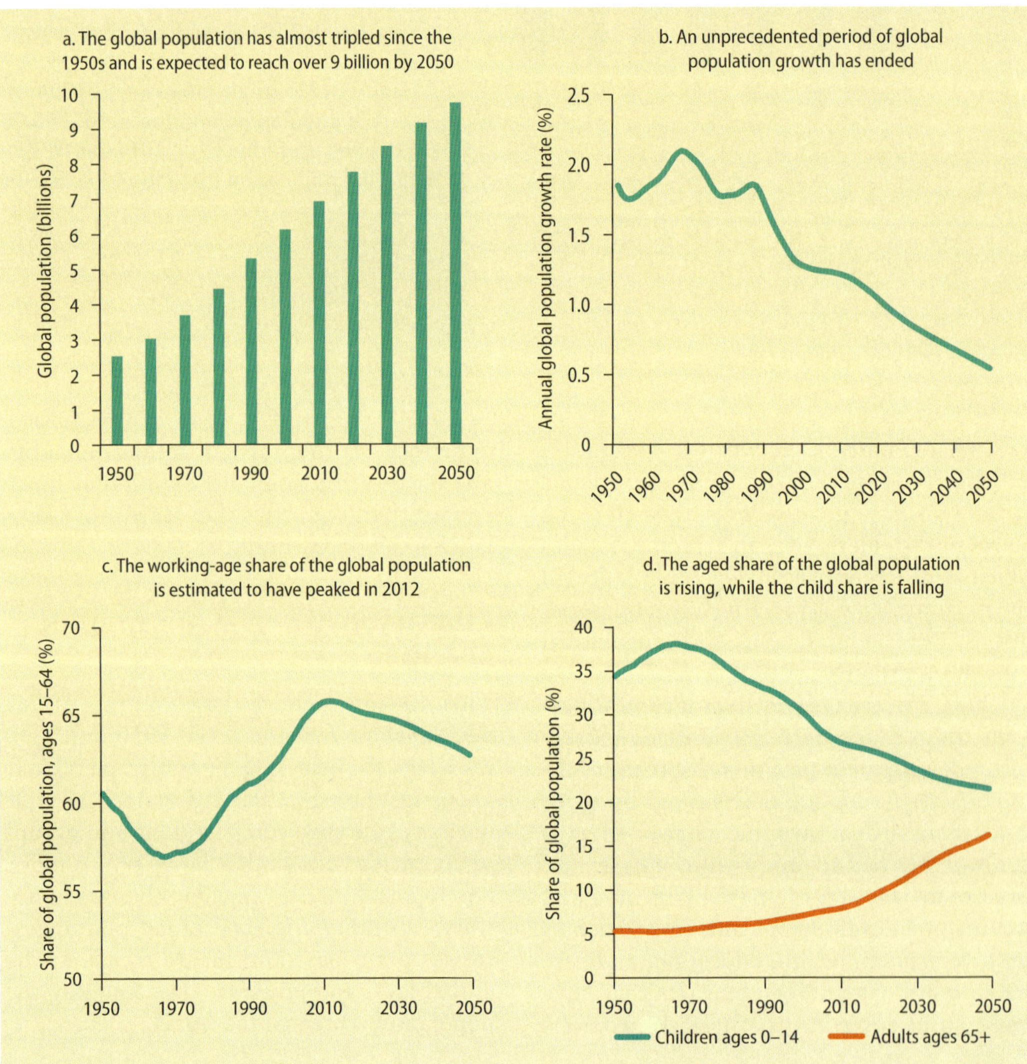

Source: World Bank calculations, based on data from UN 2015.

the working-age population reached a peak of 65.8 percent of the total population in 2012 and is expected to decline to 62.7 percent by 2050 (figure 4.1c). At the same time, children—those under age 15—represent a shrinking share of the global population, and the share of those 65 and over has been rising steadily (figure 4.1d). By 2050, the share of children in the global population is expected to have fallen to 21 percent, versus a peak of 38 percent in the late 1960s, while the aged share of the population will have expanded from 5.0 percent in 1960 to 16.0 percent. As a result of these shifts in the dependent population shares, the global total dependency ratio declined from its peak of 75.4 percent in 1965 to a low of 52.2 percent in 2010.[4] With the aged share of the global population now expanding much faster than it has in the past, the global total dependency ratio is expected to rise in the coming decades, to 59.6 percent in 2050.[5]

The world has also seen major changes in other demographic dimensions, including a halving of total fertility rates and rapid improvement in life expectancy. In the 1950s total fertility rates were about five births per woman, reaching a peak in the post–World War II period (figure 4.2).[6] Since then, fertility rates have steadily declined, falling to 2.5 births per woman as of 2015, and are projected to fall further (but remain above global replacement rates) through 2050.[7] In parallel, average life expectancy at birth has risen by more than 25 years over the past 65 years, from 46.8 years in 1950 to 71.7 years in 2015 (figure 4.3), while infant mortality has declined. Improvements in life expectancy are expected to continue, although at a much lower rate than in the past.

FIGURE 4.2 The global total fertility rate declined rapidly between the 1960s and 1990s

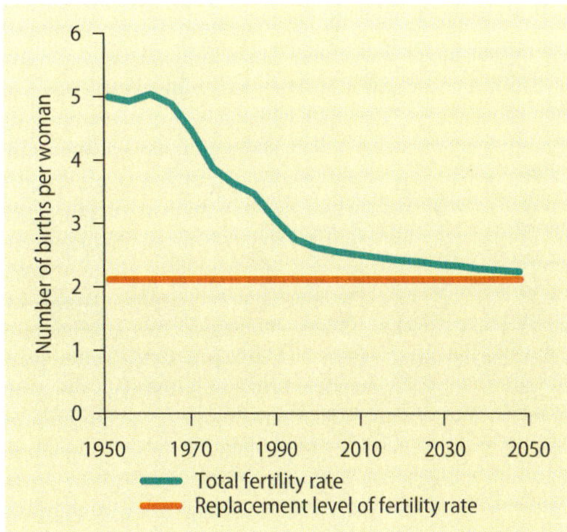

Source: World Bank calculations, based on data from UN 2015.
Note: The total fertility rate is defined as the average number of births each woman has, assuming she lives to the end of her reproductive life. The replacement level of the total fertility rate is the average number of births each woman would need to have to hold the global population constant.

FIGURE 4.3 The global population is living longer

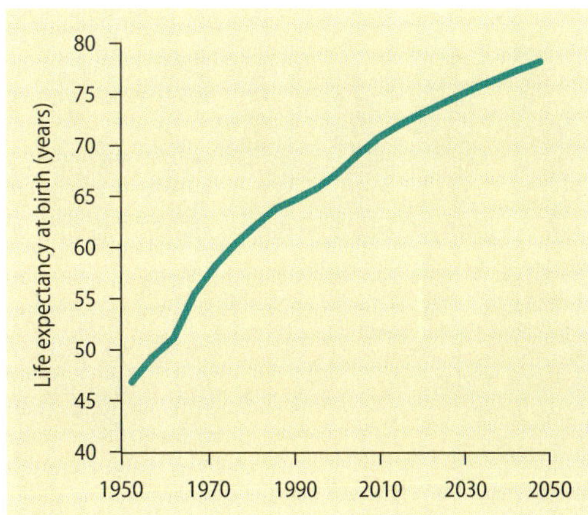

Source: World Bank calculations, based on data from UN 2015.

Disparities across countries shape global trends

The global demographic changes are mainly explained by the ongoing demographic transition in developing countries, especially the decline in mortality rates at the country level. Although mortality rates are still higher in developing than in high-income countries, they have fallen rapidly.[8] Declining mortality rates have coincided with falling infant mortality rates and longer life expectancies, most prominently for countries in East Asia and the Pacific and South Asia (figures 4.4 and 4.5). In most developing regions, infant mortality rates and life expectancies are converging on high-income country values, which have improved comparatively more slowly over the past few decades. Africa is the exception among developing regions. There,

FIGURE 4.4 Infant mortality has fallen significantly in all regions

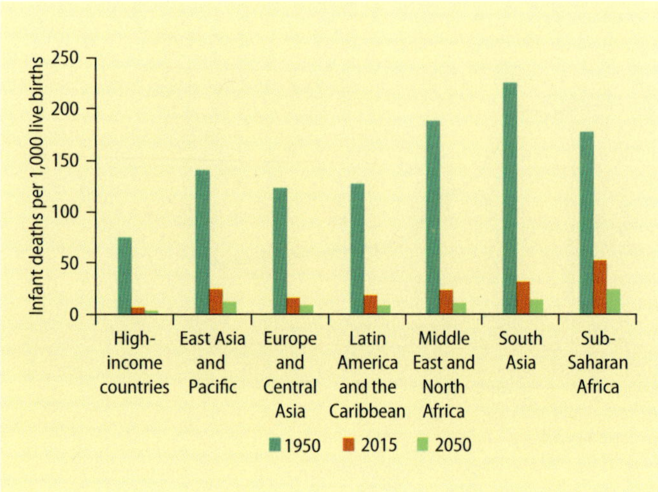

Source: World Bank calculations, based on data from UN 2015.

FIGURE 4.5 Life expectancy in Sub-Saharan Africa lags that in other developing regions

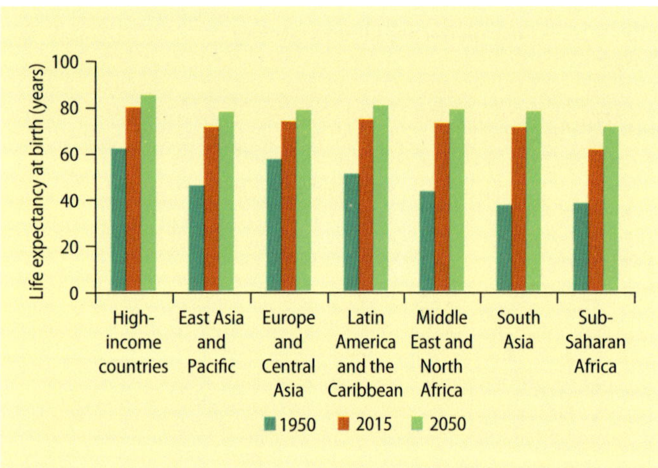

Source: World Bank calculations, based on data from UN 2015.

both mortality rates and life expectancies lag significantly behind other regions, with HIV/AIDS slowing progress (box 4.2). As of 2015, an average of 52 infants die for every 1,000 born in Sub-Saharan Africa, and the average life expectancy is 60.98 years. In contrast, in South Asia, with the second-worst indicators of mortality and life expectancy among developing regions, the average infant mortality rate is 31.4 (per 1,000) and the average life expectancy is 70.6 years.

Falling mortality and still-high fertility led to a "child bulge" in developing countries in the 1960s and 1970s, while population growth slowed in high-income countries. In many developing countries, increasing numbers of children survived past infancy in the 1950s and 1960s, even as fertility rates remained persistently high (figure 4.6).[9] Together, these two trends led to rapid population growth in developing countries (figure 4.7). This period of high population growth was accompanied by a shift in age structure, with children accounting for an increasing share of developing countries' populations. The exception was developing Europe and Central Asia, where most countries already had fertility profiles that were similar to those of high-income countries.

Falling fertility rates in developing countries led to slower population growth and in the 1970s–80s, to an increase in the working-age population share. As declining fertility rates produced smaller cohorts of babies, the cohorts born in the 1950s and 1960s formed a bulge. As the people in this bulge grew into the working-age population, they drove an increase in working-age population share in their home countries. The decline in fertility rates was observed mostly in developing countries, since aside from the mid-century baby booms, the high-income countries already had lower fertility rates.[10]

The large cohorts born in the 1950s–60s in developing countries are now increasingly contributing to global aging. This change results from the substantial improvements in life expectancy, especially in developing East Asia and Pacific, which not only had the largest child and working-age cohorts but also registered the greatest improvements in health. Between 1950 and 1970, high-income countries accounted for 55 percent of the growth in the aged population while developing East Asia and Pacific accounted for 14 percent. Between 1970 and 2000, however, high-income countries' contribution decreased to 33 percent, while that of developing East Asia and Pacific increased to 32 percent.

Falling fertility rates in developing countries have also contributed to slower global

BOX 4.2 The legacy of the HIV/AIDS pandemic on southern Africa's age structure

The HIV/AIDS epidemic in southern Africa well illustrates the negative effects of infectious diseases on life expectancies and mortality. This area has the highest prevalence of HIV/AIDS in the world. Before the pandemic, southern Africa experienced starkly different demographic trends from the rest of Sub-Saharan Africa: both fertility and mortality rates began to decline much earlier and faster and were significantly lower than those in the rest of the continent. With the advent of the HIV/AIDS pandemic in the late 1990s and early 2000s, mortality rates surged again and life expectancy at birth dropped significantly. In Lesotho, life expectancy at birth dropped from around 60 years in the early 1990s to 45 years in 2005 (Moultrie 2015). Botswana and Swaziland followed similar trends. And while life expectancy dropped less in South Africa and Namibia, it is close to the average of Sub-Saharan Africa despite the higher wealth of the two countries.

The HIV/AIDS epidemic reduced the size of the working-age population and has subsequently stalled anticipated declines in dependency ratios since 2000. Half of all deaths in southern Africa in the 2005–10 period were adults ages 20 to 49 years, compared with 21 percent in 1985–93. At the same time, population growth slowed because of the loss of so many women of childbearing age and increased infant and child mortality related to mother-to-child transmission of HIV. Thus, the overall effect of the pandemic has been to slow down the decline in the dependency ratio by reducing the size of the working-age population and by slowing the growth of the elderly population as the cohorts most affected by the pandemic reach old age.

The launch of mass-scale antiretroviral (ARV) treatment appears to have reversed the mortality trend from the middle 2000s (World Bank 2015b). Fortunately, the impact on HIV/AIDS on South Africa's population dynamics is starting to fade. According to the United Nation's Spectrum model, prevalence among adults of both sexes ages 15 to 49 in South Africa is close to its peak and is expected to decline slowly from 18.7 percent in 2015 to 16.2 percent by 2050 (Moultrie 2015). The proportion of all deaths attributable to HIV/AIDS (as distinct from all deaths among those who are HIV-positive) is expected to stabilize at around 22 percent of all deaths between 2015 and 2050. Total fertility rates did not rise in response to the surge in mortality caused by the pandemic. On the contrary, research has suggested that HIV/AIDS exerts a downward pressure on fertility in HIV-infected people and, to a lesser extent, on fertility in the general population in high-prevalence countries. The evidence thus suggests that the temporary shock might have only slowed the demographic transition rather than stopped it (Nair 2010).

population growth, with populations in some countries even expected to shrink in the future. On average, fertility rates in many developing regions converged by 2000 to levels at or below the replacement rate, that is the rate at which the population size would be constant in the long run. In many high-income countries and in developing Europe and Central Asia, fertility rates have been below replacement rates since the 1990s. In some countries, the combination of a rising share of the aged, below-replacement fertility, and emigration are expected to lead to net contractions in populations between 2015 and 2050.[11] Among high-income countries, Germany and Japan are notable in that their populations are projected to shrink by 7.7 and 15.1 percent, respectively, over this timeframe (map 4.1). Some of the most extreme population contractions, however, will be in developing countries in Europe and Central Asia. For example, Bulgaria's population is expected to shrink by 27.9 percent by 2050, owing to a combination of low fertility and high rates of net migration (World Bank 2013).

Divergences shift population centers

With a large and growing share of the global population living in developing countries, global demographic trends have been driven by changes in these countries (map 4.2). In 1950, 32 percent of the global population lived in high-income economies. Developing

FIGURE 4.6 Total fertility rates have declined, though less so in Sub-Saharan Africa

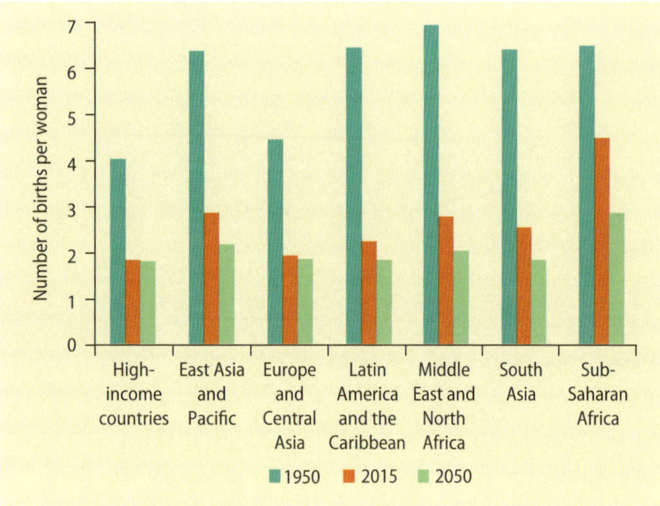

Source: World Bank calculations, based on data from UN 2015.
Note: The bars reflect the unweighted average of countries in a given group. The total fertility rate is the hypothetical number of births each woman in a given country would have, assuming she survives to the end of her reproductive life and experiences the age-specific birth rates of the given year.

FIGURE 4.7 Population growth in developing countries has been slowing since the 1970s

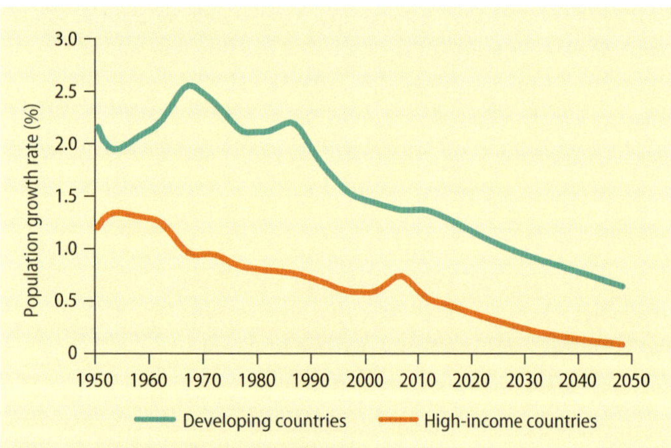

Source: World Bank calculations, based on data from UN 2015.
Note: Developing countries include low-, upper-middle-, and lower-middle-income countries.

East Asia and Pacific, the region that has seen some of the most rapid fertility declines and life expectancy improvements in recent years, accounted for 29 percent of the population, while Sub-Saharan Africa, the region with the most modest improvements, accounted for only 7 percent. By 2015, this distribution had shifted substantially, with high-income countries accounting for only 19 percent of the global population and Sub-Saharan Africa for 14 percent, while the share in developing East Asia and Pacific has remained about the same. By 2050, Sub-Saharan Africa is expected to account for almost 25 percent of the global population.

Population growth within countries, international migration, and urbanization are all changing where people live. Natural population growth—the difference between crude birth and death rates—is the key determinant of population growth in most countries. Very simply, countries that have higher (lower) natural growth rates will have increasingly higher (lower) concentrations of the global population. International migration can blunt the impact of natural growth, however. Migration occurs within countries as well, with rural-urban migration being one of the most important because it has indirect effects on national fertility rates as well.

Population growth within countries

Shifts in the location of the global population result from differences in population growth across countries, particularly between those in Africa and the rest of the world. Of the 30 countries expected to have the fastest-growing populations between 2015 and 2050, 29 are in Sub-Saharan Africa, and 13 of these countries currently have total fertility rates of 5.0 or more. Persistently high fertility rates in Sub-Saharan Africa mean that the region will have high natural growth for several decades and will account for more than half of global population growth between 2015 and 2050 (figure 4.8). The fastest-growing ten countries in the world—Burundi, Chad, The Gambia, Mali, Niger, Nigeria, Somalia, Tanzania, Uganda, and Zambia—are expected to account for 20 percent of global population growth over the same period, with Nigeria alone accounting for 2 percent of the global population growth.

Africa's high fertility and population growth will also make the region home to an increasing share of the world's children and working-age people. The number of children in Sub-Saharan Africa is expected to grow by

MAP 4.1 The populations of Europe and Central Asia will shrink substantially through 2050, while those in Sub-Saharan Africa will grow the most

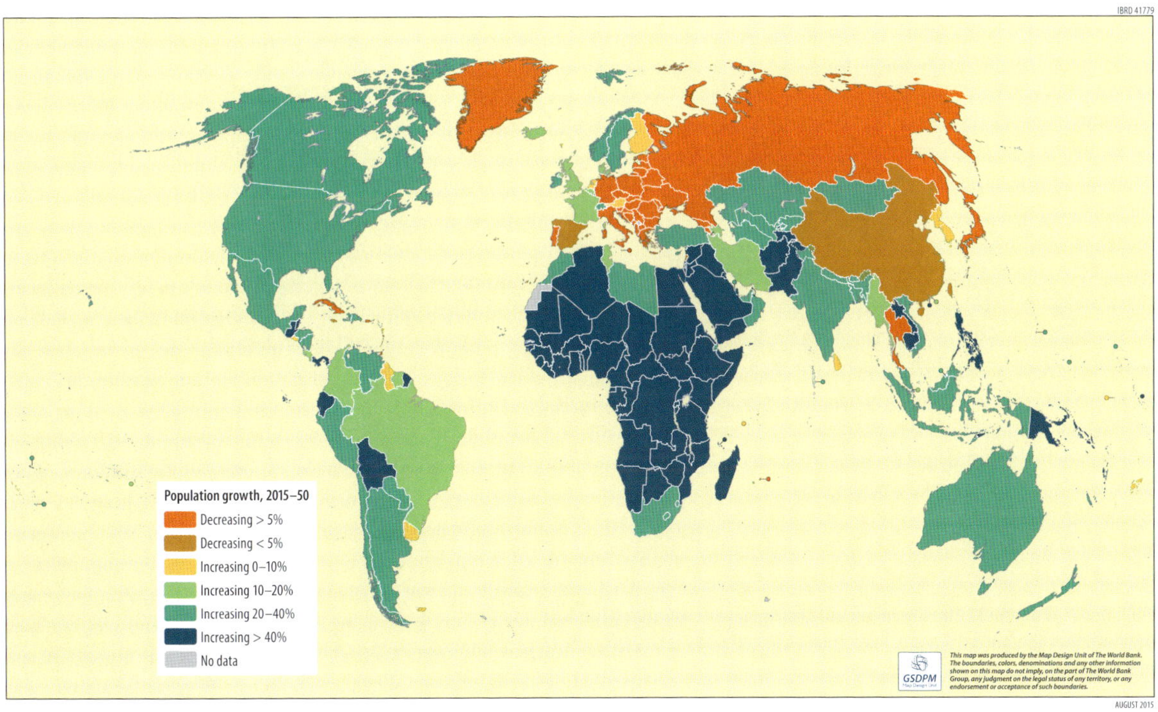

Source: World Bank calculations, based on data from UN 2015.

MAP 4.2 Developing countries account for most of the global population in 2015

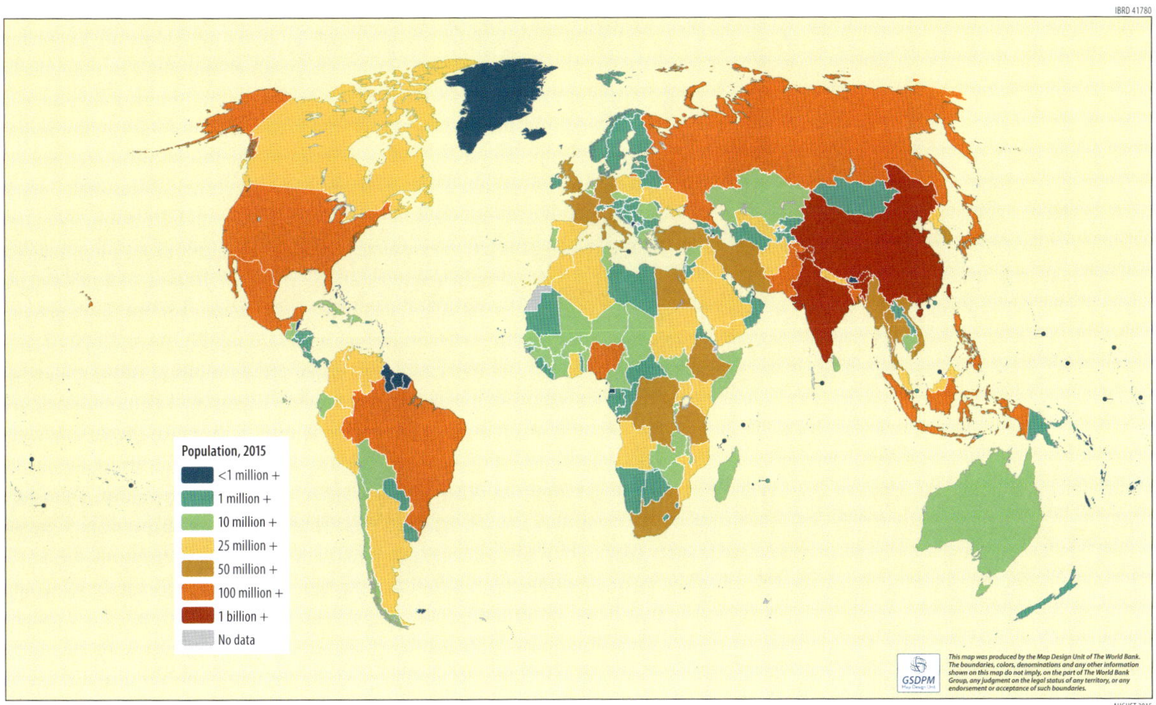

Source: World Bank calculations, based on data from UN 2015.

FIGURE 4.8 More than half of global population growth through 2050 will be in Sub-Saharan Africa

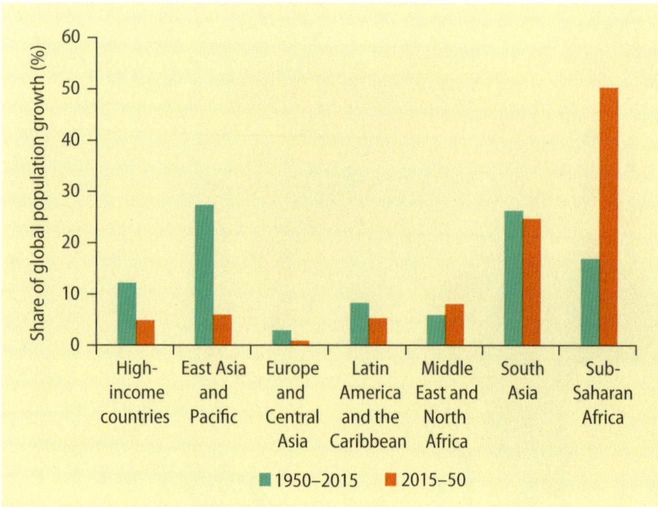

Source: World Bank calculations, based on data from UN 2015.

FIGURE 4.9 Between 2015 and 2050, children will account for 33 percent of Sub-Saharan Africa's population, versus 23 percent in the rest of the world

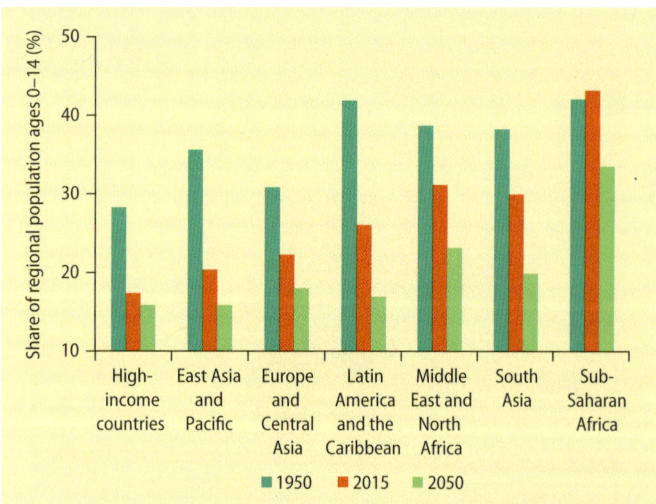

Source: World Bank calculations, based on data from UN 2015.

305 million between 2015 and 2050, whereas the number of children in the rest of the world is expected to contract by 148 million. The share of children in Africa's population is thus expected to remain above 33 percent through 2050, even as it falls to 23 percent or below in other parts of the world (figure 4.9). As Africa's children age into adulthood, they will help maintain the region's position as having the highest growth rate of the working-age population in the world, even as the working-age population in other regions of the world—developing regions included—contracts significantly (figure 4.10). In the 2015–50 period, Africa will displace East Asia and South Asia as the largest source of growth in the global working-age population, accounting for nearly two-thirds of the increase over this period (figure 4.11).

Migration

Migration directly affects the age structure of both sending and receiving countries because most international migrants are of working age. Approximately 74 percent of international migrants are in the 20 to 64 age cohort, well above the share in that same cohort in the global population (UN 2013; EUROSTAT 2015). For sending countries, the migrants' departure increases the total dependency ratio and reduces the working-age share of the population. For receiving countries, the migrants' entry and any subsequent births increase the working-age share of the population and help reduce old-age dependency. Rapid aging in Bulgaria, for example, has been accelerated by migration to other European countries (World Bank 2013). Similarly, migration from small island states in the Pacific to Australia and New Zealand has left the sending countries with extremely high total dependency ratios and higher average ages. In contrast, major destinations for migrant workers, such as Qatar, have the lowest total dependency ratios in the world despite high total fertility and low mortality rates. In Qatar, migrants account for more than three-fourths of the population, and 89.7 percent of migrants are ages 15 to 64 (UN and UNICEF 2014).

Migration, by shifting average fertility rates, can indirectly influence the population size and age structure of receiving countries. If the reproductive behavior of migrants persists after they migrate, the fertility rates of a migrant-receiving country can be either raised or reduced.[12] Evidence from Europe and the United States suggests that the average fertility rates of their migrant populations, which are predominantly from lower-income countries, tend to be higher than the national average for a generation or more (Andersson 2004; Kahn 1988; Sobotka 2008). But fertility behavior could persist even in the context of migration from higher- to lower-income countries. In Argentina, for example, the total fertility rate was 3.1 in the 1950s, close to the high-income country median of 3.6 and substantially lower than the median total fertility rate of 6.3 in the rest of Latin America.[13] The low rate in Argentina has been attributed to the large inflow of European migrants who came to Argentina in after World War II and who tended to have lower fertility rates, as was the norm in Europe (Gragnolati et al. 2015).

Urbanization

Rural-urban migration within countries has helped reduce country-level fertility rates. Urban households tend to have lower fertility rates than do rural households (figure 4.12) (Jaffe 1942; Kuznets 1974). The gap between fertility rates in urban and rural areas results in an observed inverse relationship between total fertility rates and socioeconomic development and the fact that urban areas tend to have higher levels of development (Bongaarts and Watkins 1996; Bryant 2007). As countries urbanize and populations move from rural to urban areas, overall total fertility rates can drop as the fertility profile of the previously rural migrant households converges to that of urban households. This convergence is particularly evident in China, where urbanization is estimated to have accounted for 22 percent of the decline in the country's total fertility rate between 1982 and 2008.[14] Lower-middle-income countries have experienced rapid urbanization in recent decades, with the share of the population living in urban areas rising from 29.4 percent in 1990 to 49.7 percent in 2013, with implications for their future fertility rates.

FIGURE 4.10 Working-age population growth is slowing globally but will remain high in Sub-Saharan Africa

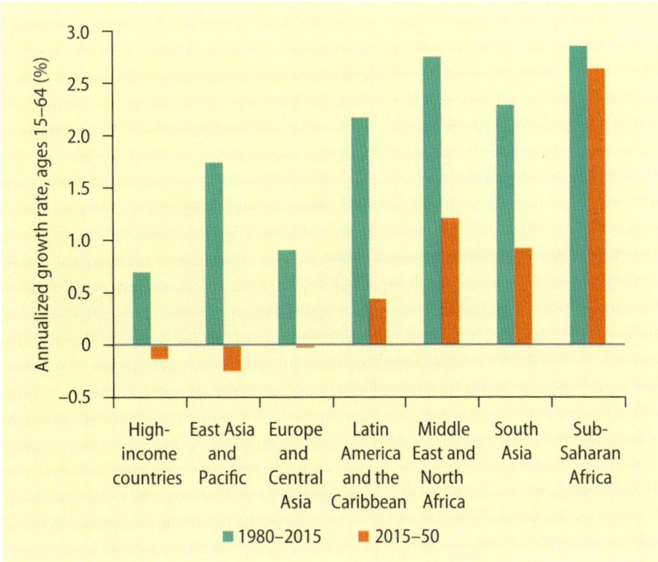

Source: World Bank calculations, based on data from UN 2015.

FIGURE 4.11 Sub-Saharan Africa will account for more than half of working-age population growth through 2050

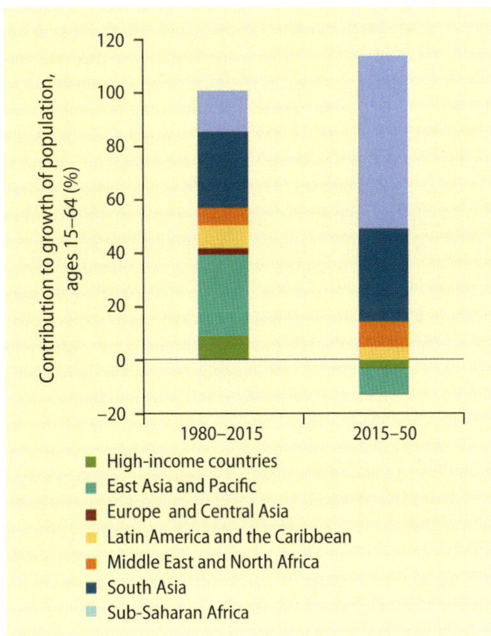

Source: World Bank calculations, based on data from UN 2015.

FIGURE 4.12 Rural households tend to have higher fertility rates than urban households

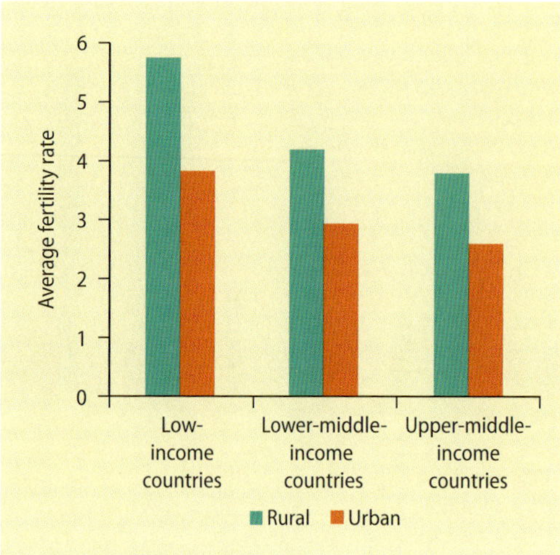

Source: World Bank calculations, based on the latest Demographic and Health Survey for each country.
Note: Average total fertility rate is the average number of births per woman. The values are unweighted averages for countries within a given group. The survey years range from 1990 to 2013 and cover 71 countries. See appendix C.2 for additional details.

Generally, countries have been urbanizing at a steady pace, although substantial disparities exist between high-income and developing economies. High-income countries urbanized rapidly in the 1960s and 1970s, with the urban share of their total populations rising from 47 percent in 1960 to 60 percent by 1980. This share has only increased slightly since then. Middle-income-countries have also urbanized rapidly, although from a much lower starting point, with 40 to 45 percent of their populations now dwelling in urban areas, up from about 18–20 percent in 1960. In contrast, populations in low-income countries remain largely rural, with only slow movement into urban areas; only 22 percent of people in these countries lived in urban areas as of 2014.

Drivers of demographic change

The three fundamental factors in changing population size and age structure—mortality, fertility, and migration across and within countries—are, in turn, closely tied to development progress. The path of birth and death rates—reflecting fertility and mortality rates—determines the natural growth of a population. But population growth is also affected by migration (both international and internal), because it influences age structure directly as people move and indirectly by affecting fertility in both the migrant-sending and migrant-receiving locations. At the same time, the dynamics of fertility and mortality in a country affect how its age structure may change over time. Mortality rates are affected by the rate of infectious disease and the availability of health care, among others, while fertility is affected not only by access to health care but to levels of education and income. Migration is influenced by income and non-income inequalities that push migrants away from their old home or pull them toward a new location. Development progress, both income- and non-income-based, is thus a critical driver over time of changes in age structure and population size.

Epidemiological trends alter mortality

The initial decline in mortality that occurs as part of the demographic transition is associated with the start of an epidemiological transition. A reduction in the mortality rate of a population is paralleled by a decline in the incidence of infectious and contagious diseases, particularly among children under age five. This decline, in turn, increases the share of the population dying from chronic and degenerative diseases. Increased use of vaccinations against fatal diseases, together with improved hygiene and sanitation and better access to clean water, typically contribute to the initial declines in mortality rates, as was first observed in Europe in the 1700s (Bloom and Williamson 1998; Cutler, Deaton, and Lleras-Muney 2006).

Mortality rates began to decline only relatively recently in developing countries and remains high in low-income countries. In low-income countries it is still driven by infectious diseases and neonatal complications (figure 4.13). Neonatal disorders, diarrhea, lower respiratory infections and other

FIGURE 4.13 Neonatal complications and infectious disease drive mortality in developing countries

Source: World Bank calculations, based on data documented in Wang et al. 2013.

infections are the cause of more than half of deaths in children under age six. In Sub-Saharan African countries, neglected tropical diseases (NTDs), malaria, HIV, and tuberculosis represented about 50 percent of deaths between 1990 and 2010.[15]

Poorer countries lag behind in achieving the development goals related to reducing infant and child mortality. In countries where the average income per capita is less than $3 a day, children under 5 accounted for 30.5 percent of deaths in 2010. In the same year, 86 percent of deaths of children under age 15 occurred in low- and lower-middle-income countries. High infant mortality in low-income countries is one reason why many of them are still in early stages of demographic transition, with high death and birth rates (World Bank 2015b). (Box 4.3 presents a model of demographic transition.)

As countries move to the later stages of demographic transition and average life expectancies rise, chronic and degenerative diseases become the primary causes of death. The epidemiological transition thus continues. While noncommunicable diseases are challenges for countries across the development spectrum, high-income country populations ages 64 or more accounted for 79 percent of deaths in 2010. These deaths occurred almost entirely from cancer, cardiovascular issues, and other chronic conditions, and these countries accounted for about 43 percent of global deaths among individuals above 80 years old. Thus, to improve life expectancy, high-income countries must focus on improving health at older ages. Addressing the chronic diseases most commonly responsible for morbidity at older ages is much more costly than addressing the infectious and contagious diseases that afflict young children in low-income countries, however, especially considering the impact on life expectancy.

Poor households tend to face higher mortality rates and worse access to health services than richer ones, regardless of income classification of the country. The bottom 40 percent (B40) of households in the wealth distribution in a given country tends to have a worse morbidity profile and higher mortality rate than families in the top 60 percent (T60) (figure 4.14).[16] This observation holds across income groupings. In low-income countries, for example, the infant mortality rate is 1.18 times higher in B40 than in T60 households; in upper-middle-income countries, the B40 rate is 1.45 times higher. In addition to their disadvantage in terms of wealth, B40 households face worse access to health facilities than T60 households (figure 4.15).

Mortality differs across countries at similar income levels and across the income distribution within countries. The variation within high-income countries illustrates this point. Although the infant mortality rate in the United States is relatively high compared with that in, for example, Western European countries, infants born to white, college-educated, married women in the United States have similar mortality rates as infants in Western Europe. In the United States, infant mortality among non-Hispanic black Americans is 12.2 (deaths per 1,000 infants born between 2008 and 2010), more than double the rate for the non-Hispanic white population of 5.3 (Chen, Oster, and Williams 2014; MacDorman et al. 2014). The large variation within counties is observed not only at the household level but also in different regions. Seattle (per capita income of $96,400) and San Jose ($86,700), two of the richest cities in the United States, have two of the lowest infant mortality rates (3.7 and 3.0 deaths per 1,000 infants born). Poorer cities, such as Cleveland ($23,400) and Detroit ($20,500), have much higher infant mortality rates (14.1 and 12.4, respectively). Mortality at older ages in the United States is also higher for people with relatively low long-term incomes and less education, and the disparity has increased in recent decades (Waldron 2007; Meara, Richards, and Cutler 2008).

Mortality rates across countries are strongly influenced by access to and supply of public health services. Different from other vital events that are subject to individual choice, death can be a consequence of several factors that are not under an individual's

BOX 4.3 The demographic transition model

The demographic transition model (DTM) describes the transition of populations from high to low fertility and mortality rates. This transition generally parallels the economic development of a country (Szreter 1993). The model consists of at least four distinct phases, with countries effectively moving from high fertility and low life expectancy to low fertility and high life expectancy as they move through the demographic transition. At the same time, they go from high proportions of children and few elderly to low proportions of children and many elderly.

Fertility rates and mortality rates are both high in the first stage, where the population tends to be younger and population growth stable but low (figure B4.3.1). If mortality rates fall but fertility rates remain high, as in the second phase, then population growth accelerates, with growing numbers of young and rising youth dependency. In the third stage, fertility rates also begin to decline, and population growth slows. During this time, the youth dependency ratios also fall and the share of the working-age population rises, boosting per capita income growth through the first demographic dividend. After a long period of lower fertility, the growth rate of the working-age population slows and the aged dependency ratio begins to rise. When fertility rates and mortality rates reach low levels, population growth also stabilizes at a low rate, in the fourth stage of the DTM.[a]

FIGURE B4.3.1 During the demographic transition, population growth first accelerates then slows as average ages rise.

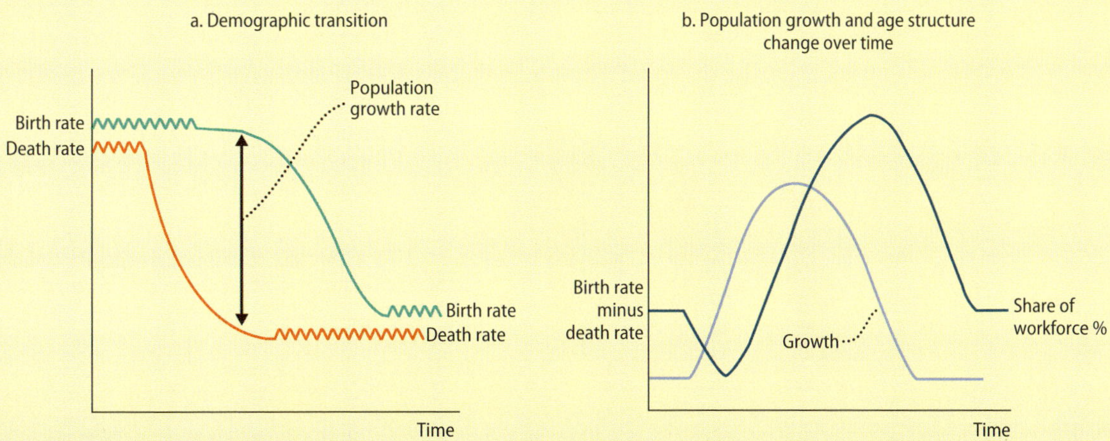

Source: Bloom and Williamson 1998.

a. Recently, some developed countries have reported increases in fertility. There is some evidence that when countries pass a threshold of human development, then fertility declines are reversed, as discussed by Myrskylä, Kohler, and Billari (2009) in a cross-country analysis of the Human Development Index and total fertility rates. Luci-Greulich and Thévenon (2014) found that economic development is likely to induce a fertility rebound for OECD members but is not sufficient to lift fertility to a significantly higher level in all countries.

control (Soares 2005). For example, East Asia experienced a particularly fast decline in child mortality, and indeed mortality at all ages, which led to an increase in life expectancy from 61.5 to 76.6 years between 1960 and 1992. Among the possible explanations for this achievement is widespread access to new public health programs and medical knowledge and technologies (Bloom and Williamson 1998). Although there is a clear association between individuals' incomes and mortality outcomes, the access to new

FIGURE 4.14 Infant mortality is higher in the bottom 40 percent of the wealth distribution than in the top 60 percent

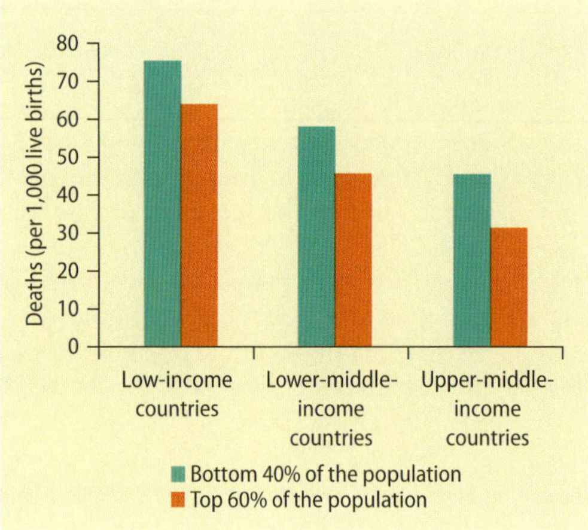

Note: Country groupings follow the standard World Bank Group income-based classification. See appendix C.2 for details.

FIGURE 4.15 The bottom 40 percent also have less access to health facilities

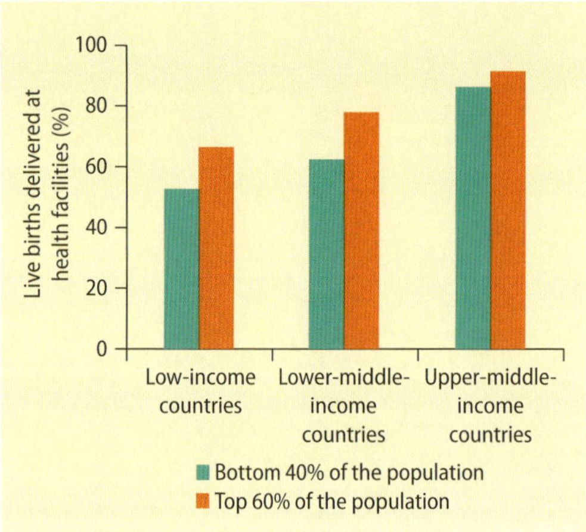

Source: World Bank calculations, using data from Demographic and Health Surveys. See appendix C.2 for additional details.

technologies and public health improvements played a key role in reducing mortality rates. Improved nutrition, quality of and access to public health, urbanization, vaccination, and medical treatments are among the main sources of reduction in infectious diseases and child mortality (Fogel 1997; Chaturvedi, De Costa and Raven 2015; Cutler, Deaton, and Lleras-Munry 2006).

Education, income, and health influence fertility

Declining infant mortality rates and increasing educational attainment, life expectancy, and income are all associated with a reduction in total fertility (figure 4.16).[17] A reduction in infant mortality rates generally has a lagged effect on reducing fertility, largely because of reproductive decisions that are based on "replacement" of deceased children and the "insurance" of having children in case some do not survive to adulthood. The intuition is that with their children more likely to survive infancy and childhood, parents will reduce their number of births to maintain the same net number of children. Improvements in child health may thus be a precursor to lower rates of fertility. In contrast, education (especially of females) and household income are negatively correlated with fertility.

There are two potential income-related mechanisms that underlie the "quality" versus "quantity" trade-off that parents face in deciding how many children to have. First, as parents' educational attainment

FIGURE 4.16 An increase in years of schooling, life expectancy, and GDP per capita and a decrease in infant mortality strongly correlate with lower fertility

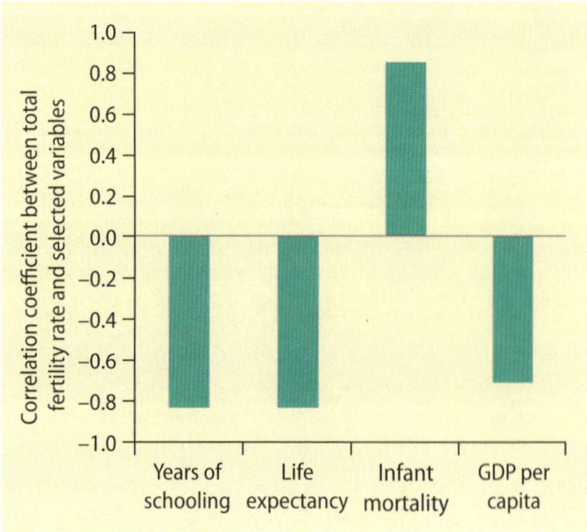

Sources: Barro and Lee (2014) for years of schooling; UN (2015) for life expectancy; WDI for the log of GDP per capita; and UN 2015 for the fertility rate.
Note: All coefficients are statistically significant at 1 percent.

rises—particularly that of women—the opportunity cost of having children rises. That alone could encourage parents to have fewer children or to delay having children (Galor and Weil 1999, 2000). Second, as incomes rise, parents could choose to have more children or invest more in the human capital of their children. Empirical evidence suggests however, that as incomes rise, families choose to have fewer but more highly educated children.[18]

The labor-market implications of rising levels of education, particularly for women, influence fertility. As women become more educated, the opportunity cost of not participating in the labor market rises, leading to either fewer or later births, although the presence or absence of gender empowerment also plays a role in the participation of women in the labor force (box 4.4). While higher educational attainment (especially of females) and higher household income are both associated

BOX 4.4 The economic benefits of gender equality

Gender equality matters not only in its own right but also as an instrument for development. There is vast potential for growth, poverty reduction, and shared prosperity via improved gender equality in the labor market, which can have large impacts on productivity. Eliminating employment segregation, as an example, would increase labor productivity by as much as 3–25 percent, while equalizing access to inputs including land and fertilizers would increase agricultural output by 2.5–4 percent (World Bank 2012). Gender equality can also help minimize the growth and fiscal impacts of aging. Gender inequality generates an average cumulative income per capita loss of 14–15.4 percent in OECD countries, considering both men and women (Cuberes and Teignier 2015). In developing countries, the average cumulative income loss is 16–17.5 percent.

Social norms and legal restrictions that largely shape the agency of women and girls are key factors underlying gender-based differences in access to opportunity. For instance, traditional roles and associated time-use patterns constrain women's economic opportunities: housework, childrearing, and elderly care are often considered primarily women's responsibility. In 2013, 128 countries had at least one legal difference between men and women, ranging from barriers to women obtaining official identification cards to restrictions on owning or using property, establishing creditworthiness, and getting a job (Klugman 2014; Klugman et al. 2014). In addition, limitations in women's and girls' agency are often explained by other disadvantages, particularly in access to education.

Addressing social norms will thus be critical to development progress. Such effort would entail both enhancing the aspirations of girls and women and changing the behavior of men and boys. Progressive constitutions and legal reforms can support the transformation of social norms surrounding agency. Increased awareness of such regulations has stimulated changes in norms and behaviors, for instance those regarding gender-based violence. Social protection and education both play major roles for women's agency. Expanding women's economic opportunities has potentially the largest positive effect for women's agency. For example, in addition to its economic benefits, Uganda's Empowerment and Livelihoods for Adolescents program, which offers girls soft skills and vocational training, has shown positive implications for the control participants exert over their sexual and reproductive health rights (Klugman et al. 2014).

A range of specific measures could help address prevailing gender gaps in economic opportunity throughout the life cycle. For children and youth, policy actions should focus on gender-specific constraints to schooling and boosting noncognitive and vocational skills. During the productive years, active labor market policies that combine training, placement, and other support to enable women to enter or reenter the workforce can increase their employment and earnings in the formal sector. Expanding access to formal child care and elder care services, and removing discrimination and disincentives in laws can also help promote female labor market inclusion in higher productivity areas. In older years, policy actions should support equitable old-age labor regulations combined with appropriate social protection (World Bank 2012). Improving women's financial access by making it easier to open accounts and obtain lines of credit would also benefit growth (Sahay et al. 2015).

FIGURE 4.17 Rising educational attainment has had the greatest impact on a fertility rates

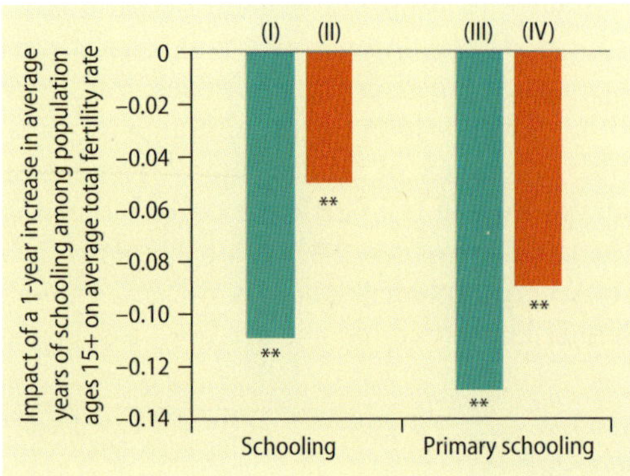

Source: Murtin 2013.
Note: Results are based on Murtin (2013) using a system GMM estimator. The estimations use long-distance lags of explanatory variables as instruments and also account for time persistence. Models I and III use lags for the birth rate while models II and IV use lags for the birth and infant mortality rates. All specifications control for lag of fertility**. Other covariates (secondary and tertiary schooling, infant mortality, death rate, and GDP per working-age adult) are not statistically significant for all specifications. ** = significant at 5 percent.

FIGURE 4.18 B40 households have higher rates of teenage parents than T60 households

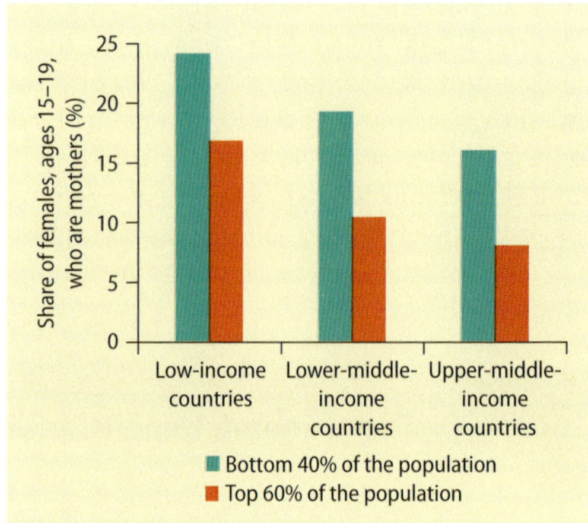

Source: World Bank calculations, based on data from Demographic and Health Surveys. See appendix C.2 for additional details.
Note: Data for B40 refers to households in the bottom 40 percent of the wealth distribution, while T60 refers to households in the top 60 of the wealth distribution.

with declines in fertility, the importance of education (particularly primary education) in affecting fertility seems to be more robust in analyses that aim to identify a causal relationship between fertility and education (figure 4.17). In regions that lag in the access to and the quality of education, and also to human development outcomes, improvements in education could be especially imporant for demographic transition.[19]

Increasing the educational attainment of girls also reduces fertility rates by increasing the age of marriage and first birth. First, more highly educated girls marry later and have lower fertility. Second, higher educational enrollment rates may increase the opportunity cost of children for household work and thereby reduce the desire for large families. Improvements in female education are positively associated with lower rates of teenage pregnancy. B40 households, which tend to have lower female educational attainment than T60 households, are also seen to have higher rates of teenage parents (figure 4.18). Higher education also increases the opportunity cost of having a child due to the potential for income from work, and so there is a delay in the first birth and marriage. A delay in the age at first birth has the effect of reducing lifetime fertility. Women living in households in the top 60 percent of the income distribution tend to have a higher median age at first birth than households in the bottom 40 percent (figure 4.19). Delaying the age at first birth also has immediate benefits beyond reducing fertility rates, such as improving maternal health (U.S. National Research Council 1989). Child marriage, in particular, can lead to substantially higher fertility (box 4.5).

Family planning and the availability of contraception vary across countries and across the income distribution but do influence fertility rates. Generally, policies that facilitate gender empowerment and reproductive health also empower households to make their own decisions regarding number of children. Relevant policies include stronger reproductive rights and ensuring adequate access to reproductive health, which can reduce the unmet need for family planning (UN 2014). Successful interventions that include the whole community, including men and community leaders, can change gender norms and support the sexual health and rights of girls and women (Klugman

FIGURE 4.19 Females in B40 households tend to have children at a younger age than those in T60 households

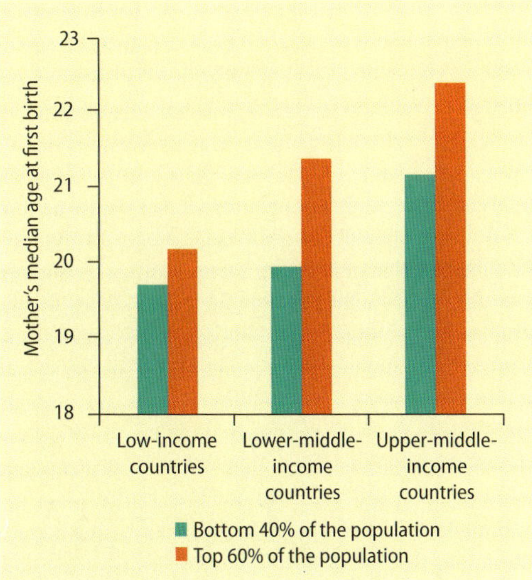

Source: World Bank calculations, based on data from Demographic and Health Surveys. See appendix C.2 for additional details.
Note: Data for B40 refers to households in the bottom 40 percent of the wealth distribution, while T60 refers to households in the top 60 of the wealth distribution.

et al. 2014; Azevedo et al. 2012). Numerous other policies that play a critical role in economic development have the added benefit of also being closely associated with falling fertility rates. For example, family planning programs alone may reduce fertility by around 0.5 to 1 birth per woman (Miller et al. 2014). Poor households, however, not only have higher fertility rates but also tend to have less access to contraceptives (figures 4.20 and 4.21). This relatively lower access to contraceptives and contraceptive methods could thus be a possible explanation for the higher rates of unplanned children in B40 households relative to T60 households, suggesting that they may have less ability to take action to implement their reproductive decisions.

Spatial contrasts drive migration

Migration, which can change age structure and population growth substantially, is driven by a range of "push" and "pull" factors. Push factors include incentives that encourage migration away from a given place (be it a country or subnational region), while pull factors are those that encourage migration to a given place. Push and pull factors include economic inequalities (differences in wages, employment prospects, or access to services) and inequalities defined more broadly (such as differences regarding security from physical harm, violation of human rights, and limitations on religious or

BOX 4.5 Economic and demographic impact of child marriage

Child marriage, defined as marrying before the age of 18, is a practice that affects mostly girls and often leads to violations of human rights for the girls who have to marry early. UNICEF (2014) estimates that over the next decade 140 million girls will marry early. Analysis of child marriage trends suggests that child marriage is declining, albeit only slowly. In 30 years the incidence of child marriage fell by only 11 percentage points, and the incidence is still high in several countries (figure B4.5.1).

Child marriage has a wide range of negative impacts on the girls who marry early, their children, communities, and society as a whole. First, child marriage and pregnancies account for a fifth of dropouts among girls in secondary schools. Each additional year of delay in the age of marriage increases schooling by 0.22 years and the likelihood of literacy by 5.6 percentage points, suggesting that reducing child marriage could have a significant impact, particularly in Africa (Field and Ambrus 2008; Lloyd and Mensch 2008; Nguyen and Wodon 2015).

Ending child marriage could result in substantially lower fertility rates for women. This, in turn, would have a large effect on demographic patterns

(box continues next page)

BOX 4.5 Economic and demographic impact of child marriage (continued)

FIGURE B4.5.1 In some developing countries, women in rural areas still tend to marry in their teens

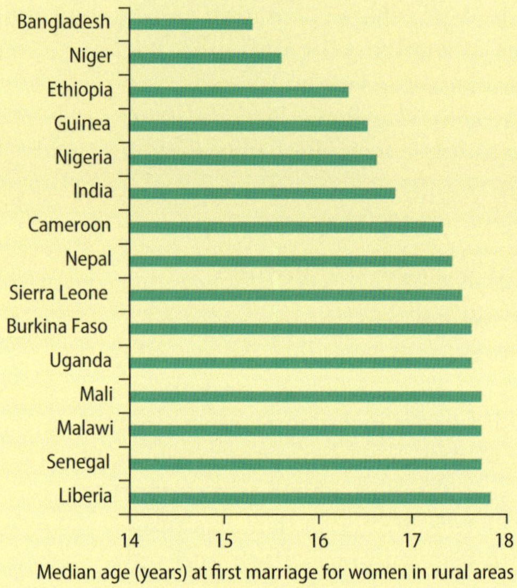

Source: World Bank calculations, based on data from Demographic and Health Surveys.
Note: The age of first marriage is based on the response provided by women ages 25 to 49 when interviewed.

and thereby on income growth. In countries with a high incidence of child marriage such as Niger, ending the practice would increase growth in gross domestic product per capita by 0.25–0.35 percentage points each year until at least 2030, thereby contributing to faster reductions in extreme poverty. Through its impact on education and fertility rates, ending child marriage could increase labor force participation and earnings for women, thereby further contributing to the reduction of extreme poverty through the generation of higher incomes for households.

The elimination of child marriage would also have strong intergenerational effects, through a reduction in child mortality and stunting. Lower prevalence of stunting as well as better educated mothers will in turn improve the education of children and their productivity and earnings later in life. Finally, ending child marriage will generate potentially important budget savings for governments in areas such as health and education, owing to the smaller population to be served (Nasrullah et al. 2014).

FIGURE 4.20 Fertility rates are higher in B40 households than in T60 households

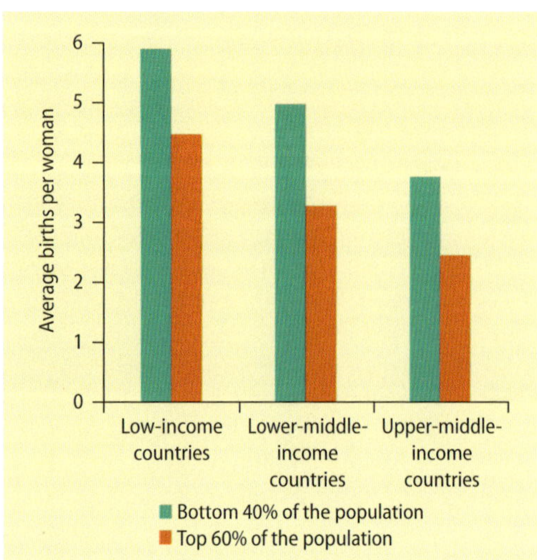

Source: World Bank calculations, based on data from Demographic and Health Surveys. See appendix C.2 for additional details.

personal freedoms) (Hansen and Spilimbergo 1999; Harris and Todaro 1970; Mayda 2010; Molho 1986).

Rural-urban migration flows can be expected to decelerate as rural-urban wage differentials diminish over time. Rural areas tend to have a surplus of labor, in that they have more workers than can be absorbed by the rural economy, as well as higher fertility rates and younger populations than urban areas. The surplus labor thus moves to urban areas where labor demand and thus wages are higher, until there is no surplus labor supply in rural areas or surplus labor demand in urban areas.[20] High-income countries went through this process in previous decades, while middle-income countries like China are experiencing it now.[21]

As migrant-sending countries develop and inequality within recipient countries declines,

FIGURE 4.21 Unmet needs for family planning are also higher in B40 households

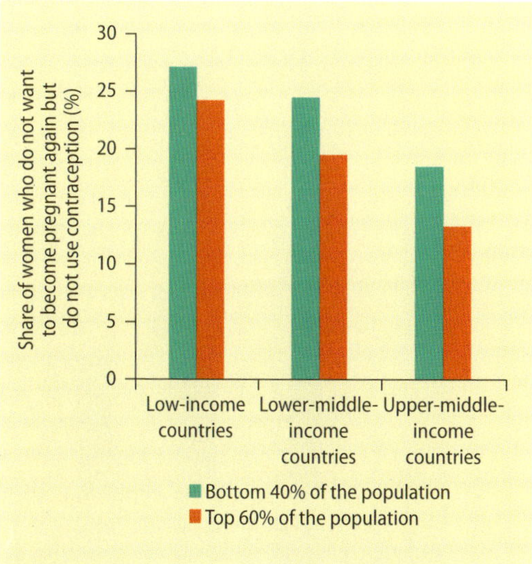

Source: World Bank calculations, based on data from Demographic and Health Surveys. See appendix C.2 for additional details.
Note: Unmet need for family planning is defined as the percentage of women who do not want to become pregnant but are not using contraception.

the economic incentives for migration could become less pronounced. High-income countries tend to be the most popular destinations for migrants, and most migrants come from developing countries (figure 4.22). The broader impact of development on migration, however, depends on the patterns of growth. If economic development does not promote employment growth, then it has the potential to exacerbate the push factors to migrate out.[22] If, on the other hand, growth in a country is on a path of eventual convergence with incomes in the high-income countries, there may be a reduction in the pull factors. In parallel, as fertility rates fall and working-age population growth slows in developing countries, push pressures for emigration might also decline.

Conflict presents another major driver of internal and international migration, with the number of forced migrants now at the highest level since World War II. Armed conflict—civil war as well as more generalized violence—can lead to migration, with people becoming refugees or asylum seekers if they are moving internationally, or internally displaced persons (IDPs) if they are moving within a country. As of 2014, there were 59.5 million forcibly displaced people in the world. Approximately two-thirds of these people were IDPs, while one-third were refugees. More than half of all refugees under the mandate of the United Nations are concentrated in only 10 countries, in descending order of refugee population size: Turkey, Pakistan, Lebanon, Islamic Republic of Iran, Ethiopia, Jordan, Kenya, Chad, Uganda, and China (UNHCR 2015). Turkey and Lebanon for example, have seen rapid increases in their refugee populations as a result of the armed conflict in the Syrian Arab Republic. Forced migration also presents a development challenge, since 90 percent of refugees are hosted in developing countries (World Bank 2014).

Conclusion

Development has a profound impact on demographic change at both the country and global level. In many countries, development has influenced the key demographic drivers of fertility, mortality, and migration. In particular, successes in infant mortality, educational attainment, poverty reduction, and gender equality have accelerated the demographic transition in many countries. These developing countries in turn have shaped the global trends. However, in Sub-Saharan Africa, continuing challenges to improving human development outcomes have left the region lagging behind the rest of the world in its demographic transition.

Demographic differences between countries are substantial, presenting tremendous scope for demography-driven spillovers as well as what is known as "chronological arbitrage." Because countries are in different stages of demographic transition, global economic integration gives them the opportunity both to take advantage of demography-driven spillovers originating in other countries and to benefit from greater globalization. Chapter 5 examines how these demographic differences are reflected in economic differences between countries and identifies the major channels for spillovers. Identifying these

FIGURE 4.22 Most migrants tend to be from developing countries but living in high-income countries

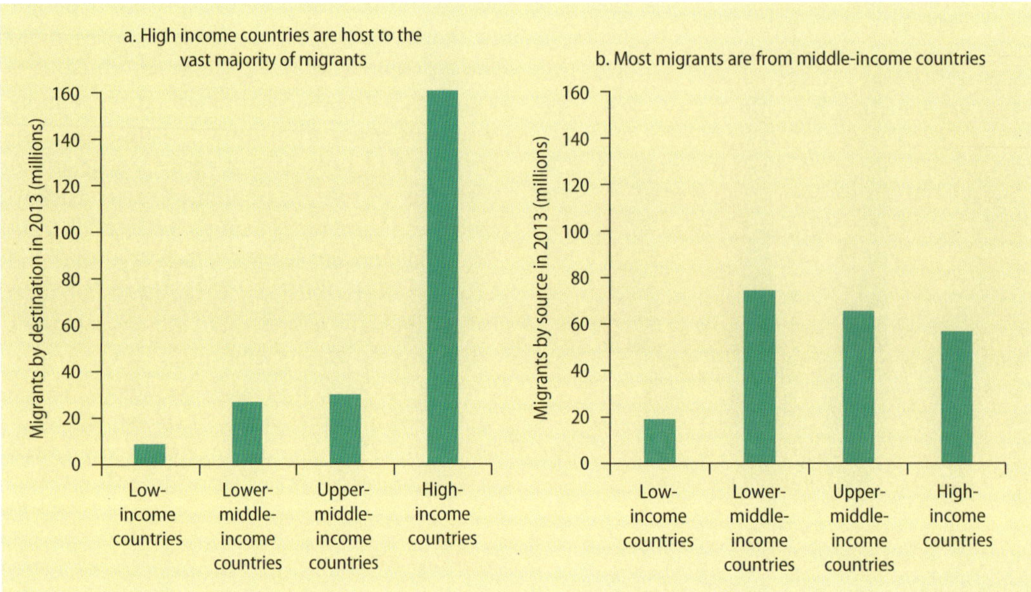

Source: World Bank calculations, based on data from UN 2013b.
Note: LIC is low-income countries, LMI is lower-middle-income countries, UMI is upper-middle-income countries, and HIC is high-income countries, following the standard World Bank Group income based classification.

channels is an important first step in harnessing these differences through chronological arbitrage, such as through trade, migration, and capital flows between countries in different demographic phases. Chapter 6 examines how chronological arbitrage through these channels could be facilitated.

Notes

1. This report considers the working-age population to be people ages 15 to 64. Recent evidence, however, suggests that in aging economies, the definition of a dependent may be changing (Sanderson and Scherbov 2010). The standard definition of the working-age population may not apply to rural, informal, or poor workers who often have to work beyond age 64 (World Bank 2015a). The issue of dependency is taken up in greater detail in chapter 5.
2. Unless specified otherwise, all population estimates and projections are based on United Nations data (UN 2015). From 2015 onward, the data are projections based on the database's medium fertility scenario. Box 4.1 explores how these global trends differ across scenarios and projection sources.
3. Unless specified otherwise, descriptions of countries as high income, upper-middle-income, lower-middle-income, low-income, or developing are based on the World Bank Group's income classification for 2016–17.
4. The total dependency ratio is commonly defined as the ratio of the dependent population, composed of children (ages 0–14) and elderly (ages 65+), to the working age population (ages 15–64).
5. Estimates of elderly dependents are subject to uncertainty arising from two sources: population projections and the definition of the age boundary for the working-age population. Unless stated otherwise, this chapter defines the working-age population as individuals ages 15–64. Other chapters consider alternative approaches.
6. The postwar increase in fertility is commonly referred to as the baby boom and was most easily recognized in the United States, peaking in the mid-1950s (Klein 2004). Other

industrial countries experienced their own baby booms at different times before the 1970s.

7. Espenshade, Guzman, and Westoff (2003) suggest that the replacement fertility rate is about 2.1 in industrial countries and can range slightly higher in developing countries where mortality rates are higher. The replacement fertility rate is the total fertility rate at which there would be no change in population size in the long run.
8. Lee (2003) provides a historical review of the health transition contributing to the demographic transition.
9. Falling mortality and infant mortality rates have a lagged impact on total fertility rates, as discussed in Reher (2011). A key factor is that as more children survive infancy and childhood, parents reduce the number of births to maintain the same number of surviving children.
10. While fertility-rates remain low in most high-income countries, there is some evidence from OECD countries that countries with high levels of human development and family-friendly policies have recently seen improvements in their fertility rates (Luci-Greulich and Thévenon 2013, 2014; Day 2012).
11. Transition economies in Europe and Central Asia are idiosyncratic in that they experienced a sharp drop in life expectancies from the 1990s until recently and a resulting increase in mortality rates (Cornia and Paniccià 2000; Kennedy, Kawachi, and Brainerd 1998; Shkolnikov et al. 1998).
12. Hervitz (1985) and Majelantle and Navaneetham (2013) provide reviews of the alternative perspectives on the impact of migration on fertility, including the idea that migration disrupts reproductive decisions, leading to lower fertility in the migrant family than in their home country.
13. The World Bank Group's high-income country grouping includes high-fertility countries like Saudi Arabia. If only high-income OECD countries were considered, the median fertility rate would be lower.
14. Guo et al. (2012) found the impact of rural-urban migration on fertility to be significant at both the national and provincial levels in China. China's implementation of the one-child policy is often discussed as being the main factor responsible for the sharp drop in fertility since the 1980s, although its fertility rates were already declining before the one-child policy was in effect.
15. NTDs refer to a group of diseases that thrive mainly among the poorest populations (WHO 2015). These diseases mainly result from four pathogens: protozoa, parasites, bacteria, and viruses.
16. The Demographic and Health Survey data used for these estimates are harmonized across countries and have extensive data on demographic and health variables. See appendix C.2 for the B40 and T60 definitions.
17. Reher (2011), Soares (2005), and Acemoglu and Johnson (2007) discuss the importance of infant mortality for fertility. The empirical literature testing the suggested three main determinants of long-term demographic transition does not converge in its conclusions, however. Murtin (2013) finds that education is more robust than infant mortality, income, and other variables in determining a fertility transition. Herzer, Strulik, and Vollmer (2012), on the other hand, suggest that mortality changes and income growth are the most important drivers of changes in fertility rate, while Angeles (2010) suggests that reductions in fertility rate are driven mostly by reductions in mortality rate.
18. This behavior would suggest that parents' elasticity of demand for quality is higher than for quantity. A large literature covers this topic, starting with Becker (1960) and Becker and Lewis (1973).
19. World Bank (2015b) argues that improvements in health, particularly child and maternal health, need to be a priority development goal and a precursor to any policy discussion regarding fertility. Improving the educational attainment of girls also helps in reducing the rate of teenage pregnancies, immediately improving health outcomes as well.
20. Lewis (1954) discussed the contribution of migration or surplus rural labor to urban areas driving growth up to a turning point

(referred to in the literature as the Lewis turning point).

21. In the case of China, reaching the Lewis turning point may also have implications for future growth since its urban manufacturing sector-led growth has benefited from the relatively low-cost labor supply from rural areas. The implications of reaching this turning point are examined more fully in Cai (2010); Das and N'Diaye (2013); and Zhang, Yang, and Whang (2011).
22. Massey (1988) provides examples of how economic development characterized by rapid structural transformation has the potential to create unemployment in rural—primarily agriculture-dependent—areas, increasing the incentives to migrate. Some of this migration reflects rural-urban movements as part of the urbanization process, but the rest reflects economic motives.

References

Acemoglu, D., and S. Johnson. 2007. "Disease and Development: The Effect of Life Expectancy on Economic Growth." *Journal of Political Economy* (115) 6: 925–85.

Andersson, G. 2004. "Childbearing after Migration: Fertility Patterns of Foreign-Born Women in Sweden." *International Migration Review* 38 (2): 747–74.

Angeles, L. 2010. "Demographic Transitions: Analyzing the Effects of Mortality on Fertility." *Journal of Population Economics: Journal of the European Society for Population Economics (ESPE)* 23 (1): 99–120.

Azevedo, J. P., M. Favara, S. E. Haddock, L. F. Lopez-Calva, M. Muller, and E. Elizaveta. 2012. *Teenage Pregnancy and Opportunities in Latin America and the Caribbean: On Teenage Fertility Decisions, Poverty and Economic Achievement*. Washington, DC: World Bank Group.

Becker, G. S. 1960. "An Economic Analysis of Fertility." In *Demographic and Economic Change in Developed Countries*. New York: Columbia University Press.

Becker, G. S., and H. G. Lewis. 1973. "On the Interaction between the Quantity and Quality of Children." *Journal of Political Economy* 81 (2): S279–S288.

Bloom, D., and J. Williamson. 1998. "Demographic Transition and Economic Miracles in Emerging Asia." *World Bank Economic Review* 12 (3): 419–56.

Bongaarts, J., and S. C. Watkins. 1996. "Social Interactions and Contemporary Fertility Transitions." *Population and Development Review* 639–82.

Bryant, J. 2007. "Theories of Fertility Decline and the Evidence from Development Indicators." *Population and Development Review* 33 (1): 101–27.

Cai, F. 2010. "Demographic Transition, Demographic Dividend, and Lewis Turning Point in China." *China Economic Journal* 3 (2): 107–19.

Chaturvedi, S., A. De Costa, and J. Raven. 2015. "Does the Janani Suraksha Yojana Cash Transfer Programme to Promote Facility Births in India Ensure Skilled Birth Attendance? A Qualitative Study of Intrapartum Care in Madhya Pradesh." *Global Health Action*, 8.

Chen, A., E. Oster, and H. Williams. 2014. "Why Is Infant Mortality Higher in the US than in Europe?" Working Paper 20525, National Bureau of Economic Research, Cambridge, MA.

Coale, A. J. 1974. "The History of Human Population." *Scientific American* 231 (3): 40–51.

Cohen, J. E. 2001. "World Population in 2050: Assessing the Projections." In *Seismic Shifts: The Economic Impact of Demographic Change*, edited by J. S. Little and R. K. Triest. Federal Reserve Bank of Boston Conference Series 46 (June).

Cornia, G. A., and R. Paniccià, eds. 2000. *The Mortality Crisis in Transitional Economies*. Oxford, UK: Oxford University Press.

Cuberes, D., and M. Teignier. 2015. "How Costly Are Labor Gender Gaps? Estimates for the Balkans and Turkey." Policy Research Working Paper 7319, World Bank, Washington, DC.

Cutler, D., A. Deaton, and A. Lleras-Muney. 2006. "The Determinants of Mortality." *Journal of Economic Perspectives* 20 (3): 97–120.

Das, M., and P. N'Diaye. 2013. *Chronicle of a Decline Foretold: Has China Reached the Lewis Turning Point?* Working Paper WP/13/26, International Monetary Fund, Washington, DC.

Day, C. 2012. "Economic Growth, Gender Wage Gap and Fertility Rebound." *Economic Record,* 88(s1), 88–99.

Espenshade, T. J., J. C. Guzman, and C. F. Westoff. 2003. "The Surprising Global Variation in Replacement Fertility." *Population Research and Policy Review* 22 (5/6): 575.

EUROSTAT. 2015. Migration and migrant population statistics. Brussels: European Commission. http://ec.europa.eu/eurostat/statistics-explained/index.php/Migration_and_migrant_population_statistics.

Field, E., and A. Ambrus. 2008. "Early Marriage, Age of Menarche, and Female Schooling Attainment in Bangladesh." *Journal of Political Economy* 116 (5): 881–930.

Fogel, R. W. 1997. "New Findings on Secular Trends in Nutrition and Mortality: Some Implications for Population Theory." *Handbook of Population and Family Economics* 1: 433–81.

Galor, O., and D. N. Weil. 1999. "From Malthusian Stagnation to Modern Growth." *American Economic Review* 89 (2): 150–54.

Galor, O., and D. N. Weil. 2000. "Population, Technology and Growth: From the Malthusian Regime to the Demographic Transition." *American Economic Review* 90 (4): 806–28.

Gerland, P., et al. 2014. "World Population Stabilization Unlikely This Century." *Science* 10 (346): 234–37.

Gragnolati, M., R. Rofman, I. Apella, and S. Troiano. 2015. *As Time Goes By in Argentina: Economic Opportunities and Challenges of the Demographic Transition.* Washington, DC: World Bank.

Guo, Z., Z. Wu, C. M. Schimmele, and S. Li. 2012. "The Effect of Urbanization on China's Fertility." *Population Research and Policy Review* 31 (3): 417–34.

Hanson, G. H., and A. Spilimbergo. 1999. "Illegal Immigration, Border Enforcement, and Relative Wages: Evidence from Apprehensions at the U.S.–Mexico Border." *American Economic Review.* 89 (05): 1337–57.

Harris, J. R., and M. P. Todaro. 1970. "Migration, Unemployment and Development: A Two-Sector Analysis." *American Economic Review* 60 (1): 126–42.

Hervitz, H. M. 1985. "Selectivity, Adaptation, or Disruption? A Comparison of Alternative Hypotheses on the Effects on Fertility: The Case of Brazil." *International Migration Review* 19 (2): 293–317.

Herzer, D., H. Strulik, and S. Vollmer. 2012. "The Long-Run Determinants of Fertility: One Century of Demographic Change, 1900–1999." *Journal of Economic Growth.* 17 (4): 357–85.

Jaffe, A. J. 1942. "Urbanization and Fertility." *American Journal of Sociology:* 48–60.

Kahn, J. 1988. "Immigrant Selectivity and Fertility Adaptation in the United States." *Social Forces* 67 (1): 108–28.

Kennedy, B. P., I. Kawachi, and E. Brainerd. 1998. "The Role of Social Capital in the Russian Mortality Crisis." *World Development* 26 (11): 2029–43.

Klein, H. S. 2004. *A Population History of the United States.* New York: Cambridge University Press.

Klugman, J. 2014. "Women's Health and Human Rights: Public Spending on Health and the Military One Decade after the African Women's Protocol: Focus: Sexual and Reproductive Health Rights and the African Women's Protocol." *African Human Rights Law Journal.* 14 (2): 705–34.

Klugman, J., L. Hanmer, S. Twigg, T. Hasan, J. McCleary-Sills, and J. Santamaria. 2014. *Voice and Agency: Empowering Women and Girls for Shared Prosperity.* Washington, DC: World Bank.

Kuznets, S. 1974. "Rural-Urban Differences in Fertility: An International Comparison." *Proceedings of the American Philosophical Society* 118 (1): 1–29.

Lee, R. 2003. "The Demographic Transition: Three Centuries of Fundamental Change." *Journal of Economic Perspectives* 17 (4): 167–90.

Lewis, W. A. 1954. "Economic Development with Unlimited Supplies of Labor." *Manchester School of Economic and Social Studies* 22: 139–91.

Lloyd, C. B., and B. S. Mensch. 2008. "Marriage and Childbirth as Factors in Dropping Out from School: An Analysis of DHS Data from Sub-Saharan Africa." *Population Studies* 62 (1): 1–13.

Luci-Greulich, A., and O. Thévenon. 2013. The impact of family policies on fertility trends in developed countries. *European Journal of Population/Revue européenne de Démographie, 29*(4), 387–416.

Luci-Greulich, A., and O. Thévenon. 2014. Does economic advancement 'Cause' a re-increase in fertility? An empirical analysis for OECD countries (1960–2007). *European Journal of Population, 30*(2), 187–221.

Lutz, W., A. Goujon, S. KC, and W. Sanderson. 2007. "Reconstruction of Populations by Age, Sex and Level of Educational Attainment for 120 Countries for 1970–2000." *Vienna Yearbook of Population Research*: 193–235.

Lutz, W., and S. KC. 2010. "Dimensions of Global Population Projections: What Do We Know about Future Population Trends and Structures?" *Philosophical Transactions of the Royal Society B: Biological Sciences* 365 (1554): 2779–91.

Lutz, W., W. Sanderson, and S. Scherbov. 2001. "The End of World Population Growth." *Nature* 412 (2): 543–45.

MacDorman M. F., T. J. Matthews, A. D. Mohangoo, and J. Zeitlin. 2014. "International Comparisons of Infant Mortality and Related Factors: United States and Europe, 2010." *National Vital Statistics Reports (CDC)* 63 (5): 1–6.

Majelantle, R. G., and K. Navaneetham. 2013. "Migration and Fertility: A Review of Theories and Evidences." *Journal of Global Economy* 1 (101): 1–3.

Massey, D. S. 1988. "Economic Development and International Migration in Comparative Perspective." *Population and Development Review* 14 (3): 383–413.

Mayda, A. M. 2010. "International Migration: A Panel Data Analysis of the Determinants of Bilateral Flows." *Journal of Population Economics* 23: 1249–1274.

Meara, E. R., S. Richards, and D. M. Cutler. 2008. "The Gap Gets Bigger: Changes in Mortality and Life Expectancy, by Education, 1981–2000." *Health Affairs* 27 (2): 350–60.

Miller E., H. L. McCauley, D. J. Tancredi, M. R. Decker, H. Anderson, and J. G. Silverman. 2014. "Recent Reproductive Coercion and Unintended Pregnancy among Female Family Planning Clients." *Contraception* 89 (2): 122–28.

Molho, I. 1986. "Theories of Migration: A Review." *Scottish Journal of Political Economy* 33 (4): 526-556.

Moultrie, T. 2015. "Demographic Profiles of Five Countries in Southern Africa and Implications for the Demographic Dividend." Background paper for the World Bank's Programmatic Economic and Sector Work "Demographics in Southern Africa," forthcoming.

Murtin, F. 2013. "Long-Term Determinants of the Demographic Transition, 1870–2000." *Review of Economics and Statistics* 95 (2): 617–31.

Myrskylä, M., H. P. Kohler, and F. C. Billari. 2009. "Advances in Development Reverse Fertility Declines." *Nature 460* (7256): 741–43.

Nair, S. P. 2010. "Population Aging in Botswana: Trends and Prospects." *Journal of African Studies and Development* 7 (2): 1–12.

Nasrullah, M., S. Muazzam, Z. A. Bhutta, and A. Raj. 2014. "Girl Child Marriage and Its Effect on Fertility in Pakistan: Findings from Pakistan Demographic and Health Survey, 2006–2007." *Maternal and Child Health Journal 18* (3): 534–43.

Nguyen, M. C., and Q. Wodon. 2015. "Early Marriage, Pregnancies, and the Gender Gap in Education Attainment: An Analysis Based on the Reasons for Dropping out of School." In *Child Marriage and Education in sub-Saharan Africa*, edited by Q. Wodon. Washington, DC: World Bank.

Reher, D. S. 2011. "Economic and Social Implications of the Demographic Transition." *Population and Development Review* 37 (Supplement): 11–33.

Sahay, R., M. Čihák, P. N'Diaye, A. Barajas, R. Bi, D. Ayala, Y. Gao, A. Kyobe, L. Nguyen, C. Saborowski, K. Svirydzenka, and S. R. Yousefi. 2015. "Rethinking Financial Deepening: Stability and Growth in Emerging Markets." IMF Staff Discussion Note 15/08, May, International Monetary Fund, Washington, DC.

Sanderson, W. C., and S. Scherbov. 2010. "Remeasuring Aging." *Science* 329 (5997): 1287–88.

Shkolnikov, V. M., G. A. Cornia, D. A. Leon, and F. Meslé. 1998. "Causes of the Russian Mortality Crisis: Evidence and Interpretations." *World Development* 26 (11): 1995–2011.

Soares, R. 2005. "Mortality Reductions, Educational Attainment, and Fertility Choice." *American Economic Review* 95 (3): 580–601.

Sobotka, T. 2008. "The Rising Importance of Migrants for Childbearing in Europe." *Demographic Research* 19 (9): 225–48.

Szreter, S. 1993. "The Idea of Demographic Transition and the Study of Fertility Change: A Critical Intellectual History." *Population and Development Review* 19 (4): 659–701.

UN (United Nations). 2013a. *International Migration Report 2013*. New York: United Nations, Department of Economic and Social Affairs, Population Division.

———. 2013b. "Trends in international migrant stock: Migrants by destination and origin." United Nations database, POP/DB/MIG/Stock/Rev.2013, Department of Economic and Social Affairs.

———. 2014. *World Contraceptive Use 2014*. New York: United Nations.

———. 2015. *World Population Prospects: The 2015 Revision, DVD Edition*, New York: United Nations, Department of Economic and Social Affairs, Population Division.

UN (United Nations) and UNICEF (United Nations Children's Fund). 2014. *Migration Profiles—Common Set of Indicators*. New York: United Nations. http://esa.un.org/MigGMGProfiles/MPCSI.htm (June 26, 2015).

UNHCR (United Nations High Commissioner for Refugees). 2015. *Global Trends: Forced Displacement in 2014*. Geneva: UNHCR.

UNICEF (United Nations Children's Fund). 2014. Ending Child Marriage: Progress and Prospects. New York: United Nations. http://www.unicef.org/media/files/Child_Marriage_Report_7_17_LR.pdf (June 26, 2015).

U.S. National Research Council. 1989. *Contraception and Reproduction: Health Consequences for Women and Children in the Developing World*. Washington, DC: National Academies Press.

Waldron, H. 2007. "Trends in Mortality Differentials and Life Expectancy for Male Social 382 Security-Covered Workers, by Socioeconomic Status." *Social Security Bulletin* 67 (3): 1–28.

Wang, H., L. Dwyer-Lindgren, K. T. Lofgren, J. K. Rajaratnam, J. R. Marcus, A. Levin-Rector, and C. J. Murray. 2013. "Age-Specific and Sex-Specific Mortality in 187 Countries, 1970–2010: A Systematic Analysis for the Global Burden of Disease Study 2010." *The Lancet*, 380 (9859): 2071–94.

Wilmoth, J. 2015. "Global Demographic Projections: Future Trajectories and Associated Uncertainty." Presentation (PPT) delivered at a Seminar of the Global Knowledge Partnership on Migration and Development, March 4, 2015.

World Bank. 1984 *World Development Report 1984*. Washington, DC: World Bank.

———. 1994 *World Population Projections*. Washington, DC: World Bank.

———. 2012. *World Development Report: Gender Equality and Development*. Washington, DC: World Bank.

———. 2013. *Mitigating the Economic Impact of an Aging Population: Options for Bulgaria*. Washington, DC: World Bank.

———. 2014. "Migration and Remittances: Recent Developments and Outlook; Special Topic: Forced Migration." Migration and Development Brief 23. Washington, DC: World Bank.

———. 015a. *Live Long and Prosper: Aging in East Asia and Pacific*. World Bank, Washington DC.

———. 2015b. *From Potential to Reality: What Will It Take to Harness a Demographic Dividend in Africa?* Washington DC: World Bank.

WHO (World Health Organization). 2015. *Investing to Overcome the Global Impact of Neglected Tropical Diseases*. Geneva: WHO.

Zhang, X., J. Yang, and S. Wang. 2011. "China Has Reached the Lewis Turning Point." http://dx.doi.org/10.1016/j.chieco.2011.07.002.

5

Implications of Demographic Change: Pathways to Prosperity

Changing age structures of populations are shaping the trajectories of development in many countries, bringing both opportunities and challenges. Rapid population growth is set to continue in the poorest countries over the coming decades, raising the share of the population that is working-age and bringing strong potential to boost growth and poverty reduction. The challenge in these centers of global poverty lies in improving human development outcomes and job creation. In contrast, countries with low fertility rates, including most high-income countries, have aging population structures. Together with opportunities to consolidate development gains, these engines of global growth are increasingly facing challenges associated with aging, including the importance of ensuring fiscal sustainability to support a growing pool of elderly.

Development opportunities and challenges stemming from demographic change vary with country circumstances. Countries with high fertility rates and low life expectancy tend to have relatively young populations with rising proportions of working-age people (between 15 and 64 years of age). However, these countries tend to have high poverty rates and face the challenge of providing services for their growing populations and ensuring productive employment for their expanding labor force. In countries where fertility rates have been below replacement level since at least the 1980s, life expectancy is typically high, and the elderly account for increasing proportions of their populations. These countries face the challenge of meeting the increasing demand for pension and health care services, while their overall economic growth may be slowing.

The world can be currently classified into four types of countries when viewed through the lens of demographic characteristics and future development potential. In the first group are high-fertility countries that are lagging in many key human development indicators. These are all low-income countries. In the second group are mostly low- and lower-middle-income countries where fertility rates have started falling recently and where changes in age structure offer tremendous opportunity for growth in the foreseeable future. The third group comprises mostly upper-middle-income countries that experienced rapid fertility declines in the 1960s, and where working-age people will be a shrinking share of the population in the coming decade. The last group is made up of mostly high-income countries that have some of the highest shares of elderly in the world and fertility rates that have been below replacement level since at least the 1980s (appendix C.3 discusses the typography in more detail).

Demographic change can boost prosperity when a greater proportion of the population is working and saving. Countries where the share of the working-age population is still rising can benefit from more workers and savers. To capitalize on these opportunities, however, policies and institutions need to be in place related to the domestic and external channels through which demography affects development. These policies relate to labor markets, human capital, savings and investment, and transfers supporting the dependent population (box 5.1).

Shifts in the population age structure can have welfare implications since the demand for public services and the patterns

BOX 5.1 Changing concepts of dependency

The total dependency ratio (TDR) is the ratio of the dependent population (children and elderly) to the working-age population that supports total consumption (working-age).

For purposes of international comparability, the working-age population is commonly defined as those aged 15–64. However, these age thresholds do not necessarily capture variations across time and regions on child-labor practices, time in school, or labor supply at older ages. For example, child labor was a common practice in the initial stage of industrialization in Europe and is still present in several developing countries (Cunningham and Viazzo 1996). Also, accumulating evidence casts doubts on a mechanical link between chronological age and the dependency rate for the elderly, and labor supply at older ages varies widely, in part reflecting the availability of public pensions and their incentive structures (Börsch-Supan 2013). Moreover, the 15–64 definition of the working-age does not necessarily identify the age cohorts that effectively support total consumption.

An alternative approach to defining the dependent population considers the age span when people do not earn enough to meet their material needs. This approach offers a more accurate measure of the share of the population that needs support to fund their consumption. It is also useful in shaping public policies, because it takes into account public transfers (such as spending on health and education). A new set of economic accounts, called National Transfer Accounts (NTAs), provides comprehensive information about how those at every age acquire and use economic resources to meet their material needs, to provide for the future, and to support others through public and private institutions (Lee and Mason 2011; UN 2013). To date these accounts have been constructed for about 40 countries.

The NTAs quantify the economic life-cycle pattern using consumption and labor income at each age. Results suggest that the ages at which people earn more through their labor than they consume varies greatly depending on economic conditions and public policy. In both high- and low-income countries, the earnings surplus begins at age 26 and ends at age 59, on average—a much shorter span than the traditional 15–64 age span (figure B5.1.1). Moreover, the extent to which those under 26 or over 59 are supporting themselves through their labor is highly variable. Consumption includes both private and public consumption. Labor income includes the earning of employees, the self-employed, and estimates of the value of labor of unpaid family workers.

The NTA-based approach suggests that rich, low-fertility countries differ from poor, high-fertility countries in four important ways:

- Children in rich countries have higher consumption than children in poor countries, even after controlling for differences in levels of income. The consumption values shown in figure B5.1.1 include public and private spending on health and education, which accounts for a substantial portion of the consumption advantage of children in rich, low-fertility countries.
- The elderly in rich countries consume more than they do in poor countries. In rich countries, consumption patterns are driven noticeably higher at

(box continues next page)

BOX 5.1 Changing concepts of dependency (continued)

FIGURE B5.1.1 Consumption and labor income by age for high and low-income countries

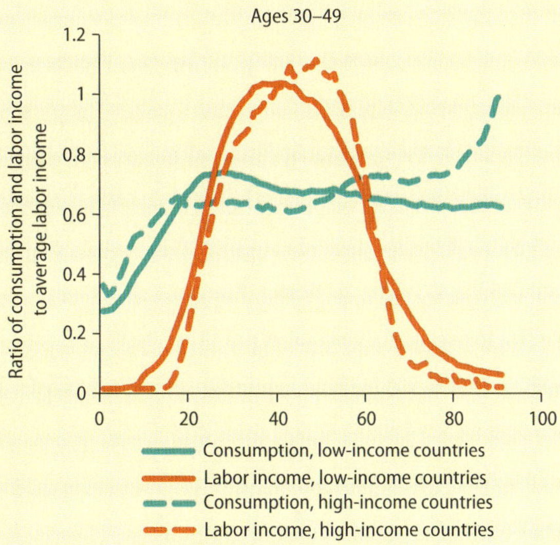

Source: National Transfer Accounts.
Note: All values are expressed relative to the average per capita labor income of persons 30–49 years of age to facilitate comparison across countries. Low-income and high-income values are based on the bottom and top quintile of NTA countries based on per capita GDP. Low-income countries: Cambodia, Ethiopia, Ghana, India, Kenya, Mozambique, Senegal, and Vietnam. High-income countries: Australia, Austria, Canada, Finland, Germany, Japan, Sweden, and the United States. All values are for a year ranging from 2003 to 2009.

older ages because of rising spending on health care. In poor countries, consumption does not turn up at older ages. Consumption among adults is much flatter in low-income countries, and the elderly consume less than do prime-age adults.

- Labor income is more highly concentrated in rich countries, with later entry to and earlier departure from the labor force. In low-income countries, labor income is noticeably higher among children and the elderly. The differences, however, are not as great as expected. Employment opportunities for teens and young adults in many low-income countries are quite limited. In addition, the elderly in low-income countries are much more likely to be in the labor force but often in very low-productivity jobs.
- The gaps between consumption and labor income for the young and elderly are substantially greater in high-income countries than in low-income countries. Dependents are more costly in high-income countries because they consume more and earn less than in low-income countries, which leads to higher life-cycle deficits. The better health of the elderly in higher-income countries does not cause them to work more or to spend less on health care than the elderly in low-income countries.

of consumption vary dramatically across a person's life. Shifting age structures can create imbalances between the resources of working-age people, for whom labor income typically exceeds consumption, and the young and old, who often produce less than they consume. The magnitude of these imbalances depends not only on demography but also on the institutions and mechanisms societies rely on to intermediate resources to the young and the old, including through family ties, government provision of services, and financial markets.

Building on the global demographic trends and the country-level differences discussed in chapter 4, this chapter examines the links between demography to development. It presents a demographic typology that classifies countries into four categories based on their fertility rates and working-age population shares. It then discusses the economic and development challenges that countries in each of the four groups face, with a particular focus on poverty and aging populations. The analysis illustrates that development progress varies with key demographic characteristics. Finally, the chapter examines how demographics impact economic growth, the achievement of development goals, and the nature of public transfers.

From demography to development: A global typology

Demographic characteristics can help or hinder economic activity, so understanding a country's demographic trends offers insight to its development prospects. Changes in the working-age share of the population can affect growth and savings and, subsequently, income per capita. For example, rising working-age population shares could lead to proportionally more income earners in the economy and thus greater growth per capita. Changes in the age structure also affect the resource constraints faced by households and the state for social spending, with potential second-order effects. For example, if households have fewer children, they would have more resources to spend on human capital and consumption. In contrast, if the share of the aging is increasing, there would not only be fewer potential workers but also higher demand for some services like health care. The exact impact of the demographic change depends on how the age-structure is changing. A typology based on the channels of impact and demographic trends can thus be used to characterize a country's development potential.

Demographic trends can produce two types of dividends

The development impact of changes in age structure occur through two mechanisms and can be classified as either a first or a second demographic dividend (Lee and Mason 2006). The first dividend is a direct and immediate consequence of the rise in the working-age share of the population. If a larger share of the population is working, average standards of living will be higher.[1] The potential benefits for poverty reduction are twofold. First, in low-income households that reduce their fertility, standards of living will rise by increasing the number of effective producers per household member. Second, improvements in public finances resulting from an increase in the number of workers in the economy will allow more resources to be devoted to low-income households. The second dividend arises when faster growth of the working-age population leads to greater savings in the short run and higher investment in human capital and investment per worker in the long run.

The first demographic dividend could persist for decades but is ultimately transitory. As fertility rates decline, child-dependency ratios fall both within households and within a population, while the share of the working-age population rises and remains high for a few generations. If the increasingly larger working-age population is productively employed, there is potential for an increase in economywide living standards. The first dividend is in large part a consequence of a given (growing) labor force supporting fewer children. For some countries, estimates suggest that the contribution of the first demographic dividend explains 9.2–15.5 percent of their per capita economic growth over the 1960–2000 period (Mason and Kinugasa 2008).

The second demographic dividend arises if changes in age structure create space for higher savings and lead to increased investment in human and physical capital. An increase in the share of workers in the economy with respect to the total population leads to higher production and more resources available in the economy, which at the same time can facilitate an increase in savings, investment, and accumulation of physical and human capital. These decisions subsequently influence the productivity of the workforce. Providing capital for a growing labor force is costly, and as labor force growth declines, a given level of investment will lead to greater capital per worker. Demographic change pushes countries toward supplying more capital, further enhancing labor productivity (Birdsall, Kelley, and Sinding 2003). Because personal assets accumulate over the lifetime of individuals, per capita household wealth rises as a population ages. Moreover, gains in life expectancy have led to an extended period of retirement, providing a powerful incentive to accumulate assets in countries where the elderly rely on funded pensions and other assets to support at least part of their old-age needs.

Countries that are too early in the demographic transition face challenges to activating the first demographic dividend, while countries late in the transition face challenges in sustaining the second dividend. Where total fertility rates are high, the child-dependency ratio will likely be too high and the working-age population share too low to realize the first demographic dividend, as in the case of some high-fertility, low-income countries. In contrast, countries with rapidly shrinking working-age population shares face the challenge of maintaining the pace of physical and human capital accumulation needed to maintain labor productivity growth. In such countries—as in many low-fertility, high-income countries today—demographic conditions can strain public services, especially health and pension.

Trends and potential form basis of a new typology

Viewed through the lens of demography, the world has four types of countries, each type with measures it can take to maximize future economic potential (map 5.1).[2] *Pre-dividend countries* lag in key human development indicators and have fertility rates greater than four births per woman. Their high dependency ratios are expected to decline as the fertility transition proceeds. *Early-dividend countries* have progressed further in the fertility transition, with fertility rates below four births per woman and the working-age share in the population likely to rise considerably in the future. Priorities for these countries are realizing the first demographic dividend and laying the groundwork for the second dividend. *Late-dividend countries* have shrinking working-age shares, but their overall age structures are still favorable for the first demographic dividend. However, they may experience rapid aging in coming decades, so realizing the second dividend is key. Finally, *post-dividend* countries are those where fertility transitioned below replacement levels three decades ago and that have shrinking working-age population shares and high shares of elderly. They are too late in the transition to gain additional benefits from the first demographic dividend but could still be realizing the second dividend.

MAP 5.1 World through the lens of the demographic typology

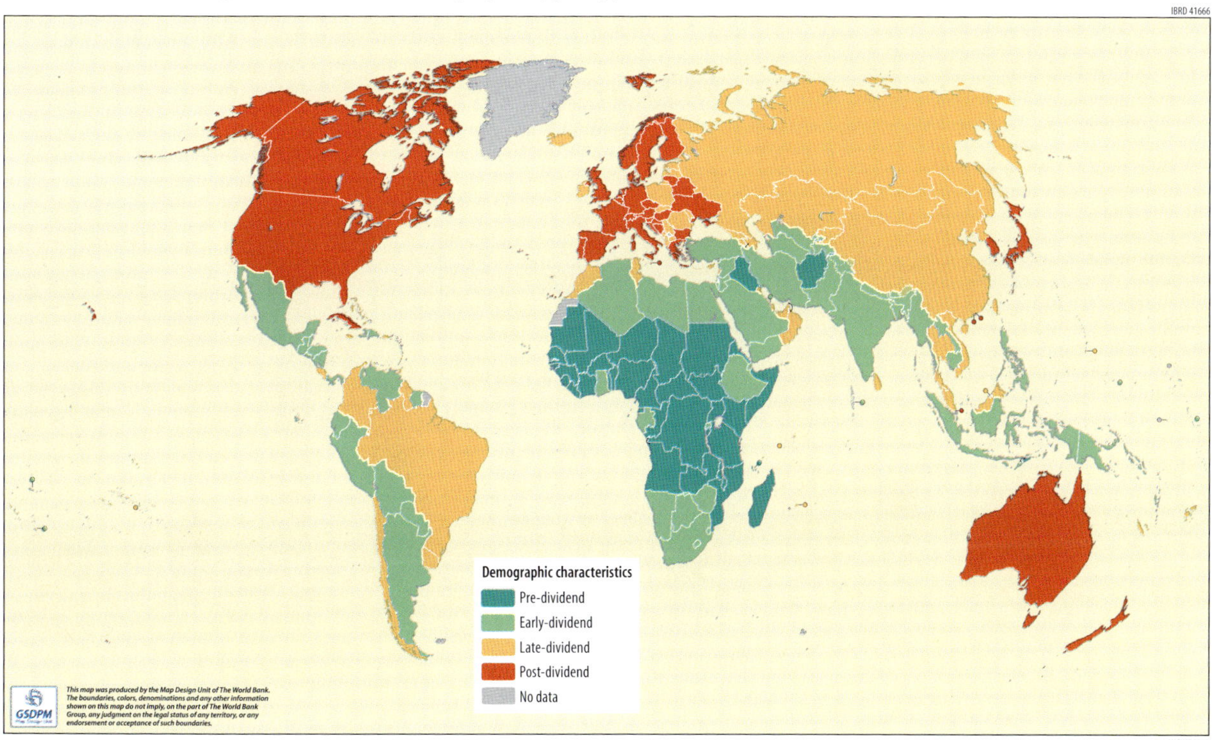

Source: World Bank calculations, based on data from UN 2015.

FIGURE 5.1 The different demographic country types correspond to countries in different stages of demographic transition

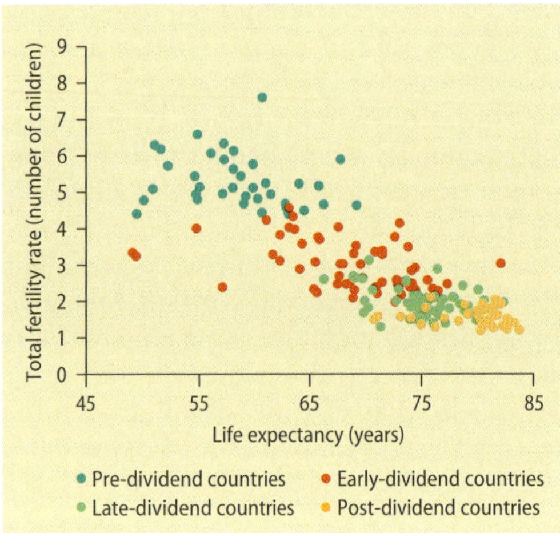

Source: World Bank calculations, based on data from UN 2015.
Note: The total fertility rate is the average number of births a woman in a given country has, assuming she lives to the end of her reproductive life. Details on the typology can be found in appendix C.3.

The demographic typology reflects the different stages of demographic transition. The first demographic indicator considered in the typology, fertility rate, is a main determinant of demographic transition (see chapter 4). At the start of demographic transition, countries typically have high fertility and mortality rates. As transition proceeds, the mortality rate begins to decline while the fertility rate remains high, resulting in rising life expectancy. Later, the birth rate begins to decline as well, until finally fertility and mortality rates both level off at low rates. Indeed, the pre-dividend countries have the low life expectancy and high fertility rates of countries of the early stages of demographic transition, post-dividend countries have the high life expectancy and low fertility of countries in the final stages of demographic transition, and early- and late-dividend countries lie somewhere in between (figure 5.1). The second indicator considered in the demographic typology developed in this report, working-age population share, is an outcome of demographic transition and the conceptual basis of the demographic dividend model.

More than half of the global population lives in pre- and early-dividend countries, and more than a third lives in late-dividend countries (figure 5.2). Interestingly, most of

FIGURE 5.2 Income level is correlated with the stage of demographic transition

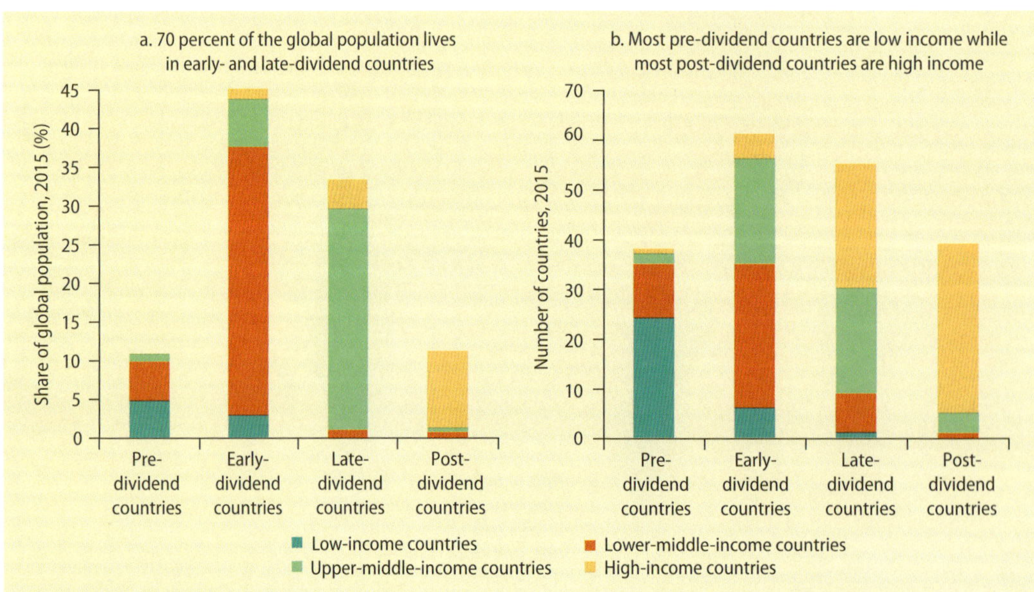

Source: World Bank calculations, based on data from UN 2015.
Note: See appendix C.5 for the World Bank Group classifications of country groupings.

the early-dividend population lives in lower-middle-income countries, which includes Bangladesh and India. Similarly, most of the late-dividend population lives in upper-middle-income countries, which include China. Pre-dividend countries, which account for less than 11 percent of the global population, are mostly low-income countries and are mostly in Sub-Saharan Africa. Post-dividend countries, accounting for another 11 percent of the global population, are predominantly high-income countries, mostly in North America and Europe.

Pre-dividend countries will account for most of the global population growth through 2050. The fertility rates of pre-dividend countries will remain above replacement for several decades, leading to rapid population growth and slower changes in age structure. By definition, the total fertility rate of pre-dividend countries is currently above four. The rate is falling only slowly in the countries in this group, and their younger age cohorts will continue to swell in the coming decades. As a result, the population of this group of countries will grow by 49 percent (or 413 million people) by 2030 and by 132 percent (or 1.1 billion people) by 2050. Children as a share of the population will remain above 40 percent until 2030 and above 34 percent until 2050.

Challenging starting points

Cross-country differences in development are reflected by differences in demographics. As figure 5.2 suggests, poorer countries tend to be earlier in their demographic transition, while richer countries tend to be further along. Pre- and early-dividend countries are earlier in their demographic transition and they tend to perform poorly in several development indicators, including the poverty headcount rate. At the same time, late- and post-dividend countries tend to be richer, have larger economies, and are currently major sources of global economic activity. This section describes development progress and then the distribution of economic activity across the different demographic-types.

Poverty persists in pre- and early-dividend countries

About 87 percent of the world's poor live in pre- and early-dividend countries (figure 5.3). Pre-dividend countries, where 44 percent of the population lives below the poverty line on average, account for 37 percent of the global poor. Early-dividend countries have a much lower poverty rate of 16 percent but account for 50 percent of the global poor, largely because this group includes Bangladesh and India, which together are home to 33 percent of the world's poor. The late-dividend group of countries has an average poverty headcount of only 3 percent, but one member of this group, China, accounts for almost 10 percent of global poverty.

The pre- and early-dividend countries with the highest poverty rates also face extremely fast population growth, with populations expected to double in coming decades. The five countries expected to have the most rapid population growth between 2015 and 2050

FIGURE 5.3 Pre- and early-dividend countries account for most global poverty

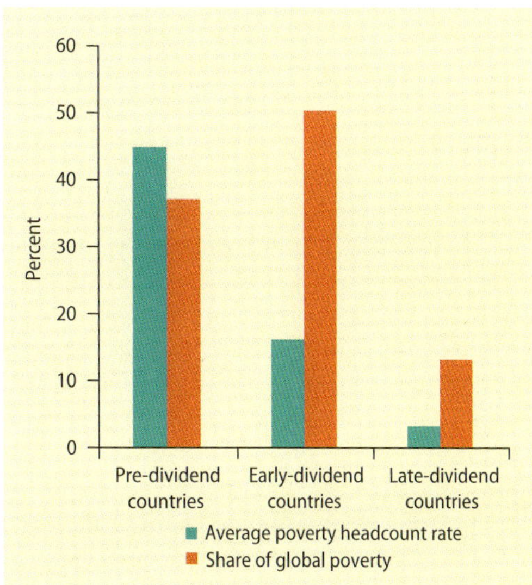

Source: World Bank calculations.
Note: Data are for 2012 and are based on a poverty line of $1.90 a day for all countries listed in appendix table C5.1 The average poverty headcount rate is the unweighted average across countries in a given group. The sample of countries depicted in the figure includes 31 pre-dividend countries, 48 early-dividend countries, 34 late-dividend countries, and 4 post-dividend countries.

are all pre-dividend countries in Sub-Saharan Africa: Angola, Mali, Niger, Uganda, and Zambia. These countries are very poor, with 2012 poverty rates that ranged from 29 to 62 percent. Without improvements in their poverty headcount rates, these countries will experience even greater concentrations of poverty in the future.

Early- and late-dividend countries, where much of the global poverty reduction over the past two decades occurred, also experienced a fertility transition over this period. Between 1990 and 2012, the global poverty headcount rate fell from 37.1 percent to 12.7 percent, representing a reduction in the number of global poor by more than 1.06 billion. By virtue of their large populations and high poverty headcount rates, China and India accounted for much of the reduction in global poverty. These countries now not only have lower poverty headcounts but also lower population growth rates, having lowered their fertility rates over time. Bangladesh and Indonesia, which together accounted for another 10 percent of global poverty in 2012, have also experienced slowing population growth rates. Poverty reduction successes in these countries would thus have a diminishing impact on global poverty reduction.

Ninety percent of countries that met the Millennium Development Goal (MDG) target of halving poverty rates were early- and late-dividend countries.[3] As of 2012, 40 percent of early-dividend and 68 percent of late-dividend countries were able to halve their poverty headcount rates from their 1990 levels. In contrast, only 2 percent of pre-dividend countries were able to achieve similar reductions in their poverty rates. Given that pre-dividend countries also typically have faster population growth rates than countries at more advanced stages of demographic transition, a reduction in the poverty headcount rate may not necessarily imply a reduction in the absolute number of poor people (Herrmann 2015). For example, Mali reduced its poverty headcount rate by a third between 1990 and 2012, but because of its high population growth, the number of poor still rose by 13 percent. The countries that have had the most success in reducing poverty are those where the working-age share of the population has peaked or is close to peaking and where population growth has decelerated in parallel to improvements in life expectancy, infant mortality, and fertility.

Progress on other development goals also varies across countries at different stages of demographic transition. On MDG 4, only 17 and 25 percent of pre- and early-dividend countries were able to reduce under-five child mortality rates by three-fourths from 1990 to 2013. Late-dividend countries were slightly more successful in this regard. On MDG 5, only 10 percent of the countries succeeded in reducing the maternal mortality rate by three-fourths between 1990 and 2013. Progress has been made toward MDG 6 on combating HIV/AIDS, especially with the wider access to retrovirals in the new millennium.

As more and more people live in urban areas, progress in reducing the shares of urban populations living in slums has been modest (box 5.2). Overall, the shares of populations in pre-, late-, and post-dividend countries living in urban areas stayed relatively stable between 1990 and 2013 (figure 5.4). However, early-dividend countries have seen rapid urbanization over this period, a shift that is driving global urbanization trends. Rising urbanization has been paralleled by an increase in the number of those living in slums (figure 5.5). Large cities in developing countries, such as Baghdad, Caracas, Johannesburg, Karachi, Lagos, Lima, Mumbai, Nairobi, and Rio de Janeiro, have large slums, some of them with estimated populations of more than 500,000. Lack of access to public services in these slums has the potential to lead new generations of urban slum residents into poverty traps (Marx, Stoker, and Suri 2013).

Low educational attainment in pre-dividend countries has implications for the future global labor supply. In pre-dividend countries, just 35 percent of those enrolled completed lower-secondary education, compared with 72 percent in early-dividend countries and 90 percent in late-dividend countries.[4] These pre-development countries will

BOX 5.2 Rapid urbanization connected to demographic change presents a development challenge

Internal migration and the rise of large urban agglomerations in developing countries are essential parts of the story of demographic change. Higher population growth in rural areas tends to translate into rural-urban migration. Studies suggest that about half of the urbanization growth in the world results from the internal rural-to-urban migration and area reclassifications (UN 2008). People moving to cities are attracted by the various job opportunities, higher (real) wages, the many local amenities such as cultural and recreational offerings, and the availability of public utilities and transportation facilities. The existence of very large cities around the world suggest that these attractions more than compensate for the congestion that arises in densely populated areas (Krugman 1991). Urbanization is rising fast in developing countries, where 7 of the 10 largest urban areas in the world are currently located, including Cairo, Jakarta, Karachi, and Mexico City (UN-Habitat 2003).

In many developing countries, big cities are characterized by the presence of very large slums (figure B5.2.1). About a third of the urban population in developing countries lives in slums. These slums can be transitory if they are the by-product of rapidly growing economies, but many of them are located in countries with slow or stagnant growth. Overall living conditions can be worse than in rural areas (Bradley et al. 1992; Duflo, Galiani, and Mobarek 2012).

By 2030, around 2 billion people will be living in slums—twice as many as today and a direct consequence of unprecedented urban growth. About 90 percent of the urban growth in the next 15 years will be concentrated in Asia and Sub-Saharan Africa. Already home to most of the world's slum population, these two regions are expected to see a significant increase in those numbers.

The presence and persistence of these slums pose many challenges to the process of urbanization and development in general (Marx, Stoker, and Suri 2013). Improving the quality of life of the people living in slums requires policies that cover many dimensions, from access to potable water and sanitation to continuous access to electricity, transport infrastructures, and job opportunities (Banerjee, Pande, and Walton 2012). An additional challenge is to prevent these slums from expanding. Policies to remove or relocate slums or to upgrade the services available have shown limited success in reducing their size or limiting their sprawl. Improving local governance, engaging in land reform, and launching major public investments in urban areas may be the most promising policies for limiting the sprawl of slums.

FIGURE B5.2.1 Substantial shares of urban populations in major developing countries still live in slums

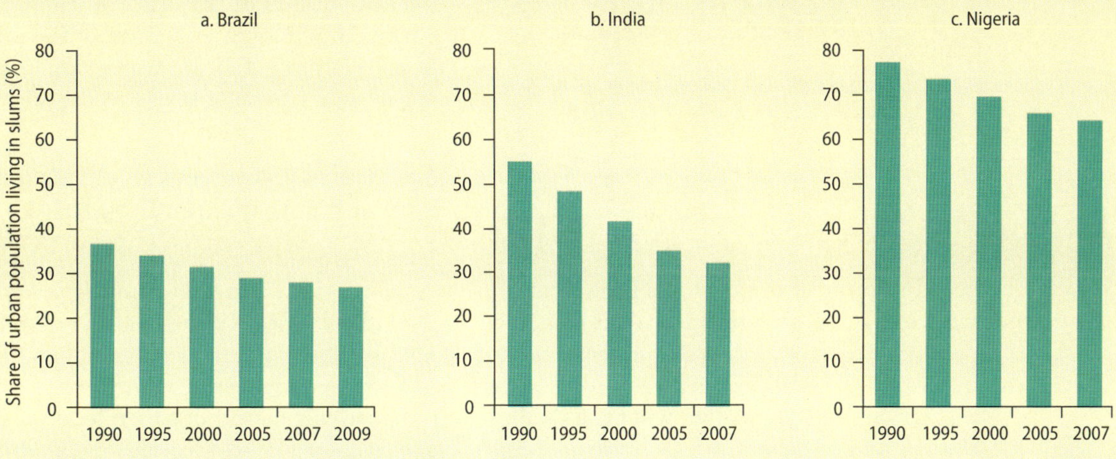

Source: World Bank calculations, based on data from UN-Habitat Urban Data.

FIGURE 5.4 Early-dividend countries are urbanizing rapidly

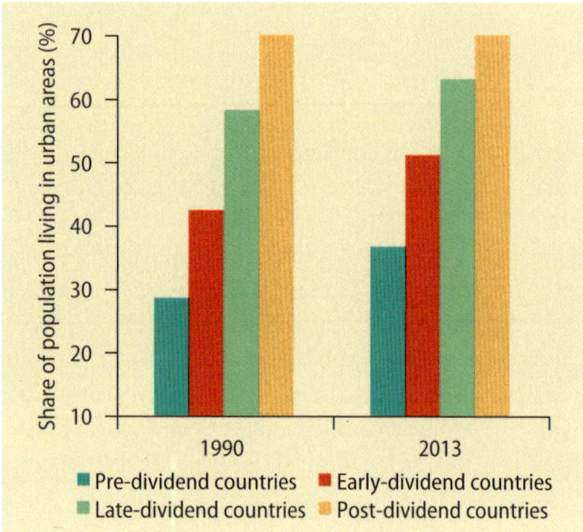

Source: World Bank calculations, based on World Bank World Development Indicators, Millennium Development Goals database, and UN 2015.
Note: Data reflect unweighted averages for the different country groups.

FIGURE 5.5 A large share of the population of early- and late-dividend countries still lives in slums

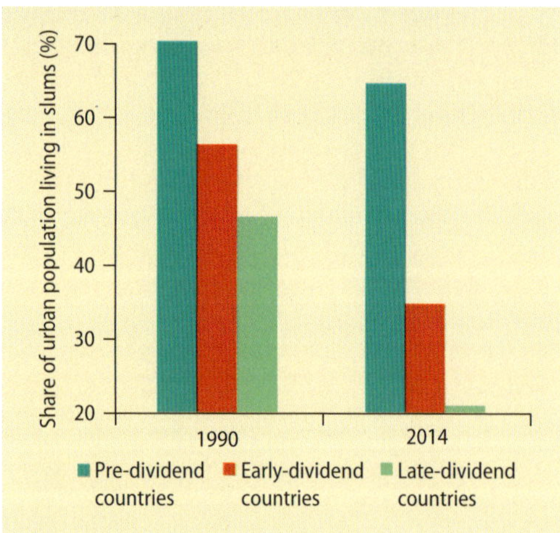

Source: World Bank calculations, based on World Bank World Development Indicators, Millennium Development Goals database, and UN 2015.
Note: Data reflect unweighted averages for the different country groups.

account for most of the global growth in the working-age population over the next few decades; if their education attainment rates do not improve, the global average skill level of the working-age population will be in doubt.[5]

Pre- and early-dividend countries present a high demand for services for children, including education. Education is a critical

FIGURE 5.6 Education expenditure per capita is negatively correlated with child-dependency ratio

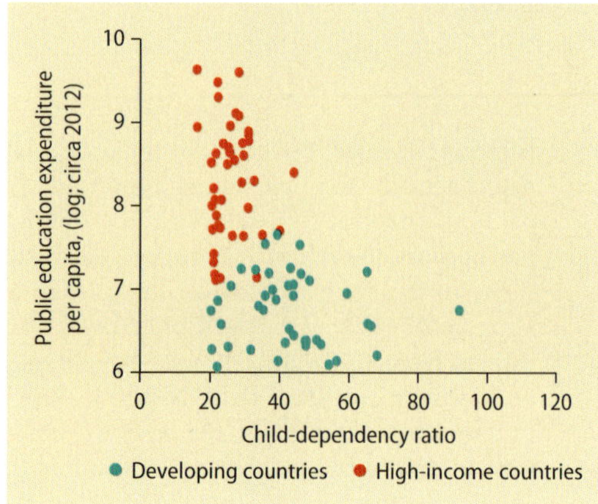

Source: World Bank calculations, based on data from UN 2015 and World Bank World Development Indicators.

component of early childhood development, with long-term implications not only for human capital accumulation and future income, but also for socialization and health (Heckman, Pinto, and Savelyev 2013).[6] However, low- and middle-income countries generally have lower public spending per capita on education, while having substantially greater child-dependency ratios than high-income countries (figure 5.6). These countries thus face the challenge both of increasing the quality of their education through improvements in per capita spending and expanding their spending to accommodate a larger child population in the near future. In pre-dividend countries, in particular, children as a share of the population are projected to stay almost the same (or rise in some cases) for several decades.

Economic dynamism is weakening in late- and post-dividend countries

Late-dividend countries have experienced demographic change at a much faster pace than many post-dividend countries did. By the 1940s, most post-dividend countries already had low fertility rates, which briefly rose in the post-war period but then fell and generally remained low. In the 1950s, late-dividend countries had almost double the fertility rates of post-dividend countries, and average life

FIGURE 5.7 Fertility rates in late-dividend countries have converged to those of post-dividend countries since the 1950s

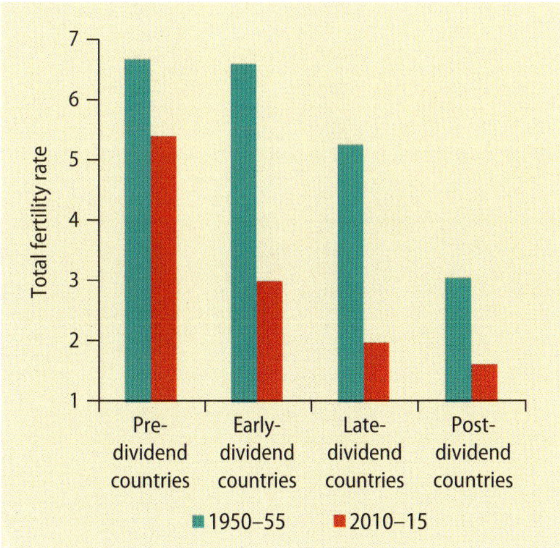

Source: World Bank calculations, based on data from World Bank World Development Indicators, Millennium Development Goals database, and UN 2015.
Note: Data reflect unweighted averages for the different country groups. The total fertility rate is the average number of births per woman.

FIGURE 5.8 Differences in life expectancy across typologies of countries have narrowed

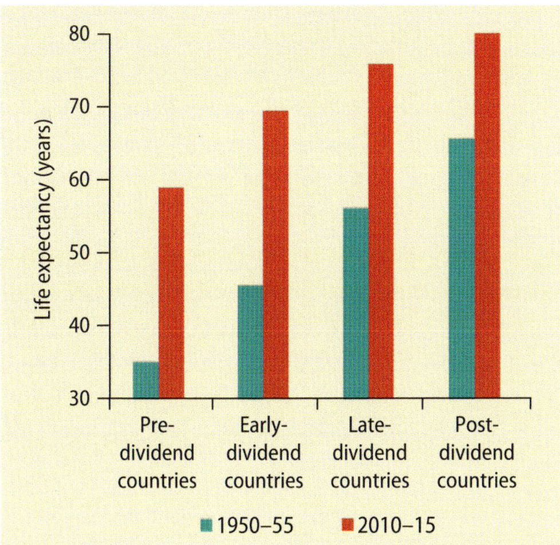

Source: World Bank calculations, based on data from World Bank World Development Indicators, Millennium Development Goals database, and UN 2015.
Note: Data reflect unweighted averages for the different country groups.

expectancies were shorter by nine years (figures 5.7, 5.8). However, late-dividend countries have since made substantial improvements in these metrics, with extremely rapid improvements in life expectancy. Several factors fed into this faster pace of improvement, all having to do with the importance of these countries in the global economy. As a result, late-dividend countries are expected to have the same age structure as post-dividend countries by 2050 (figure 5.9).

At the same time, late-dividend countries accounted for 36 percent of global GDP growth in 2000–14 (figure 5.10). Growth in many of these countries was rapid. Brazil and China alone, for example, contributed

FIGURE 5.9 Late-dividend countries are aging rapidly

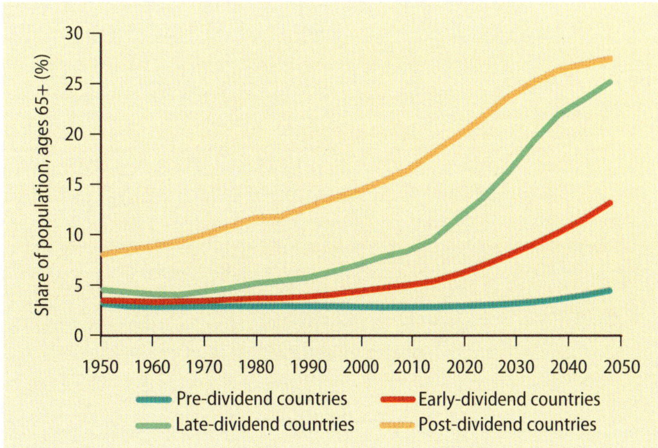

Source: World Bank calculations, based on UN 2015 and World Bank World Development Indicators.

FIGURE 5.10 Aging countries accounted for most of global growth, 2000–14

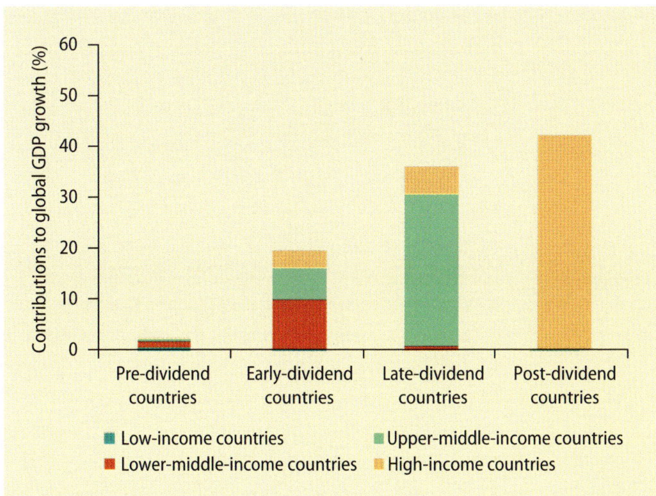

Source: World Bank calculations, based on UN 2015 and World Bank World Development Indicators.

a quarter of global growth over the period. Brazil and China grew at average annual real GDP growth rates of 3.5 and 10 percent, respectively, over this period. However, in late-dividend countries, both the number of working-age people and their share of the population will contract over the next few decades, suggesting demographic change is likely to dampen their contribution to future global growth.

Post-dividend countries' contributions to global growth have been slowing down, with potential spillovers for other countries (chapter 3 of this report; IMF 2015). These countries account for 59.8 percent of global economic activity in 2014, and 42 percent of global GDP growth. Post-dividend economies are also the major export destinations for pre- and early-dividend countries and account for two-thirds of global import demand. While other post-dividend and late-dividend countries meet most of this demand, the post-dividend countries are the preeminent markets for exports from pre- and early-dividend countries, mainly textiles, clothing, and other light manufactures, as well as commodities. If growth in post-dividend countries slows, early- and pre-dividend countries will need to find alternative export markets. In addition, as post-dividend economies age, their national savings rates are expected to fall, leading to a possible slowdown in capital flows to the rest of the world.[7]

In some late- and post-dividend countries, pension systems are increasingly stressed as the number of beneficiaries rises relative to the numbers the systems were designed to support (Bogetic et al. 2015). Late- and post-dividend countries will have a combination of shrinking shares of working-age population combined with an increase in the share of aged people, potential candidates for public pension (Bonoli and Shinkawa 2005). As populations age, pension systems need to adapt to demographic and occupational changes to avoid generosities and incentives that encourage early retirement and thus long retirement periods (World Bank 2015b). In 2012, one-fourth of the European Union's (EU's) population—130 million people—received at least one pension. The EU spent about €1.71 billion on pensions in 2012, which represents about 13.3 percent of its GDP.

FIGURE 5.11 Health expenditure per capita is positively correlated with aged dependency ratio

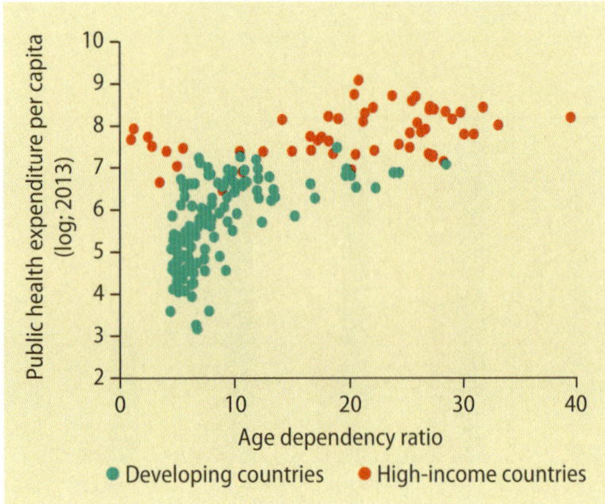

Source: World Bank calculations, based on data from UN 2015 and World Bank World Development Indicators.

Some high-income countries are experiencing a rapid rise in health care costs as their populations age (figure 5.11). Health care spending generally increases with age, with a notable jump in spending between the ages of 55 and 60, reflecting changes in morbidity (EC 2015). In Organisation for Economic Co-operation and Development (OECD) countries, health care spending on those 65 and older is expected to jump from 40 percent in 2010 to 60 percent by 2060 (de la Maisonneuve and Martins 2013). In the United States, health spending is expected to rise faster than GDP and account for 19.6 percent of GDP by 2024, up from 17.4 percent in 2013 (CMS 2015a). The cost of Medicare (the public health insurance for people 65 or older) is expected to increase substantially, moving from $256.5 billion in 2002 to $489.4 billion in 2010 (CMS 2015b). The aging of baby boomers in the coming years will lead to an unprecedented increase in the size and composition of the elderly population in the program (Lassman et al. 2014).

Pathways to future prosperity

Demographic change can affect future prosperity in three ways. The first way is through changes in the working-age share of the population that affect income growth and savings. The second way is through changes in the age structure of households that directly affect poverty, human capital investments, and decisions about how dependents will be supported. In poor households with high fertility, these changes in age structure typically involve behavioral changes that lead to lower fertility. The third way is through the changes in the means by which aging populations support themselves around the world. This section addresses each of these pathways to future prosperity in further detail.

Rising working-age shares can raise growth

An increase of 1 percentage point in the working-age population share is estimated to boost GDP per capita by 1.1 to 2.0 percentage points, on average (see appendix C.4 for details). More generally, growth in the working-age share is associated with higher per capita income growth (see also figure 5.12).[8] The causality underpinning this association is complex and occurs through multiple pathways, including through an increase in the supply of workers relative to the total population; a rise in the capacity to save, which leads to a higher capital per worker ratio; and more investment in human capital (table 5.1).[9] While these channels can work simultaneously, the differentiation between the first and second dividends is informed not only by the transmission mechanisms but also by the time horizon through which they are at work.

FIGURE 5.12 A rising working-age population share is positively correlated with GDP per capita growth

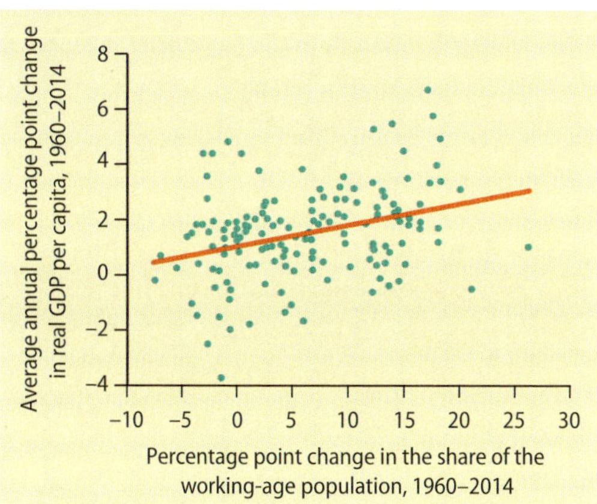

Source: World Bank calculations, based on World Bank World Development Indicators and UN 2015.

The contribution of the second demographic dividend to growth is potentially greater than the first (Mason 2005). For example, for East Asia, during the 1970–2000 period, the contribution from the second demographic dividend on GDP growth was 2.22 times larger than the first demographic dividend. For some countries, estimates suggest that the contribution of the first demographic dividend explains between 9.2 and 15.5 percent of their per capita economic growth over the 1960–2000 period (Mason and Kinugasa 2008).

An increase of 1 percentage point in the share of working-age population is associated with an increase of 0.6 to 0.8 percentage point in savings (appendix C.4). National private-savings rates have been found to depend on the age composition of the population: individuals are typically net savers when they are working age and continue to save in old age, on average, but they tend to be predominantly consumers when they are children. This outcome is associated with the second demographic dividend, where declining dependency ratios, led by a lower share of children in the population, tend to boost domestic savings and investment.[10]

Increases in aged dependency ratios do not necessarily lead to lower savings. Since people expect to live longer, they tend to save more during the economically active portion of their lives (Kinugasa and Mason 2007). Retirement lengthens with gains in life expectancy, increasing demand for pension wealth. In countries where funded pensions are important, pension assets have increased very substantially (Towers Watson 2012; Saez and Zucman 2014). This positive effect on savings associated with aging could lead to capital deepening, although the net effect of aging on savings is unclear.[11]

Changes in age structure can lead to higher investment in human capital, a key condition for realizing the second demographic dividend. The quantity-quality trade-off is one of

TABLE 5.1 Demographic dividends in a nutshell

Channel	Transmission mechanisms	Demographic dividend	Stage of demographic transition
Labor force	Increase in the support ratio (ratio of effective labor to effective consumers) holding constant other factors, including saving and income per effective worker.	First	Early stage (pre- and early-dividend countries)
Savings	Changes in saving and capital per effective worker influence income, from labor and assets, per effective worker.	Second	Late stage (late- and post-dividend countries)
Human capital	Lower fertility and the quantity-quality trade-off lead to greater spending on health and education for children.	Second	Late stage (late- and post-dividend countries)

Source: GMR team elaboration, based on Lee and Mason 2006.
Note: For both the first and second demographic dividends, changes in the factor given in the first column of the table, through the transmission mechanism described in the second column, results in a boost to growth.

the most widely confirmed linkages between population and economic decision making (Becker 1960; Becker and Lewis 1973). People who have fewer children spend more per child. The quantity-quality trade-off is particularly strong when it comes to human-capital spending. Moreover, the quantity-quality trade-off was found to be as strong for public spending as for private spending. The increased spending on education can take the form of both improving coverage of children, as well as increasing spending per child.

The correlates between demography and development are strong, but favorable demographic change does not guarantee improvement in development conditions. A rising working-age population share, for instance, has the potential to improve the welfare of the poorest members of society (box 5.3). Early- and pre-dividend countries, where

BOX 5.3 Making the most out of demographic change

An increase in the share of the working-age population has the potential to boost economic growth through a range of channels and to help a country reap demographic dividends. First, a rising working-age population has the potential to increase the number of people employed as a share of the population. Second, it has the potential to increase national savings and hence the investment rate, since income-earners would become a greater share of the population. Third, it can lead to faster productivity growth since households might have more resources to invest in fewer children, and it might be easier for mothers with lighter child-rearing responsibilities to enter the labor market.

However, certain enabling conditions are necessary for an increase in the share of the working-age population to boost economic growth (Barro 2003; Kremer 1993; Lucas 1988). These conditions include measures that help new labor market entrants find productive employment and that facilitate investments in human and physical capital. Under a baseline scenario that considers the impact of projected demographic change on the working-age population and on savings and investment, simulation results suggest an average annual GDP per capita growth rate for the global economy of 2.1 percentage points over 2015–30 (figure B5.3.1).

Demographic change can boost per capita income growth in pre- and early-dividend countries, but it may dampen growth prospects in aging countries and for the global economy. In pre- and early-dividend countries, where the share of working-age population will increase, demographic change could account for 0.5 to 0.8 percentage point of annual GDP per capita growth, over 2015–30 given the right enabling conditions. At the same time, even though per capita growth is expected to be high in late-dividend countries,

(box continues next page)

BOX 5.3 Making the most out of demographic change (continued)

including China, demographic change in the absence of countervailing policies could reduce annual growth by 0.2 to 0.4 percentage point in late- and post-dividend countries, where working-age population shares are expected to decline.[a] Aging in post-dividend countries is expected to slow both their own growth and global growth, because post-dividend countries account for such a high share of global economic activity.

Global poverty could thus drop from 11.4 percent in 2015 to 4.4 percent in 2030 if potential benefits from demographic change are realized (figure B5.3.2). This reduction is equivalent to a drop in the number of poor from 729.2 million in 2015 to 325.9 million by 2030. Even without these benefits, poverty would likely drop in pre- and early-dividend countries where the child share of the population is expected to decline and the share of income earners to rise. These age shifts can reduce poverty regardless of changes in average income. The demographic dividend has the potential to help to lift an additional 38.7 million people in pre-dividend countries and 24.4 million people in early-dividend countries out of poverty by 2030. Added together, the extreme poverty headcount would be 16.2 percent lower in 2030 than it would have been without changes in age structure and the benefits of enabling conditions (figure B5.3.3).

FIGURE B5.3.1 Demographic change could account for substantial growth in pre- and early-dividend countries if enabling conditions help create jobs and convert savings to investment

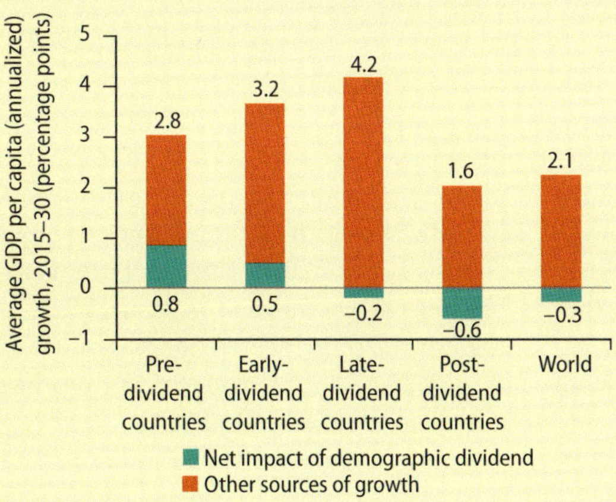

FIGURE B5.3.2 Global poverty rate could fall substantially but not enough to reach the 3 percent global World Bank target

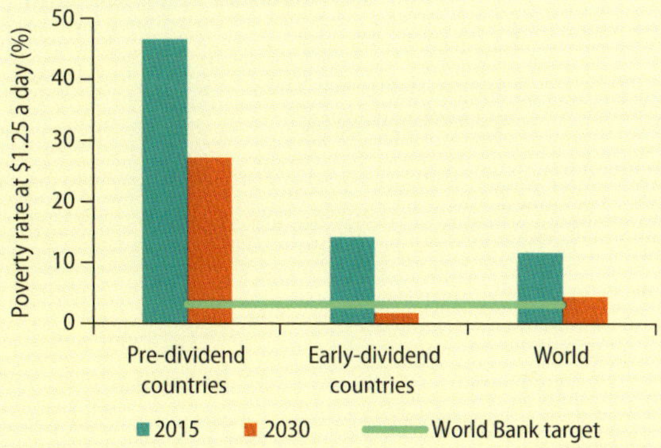

FIGURE B5.3.3 Global poverty headcount could be 16.2 percent lower due to demographic change

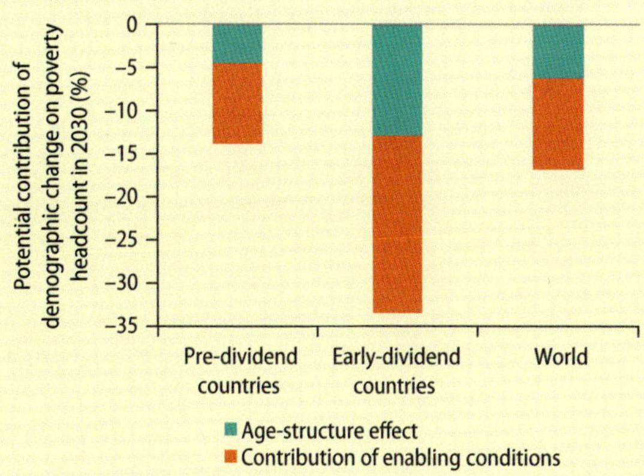

Source: World Bank calculations.

Note: See appendixes D.1 and D.2 for details. Poverty estimations are based on the $1.25 poverty line and the 2005 PPP prices. The differences in poverty headcount in 2030 due to age-structure changes and the contribution of enabling condition are estimated by comparing the baseline scenario with counterfactuals changing the structure of the population (2015 versus 2030) and the number of jobs. Age-structure effect measures the difference in the poverty rate by assuming the same population structure as in 2015. Contribution of enabling conditions is the impact of job growth keeping pace with growth in the share of working-age population and aggregate savings being converted to investment.

a. This result is broadly in line with those of other studies. Manyika et al. (2015) consider the impact of demographic change on growth for a longer time horizon and estimate that the declining working-age population share could reduce the global average income per capita by 20 percent over 2015–65. Simulation analysis by Batini, Callen, and McKibbin (2006) finds that the demographic transition can help raise developing countries' GDP 2 percent higher by 2025 than if demographic transition does not occur. This compares with our estimates of 1.1 percent increase in developing-country GDP from demographic transition over 2015–30. McKibbin (2006) conducts a similar analysis for several economies and finds that demographic change can lead to lower GDP for many high-income countries. For example, Japan's GDP in 2050 is projected to be 28 percent smaller than it was in 1985. Our estimate for Japan is a decline of 6 percent over 2015–30. Tyers and Shi (2007) find that demographic transition could increase GDP in Sub-Saharan Africa by 15 percent over 1995–2030. This is in line with our estimates of 8 percent over 2015–30.

fertility rates are still falling to replacement levels and where working-age population shares are still rising, are in precisely this position. They will experience the first demographic dividend, however, only if they are able to successfully absorb new entrants to the labor force—that is, if growth in the number of jobs is at least as high as growth in labor supply, and if people with the necessary skills for available jobs are able to find those jobs. Similarly, the second demographic dividend can be obtained by post-dividend countries only if they are able to mobilize savings that their current cohorts of elderly had saved and invested when they were younger.

Changing demographics can step up development

As fertility rates fall, the demographic structures of households change and directly affect poverty and shared prosperity, particularly in poor households. Because of the association between fertility and education, income, and life expectancy, households in the top 60 percent (T60) of the income distribution tend to have lower child-dependency ratios and to pass through the demographic transition before households in the bottom 40 percent (B40) in almost all countries (figure 5.13).

A reduction of 1 percentage point in the child dependency ratio is associated with a reduction of 0.38 percentage point in the poverty rate (figure 5.14).[12] An increase in the share of working-age population can also lead to a decline in the poverty rate. If fertility declines are concentrated among the B40, the economic benefits of lower dependency rates and more income earners as a share of the population will accrue to the poorest. As the household's child-dependency ratio falls and the share of working-age people increases, per capita income is likely to increase, which relaxes the social and household budget constraints. Families who have fewer children will have more per capita resources at their disposal for consumption, as well as investment.

The realization of the first demographic dividend, led by a reduction in the child-dependency ratio, could facilitate the eradication of global poverty. In 1990, East Asia had a higher average poverty headcount than South Asia (figure 5.15). As it reduced its child-dependency ratio, it was able to reduce its poverty more than the other regions. Evidence from Bangladesh suggests that demographic factors, including age structure, gender, and regional distributions of populations, accounted for a quarter of the rapid reductions in poverty that occurred between 2000 and 2010 (World Bank 2013b). Bangladesh halved its fertility rate between 1971 and 2004, going from more than six children per woman to about three, and is on track to reach replacement rates in the coming decades. Bangladesh has also managed to reverse the infamous gender inequality in infant mortality that characterizes most South Asian countries.

Aging populations are changing what it means to be dependent

While children's consumption relies most on transfers from within the household, elderly people's consumption is supported by transfers from a range of sources, including their own income (box 5.4). Aged individuals can support their consumption by dissaving or extending their working life. The capacity to generate savings is associated with their productivity during their working life. Individuals with low human capital who have (or had) low-paid jobs, or who experienced long periods of unemployment during their working life, would have challenges in supporting their own consumption in later years. The greater the investment in human capital, and the earlier that investment begins, the higher return to society throughout a worker's productive life (Heckman 2008).

It is not unusual for labor income to support half or more of a person's consumption at age 65 (figure 5.16).[13] That is not the case in high-income economies such as Germany, Hungary, Japan, Slovenia, and Taiwan, China. But low reliance on labor income does not necessarily mean that those over 65 have left the labor market. In Japan, for example, labor force participation among the 65-year-old population is quite high, although labor income per worker is low. By age 75 labor

FIGURE 5.13 T60 households tend to have lower child-dependency ratios than B40 households in countries in all income categories

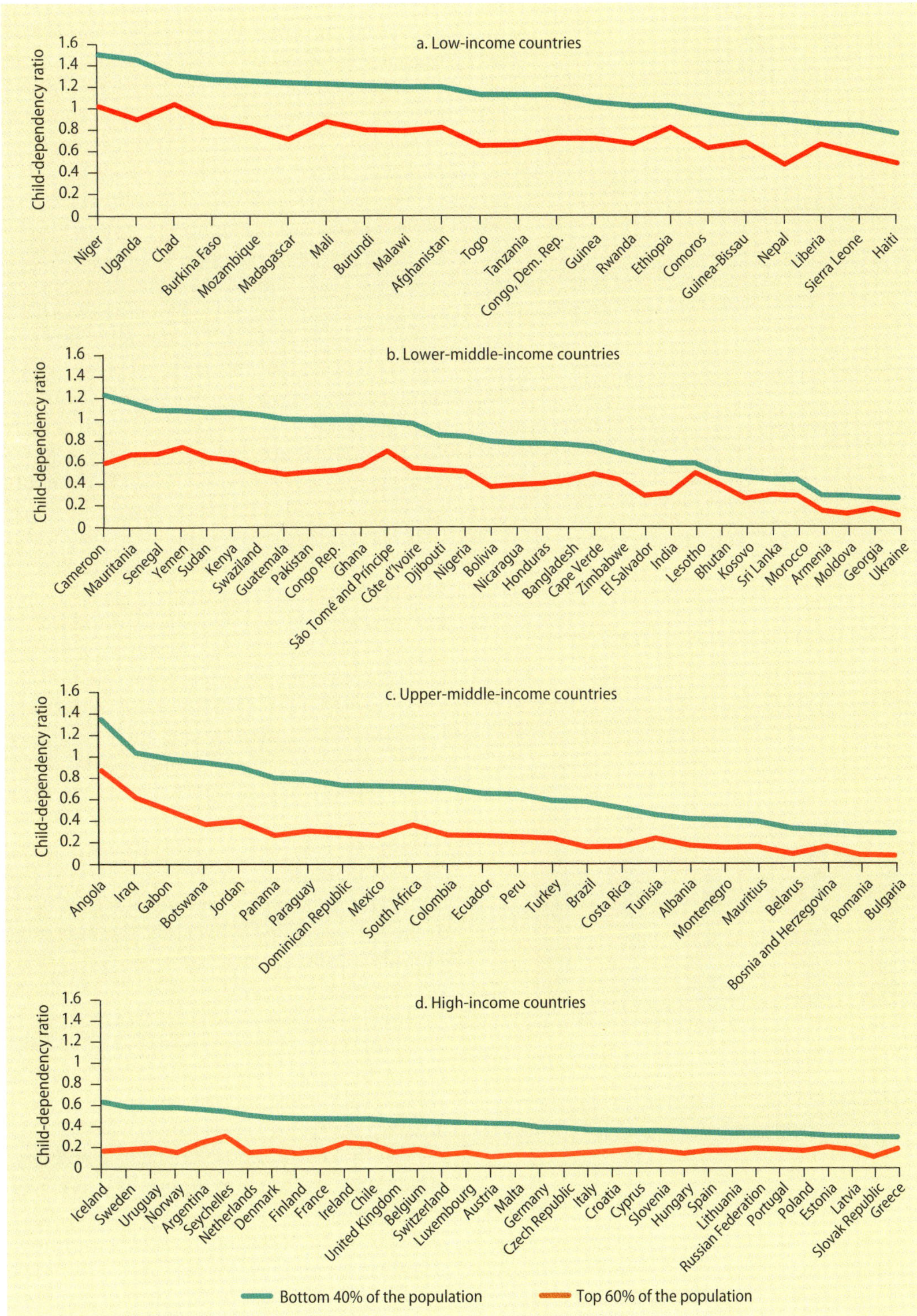

Source: World Bank calculations, based on data from household surveys, circa 2012, but including the latest available data from 2004–13.
Note: The sample covers 34 high-income; 24 upper-middle-income; 32 lower-middle-income; and 22 low-income countries.

FIGURE 5.14 Demographic change can have substantial impacts on poverty

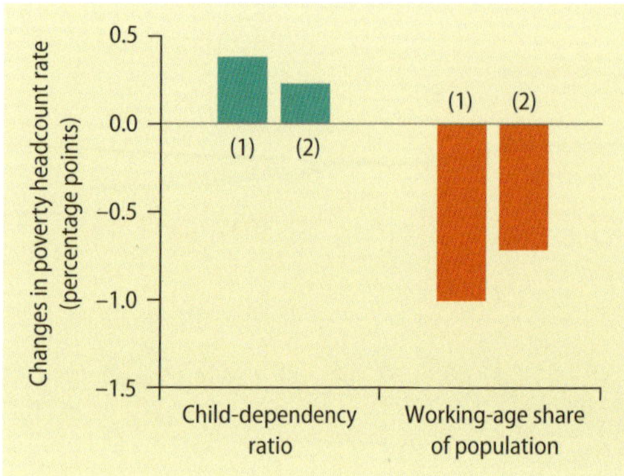

Source: World Bank calculations.
Note: Data are from UN (2015), Penn World Tables, and WDI. Results are based on the first-difference estimator over the 1980-2012 period (5-year average), covering 103 countries. Specification 1 has changes in the poverty headcount rate as a function of changes in the child-dependency ratio (CDR), controlling for regional and time-fixed effects. Specification 2 also controls for changes in the GDP per capita, latitude, and institutions (e.g., former colonies). The same exercise is repeated with the working-age share of population (WAsP), instead of the child-dependency ratio. All estimates are significant at the 5 percent level. The bars show the change in the poverty headcount rate associated with a 1 percentage point reduction on CDR or WAsP.

FIGURE 5.15 Lower child-dependency ratios are associated with lower poverty rates

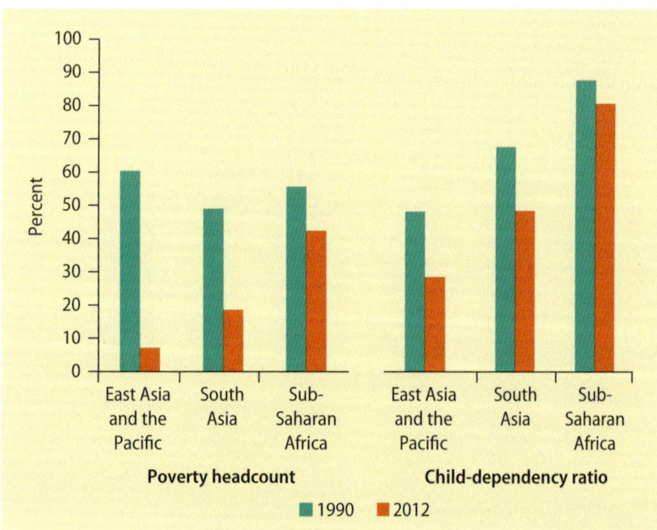

Source: World Bank calculations.

income as a share of consumption drops substantially across countries for which data are available. Labor income at age 75 is close to or greater than 20 percent of consumption in only a few early- and late-dividend countries, including China, India, Indonesia, Mexico, and the Philippines. Increases in life expectancy in these countries would require increased reliance on either labor income (retiring at a later age) or asset-based flows (saving more while working or reducing bequests) if current levels of labor income and asset-based flows are to be maintained.

The importance of net public transfers varies greatly across countries, with the highest levels found in Europe and Latin America and in China, Japan, and the Republic of Korea in Asia.[14] At age 65 private transfers are important in many economies, but the elderly are providing support rather than receiving it. At age 65 net public transfers are equivalent to less than 15 percent of consumption in China; Mexico; Taiwan, China; and the United States. For several developing countries—India, Indonesia, the Philippines, South Africa, and Thailand—the elderly pay more in taxes than they receive in benefits.[15] By age 75, net public transfers are more important in almost every country. The regional patterns persist, however, with the largest net public transfers found in Europe and Latin America. In several countries, including South Africa and early-dividend Asian countries, the elderly receive very little in the way of public support even at age 75.

In most late- and post-dividend countries, the elderly rely heavily on assets to support their consumption. Asset-based reallocations tend to be more important in the early-dividend countries where on average they support almost 60 percent of consumption. In late-dividend countries, asset-based flows amount, on average, to 40 percent of consumption by the elderly, and in post-dividend countries to approximately 25 percent. At age 75, asset-based inflows are nearly as high in early-dividend countries as they are at age 65. In late- and post-dividend countries, these flows are equal to about 30 percent of consumption.

Because the elderly support their consumption through multiple sources and at different shares of those sources, the growing cohort of elderly will have diverse fiscal impacts

BOX 5.4 Funding the difference between consumption and production over the life cycle

The life-cycle deficit, the gap between what is consumed and what is produced, must be funded. For children, the support system is dominated by public and private transfers. Public transfers to children rise with the level of a country's income (figure B5.4.1 compares public transfers in Germany and the Philippines). The identification of the sources of transfer to support the consumption of the dependent population across the life cycle is a key information to analyze the potential effect of demographic change on public finance (Lee et al. 2014).

Support systems are generally more complex for the elderly than for children. The elderly rely on assets in addition to public and private transfers to fund their life-cycle deficits. The elderly may own their own home, a farm, or business, or participate in a funded pension system.

Old-age support systems are highly varied around the world. Among high-income countries, net private transfers to the elderly are very small and often negative—the elderly as a group provide more to their descendants than they receive. The key trade-off for the elderly is between relying on net public transfers and relying on assets. In some European countries, such as Finland, Germany, and Sweden, net public transfers are sufficient to fund all or nearly all of their old-age life-cycle deficits. The elderly in other rich countries, such as Japan, the United Kingdom, and the United States rely much less on public transfers and much more on assets to fund their old-age needs.

Variation is also great among low- and middle-income countries. The elderly in developing countries in Asia, such as India, the Republic of Korea, the Philippines, and Thailand, are more likely to depend on private transfers and on assets than on public transfers. The elderly in many Latin American countries rely much more heavily on public transfers and less on private transfers and assets.

FIGURE B5.4.1 Public transfers to dependents are greater in Germany than in the Philippines

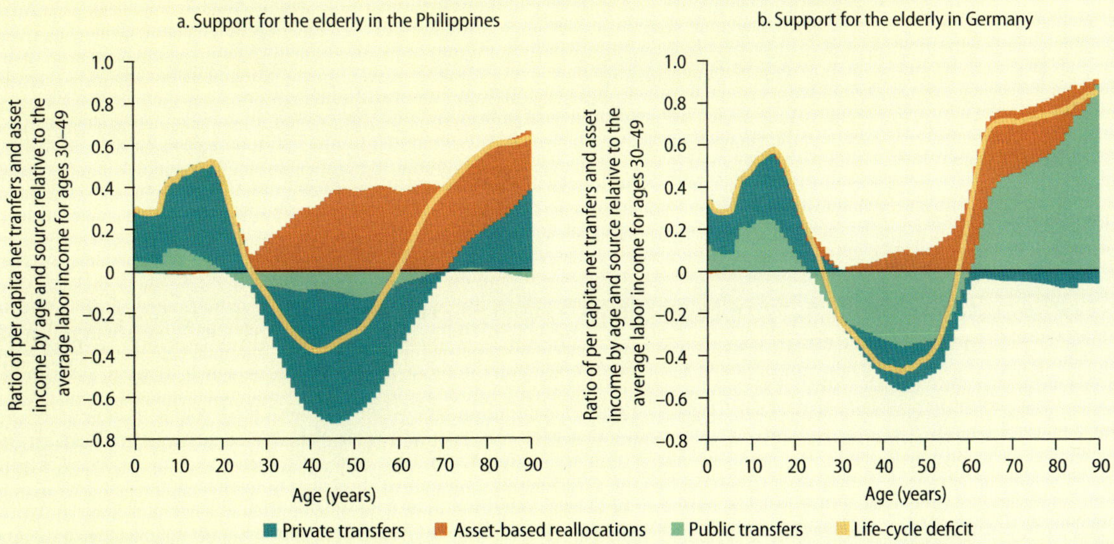

Source: National Transfer Accounts.
Note: Philippines, 1999; Germany: 2003. Positive transfers suggest that a person of a given age is a net recipient of transfers. Positive life-cycle deficit suggests that consumption at a given age is supported mostly by transfers and asset income. Values all expressed relative to the average labor income of persons ages 30–49.

from country to country. In countries with generous public pension systems, such as Finland, Germany, and Sweden, net public transfers are sufficient to fund all or nearly all consumption by the elderly, while in Japan, the United Kingdom, and the United States, the elderly rely more on private assets to fund their old-age needs. In Asian countries like

FIGURE 5.16 Labor income still supports substantial consumption for 65-year olds, while 75-year-olds rely mostly on public transfers or asset-based flows

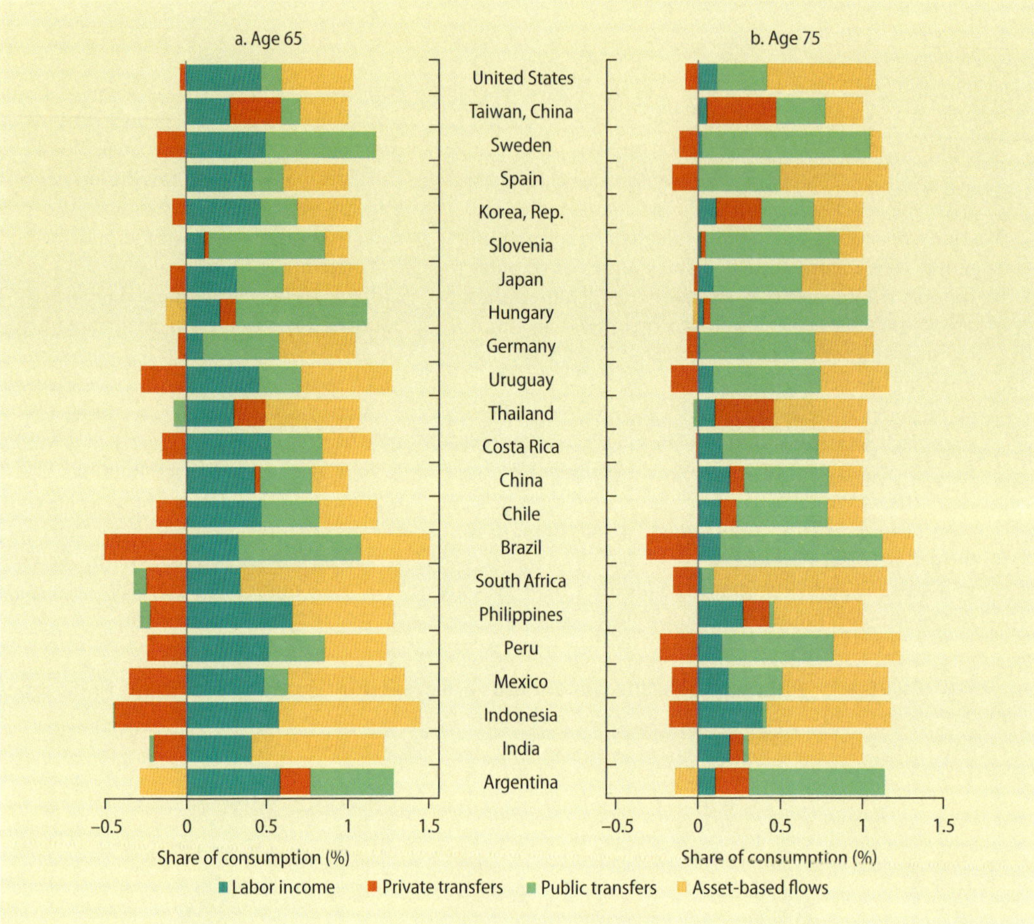

Source: World Bank calculations, based on the National Transfer Accounts database.

China, the Republic of Korea, and Thailand, private transfers are the major source of funding for old-age support.[16] In these latter two groups of countries where old-age support is financed privately, the growing shares of elderly place a smaller burden on fiscal balances than they do in other countries with more mature public-pension systems.

Conclusion

Demographic change presents both opportunities and challenges to development. Although demography is by no means the only force that shapes the economy, it has direct effects on the availability of key resources for development and, at the same time, impacts the demand for public services. Slow progress in human development in pre-dividend countries has contributed to persistently high fertility rates, which in turn limit these countries to increase investment in human capital. Pre- and early-dividend countries also face the challenge of creating enough jobs for the growing working-age population share and in investing sufficiently in raising their skill levels. Late- and post-dividend countries face possible growth slowdowns as a growing share of the working-age progresses to retirement, requiring an increasingly large share of capital simply to maintain or improve their welfare.

Demographic transition in large economies can have substantial spillovers to the global economy. There is evidence that aging in late- and post-dividend countries could slow potential future growth, leading to negative global spillovers through channels such as the demand for imports and foreign direct investment (see chapter 3). At the same time, the realization of demographic dividends in large economies can have positive spillovers to other economies. For example, China's rapid GDP growth has been supported not just by a larger share of working-age population but also by deeper integration into the global economy through trade links.

The realization of demographic dividends stands to have global environmental externalities, another critical spillover (box 5.5). An increase in the consumption per capita associated with the realization of demographic dividends will lead to an increase of carbon dioxide emissions, keeping constant

BOX 5.5 Current demographic trends could lead to greater greenhouse gas emissions in some countries

Population growth is a central factor that affects greenhouse gas emissions and subsequently climate change. The relevance of population trends for environmental policy has been increasingly acknowledged, and empirical research on these interactions has grown in recent years (Harper 2013). Models used in climate-change studies are based on the premise that greenhouse gas emissions growth is the product of population growth, economic growth, and the carbon intensity of energy consumption in the economy (Pachauri and Reisinger 2007).

Various statistical analyses confirm that population growth has driven emissions growth over the past several decades (O'Neill et al. 2010). A 1 percentage point increase in population has been associated with a similar increase in carbon emissions (O'Neill 2009). As a result, and based on UN projections, if the world's population follows a low, rather than a medium, growth path, global emissions could be expected to fall by 15 percent in 2050 and by 40 percent in 2100. On the other hand, a high population growth path could increase emissions by 17 percent in 2050 and by 60 percent in 2100 (O'Neill et al. 2012). Other estimates show that slower population growth could account for as much as 16–29 percent of the reduction in emissions that would be necessary to avoid dangerous climate change by 2050 (O'Neill et al. 2010).

Demographic characteristics beyond population size will also play a more relevant role for future carbon emissions in the future. These include the age, education, and sex distribution of the population; the place of residence; and household size (O'Neill et al. 2010; Lutz and Striessing 2015). It has been found, for instance, that shifts in the age and cohort composition of the population drove some of the observed increase in carbon emissions in high-income countries in the past (Menz and Welsch 2012). China, India, and other developing countries are expected to experience the most pronounced shift toward urbanization, while countries in the European Union and Latin America will undergo significant changes in the age composition of households (O'Neill et al. 2010).

In the future, population trends will largely shape each country's contribution to global greenhouse gas emissions. As an example, and based on the expected demographic trends highlighted above, projections show that aging could reduce emissions in the long term by up to 20 percent, particularly in industrialized country regions. At the same time, urbanization could increase projected emissions by more than 25 percent, particularly in developing countries (O'Neill et al. 2010). However, urbanization is also associated with higher income growth, which in turn may lead to a reduction in emissions. Thus a better understanding of possible changes in consumption preferences associated with income growth and the urbanization process, as two potentially offsetting forces, will be required to adequately assess future global and country patterns in greenhouse gas emissions (O'Neill et al. 2012).

The emission intensity of growth varies across countries and explains differential contributions to global environmental changes moving forward (map B5.5.1). Countries with low population growth can

(box continues next page)

BOX 5.5 Current demographic trends could lead to greater greenhouse gas emissions in some countries (continued)

still account for increasing shares of emissions if their economic growth model is highly dependent on fossil fuels–based energy consumption. For instance, annual emissions per capita were much higher in the United States (17.6 tons in 2010–14) than in China (slightly above 6 tons), and above the world average of 4.5 tons per person annually (World Development Indicators). However, in general, environmental degradation is associated with the development stage of countries, following a U-shaped inverted curve. In largely agricultural economies and highly developed countries, environmental damage is minimal, while in industrializing countries pollutant emissions are highest (Aznar-Marquez and Ruiz-Tamarit 2005).

MAP B5.5.1 High-income countries with slower population growth have higher greenhouse gas emissions intensities

World CO_2 emissions per capita, metric tons per capita

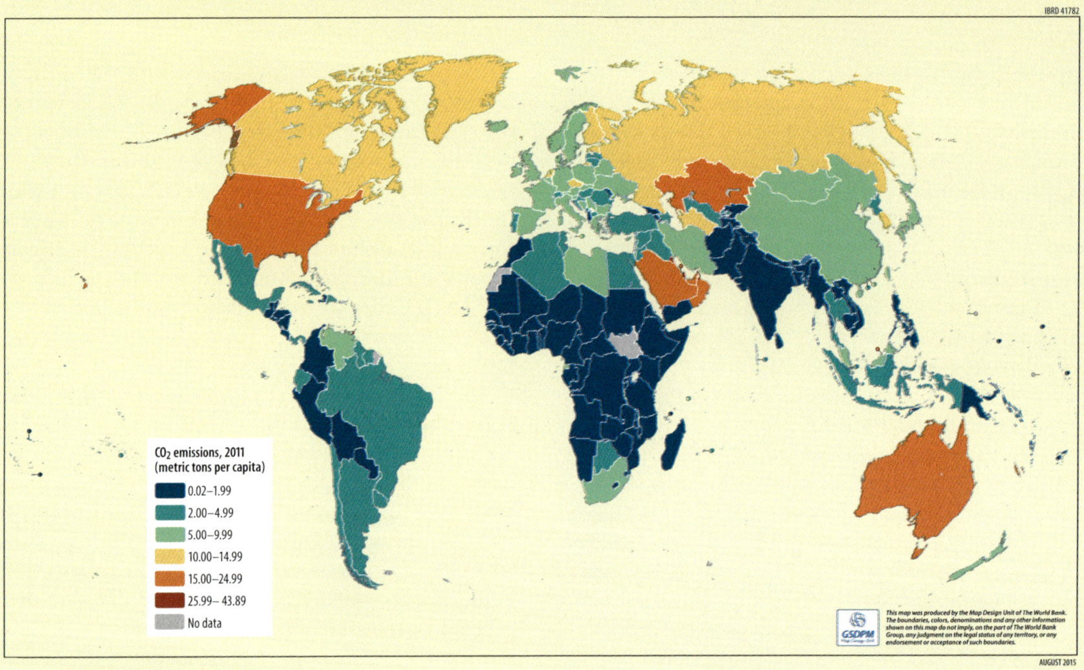

Source: World Development Indicators.

technology and consumers' behavior. The growth in per capita consumption in large, fast-growing, emerging-market economies has increased the global demand for goods and services, with subsequent implications for environmentally sustainable growth. If per capita consumption of renewable and nonrenewable resources (such as fossil fuels, water, forest resources) in developing countries follows the same profile as that in developed countries, then there may be challenges to the sustainability of global growth.

Countries can take advantage of not just their own demographic contexts but also demographic disparities across countries. The opportunities to be realized depend on the demographic stage of the country, however. Whatever the stage of transition, policies will be needed to provide the necessary conditions for an effective and productive allocation of these resources. Chapter 6 focuses on policy recommendations that will be useful in this regard.

Notes

1. Assuming a constant output per worker, if the effective number of producers (workers) grows at the same rate as the number of effective consumers (total population), there would be no change in welfare in per capita terms. For example, pre-dividend countries with very high fertility rates might have a positive growth in their GDP that does not lead to improvements in their welfare per capita, because the dependent population could be growing faster than the working-age population.
2. Appendix C3 discusses the specifics of how the typology is constructed.
3. Based on the $1.90 a day poverty line data from Povcalnet. The sample of countries included 31 pre-dividend countries, 48 early-dividend countries, 34 late-dividend countries, and 4 post-dividend countries.
4. Based on data for 191 countries from World Development Indicators; the data are for the latest year available between 2011 and 2012.
5. This projection is equivalent to the constant enrollment rate assumption in the most pessimistic education projection scenarios of KC et al. (2010).
6. Early childhood development consists of measures beyond education with clear implications for multidimensional poverty reduction (World Bank 2015a).
7. Börsch-Supan, Ludwig, and Winter (2002) and the World Bank (2013a) suggest that capital flows from fast-aging economies to younger economies could be substantial in the future.
8. The extensive literature on this includes but is not restricted to Bloom and Williamson (1998), Bloom et al. (2009), Bloom and Canning (2004), Higgins and Williamson (1997), Eastwood and Lipton (2011), Kelley and Schmidt (1995, 2005, 2007), and Rosenzweig (1990).
9. National private-savings rates have been found to depend on the age composition of the population: individuals are typically net savers when they are working age but tend to be predominantly consumers when they are young or old. Empirically, declining dependency ratios tend to boost domestic savings and investment (Loayza, Schmitt-Hebel, and Servén 2000).
10. An extensive literature on this includes Kelley and Schmidt (2005), Higgins (1998), Higgins and Williamson (1997), and Kinugasa and Mason (2007).
11. Several studies suggest that declining dependency ratios tend to boost domestic savings and investment (Loayza, Schmitt-Hebel, and Servén 2000), but others suggest that some of these findings are not plausible within the life-cycle savings model on which this empirical analysis relies. Lee, Mason, and Miller (2003) and Kinugasa and Mason (2007) suggest that some impact of the dependency ratio on saving is most pronounced in countries experiencing rapid fertility decline, rapid economic growth, and shifts away from reliance on family transfers for old-age support.
12. Due to the potential endogeneity issues described in appendix C.4, the econometric results showing the association between demographic change and the poverty rate should be interpreted cautiously, as correlations may not reflect causality.
13. The analysis in this section is based on data from the National Transfer Accounts (NTAs).
14. Net public transfers are defined in NTAs as public transfer inflows less public transfer outflows. Public transfer inflows are broadly defined to include cash and all in-kind transfers, such as education, publicly funded health care, and other forms of public consumption. Public transfer outflows are defined as the taxes imposed, including indirect taxes, to fund public transfer inflows. Inflows and outflows are assigned to age groups using administrative records, household surveys, and tax-incidence rules that are described in more detail in Lee and Mason (2011) and UN (2013)
15. Employment-based pensions paid to retirees, including payments to public sector retirees, are not transfers. They are a form of deferred compensation. To the extent that the elderly are supported through transfers, it is in the form of health and other in-kind

transfers. Taxes assessed on pension income may be small in a country, but transfer outflows include taxes on profits, rent, interest, and consumption including value added taxes.

16. Based on these differences, World Bank (2015b and Bussolo, Koettle, and Sinnott (2015) argue that countries with less mature public-pension systems have an opportunity to reform these systems before the beneficiaries grow old.

References

Aznar-Marquez, J., and J. R. Ruiz-Tamarit. 2005. "Democratic Transition, Environmental Concern and the Kuznets Curve." Département des Sciences Économiques de l'Université catholique de Louvain, Belgium.

Banerjee, A., R. Pande, and M. Walton. 2012. "Delhi's Slum Dwellers: Deprivation, Preferences and Political Engagement among the Urban Poor." Working Paper, International Growth Centre, London.

Barro, R. J. 2003. "Determinants of Economic Growth in a Panel of Countries." *Annals of Economics and Finance* 4 (2): 231–74.

Batini, N., T. Callen, and W. McKibbin. 2006. "The Global Impact of Demographic Change." IMF Working Paper, WP 06/09. International Monetary Fund, Washington, DC.

Becker, G. S. 1960. "An Economic Analysis of Fertility." In *Demographic and Economic Change in Developed Countries*. New York: Columbia University Press.

Becker, G. S., and H. G. Lewis. 1973. "On the Interaction between the Quantity and Quality of Children." *Journal of Political Economy* 81 (2).

Birdsall, N., A. Kelley, and S. Sinding, eds. 2003. *Demographic Change, Economic Growth, and Poverty in the Developing World*. Oxford, U.K.: Oxford University Press.

Bloom, D., and D. Canning. 2004. "Global Demographic Change: Dimensions and Economic Significance" in *Global Demographic Change: Economic Impacts and Policy Challenges*, proceedings, Federal Reserve Bank of Kansas City, "Economic Policy Symposium—Jackson Hole, Wyoming, August 26–28, pp 9–26.

Bloom, D., D. Canning, G. Fink, and J. E. Finlay. 2009. "Fertility, Female Labor Force Participation, and the Demographic Dividend." *Journal of Economic Growth* 14 (2): 79–101.

Bloom, D., and J. Williamson. 1998. "Demographic Transition and Economic Miracles in Emerging Asia." *World Bank Economic Review* 12 (3): 419–56.

Bogetic, Z., H. Onder, A. Onal, E. Skrok, E. Schwartz, and H. Winkler. 2015. "Fiscal Policy Issues in the Aging Societies." MFM Discussion Paper 1, World Bank, Washington, DC.

Bonoli, G., and T. Shinkawa. 2005. *Aging and Pension Reform around the World: Evidence from Eleven Countries*. Edward Elgar Publishing.

Börsch-Supan, A. 2013. "Myths, Scientific Evidence and Economic Policy in an Aging World." *Journal of the Economics of Ageing* 1–2: 3–15.

Börsch-Supan, A., A. Ludwig, and J. Winter. 2002. "Ageing and International Capital Flows." In *Ageing, Financial Markets and Monetary Policy*, edited by A.J. Auerback and H. Herrmann, chapter 2. Berlin: Springer.

Bradley, D., C. Stephens, T. Harpham, and S. Cairncross. 1992. "A Review of the Environmental Health Impacts in Developing Country Cities." Urban Management Program Discussion Paper 11101, World Bank, Washington, DC.

Bussolo, M., J. Koettl, and E. Sinnott. 2015. *Golden Aging: Prospects for Healthy, Active, and Prosperous Aging in Europe and Central Asia*. Washington, DC: World Bank.

CMS (Centers for Medicare and Medicaid Services). 2015a. *Health Expenditure Projections 2014–2024 Forecast Summary*. Washington, DC: Centers for Medicare and Medicaid Services.

———. 2015b. *Health Expenditures by Age and Gender*. Washington, DC: Centers for Medicare and Medicaid Services.

Cunningham, H., and P. Viazzo. 1996. *Child Labor in Historical Perspective—1980–1985: Case Studies from Europe, Japan and*

Colombia. Florence: UNICEF International Child Development Center.

de la Maisonneuve, C., and J. O. Martins. 2013. "A Projection Method for Public Health and Long-Term Care Expenditures." Economics Department Working Papers 1048, Organisation for Economic Co-operation and Development, Paris.

Duflo, E., S. Galiani, and M. Mobarak. 2012. "Improving Access to Urban Services for the Poor: Open Issues and a Framework for Future Research Agenda." J-Pal Urban Services Review Paper, Cambridge, MA.

Eastwood, R., and M. Lipton. 2011. "Demographic Transition in Sub-Saharan Africa: How Big Will the Economic Dividend Be?" *Population Studies* 65(1): 9–35.

EC (European Commission). 2015. *The 2015 Ageing Report. Economic and Budgetary Projections for the 28 EU Member States (2013–2060)*. Brussels: European Commission.

Harper, S. 2013. "Population–Environment Interactions: European Migration, Population Composition and Climate Change." *Environmental and Resource Economics* 55 (4): 525–41.

Heckman, J. 2008. "Schools, Skills, and Synapses." *Economic Inquiry* 46 (3): 289–324.

Heckman, J., R. Pinto, and P. Savelyev. 2013. "Understanding the Mechanisms through Which an Influential Early Childhood Program Boosted Adult Outcomes." *American Economic Review* 103 (6): 2052–86.

Herrmann, M., ed. 2015. *Consequential Omissions. How Demography Shapes Development—Lessons from the MDGs for the SDGs*. Berlin: Berlin Institute for Population and Development.

Higgins, M. 1998. "Demography, National Savings, and International Capital Flows." *International Economic Review* 39: 343–69.

Higgins, M., and J. G. Williamson. 1997. "Age Structure Dynamics in Asia and Dependence on Foreign Capital." *Population and Development Review* 23 (2): 261–93.

IMF (International Monetary Fund). 2015. *World Economic Outlook: Uneven Growth—Short- and Long-Term Factors*. Washington, DC: International Monetary Fund.

KC, S., B. Barakat, A. Goujon, V. Skirbekk, W. Sanderson, and W. Lutz. 2010. "Projection of Populations by Level of Educational Attainment, Age, and Sex for 120 Countries for 2005–2050." *Demographic Research* 22 (15): 383–472.

Kelley and Schmidt 1995. "Aggregate Population and Economic Growth Correlations: The Role of the Components of Demographic Change." *Demography* 32 (4): 543–55.

———. 2005. "Evolution of Recent Economic-Demographic Modeling: A Synthesis." *Journal of Population Economics* 18 (2): 275–300.

———. 2007. "A Century of Demographic Change and Economic Growth: The Asian Experience in Regional and Temporal Perspective." In *Population Change, Labor Markets and Sustainable Growth: Towards a New Economic Paradigm*, edited by A. Mason and M. Yamaguchi, 39–74. Amsterdam: Elsevier.

Kinugasa, T., and A. Mason, A. 2007. "Why Countries Become Wealthy: The Effects of Adult Longevity on Saving." *World Development* 35 (1): 1–23.

Kremer, M. 1993. "Population Growth and Technological Change: One Million BC to 1990." *Quarterly Journal of Economics* 681–716.

Krugman, P. 1991. "Technology, Trade and Factor Prices." *Journal of International Economics* 50 (1): 51–71.

———. 1994. "The Myth of Asia's Miracle." *Foreign Affairs* 73 (6): 62–78.

Lassman, D., M. Hartman, B. Washington, K. Andrews, and A. Caitlin. 2014. "US Health Spending Trends by Age and Gender: Selected Years 2002–10." *Health Affairs* 33 (5): 815–22.

Lee, R., A. Mason, and T. Miller. 2003. "From Transfers to Individual Responsibility: Implications for Savings and Capital Accumulation in Taiwan and the United States." *Scandinavian Journal of Economics* 105(3): 339–57.

Lee, R., and A. Mason. 2006. "What Is the Demographic Dividend?" *Finance and Development* 43 (3).

———. eds. 2011. *Population Aging and the Generational Economy: A Global Perspective*. Cheltenham, U.K.: Edward Elgar.

Lee, R., et al. 2014. "Is Low Fertility Really a Problem? Population Aging, Dependency, and Consumption." *Science* 346 (6206): 229–34.

Loayza, N., K. Schmitt-Hebel, and L. Servén. 2000. "What Drives Private Saving across the World?" *Review of Economics and Statistics* 82 (2): 165–81.

Lucas Jr., R. 1988. "On the Mechanics of Economic Development." *Journal of Monetary Economics* 22(1): 3–42.

Lutz, W., and E. Striessing. 2015. Demographic Aspects of Climate Change Mitigation and Adaptation. *Population Studies* 69 (supp 1): S69–S76.

Manyika, J., J.Woetzel, R. Dobbs, J. Remes, E. Labaye, and A. Jordan. 2015. *Global Growth: Can Productivity Save the Day in an Aging World?* New York: McKinsey Global Institute.

Marx, B., T. Stoker, and T. Suri. 2013. "The Economics of Slums in the Developing World." *Journal of Economic Perspectives* 27 (4): 187–210.

Mason, A. 2005. "Demographic Transition and Demographic Dividends in Developed and Developing Countries." In *United Nations Expert Group Meeting on Social and Economic Implications of Changing Population Age Sstructures*, vol. 31.

Mason, A., and T. Kinugasa. 2008. "East Asian Economic Development: Two Demographic Dividends." *Journal of Asian Economics* 19 (5): 389–99.

McKibbin, W. J. 2006. "The Global Macroeconomic Consequences of a Demographic Transition." *Asian Economic Papers* 5 (1): 92–134.

Menz, T., and H. Welsch. 2012. "Population Aging and Carbon Emissions in OECD Countries: Accounting for Life-cycle and Cohort Effects." *Energy Economics* 34 (3): 842–49.

O'Neill, B. C. 2009. "Climate Change and Population Growth." In *Population, Justice and the Environmental Challenge*, edited by L. Mazur. Washington, DC: Island Press.

O'Neill, B. C., X. Ren, L. Jiang, et al. 2012. "The Effect of Urbanization on Energy Use in India and China in the Ipets Model." *Energy Economics* 34 (Supplement 3): S339–S345.

O'Neill, B. C., et al. 2010. "Global Demographic Trends and Future Carbon Emissions." *Proceedings of the National Academy of Sciences of the United States of America* 107: 17521–26.

Pachauri, R. K., and A. Reisinger, eds. 2007. *Climate Change 2007 Synthesis Report: Summary for Policymakers.* IPCC Secretariat.

Rosenzweig, Mark R. 1990. "Population Growth and Human Capital Investments: Theory and Evidence." *Journal of Political Economy* 98 (5): 38–70.

Saez, E., and G. Zucman. 2014. "Wealth Inequality in the United States since 1913: Evidence from Capitalized Income Tax Data." Working Paper, National Bureau of Economic Research, Cambridge, MA.

Towers Watson. 2012. *Global Pension Assets Study 2012*. London: Towers Watson.

Tyers, R., and Q. Shi. 2007. "Demographic Change and Policy Responses: Implications for the Global Economy." *World Economy* 30 (4): 537–66.

UN (United Nations). 2008. *Urbanization, Internal Migration and Development: An International Perspective.* New York: United Nations.

———. 2013. *National Transfer Accounts Manual: Measuring and Analysing the Generational Economy.* New York, United Nations.

———. 2015. *World Population Prospects: The 2015 Revision,* New York: United Nations, Department of Economic and Social Affairs, Population Division.

UN-Habitat. 2003. *The Challenges of Slums: Global Report on Human Settlements 2003.* London and Sterling, VA: Earthscan Publications.

World Bank. 2013a. *Global Development Horizons: Capital for the Future.* Washington, DC: World Bank.

———. 2013b. *Poverty Assessment: Assessing a Decade of Progress in Reducing Poverty 2000–2010.* Washington, DC: World Bank.

———. 2015a. *World Bank Support to Early Childhood Development: An Independent Evaluation.* Washington, DC: World Bank.

———. 2015b. *Aging in East Asia and Pacific: Capitalizing on the Demographic Transition.* Washington, DC: World Bank.

6

Policy Priorities in an Era of Demographic Change

Demographic change is a major factor shaping the trajectory of development for countries at all income levels. It offers opportunities where the share of working-age people in the population is rising. It can pose challenges where fertility rates are persistently high or where the population is aging rapidly. Navigating these dynamics will require sound policies informed by a long-run perspective and tailored to a nation's demographic context. Effective policies will leverage demographic transitions both within a country and across borders. Demography-informed policies can cover a wide range of areas, including human, private sector, financial development, and governance. Such policies can play important parts in achieving the development goals.

Demographic change can support development if governments implement demography-informed policies. As detailed in chapter 5, countries moving from high to low fertility can benefit from a growing working-age population share. These countries have the potential to realize the first and second demographic dividends beneficial to poverty reduction and shared prosperity, as well as to overall growth and development. Half of the world's population—and most of the world's poor—lives in countries where the working-age population share is rising. Whether a rising working-age share is beneficial depends on the extent to which governments ensure that policies and institutions take advantage of these trends. The other half of the world's population lives in countries where the population is aging, and the working-age share is dwindling. In these countries, policies will need to be adapted to these demographic changes if welfare is to be maintained or improved. It is worth noting that demographic change has significant implications for the political economy of policy making because changing age structures affect both political pressures and preferences (box 6.1).

Country-level priorities will depend on the country's stage of demographic transition. In terms of the country typology set out in chapter 5, policies in pre-dividend countries need to *spark demographic transition* by addressing human development challenges and speeding up the fertility declines necessary to raise the working-age share of the population and boost economic growth. In early-dividend countries, the priority is to *accelerate job creation* by investing in human

BOX 6.1 The impact of demographic change on political economy

Demographic change may exert a powerful impact on political forces. The nascent fields of "political demography" and "political economy of demography" seek to deepen the understanding of these impacts, and how policy choices, especially those that have distributional implications, will be affected by changes in demographic patterns (Null 2015). At the country level, three channels of impact are salient: the impact of a "youth bulge" on politics, the effect of an increase in the age of the median voter on demands for more open democratic representation, and the role of aging in shaping the prospects for pension reform. At the international level, cross-border spillovers from country-level effects of demographic change can be significant, and global economic and security arrangements may become less stable because of the aging and anticipated declines in the populations of countries that have played a pivotal role in upholding these frameworks in the past. Finally, the effect of demographic change on political preferences also plays a role in shaping the prospects for implementing policies that will be central to making the most of opportunities while mitigating the risks associated with evolving demography.

Impact on political economy at the country level

Ensuring that the youth bulge—relatively large cohorts of youth entering the labor force—is productively employed is essential for political stability. While accelerating demographic transitions to low fertility and mortality give rise to potential demographic dividends, these can be realized only if the youth bulge can find gainful employment. If employment opportunities are limited because of labor market rigidities or other factors, the risk of discontent grows. In countries within the "demographic arc of instability," defined as having a population with a median age of less than 25, the chances of conflict are 2.5 times higher than for other countries (Cincotta 2010). Based on the projection of population age structures to 2030, elevated risks of fragility and conflict become concentrated in Sub-Saharan Africa (where the median age remains low), potentially jeopardizing decades of hard-won development gains.

Populations with higher median ages tend to press for more political openness. Political demography suggests that, when the median age of the population reaches 25–35, the tolerance for authoritarianism to ensure stability falls, and the demand for liberal democracy and more openness grows (Cincotta 2011). The focus shifts to improving the investment climate and increasing openness, enabling business, and boosting employment creation.

The evidence on the impact of aging on political pressures for generous pensions is mixed. Rapid aging of populations in many countries is heightening concerns about the sustainability of pension and social protection systems, especially if a graying of the median voter bolsters political preferences for more pension spending at the expense of other priorities. The evidence for this is mixed. For example, older age cohorts in Europe tend to prefer more spending on pensions and less on education (Bussolo, Koettl, and Sinnott 2015). In the United States, this preference for lower spending extends to lower spending on a per child basis (Cattaneo and Wolter 2007; Oberndorfer and Steiner 2006; Poterba 1996). While the success of "gray interest" political parties across Europe has been mixed, older people are also more likely to vote and may increasingly frustrate pension reforms aimed at ensuring sustainability. Other evidence from OECD countries, however, suggests that an aging median voter does not lead to higher benefits per retiree, including health benefits (Hollanders and Koster 2012). Well-designed systems can also be implemented that cut across particular political interest groups (Góra 2013). In developing East Asia and Pacific, aging does not pose insurmountable challenges for public spending, especially where it is addressed through proactive public policy and political leadership (World Bank 2015b).

Impact on political economy at the global level

The contributions of demographic change to conflict, pressure for liberal democracy, or increased pension spending can lead to significant international spillovers. The potential for such spillovers is more pronounced than ever before given increasing interconnectedness and the accelerating pace of globalization

(box continues next page)

BOX 6.1 The impact of demographic change on political economy (continued)

in recent decades. For example, whether stemming from countries with low median ages in conflict, or countries with intermediate median ages in the throes of establishing more open political systems, the instability in the Middle East and North Africa has prompted a large influx of migrants and refugees to Western Europe. Similarly, increased demands for pension spending—in countries with aging populations that are typically higher income—affect the savings available for investment in emerging markets and sharpens the competition official development assistance faces for public funds.

Demographic change may have implications for international trade and security arrangements. Population aging may be weakening support for international systems in many countries that traditionally played an important role in upholding these arrangements. For example, the workforces of Germany, Japan, and the Russian Federation are shrinking and the demands for entitlement spending are rising, helping reduce their relative economic heft and shift national spending priorities. These trends will affect their capacity to bolster international political and economic systems (Goldstone, Kauffman, and Toft 2012). The shift in influence and responsibility toward developing countries for ensuring strong global economic and political relationships is already evident with the establishment of additional multilateral development banks led by the largest emerging market economies.

Implications for policy implementation

The feasibility of implementing policies informed by demography is affected by demographic change, but as noted, the findings are mixed. With the aging of the median voter, there are concerns that implementing key policies to reflect demographic change may become more difficult, "locking in" unsustainable pension systems, for example. However, in some cases the maturing median age voter appears to prefer the needed policies, such as investing in human capital, ensuring labor market flexibility, and promoting job creation in early-dividend countries. The role of demographic change is mixed even regarding politically charged issues like immigration. For example, there is strong evidence that today's elderly hold less favorable views of immigration than the average survey respondent in much of Europe; however, there is no strong reason to think that today's younger cohorts will become less supportive of migration in the future when they become the elderly (Bussolo, Koettl, and Sinnott 2015). Hence, with leadership and a strong evidence base, sound policies that reflect demographic considerations may find the necessary political support to move forward.

capital and ensuring an enabling environment for private sector development to help realize the first demographic dividend and lay the groundwork for the second dividend. In late-dividend countries, in which fertility rates are low and the working-age share of the population is high (but shrinking), the key challenge is to *sustain productivity growth* by mobilizing savings for productive investment while also preparing for aging. Finally, in post-dividend countries, the policy priority is to *adapt to aging* through efforts to maintain welfare and accommodate changing demands for services while encouraging a rise in fertility rates toward the replacement level.

Countries face opportunities to arbitrage demographic differences across borders. Taking cross-country demographic differences into account adds to the benefits of liberalizing trade in goods, services, and capital, as well as ensuring that supplies of migrant labor can meet demands through transparent and legal channels. Realizing these benefits may require closer international economic cooperation, as well as appropriate domestic interventions on trade, migration, and capital flow issues. These measures will permit countries to take advantage of opportunities arising from the heterogeneous demographic trends across countries by ensuring that cross-border economic exchange reflects the comparative advantages that are shaped by demography.

Building on the exposition of demographic trends and their channels of impact in chapters 4 and 5, this chapter highlights key policy priorities tailored to demographic features. The chapter first identifies policies to realize opportunities and mitigate risks from demographic change at the country level. It then discusses those interventions that can help make the most of the varieties of demographic change around the world.

Leveraging demographic change within countries

Analytical work and evidence from country experiences show that demographic change can inform the policies countries implement to boost growth and reduce poverty.[1] A brief summary of policy priorities within countries is presented in table 6.1. These policies enable countries to absorb additional labor in the case of the first demographic dividend and to facilitate investment in human and physical capital in the case of the second dividend. For example, in the 1960s, policies in support of investment in human capital along with openness to trade and foreign direct investment (FDI) helped East Asia take advantage of its rapid demographic transition (Bloom and Williamson 1998).

Sparking demographic transition in pre-dividend countries

Pre-dividend countries are characterized by deprivations in human development that have contributed to their slow demographic transition. Most pre-dividend countries are in Sub-Saharan Africa (see appendix C.3 for a list of countries by typology). For these countries,

TABLE 6.1 Policy priorities for leveraging demographic change at the country level

Country type	Issues	Recommendations
Pre-dividend	*Sparking demographic transition* Improving human development outcomes to reduce fertility rates.	Improve maternal and child health by strengthening provision of basic health care services. Expand education without letting girls fall behind. Empower women, and give them access to comprehensive family planning services.
Early-dividend	*Accelerating job creation* Creating productive jobs for the growing share of the population in working age to reap the first demographic dividend.	Invest in human capital, including vocational and technical training. Enhance labor market mobility. Reduce barriers to female labor force participation. Strengthen conditions conducive to savings and job creation (public services underpinning private sector activity, contract enforcement, financial inclusion, protection of labor rights).
Late-dividend	*Sustaining productivity growth* Creating conditions necessary to reap the second demographic dividend and beginning to prepare for aging.	Continue mobilization of savings for productive investment. Ensure that public policies across the board encourage labor-force participation of both sexes. Design cost-effective and sustainable systems for welfare and human development that address current needs (including health, child care, education, and support to vulnerable elderly) and that can be adapted to meet the needs that emerge as aging proceeds.
Post-dividend	*Adapting to aging* Maintaining and improving welfare in the context of a declining working-age share and growing old-age share.	Complete reforms of welfare systems—including pensions, health care, and long-term care—that ensure fiscal sustainability and, as part of integrated approaches, protection of the vulnerable, elderly and others, and encouragement of work among those who are able. Raise labor force participation and productivity (including incentives for participation targeted at women and older cohorts; and lifelong learning for all). Pursue policies that encourage a rebound of fertility, among other things by making it easier for men and women to combine child rearing and participation in the labor market.

Source: GMR team elaboration.

current outcomes are discouraging according to most development indicators, including poverty, infant mortality, educational attainment, health, and labor productivity. Because of high youth-dependency ratios, high fertility rates, and other factors, their projected population growth is high (World Bank 2015a).

Policy action focused on human development may help pre-dividend countries progress to the next stage in the demographic transition. Fertility (and child mortality) rates are influenced by policies that improve maternal and child health services, expand education coverage (particularly to girls), and empower women in the household and in the labor force (Bloom et al. 2009; Soares and Falcão 2008; World Bank 2015a). Given their potential to reduce total fertility rates and lower child mortality, these policy areas can be considered "interactive accelerators" of demographic transition, in addition to being important development goals in their own right. Concluding the unfinished Millennium Development Goals (MDGs) agenda related to these policies should be considered a priority for pre-dividend countries. Simulations for Niger, a pre-dividend country, point to the costs of inaction that stalls fertility decline: if total fertility remains at the 2015 rate of around 7 children per woman through 2050 instead of gradually declining to 4.7, the extreme poverty rate in 2050 would be substantially higher, 20 percent instead of 14 percent. (Additional analysis of Niger is found in the Country Spotlights at the end of this chapter.)

A first area of policy focus for pre-dividend countries is the improvement of health outcomes, particularly for women and children. The exact mechanisms by which maternal and child health can be improved depend on the country context. Broadly, they include measures to strengthen national health systems, including improvements in their human resource and infrastructure capacity for service delivery. Priority services areas include immunization programs, enhanced growth monitoring of children, and services targeted at women during pregnancy and after giving birth.[2] Several multilateral initiatives embrace such a multipronged approach, as illustrated by the multilateral African Road Map for reducing maternal and newborn mortality. A number of countries are strengthening the newborn components of existing child health plans as part of the World Health Organization's Every Newborn Action Plan (WHO and UNICEF 2015). Immunization coverage can also be expanded by taking advantage of multilateral initiatives, such as the Global Vaccine Action Plan, and public-private partnerships such as the Global Alliance for Vaccines and Immunizations.

A second area of policy focus is to improve educational outcomes, paying particular attention so that girls do not fall behind. Given low levels of educational attainment in pre-dividend countries, gains in educational attainment yield a future labor force that better contributes to accelerated growth by being more productive in a wider range of sectors. Schooling of girls is particularly important since improvements in their educational attainments are also associated with lower fertility rates. For example, in Ethiopia, a country that recently proceeded to the early-dividend stage, women with more education have lower fertility rates than women who are less educated. The scope for improving female education, reducing fertility, and lowering child-dependency ratios is particularly large among poorer households, thus offering a path toward accelerated poverty reduction for these groups and faster per capita growth overall as the working-age share of the population is increased.

A third area of policy focus is that of giving females greater agency and voice. These are valuable development goals on their own, and they can also contribute to lower fertility. Surveys often find that women in Africa would prefer to have fewer children than their male partners (Voas 2003). Access to comprehensive family-planning services is important for women to achieve their desired fertility levels (World Bank 2014d). Yet imbalances in household bargaining power reduce use of contraceptives and family planning, raising fertility rates above levels preferred by women. These power imbalances are also linked to the incidence of child marriage. For example, about 75 percent of girls ages 18 or younger are married in Niger, 68 percent in Central African Republic and Chad, and more than 50 percent in Burkina Faso, Guinea, Malawi, Mali, and South Sudan (World Bank 2014a). Since early marriage is associated with, and most likely contributes to, weaker educational outcomes, delayed marriage may help improve education of girls, with potential growth and poverty reduction payoffs (see the section on Niger in the Country Spotlights at the end of this chapter).

Accelerating job creation in early-dividend countries

Early-dividend countries have growing working-age population shares, and their total fertility rates have been steadily declining in recent decades. These countries currently have average fertility rates of under 4 births per woman, and many are expected to approach the replacement fertility rate of 2.1 births per woman by 2030. These predominantly middle-income countries—including several large economies, such as India and Mexico—are home to a third of the global population. Declining fertility and mortality rates and growing working-age population shares in early-dividend countries create the conditions needed to realize the first demographic dividend: a transitory boost to growth as labor supply, labor participation, and per capita savings increase.

To realize and maximize demographic dividends, early-dividend countries need to focus on interventions that help absorb new workers into productive jobs. The first demographic dividend arises only to the extent that the economy is able to create productive jobs at a rate that exceeds the rate of population growth. Such job creation may be sped up by progress in several areas: investments in human capital (including vocational and technical training), maintenance of macroeconomic stability, financial inclusion, and labor-market policies that allow all socioeconomic groups to benefit from favorable population dynamics (Fox and Sohnesen 2012; Lee and Mason 2006; Troiano 2015). Policies that improve labor mobility, for example, will make it easier for workers to find jobs where they are most needed, contributing to rural-urban migration and relocation from regions with labor surpluses to regions with shortages (World Bank 2009).

Policies and institutions also need to ensure that supply and demand for workers are consistent with rapid employment growth. Scenario analysis for Ethiopia, an early-dividend country, was used to assess the likely effects of a policy package aimed at making better use of the country's rapidly growing labor force through improved education, higher private savings, and more rapid total factor productivity (TFP) growth during the period 2015–30 (see the section on Ethiopia in the Country Spotlights at the end of this chapter). The results indicate that, over a 15-year horizon, higher private savings (channeled into higher private investment) and more rapid TFP growth can make a significant difference.

In many countries, persistent low female labor-force participation is an obstacle to the realization of the first demographic dividend. Gender gaps in labor force participation have generally persisted (based on figure 6.1, the gender gap in labor-force participation is smaller in 2013 than in 1990), especially in some demographic types and in some regions. In the Middle East and North Africa region, for example, the average female participation rate is 32 percent, and several countries have rates below 20 percent, including Algeria, the Islamic Republic of Iran, Iraq, and Jordan. Facilitating the access of females to the labor market has simultaneous effects on demography, human capital, and growth, and is needed to realize the first demographic dividend (Galor 2012). Causality may also go in other directions because high fertility rates may limit female education and labor-force participation: studies suggest that a single birth reduces a woman's labor supply by almost 2 years during her reproductive life (Bloom et al. 2009).

FIGURE 6.1 Gender gaps in labor-force participation have persisted since the 1990s across all countries

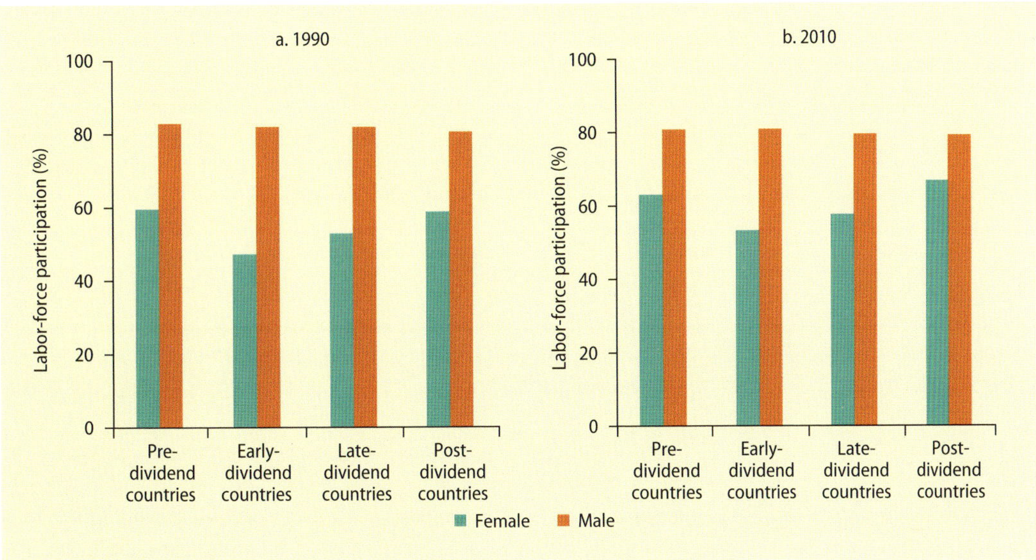

Source: World Bank calculations, based on UN 2015 and the World Bank's World Development Indicators database for 2015.
Note: Labor-force participation includes both men and women ages 15–64.

Early-dividend countries also need to implement policies that will facilitate the second demographic dividend in the future. Such policies should encourage savings and their channeling into productive investments in human and physical capital. Their potential payoffs start to become significant when the decline in fertility rates sets in; that is, even though policies in this area remain important at later demographic stages, a late start may come at the cost of foregone growth. In the case of human capital, family planning programs that have been found to contribute to fertility declines are also positively associated with increases in human capital investment (Joshi and Schultz 2013). For physical capital investment and asset accumulation in general, policy should ensure that when the population begins to age, those retiring workers who will be the future elderly have been saving and accumulating assets throughout their lives. If governments wait until the population has already begun to age before encouraging and facilitating saving, then it may be too late, since the retiring and retired workers may not have as many assets and will have to rely on family or public transfers, coming out of current labor income.[3]

Sustaining productivity growth in late-dividend countries

Thanks to their still large (albeit often shrinking) working-age population shares, late-dividend countries have the ability to extract a substantial second demographic dividend.[4] Many countries in Eastern Europe, East Asia, and Latin America belong to this group. The reasons for projected growth-dampening declines in the working-age share of the population vary across countries. In most Eastern European countries, these declines have been driven mainly by declining fertility and, to a lesser extent, by increases in longevity. For countries in Latin America and East Asia, fertility declines and increased longevity have both been important. East Asia is aging more rapidly than any other region in history, with Vietnam and Thailand, two late-dividend countries, representing extreme cases (Cotlear 2011; World Bank 2015a). However, a slowdown in economic growth resulting from shrinking working-age shares is not inevitable if countries boost productivity growth through the second demographic dividend. Because of their still sizable working-age shares, high aggregate savings and investment are feasible. The fact that longevity typically is increasing in these countries adds to the incentives for people to save for their retirement (Lee and Mason 2006).

Policies in support of higher aggregate savings to facilitate greater investments in human and physical capital is a top priority for late-dividend countries. A financial sector that is inclusive, reaching across regions and income groups, and that provides adequate incentives is needed to raise savings and channel them to productive investments in physical capital. Investments in human capital may similarly be facilitated by incentives in the form of wage gains in a well-functioning labor market and the presence of a financial sector that encourages savings for future education; however, the latter would need to be underpinned by a strong educational sector, typically including a mix of public and private services. The realization of the second dividend is particularly important since it may add to the future productivity of an increasingly scarce labor force in at least two ways: by directly adding to its skills and flexibility and by reducing the ratio of labor to physical capital.

The long-run benefit of increased physical and human capital accumulation may be reinforced by complementary labor and commercial policies. The policies that most effectively support growth are context specific. However, increased education for females often may boost female labor-force participation. So too can improved access to formal child and elderly health care, given the typical role of women as family caregivers (Bussolo, Koettl, and Sinnott 2015). For the growing old-age population, labor-force participation may be encouraged by policies that contribute to better health (enabling them to work) and by supportive incentives (encouraging them to work, for example by carefully designed pension systems) (World Bank 2015a). For countries (especially in Eastern Europe) that experience significant emigration by young workers despite increased aging and labor scarcity, many policies that make it attractive for women and elderly to work may also, to the extent that they involve a general improvement in work incentives, discourage emigration and encourage immigration by returning nationals and others (Bussolo, Koettl, and Sinnott 2015).

Population aging will also generate growing demands for pensions, health care, long-term care, and social protection (for the vulnerable), long-term care, and health services. Given that the share of the elderly is still relatively small, the short-run repercussions of the specific policy choices in this area are relatively limited. Given that the share of the old will grow, however, the initial design of policies in this area is extremely important considering their fiscal consequences and the difficulty of changing behavioral and institutional patterns. The lessons from countries that currently have reached the post-dividend stage suggest that it may be particularly important to ensure that long-term care is, as much as possible, offered at home or within the community, rather than in nursing homes and hospitals, which tend to be costlier. In addition, rules for pension systems should be consistent with working at an older age as life expectancy increases (raising overall living standards) (World Bank 2015a).

Policies that influence savings, labor force participation, and labor productivity may also yield substantial long-run gains. Brazil, for example, faces the challenge of finding ways to increase output per worker while protecting the living standards of its rapidly growing elderly population and maintaining sustainable fiscal balances. Scenario analysis suggests that, by boosting savings to the levels of comparable countries, ensuring increased labor-force participation and moderately raising labor-specific productivity, the country could raise average annual GDP per-capita growth between 2016 and 2050 by 1 percentage point (doubling the growth rate) and improving other development outcomes (see the section on Brazil in the Country Spotlights at the end of this chapter).

Adapting to aging in post-dividend countries

For post-dividend countries, characterized by a large share of the population age 65 or older, the challenge is to adapt to aging so that living standards can be maintained and improved.[5] Post-dividend countries are characterized by a substantial decline in mortality and fertility rates, leading to a fall in their working-age population and its share in the total population. The dependent populations have shifted from the young to the old and inactive. These trends are likely to exert upward pressure on public spending while slowing potential output growth. Despite the major challenges that an aging population presents, increased longevity can be an economic boon if it translates into longer working lives and higher productivity per worker.

A top priority for these countries is to fine-tune welfare, health, and education policies to ensure successful adaptation to aging while enhancing and maintaining fiscal sustainability. Given considerable lags in the adaptation of policies, behavior, and institutions to new realities, this task is urgent. The job is easier where countries have inherited good policies and their effects from earlier stages of demographic transition. The reforms that may be of high priority will vary from one country to another and may be guided by analysis of how a country, considering its median age, performs compared with other countries according to indicators such as expected years of healthy life at birth, labor force participation rates for different groups, savings, net migration, labor productivity, relative old-age poverty, total fertility rate, and public debt (Bussolo, Koettl, and Sinnott 2015).

Policies will need to help raise employment rates among those who are above today's typical retirement ages and encourage savings channeled to productive physical investments. The design of policies in a wide range of areas, including education, health, and pensions, may contribute to the long-run achievement of this objective (box 6.2 discusses pension reform from a European perspective). In education, a comprehensive high-quality system is needed both for the young and, in a manner integrated with work, for adults throughout the life cycle. Among the elderly, a strong educational background will likely increase the incentives to work since it tends to raise wages and improve employment prospects. In health, preventive care, and a healthy living style help ensure that people age in good health and remain able to work. Pension systems may be designed to encourage late retirement, by imposing higher minimum retirement ages and offering incentives to delay retirement. In a setting with a well-functioning financial system, high employment rates among the elderly, and the expectation of living long, aging need not be associated with a decline in private savings rates.

Public policy may also help raise low fertility rates by making it easier to combine child rearing and labor-market engagement and by reducing financial burdens of having children. Given that low fertility rates are the main source behind the emerging aging challenge, it is important to design policies that can change this situation. In fact, there is no strong reason to take for granted that the societies that today have rates below replacement rates are destined to remain in this situation forever: fertility rates have recently changed drastically during a short time period, countries at similar income levels show significant differences, and in some post-dividend countries, increases have been recorded in recent years. In Europe, countries with the highest female labor-force participation and employment rates also have high fertility rates, demonstrating that parenthood can be reconciled with work (Myrskylä et al. 2009). Compared with observed total fertility rates for 1985–90, the projected rates for 2015–20 show increases of more than 0.1 for 7 post-dividend countries, all in Europe: Belgium, Denmark, Finland, France, Italy, Luxembourg, and the Netherlands (UN 2015).

Scenario analysis for Japan up to the year 2100 demonstrates the importance of some

BOX 6.2 Pension System Reform: The perspective of European countries

Population aging, driven by increasing longevity and low fertility, poses a persistent long-term challenge.[a] Many European countries, already facing an increased debt burden resulting from the economic crisis, have adopted reforms to deal with this challenge and, as a result, public pension spending as a share of GDP is expected to remain more or less stable in Europe (EU28) until 2060.

Many of the reforms lengthened working lives so that individuals contribute more to improve the sustainability of the system. Some countries implemented increases in minimum contributory periods while limiting the effect of career breaks and part-time work. Most pension reforms, however, are focused on prolonging working lives at the end of the career through increases in the statutory retirement age; a tightening of early retirement provisions, including higher penalties for early benefit withdrawals; and greater financial incentives to work beyond the pensionable age.

Retirement age is probably the most contentious pension parameter. Increasing it is a politically sensitive issue in many countries, and winning approval for it has generally been difficult. Still, Hungary, Ireland, the Netherlands, Portugal, Spain, and the United Kingdom have all raised retirement ages, sometimes beyond 65, generally the norm in most countries for the past decade. A few countries—Greece, Italy, Slovenia, and Poland—have equalized the retirement age of men and women. The majority of the legislated increases are phased in over several years and often apply to future cohorts of workers.

Some countries, including France and Luxembourg, have increased the minimum periods workers must contribute to a pension plan before being permitted to draw benefits. Other countries have opted for automatic adjustment of pension systems based on gains in life expectancy, or in some cases on economic developments. Automatic adjustments can be politically appealing, but their design benefits can be a challenge if financial sustainability is enhanced at the expense of lower benefits for already financially precarious population groups.

Austria, Belgium, Denmark, Portugal, and Spain have all made access to early retirement more restrictive. Access to disability pensions has been tightened in Finland, Hungary, and Poland. Financial incentives to encourage people to work longer have been strengthened in the Netherlands, Portugal, and Sweden and have often been accompanied by increasing flexibility to combine pension benefit withdrawal with work. In contrast, full pension benefits (without penalties) will be awarded below the legal retirement age to people who started their career early in France and Germany.

a. This box was contributed by the OECD, and is based on OECD 2014.

of the policy interventions discussed here. Japan's experience exemplifies the difficulties of raising fertility rates; evaluations of its pronatalist initiatives since the early 1990s found that they had almost no effect on fertility.[6] Nevertheless, learning from experience and continuing the pursuit of policies in this area are critical given that Japan must raise fertility in the very long run if it wants to avoid a constantly shrinking population. Scenario analysis analyzes effects of a combination of policy interventions, including increases in fertility, migration, and labor-force participation up to 2100, indicating that they may increase both total and per capita GDP substantially (see the section on Japan in the Country Spotlights at the end of this chapter).

While higher labor force participation may have a lasting impact on GDP per capita and total GDP, greater legal migration and fertility primarily affect total GDP and not GDP per capita, since they result in increases in total population. One way to alleviate the labor market pressures is to a focus on a better allocation of skills by fostering internal mobility (an issue that may be especially important within Europe); a better use of migrants' skills; and the development of migrants' skills (box 6.3).

The age composition of the population is not the only determinant of living conditions

BOX 6.3 Migration and labor-market-policy reform from the perspective of high-income countries

All the members of the Organisation for Economic Co-operation and Development (OECD) are confronted with the effects of population aging, but the European Union (EU) and Japan will be affected first and most severely.[a] The EU28 working-age population (15–64) is projected to decline by 2.2 percent between 2013 and 2020. Without migration, the working-age population of the 28 EU countries is expected to decline by more than 11 million by 2020 (80 million by 2050). Under this scenario, the working-age population in Germany, Italy, and Poland will shrink by more than 1.5 million by 2020. Similar trends will be observed in Japan (-8 million) and, to a lesser extent, Canada (–1 million). In the United States and Australia, the working-age population will remain stable. The short- and medium-term effects of demographic changes on the labor force are not clear-cut however, because of changes in labor-participation rates by gender, age, and education level. Further progress in tackling the gender gap in employment, addressing the problems of disadvantaged youth, and increasing the employment rates of older workers would significantly increase the labor force.

Taking migration into account transforms the picture. At current projected levels of net migration and participation, the European labor force will increase slightly by 1.2 percent between 2010 and 2020. Moreover, if immigrants participated at the same rates as their native-born counterparts with similar characteristics, an additional 1 million workers would be added to the rolls in the EU.

To reap the full potential of migration, a three-pronged approach is needed: a focus on a better allocation of skills by fostering internal mobility, notably within Europe; a better use of migrants' skills; and the development of migrants' skills. Given the large differences in labor-market conditions across European countries (which were further amplified during the financial crisis), internal labor mobility could make a significant contribution to overall employment growth. To improve the use of the potential of intra-EU migration, efforts to reduce barriers to mobility need to be stepped up. As part of a broader mobility strategy, skills-matching tools within the EU need to be strengthened and the learning of relevant languages promoted.

Immigrants tend to be overrepresented on both ends of the qualification scale, but on average they have slightly fewer years of education than the native-born. Labor market disparities between the foreign-born and their native-born peers widen with educational attainment, however, and returns to foreign qualifications are lower than returns to host-country qualifications, in terms of employment, job quality, and earnings.

Not only are the skills of immigrants often underutilized but so too are those of their children who have been raised and trained in the host country. Strengthening integration and antidiscrimination policies will be necessary to address this issue. Efficient use of the skills of immigrants and development of their potential requires a series of measures, including increasing the availability of information and recognition of foreign qualifications; ensuring that immigrants have access to effective, active, labor-market programs; putting immigrants more directly in contact with employers; making sure that children of immigrants have access to early childhood education and care; and providing language training adapted to migrants' skills in destination countries.

a. This box was contributed by the OECD and is based on OECD-EU 2014.

for post-dividend countries. The policies that determine how countries adapt to aging may in fact be far more important. With proper incentives and good health at higher ages (already experienced by many in post-dividend countries), nothing prevents people from working and saving beyond the age limits that have been observed to date. The changing roles of women in the labor market in recent decades show that gender differences need not be significant. Contrary to common perceptions, the share of the population in different age cohorts is not a good predictor of health costs. In fact, the highest annual costs are incurred during the last few years (especially the last year) in the lives of most of the aging. Moreover, health costs are to a large extent a function of the choices that society and individuals have made during several decades, influencing the health of the aging, which depends on lifestyle choices and the organization of the health system. However, time lags in health and education may be long, and it is difficult to quickly adapt policies to match new realities.

The welfare system and human development policies should be designed to provide adequate protection for the vulnerable, including the elderly poor. The welfare system should aim to ensure that no one is left behind throughout the different stages of the life cycle: provision of child care to reconcile work and parenthood; education at different stages of life; health care; and long-term care complementing the care provided by families, pensions, and a social safety net that catches those that otherwise would risk falling into poverty (OECD 2013b).

Decisions to maximize service coverage in a wide range of areas, including a strong welfare system, must carefully consider the fiscal consequences of different options. The choices that are made should reflect societal preferences and awareness of the consequences of different decisions. Fortunately, a rich set of options is available in many areas. The different institutional options for health and long-term care already available in the late-dividend stage are also relevant for post-dividend countries, where these options may have vastly different cost implications. In several areas, different degrees of targeting of public spending on groups that are particularly needy may be considered. In this context, it is important to reiterate that costs tend to be easier to control over time if the initial design is fiscally sound and avoids the creation of behavior and expectations that cannot be sustained. For example, pension systems with minimum retirement ages that increase with life expectancy may offer an effective means of containing costs, in contrast to systems that permit retirement after a certain number of service years irrespective of age and without any penalty.

Leveraging demographic differences across countries

Variation in demographic change among countries creates opportunities for cross-border exchanges and international cooperation. Differences in the demographic dynamics at the country level are producing important spillovers, changing the comparative advantages that underpin trade and the returns to labor and capital. To benefit from these changes, countries typically need to implement policies that enhance trade in goods and services and promote greater factor mobility.[7] As a result, some labor-intensive production may shift from East Asia to South Asia and Africa, or migration may increase from countries with growing working-age populations to countries where the number of workers is falling, with migrants often helping deliver nontradable services, such as elderly care. A brief summary of policy priorities across countries is presented in table 6.2. Global demographic change is also related to environmental sustainability, a crucial challenge that countries must tackle together (box 6.4).

The complementary relationship among migration, trade, and capital flows implies that all of these factors may play a role in the adjustment to changing demographic patters. The World Bank Africa-Asia Trade and Investment Survey, as well as business case studies, clearly identify such complementarities in China and India's trade and investment ties with African countries.[8] Most studies also find a mutually reinforcing effect between trade and investment flows on the one hand and technology transfers on the other, suggesting that policies facilitating cross-border flows are likely to accelerate the pace of technological diffusion, contributing to growth and poverty eradication.[9]

Supporting international trade

Supported by policies that facilitate trade, developing countries could benefit from differing demographic trajectories that are contributing to shifts in trade patterns. Countries at the early stage in their demographic transition are expected to raise their share of global

TABLE 6.2 Policy priorities for leveraging the differences in demographic change across countries

Area of focus	Issues	Recommendations
International trade	Promoting foreign provision of education services to boost educational opportunities in countries with a high share of young population or to facilitate lifelong learning for aging countries.	Ease visa requirements for the free flow of international students and academics; address qualification recognition issues; reduce limits on foreign ownership; and increase transparency of government education regulations.
	Using foreign providers to meet demand for health services in aging countries.	Address restrictions affecting the physical presence of foreign suppliers, foreign equity ceilings, or barriers on the movement of health care professionals across borders.
	Supporting comparative advantage in producing labor-intensive products in labor-abundant countries.	Streamline customs, border, and transit performance; improve logistics and transport services and extend physical infrastructure; tackle remaining tariff and nontariff barriers on goods trade.
Migration	Promoting legal migration flows to counteract the decline in working-age populations in aging countries and to mitigate labor market pressures in labor-abundant countries.	Formulate clear migration policies; enforce minimum wage laws; provide adequate information to migrants about their rights and obligations; facilitate their contribution to and benefits from social protection schemes and public services; sanction potential abuses by firms.
	Reducing the burden of brain drain in sending countries.	Develop comprehensive and targeted policies to retain, and attract talent; encourage return migration.
International finance	Attracting international capital flows to young, labor-abundant countries.	Create favorable investment climate; strengthen macroeconomic stability, the financial sector, and governance.
	Addressing challenges posed by large and volatile capital flows to developing countries.	Undertake measures to relax investment barriers at the domestic, regional, and global level.
	Supporting opportunities for capital-abundant countries to increase returns and diversify investment portfolios.	Introduce macroeconomic policies to address risks from volatile capital inflows, supervision, regulation, and strong institutions.
		Provide investment guarantees or technical assistance.

Source: GMR team elaboration.

BOX 6.4 Environmental sustainability and demographics

The global demographic transition under way has been influenced by a parallel environmental transition that may slow down development progress. Changes in the size, composition, density, and distribution of the population over the past three centuries in combination with the associated shift toward industrialization, urbanization, and higher consumption throughout the world have important implications for environmental sustainability. For instance, it has been shown that greenhouse gas emissions increase with population size, and that these emissions vary depending on the stage of a country's development.[a] In turn, environmental changes can slow development progress through a wide range of channels including health, water supply, food security and agriculture, infrastructure, and services provision, thus affecting demographics, especially migration patterns. Such negative effects already can be observed in different parts of the world, including countries in Asia and Central America.[b]

Urbanization and aging deserve greater attention in emissions projections. Population aging, urbanization, household size, land and energy use, technology, and climate policy may have a more significant impact on emissions in the future than population growth per se.[c] Urbanization and aging may be especially important in China, India, the United States and the European Union.[d] Urbanization will also become increasingly important in Sub-Saharan Africa, where almost half of the population is expected to live in cities by 2030.[e] Projections suggest that household size decreases as populations age, a change that leads to higher emissions due to a loss in economies of scale in energy consumption.[f] The effects of urbanization, however, are less clear. This trend increases economic activity through a higher concentration of production and consumption but also allows for economies of scale and greater energy efficiency.[g]

(box continues next page)

BOX 6.4 Environmental sustainability and demographics (continued)

In short, demographic trends and related policies will have implications for the global environment and for the effectiveness of adaptation and mitigation strategies. Family planning and reproductive health policies may help mitigate the negative effects of climate change by reducing population growth, especially in pre- and early-dividend countries. Education is not only likely to lower fertility, it can also have a major impact on the effectiveness of measures aimed at tackling the negative effects of climate change. Among other things, it may improve the adaptive capacity of individuals and raise awareness of the implications of consumption patterns, leading to changes in lifestyles and behaviors. In rapidly urbanizing areas, the next decades offer a window of opportunity for mitigation through policies that improve access to public transport and consider environmental aspects of the location of high-density residential and employment areas.

The links between demography, environmental sustainability, and development goals raise complex issues that have to be taken into account in policy making. Global efforts may be the only way to adequately address most of these issues. Reaching agreements on the best way forward is challenging, however; outcomes that are seen as equitable may have the highest potential to be adopted. Developing countries that have high fertility rates or undergo rapid urbanization and industrialization, or both, have contributed least to climate change and are disproportionately affected by its negative consequences. They often have limited capacity to develop and implement adaptation and mitigation strategies. Indeed, poor and vulnerable populations are particularly exposed to climate risks through higher temperatures, water stress, rising sea levels, loss of agricultural production, and the spread of diseases.

a. Liddle 2011, 2013; Liddle and Lung 2010; O'Neill et al. 2012; Zagheni 2011.
b. Harper 2013.
c. IPCC 2014; Jiang and Hardee 2009; Stephenson et al. 2013.
d. O'Neill 2009; O'Neill et al. 2012.
e. Black et al. 2008.
f. Dalton et al. 2008; Jiang and O'Neill 2007; Zeng et al. 2008.
g. Sadorsky 2013.

trade, which can boost incomes if supported by appropriate policies. Facilitating and enabling trade in products and services that are growing in importance, especially those that are most closely related to demographic change, such as health care and education, can play an important role. Knowledge transfers from trade in health and education products and services contribute significantly to the achievement of development goals, while medical imports are systematically associated with lower mortality rates (Papageorgiou, Savvides, and Zachariadis 2007; World Bank and WTO 2015). Trade openness in general is positively linked with faster mortality reduction in developing countries (Jamison, Sandbu, and Wang 2001; Owen and Wu 2007).

How does trade relate to demography?

Global trade flows are projected to shift toward countries that are in the early stages of their demographic transition. The average annual economic growth rates of pre- and early-dividend countries are expected to be higher than those of late- and post-dividend countries, which will contribute to a further decline in the importance of the latter groups as global export destinations. Post-dividend countries' share of global exports is expected to decline from 61 percent in 2015 to 52 percent in 2030, with the bulk of the matching increases shared evenly between early- and late-dividend countries (figure 6.2).[10] However, post-dividend countries are expected to remain the most important export market in the world, in part reflecting the fact they will still account for more than half of global economic activity in the future.

Differences in demographic change among countries contribute to changes in comparative advantages that, in turn, influence trade patterns. Countries with relatively slow

FIGURE 6.2 Pre-, early-, and late-dividend countries become more important export markets

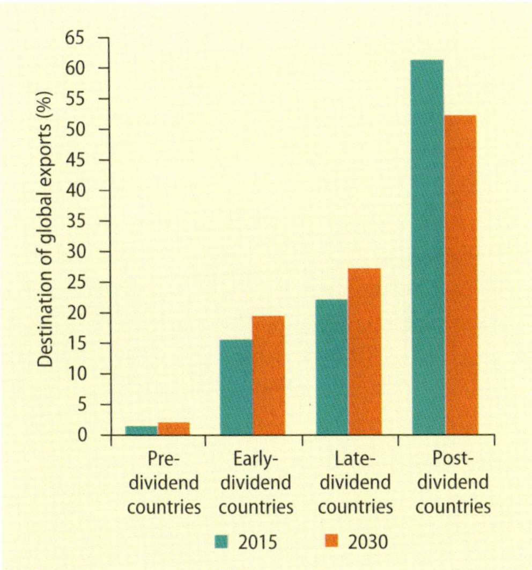

Source: World Bank classifications, based on simulations with the LINKAGE model (see appendix D).

population growth tend to become relatively more capital abundant over time, while countries with relatively faster population growth become relatively more labor abundant. As a result, pre-dividend countries' exports are mainly concentrated in agricultural and natural resource products, which accounted for 75 percent of their total exports in 2015. By 2030, their specialization in agricultural goods and labor-intensive manufacturing is expected to increase at the expense of natural resource products. In 2015, manufactured and natural resource goods accounted for 46 and 36 percent, respectively, of early-dividend exports, whereas the respective shares of late-dividend countries were 71 and 19 percent. By 2030, exports of manufactured goods and services are projected to represent a larger share in both early- and late-dividend countries (figure 6.3).

How can trade policy leverage demographic differences?

Trade policy measures can be powerful tools as countries adapt to the opportunities and challenges brought about by demographic change. Agricultural trade is still distorted by significant barriers, such as high tariffs, nontariff barriers, export subsidies, and domestic support measures (WTO 2014). These measures harm poor rural producers by eroding

FIGURE 6.3 Labor-intensive goods will continue to account for greater shares of exports from pre- and early-dividend countries

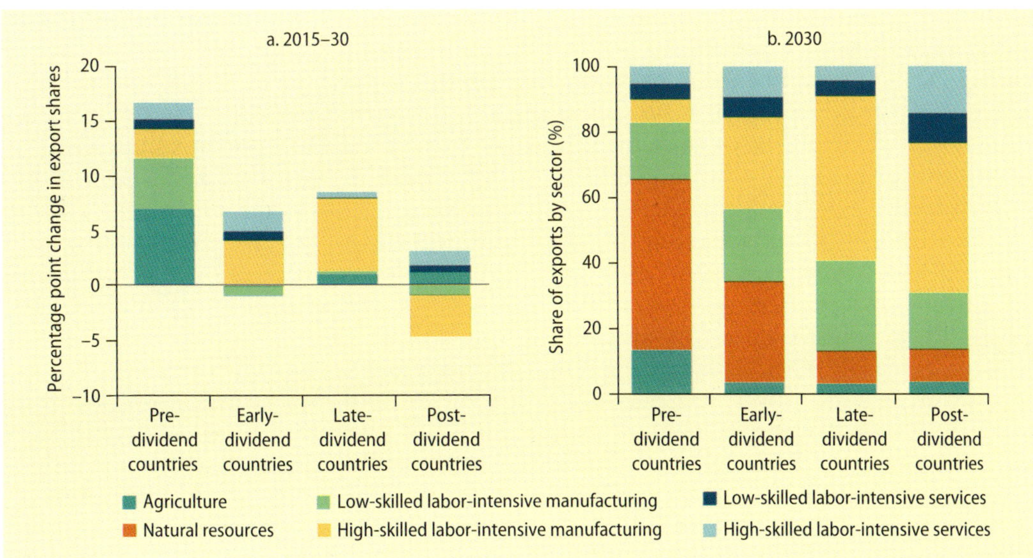

Source: World Bank classifications, based on simulations with the LINKAGE model (see appendix D).

their competitiveness and reducing the prices they receive in international markets (Anderson, Ivanic, and Martin 2013). While average tariffs on manufactured goods have been declining over time, significant tariff and nontariff barriers continue to slow or block the free flow of goods between countries (UNCTAD 2013; WTO 2012). Out of nontariff measures, technical barriers to trade and sanitary and phytosanitary measures are the most commonly used, affecting on average about 30 and 15 percent of trade, respectively. The high incidence of such barriers affects the exports of developing countries disproportionally more because the cost of compliance is higher (UNCTAD 2013).

Demographic change is expected to affect capital-labor ratios across the globe, helping developing countries to specialize in labor-intensive goods. Reductions of trade barriers, coupled with policy measures to improve trade facilitation, could create incentives for firms to relocate production to relatively more labor-abundant countries and allow developing countries to take full advantage of their growing labor forces. Rising wages and product upgrading in China that could lead to the relocation of labor-intensive production create opportunities for African countries to double employment in manufacturing (Chandra, Lin, and Wang 2012). By reducing the cost of trade in pre- and early-dividend countries, substantial potential improvements in trade flows, income, and poverty reduction can be achieved (box 6.5).

Countries that take steps to reduce the costs of trade may be able to achieve substantial increases in exports and income. Improving connectivity, making trade-related institutions and policy frameworks more effective, and providing a supportive enabling environment can help improve gains from trade for the poor, especially in rural areas. Efforts to integrate markets are critical, using measures in key areas, such as tariff and nontariff barriers, infrastructure and trade facilitation, access to trade-related technology, and trade finance (World Bank and WTO 2015).[11] While there is a vast empirical literature on supporting international trade in developing countries, covering policy recommendations in each of the above areas, this section has a narrow focus on policy recommendation in health and education services as they are directly linked to the changing demographic structure of the world population.

Trade can help meet the demand for health services in aging countries and the demand for education services in young countries. Both health care and education are only lightly traded across borders, in part because of policy constraints on service providers and on the movement of people across borders. Cross-border supply of health services (Mode 1 of the General Agreement on Trade in Services) is still quite small, although increasing numbers of people are seeking medical treatment abroad (Mode 2), and significant numbers of health professionals are practicing somewhere other than their home country (Mode 4) (Blouin, Drager, and Smith 2006; Smith, Chanda, and Tangcharoensathien 2009). Given the links with other service sectors, such as telecommunications and audiovisual services, as well as with the movement of people across borders, the liberalization of education services should be addressed as part of an effort to liberalize services more generally.

Domestic services liberalization and international law regulating health and education services are needed to ensure further expansion of international trade. In the case of health services, efforts are urgently needed to lower barriers affecting the physical presence of foreign suppliers, the maximum share of equity that can be owned by foreigners, and the movement of health professionals across borders. International agreements on various regulations, such as those pertaining to licensing and qualification requirements, could play a key role in enabling international providers to supply health services in domestic markets. The most significant measures affecting trade in education services are barriers to using the Internet and restrictions on the import of educational materials (Mode 1); visa requirements against the free flow of international students and qualification recognition issues (Mode 2);

BOX 6.5 Trade facilitation can help leverage demographic transition

Simplifying and harmonizing international trade procedures can help countries take greater advantage of their demographic differences through trade. In both developed and developing countries, there is substantial scope for this simplification and harmonization (trade facilitation) to reduce costs. In developed countries, simplification of procedures could account for 5.4 percent of potential trade cost savings, followed by advance rulings (3.7 percent), automation (2.7 percent), and fees and charges (1.7 percent). In developing countries, the contribution of each indicator varies, but total trade cost reduction amounts to 14.5 percent for low-income countries, 15.5 percent for lower-middle-income countries, and 13.2 percent for upper-middle-income countries (Moïsé, Orliac, and Minor 2011; Moïsé and Sorescu 2013). This box explores the growth and poverty impacts of reducing trade costs by 15 percent in pre- and early-dividend countries.

By reducing the costs of trade for pre- and early-dividend countries, substantial potential increases in trade flows and expansion of labor-intensive manufacturing can be achieved. Lower trade costs result in additional income gains in pre- and early-dividend countries, amounting, respectively, to 3.6 percent and 2.5 percent of GDP in 2030 (figure b6.5.1). The benefits could lift an additional 13 million people out of poverty (figure b6.5.2).[a] Faster income growth is driven by substantially higher values of trade and some production upgrading. In pre-dividend countries, the share of low-skilled and high-skilled labor-intensive manufacturing products in total exports could increase, at the expense of agriculture and natural resources, by an additional 8 and 3 percentage points, respectively. In early-dividend countries, reduced trade costs could boost the share of these products in total exports by 5 and 10 percentage points, respectively.

Trade facilitation entails streamlining customs, border, and transit procedures; improving logistics and transport services; and extending physical infrastructure. In developed countries, the policy areas that could have the greatest impact on trade performance are related to advanced rulings in determining classification and value of goods, fees and charges, processes, and procedures. Low-income countries would benefit most from simplifying documentation requirements, automating processes, and making trade-related information available. Lower-middle-income countries are expected to gain the most from the simplification of documentation formalities, streamlining of procedures, and automation. Finally, upper-middle-income countries would benefit most from streamlining procedures, automation, and advance rulings.

FIGURE B6.5.1 Trade facilitation can boost income growth in pre- and early-dividend countries

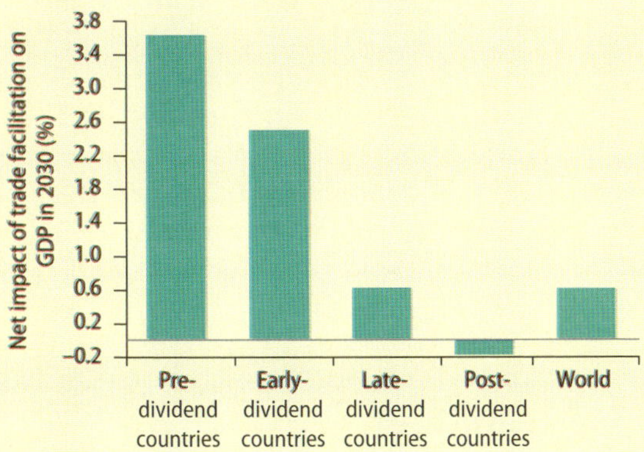

FIGURE B6.5.2 Lowering trade costs can contribute to poverty reduction

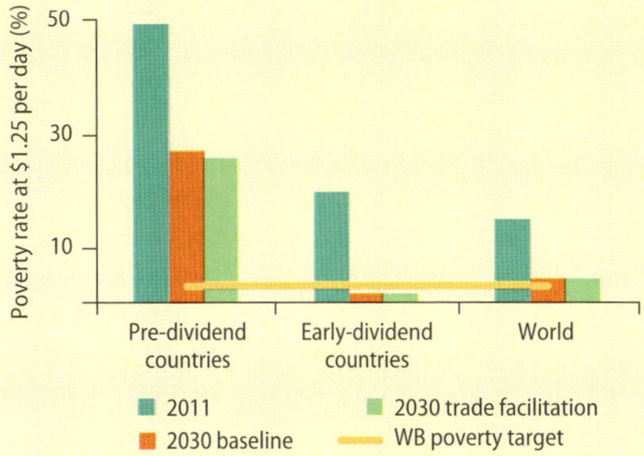

Source: UN 2013a; Medium Fertility Scenario; and World Bank calculations (see appendix D).
Note: Pre-, early-, late- and post-dividend refer to stages of demographic transition of countries.

a. At $1.25 a day based on 2005 purchasing power parity.

limits on foreign ownership and lack of transparency of government education regulations (Mode 3); and visa requirements on the free flow of academics (Mode 4).

Facilitating legal international migration

Legal migration can help the world adjust to uneven demographic change. Given the generally high level of restrictions on the movement of people from one country to another, the potential for gains from more regular and safe migration is large. Demographic disparities are amplifying these potential gains.

How does migration relate to demography?

Demographic differences contribute to migration flows. Although South-South migration flows have grown rapidly, the major migration flows are from young developing countries to aging high-income countries. Between 1990 and 2013, the stock of migrants from pre- and early-dividend countries residing in late- and post-dividend countries increased by more than 150 percent. In 2013, close to 55 percent of all international migrants (slightly more than 125 million people) lived in post-dividend countries, while 21 percent lived in early-dividend countries and 19 percent in late-dividend countries (figure 6.4). Post-dividend countries are host to the most diverse group of migrants. Most migrants in pre- and early-dividend countries come from countries in the same group.[12] As early- and pre-dividend countries make development progress, the impetus to migrate from these countries may fall. The broader impact of development on migration, however, depends on the patterns of growth. Economic development that does not promote employment growth has the potential to exacerbate the factors that push people to migrate out of their home countries (Massey 1988).

International migration flows may mitigate the decline in working-age population shares in aging countries. Younger immigrants can help rebalance the decline in the working-age population relative to the number of older people in late- and post-dividend

FIGURE 6.4 Post-dividend countries tend to receive the most migrants

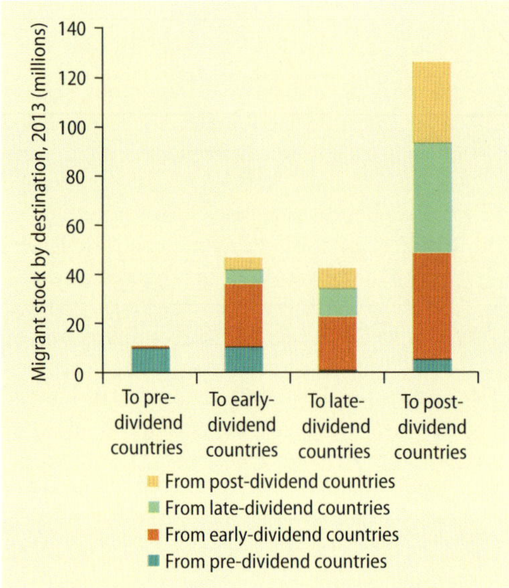

Source: World Bank staff calculations, based on data from UN 2013c.

countries, as several aging, high-income countries have already experienced (see box 6.3). Migration flows can thus play a central role in improving the growth prospects and ensuring the sustainability of public finances in destination countries. Existing estimates suggest that the potential net benefits from reducing barriers to international migration are large (Borgy et al. 2010; Tyers and Shi 2007; Walmsley, Winters, and Ahmed 2007; World Bank 2006) and a multiple of the gains from further trade liberalization (Anderson and Winters 2008, Clemens 2011). A rise in migration sufficient to increase the labor force of high-income countries by 3 percent phased in over a 10-year period would yield a global gain of real income of $674 billion (World Bank 2006).

How can migration leverage demographic differences?

Countries of origin and countries of destination could implement a wide range of policies to facilitate legal and mutually beneficial migration. During the past 10 years, many countries have revised their migration laws in response to changes in labor market conditions, demography, and political contexts (OECD 2013a). Different types of policies affect different stages of the migration process (before departure, during migration, and return), as well as different aspects under each stage (financial and social protection, employment, and remittances). Pre-departure orientation and training programs, measures that protect the rights and prevent the abuse of migrants, integration and language programs, and policies that lower remittance costs or remove regulatory and bureaucratic barriers against return migration are all important in enhancing the development benefits and reducing the potential costs associated with international migration. Several developed countries have implemented temporary migration programs with varying degrees of success (UN 2013b).

Policies have the potential to make migration more beneficial for all parties involved.[13] These include the formulation of clear migration policies in consultation with all relevant parties, foreign-worker levies paid by companies rather than workers, enforcement of minimum wage laws, provision of adequate information to migrants about their rights and obligations, facilitation of their contribution to and benefits from social protection schemes and public services, and sanctions against abuses by employers (Ahsan et al. 2014). Measures aiming to reduce the transfer cost of remittances are motivated by mounting empirical evidence on the positive impacts remittances have on development (Adams and Page 2005).[14] Financial education can also reduce the risk of using or switching to costlier remittance products (Gibson, McKenzie, and Zia 2014). Bilateral or multilateral migration agreements between countries of origin, transit, and destination can help achieve policy coherence across countries (Naik, Koehler, and Laczko 2008; World Bank 2006).

Migration benefits sending countries through social as well as financial remittances, but policy actions are needed to help reduce the burden of brain drain. Social remittances include transfers of knowledge back to the home country, the application of newly acquired skills from abroad, and the development of networks that facilitate trade and political links between countries. The benefits of remittances are not automatic, however, and outward migration can have negative effects, especially in countries where large numbers of high-skilled workers emigrate. In these cases, a combination of comprehensive and targeted polices may be able to retain, attract, or reattract talent. Comprehensive policies that boost productivity and growth are critical, especially education policies that foster the supply of skills and growth policies that boost the demand for skills.[15]

Encouraging global capital flows

International capital flows benefit countries in different ways, depending where they are on the demographic dividend continuum. Countries in the early stages of their demographic transition need to boost investment, while those in the later stages seek higher returns on investment than may be available domestically, creating a potential win-win situation. The benefits of these flows will not be automatic. Appropriate policies, including efforts to enhance institutional quality, deepen the financial sector, and introduce sound financial supervision and regulation, along with making greater use of international investment agreements can all help ensure the full realization of benefits of capital flows. Together, such policies could help catalyze FDI and other forms of financing that are essential for reaching development goals.

How do capital flows relate to demography?

Facilitating international capital flows would allow young, labor-abundant countries to attract much-needed capital. In the initial stages of demographic transition, countries with relatively high dependency ratios tend to have excess demand for investment relative to savings, stimulating current account deficits. In countries in more advanced stages of demographic transition, higher life expectancy increases savings for retirement, while

FIGURE 6.5 Countries with low working-age population shares tend to run current account deficits

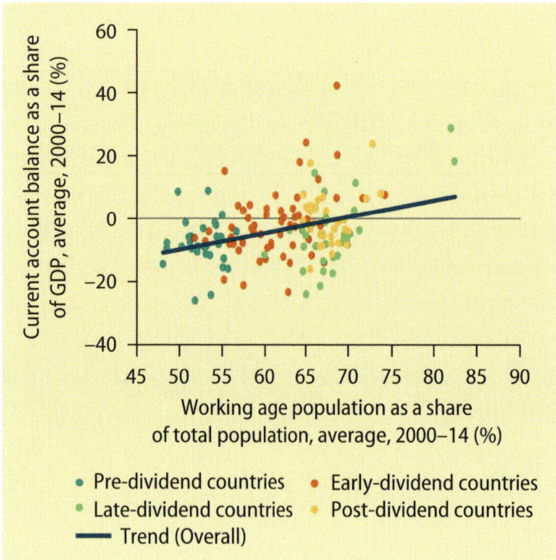

Source: World Bank calculations, based on World Bank World Development Indicators database.

shrinking labor forces reduce investment demand, encouraging net capital outflows. In addition to these fundamental drivers of capital flows, lower working-age population shares, typical for countries in earlier stages of demographic transition, are associated with current account deficits (figure 6.5).[16] Capital flows could generate an increase in labor productivity and wages, and thus spur faster growth in young, labor-abundant countries. For sending countries, increasing investment in "young" economies can provide much-needed opportunities to raise capital returns and diversify investment portfolios, especially if labor-abundant countries create favorable investment climates, ensure macroeconomic stability, deepen their financial sectors, and strengthen governance.

How can capital flows leverage demographic differences?

Improvements in institutional quality and financial sector development could contribute significantly to capital flows to pre-, early- and late-dividend countries. Potential increases are driven by rapid economic growth, demographic changes that support growing consumer and investment demand, and improvements in the business environment (World Bank 2013a).[17] With rapid improvements in the business environment, the net capital flows to pre-, early- and late-dividend countries could increase to $13.4 trillion in 2030 (up from $6.4 trillion with no policy changes) and could account for 62 percent of total capital flows, up from 26 percent of the total in 2011 (figure 6.6).[18] Low- and middle-income countries would be the main beneficiaries of the increased capital flows under this rapid convergence scenario.[19]

Countries early in the demographic transition are expected to account for a growing share of gross capital inflows. These countries tend to register net capital inflows if they offer opportunities for healthy economic growth along with strong institutions, favorable business environment, and potential for financial sector deepening. For example, India and Sub-Saharan Africa are projected to run current account deficits averaging 2.4

FIGURE 6.6 By 2030, a larger share of capital flows may go to countries in earlier stages of demographic transition

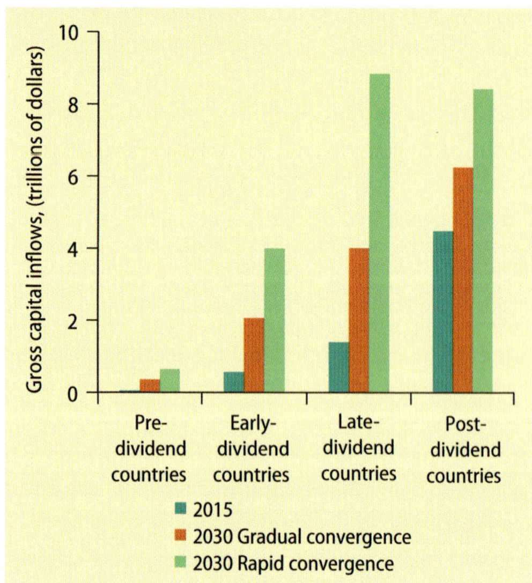

Source: World Bank 2013a and staff calculations.
Note: Inflows are in nominal U.S. dollars, assuming a constant 3.5 percent world inflation rate based on the 2003–07 five-year average from the World Bank Global Economic Monitor database. The gradual and rapid convergence scenarios predict average global annual GDP growth of 2.5 and 3.1 percent, respectively, between 2015 and 2030. GDP growth in pre-, early-, late- and post-dividend countries is projected to average 5.5, 4.0, 4.9, and 0.9 percent, respectively, in the gradual convergence scenario, and 6.3, 4.7, 6.1, and 0.8 percent in the rapid convergence scenario.

percent and 3.2 percent of GDP, respectively, over 2015–30 (World Bank 2013a). These capital inflows will likely come from post-dividend countries, but the contributions from early- and late-dividend East Asian countries, most notably China, are likely to continue to rise.

Countries early in their demographic transition could promote foreign direct investment by reducing the economic, political, and legal risks facing investors. To attract FDI, host countries need to relax investment barriers. These come in many forms: the exclusion of foreign investors from certain economic activities, quantitative limitations in the form of quotas, foreign ownership caps, joint venture requirements, and discriminatory tax treatment. Home countries can further promote outflows of FDI with policies such as investment guarantees or technical assistance.

At the global level, reforms are needed to take full advantage of international investment agreements. Although an estimated 3,271 international investment agreements were in place in 2015, many of these required additional reforms (UNCTAD 2015). Other important areas for policy making include protections of a country's right to regulate investment (such as clarifying most-favored-nation treatment provisions); more efficient dispute-settlement procedures; greater compliance with domestic laws and corporate social responsibility requirements; improving the consistency of the international investment agreements; and linking reforms of the agreements with the domestic policy agenda would also be useful. Measures in these areas could be further complemented with the consolidation and harmonization of multilateral investment rules.

In addition to sound financial supervision and regulation and strong institutions, macroeconomic policies need to play a key role in addressing risks from volatile capital inflows. Under certain circumstances, capital flow management measures can be useful. They should not, however, be a substitute for warranted macroeconomic adjustment. In addition, macroprudential measures are at times necessary to address the challenges posed by large and volatile capital flows.[20] Financial and institutional development can reduce the riskiness of financial liberalization (Sahay et al. 2015), although a sequenced approach that builds resilience to large and volatile capital flows through macroeconomic policies and regulation is preferred (IMF 2012). Furthermore, international regulatory coordination would be beneficial both at the bilateral and multilateral levels, including measures such as strengthening and institutionalizing the swap lines that provide liquidity for less commonly traded currencies.

As pre-, early-, and late-dividend countries are expected to account for a growing share of capital flows, their policies on exchange rates and capital flows will become more important. Reliance on fixed exchange rates pegged to a single currency could pose difficult choices for countries with increasing inflows, whereas an exchange rate pegged to a basket of currencies may be better able to smooth currency volatility. In addition, the accumulation of reserves among developing countries is expected to decelerate as more adapt floating exchange rate regimes and capital markets become more open (World Bank 2013a).

Conclusion

Demographic change can shape development trajectories, and policies that reflect a country's specific circumstances can help it to benefit from opportunities that are offered. Policies also need to respond to the significant differences across countries in the direction and speed of demographic change. The challenge, at both the country and global levels, is to prepare for the demographic landscape of the future. At the country level, policy makers and stakeholders need to address expected demographic advantages and challenges, depending on whether their countries are pre-dividend, early-dividend, late-dividend, or post-dividend. Collectively, all countries—from low- to high-income—can benefit from pronounced differences in demographic change through enhanced trade, migration, and capital flows across borders. Collective action is also needed to meet the global environmental sustainability challenge.

Policies can improve development outcomes by taking advantage of demographic factors. Strong economic growth that is economically, socially, and environmentally sustainable is a prerequisite for achieving development goals. Demographically informed policy can both add to and take advantage of economic growth through policies in several critical areas: labor markets, education, health, pensions and other social transfers, international migration, trade, and capital flows. A number of policy interventions have significant fiscal costs, requiring that attention be paid to fiscal sustainability. Getting policies right in light of demographic trends could well be the difference between eliminating extreme poverty, boosting shared prosperity, and reaching broader development goals by 2030 and falling short and leaving major gaps in the development agenda for the next generation.

Country Spotlights: Policy challenges at different stages of demographic transition

This spotlight presents analyses of major policy challenges facing four countries, each representative of the demographic group to which it belongs: Niger (pre-dividend), Ethiopia (early-dividend), Brazil (late-dividend), and Japan (post-dividend). The analysis is based on simulations with a computable general equilibrium (CGE) model, applied to country databases developed for this report.[a]

Sparking demographic transition in Niger: Child marriage and fertility

As indicated by its low per-capita income, high poverty, low human development, and fragile environment (physical, political, and military), Niger, a pre-dividend country faces a long list of challenges. Between 1991 and 2015, its population more than doubled (from 8 to 19 million) and is expected to reach 69 million by 2050. Its current total fertility rate (TFR) of 7 (average births per woman) is among the highest in the world and is expected to fall to 4.7 by 2050. This current high rate is both a cause and a consequence of Niger's low scores on most development indicators. It is partly driven by one of the highest rates of child marriage in the world—74 percent of Nigerien girls marry before turning 18 (World Bank 2014b)—high adolescent fertility rates, low per-capita incomes, and low levels of education (including high female school dropout rates). Figure 6.7 illustrates the dramatic trends in total fertility and dependency rates facing Niger.

To determine the effects of reduced child marriage on fertility, female labor-force participation, and female education in Niger, a set of scenarios was analyzed for the period 2015–50. Under the base scenario, GDP per capita is projected to grow at an average rate of around 2 percent a year; for the indicator most directly affected by child marriage, the fertility rate (FR) of women ages 15–19, the United Nations (UN) medium-variant projection of a decline is used (from around 0.20 births a year per woman ages 15–19 in 2015 to 0.08 in 2050). Three non-base simulations are used to test effects of alternative trajectories to the base for the 15–19 FR: a gradual cut to zero by 2050 (f-), an immediate cut (in 2016) to zero (f--), and no cut (the 2015 rates stay in place up to 2050; fconst). The case of a gradual cut is combined with a 10 percentage point increase in the rates of labor force participation for women who delay their marriages (f-l+), and a 10 percentage point increase in the share within this group of women who achieve 9 or more years of education (f-l+e+).[b]

Reducing the fertility rates for women ages 15–19 can lead to improvements in several

FIGURE 6.7 Fertility and dependency rates in Niger, 2015–50

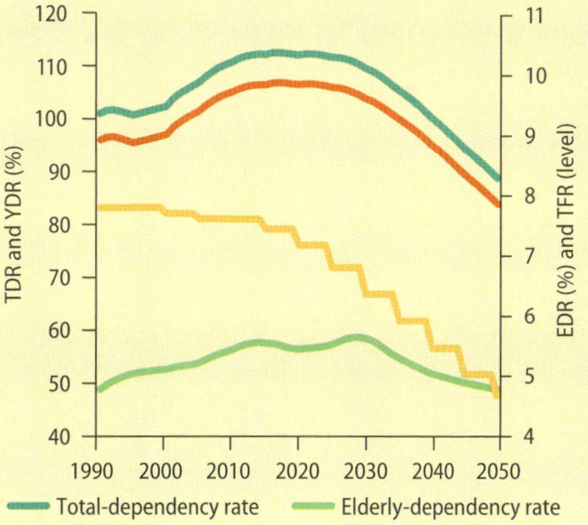

Source: World Bank calculations, based on medium variant in UN (2013b).

FIGURE 6.8 Niger's GDP per capita growth under alternative scenarios, 2016–50

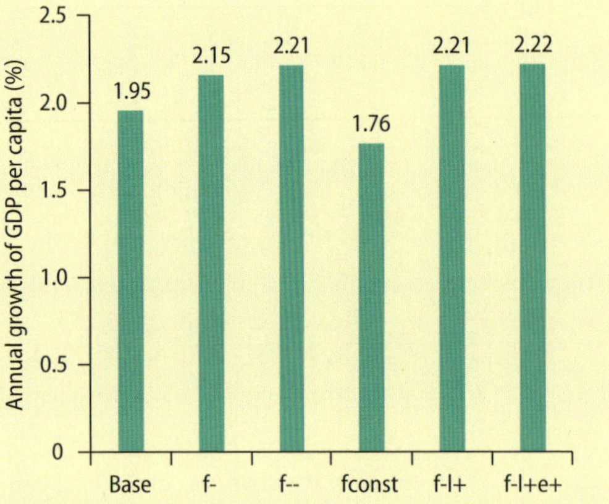

Source: World Bank estimates using MAMS simulation results.
Note: Base = benchmark (no change), f- = gradual elimination of 15–19 year fertility, f-- = immediate elimination of 15–19 year fertility, fconst = constant 15–19 year fertility (2015 rate), f-l+ = f- plus increased labor-force participation, f-l+e+ = f-l+ plus increased education.

human development indicators, such as health and education, while also benefiting overall income. Compared with the base scenario, gradual and immediate cuts in FR (f- and f--) raise average growth in GDP per capita by 0.2 and 0.3 percentage point respectively, while a constant FR reduces this growth rate by 0.2 percentage point (fconst) (figure 6.8). Per-capita household consumption in 2050 is 15 percent higher for f-- compared with fconst. The main reason for the gain is that a lower FR accelerates growth in per capita labor and capital endowments; for example, for f-- the percentage point increases are 0.2 for labor and 0.4 for capital. By comparison, the likely macroeconomic impact of plausible changes in labor-force participation and education rates due to reduced fertility is minor from the perspective of the economy as a whole, but likely very important for the individuals who are able to have fewer children. Extreme poverty declines from 49 percent in 2015: by 2030, poverty rates fall to 29 percent under the base scenario, compared with 23, 26, and 30 percent for f--, f-, and fconst, respectively.

The policies needed to speed up the decline in child marriage and adolescent fertility in Niger and other countries in a similar situation include actions aimed at improved education outcomes for girls at the primary and secondary levels and greater access to reproductive health services (ICRW 2007; World Bank 2014d). Irrespective of concerns related to child marriage and fertility, such actions should already be on the agenda. Their payoff depends on the broader context, including the ability of the economy to generate growth sufficient to offer jobs with attractive wages.

Accelerating job creation in Ethiopia: Education, savings, and productivity

Over the past decade, Ethiopia has managed to maintain rapid per capita growth, delivered by appropriate policies and facilitated by a strong fertility decline. For 2004–13, Ethiopia's average annual GDP per capita growth was very high, at 8.1 percent. Since 2000, per-capita growth has likely been boosted by a strong decline in the total dependency rate (TDR), driven by a declining total fertility rate; these demographic trends will continue up to 2030 and beyond (Ahmed et al. 2014; figure 6.9). Growth has been driven to a large extent by public investment while private investment has been low (Moller and Wacker 2015). Judging from the record of other successful countries, Ethiopia faces the structural

FIGURE 6.9 Fertility and dependency rates in Ethiopia, 1990–2030

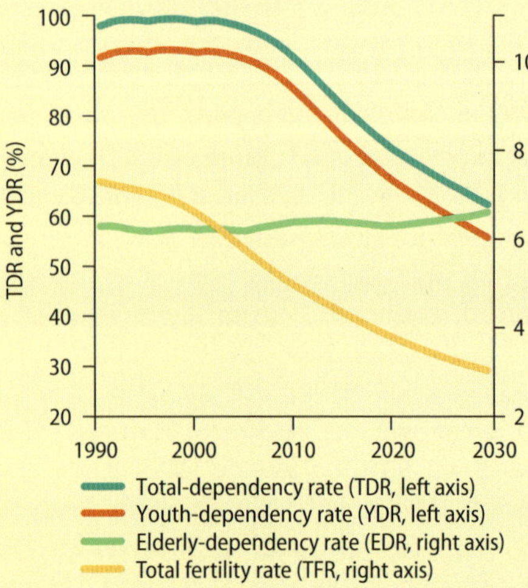

Source: World Bank calculations, based on medium variant in UN (2013b).

challenge of finding a prominent role for the private sector.[c] The World Bank's Doing Business Indicators show that Ethiopia does well in general but lags in the areas of credit access in the private sector and contract enforcement, the two indicators that may matter most for growth (Hanusch 2012; World Bank 2014a).

The scenarios for Ethiopia assess effects of a policy package aimed at making good use of its rapidly growing labor force through improved education, higher private savings, and more rapid total factor productivity (TFP) growth during the period 2015–30. The base scenario, which serves as a benchmark, represents business-as-usual conditions, including a projected annual per capita GDP growth rate of 4.0 percent up to 2030; this rapid growth is fueled by a projected continuing decline in the total dependency rate and 3 percent annual growth of the labor force. The scenario educ+, is based on an projection for a "fast-tracked" improvement in educational attainment, generating by 2030 an increase in the number of workers with nine or more years of education by 7 percent compared with the base.[d] Under this scenario, the share of total labor force with nine years of education or more in 2030 increases modestly to 9.0 percent, compared with 8.4 percent for the base. To close part of Ethiopia's private savings gap compared with similar countries, the savings scenario (sav+) gradually raises private savings by roughly 4 percent of GDP between 2015 and 2030, a change that replicates increases in the national savings rate during the last few years. In the scenario with increased TFP growth (tfp+), annual factor-neutral TFP growth is increased by 0.5 percentage point (which may be compared to an annual TFP growth rate of 1.9 percent under the base scenario). In the final scenario, changes in these three areas are introduced together (combo+).

While interventions in each of the three areas would accelerate growth, poverty reduction, and shared prosperity, the strongest impacts would stem from TFP growth and private investment. Compared with the base, higher educational attainments raise annual GDP growth by a mere 0.1 percent, reflecting the fact that feasible additional changes in labor force educational composition within a 15-year period are quite limited (figure 6.10). The growth gains are higher (0.5–0.7 percentage point) for tfp+ and sav+, because they immediately add to stocks of employed factors and their productivity. Combo+ brings about a growth gain of 1.3 percentage points. Under the base, extreme poverty declines drastically, from 27.8 percent in 2015 to 9.6 percent in 2030; the strongest additional decline is for combo+, with a poverty rate of just 5.5 percent in 2030.

FIGURE 6.10 Ethiopia's GDP per capita growth under alternative scenarios, 2016–30

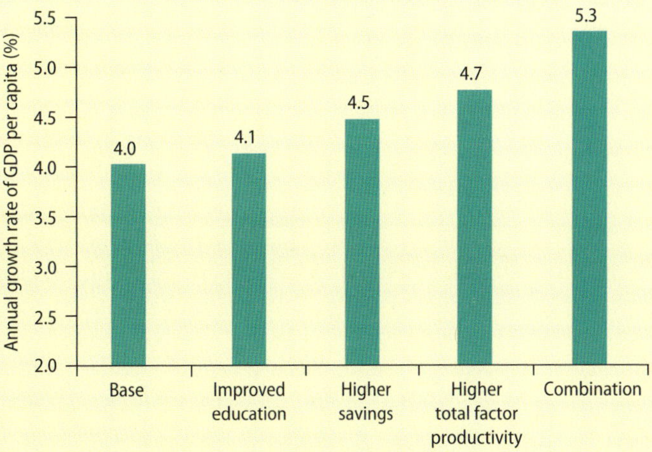

Source: World Bank calculations, based on MAMS simulation results.
Note: Scenarios include base = benchmark (no change); educ+ = improved education; sav+ = higher savings; tfp+ = higher total factors of production; and combo+ = combination of all three.

These findings suggest that, in the long run, continued rapid growth may require stronger emphasis on the private sector. While recognizing the impressive progress that Ethiopia has made in recent years, recent World Bank analysis (Eden and Kraay 2014; Gable, Lofgren, and Osario-Rodarte 2015; Moller and Wacker 2015) suggests that, as public investment manages to close the most urgent infrastructure gaps over time, a rebalancing with increased emphasis on private investment may be most conducive to continued rapid growth. The results indicate that growth and shared prosperity could benefit strongly from policies that raise and effectively channel private savings to productive investment and improve the business climate for the private sector, making continued productivity gains feasible; together, such steps could make it easier to absorb the growing labor force at improving wages.

Sustaining productivity growth in Brazil: Savings, labor, and pensions

Brazil, a country in the late-dividend group, faces the challenge of increasing output per worker while protecting the living standards of its rapidly growing elderly population. Around 2020, Brazil's total dependency rate is expected to end more than 50 years of decline as the increase in the elderly dependency rate begins to exceed the decline in the youth dependency rate. After a longer period of decline, the total fertility rate is expected to stabilize well below the replacement level (figure 6.11). The population ages 15–64 is expected to peak around 2020, and the total population some time before 2050 (at around 230 million). To improve living standards, output per worker will have to rise. That will require increases in the private capital stock per worker and improved worker skills.

The scenarios for Brazil use a policy package that helps increase private savings, labor force participation, and labor productivity to test how growth might be sustained for the period 2015–50. The benchmark base scenario assumes relatively unchanged GDP shares for private investment, taxation, and government spending, the latter requiring pension reform given rapid aging. A GDP per capita growth rate of 1 percent is imposed for this scenario, an improvement from growth rates near zero during the past few years. In the alternative scenarios, the private savings rate is raised gradually to match the GDP shares of peer country comparators starting by 2030 (sav+); the labor force participation rate (labor force as a share of population ages 15–64) is raised from 77 to 87 percent, enough to permit labor force growth to match population growth (lfp+); and a moderate increase of 0.5 percent in labor-specific productivity growth is imposed (lprd+), sufficient to bring about a moderate increase in TFP growth of 0.3 percentage point (to 0.8 percent a year). The scenario combo+ combines all of these changes.

The results suggest that changes in savings, labor force participation, and labor productivity combine to raise the annual GDP per capita growth rate by 1 percentage point in the 2016–50 period. The results show levels for 2015–50 and growth for 2016–50 (since growth by definition is compared to a preceding year). An increase in private savings and investment of around 7 percent of GDP, sufficient to close Brazil's savings gap (IMF 2013), generates an increase in annual GDP growth of 0.3 percentage point (sav+; figure 6.12). Similar growth gains follow from increases in labor productivity (lprd+) and labor force participation (lfp+); the required participation increase could be almost fully realized if female participation rose to the male level (which already is close to 87 percent), but a delayed retirement age could also contribute. The impact of combining the three shocks is a doubling of GDP per capita growth from 1 to 2 percent, with two-thirds of the gain due to increased factor employment and one-third due to increases in TFP. In the base scenario, population in extreme poverty declines from 4.8 percent in 2015 to 3.6 in 2030 and to 2.2

FIGURE 6.11 Fertility and dependency rates in Brazil, 1990–2030

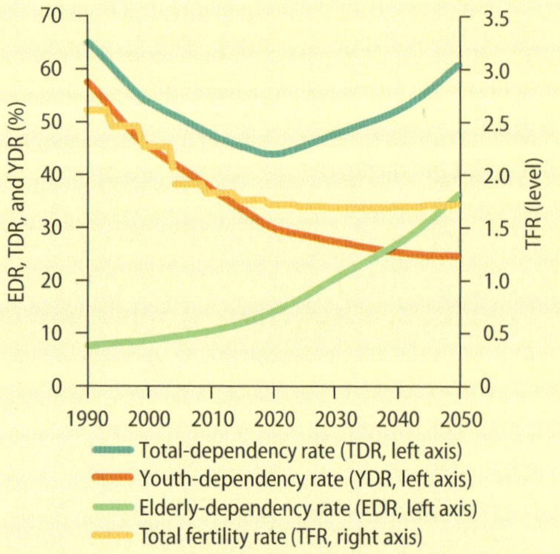

Source: World Bank calculations, based on medium variant in UN (2013b).

FIGURE 6.12 Brazil's per capita GDP growth under alternative scenarios, 2016–30

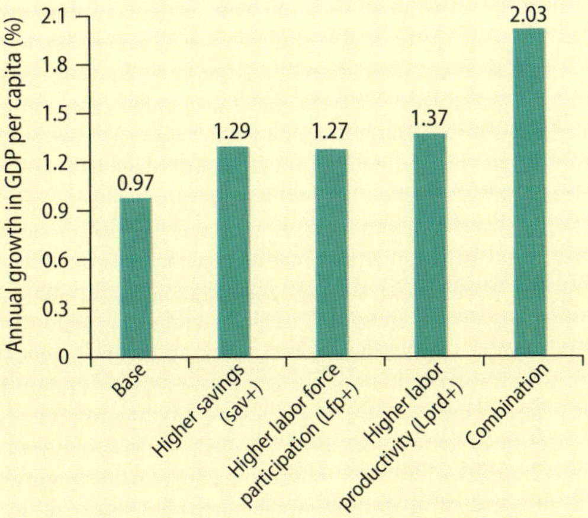

Source: World Bank calculations, based on MAMS simulation results.
Note: Scenarios include base = benchmark (no change), sav+; Lfp+; Lprd+; and combo+ = combination of all three.

in 2050. For combo+, a mere 0.7 percent remain extremely poor in 2050. Per capita consumption growth ranges between 0.9 percent for base and 1.6 percent for combo+.

These gains require reforms in the pension and education systems, the labor market, and the business environment. The reforms in the pension system, implicit in the freezing of public pension spending at the 2015 GDP share, may be the most difficult challenge since it may imply a considerable decline in pension per beneficiary toward levels comparable to that of major OECD economies (Economist 2012). If current benefits were kept in place and adjusted for per capita consumption growth, likely increases in spending and taxation would exceed 10 percent of GDP. A microeconomic perspective is needed to assess the impact of higher taxes and redistribution on growth, including savings.[e] A substantial body of research looks at potential reforms that could address policies related to aging (Gragnolati et al. 2011) and other areas, including Brazil's educational system (Bruns, Evans, and Luque 2012; OECD 2012), and business environment, indicated by a ranking of 40 among the 51 upper-middle-income countries covered by the Doing Business Indicators (World Bank 2014a).

Adapting to aging in Japan: Labor force participation and immigration

The demography of Japan, a post-dividend country that has reached an advanced stage of aging, imposes severe challenges to maintaining its high living standards. Japan's total fertility rate is 1.3 percent, one of the lowest in the world, and its aging population (65 and over) stands at 26 percent, the largest in the world. Although fertility is projected to increase, Japan's population is expected to shrink from a current level of around 125 million to 85 million in 2100 (figure 6.13). Dependency ratios will not change over this period, reflecting a convergence of the growth rates of each population group to negative values.

The scenario analysis for Japan assesses the impact of a policy package that includes actions aimed at raising the total fertility rate, labor force participation, and immigration for the period 2015–2100. The base scenario is designed to represent a business-as-usual case, with no change in government policies.[21] Labor force participation and savings depend on age-specific and, for labor, gender-specific rates. In the alternative scenarios, the

FIGURE 6.13 Fertility and dependency rates in Japan, 1990–2100

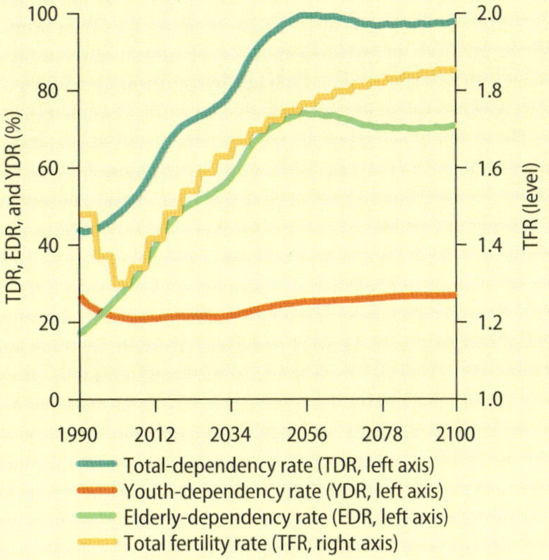

Source: World Bank calculations, based on medium variant in UN (2013b).

TFR is increased to the replacement level of 2.1 percent (fert+), and labor force participation is raised by bringing females to the male level and delaying by a decade the decline that starts at age 55 (lfp+); both fertility and labor force changes are introduced gradually from 2016 to 2035. During the same period, the scenario migr+ brings an annual flow of around 200,000 immigrants in their 20s—a number slightly above what is needed to eliminate the projected population decline for this age group and proposed in a recent government report (Economist 2014; Japan Times 2014). Starting in 2036, the number of new immigrants declines gradually, becoming insignificant by 2100. The immigrants are evenly split between men and women, and they take on the demographic and economic characteristics of the resident population except for that they remit 10 percent of their incomes to their home country.

The results indicate that such a policy package could both improve living standards and limit the decline in Japan's share in the world economy in the long run. In the long run, higher fertility (fert+) or immigration (migr+) reduce the total dependency ratio and raise the population; together, they bring about positive population growth (figures 6.14, 6.15) and raise total GDP. However, the impact of these two scenarios on GDP per capita is insignificant given similar gains in population and labor force growth, leaving population growth in excess of labor growth (figure 6.16). Higher labor force participation (lfp+) raises growth in employment and GDP without affecting population growth, thereby

FIGURE 6.14 Higher fertility and migration rates would reduce total dependency rates in Japan

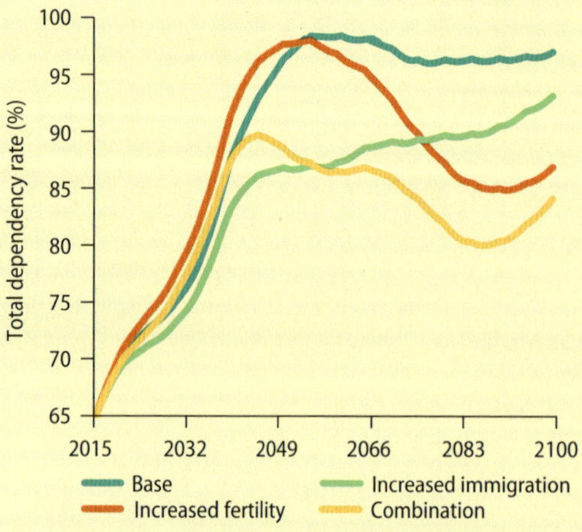

Source: World Bank calculations, based on MAMS simulation results.
Note: base = benchmark (no change); fert+ = increased fertility; migr+ = increased immigration; and combo+ = combination of the two.

FIGURE 6.15 Combined, higher fertility rates and immigration could raise Japan's population

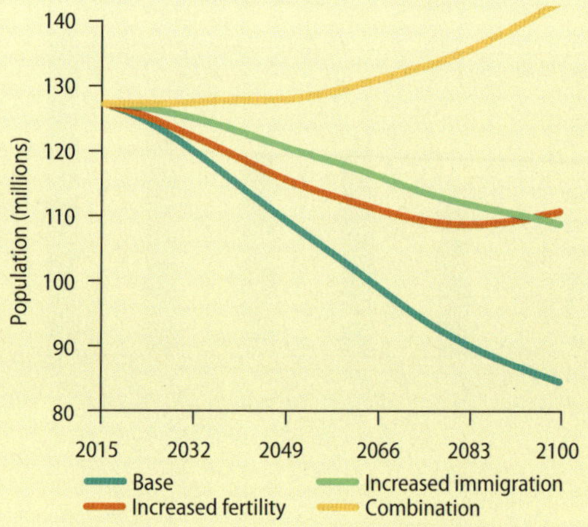

Source: World Bank estimates based on MAMS simulation results.
Note: Base = benchmark (no change); fert+ = increased fertility rate; migr+ = increased immigration; and combo+ = combination of the two.

FIGURE 6.16 Higher labor force participation in Japan could have the biggest impact on GDP per capita growth

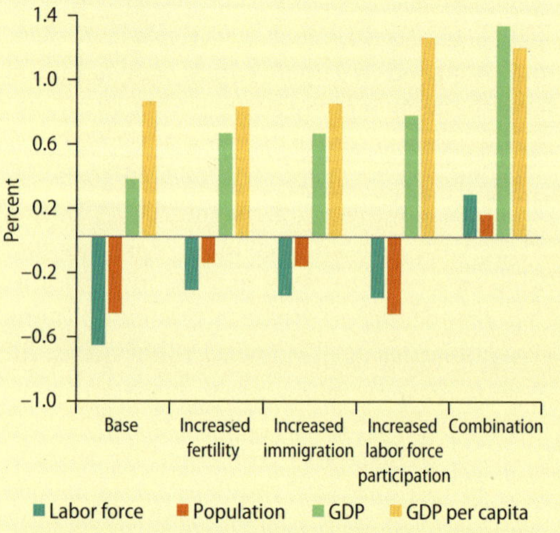

Source: World Bank calculations, based on MAMS simulation results.
Note: base = benchmark (no change); fert+ = increased fertility rate; migr+ = increased immigration; and combo+ = combination of the two.

raising GDP per capita. In the background, the changes in age composition and labor force participation raise savings and capital accumulation, with the strongest impact for the scenario lfp+.

The changes in fertility, labor force participation, and migration that underpin these simulations may be difficult to realize and depend on changes in behavior and policy. Japan's demographic challenges are a longstanding concern. Policy measures tend to stress the need to encourage work, reduce financial and career-related burdens of child rearing, and facilitate integration of immigrants into Japanese society.[f] Limited success to date in bringing about these changes suggests that the issues are difficult and depend on attitudes and social processes that respond to policy only very slowly.

Notes for Country Spotlights

a. The model that is used, MAMS, is described in appendix D. For a basic reference, see Lofgren, Cicowiez, and Diaz-Bonilla 2013.

b. The parametric changes in labor force participation and educational attainment are based on findings from ongoing research (Wodon 2015).

c. In 2011, Ethiopia had the 3rd highest public investment level in the world and the 6th lowest private investment rate in the world, 18.6 and 6.9 percent of GDP, respectively; these figures reflect the pursuit, since the late 1990s, of a development strategy based on a "big push" in public infrastructure investment as the engine of growth (World Bank 2013c).

d. The International Institute for Applied Systems Analysis has produced alternative projections for educational attainment up to 2050 for 120 countries, including Ethiopia with a scenario that reflects current trends (part of base) and a fast-track scenario with accelerated but still plausible gains in educational attainments (part of educ+); see KC et al. (2010).

e. Research is not settled in these areas and there may be trade-offs between growth and equity. For different findings on savings in Brazil, compare Rocha 2010 and Jorgenson 2011; for a cross-country perspective on taxes, see Ostry, Berg, and Tsangarides 2014.

f. Among international institutions, the IMF and the OECD have produced an extensive body of research on issues related to growth, the labor market, and gender issues in Japan. For an up-to-date perspective, see for example Botman, Danninger, and Schiff 2015.

Notes

1. This section draws heavily on recent World Bank reports on demography with a regional or country focus, including Cotlear 2011; Gragnaloti et al. 2011, 2015; Bussolo, Koettl, and Sinnott 2015; World Bank 2015b, 2015c, 2015d.
2. The first 1,000 days, starting from conception, are critical for infant and child health. Improving the nutrition and health of expecting mothers reduces the incidence of health complications for newborns and infants.
3. World Bank (2015b) argues that developing countries that have just started to age and that do not already have well-established public pension systems have an opportunity to develop fiscally sustainable support systems. In this, they are at an advantage compared with high-income countries at an advanced stage of aging that often have to undertake politically difficult reforms in costly and unsustainable aged-support systems.
4. Issues related to demography in late-dividend countries are addressed in detail in Gragnaloti et al. 2011, 2015; Bussolo, Koettl, and Sinnott 2015; and World Bank 2015a, 2015d.
5. Issues related to demography in post-dividend countries are addressed in detail in Bussolo, Koettl, and Sinnott 2015 and World Bank 2015a, 2015d.
6. For surveys of issues related to fertility and policy in East Asia, including Japan, see Frejka, Jones, and Sardon 2010, and Abbasi-Shavazi and Gubhaju 2014.
7. Under perfect competition, the removal of impediments to the movement of factors and trade goods across countries creates opportunities for mutual gain as agents take advantage of price differences and reallocate resources across and within countries. In the presence of imperfect competition or various market failures, however, the domestic policy needs to play a significant role in improving institutions, infrastructure, human capital, and the like.
8. Broadman 2007 found that accelerating Asian trade and investment in Africa can have significant impacts on Africa's economic growth and development.
9. Long-term trends in trade, migration, and capital flows are discussed in Solimano and Watts 2005 and WTO 2014.
10. These results were obtained through a simulation of the World Bank's LINKAGE model. Appendix D discusses the methodology and model results.
11. Measures in all of these areas are also key in supporting the integration of Sub-Saharan Africa into global value chains (IMF 2015).
12. From a regional perspective, migration in Africa, Asia, and the Commonwealth of Independent States is predominantly within each region; for example, intraregional flows account for two-thirds of all migration within Sub-Saharan Africa and for two-thirds within Europe and Central Asia (Ratha and Shaw 2014; WTO 2013).
13. Empirical evidence on the effectiveness of individual policy measures on migration is generally limited (McKenzie and Yang 2015).
14. Some studies also caution about the risk of Dutch Disease (Acosta, Lartey, and Mandelman 2009; Lartey, Mandelman, and Acosta 2012).
15. Malaysia provides two examples of targeted approaches: A returning expert program offers Malaysian professionals working abroad a (lower) flat income tax rate of 15 percent for 5 years if they return to work in Malaysia. A second program, targeted at migrants to Malaysia, offers foreign workers residence passes for up to 10 years, which allow these workers to freely change employers (World Bank 2011).
16. Several studies have examined this, including Attanasio and Violante 2000; Chinn and Prasad 2003; Feroli 2003; Higgins 1998); IMF 2004; and Luhrmann 2003.
17. These are key features under the "rapid convergence scenario" of World Bank 2013a and Bussolo et al. 2014, in which half of the gap in structural determinants of capital flows between developing countries and the United States is closed by 2030. This scenario implies, for example, that financial development in Brazil, India, and the Middle East in

2030 reaches the level of financial development in the United States in the 1980s.

18. The simulation results do not distinguish between FDI and portfolio flows. Full details of these simulations are provided in Bussolo et al. 2014.
19. In the absence of frictions, most theoretical models will render net capital flows in a North-South direction, a result of the higher marginal product of capital in developing countries. In reality, capital has, somewhat paradoxically, been flowing from the South to the North (Lucas 1990). This paradox is explained by the differences in fundamentals affecting the production structure of the economy on the one hand and international capital market imperfections on the other. The rapid convergence scenario leads to a reversal of the deficit (surplus) position of high-income (developing) countries, which suggests a modest reversal of the Lucas paradox.
20. Macroprudential measures include tools to address threats to financial stability arising from excessive credit expansion and asset price booms, to address key amplification mechanisms of systemic risk linked to leverage and maturity mismatches, and to mitigate structural vulnerabilities in the system and limit systemic spillovers in times of stress (Financial Stability Board 2011; IMF 2014). Capital flow management policies can be residency-based (capital controls), or they can be structured not to discriminate based on residency but still aim to influence cross-border capital flows (such as reserve requirements on foreign exchange deposits).
21. The business-as-usual scenario is calibrated to replicate IMF growth projections up to 2020, after which annual per capita growth continues at a rate of 0.8 percent.

References

Abbasi-Shavazi, M. J., and B. Gubhaju. 2014. "Different Pathways to Low Fertility in Asia: Consequences and Policy Implications." Population Division Expert Paper 2014/1. United Nations, Geneva.

Acosta, P., E. Lartey, and F. Mandelman, 2009. "Remittances and the Dutch Disease." *Journal of International Economics Volume* 79 (1): 102–16.

Adams, R. H., and J. Page. 2005. "Do International Migration and Remittances Reduce Poverty in Developing Countries?" *World Development* 33 (10): 1645–69.

Ahmed, S. A., M. Cruz, D. S. Go, M. Maliszewska, and I. Osorio-Rodarte. 2014. "How Significant Is Africa's Demographic Dividend for its Future Growth?" Policy Research Working Paper 7134, World Bank, Washington, DC.

Ahsan, Ahmad, Manolo Abella, Andrew Beath, and Hua. 2014. "International Mitigation and Development in East Asia and the Pacific. World, Bank, Washington, DC. http://documents.worldbank.org/curated/en/2014/01/20306813/international-mitigation-development-east-asia-pacific.

Anderson, K., M. Ivanic, and W. Martin. 2013. "Food Price Spikes, Price Insulation, and Poverty." Policy Research Working Paper 6535, World Bank, Washington DC.

Anderson, K., and L. A. Winters. 2008. "The Challenge of Reducing International Trade and Migration Barriers." Policy Research Working Paper 4598, World Bank, Washington DC.

Attanasio, O. P., and G. L. Violante. 2000. "The Demographic Transition in Closed and Open Economy: A Tale of Two Regions." Working Paper 412, Research Department, Inter-American Development Bank, Washington, DC.

Black, R., D. Kniveton, R. Skeldon, D. Coppard, A. Murata, and K. Schmidt-Verkerk. 2008. "Demographics and Climate Change: Future Trends and Their Policy Implications for Migration." Working Paper T-27. Development Research Centre on Migration, Globalisation and Poverty.

Bloom, D. E., D. Canning, G. Fink, and J. E. Finlay. 2009. "Fertility, Female Labor Force Participation, and the Demographic Dividend." *Journal of Economic Growth* 14 (2): 79–101.

Bloom, D. E., and J. G. Williamson. 1998. "Demographic Transitions and Economic Miracles in Emerging Asia." *World Bank Economic Review* 12 (3): 419–56.

Blouin, C., N. Drager, and R. Smith, eds. 2006. *International Trade in Health Services and the GATS: Current Issues and Debates.* Washington, DC: World Bank.

Borgy, V., X. Chojnicki, G. Le Garrec, and C. Schwellnus. 2010. "Macroeconomic Consequences of Global Endogenous Migration: A General Equilibrium Analysis." *Annals of Economics and Statistics* 97/98: 13–39.

Botman, D., S. Danninger, and J. A. Schiff, eds. 2015. *Can Abenomics Succeed? Overcoming the Legacy of Japan's Lost Decades.* Washington, DC: International Monetary Fund.

Bruns, B., D. Evans, and J. Luque. 2012. *Achieving World-Class Education in Brazil: The Next Agenda.* Directions in Development. Washington, DC: World Bank.

Bussolo, M., J. Koettl, and E. Sinnott. 2015. *Golden Aging: Prospects for Healthy, Active, and Prosperous Aging in Europe and Central Asia.* Washington, DC: World Bank

Bussolo, M., J. Lim, M. Maliszewska, H. Timmer. 2014. "Capital Will Not Become More Expensive as the World Ages." Policy Research Working Paper 6989. World Bank, Washington, DC.

Cattaneo, A., and S. C. Wolter. 2007. "Are the Elderly a Threat to Educational Expenditures?" Economics of Education Working Paper 0003, University of Zurich, Institute for Strategy and Business Economics .

Chandra, U., J. Y. Lin, and Y. Wang. 2012. "Leading Dragons Phenomenon: New Opportunities for Catch-up in Low Income Countries." Policy Research Working Paper, World Bank, Washington, DC.

Chinn, M. D., and E. S. Prasad. 2003. "Medium-Term Determinants of Current Accounts in Industrial and Developing Countries: An Empirical Exploration." *Journal of International Economics* 59 (January): 47–76.

Cincotta, R. 2010. "Whither the Demographic Arc of Instability?" *New Security Beat* Blog, December 14.

———. 2011. "Tunisia's Shot at Democracy: What Demographics and Recent History Tell Us." *New Security Beat* Blog, January 25.

Clemens, M. A. 2011. "Economics and Emigration: Trillion-Dollar Bills on the Sidewalk?" *Journal of Economic Perspectives* 25 (3): 83–106.

Cotlear, C., ed. 2011. *Population Aging: Is Latin America Ready.* Washington, DC: World Bank.

Dalton, M., B. O'Neill, A. Prskawetz, L. Jiang, and J. Pitkin. 2008. "Population Aging and Future Carbon Emissions in the United States." *Energy Economics* 30 (2): 642–75.

EC (European Commission). 2015. *The 2015 Aging Report. Economic and Budgetary Projections for the 28 EU Member States (2013-2060).* Brussels: European Commission.

Economist, The. 2012. "Brazil's Pension System—Tick, Tock." March 24.

———. 2014. "Japan's Demography: The Incredible Shrinking Country. For the First Time, a Proper Debate is Starting about Immigration." May 31.

Eden, M., and A. Kraay. 2014. "Crowding In and the Returns to Government Investment in Low-Income Countries: Policy Implications for Ethiopia." World Bank, Washington, DC, February 14.

Feroli, M. 2003. "Capital Flows among the G-7 Nations: A Demographic Perspective." Finance and Economics Discussion Series 2003–54, Federal Reserve Board, Washington, DC.

Financial Stability Board. 2011. "Macroprudential Policy Tools and Frameworks: Progress Report to G20." Financial Stability Board, International Monetary Fund, and Bank for International Settlements.

Fox, L., and T. P. Sohnesen. 2012. "Household Enterprises in Sub-Saharan Africa: Why They Matter for Growth, Jobs, and Livelihoods." Policy Research Working Paper 6184. World Bank, Washington, DC.

Frejka, T., G. W. Jones, J.-P. Sardon. 2010. "East Asian Childbearing Patterns and Policy Developments." *Population and Development Review* 36 (3): 579–606.

Gable, S., H. Lofgren, and I. Osorio-Rodarte. 2015. "Country Development Diagnostics Post-2015: Ethiopia at a Glance." Background document for the Third International Financing for Development Conference in Addis Ababa, July. World Bank, Washington, DC.

Galor, O. 2012. "The Demographic Transition: Causes and Consequences." *Cliometrica* 6 (1): 1–28.

Gibson, J., D. McKenzie, and B. Zia. 2014. "The Impact of Financial Literacy Training For Migrants." *World Bank Economic Review* 28 (1): 130–61.

Goldstone, J. A., E. Kauffman, and M. D. Toft, eds. 2012. *Political Demography: How Population Changes are Reshaping International Security and National Politics*. Boulder, CO: Paradigm Publishers.

Góra, M. 2013. "Political Economy of Pension Reforms: Selected General Issues and the Polish Pension Reform Case." *IZA Journal of Labor & Development* 2 (2).

Gragnolati, M., O. H. Jorgensen, R. Rocha, and A. Fruttero. 2011. *Growing Old in an Older Brazil: Implications of Population Aging on Growth, Poverty, Public Finance, and Service Delivery*. Washington, DC: World Bank.

Gragnolati, M., R. Rofman, I. Apella, and S. Troiano. 2015. *As Time Goes By in Argentina: Economic Opportunities and Challenges of the Demographic Transition*. Washington, DC: World Bank.

Hanusch, M. 2012. "The Doing Business Indicators, Economic Growth and Regulatory Reform." Policy Research Working Paper 6176, August. World Bank, Washington, DC.

Harper, S. 2013. "Population–Environment Interactions: European Migration, Population Composition and Climate Change." *Environmental and Resource Economics* 55 (4): 525–41.

Higgins, M. 1998. "Demography, National Savings, and International Capital Flows." *International Economic Review* 39 (2): 343–69.

Hollanders, D., and F. Koster. 2012. "The Greying of the Median Voter." CentER Discussion Paper Series 2012-061, July.

ICRW (International Center for Research on Women). 2007. "How to End Child Marriage: Action Strategies for Prevention and Protection." Washington, DC.

IMF (International Monetary Fund). 2004. WEO. "How Will Demographic Change Affect the Global Economy?" International Monetary Fund, Washington, DC.

———. 2012. "The Liberalization and Management of Capital Flows: An Institutional View." International Monetary Fund, Washington, DC.

———. 2013. Brazil 2013 Article IV Consultation. Selected Issues. IMF Country Report 13/313. International Monetary Fund, Washington, DC.

———. 2014. "Staff Guidance Note on Macroprudential Policy—Considerations for Low Income Countries." International Monetary Fund, Washington, DC.

———. 2015. "Sub-Saharan Africa: Navigating Headwinds." Regional Economic Outlook Series. International Monetary Fund, Washington, DC (April).

IPCC (Intergovernmental Panel on Climate Change). 2014. *Climate Change 2014: Synthesis Report. Contribution of Working Groups I, II and III to the Fifth Assessment Report of the Intergovernmental Panel on Climate Change*. Geneva.

Jamison, D. T., M. Sandbu, and J. Wang. 2001. "Cross-country Variation in Mortality Decline, 1962–87: The Role of Country-Specific Technical Progress." CMH Working Paper Series, Paper WG1:4.

Japan Times. 2014. "Japan May Boost Immigrant Numbers." March 14.

Jiang, L., and K. Hardee. 2009. "How Do Recent Population Trends Matter to Climate Change?" Population Action International.

Jiang, L., and B. C. O'Neill. 2007. "Impacts of Demographic Trends on U.S. Household Size and Structure." *Population and Development Review* 33 (3): 567–591.

Jorgensen, O. H. 2011. "Macroeconomic and Policy Implications of Population Aging in Brazil." Policy Research Working Paper 5519. World Bank, Washington, DC.

Joshi, S., and T. P. Schultz. 2013. "Family Planning and Women's and Children's Health: Long-Term Consequences of an Outreach Program in Matlab, Bangladesh." *Demography* 50 (1): 149–80.

KC, S., B. Barakat, A. Goujon, V. Skirbekk, W. Sanderson, and W. Lutz. 2010. "Projection of Populations by Level of Educational Attainment, Age, and Sex for 120 Countries for

2005–2050." *Demographic Research* 22 (15): 383–472.

Lartey, E., F. Mandelman, and P. Acosta. 2012. "Remittances, Exchange Rate Regimes and the Dutch Disease: A Panel Data Analysis." *Review of International Economics* 20 (2): 377–95.

Lee, R., and A. Mason. 2006. "What Is the Demographic Dividend?" *Finance and Development* 43 (3).

Liddle, B. 2011. "Consumption-Driven Environmental Impact and Age Structure Change in OECD Countries: A Cointegration-STIRPAT Analysis." *Demographic Research* 24 (30): 749–70.

———. 2013. "Population, Affluence, and Environmental Impact across Development: Evidence from Panel Cointegration Modeling." *Environmental Modelling and Software* 40: 255–66.

Liddle, B., and S. Lung. 2010. "Age-Structure, Urbanization, and Climate Change in Developed Countries: Revisiting STIRPAT for Disaggregated Population and Consumption-Related Environmental Impacts." *Population and Environment* 31 (5): 317–43.

Lofgren, H., M. Cicowiez, and C. Diaz-Bonilla. 2013. "MAMS—A Computable General Equilibrium Model for Developing Country Strategy Analysis." In *Handbook of Computable General Equilibrium Modeling*. Vol. 1A, edited by P. B. Dixon and D. W. Jorgenson. North Holland, Elsevier B.V.

Lucas, Robert E., Jr. 1990. "Why Doesn't Capital Flow from Rich to Poor Countries?" *American Economic Review* 80(2): 92–96.

Luhrmann, M. 2003. "Demographic Change, Foresight, and International Capital Flows." Mannheim University, Mannheim, Germany.

Massey, D. S. 1988. "Economic Development and International Migration in Comparative Perspective." *Population and Development Review* 14 (3): 383– 414.

McKenzie, D., and D. Yang. 2015. "Evidence on Policies to Increase the Development Impacts of International Migration." *World Bank Research Observer*. World Bank, Washington, DC.

Moïsé, E., T. Orliac, and P. Minor. 2011. "Trade Facilitation Indicators: The Impact on Trade Costs." OECD Trade Policy Papers 118, OECD Publishing, Paris.

Moïsé, E., and S. Sorescu. 2013. "Trade Facilitation Indicators: The Potential Impact of Trade Facilitation on Developing Countries' Trade." OECD Trade Policy Papers 144, OECD Publishing, Paris.

Moller, L. C., and K. M. Wacker. 2015. "Ethiopia's Growth Acceleration and How to Sustain It: Insights from a Cross-Country Regression Model." Policy Research Working Paper 7292, World Bank, Washington, DC.

Myrskylä, M., H. P. Kohler, and F. C. Billari. 2009. "Advances in Development Reverse Fertility Declines." *Nature* 460 (7256): 741–43.

Naik, A., J. Koehler, and F. Laczko. 2008. "Migration and Development: Achieving Policy Coherence." No. 34. International Organization for Migration, Geneva.

Null, S. 2015. "The Future of Political Demography and Its Impact on Policy." New Security Beat Blog, March 9.

Oberndorfer, U., and V. Steiner. 2006. "Intergenerational Conflict, Partisan Politics, and Public Higher Education Spending: Evidence from the German States." IZA Discussion Papers 2417, Institute for the Study of Labor, Bonn.

OECD (Organisation for Economic Co-operation and Development). 2012. "Brazil Country Note—Programme for International Student Assessment (PISA): Results from PISA 2012." OECD Publishing, Paris.

———. 2013a. *International Migration Outlook 2013*. Paris: OECD Publishing.

———. 2013b. *Pensions at a Glance 2013: OECD and G20 Indicators*. Paris: OECD Publishing.

———. 2014. *OECD Pensions Outlook 2014*. Paris: OECD Publishing.

OECD–EU (Organisation for Economic Development and Co-operation and European Union). 2014. *Matching Economic Migration with Labour Market Needs*. Paris: OECD Publishing.

O'Neill, B. C. 2009. "Climate Change and Population Growth." In *A Pivotal Moment: Population, Justice and the Environmental Challenge*, edited by L. Mazur. Washington, DC: Island Press.

O'Neill, B. C., X. Ren, L. Jiang, and M. Dalton. 2012. "The Effect of Urbanization on Energy Use in India and China in the iPETS Model." *Energy Economist* 34 (S3): 339–45.

Ostry, J. D., A. Berg, and C. G. Tsangarides. 2014. "Redistribution, Inequality, and Growth." IMF Staff Discussion Note, International Monetary Fund, Washington, DC.

Owen, A. L., and S. Wu. 2007. "Is Trade Good for Your Health?" *Review of International Economics* 15 (4): 660–82.

Papageorgiou, C., A. Savvides, and M. Zachariadis. 2007. "International Medical Technology Diffusion." *Journal of International Economics* 72 (2): 409–27.

Poterba, J. 1996. "Demographic Structure and the Political Economy of Public Education." NBER Working Paper 5677, National Bureau of Economic Research, Cambridge, MA (July).

Ratha D., and W. Shaw. 2014. "South-South Migration and Remittances." Policy Research Working Paper 102. World Bank, Washington, DC.

Rocha, R. 2010. "Savings, Poverty and Lifecycle in Brazil." *Quarterly Knowledge Report.* World Bank, Brasilia (August).

Sadorsky, P. 2013. "Do Urbanization and Industrialization Affect Energy Intensity in Developing Countries?" *Energy Economics* 37 (May): 52–59.

Sahay, Ratna, Martin Čihák, Papa N'Diaye, Adolfo Barajas, Ran Bi, Diana Ayala, Yuan Gao, Annette Kyobe, Lam Nguyen, Christian Saborowski, Katsiaryna Svirydzenka, and Seyed Reza Yousefi. 2015. "Rethinking Financial Deepening: Stability and Growth in Emerging Markets." IMF Staff Discussion Note 15/08, International Monetary Fund, Washington, DC (May).

Smith, R. D., R. Chanda, and V. Tangcharoensathien. 2009. "Trade in Health-Related Services." *The Lancet* 373.9663: 593–601.

Soares, Rodrigo R., and B. L. S. Falcão. 2008. "The Demographic Transition and the Sexual Division of Labor." *Journal of Political Economy* 116 (6): 1058–104.

Solimano A., and N. Watts. 2005. "International Migration, Capital Flows and the Global Economy: A Long Run View." UN CEPAL, Economic Development Division, Santiago, Chile.

Stephenson, J., S. F. Crane, C. Levy, and M. Maslin. 2013. "Population, Development, and Climate Change: Links and Effects on Human Health." *The Lancet* 382 (9905): 1665–73.

Troiano, S. 2015. "Population Dynamics and the Implications for Economic Growth, Poverty and Inequality—What Is Relevant for Southern Africa." World Bank, Washington, DC.

Tyers R., and Q. Shi. 2007. "Demographic Change and Policy Responses: Implications for the Global Economy." *World Economy* 30 (4): 537–66.

United Nations. 2013a. *World Population Prospects: 2013 Revision.* Geneva: United Nations.

———. 2013b. "Global Migration: Demographic Aspects and Its Relevance for Development." Technical Paper 2013/6. Department of Economic and Social Affairs Population Division, United Nations, Geneva.

———. 2013c. "Trends in International Migrant Stock: Migrants by Destination and Origin." United Nations database, POP/DB/MIG/Stock/Rev.2013, Department of Economic and Social Affairs.

———. 2015. *World Population Prospects; The 2015 Revision.* Geneva: United Nations.

UNCTAD (United Nations Conference on Trade and Development). 2013. *Non-Tariff Measures to Trade: Economic and Policy Issues for Developing Countries.* Geneva: United Nations.

———. 2015. *World Investment Report 2015: Reforming International Investment Governance.* Geneva: United Nations.

Voas, D. 2003. "Conflicting Preferences: A Reason Fertility Tends to Be Too High or Too Low." *Population and Development Review* 29 (4): 627–46.

Walmsley, T. L., L. A. Winters, and S. A. Ahmed. 2007. "Measuring the Impact of the Movement of Labor Using a Model of Bilateral Migration Flows." GTAP Technical Paper 28. Center for Global Trade Analysis, Purdue University.

Wodon, Q. 2015. Personal communication of results from ongoing research on child marriage in Niger.

World Bank. 2006. *Global Economic Prospects 2006: Economic Implications of Remittances and Migration.* Washington DC: World Bank.

———. 2009. *World Development Report: Reshaping Economic Geography*. Washington DC: World Bank.

———. 2011. *Malaysia Economic Monitor: Brain Drain*. Washington, DC: World Bank.

———. 2013a. *Capital for the Future: Saving and Investment in an Interdependent World*. Global Development Horizons. Washington, DC: World Bank.

———. 2013b. *World Development Report: Jobs*. Washington, DC: World Bank.

———. 2013c. *Ethiopia Economic Update II: Laying the Foundation for Achieving Middle Income Status*. Washington, DC: World Bank.

———. 2014a. Doing Business Indicators. http://www.doingbusiness.org/rankings.

———. 2014b. "Economic Impacts of Child Marriage: Conceptual Framework and White Paper." World Bank and the International Center for the Research on Women.

———. 2014c. *Ethiopia Economic Update II: Laying the Foundation for Achieving Middle Income Status*. Washington, DC: World Bank.

———. 2014d. *Voice and Agency: Empowering Women and Girls for Shared Prosperity*. Washington, DC: World Bank.

———. 2015a. *From Potential to Reality: What Will It Take to Harness a Demographic Dividend in Africa?*, Washington DC: World Bank.

———. 2015b. *Live Long and Prosper: Aging in East Asia and the Pacific*. Washington, DC: World Bank.

———. 2015c. "Russian Federation: Aging and Prosperity." Forthcoming.

———. 2015d. *What's Next in Aging Europe: Aging with Growth in Central Europe and the Baltics*. Washington, DC: World Bank.

WHO and UNICEF (World Health Organization and United Nations Children's Fund). 2015. *Every Newborn Action Plan Progress Report*. Geneva: World Health Organization.

World Bank and World Trade Organization. 2015. *The Role of Trade in Ending Poverty*. Geneva: World Trade Organization.

WTO (World Trade Organization). 2012. *World Trade Report 2012; Trade and Public Policies: a Closer Look at Non-Tariff Measures in the 21st Century*. Geneva: World Trade Organization.

———. 2013. *World Trade Report 2013; Factors Shaping the Future of World Trade*. Geneva: World Trade Organization.

———. 2014. *World Trade Report 2014; Trade and Development: Recent Trends and the Role of the WTO*. Geneva: World Trade Organization.

Yang, D. 2011. "Migrant Remittances." *Journal of Economic Perspectives* 25 (3): 129–51.

Zagheni, E. 2011. "The Leverage of Demographic Dynamics on Carbon Dioxide Emissions: Does Age Structure Matter?" *Demography* 48: 371–99.

Zeng, Y., W. Zhenglian, J. Leiwen, and G. Danan. 2008. "Projection of Family Households and Elderly Living Arrangement in the Context of Rapid Population Aging in China—A Demographic Window of Opportunity until 2030 and Serious Challenges Thereafter." *Genus* 64 (1–2): 9–36.

Appendixes

A. Millennium Development Goals Report Card

B. The Role of Multilateral Development Banks: From Millennium Development Goals to Sustainable Development Goals

C. Data Sources

D. Methodology

Goals and Targets from the Millennium Declaration

GOAL 1	**ERADICATE EXTREME POVERTY AND HUNGER**
Target 1.A	Halve, between 1990 and 2015, the proportion of people whose income is less than $1.25 a day
Target 1.B	Achieve full and productive employment and decent work for all, including women and young people
Target 1.C	Halve, between 1990 and 2015, the proportion of people who suffer from hunger
GOAL 2	**ACHIEVE UNIVERSAL PRIMARY EDUCATION**
Target 2.A	Ensure that by 2015, children everywhere, boys and girls alike, will be able to complete a full course of primary schooling
GOAL 3	**PROMOTE GENDER EQUALITY AND EMPOWER WOMEN**
Target 3.A	Eliminate gender disparity in primary and secondary education, preferably by 2005, and at all levels by 2015
GOAL 4	**REDUCE CHILD MORTALITY**
Target 4.A	Reduce by two-thirds, between 1990 and 2015, the under-five mortality rate
GOAL 5	**IMPROVE MATERNAL HEALTH**
Target 5.A	Reduce by three-quarters, between 1990 and 2015, the maternal mortality ratio
Target 5.B	Achieve by 2015 universal access to reproductive health
GOAL 6	**COMBAT HIV/AIDS, MALARIA, AND OTHER DISEASES**
Target 6.A	Have halted by 2015 and begun to reverse the spread of HIV/AIDS
Target 6.B	Achieve by 2010 universal access to treatment for HIV/AIDS for all those who need it
Target 6.C	Have halted by 2015 and begun to reverse the incidence of malaria and other major diseases
GOAL 7	**ENSURE ENVIRONMENTAL SUSTAINABILITY**
Target 7.A	Integrate the principles of sustainable development into country policies and programs and reverse the loss of environmental resources
Target 7.B	Reduce biodiversity loss, achieving by 2010 a significant reduction in the rate of loss
Target 7.C	Halve by 2015 the proportion of people without sustainable access to safe drinking water and basic sanitation
Target 7.D	Have achieved a significant improvement by 2020 in the lives of at least 100 million slum dwellers
GOAL 8	**DEVELOP A GLOBAL PARTNERSHIP FOR DEVELOPMENT**
Target 8.A	Develop further an open, rule-based, predictable, nondiscriminatory trading and financial system (including a commitment to good governance, development, and poverty reduction, both nationally and internationally)
Target 8.B	Address the special needs of the least-developed countries (including tariff- and quota-free access for exports of the least-developed countries; enhanced debt relief for heavily indebted poor countries and cancellation of official bilateral debt; and more generous official development assistance for countries committed to reducing poverty)
Target 8.C	Address the special needs of landlocked developing countries and small island developing states (through the Programme of Action for the Sustainable Development of Small Island Developing States and the outcome of the 22nd special session of the General Assembly)
Target 8.D	Deal comprehensively with the debt problems of developing countries through national and international measures in order to make debt sustainable in the long term
Target 8.E	In cooperation with pharmaceutical companies, provide access to affordable essential drugs in developing countries
Target 8.F	In cooperation with the private sector, make available the benefits of new technologies, especially information and communications

A

Millennium Development Goals Report Card

Since the Millennium Development Goals (MDGs) were articulated in the United Nations Millennium Declaration in 2000, substantial progress has been made, but a large unfinished agenda remains. The global target on poverty was met five years ahead of the 2015 deadline, and several other MDGs have been met or are likely to be met, such as gender parity in primary and secondary school enrollment. MDGs covering other areas like maternal mortality, however, are out of reach and will not be met this year, nor are they expected to be met globally in the near future. Progress has also been uneven across countries and regions (Sub-Saharan Africa is the only region that will not meet any of the targets by 2015) and socioeconomic boundaries.

In many developing countries, population growth has made it more difficult to achieve some goals and targets. Many targets are specified as proportions or rates, using the ratio of two numbers. The population, or a subgroup of the population, is often the denominator—so when the population grows, achieving a fall in the rate will require a correspondingly large fall in the numerator. If a target is mainly for specific age groups (such as targets related to child malnutrition, primary completion, child mortality, and maternal mortality), the population growth within the age groups can make it more difficult to achieve the target. The growth in populations of school-age children and women of child-bearing age has been significant in the past quarter century, especially in Sub-Saharan Africa.

The MDGs have been instrumental in spurring a push for better data and enhanced monitoring. One important aspect of the MDGs has been their focus on measuring and monitoring progress; this focus has presented a clear challenge to improve the quality, frequency, and availability of relevant statistics. Much has been done to strengthen the national statistical systems where most data originate, but weaknesses remain in the coverage and quality of many indicators in the poorest countries, where resources are scarce and careful measurement of progress may matter the most. Based on the most recent data available, the MDG Report Card in this appendix presents a goal-by-goal analysis on the progress toward the MDGs, which is complemented by online progress charts at http://data.worldbank.org/mdgs.

MDG 1

Eradicate extreme poverty and hunger

Evaluated at $1.25 a day in 2005 purchasing power parity (PPP), the world met the MDG target of halving the proportion of the population in extreme poverty five years ahead of the 2015 deadline (World Bank 2015). The proportion of people in the world living on less than $1.25 a day fell from 36.4 percent in 1990 to 14.5 percent in 2011. Forecasts based on country-specific growth rates over the past 10 years indicate a fall in the global extreme poverty rate to 11.5 percent by 2015 (figure A.1), a drop of more than two-thirds from the baseline.

Progress toward reducing poverty across regions has been uneven. East Asia and the Pacific experienced the fastest rate of poverty reduction, slashing its share of people living on less than $1.25 a day from 58.2 percent in 1990 to 7.9 percent in 2011 and reaching the target well ahead of the deadline. Europe and Central Asia, Latin America and the Caribbean, and the Middle East and North Africa all reached the target by 2010. South Asia achieved the target by 2011, following a strong acceleration after 2008. This reduction was mainly brought about by populous India, whose poverty trajectory strongly influenced the trend for the whole South Asian region. By contrast, Sub-Saharan Africa still lags behind and is not expected to meet the target by 2015.

Progress in reducing the absolute number of poor people was weaker, especially in regions and countries with rapid population growth. In Sub-Saharan Africa, the number of extremely poor people actually increased from 290 million in 1990 to 415 million in 2011, as a result of a very fast-growing population (figure A.2).

The global achievement of the MDG 1 poverty target was aided by the strong performance of China and India, the two countries in the world in 1990 with the highest population and also the largest number of extremely poor. China has been a driving force for poverty reduction worldwide as well as in its own region. China's extreme poverty rate declined from 60.7 percent in 1990 to 6.3 percent in 2011. Still, it had 8.3 percent of the world's extremely poor in 2011, the world's third-largest share. India more than halved its extreme poverty rate, reducing it from 51.4 percent in 1990 to 24.7 percent in 2011. Still, it was home to nearly a third of the world's total of extremely poor people in 2011. While these countries have achieved the poverty target, their task of eradicating extreme poverty remains critical, especially when confounded by population growth.

Based on current trends, nearly half of the 145 developing countries have already achieved the poverty target of MDG 1. However, 27 countries are seriously off track, meaning that at the current pace of progress, they will not be able to halve their 1990 extreme poverty rates even by 2030. All but six of these 27 countries are in Sub-Saharan Africa (World Bank MDG Data Dashboard).[1]

MDG 1 also aims to halve hunger and malnutrition rates by 2015. The prevalence of malnutrition among children under age five in developing countries has dropped substantially, falling from 25 percent in 1990 to 16 percent in 2014. However, developing countries as a whole may not be able to meet the target by 2015, nor will South Asia or Sub-Saharan Africa (figure A.3). In part, the target will be missed because of the significant growth in the under-five population in Sub-Saharan Africa, which grew nearly 75 percent between 1990 and 2014. In other developing regions, the under-five population either dropped considerably (East Asia and the Pacific, Europe and Central Asia, and Latin America and the Caribbean) or grew only moderately (Middle East and North Africa and South Asia). Sub-Saharan Africa is also the only developing region that has seen a steady upward trend in the number of underweight children under the age of five, from 27.5 million in 1990 to 31.4 million in 2014 (one-third of the developing world's underweight children under age five).

FIGURE A.1 Share of people living on less than $1.25 a day, by region, 1990–2015

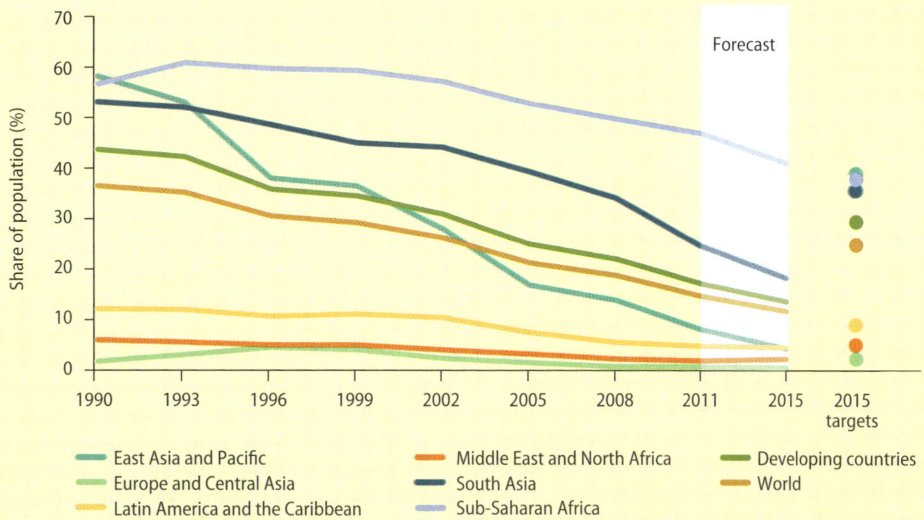

Source: World Bank PovcalNet (http://iresearch.worldbank.org/PovcalNet).
Note: Based on 2005 purchasing power parity.

FIGURE A.2 Number of people living on less than $1.25 a day, by region, 1990–2015

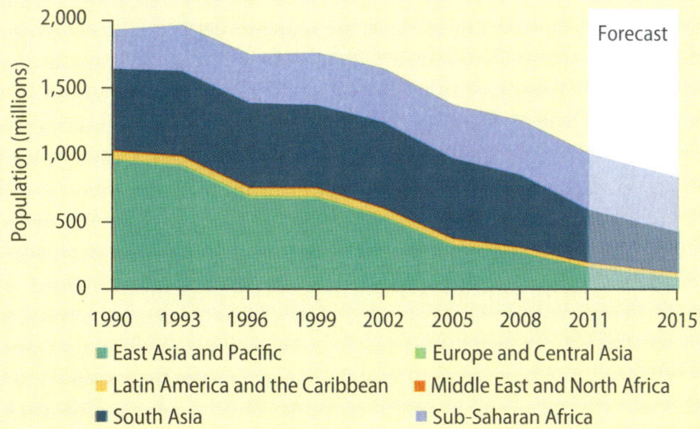

Source: World Bank PovcalNet (http://iresearch.worldbank.org/PovcalNet).
Note: Based on purchasing power parity.

FIGURE A.3 Percentage of children under five who are underweight, by region, 1990–2015

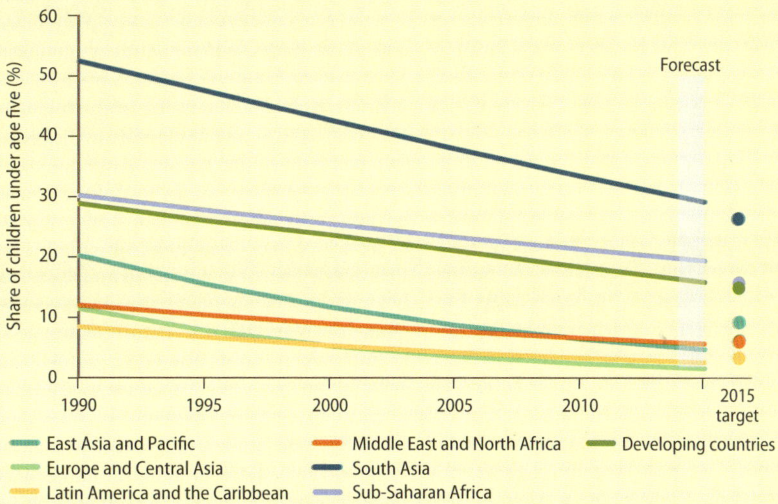

Source: UNICEF, WHO, and World Bank 2015.

MDG 2

Achieve universal primary education

MDG 2 focuses solely on the effort to ensure that all children, boys and girls alike, can complete a full course of primary education by 2015. This target is measured by the primary school completion rate—the proportion of children completing the last grade of primary education, regardless of age—and is not likely to be met by developing countries as a whole by 2015.

The primary completion rate in developing countries increased from about 79 percent in 1990 to 91 percent in 2013 (figure A.4). This is an impressive gain, especially when considering that the number of students in the last grade of primary education in developing countries grew from 88 million in 1990 to 103 million in 2013. This increase means that, during the past two decades or so, nearly 25 million more children were able to complete a full course of primary education. Even though the primary completion rate has remained at 91 percent since 2009 for developing countries, 1 million more children were added to the group of primary school graduates over the past five years.

Among the six developing regions, East Asia and the Pacific, Europe and Central Asia, and Latin America and the Caribbean have reached the target. However, the other regions are not expected to reach the target. The challenge faced by Sub-Saharan Africa is especially daunting: despite a substantial increase in the primary completion rate, from 54 percent in 1990 to 69 percent in 2013, it is still the lowest among all regions; in 2013 it was nearly 20 percentage points below the average rate for all developing countries. At the same time, Sub-Saharan Africa has the fastest-growing population of primary-school-age children among all regions, placing more pressure on its education system.

Regional averages often conceal variations in performance across countries. For example, although East Asia and the Pacific, Europe and Central Asia, and Latin America and the Caribbean have achieved the MDG 2 target, 18 countries in these regions are seriously off track and are unlikely to achieve the target even by 2030. On the other hand, the target has been achieved in 9 countries in Sub-Saharan Africa, although the region as a whole has lagged (World Bank MDG Data Dashboard).

Variations are captured not only across countries but also within countries—between the rich and the poor and between urban and rural residents. Children in poor families and those living in rural areas are less likely to enroll or remain in school. In Senegal, for example, 73 percent of children from households whose incomes were in the richest quintile completed primary education in 2012, compared with 51 percent of children from the poorest quintile. While 83 percent of children in urban areas completed primary school, only 57 percent of children in rural areas did so (figure A.5). Ensuring equitable access to education is a key challenge in achieving universal primary education.

To complete a course of education, children need to enroll and stay in school. However, many children either never attend school, start school but attend intermittently, or drop out before completion. The number of primary-school-age children not attending school has been halved to 56 million since peaking in 1997. South Asia substantially reduced the number of primary-school-age children not in school, driven by significant progress in India. Sub-Saharan Africa decreased the number of out-of-school children by about 8 million between 1990 and 2013. But the population growth of primary-school-age children in the region—a 77 percent increase from 87 million to 153 million during the same period—made it all the more challenging for countries in the region to make a larger reduction. Consequently, about 60 percent of the developing world's out-of-school children live in Sub-Saharan Africa (figure A.6).

FIGURE A.4 Primary school completion rate, by region, 1990–2013

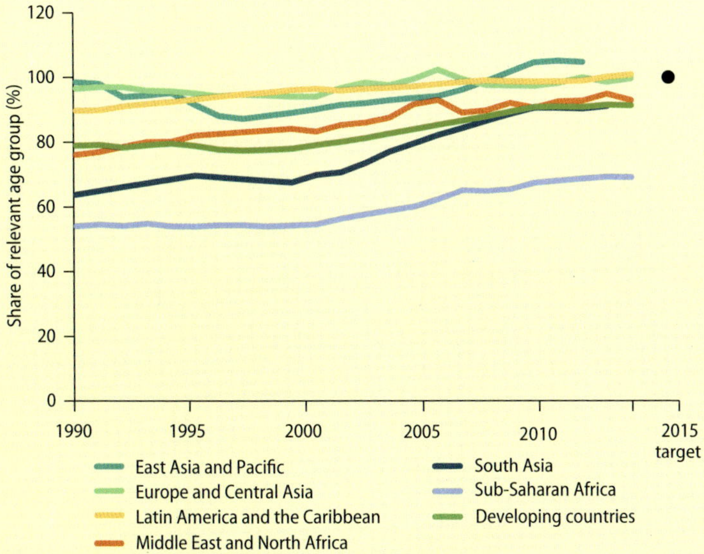

Source: United Nations Educational, Scientific and Cultural Organization Institute for Statistics.

FIGURE A.5 Primary completion rate by income quintile and residence, Senegal, 2012

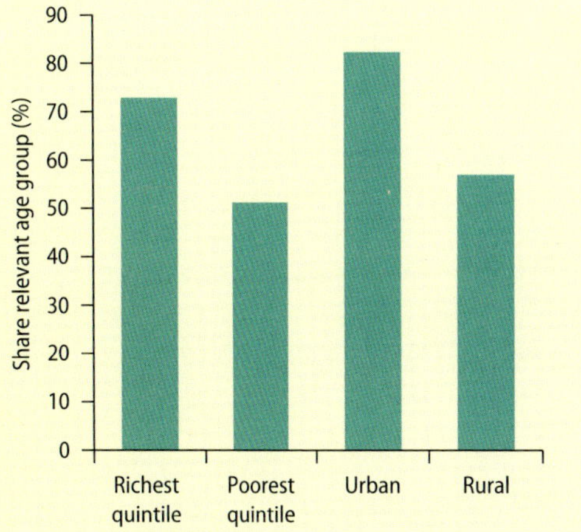

Source: World Bank EdStats Database. World Bank calculations, based on Demographic and Health Surveys.

FIGURE A.6 Number of primary-school-age children out of school, by region, 1990–2013

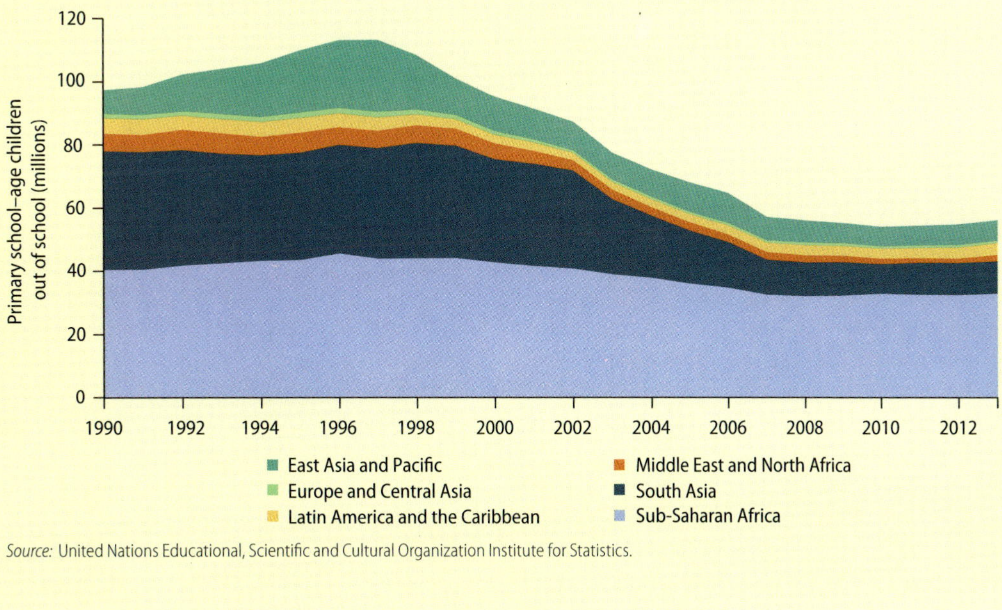

Source: United Nations Educational, Scientific and Cultural Organization Institute for Statistics.

MDG 3

Promote gender equality and empower women

MDG 3 is aimed at promoting gender equality and empowering women by enhancing women's social, economic, and political participation. Expanding opportunities for girls and women in these areas benefits them directly as well as society as a whole.

The target associated with MDG 3 is to eliminate gender disparity at all levels of education by 2015. Developing countries as a whole are likely to reach gender parity in primary and secondary enrollment, defined as having a ratio of girls to boys in primary and secondary education at 97–103 percent, according to UNESCO (2004). The ratio of girls to boys enrolled in primary and secondary schools increased from 83 percent in 1990 to 97 percent in 2013 (figure A.7). The ratio in tertiary education has increased even more, from 72 percent to 103 percent in the same period.

Nearly half of the 145 countries have achieved gender parity in primary and secondary enrollment. However, 25 countries are seriously off target. While 11 countries are in the Middle East and North Africa and Sub-Saharan Africa, 12 are in Europe and Central Asia and Latin America and the Caribbean, regions that have achieved gender parity on the whole (World Bank MDG Data Dashboard).

Across developing regions, there are substantial differences in progress. Besides economic and policy factors that influence gender parity in education (such as economic growth, investment in infrastructure and education, and more direct policy interventions), demography and the evolution of school-age populations in each region may also underlie some of the uneven progress. South Asia made the most remarkable progress among regions, closing the gender gap in primary and secondary enrollment by more than 30 percentage points between 1990 and 2013 to reach gender parity. In 1990, South Asia's ratio of girls to boys in school enrollment was only 68, 12 percentage points lower than in the Middle East and North Africa (the next lowest region). South Asia achieved parity even though the region added 47 million school-age boys and 41 million school-age girls in the period, pressuring school systems to educate more children. East Asia and the Pacific and Europe and Central Asia had already reached gender parity in primary and secondary school enrollment by 2013. These regions have experienced a decline in the school-age population since the early 2000s, which may have enabled them to make more resources available for children. Sub-Saharan Africa and the Middle East and North Africa saw fast progress, but they continue to have the largest gender disparities in primary and secondary enrollment rates among all developing regions and are unlikely to meet the target of eliminating these disparities by 2015. The task has been more challenging for Sub-Saharan Africa because its school-age population has grown steadily since 1990, imposing increased pressure on its educational systems.

While tremendous progress was made regarding gender parity in tertiary education (figure A.8), regional disparities are quite stark. Four of the six regions have achieved gender parity in tertiary education, including the Middle East and North Africa, which is struggling to achieve gender parity in primary and secondary education. South Asia has made accelerated progress since 2010 and is on track to reach gender parity in tertiary enrollment. As of 2013, however, the female-to-male tertiary enrollment ratio remained very low in Sub-Saharan Africa (73 percent).

Gender disparities in the labor market and in the political arena are also critical, and associated indicators are used for monitoring progress there as well. Women work long hours and contribute considerably to their families' economic well-being, but many engage in low-paying and less productive jobs. The share of women's paid employment in the nonagricultural sector is less than 20 percent in the Middle East and North Africa, having risen only marginally over the years. The share of women in wage employment is the highest in Europe and Central Asia, almost equal to men's at 45 percent (figure A.9).

Women also lag men in participating in public life and decision making at the highest levels, as measured by the proportion of parliamentary seats held by women. As of 2014, Latin America and the Caribbean led developing-country regions, with 29 percent of the seats held by women, followed closely by Sub-Saharan Africa at 22 percent. Overall, women's presence has improved compared with 1990 levels. The biggest change has occurred in the Middle East and North Africa, where the proportion of seats held by women more than quadrupled between 1990 and 2014 (figure A.10).

FIGURE A.7 Ratio of girls to boys in primary and secondary education, by region, 1990–2013

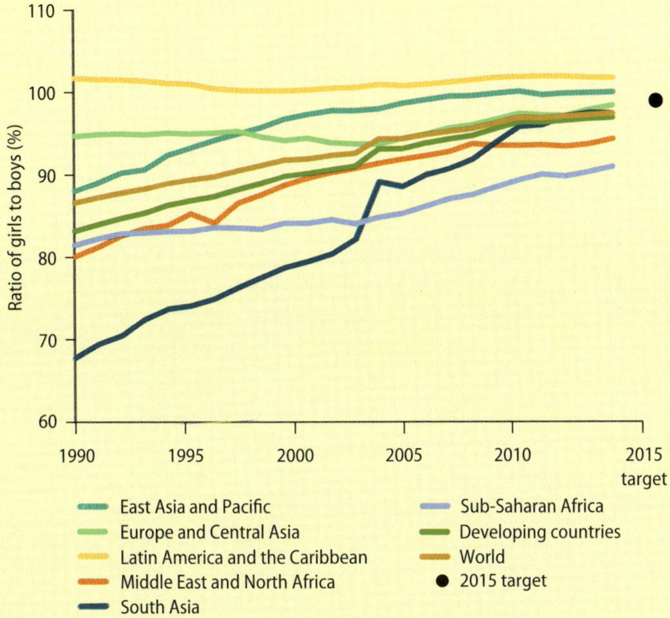

Source: United Nations Educational, Scientific and Cultural Organization Institute for Statistics.

FIGURE A.8 Ratio of girls to boys in tertiary education, by region, 1990–2013

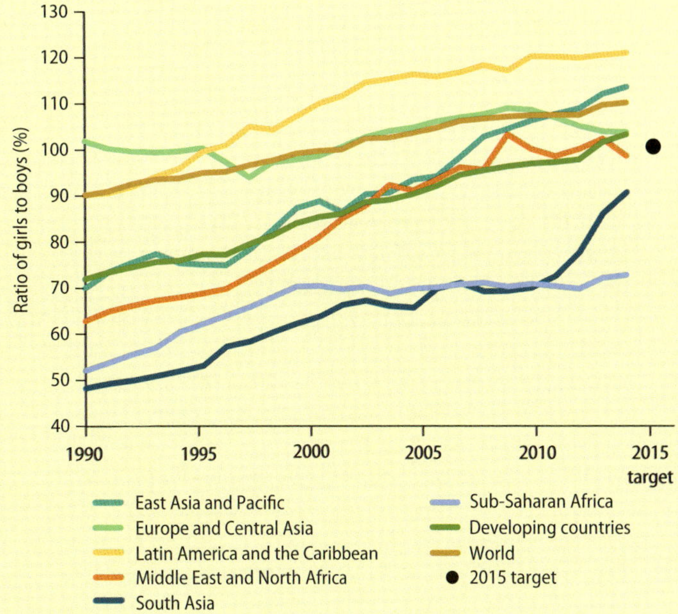

Source: United Nations Educational, Scientific and Cultural Organization Institute for Statistics.

FIGURE A.9 Share of women in wage employment in the nonagricultural sector, 2009–13

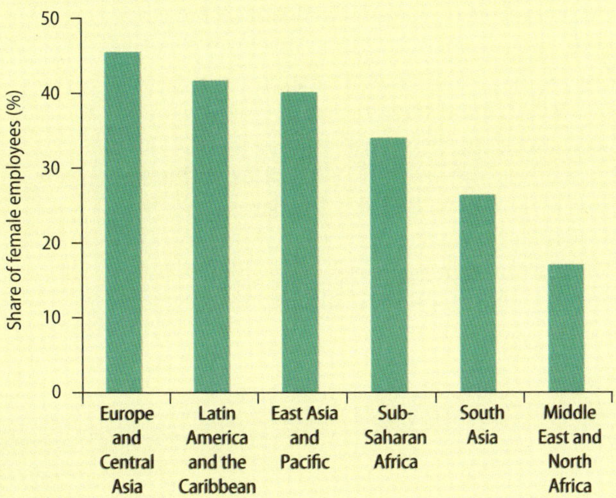

Source: International Labour Organization.
Note: The percentage for each region is the median for the region's countries for the most recent year available between 2009 and 2013.

FIGURE A.10 Proportion of seats held by women in national parliaments, by region, 2000–14

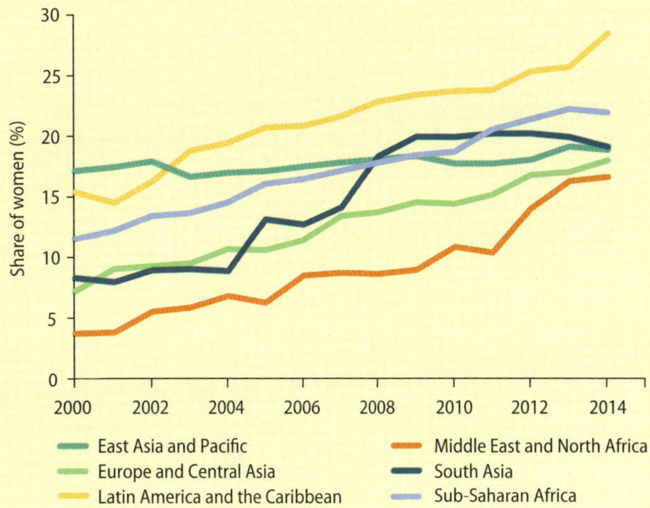

Source: Inter-Parliamentary Union.

MDG 4

Reduce child mortality

In the past two decades, the number of children across the globe who die each year before their fifth birthday has been cut by more than half, falling from 13 million in 1990 to 6 million in 2015. At the end point of the MDGs, at least 16,000 fewer children die each day compared with 1990.

In 2015, the global average rate of child mortality declined to 43 deaths per 1,000 live births, about half its 1990 level of 91 deaths per 1,000 live births. Although a significant achievement, based on the current trend, the world as a whole fell short of the MDG 4 target of reducing the under-five mortality rate by two-thirds between 1990 and 2015. The average annual rate of decline of the global under-five mortality rate accelerated from 1.8 percent over 1990–2000 to 3.9 percent over 2005–15. If the more recent rate of decline had started in 1990, the target for MDG 4 would likely have been achieved by 2015. And if this recent rate of decline continues, the target will be achieved in 2026 (United Nations Interagency Group for Child Mortality Estimation 2015).

Sub-Saharan Africa and South Asia bear the highest child mortality rates, despite rapid improvements since 2000 (figure A.11). In Sub-Saharan Africa, the rate declined by more than half between 1990 and 2015 but still remained high at 83 deaths per 1,000 live births. At the same time, the number of under-five deaths declined by only 24 percent largely because of the large increase (nearly 76 percent) in the under-five population in the region.

East Asia and the Pacific and Latin America and the Caribbean have achieved the MDG 4 target. Among the 145 countries evaluated, 57 have already met the child mortality target by 2015. Based on recent trends, 35 countries are seriously off track, and more than one-third of these countries are in Sub-Saharan Africa (World Bank MDG Data Dashboard).

In 2015 around 4.3 million under-five deaths, or about 73 percent of all such deaths worldwide, occurred in 20 developing countries. Most of these countries are characterized by large populations, often with high birthrates. Many have substantially reduced mortality rates over the past two decades. Of these 20 countries, Bangladesh, Brazil, China, the Arab Republic of Egypt, Ethiopia, Indonesia, Malawi, Mozambique, Niger, Tanzania and Uganda achieved a two-thirds reduction in their under-five mortality rate by 2015. Had the mortality rates of 1990 prevailed in 2015, 4.2 million more children would have died in these 11 countries, and another 6.9 million would have died in the remaining 9 countries (figure A.12).

Urbanization is associated with lower levels of child mortality (World Bank 2013). Figure A.13 shows that child mortality rates tend to be lower in countries with a larger share of the population living in urban areas. These lower rates may be because urban residents tend to be more affluent or have better access to health facilities and more cost-effective interventions. In urban areas, women also tend to be better educated and have better access to contraceptive methods than their rural counterparts, which in turn contributes to lower fertility rates and better health for the mother and child (Müller et al. 2015). This is not always the case, however. Child mortality tends to be very high in countries where the majority of the urban population lives in slums.[2]

FIGURE A.11 Under-five mortality rate (per 1,000 live births), by region, 1990–2015

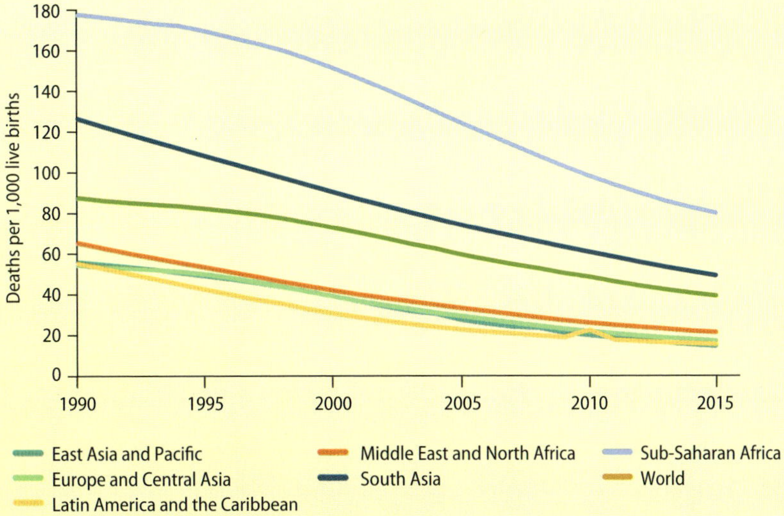

Source: United Nations Inter-agency Group for Child Mortality Estimation.

FIGURE A.12 Number of deaths of children under age five in 2015, selected countries

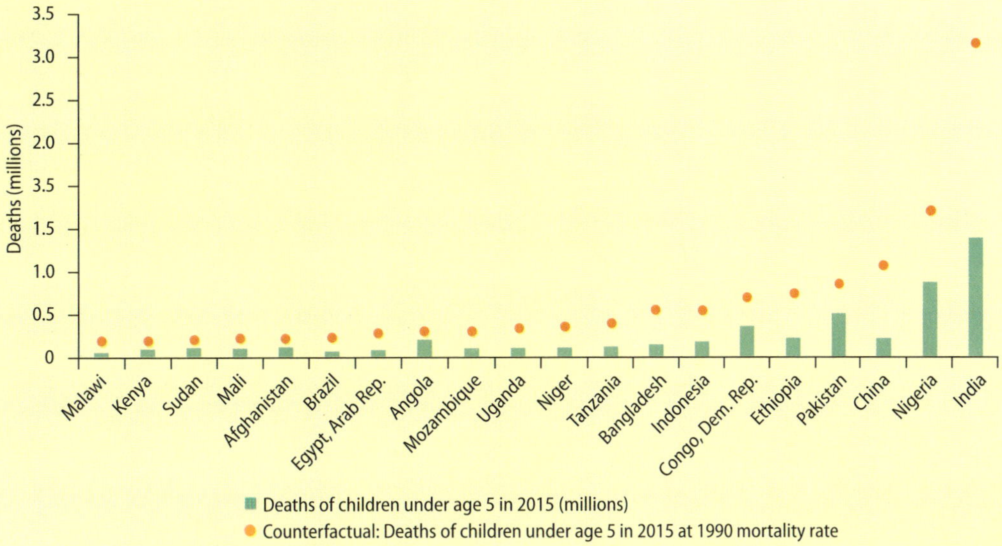

Source: World Bank calculations.

FIGURE A.13 Child mortality and urbanization, 2015

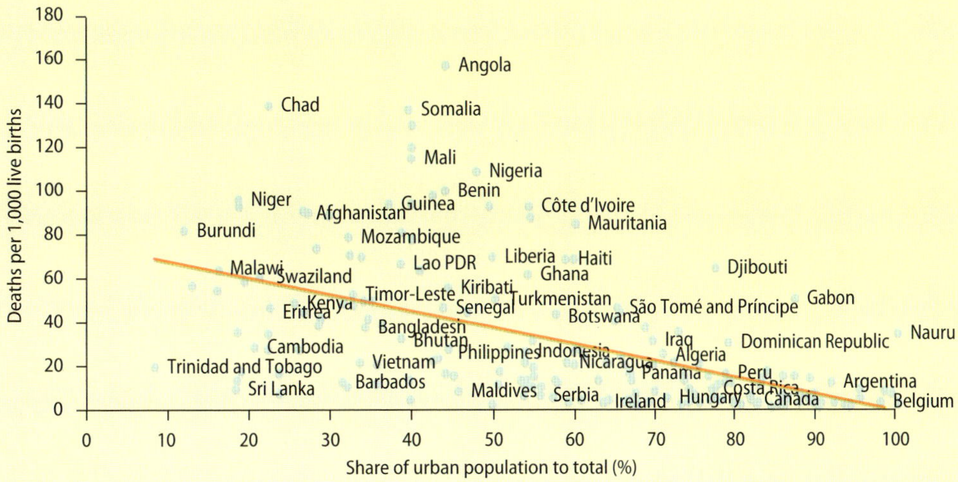

Source: World Development Indicators database.

MDG 5

Improve maternal health

Every day, around 800 young women lose their lives before, during, or after childbirth. Most of these deaths are avoidable (WHO 2014b]. Maternal deaths are heavily concentrated in poor areas of the world. Globally, an estimated 289,000 women died from maternal causes in 2013, 99 percent of which occurred in developing countries. Sub-Saharan Africa experienced disproportionately high maternal deaths, accounting for 62 percent of the global total, followed by South Asia, which accounted for 24 percent.

The MDG 5 target calls for reducing the maternal mortality ratio (MMR) by 75 percent between 1990 and 2015, the highest percentage reduction among all MDG targets. The MMR is calculated based on the number of maternal deaths per 100,000 live births. During the period 1990–2013, the MMR came down substantially in developing countries as a whole, declining from 430 maternal deaths per 100,000 live births in 1990 to 230 maternal deaths in 2013 (figure A.14). Despite this very significant progress, most developing countries are not likely to achieve this MDG target. According to recent data, only 18 countries (12 percent) have already achieved or are likely to achieve the target (World Bank MDG Data Dashboard). The majority of developing countries (88 countries, 61 percent) are seriously off target.

Even though many countries are unlikely to achieve the target, most of these countries have experienced a large reduction in their MMR since 1990. A decline in the MMR itself, however, does not necessarily mean that the number of maternal deaths has declined. In Niger, for example, the MMR declined by 37 percent between 1990 and 2013, but the number of maternal deaths increased by 30 percent. Because the number of reproductive-age women (15–49 years) more than doubled between 1990 and 2013, and because the total fertility rate remained very high at 7.6 births per woman, the number of live births not only increased rapidly but also outpaced the decline of the MMR.

Improved maternal health care is found to be associated with lower maternal mortality. However, less than 50 percent of women in South Asia and Sub-Saharan Africa are able to meet the World Health Organization's recommendation of at least four prenatal care services during each pregnancy. Moreover, only half of all births in these two regions are assisted by skilled birth attendants such as doctors, nurses, and trained midwives (figure A.15).

Reducing maternal deaths requires a comprehensive approach to women's reproductive health services, particularly through better access to contraception. Women with more than four children tend to have an increased risk of maternal deaths (WHO 2013). A higher prevalence of contraceptive use can reduce the number of pregnancies, leading to a lower risk of maternal deaths. Moreover, contraceptive use can reduce the likelihood of unwanted pregnancies and therefore unsafe abortions, which are one of the main causes of maternal deaths. There is a negative correlation between the MMR and the contraceptive prevalence rate (CPR) (Ahmed and others 2012) (figure A.16). Most Sub-Saharan African countries have low CPRs and very high MMRs compared with other developing countries.

Lower fertility rates for adolescent women (ages 15–19 years) are also associated with lower maternal mortality ratios (Conde-Agudelo, Belizán, and Lammers 2005). Women who give birth at early ages are likely to bear more children and are at greater risk of death or serious complications from pregnancy. The adolescent fertility rate remained high in Sub-Saharan Africa, although it declined by about 26 percent between 1990 and 2014, from 140 to 103 per 1,000 adolescent women (figure A.17). In contrast, during the same period in South Asia, the adolescent fertility rate declined by two-thirds, from 103 to 35 per 1,000 adolescent women.

FIGURE A.14 Maternal mortality ratio, by region, 1990–2013

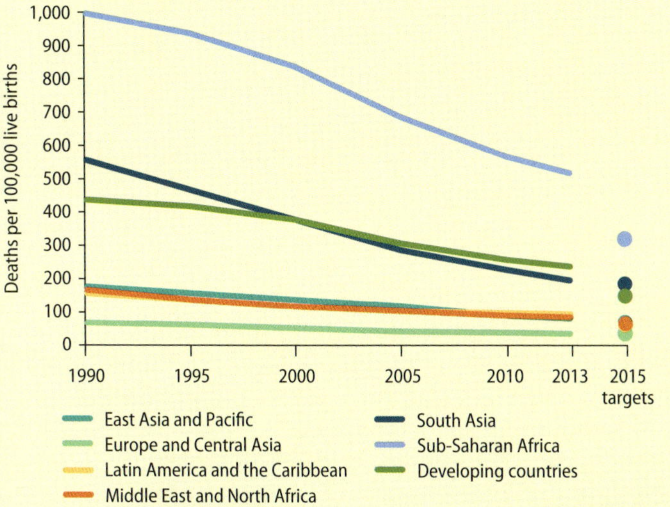

Source: United Nations Maternal Mortality Estimation Inter-agency Group, modeled estimates.

FIGURE A.15 Share of births attended by skilled health staff, by region

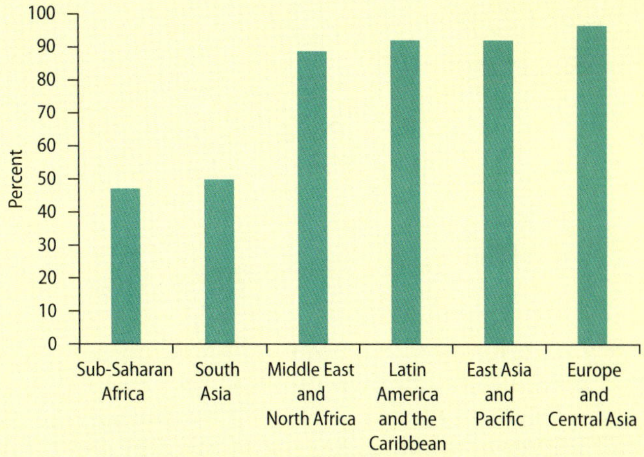

Source: United Nations Children's Fund and household surveys (including Demographic and Health Surveys and Multiple Indicator Cluster Surveys).
Note: The percentage for each region is the average for the region's countries for the most recent year available between 2008 and 2014.

FIGURE A.16 Comparison of contraceptive prevalence rate (CPR) and maternal mortality ratio (MMR), by region

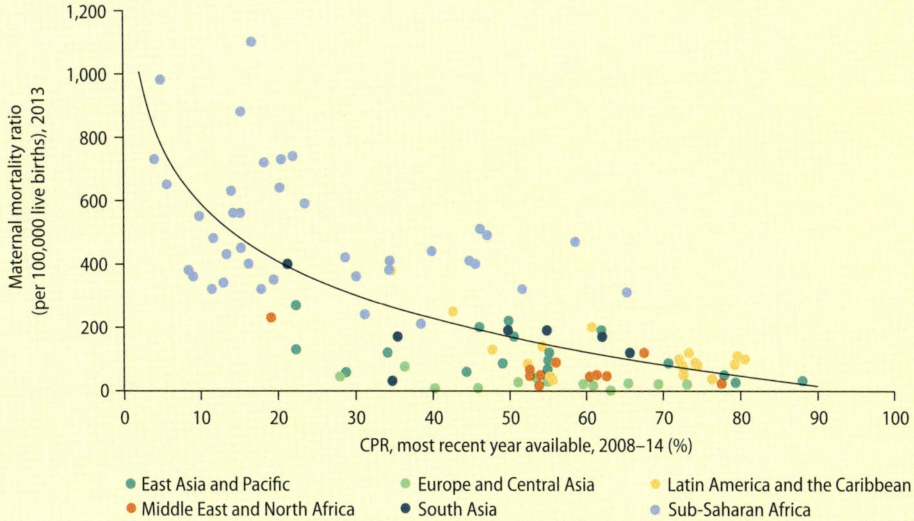

Source: United Nations Maternal Mortality Estimation Inter-agency Group, United Nations Children's Fund, and household surveys (including Demographic and Health Surveys and Multiple Indicator Cluster Surveys).

FIGURE A.17 Adolescent fertility rate, by region, 1990–2014

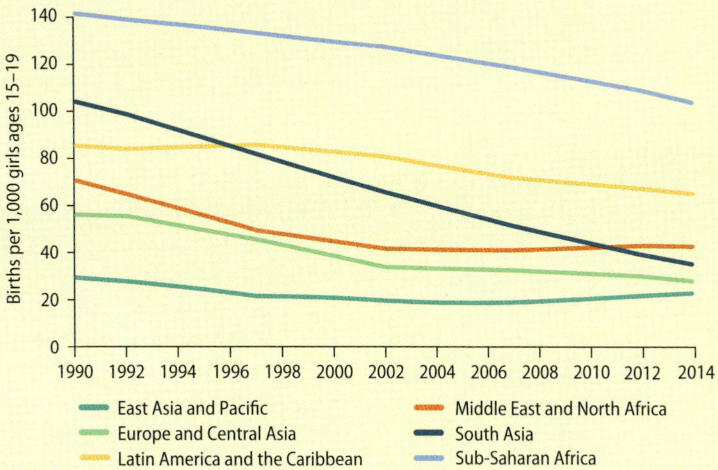

Source: United Nations Population Division.

MDG 6

Combat HIV/AIDS, malaria, and other diseases

HIV/AIDS, malaria, and tuberculosis are among the world's deadliest infectious diseases. The targets of MDG 6 are to halt and begin to reverse the spread and incidence of these diseases by 2015. In Sub-Saharan Africa, the spread of HIV/AIDS brought to a standstill decades of steady increases in life expectancy: the region's average life expectancy at birth increased from 40 years in 1960 to 50 years in 1990 but stagnated in the 2000s. HIV/AIDS has also left millions of children orphaned. Tuberculosis killed 1.1 million people worldwide in 2013, most of them ages 15–45, and sickened millions more. Malaria has taken a large toll as well, being one of the leading causes of death among young children, and at the same time it has undermined the health of millions of adults at a high cost to their productivity.

Across the world, an estimated 37 million people were living with HIV/AIDS in 2014. The number of people newly infected with HIV is continuing to decline in most parts of the world: 2 million people contracted the disease in 2014, down 33 percent from 2001 and 13 percent from 2011. The spread of new HIV infections has slowed, in line with the target of halting and reversing the spread of HIV/AIDS by 2015. However, the proportion of adults living with HIV worldwide has stayed around 0.8 percent since 2000. Sub-Saharan Africa remains the center of the HIV/AIDS epidemic, with about 70 percent of the world's adults living with HIV. The HIV prevalence rate was 4.5 percent in Sub-Saharan Africa in 2014, compared with less than 1 percent in other regions that have data available.

Despite the progress in stabilizing the proportion of adults living with HIV worldwide, continued population growth means that the absolute number of adults with HIV is increasing (figure A.18). Their number increased from 29 million in 2005 to 34 million in 2014 worldwide, and from 20 million to 24 million in Sub-Saharan Africa alone. This dynamic poses additional challenges to expanding coverage in access to antiretroviral drugs, which have dramatically improved the survival rates for those living with HIV. In 2015, 15 million people worldwide are receiving antiretroviral drugs. The percentage of people living with HIV who are not receiving antiretroviral therapies has fallen from 90 percent in 2006 to 60 percent in 2014 (UNAIDS 2015).

Slowing and reversing the HIV epidemic require changes in behaviors based on understanding the causes and transmission mechanisms of the disease, as well as on effective steps to avoid infection. Survey results show that wide knowledge gaps persist. Many young people appear to be ill-informed about HIV and engage in risky behaviors. Of the 10 countries with the highest HIV prevalence rates, 2013 survey participants in Namibia and Swaziland were the most informed, with more than 50 percent of the sampled men and women ages 15–24 able to list two ways to prevent HIV, as well as to reject three common misconceptions about HIV. In Kenya and Mozambique, men scored above 50 percent, but women fell short, while in Zimbabwe the opposite was the case. In the remaining five countries (Lesotho, Malawi, South Africa, Uganda, and Zambia), both men and women scored less than 50 percent.

In 2013, there were 9 million new tuberculosis cases in the world and 1.1 million deaths. However, the incidence and prevalence of tuberculosis, as well as the rate of deaths resulting from it, are falling: incidence fell 41 percent between 1990 and 2013, and the death rate fell 45 percent (WHO 2014a). Globally, the target of halting and reversing tuberculosis incidence by 2015 has been achieved. Despite population growth, the absolute numbers of tuberculosis cases and deaths have dropped because of the decline in the incidence and death rates (figure A.19).

Globally, an estimated 214 million cases of malaria occurred in 2015, which led to 438,000 deaths. An estimated 3.2 billion people are at risk of being infected with malaria and developing the disease. Since 2000, there have been substantial reductions in both the number of malaria cases and deaths. It is evident that the target of halting and reversing the incidence of malaria has been met (WHO and UNICEF 2015). Country-level data suggest that there has been progress against malaria over time, although consistent data needed to monitor trends globally are limited. Malaria occurs in all regions, but the most lethal form of the malaria parasite is concentrated mainly in Sub-Saharan Africa. Insecticide-treated bed nets have proven an effective preventative, and their use by children in the region is growing (figure A.20). Better testing and the use of combination drug therapies are improving the effectiveness of treatment.

FIGURE A.18 Prevalence of HIV in adults and number of adults living with HIV, by region, 1990–2014

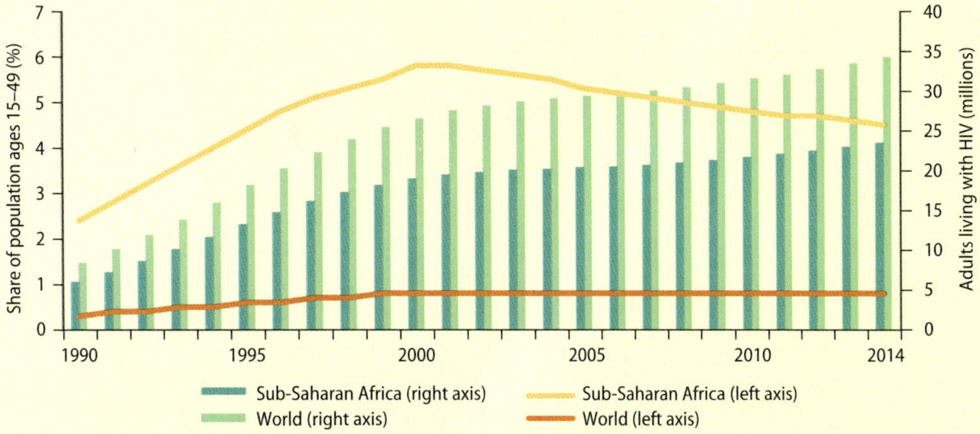

Sources: Joint United Nations Programme on HIV/AIDS and World Development Indicators Database.

FIGURE A.19 Rate and numbers of tuberculosis prevalence, incidence, and death in the world, 1990–2013

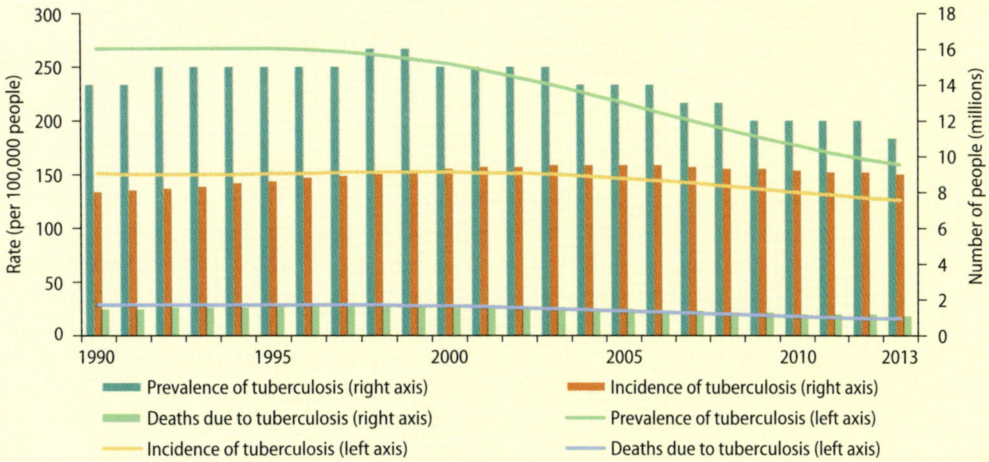

Sources: World Health Organization and World Development Indicators Database.
Note: Incidence of tuberculosis is the estimated number of new pulmonary, smear-positive, and extrapulmonary tuberculosis cases. Incidence includes patients with HIV. Prevalence includes both new cases and those who contracted the disease in the past and are still surviving.

FIGURE A.20 Use of insecticide-treated bed nets, Sub-Saharan Africa

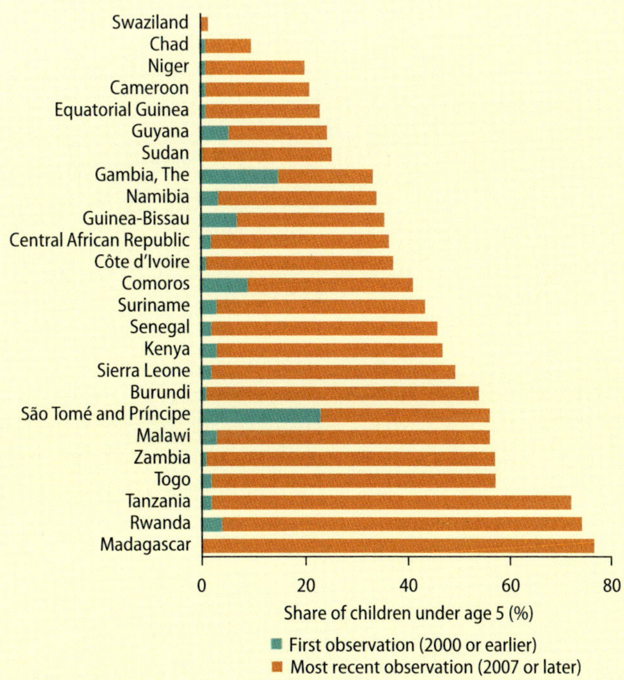

Source: Household surveys (including Demographic and Health Surveys, Malaria Indicators Surveys, and Multiple Indicator Cluster Surveys). Data are compiled by UNICEF.

MDG 7

Ensure environmental sustainability

MDG 7 seeks to promote environmental sustainability by focusing on several key targets: reversing the loss of natural resources, preserving biodiversity, increasing access to safe water and sanitation, and improving the living conditions of people in slums. The aim is to achieve these goals in a sustainable manner, whereby people's lives can improve without depleting natural and manmade capital stocks.

The loss of forests threatens the livelihood that poor people depend upon, destroys the habitat that harbors biodiversity, and eliminates an important carbon sink that helps moderate the climate. Net losses since 1990 have been substantial, especially in Latin American and the Caribbean and Sub-Saharan Africa. The losses have only been partly compensated by gains elsewhere, mainly in the East Asia and Pacific region and in high-income countries (figure A.21). The rate of deforestation has slowed over the past decade, but with current trends, zero net losses will not be reached for another two decades.

The protection of forests and other terrestrial and marine areas is essential to preserving plant and animal habitats, as well as the diversity of species.[3] By 2012, more than 14 percent of the world's land and more than 12 percent of its oceans were protected, an improvement of 6 percentage points in both categories since 1990 (figure A.22).

Failure to limit greenhouse gas emissions leaves billions of people vulnerable to the adverse effects of climate change, with developing countries being hit hardest. Higher temperatures, changes in precipitation patterns, rising sea levels, and more frequent weather-related disasters pose risks for agriculture, food, and water supplies. Carbon dioxide emissions rose by about 60 percent between 1990 and 2013, reaching an unprecedented level of 36 billion metric tons. The average annual growth rate in emissions has slowed to 2.3 percent since 2010, slightly lower than the annual average growth rate of 3 percent during the 2001–11 period (figure A.23).

The water target of MDG 7 calls for halving the proportion of the population without access to improved water and sanitation sources by 2015. The share of people worldwide without access to an improved water source declined from 23.9 percent in 1990 to 9.0 percent in 2015, achieving the target ahead of time (figure A.24). The result is especially impressive given that world population grew from 5.3 billion to 7.3 billion during this period, creating more demand for improved water access. Not only was coverage extended to more than half of the 1.3 billion people without access in 1990, but a large portion of newly added population was also able to access improved water sources. By 2015, the absolute number of people without access to improved water sources worldwide dropped to 658 million people—a 48 percent reduction compared with 1990. Progress varies across regions, with Sub-Saharan Africa continuing to lag—about 32 percent of its population lacks access. East Asia and the Pacific managed to make impressive improvements, moving from a starting position of only 69 percent coverage in 1990 to 94 percent in 2015. The other regions have access rates of more than 92 percent.

In 1990, only 53 percent of the world's population had access to improved sanitation facilities. By 2015, this proportion had risen to 68 percent, but this still leaves 2.4 billion people worldwide lacking access to improved sanitation facilities. For the world to meet the 2015 MDG target on sanitation, 76 percent of the population needs access to improved sanitation. This target was not met on time. Coverage is worse in rural areas, where 50 percent of the world population lacked access in 2015, compared with 18 percent in urban areas. This large disparity, especially in South Asia and Sub-Saharan Africa, is the main reason that the sanitation target was not met on time. Given the connections between sanitation and other MDGs, such as infant mortality, expanding access to sanitation remains a critical part of the development agenda.

FIGURE A.21 Change in forest area, by region, 1990–2012

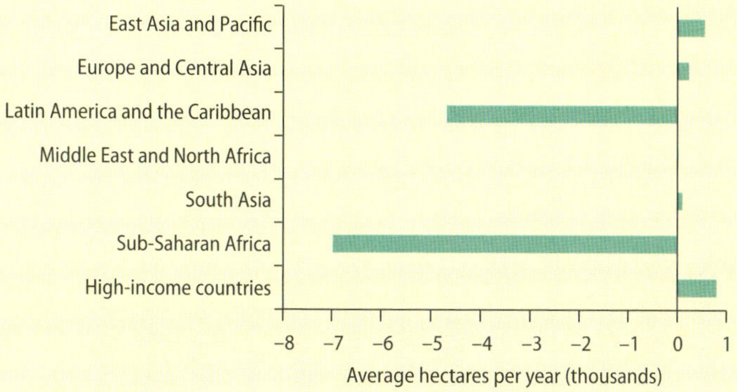

Sources: World Development Indicators Database and Food and Agriculture Organization.

FIGURE A.22 Territorial and marine protected areas, by country income group, 1990–2012

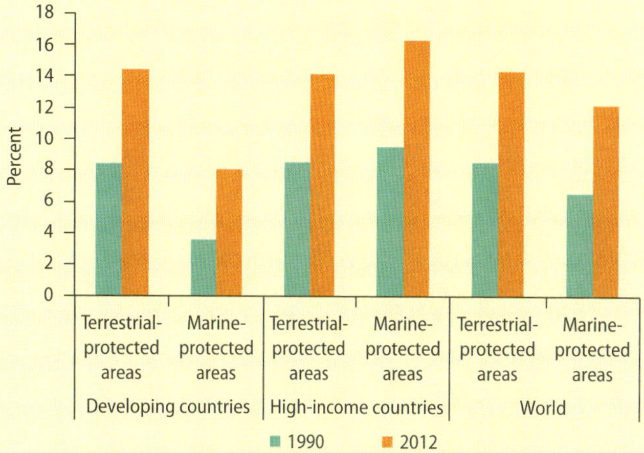

Source: World Development Indicators Database derived from UNEP and WCMC databases.

FIGURE A.23 Carbon dioxide emissions from fossil fuel, by country income group, 1990–2011

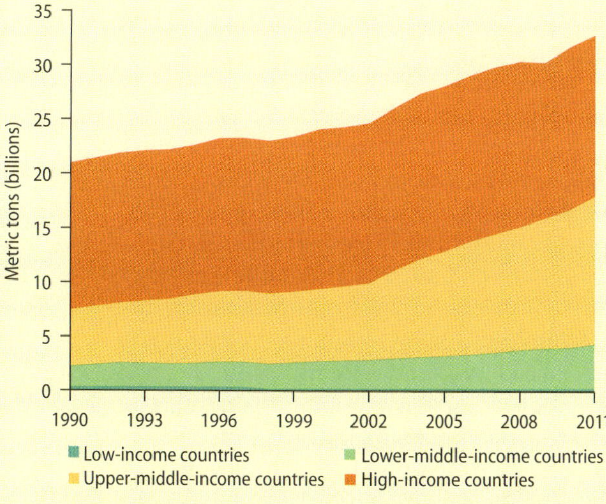

Sources: Carbon Dioxide Information Analysis Center and World Development Indicators Database.

FIGURE A.24 Access to an improved water source, by region, 1990–2015

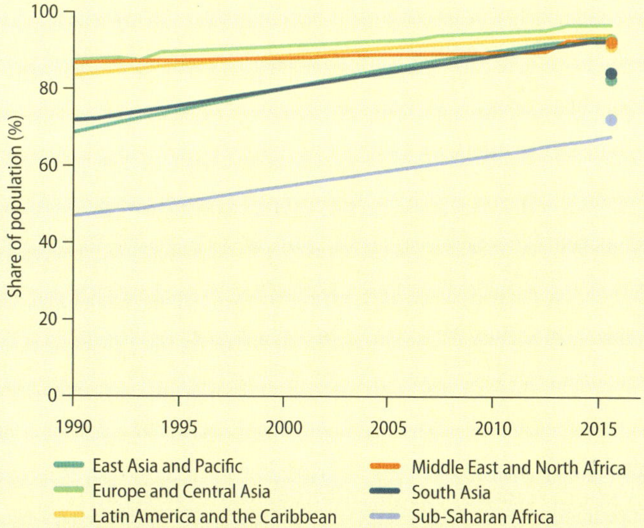

Sources: WHO/UNICEF Joint Monitoring Programme for Water Supply and Sanitation and World Development Indicators Database.

MDG 8

Develop a global partnership for development

MDG 8 focuses on the need to create a global environment that is conducive to promoting development and eliminating poverty. Consequently, this goal highlights the need to establish a fairer multilateral trading and financial system, deal comprehensively with debt problems of developing countries, and address the special needs of low-income countries, including landlocked and small island developing states. The goal recognizes that building and sustaining a partnership is an ongoing process that does not stop on a given date or when a specific target is reached. Moreover, the goal highlights the need to support infrastructure development and to provide affordable access to new technologies and essential medicines.

Official development assistance (ODA) by the Development Assistance Committee (DAC) members of the Organisation for Economic Co-operation and Development (OECD) reached a high of $135 billion in 2013, 6.1 percent higher than in 2012 in real terms. This increase came after two successive years of decreases in 2011 and 2012 in real terms (figure A.25). The rebound in 2013 happened because several members stepped up spending on foreign aid, despite continued budget pressures, and five new member countries joined the DAC: the Czech Republic, Iceland, Poland, the Slovak Republic, and Slovenia. The 0.7 percent target of ODA as a share of gross national income (GNI) was met and exceeded only by Denmark, Luxembourg, Norway, and Sweden, while the Netherlands fell below this target for the first time since 1974. On the other hand, the top five ODA contributors by volume were the United States, the United Kingdom, Germany, Japan, and France.

The debt burden of developing economies, measured as the proportion of external debt service to export receipts, fell to half its 2000 levels in 2013. This improvement is linked to greater external debt servicing capacity due to increased export earnings, better debt management, and enhanced debt restructuring, as well as to more favorable borrowing conditions on international capital markets in recent years. The poorest and most highly indebted countries have also benefited from extensive debt relief: 35 of the 39 countries eligible for the Heavily Indebted Poor Country Initiative and the Multilateral Debt Relief Initiative have completed the process. The debt service to export ratio averaged 11 percent in 2013, half its 2000 level, but with wide disparity across regions (figure A.26). The ratio is likely to rise going forward because of the fragile global economic outlook, soft commodity prices, and projected 20 percent rise in developing countries' external debt service over the next two to three years, following the 33 percent increase in their combined external debt stock since 2010.

With the rapid development and adoption of mobile telephone services and the global expansion of the Internet, information and communication technologies are recognized as essential tools of development, contributing to global integration and enhancing public sector effectiveness, efficiency, and transparency. Further spreading the use of advanced technology for reducing disaster risk, managing communicable disease outbreaks, and addressing the impacts of climate change carries enormous promise.

Global partnership also includes cooperation with the private sector, and making available the benefits of new technologies, especially information and communications. Mobile cellular subscriptions reached almost 7 billion worldwide in 2014. Developing countries' share of global mobile cellular subscriptions rose from 26 percent in 2000 to 75 percent in 2014. High-income economies had more than 1 mobile cellular subscription per person in 2014, with 123 subscriptions per 100 people, and upper-middle-income economies also reached 101 subscriptions per 100 people. For lower-middle-income economies, the number is 87, while low-income economies lagged with 57 subscriptions per 100 people in 2014 (figure A.27). In part, mobile cellular phones have replaced fixed-line telephone systems: the fixed telephone subscription rate in the world has been falling gradually, from 19 in 2005 to 15 subscriptions per 100 people in 2014.

Similarly, Internet use in developing countries appears to be increasing quickly. Internet use spread rapidly in high-income economies in the 1990s but was barely under way in developing-country regions. Since 2000, the number of Internet users per 100 people in developing countries has grown an average of 26 percent a year. The percentage of the population with Internet access more than doubled in South Asia between 2010 and 2014, with 17 percent of the population having access in 2014. However, large gaps still exist around the world. For example, the low-income countries of South Asia and Sub-Saharan Africa alone account for about half of the approximately 4 billion people who are not yet using the Internet (figure A.28).

FIGURE A.25 Official development assistance from Development Assistance Committee members, 1990–2013

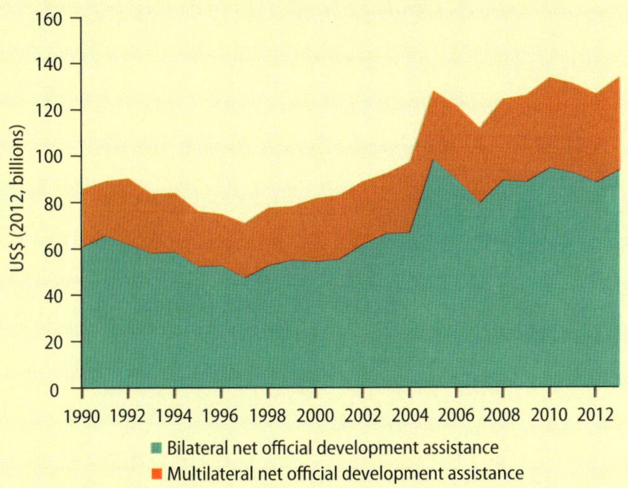

Sources: Organisation for Economic Co-operation and Development, StatExtracts.

FIGURE A.26 Total debt service, by region, 1990–2013

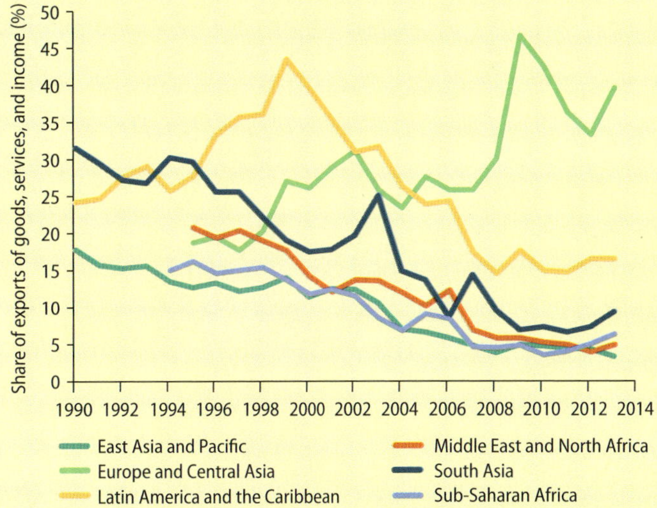

Source: World Development Indicators Database.

FIGURE A.27 Mobile cellular subscriptions, by income group, 2000–14

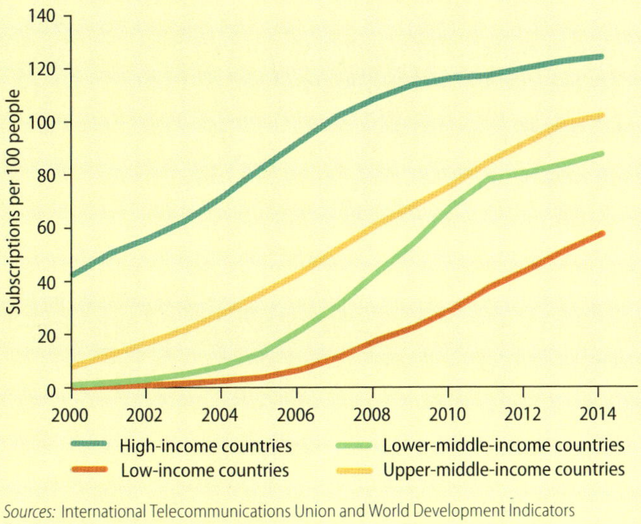

Sources: International Telecommunications Union and World Development Indicators Database.

FIGURE A.28 Internet users, by region, 2000–14

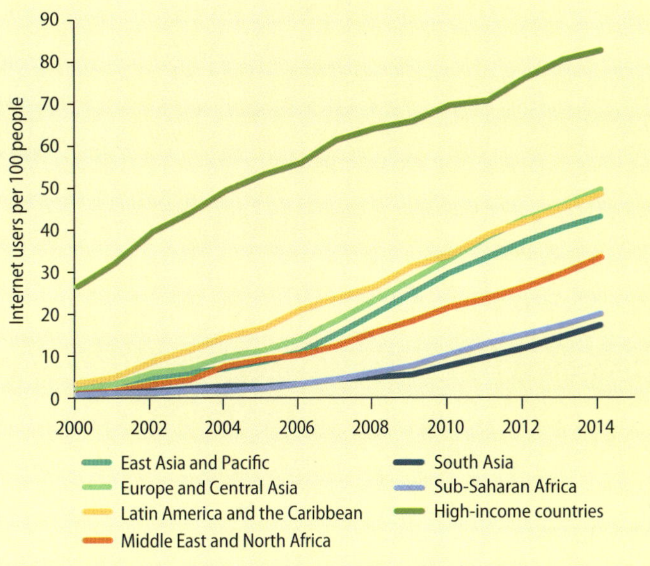

Sources: International Telecommunications Union and World Development Indicators Database.

Notes

1. MDG Dashboard is available at: http://data.worldbank.org/mdgs.
2. As in Angola, Central Africa Republic, Chad, Democratic Republic of Congo, Guinea-Bissau, Nigeria, Mali, Sierra Leone, and Somalia, for example.
3. Protected areas are defined as terrestrial, freshwater, or marine areas that are recognized, dedicated, and managed, through legal or other effective means, to achieve the long-term conservation of nature with associated ecosystem services and cultural values. This definition includes, for example, national parks and nature reserves (United Nations Environmental Programme—World Conservation Monitoring Centre).

References

Ahmed, S., Q. Li, L. Liu, and A. O. Tsui. 2012. "Maternal Deaths Averted by Contraceptive Use: An Analysis of 172 Countries." *The Lancet* 380 (9837): 111–25.

Conde-Agudelo, A., J. M. Belizán, and C. Lammers. 2005. "Maternal-Perinatal Morbidity and Mortality Associated with Adolescent Pregnancy in Latin America: Cross-Sectional Study." *American Journal of Obstetrics and Gynecology* 192 (2): 342–49.

Müller, R., T. Kiziak, R. Klingholz, and M. Herrmann. 2015. *Consequential Omissions. How Demography Shapes Development: Lessons from the MDGs for the SDGs*. Berlin: Berlin-Institut für Bevölkerung und Entwicklung. http://nbn-resolving.de/urn:nbn:de:101:1-201504135086.

UNAIDS (Joint United Nations Programme on HIV/AIDS). 2015. *How AIDS Changed Everything*. Geneva: UNAIDS.

UNESCO (United Nations Educational, Scientific and Cultural Organization). 2004. *Education for All Global Monitoring Report 2003/4: Gender and Education for All—The Leap to Equality*. Paris: UNESCO.

UNICEF, WHO, and World Bank (United Nations Children's Fund, World Health Organization, and World Bank). 2015. *2014 Joint Child Malnutrition Estimates—Levels and Trends*. New York: UNICEF. http://www.who.int/nutgrowthdb/estimates2014/en/.

United Nations Inter-agency Group for Child Mortality Estimation. 2015. "Levels & Trends in Child Mortality: Report 2015." UNICEF, New York.

WHO (World Health Organization). 2013. "Family Planning." Fact Sheet 351, Geneva. http://www.who.int/mediacentre/factsheets/fs351/en/.

———. 2014a. *Global Tuberculosis Report 2014*. Geneva: World Health Organization.

———. 2014b. "Maternal Mortality." Fact Sheet 348, Geneva. http://www.who.int/mediacentre/factsheets/fs348/.

WHO and UNICEF (World Health Organization and United Nations Children's Fund). 2015. *Achieving the Malaria MDG Target: Reversing the Incidence of Malaria 2000–2015*. Geneva: WHO.

World Bank. 2013. *Global Monitoring Report 2013: Rural-Urban Dynamics and the Millennium Development Goals*. Washington, DC: World Bank.

World Bank. 2015 *World Development Indicators 2015*. Washington, DC: World Bank.

B

The Role of Multilateral Development Banks: From Millennium Development Goals to Sustainable Development Goals

In reflecting on the role of policies and institutions needed to make progress toward development goals, it is useful to consider the contributions made by the multilateral development banks (MDBs). Development hinges on the efforts of multiple stakeholders at the country and global levels, including the engagement of the MDBs. This appendix conveys reflections from the World Bank Group, the African Development Bank (AfDB), the Asian Development Bank (ADB), the European Bank for Reconstruction and Development (EBRD), and the Inter-American Development Bank (IDB) on their experiences with the Millennium Development Goals (MDGs), and describes lessons learned for the Sustainable Development Goals (SDGs). Each MDB section answers two questions:

- How has it been supporting progress toward the MDGs?
- What lessons can be drawn from its experience with the MDGs, in terms of what worked and what was less effective, for designing our future engagements on the SDGs?

The experience of the MDBs in supporting efforts toward the MDGs spans the globe and is highly contextual, based on specific country circumstances. Still, several themes emerge that will be useful to inform efforts toward the SDGs. With so much of development driven by country-level stakeholders, ensuring that they retain full ownership is essential. Given the range of country circumstances, the approach to the MDGs needs to be country specific. Finally, implementation arrangements, including adequate policy focus and financing (the MDBs have made commitments of over $400 billion for the period 2016–18) are key to progress. These lessons and others will facilitate the transformative progress envisioned by the SDGs.

The World Bank Group

The World Bank Group has worked closely with clients endeavoring to achieve the MDGs and, building on this experience, seeks to contribute strongly to the SDG agenda. Through numerous MDG-related engagements at the global and country levels, the World Bank Group has supported a broad range of client efforts. Based on continual assessment of this experience, the World Bank Group has implemented institutional and financial changes aimed at enhancing effectiveness and deepening engagement on the 2030 agenda.

Supporting progress toward the MDGs

Numerous findings emerge from the World Bank Group's extensive MDG-related activities, which will help shape the institution's engagement on the SDG agenda. The complexity of development and the wide range of stakeholders make attribution and identification of cause and effect difficult. Still, a review of the World Bank Group's strategies, partnerships, and institutional changes during the MDG period yields five key findings (World Bank 2015):

- The World Bank Group integrated the MDGs into its strategies at both at the corporate and the country levels.
- The analytical and advisory services provided by the World Bank Group contributed meaningfully to the evolution of development thinking in support of the MDGs.
- The country-based model was essential to ensure that the MDGs agreed upon at the global level are fully reflected in country development programs.
- Given that development is a collaborative effort, the World Bank Group has sought to work closely with other development partners and stakeholders in supporting the MDGs.
- More needs to be done to articulate a results chain than translates the World Bank Group's activities and approaches into contributions toward progress on the MDGs.

Integrating the MDGs into World Bank Group Strategies

The World Bank integrated MDG-related initiatives into its core strategies, while increasing emphasis on institutions, governance, and global public goods. It formally endorsed the MDGs through the 2001 Strategic Framework Paper, emphasizing the importance of the results-based framework of the MDGs in helping to monitor development impact, as well as the role of the MDGs in facilitating enhanced donor coordination and engagement with country counterparts. In the course of the MDG period, the World Bank Group boosted MDG-related activities, scaling up engagement on basic education, agriculture, and infrastructure, while focusing on results management and putting more resources into impact evaluations. In the process, the institution developed a selectivity framework that sought to channel its resources into areas where additional resources were urgently needed and could best make a difference, mindful that other entities may be better placed to support development efforts in various areas.

The share of World Bank Group lending for the MDGs has remained broadly stable at about 40 percent (figure B.1). This level reflects a prioritization of development objectives that was broadly consistent with the MDGs already in the 1990s, and with the expansion of total commitments, the World Bank Group continued to focus on MDG areas, especially the social sectors. The bulk of lending commitments were in the form of investment loans, rather than budget support. In many instances, the World Bank Group sought to implement multisectoral approaches, emphasizing public administration in many education and health projects, for example. In other cases, even if a multisectoral approach was not evident at the project level, the majority of countries with health and nutrition projects also had water and sanitation projects. More work is needed to ensure that multisectoral approaches deliver expected results.

Contributing to the knowledge base underpinning the MDGs

The World Bank Group's analytical work been a central part of the institution's engagement on development, influencing strategy and the results agenda. The share of analytical and advisory work related to the MDGs has grown steadily during the MDG period (figure B.2). The nonlending technical assistance component has risen particularly quickly. The production of impact evaluations also rose strongly during the MDG period, and more needs to be done to put good feedback loops in place to ensure adequate learning from these outputs.

FIGURE B.1 MDG-related World Bank Group commitments and composition

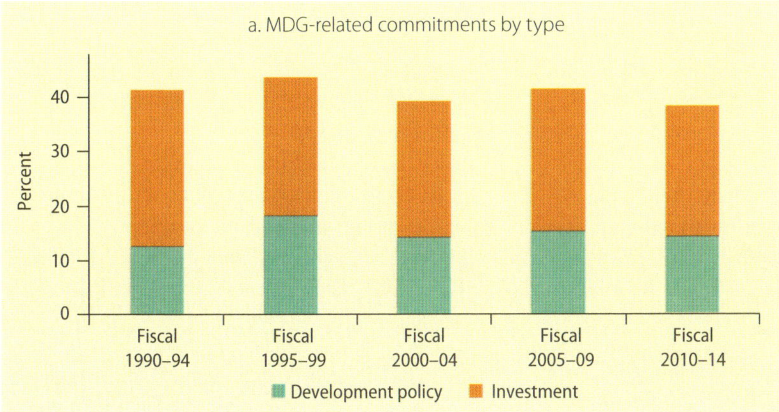

b. Composition of MDG-related commitments

Percent

	Fiscal 1990–2001	Fiscal 2002–14
MDG 1	9	7
MDG 2	5	10
MDG 3	7	11
MDG 4	1	2
MDG 5	1	1
MDG 6	1	3
MDG 7	31	27
MDG 8	45	38
Total	**100**	**100**

Source: Business Warehouse, World Bank 2015.
Note: MDG-related commitments are determined using Operations Policy and Country Services classification, which maps the Bank's theme codes to specific MDGs.

FIGURE B.2 MDG-related analytical and advisory activities and composition

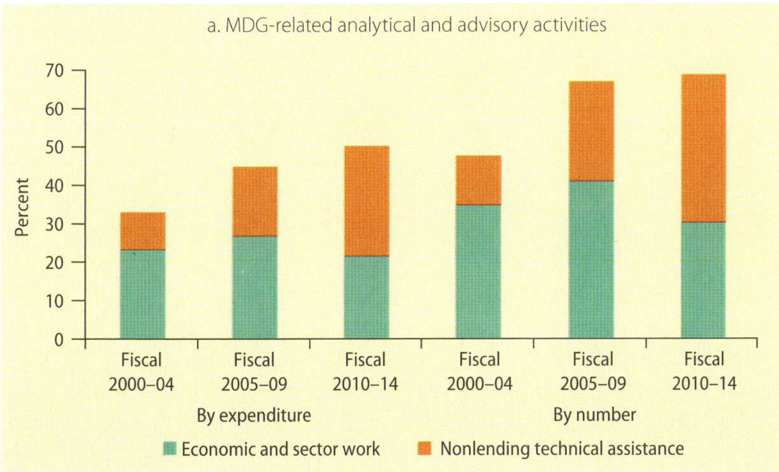

b. Composition of MDG-related analytical and advisory activities

Percent

	Fiscal 1990–2001	Fiscal 2002–14
MDG 1	2	10
MDG 2	12	3
MDG 3	14	8
MDG 4	0	1
MDG 5	0	1
MDG 6	2	3
MDG 7	22	23
MDG 8	48	51
Total	**100**	**100**

Source: Business Warehouse World Bank 2015.
Note: MDG-related analytical and advisory activities are determined using Operations Policy and Country Services classification, which maps the Bank's theme codes to specific MDGs.

The application of a combination of World Bank Group instruments at the country level can generate synergies for good results. In Bangladesh, the program of analytic work, policy-based lending (in support of policy and institutional reforms), investment lending, and capacity-building nonlending technical assistance played a meaningful role in achieving better social protection outcomes. Similarly, in Brazil, broad-based engagement helped the government target social policies, and then monitor results.

Supporting progress toward the MDGs through the country-based model

The country-based model has been at the center of the World Bank Group's engagement on the MDGs, but it can complicate integration of sector and corporate strategies. The 2002 Monterrey Consensus notes that "each country has primary responsibility for its own economic and social development" (UN 2002). This is essential for country ownership and underpins the World Bank Group's country-based model. To better deliver on this approach, several key organizational changes were implemented during the MDG period, including extensive decentralization of staff to the field and matrix management.

MDG themes were reflected in country strategies. While the MDGs were not always explicitly noted, closer analysis of a cross-section of 40 country engagements shows that more than 80 percent of the strategic pillars underpinning the World Bank Group's country strategies were related to MDG themes (World Bank 2015). In some instances, the strategy focused explicitly on supporting efforts toward MDGs that the country was not expected to meet, for example in relation to education and gender equality in the Republic of Yemen. While the country-based model has proven effective, it could be strengthened further to ensure integration with sector and corporate strategies.

Building partnerships for achieving the MDGs

The complexity of development means that effective progress depends on partnerships and selectivity based on institutional comparative advantage. The global endorsement of the MDGs provided a platform to help align the efforts of the development community toward shared objectives. To support this improved alignment, the World Bank Group prepared a selectivity framework that emphasizes comparative advantage, strategic relevance, and expected benefits. It has also sought to deepen partnerships at numerous levels, although more could be done. Strong partnerships boosted trust-funded activities to complement various World Bank Group efforts toward the MDGs, centered on specific thematic areas. For example, the Education for All – Fast Track Initiative channeled funds into primary education, and enabled the World Bank Group to put its resources into other aspects of service delivery and connections between education and the labor market. In some cases, the funds managed and supervised by the World Bank Group far exceeded its own resources. For example, the Global Fund to Fight Aids, Tuberculosis and Malaria, disbursed about $26.7 billion from 2002 to 2014, nearly five times the World Bank Group's related commitments during this period.

Articulating a results chain for the World Bank Group

While the World Bank Group has consistently sought to increase its results focus, including by supporting statistical capacity building in client countries, connecting specific interventions to MDG outcomes remains challenging. The focus on results is mainstreamed in the activities of the World Bank Group, as reflected in results-based country strategies and the deployment of new financing instruments, such as the Program for Results, which links financing to predetermined results in stages. In support of sound monitoring frameworks, the World Bank Group provided assistance for statistical capacity building in many client countries. Establishing a clear results chain from interventions to intermediate outcomes to results remains difficult, and more needs to be done to put in place effective feedback loops that sharpen the focus on specific MDG areas that may need additional attention at the country level.

Supporting progress toward the SDGs with learning from the MDGs

Translating the SDGs articulated at the global level into effective development programs at the country level is the central implementation challenge. It will be challenging for many governments and other stakeholders to bring the wide-ranging and integrated SDG agenda into effective development programs that also match country-level priorities. The World Bank Group will seek to support clients in this process, based on lessons learned from the MDG experience and recommendations from assessments (Schmaljohann, Prizzon, and Rogerson 2015; World Bank 2015). The institution will focus on its core strengths, including the provision of long-term country level engagements, integrated development solutions, a full menu of services (knowledge and financing), and platforms for cross-border initiatives (World Bank 2015).

The World Bank Group supports the integrated set of SDGs and will intensify efforts on four cross-cutting "prerequisites" that are essential enablers for the wider SDG agenda in many countries. These prerequisites include supporting countries to transition from fragility and conflict to development, to scale up infrastructure investment, to mitigate climate change, and to join the data revolution (World Bank 2015). Making gains in these cross-cutting areas generally hinges on working at the international level with a wide range of stakeholders. The World Bank Group will seek to contribute meaningfully on related initiatives.

The World Bank Group is implementing institutional and financing changes to boost effectiveness and impact. While still applying the country-based model, the World Bank Group seeks to support progress on the SDGs with better knowledge flows and integrated development solutions, as well as new operational instruments. Stretched and leveraged balance sheets are enabling greater financing volumes to clients. These efforts will also be essential to making progress toward the World Bank Group's goals of eliminating extreme poverty and boosting shared prosperity.

African Development Bank

Progress toward MDG attainment

Despite a weak start, the pace of progress toward the attainment of the MDGs in Africa accelerated after 2003. The continent started from a relatively low base on virtually all MDGs, requiring large investments and much effort to catch up with comparator regions. Despite these efforts, progress has been slow in a number of countries. During the new SDG era, the AfDB's overarching goal will remain poverty reduction, but the institution will also seek to ensure that growth is more inclusive. Inclusive growth will be underpinned by enhancing the capacity of Africans to sustainably manage and leverage their natural resources to drive their development efforts in a peaceful manner.

The AfDB supports progress toward the MDGs through country-level interventions that are directly aligned with the countries' national development efforts. The analysis presented here is based on the AfDB's 2014 Annual Report, its 2014 Development Effectiveness Review, and data from the 2014 MDG report jointly produced with the African Union, the United Nations Economic Commission for Africa, and the United Nations Development Programme, where it was found that Africa's progress toward the achievement of MDGs has been mixed. The analysis found variations across countries and regions, with some countries making significant progress toward the targets while others have not. Table B.1 highlights the best-performing countries for selected targets and indicators.

AfDB's engagements during the new SDG era

Africa has enjoyed high levels of average growth—above 5 percent—during the MDG era, but with wide variations at the country level. In 2015 and beyond, the prospects for Africa are significantly brighter than they were at the turn of the millennium. Its performance on MDGs has been muted, however, with the continent off track in achieving five of the eight MDGs by 2015. The new era of SDGs presents a unique opportunity for Africa to articulate its common priorities, opportunities, and challenges. African governments need to develop a strong vision for monitoring and accountability, with clear plans for financing and implementation of the strategies.

The AfDB remains a significant financier of infrastructure projects, with a cumulative contribution of $45 billion from 1967 to 2014. In line with its Ten-Year Strategy (2013–22), and through its lending, technical expertise, and policy advocacy, the AfDB plans to support Africa's development in five priority areas: infrastructure, regional integration, private sector development, skills and technology, and governance and accountability. The institution's support will

TABLE B.1 Africa's recent MDG performance: Selected targets and indicators

Goals	Targets and indicators	Best-performing countries[a]
Goal 1: Eradicate extreme poverty and hunger	Target 1A: Halve (between 1990 and 2015), the proportion of people whose income is less than $1.25 a day per person.	Egypt, Arab Rep.; Gabon, Guinea; Morocco; Tunisia.
	Target 1B: Achieve full and productive employment and decent work for all, including women and young people.	Burkina Faso, Ethiopia, Togo, Zimbabwe.
	Target 1C: Halve (between 1990 and 2015) the proportion of people who suffer from hunger.	Algeria; Benin; Egypt, Arab Rep.; Ghana; Guinea-Bissau; Mali; South Africa; Tunisia.
Goal 2: Achieve universal primary education	Indicator 2.1: Increase net enrollment ratio in primary. education by 1.5 percent annually.	Algeria; Egypt, Arab Rep.; Rwanda; São Tomé and Príncipe.
	Indicator 2.2: Proportion of pupils starting grade 1 who reach last grade of primary education.	Ghana, Morocco, Tanzania, Zambia.
Goal 3: Promote gender equality and empower women	Indicator 3.1: Ratio of girls to boys in primary, secondary and tertiary education.	The Gambia; Ghana; Mauritius; Rwanda; São Tomé and Príncipe.
	Indicator 3.2: Share of women in wage employment in the non-agricultural sector.	Botswana, Ethiopia, South Africa.
	Indicator 3.3: Proportion of seats held by women in national parliament.	Angola, Mozambique, Rwanda, Seychelles, South Africa.
Goal 4: Reduce child mortality by two-thirds	Indicators 4.1 and 4.2: Under-five mortality and infant (under-one) mortality rates.	Egypt, Arab Rep.; Ethiopia; Liberia; Libya; Malawi; Rwanda; Seychelles; Tanzania; Tunisia.
Goal 5: Improve maternal health	Target 5A: Reduce by three-quarters, the maternal mortality ratio between 1990 and 2015.	Equatorial Guinea; Egypt, Arab Rep.; Eritrea; Libya; Mauritius; Rwanda; São Tomé and Príncipe; Tunisia.
	Target 5B: Achieve by 2015 universal access to reproductive health.	Egypt, Arab Rep.; Ghana; Guinea-Bissau; Rwanda; South Africa; Swaziland.
Goal 6: Combat HIV/AIDS, malaria, and other diseases	Target 6A: To have halted by 2015 and begun to reverse the spread of HIV/AIDS and other diseases.	Côte d'Ivoire, Namibia, South Africa, Zimbabwe.
	Target 6B: Achieve by 2010 universal access to treatment of HIV/AIDS for all those who need it.	Botswana, Comoros, Namibia, Rwanda.
	Target 6C: To have halted by 2015 and begun to reverse the incidence of malaria and other major diseases.	Algeria; Cabo Verde; Egypt, Arab Rep.; Libya; Mauritius; São Tomé and Príncipe; Sudan; Tunisia.
Goal 7: Ensure environmental sustainability	Target 7A: Integrate the principles of sustainable development into country policies and programs and reverse the loss of environmental resources.	Egypt, Arab Rep.; Gabon; Morocco; Nigeria.
	Target 7C: Reduce by half the proportion of people without sustainable access to safe drinking water and basic sanitation, by 2015.	Algeria; Botswana; Egypt, Arab Rep.; Libya; Mali; Mauritius; Namibia; Rwanda; Swaziland.
Goal 8: Global partnership for development	Target 8F: In cooperation with the private sector, make available the benefits of new technologies, especially information and communications technology.	Kenya, Libya, Rwanda, Seychelles, Sudan, Uganda, Zambia.

Source: African Development Bank Group 2014 Annual Report.
a. Those countries that, with respect to each target/indicator, have made the greatest improvements from their initial conditions (not necessarily those that have reached the targets).

help to create the conditions in which Africans can identify and implement innovative solutions to their development challenges.

Infrastructure

Infrastructure remains the AfDB's highest priority, absorbing the lion's share of its resources. The AfDB invests heavily in transport infrastructure, helping to put in place the backbone highway network to link African countries to each other and the feeder roads that link businesses and households to markets and services. Over the past two years, the AfDB has built or rehabilitated over 6,000 kilometers of road and provided 32 million people with improved access to transport. Projects like the 175-kilometer road between Wacha and Maji in Ethiopia have dramatically reduced transportation costs for farmers, raising rural incomes. The AfDB is also investing in railways, airports, and port facilities. In the energy sector, it has funded over 1.3 gigawatts of new power-generation capacity, while providing 10 million people with electricity connections. The AfDB is also making substantial investments in renewable energy, such as Africa's largest wind power project in Lake Turkana in Kenya, and is helping African countries to access international climate funds and leverage private sector finance for clean energy projects. The AfDB's investments in water and sanitation have benefited more than 4 million people. To boost water security, the AfDB also has a strong focus on the management of water resources.

Regional integration

Under its new Strategy for Regional Integration 2014–23, the AfDB is prioritizing the development of regional infrastructure (along with the institutions required to manage it) and the promotion of industrialization and trade. In the past two years, it has built 680 kilometers of cross-border roads, together with improved border infrastructure. It has ongoing investments in cross-border power transmission lines, and is helping to link national power grids into more efficient regional power pools. Many AfDB regional initiatives have an explicit focus on promoting peace and security, such as the support for the International Conference on the Great Lakes Region.

Private sector development

The AfDB also aims to build an environment in which African businesses can innovate and flourish. Its Private Sector Strategy 2013–17 focuses on improving Africa's business climate and promoting enterprise development. Through its budget support operations and technical assistance, the AfDB is helping African countries to modernize their business regulations and to make their tax systems more effective. Improved governance allows for more frequent use of public-private partnerships as an effective methodology to deliver critical infrastructure, with a good number of successful transactions recently completed, such as the Henri Konan Bédié Bridge in Abidjan, Côte d'Ivoire. The AfDB is also helping to create a sustainable market in microfinance for household enterprises and small businesses. Over the past two years, it has provided 17,900 microcredits and created 1.2 million jobs, of which 340,000 were for women. The AfDB's private sector window continues to provide finance so that African businesses can innovate and flourish throughout the continent.

Skills and technology

The AfDB is investing in the technical and vocational skills of young Africans to equip them for gainful employment and successful entrepreneurship. Its support has a strong focus on science and technology to promote more innovative, knowledge-based economies. Over the past two years, the AfDB has provided vocational training to 5,430 young people and constructed over 1,480 classrooms and educational support facilities. It is rapidly expanding its investments in this area with projects to transform systems of vocational training in the Democratic Republic of Congo, Mauritania, Morocco, Rwanda, Tanzania, and Zimbabwe. It is also supporting a network of centers of excellence in biomedical science to help address the skills gap.

Governance and accountability

The AfDB's new Governance Strategic Framework and Action Plan 2014–2018 sets out how it will help tackle Africa's governance deficits. Its main focus is on economic and financial governance. The AfDB is also helping to strengthen the business environment through improved regulation. For example, it helped Mozambique to establish a one-stop shop for business registration. In this way, the AfDB is investing in more inclusive and sustainable financial systems, supporting many African countries on budgeting and financial management, and helping them to raise revenues and to target their spending on development priorities, guided by the principles of transparency and accountability. In the Comoros, for example, the AfDB helped to strengthen the management of the energy sector, while supporting the work of anticorruption agencies. In Sierra Leone, it is supporting wide-ranging public financial management reforms, including improved governance of the energy and extractive sectors. The AfDB's projects are promoting innovations in governance, such as the use of e-governance and improved engagement with civil society and communities.

In addition to these five core priorities, during the new SDG era, the AfDB will also place special emphasis on issues related to fragility, food security, and women's economic empowerment.

Asian Development Bank

ADB's support to the MDGs

The ADB has been supporting the MDGs since their adoption in 2000. Successive corporate-level strategies, individual country partnership strategies, and lending and nonlending operations have helped integrate support for MDGs at both the strategic and the operational levels at the ADB, complementing efforts of its developing member countries toward progress and monitoring their achievement.

The ADB's Poverty Reduction Strategy of 1999 guides the bank's mandate on poverty reduction (MDG 1) in the East Asia and Pacific region. Poverty reduction remained the ADB's key mission under its Long-Term Strategic Framework of 2001, which also emphasized inclusive social development, basic social services, gender empowerment, and environmental sustainability—priority areas in alignment with the MDGs. The ADB's Enhanced Poverty Reduction Strategy of 2004 and its Medium-Term Strategy II for 2006–08 continued to emphasize poverty reduction and progress on the MDGs.

The ADB's Strategy 2020, approved in 2008, delivered a vision of an East Asia and the Pacific free of poverty and underlined that progress on poverty reduction in the region was critical for meeting the MDGs (ADB 2008). The three key complementary agendas of Strategy 2020—inclusive economic growth, environmentally sustainable growth, and regional integration—are closely linked to MDG achievement. Strategy 2020 underlined the need for mobilization of resources and made the commitment that the ADB, in addition to providing financial and other assistance, would closely monitor and track the progress of its developing member countries on the MDGs. To that end, the ADB's corporate results framework, put in place in 2008, with successive periodic refinements, reports annually on progress made by the East Asia and the Pacific region on the achievement of the MDGs. A Midterm Review of Strategy 2020 completed in 2014 committed the ADB to expand support to sectors and areas of direct relevance to the MDGs (ADB 2014).

A country partnership strategy—the main articulation of ADB strategic directions and support at the country level—aligns ADB assistance with country priorities, the ADB's corporate strategic directions, and international development agreements (including on MDGs). Each strategy presents agreed priorities for the ADB's support that will help the country reduce poverty and achieve inclusive and sustainable economic growth. The strategy also provides for monitoring and reporting on progress toward the MDGs.

Pursuant to the country partnership strategies, the ADB provides lending and nonlending support to developing member countries. A large part of its lending assistance supports development of sustainable infrastructure. In 2011–13, infrastructure projects—which contributes directly to MDG 1 by promoting inclusive economic growth, supporting reduction in poverty, and creating employment and other economic opportunities—accounted for $24.8 billion, or 69 percent, of sovereign approvals. Support for agriculture and irrigation projects contributes to poverty reduction through its impact on farm productivity, food security, and mitigation of malnutrition. The volume of ADB-assisted education projects, which support progress on MDG 2, is projected to increase from 4 percent during 2011–13 to 6 percent during 2015–17. The ADB also plans to increase health sector operations to meet its target of 3–5 percent of annual approvals. Clean energy and sustainable transportation projects directly support MDG 7 by strengthening environmental sustainability and managing climate change by lowering carbon emissions. In 2014, the ADB already surpassed its 2016 targets to incorporate climate change in 45 percent of its operations and in 50 percent of its operations to support environmental sustainability. The ADB also assists with water supply and sanitation-related projects in urban and rural areas, which directly support MDG 7 by increasing the proportion of the population with access to safe drinking water and sanitation facilities.

In addition to direct support, infrastructure projects also indirectly support progress on other non-income MDGs. For example, ADB-supported transport projects, including rural roads, improve access to schools and hospitals across genders, necessary for progress on MDG 2 on universal primary education, MDG 3 on eliminating gender disparities in education, and MDGs 4 and 5 on reducing child mortality and improving maternal health. ADB-assisted water supply and sanitation projects also contribute to progress on the health-related MDGs (ADB 2015a). A number of examples of ADB support are presented in the ADB publication *Together We Deliver*.

To raise awareness about the MDGs in the region, support regular monitoring and progress, and develop the institutional capacity of developing member countries to achieve the MDGs, the ADB entered into a long-term partnership with the United Nations Development Programme and the United Nations Economic and Social Commission for Asia and the Pacific, which produces the regular series of regional MDG reports (UNESCAP, ADB, and UNDP 2015). The reports show that the region has made big gains in reducing poverty—as measured by the reduction in the number and share of people living on less than $1.25 a day purchasing power parity—and has made good progress on other MDGs. Some MDGs have been achieved ahead of 2015, the target year: gender equality in education, reducing HIV prevalence, stopping the spread of tuberculosis, increasing forest cover, reducing consumption of ozone-depleting substances, and halving the proportion of people without access to safe drinking water.

Lessons from East Asia and the Pacific and the post-2015 agenda

The MDGs were effective in East Asia and the Pacific in influencing local priorities, shaping national budgets, and protecting social expenditures. Many countries in the region have adapted the goals to meet their specific needs. The MDGs have influenced national development planning frameworks in nine East Asia-Pacific countries including Bangladesh, Cambodia, India, Indonesia, the Lao People's Democratic Republic, Mongolia, Nepal, Timor-Leste, and Vanuatu (ADB, UNESCAP, and UNDP 2013). However, the articulation of the MDGs as stand-alone goals led to a fragmented approach to public policy and planning, monitoring, and assessing contributions toward achieving the goals. Moreover, some development challenges, like unplanned urbanization and the rising threat of climate change, were not considered when the MDGs were formulated. Data requirements that escalated with MDG monitoring were inadequately backed by resources. The post-2015 development goals should recognize the importance of customization and that their inherent interdependence will require coordinated action across ministries, the importance of data for monitoring, the cross-cutting nature of infrastructure, and the key role of policy and knowledge support for sustainable development.

While strong economic dynamism has driven regional success in income poverty reduction, challenges remain on inclusion-related issues in the region and within developing member countries. High levels of hunger remain, fast-growing developing member countries continue to lose shocking numbers of children before their fifth birthday, and thousands of mothers die in childbirth. Striking disparities remain between and within subregions, countries, and even social groups in their progress toward the MDGs. For instance, South Asia as a whole is on track for just nine MDG indicators, but Sri Lanka is on track for 15 and generally outperforms the subregion. Within developing member countries, disparities between men and women, between social and ethnic groups, and between regions hold back large sections of the population from achieving the MDGs. Issues that remain important—and should therefore help define the Post-2015 Development Agenda—include inequality, lack of decent and productive jobs, continuing hunger and food insecurity, gender discrimination, limited achievements in health, low-quality education, heightened vulnerability and economic insecurity, rapid demographic change, unplanned urbanization, pressure on natural resources, exposure to disasters, and the rising threat of climate change.

The changing development finance landscape makes it clear that all sources of finance, public and private, need to be harnessed to achieve sustainable development. Growing domestic public resources in the region will continue to be the most important source of development finance. At the same time, international public flows—like official development assistance—are critical for low-income and fragile countries and a signal of the development community's commitment to shared development agendas. The largest sums are increasingly in private hands, however, and are not directly programmable or available for development. While governments have the primary role in drawing in these funds, as well as in influencing the course of private activities on economies, societies, and the environment in line with sustainable development, they will need assistance to create a supportive environment to mobilize private investment.

While MDG monitoring in the region reveals improvement in the availability of data in recent years, it also highlights large data gaps that strain national capacities for producing, disseminating and using quality statistics for MDG monitoring. The post-2015 agenda will bring renewed demand for new indicators to measure other dimensions of environmental, economic and social progress. Resources will be needed to increase support for national statistical systems along with actions to promote open access and use of data.

ADB focus and preparedness for the Post-2015 Development Agenda

The ADB has taken early steps in readying for the proposed SDGs in line with priorities identified in its *Strategy 2020 Midterm Review*. The mid-term review of the ADB's corporate Strategy 2020 confirms alignment with the new SDGs to be finalized in September 2015 by United Nations member states, including ADB clients and shareholders (ADB 2014). The review concluded that Strategy 2020 remains valid in its broad strategic directions to address the development challenges of a transforming Asia and Pacific. It found that the ADB's 10 strategic priorities respond to the SDGs in a manner consistent with realities of country-level implementation. The 10 priorities are poverty reduction and inclusive economic growth, environment and climate change, regional cooperation and integration, infrastructure development, middle-income countries, private sector development and operations, knowledge solutions, financial resources and partnerships, delivering value for money, and organizing to meet new challenges. The ADB has also initiated work on a new strategy to guide it over the longer term and that will reflect the SDGs once approved.

The ADB recognizes that the new global sustainable development agenda will need new thinking on financing and the capacity to tap all sources of funds. In its 2015 report *Making Money Work: Financing a Sustainable Future in Asia and Pacific,* ADB offers insights on the scale of the region's increased financing needs and the importance of harnessing all sources of finance, public and private (ADB 2015b). The report looks at both sides of making money work: shifting money toward investments in sustainable development, and boosting the ability of developing member countries to attract more money from a wider range of sources for such investments.

The ADB is enhancing its own capacity to provide finance for poverty eradication and sustainable development. The ADB Board of Governors recently approved a groundbreaking initiative to combine the lending operations of the bank's Asian Development Fund with its ordinary capital resources balance sheet. The merger will boost ADB's total annual lending and grant approvals to as high as $20 billion—50 percent more than the current level. ADB assistance to poor countries will rise by up to 70 percent. Together with cofinancing, the ADB's annual assistance will reach as high as $40 billion in coming years, up from $23 billion in 2014. Poor countries currently eligible for development fund loans will continue to receive concessional loans from expanded ordinary capital resources on the same terms and conditions as current Asian Development Fund loans. The fund will be retained as a grant-only donor fund to provide assistance to eligible countries.

In addition to making more funds available, the ADB is also helping to strengthen the capacity of its developing member countries to draw in money toward sustainable development. The Asia Pacific Project Preparation Facility approved in November 2014 will help prepare a pipeline of "ready to finance" infrastructure investments and place these with investors for public-private partnerships. The ADB is also assisting its developing member countries to access climate finance sources from funds such as the Global Environment Facility, Climate Investment Funds, and the Green Climate Fund for projects with sustainable development benefits.

In responding to the financing needs of the proposed SDGs, the ADB's priority will be to direct resources to human needs, infrastructure, and cross-border public goods. These categories are synergistically interlinked and together can strengthen sustainable development results. While infrastructure deficits are a continuing bottleneck affecting most MDGs, matters related to financing, implementation, accountability, and the role of partnerships are claiming center stage as developing member countries and their development partners explore the Post-2015 Development Agenda.

European Bank for Reconstruction and Development

With their focus on poverty reduction and social development, the MDGs have limited overlap with the EBRD's economic transition and private sector–focused mandate. Nevertheless, there are links between the EBRD's activities and the MDG targets in the areas of gender equality, water and sanitation, and environmental sustainability.

Gender equality (MDG 3)

With its commitment to gender equality through its Strategic Gender Initiative, approved in April 2013, the EBRD has contributed to the overarching gender equality goal, particularly with respect to the economic empowerment dimension of MDG 3, which is the EBRD's niche within gender equality. During the implementation of the initiative, the EBRD has contributed to an increase in the share of women in nonagricultural wage employment. Through the development of Equal Opportunities projects, solutions have been designed to respond to the challenges of barriers for women in employment, especially in countries where labor force participation is low (such as Turkey) and even declining such as in Jordan and the Arab Republic of Egypt.

Of the 16 new projects signed in the past two years, 94 percent are in the initiative's target regions (Central Asia, the Middle East, and Turkey); 50 percent develop measures to improve women's access to finance; and 20 percent improve women's access to employment and skills. The remaining 30 percent are projects to provide solutions to improve women's access to services.

With respect to increasing access to resources, and finance in particular, three teams within the EBRD developed a new product called the "Women in Business Framework." Launched first in Turkey, and subsequently in the Western Balkans and Egypt (with Croatia, the Eastern Partnership, and Kazakhstan under development for 2015), the framework brings together three critical components to support women's access to finance: donor financing to partner banks for the provision of dedicated financing for women, including a first loss guarantee for women-led small and medium enterprises; technical assistance to support the partner banks to adjust their business models and delivery mechanisms and to develop new financial products for women; and an advisory services component targeting women entrepreneurs, who in turn will become the partner banks' potential client base. Overall, €460 million of credit lines are expected to be channeled through up to 40 partner banks in 16 EBRD countries of operation for on-lending to eligible women-led small and medium enterprises.

Water and sanitation (MDG 7)

The EBRD aims to achieve the sustainable delivery of essential services, notably in water and wastewater, public transport, urban roads and lighting, solid waste management, and district heating and energy efficiency, throughout its region. To reach this goal, the EBRD centers its operations on decentralization of decision making to the local level, commercialization of services for affordability and effectiveness, and improvement of the environment.

From 2010 to 2014, the EBRD's Municipal and Environmental Infrastructure team invested in 177 projects worth a collective €2.9 billion. In 2013 and 2014, water and wastewater projects contributed to a reduction of a combined 166,000 tons of carbon dioxide (CO_2) equivalent. Over the same period, solid waste projects achieved a reduction of 197,000 tons of CO_2 equivalent.

Environmental sustainability (MDG 7)

The EBRD addresses the challenges of climate change and energy efficiency by integrating these issues into all of its operations as a core strategic component and competence. Through its work, it helps countries from Central Europe to Central Asia secure sustainable energy supplies, and it finances the efficient use of energy that will cut demand and imports, reduce pollution, and mitigate the effects of climate change. The focal point for these operations is the Sustainable Energy Initiative. Launched in May 2006, this initiative addresses the twin challenges of energy efficiency and climate change in the EBRD region—which is one of the most energy intensive in the world. The initiative is assisted by strong funding support from donor governments and the EBRD Shareholder Special Fund. Since 2006, the EBRD has invested €8.8 billion under the initiative through 464 projects in 29 countries with a total project value of €46.9 billion. The EBRD is now building on the initiative's success by expanding its remit to include not only energy but also water and material efficiency projects. As part of its policy dialogue activities, the Sustainable Energy Initiative also works with governments to support the development of strong institutional and regulatory frameworks that are the prerequisite to deliver sustainable resource investments.

The EBRD implements its environmental and sustainable development mandate by

- Incorporating environmental and social requirements into the appraisal and

implementation of all EBRD-funded projects based on EU standards and international best practice;
- Providing finance and technical assistance specifically aimed at environmental issues such as sustainable energy, climate change, environmental infrastructure, and nuclear safety;
- Promoting social inclusion through investment and other forms of support for microenterprises and by increasing access to community services such as water and public transport;
- Supporting projects that promote gender equality; and
- Encouraging public participation for pre-investment consultation and disclosure, together with maintaining regular strategic dialogue with civil society organizations.

The broader SDG agenda, to be agreed in 2015, is likely to broaden the scope of the EBRD's involvement in the global development agenda. Many of the headline goals, such as those involving infrastructure, agriculture, climate change, and access to energy, represent areas of work in which the EBRD has been engaged for years. In some cases, there is significant room for scaling up activities that can have real development impact. Given its unique mandate, the EBRD is eager to share lessons learned in how to approach and mobilize private sector finance. Together, MDBs can also forge joint initiatives in this regard, building upon their competitive advantages built from decades of regional experience.

Inter-American Development Bank

The conclusion of the MDG target period at the end of 2015 and the initiation of a new, more ambitious set of SDGs in 2016 will be a milestone for all nations, but in particular for Latin America and the Caribbean. The region has made significant social progress since the MDGs were established in 2000. The region has achieved several MDGs and several others are expected to be achieved by the end of 2015. Indicators of social development have shown impressive results since the beginning of the millennium—including poverty, the size of the middle class, income inequality, education, child malnutrition, and maternal and infant mortality. While these achievements were facilitated by favorable terms of trade, the responsible management of domestic economic policies, and reforms of social policies over a two-decade period, commitment to the well-defined MDGs was an important determinant as well. Moving forward, the region now faces the double challenge of achieving the new SDGs while sustaining and deepening recent social achievements.

The Inter-American Development Bank made its own contribution to meeting the MDGs through technical assistance, operational tools, socioeconomic research, country strategies, dialogue with governments, and other instruments and activities. The IDB's Institutional Strategy closely mirrored the MDGs. In 2010 the Ninth General Increase in the Resources of the IDB established two overarching objectives: poverty and inequality reduction, and sustainable growth. The institutional strategy also placed a high priority on tracking results and promoting development effectiveness in all of the IDB's work. The IDB's Corporate Results Framework serves as the primary tool for monitoring and measuring the IDB's performance and the achievement of its strategic objectives. To assist the region in facing new challenges going forward, the IDB recently updated its Institutional Strategy, approved by the Board of Governors in 2015, again placing special emphasis on reduction of poverty and inequality and on sustained growth.

The Social Strategy for Equity and Productivity provides a set of detailed guidelines designed to assist countries in responding more effectively to the challenges of sustainability and inclusiveness. It focuses on increasing access to comprehensive child development services (essential nutrition, early stimulation, family education) for children from poor households in order to prevent developmental delays and prepare children for entry into the school system; increasing the quality, equity, and relevance of education; equitably improving health outcomes; protecting households against risks; redistributing income effectively while fostering increases in labor productivity; enhancing labor market performance, as indicated by the capacity to create jobs with higher wages and social security coverage; building a new generation of social programs that foster equality of opportunities regardless of labor status, race, ethnicity or gender; and tackling cross-cutting gender and diversity issues.

Recognizing that governments alone cannot tackle the many remaining development challenges, the IDB has encouraged and participated in a number of public-private partnerships aimed at tapping resources from a variety of sources, including nonprofit groups, company foundations, donor-nation funds, and local governments. Emblematic of this new form of collaboration is the Mesoamerican Health Initiative, an innovative partnership designed to narrow the equity gaps in health experienced by population segments in extreme poverty. It was jointly created in 2010 by the Bill & Melinda Gates Foundation, the Instituto Carlos Slim de la Salud, the governments of Spain, Belize, El Salvador, Guatemala, Nicaragua, Honduras, Panama, and Costa Rica, the Mexican state of Chiapas, and the IDB. Its goal is to support regional governments' efforts in achieving the health-related MDGs through investments in interventions of proven effectiveness among the poorest 20 percent of the population, focusing on women and children under five years of age.

This partnership implements transformative solutions through extending the coverage, quality, and use of basic reproductive health services for mothers, newborns, and toddlers as well as by promoting maternal and child nutrition and vaccination. This collaboration has allowed the IDB to leverage valuable knowledge and experience from different partners to tackle the challenging issues of maternal and child health care service delivery in the region's most remote areas. Further, the partnership has allowed for the application of results-based financing mechanisms that use predetermined performance indicators and independent measurement of achievements to help drive country performance.

Despite recent progress in reducing inequality, it remains high in Latin America and the Caribbean. The MDGs measure progress in terms of country-level averages; however, averages can mask steep differences within countries. For example, in Guatemala almost 50 percent of children are chronically malnourished, and the fraction of children who are malnourished is five times as high among children in the poorest income quintile as it is among children in the richest income quintile. As inequality continues to present significant challenges in the region, looking beyond averages is crucial to ensuring that no one is left behind.

To support these efforts, the IDB plans to support countries in building statistical capacity, including the ability to disaggregate data by such characteristics as subnational geography or gender. Along with other MDBs, the IDB has signed a memorandum of understanding with the United Nations to enhance collaboration in supporting the strengthening of country statistical capacity. The IDB is also working to support governments in the region in adopting evidence-based policies and in monitoring progress in meeting post-2015 development goals. Emphasis is being placed on four areas: strengthening the institutional capacity of national statistics offices; strengthening the quality of basic statistics (population and housing censuses, agricultural censuses, household surveys and administrative records); promoting the use of statistics in decision making and in the design and management of interventions by strengthening the end-users' data capabilities; and optimizing the use of modern technologies in production processes, access, and dissemination of statistical information.

The IDB also will help to close financing gaps by exploring ways to improve domestic resource mobilization, tap innovative sources of finance, and better leverage the private sector. Finally, as the leading source of development financing in the region, the IDB can utilize its strong relationships with diverse stakeholders (such as ministries of finance, planning and development, and civil society organizations) to facilitate country and regional dialogues to translate the SDGs into targets and interventions at the country level.

References

ADB (Asian Development Bank). 2008. *Strategy 2020: The Long-Term Strategic Framework of the Asian Development Bank, 2008–2020.* Manila.

———. 2014. *Midterm Review of Strategy 2020: Meeting the Challenges of a Transforming Asia and Pacific.* Manila.

———. 2015a. *Together We Deliver: From Knowledge and Partnerships to Results.* Manila.

———. 2015b. *Making Money Work: Financing a Sustainable Future in Asia and the Pacific.* Manila.

ADB, UNESCAP, and UNDP (Asian Development Bank, United Nations Economic and Social Commission for Asia and the Pacific, United Nations Development Programme). 2013. *Asia-Pacific Aspirations: Perspectives for a Post-2015 Development Agenda.* Asia-Pacific Regional MDGs Report 2012/13, Bangkok.

Schmaljohann, M., A. Prizzon, and A. Rogerson. 2015. "The Role of the World Bank Group in the Post-2015 agenda." Policy Note, Deutsche Gesellschaft für Internationale Zusammenarbeit (GIZ), April.

UNESCAP, ADB, and UNDP (United Nations Economic and Social Commission for Asia and the Pacific, Asian Development Bank, and United Nations Development Programme). 2015. *Making It Happen: Technology, Finance and Statistics for Sustainable Development in Asia and the Pacific.* Asia Pacific Regional MDGs Report 2014/15, Bangkok.

UN (United Nations). 2002. *Monterrey Consensus on Financing for Development.* New York: United Nations.

World Bank. 2015. *Results and Performance of the World Bank Group 2014: An Independent Evaluation. Vol. 1*: Main Report. Washington, DC: World Bank.

C

Data Sources

1. Shared prosperity data

TABLE C.1 Shared prosperity estimates by country based on the latest surveys available from the Global Database of Shared Prosperity

			Annualized growth per capita[c,d]		Mean consumption or income per capita[c]				
					Baseline		Most recent year		
Country	Period[a]	Type[b]	Bottom 40 %	Total population (%)	Bottom 40% $ a day (PPP)	Total population $ a day (PPP)	Bottom 40% $ a day (PPP)	Total population $ a day (PPP)	PPP year
Albania	2008–12	C	−1.22	−1.31	4.28	7.81	4.08	7.41	2011
Argentina[e]	2007–12	I	6.43	3.13	5.62	18.16	7.67	21.19	2011
Armenia	2008–13	C	−1.49	−1.05	3.40	6.28	3.15	5.95	2011
Australia	2003–10	I	4.39	4.65	—	—	—	—	2011
Austria	2007–12	I	0.37	0.39	27.78	52.68	28.31	53.73	2011
Bangladesh	2005–10	C	1.73	1.37	0.83	1.59	0.91	1.70	2005
Belarus	2006–11	C	9.13	8.14	6.51	11.65	10.08	17.23	2011
Belgium	2007–12	I	1.14	0.44	25.79	46.88	27.29	47.92	2011
Bhutan	2007–12	C	6.53	6.47	2.57	5.88	3.53	8.04	2011
Bolivia	2007–12	I	10.10	4.29	2.29	9.82	3.70	12.12	2011
Brazil	2007–12	I	6.93	4.54	3.45	13.99	4.82	17.46	2011
Bulgaria	2008–13	I	1.29	1.37	6.77	14.70	7.22	15.73	2011
Cambodia	2007–12	C	8.53	4.09	1.10	2.35	1.65	2.88	2005
Canada	2004–10	I	2.14	1.93	—	—	—	—	2011
Chile	2006–11	I	3.87	2.83	5.49	18.14	6.63	20.86	2011
China	2005–10	C	7.23	7.86	—	—	—	—	2011
Colombia	2008–12	I	5.99	3.59	2.79	11.57	3.52	13.32	2011
Congo, Dem. Rep.	2004–12	C	7.81	7.20	0.33	0.89	0.58	1.50	2011
Congo, Rep.	2005–11	C	7.22	4.29	1.00	2.96	1.52	3.81	2011
Costa Rica	2010–13	I	1.33	3.15	6.62	20.34	6.88	22.32	2011
Croatia	2004–10	C	1.59	0.25	11.67	21.85	12.83	22.18	2011
Cyprus	2007–12	I	−2.75	−1.58	27.10	50.79	23.57	46.91	2011
Czech Republic	2008–13	I	0.15	0.37	15.70	25.81	15.82	26.30	2011
Denmark	2007–12	I	−0.75	0.32	28.65	48.29	27.58	49.05	2011
Dominican Republic	2007–12	I	1.79	−0.20	3.83	11.93	4.19	11.82	2011
Ecuador	2007–12	I	5.51	0.97	2.87	10.74	3.75	11.27	2011
El Salvador	2007–12	I	0.21	−1.49	3.60	9.89	3.64	9.17	2011
Estonia	2008–13	I	−2.10	−1.24	12.84	24.56	11.55	23.07	2011
Ethiopia	2004–10	C	−1.45	−0.09	1.51	2.69	1.38	2.68	2011
Finland	2007–12	I	1.55	1.07	26.72	46.79	28.86	49.35	2011
France	2007–12	I	0.19	0.39	26.58	51.51	26.83	52.53	2011
Georgia	2008–13	C	2.91	2.63	2.12	5.34	2.45	6.08	2011
Germany	2006–11	I	1.35	0.14	26.51	52.41	28.35	52.79	2011
Greece	2007–12	I	−10.02	−8.40	16.32	34.68	9.63	22.36	2011
Guatemala	2006–11	I	−1.85	−4.57	2.75	10.87	2.50	8.60	2011
Honduras	2007–12	I	−3.22	−2.68	2.10	8.92	1.78	7.79	2011
Hungary	2008–13	I	−1.93	−0.67	10.89	19.32	9.88	18.69	2011
Iceland	2007–12	I	−3.85	−4.56	33.07	58.69	27.17	46.47	2011
India	2004–11	C	3.20	3.70	1.46	2.81	1.82	3.63	2011
Indonesia	2011–14	C	3.82	3.39	2.11	4.82	2.36	5.33	2011
Iran, Islamic Rep.	2009–13	C	3.05	−1.20	2.63	17.41	2.96	16.59	2011
Iraq	2007–12	C	0.33	0.98	—	—	—	—	2011
Ireland	2007–12	I	−4.38	−3.88	26.17	50.03	20.92	41.05	2011
Israel	2005–10	I	1.88	2.46	—	—	—	—	2011
Italy	2007–12	I	−2.86	−1.82	21.24	43.54	18.37	39.72	2011
Jordan	2006–10	C	2.70	2.57	3.21	6.37	3.58	7.05	2005
Kazakhstan	2009–13	C	8.92	7.56	5.06	8.96	7.13	11.99	2011
Kyrgyz Republic	2008–12	C	−0.13	−2.35	3.33	6.62	3.31	6.02	2011
Lao PDR	2007–12	C	1.25	1.96	0.98	1.98	1.04	2.18	2005
Latvia	2008–13	I	−3.04	−4.33	9.69	22.38	8.31	17.94	2011

(Table continues next page)

TABLE C.1 Shared prosperity estimates by country based on the latest surveys available from the Global Database of Shared Prosperity (continued)

			Annualized growth per capita[c,d]		Mean consumption or income per capita[c]				
					Baseline		Most recent year		
Country	Period[a]	Type[b]	Bottom 40 %	Total population (%)	Bottom 40% $ a day (PPP)	Total population $ a day (PPP)	Bottom 40% $ a day (PPP)	Total population $ a day (PPP)	PPP year
Lithuania	2008–13	I	−1.77	−1.16	10.14	20.99	9.28	19.79	2011
Luxembourg	2007–12	I	−2.67	−0.54	38.29	72.80	33.44	70.85	2011
Madagascar	2005–10	C	−4.49	−3.52	0.78	1.74	0.62	1.45	2011
Malawi	2004–10	C	−1.84	1.27	0.78	1.77	0.70	1.90	2011
Mali	2006–09	C	2.25	−1.47	1.10	2.53	1.20	2.38	2011
Mauritania	2008–14	C	3.25	1.62	2.36	5.47	2.86	6.03	2011
Mauritius	2006–12	C	0.76	0.86	5.31	11.02	5.54	11.56	2011
Mexico	2008–12	I	1.15	−0.22	3.39	11.27	3.54	11.17	2011
Moldova	2008–13	C	4.99	1.81	4.23	8.77	5.40	9.59	2011
Montenegro	2008–13	C	−4.81	−3.64	8.86	16.35	6.92	13.59	2011
Nepal	2003–10	C	7.47	4.08	1.21	2.97	2.00	3.91	2011
Netherlands	2007–12	I	−0.01	−0.99	28.06	51.72	28.05	49.21	2011
Nigeria	2003–09	C	0.12	1.12	0.93	2.33	0.94	2.49	2011
Norway	2007–12	I	3.17	2.39	33.37	58.45	39.00	65.77	2011
Pakistan	2004–10	C	3.76	2.69	1.82	3.40	2.27	3.99	2011
Panama	2008–12	I	4.14	3.63	4.58	17.18	5.39	19.82	2011
Paraguay	2007–12	I	7.21	5.20	3.39	11.75	4.80	15.15	2011
Peru	2007–12	I	8.57	3.99	3.06	11.19	4.62	13.61	2011
Philippines	2006–12	C	1.15	0.41	2.05	5.58	2.20	5.72	2011
Poland	2007–12	C	1.99	1.44	7.57	15.21	8.35	16.34	2011
Portugal	2007–12	I	−1.99	−2.14	12.89	27.97	11.65	25.11	2011
Romania	2008–13	C	0.58	−0.28	4.81	8.89	4.95	8.76	2011
Russian Federation	2007–12	C	5.86	5.27	7.60	19.42	10.10	25.11	2011
Rwanda	2005–10	C	5.04	3.89	0.72	2.27	0.92	2.75	2011
Senegal	2005–11	C	−0.23	0.31	1.31	3.10	1.29	3.16	2011
Serbia	2007–10	C	−1.76	−1.33	7.32	13.37	6.94	12.84	2011
Slovak Republic	2008–13	I	5.48	6.67	12.46	20.27	16.27	28.00	2011
Slovenia	2008–13	I	−0.84	−0.28	20.64	33.44	19.79	32.97	2011
South Africa	2006–11	C	4.09	4.38	1.73	9.50	2.12	11.78	2011
Spain	2007–12	I	−1.32	0.00	17.14	36.25	16.04	36.25	2011
Sri Lanka	2006–12	C	2.21	1.66	2.96	6.80	3.37	7.51	2011
Sweden	2007–12	I	2.04	2.25	26.22	45.14	29.01	50.46	2011
Switzerland	2007–12	I	2.43	0.93	30.49	63.18	34.38	66.19	2011
Tanzania	2007–11	C	3.54	1.59	1.01	2.40	1.20	2.58	2011
Thailand	2008–12	C	4.78	3.95	5.15	12.45	6.21	14.54	2011
Togo	2006–11	C	−2.17	0.95	0.99	2.50	0.89	2.63	2011
Tunisia	2005–10	C	3.45	2.63	3.72	8.44	4.40	9.61	2011
Turkey	2007–12	C	4.33	4.81	5.40	12.92	6.67	16.34	2011
Uganda	2009–12	C	3.90	2.95	1.23	3.14	1.39	3.43	2011
Ukraine	2008–13	C	3.47	2.27	6.81	11.60	8.08	12.97	2011
United Kingdom	2007–12	I	−1.67	−2.78	23.89	51.10	21.96	44.38	2011
United States	2007–13	I	−0.16	−0.43	—	—	—	—	2011
Uruguay	2007–12	I	7.87	4.33	6.00	18.63	8.75	23.03	2011
Vietnam	2004–10	C	6.22	7.81	2.13	5.03	3.07	7.89	2011

Source: Global Database of Shared Prosperity 2015.
Note: — = Not available.
a. Refers to the years in which the underlying household survey data were collected; in cases for which the data collection period bridged two calendar years, the year in which most of the data were collected is reported. The initial year refers to the nearest survey collected five years before the most recent survey available; only surveys collected between three and seven years before the most recent survey are considered. The final year refers to the most recent survey available between 2010 and 2014.
b. Denotes whether the data reported are based on consumption (C) or income (I) data. Capital letters indicate that grouped data were used.
c. Based on real mean per capita consumption or income measured at 2011 and 2005 purchasing power parity (PPP) using the PovcalNet (http://iresearch.worldbank.org/PovcalNet). For some countries, means are not reported because of grouped and/or confidential data.
d. The annualized growth rate is computed as (Mean in year 2/Mean in year 1)^(1/(Year 2 – Year 1)) – 1.
e. Covers urban areas only.

2. Demographic and health surveys

Part II of this report draws extensively on the Demographic and Health Surveys (DHSs). These are nationally representative household surveys that provide data for a wide range of monitoring and impact evaluation indicators in the areas of population, health, and nutrition.

The analyses presented in this report use only the latest data available in the DHS program, which have survey-year ranges from 1985 to 2014. The DHS database included 88 countries as of May 2015.[1] For certain indicators, some countries may not be included. For the figures in chapter 4 that use the DHS data, a simple average was used to aggregate selected indicators by income level and by typology.

The DHS wealth index was used to illustrate the difference between the bottom 40 (B40) percent and the top 60 (T60) percent of the income distribution in a country. The wealth index, which measures a household's composite living standard, has five levels and is calculated using easy-to-collect data on a household's ownership of selected assets, such as televisions and bicycles; materials used for housing construction; and types of water access and sanitation facilities. To illustrate the demographic difference between the B40 and T60 percent, we combined the DHS's "lowest" and "second" levels as the B40 percent and its "middle," "fourth," and "highest" as the T60 percent.

To illustrate within-country demographic variance, the following indicators are used in each figure:

Figure 4.12 compares the total fertility rate in rural and urban areas. The values refer to the total fertility rate for the three years preceding the survey (DHS indicator: 20171000). Similarly, figure 4.20 uses the same fertility indicator but compares the rates for the B40 and T60 populations according to the DHS wealth index.

Figure 4.14 compares the infant mortality rate for the B40 and T60 of the same wealth index. Infant mortality rate (DHS indicator: 70254002) refers to the probability of dying before the first birthday in the period 1–60 months (and 1–120 months for background characteristics) preceding the survey per 1,000 live births.[2]

Figure 4.15 compares health facility access for the B40 and the T60 of the DHS wealth index. Live births delivered at health facilities (indicator: 77282000) denotes the percentage of live births in the three/five years preceding the survey delivered at a health facility.[3]

Figure 4.18 compares the share of teenagers who are mothers (DHS indicator: 29169000) for the B40 and the T60 of the DHS wealth index. This variable is defined as percentage of women ages 15–19 who are mothers or pregnant with their first child by selected background characteristics.

Figure 4.19 compares women's median age at first birth (DHS indicator: 55166000) for the B40 and the T60 of the wealth index. This variable refers to women between 25 and 49 years of age.

Figure 4.21 compares unmet needs for family planning (DHS indicator: 216236002) for women in the B40 and T60. This variable is defined as the percentage of women who do not want to become pregnant but are not using contraception following the DHS definition.[4]

Figure B4.5.1 shows the median age at first marriage for women in rural areas for selected countries (DHS indicator: 55166000). The age at first marriage is based on the responses provided by women ages 25 to 49 when interviewed.

Notes

1. Albania; Angola; Armenia; Azerbaijan; Bangladesh; Benin; Bolivia; Botswana; Brazil; Burkina Faso; Burundi; Cambodia; Cameroon; Cabo Verde; Central African Republic; Chad; Colombia; Comoros; Congo, Rep.; Congo, Dem. Rep.; Cote d'Ivoire; Dominican Republic; Ecuador; Egypt, Arab Rep.; El Salvador; Eritrea; Ethiopia; Gabon; Gambia, The;

Georgia; Ghana; Guatemala; Guinea; Guyana; Haiti; Honduras; India; Indonesia; Jamaica; Jordan; Kazakhstan; Kenya; Kyrgyz Republic; Lesotho; Liberia; Madagascar; Malawi; Maldives; Mali; Mauritania; Mexico; Moldova; Morocco; Mozambique; Namibia; Nepal; Nicaragua; Niger; Nigeria; Pakistan; Paraguay; Peru; Philippines; Romania; Rwanda; São Tomé and Príncipe; Senegal; Sierra Leone; South Africa; Sri Lanka; Sudan; Swaziland; Tajikistan; Tanzania; Thailand; Timor-Leste; Togo; Trinidad and Tobago; Tunisia; Turkey; Turkmenistan; Uganda; Ukraine; Uzbekistan; Vietnam; Yemen, Rep.; Zambia; Zimbabwe. DHS surveys are carried out only in less-developed countries and/or countries receiving U.S. foreign aid. Further details on country coverage of DHS surveys are available at http://dhsprogram.com/.

2. The Gambia was not included because of lack of data.
3. Botswana, The Gambia, Mexico, Sri Lanka, Sudan, Thailand, Trinidad and Tobago, and Tunisia were not included because of lack of data.
4. Angola, Botswana, Cabo Verde, Ecuador, El Salvador, The Gambia, Georgia, Jamaica, Mexico, Romania, Sri Lanka, Sudan, Thailand, Trinidad and Tobago, and Tunisia were not included because of lack of data.

3. Demographic typology

Evidence shows that changes in age structure can affect GDP, with the exact impact depending on the nature of the change. Lee and Mason (2006), among others, have identified two "demographic dividends" associated with changes in the working-age population share in different stages of demographic transition. After an initial decline in mortality, countries tend to transition from high to low fertility. During this phase, the population share of children declines and the share of people of working age increases, while the share of elderly remains small. As a result, these countries potentially experience a boost to aggregate economic growth, a phenomenon referred to as the "first demographic dividend." Subsequently, as the population share in working age continues to increase, countries are in a position to realize high rates of savings and investment, building up large stocks of human and physical capital. The contribution of this capital to production, which may be long term, is considered a "second demographic dividend." The demographic dividends are potential economic outcomes associated with a country's demographic context. The extent to which countries reap these dividends varies. The demographic typology in this report classifies countries on the basis of the economic implications of their demographic characteristics.

A few criteria are used to identify whether the potential for a first demographic dividend is in a country's past, present, or future. The first criterion is whether the working-age share is likely to be rising or not during 2015–30—the time horizon for several development goals. This criterion differentiates two broad groups of countries.

The first broad group is made up of countries for which the working-age share is projected to decrease or stay unchanged during 2015–30; for this group of countries, the potential for the first demographic dividend has either already passed or is passing. To distinguish two subgroups within this broader group, the fertility rate from 1985, 30 years ago, is used to identify how far along countries are in the final phase of demographic transition, which is characterized by low rates of both fertility and mortality. Thirty years describes the ballpark length of a generation from the birth of a parent to the birth of a child, although the exact length would vary by country and across time. Countries whose fertility rate in 1985 was below replacement are most likely to be the furthest along in their demographic transition, with the potential for a first demographic dividend being part of their past. These countries are classified as *post-dividend*. Countries whose fertility rate in 1985 was at or above replacement are likely to have entered the final phase of demographic transition more recently; they may still be reaping the first demographic dividend but are at the tail end of that window. These countries are classified as *late-dividend* countries.

The second broad group includes countries whose working-age population shares are growing. On the basis of the current total fertility rate, two subgroups are considered: those for which the window for the first demographic dividend was open recently and those for which it will open in the future. If a country's total fertility is below four births per woman, then it is likely that the country has been progressing through the demographic transition model and will be experiencing rapid reductions in the population share of its youth. These are the *early-dividend* countries. Countries whose current fertility rates are four births per woman or higher are most likely at an earlier stage of demographic transition and have yet to experience most of the decline in the child population share that makes the first demographic dividend possible. These are the *pre-dividend* countries. It should be noted that the selection of the specific value of four births per woman as the cutoff is arbitrary and that the classification of some countries would change if a slightly different value had been selected.

These criteria—summarized in table C.2—are applied to 191 economies covered by both the United Nations World Population Prospect: The 2015 Revision (WPP) (UN 2015) and the World Development Indicators, to yield the typology illustrated in map 5.1 and listed below in table C.3. The population data for 1950–2013 are the historical estimates of the WPP. The population data from 2013 onward are from the WPP's medium-fertility scenario. As noted in box 4.1, population projections differ across alternative databases and WPP scenarios, so the typology of countries may vary slightly depending on the source of the projections because of possible differences in growth of the working-age populations in 2015–30. As also noted in box 4.1, however, substantial changes in working-age population growth across countries are unlikely because of the short time horizon.

TABLE C.2 Criteria for typology

Growth of working-age population share, 2015–30	Total fertility rate, 1985		Total fertility rate, 2015	
	< 2.1	≥ 2.1	< 4	≥ 4
≤ 0	Post-dividend	Late-dividend		
> 0			Early-dividend	Pre-dividend

Note: The working-age population is defined as the share of the population aged between 15 and 64 years. Total fertility rate is the average number of births per woman in her lifetime.

TABLE C.3 Economies by World Bank Group classification and demographic typology

Name	World Bank Group income classification	Demographic type	Percent change in working-age population share, 2015–30	Total fertility rate, 1985–90	Total fertility rate, 2015–20
Afghanistan	LIC	Pre-dividend	17.53	7.47	4.25
Albania	UMC	Late-dividend	−10.69	3.15	1.78
Algeria	UMC	Early-dividend	0.99	5.30	2.62
Angola	UMC	Pre-dividend	6.56	7.25	5.79
Antigua and Barbuda	HIC	Post-dividend	−2.78	2.07	2.03
Argentina	HIC	Early-dividend	1.13	3.05	2.27
Armenia	LMC	Late-dividend	−8.09	2.58	1.51
Aruba	HIC	Late-dividend	−8.13	2.30	1.62
Australia	HIC	Post-dividend	−6.42	1.86	1.86
Austria	HIC	Post-dividend	−9.17	1.45	1.53
Azerbaijan	UMC	Late-dividend	−7.88	2.95	2.22
Bahamas, The	HIC	Late-dividend	−6.78	2.65	1.83
Bahrain	HIC	Early-dividend	1.45	4.08	1.98
Bangladesh	LMC	Early-dividend	6.15	4.98	2.08
Barbados	HIC	Post-dividend	−8.53	1.77	1.80
Belarus	UMC	Post-dividend	−8.41	2.00	1.64
Belgium	HIC	Post-dividend	−6.77	1.56	1.83
Belize	UMC	Early-dividend	4.65	4.70	2.46
Benin	LIC	Pre-dividend	7.60	6.88	4.50
Bhutan	LMC	Early-dividend	4.47	6.11	1.93
Bolivia	LMC	Early-dividend	4.99	5.09	2.83
Bosnia and Herzegovina	UMC	Post-dividend	−9.86	1.91	1.23

(Table continues next page)

TABLE C.3 Economies by World Bank Group classification and demographic typology (continued)

Name	World Bank Group income classification	Demographic type	Percent change in working-age population share, 2015–30	Total fertility rate, 1985–90	Total fertility rate, 2015–20
Botswana	UMC	Early-dividend	4.39	5.11	2.67
Brazil	UMC	Late-dividend	−1.41	3.10	1.74
Brunei Darussalam	HIC	Late-dividend	−3.21	3.72	1.82
Bulgaria	UMC	Post-dividend	−4.91	1.95	1.60
Burkina Faso	LIC	Pre-dividend	8.18	7.07	5.23
Burundi	LIC	Pre-dividend	3.67	7.59	5.66
Cabo Verde	LMC	Early-dividend	4.30	5.63	2.19
Cambodia	LIC	Early-dividend	2.39	5.99	2.53
Cameroon	LMC	Pre-dividend	8.25	6.60	4.46
Canada	HIC	Post-dividend	−10.27	1.62	1.56
Central African Republic	LIC	Pre-dividend	7.15	5.90	4.02
Chad	LIC	Pre-dividend	7.99	7.21	5.79
Chile	HIC	Late-dividend	−4.98	2.60	1.73
China	UMC	Late-dividend	−7.12	2.75	1.59
Colombia	UMC	Late-dividend	−0.93	3.18	1.83
Comoros	LIC	Pre-dividend	6.34	6.70	4.23
Congo, Dem. Rep.	LIC	Pre-dividend	7.15	6.98	5.66
Congo, Rep.	LMC	Pre-dividend	6.23	5.55	4.64
Costa Rica	UMC	Late-dividend	−2.89	3.31	1.76
Côte d'Ivoire	LMC	Pre-dividend	4.49	6.85	4.77
Croatia	HIC	Post-dividend	−6.58	1.72	1.48
Cuba	UMC	Post-dividend	−9.04	1.85	1.58
Cyprus	HIC	Late-dividend	−5.01	2.43	1.42
Czech Republic	HIC	Post-dividend	−5.85	1.90	1.54
Denmark	HIC	Post-dividend	−5.12	1.54	1.76
Djibouti	LMC	Early-dividend	4.93	6.18	2.99
Dominican Republic	UMC	Early-dividend	2.71	3.65	2.38
Ecuador	UMC	Early-dividend	1.28	4.00	2.44
Egypt, Arab Rep.	LMC	Early-dividend	3.29	5.15	3.16
El Salvador	LMC	Early-dividend	2.51	4.17	1.87
Equatorial Guinea	HIC	Pre-dividend	1.32	5.89	4.52
Eritrea	LIC	Pre-dividend	12.43	6.51	4.02
Estonia	HIC	Late-dividend	−5.97	2.20	1.66
Ethiopia	LIC	Early-dividend	12.05	7.37	3.99
Fiji	UMC	Late-dividend	−0.28	3.47	2.48
Finland	HIC	Post-dividend	−7.05	1.66	1.77
France	HIC	Post-dividend	−5.44	1.81	1.99
French Polynesia	HIC	Late-dividend	−5.51	3.64	1.99
Gabon	UMC	Early-dividend	7.18	5.58	3.68
Gambia, The	LIC	Pre-dividend	6.25	6.14	5.53
Georgia	LMC	Late-dividend	−7.19	2.26	1.82
Germany	HIC	Post-dividend	−10.74	1.43	1.44
Ghana	LMC	Early-dividend	6.42	5.88	3.95
Greece	HIC	Post-dividend	−2.46	1.53	1.30
Grenada	UMC	Early-dividend	0.92	4.14	2.08
Guam	HIC	Late-dividend	−4.48	3.14	2.32
Guatemala	LMC	Early-dividend	8.10	5.50	3.03

(Table continues next page)

TABLE C.3 Economies by World Bank Group classification and demographic typology (continued)

Name	World Bank Group income classification	Demographic type	Percent change in working-age population share, 2015–30	Total fertility rate, 1985–90	Total fertility rate, 2015–20
Guinea	LIC	Pre-dividend	6.57	6.63	4.73
Guinea-Bissau	LIC	Pre-dividend	6.01	6.68	4.56
Guyana	LMC	Late-dividend	−3.02	3.77	2.47
Haiti	LIC	Early-dividend	6.11	5.70	2.85
Honduras	LMC	Early-dividend	7.02	5.37	2.25
Hong Kong SAR, China	HIC	Post-dividend	−17.53	1.36	1.30
Hungary	HIC	Post-dividend	−4.48	1.86	1.40
Iceland	HIC	Late-dividend	−6.25	2.12	1.90
India	LMC	Early-dividend	3.11	4.27	2.34
Indonesia	LMC	Early-dividend	1.40	3.40	2.36
Iran, Islamic Rep.	UMC	Early-dividend	1.48	5.62	1.62
Iraq	UMC	Pre-dividend	5.10	6.09	4.35
Ireland	HIC	Late-dividend	−1.78	2.18	2.00
Israel	HIC	Early-dividend	0.27	3.07	2.93
Italy	HIC	Post-dividend	−7.83	1.35	1.49
Jamaica	UMC	Late-dividend	−3.36	3.10	1.99
Japan	HIC	Post-dividend	−5.68	1.66	1.46
Jordan	UMC	Early-dividend	7.74	6.02	3.20
Kazakhstan	UMC	Late-dividend	−2.03	3.03	2.53
Kenya	LMC	Pre-dividend	8.34	6.54	4.10
Kiribati	LMC	Early-dividend	2.21	4.80	3.58
Korea, Dem. People's Rep.	LIC	Late-dividend	−1.47	2.36	1.94
Korea, Rep.	HIC	Post-dividend	−13.45	1.60	1.33
Kuwait	HIC	Late-dividend	−2.00	3.15	2.04
Kyrgyz Republic	LMC	Late-dividend	−0.74	4.02	2.93
Lao PDR	LMC	Early-dividend	6.81	6.27	2.77
Latvia	HIC	Late-dividend	−5.61	2.13	1.55
Lebanon	UMC	Late-dividend	−1.84	3.23	1.71
Lesotho	LMC	Early-dividend	4.97	5.14	3.01
Liberia	LIC	Pre-dividend	7.82	6.72	4.47
Libya	UMC	Early-dividend	7.10	5.71	2.32
Lithuania	HIC	Post-dividend	−7.62	2.06	1.63
Luxembourg	HIC	Post-dividend	−6.68	1.47	1.61
Macao SAR, China	HIC	Post-dividend	−16.77	1.94	1.34
Macedonia, FYR	UMC	Late-dividend	−6.94	2.27	1.55
Madagascar	LIC	Pre-dividend	4.74	6.30	4.21
Malawi	LIC	Pre-dividend	9.24	7.30	4.88
Malaysia	UMC	Late-dividend	−1.75	3.59	1.90
Maldives	UMC	Early-dividend	3.66	6.66	1.98
Mali	LIC	Pre-dividend	8.38	7.15	5.92
Malta	HIC	Post-dividend	−7.59	2.01	1.49
Mauritania	LMC	Pre-dividend	5.82	6.09	4.39
Mauritius	UMC	Late-dividend	−5.64	2.31	1.44
Mexico	UMC	Early-dividend	2.42	3.75	2.14
Micronesia, Fed. Sts.	LMC	Early-dividend	1.22	5.20	3.08
Moldova	LMC	Late-dividend	−7.08	2.64	1.23
Mongolia	UMC	Late-dividend	−1.48	4.84	2.54

(Table continues next page)

TABLE C.3 Economies by World Bank Group classification and demographic typology (continued)

Name	World Bank Group income classification	Demographic type	Percent change in working-age population share, 2015–30	Total fertility rate, 1985–90	Total fertility rate, 2015–20
Montenegro	UMC	Late-dividend	−4.46	2.11	1.65
Morocco	LMC	Late-dividend	−0.95	4.45	2.38
Mozambique	LIC	Pre-dividend	7.28	6.33	5.12
Myanmar	LMC	Early-dividend	3.22	3.80	2.13
Namibia	UMC	Early-dividend	4.45	5.55	3.31
Nepal	LIC	Early-dividend	10.01	5.33	2.09
Netherlands	HIC	Post-dividend	−8.89	1.55	1.77
New Caledonia	HIC	Late-dividend	−2.95	3.03	2.04
New Zealand	HIC	Post-dividend	−6.56	2.03	1.99
Nicaragua	LMC	Early-dividend	4.70	5.00	2.16
Niger	LIC	Pre-dividend	1.75	7.69	7.46
Nigeria	LMC	Pre-dividend	6.15	6.60	5.41
Norway	HIC	Post-dividend	−5.43	1.80	1.81
Oman	HIC	Late-dividend	−4.18	7.85	2.51
Pakistan	LMC	Early-dividend	5.51	6.30	3.38
Panama	UMC	Early-dividend	0.27	3.24	2.36
Papua New Guinea	LMC	Early-dividend	6.18	4.97	3.58
Paraguay	UMC	Early-dividend	2.65	4.77	2.45
Peru	UMC	Early-dividend	1.69	4.10	2.35
Philippines	LMC	Early-dividend	2.40	4.53	2.87
Poland	HIC	Late-dividend	−8.38	2.16	1.33
Portugal	HIC	Post-dividend	−5.92	1.62	1.24
Puerto Rico	HIC	Late-dividend	−3.09	2.26	1.59
Qatar	HIC	Late-dividend	−2.27	4.41	1.95
Romania	UMC	Late-dividend	−3.79	2.22	1.53
Russian Federation	HIC	Late-dividend	−8.60	2.12	1.72
Rwanda	LIC	Early-dividend	11.47	7.99	3.62
Samoa	LMC	Early-dividend	3.99	5.35	3.90
Saudi Arabia	HIC	Early-dividend	3.09	6.22	2.59
Senegal	LMC	Pre-dividend	7.23	6.88	4.83
Serbia	UMC	Late-dividend	−4.38	2.23	1.59
Seychelles	HIC	Late-dividend	−2.97	2.94	2.21
Sierra Leone	LIC	Pre-dividend	10.04	6.66	4.28
Singapore	HIC	Post-dividend	−12.12	1.70	1.26
Slovak Republic	HIC	Late-dividend	−8.71	2.15	1.44
Slovenia	HIC	Post-dividend	−10.57	1.65	1.65
Solomon Islands	LMC	Early-dividend	9.87	6.13	3.76
Somalia	LIC	Pre-dividend	4.81	7.26	6.12
South Africa	UMC	Early-dividend	2.73	4.00	2.28
South Sudan	LIC	Pre-dividend	6.75	6.83	4.73
Spain	HIC	Post-dividend	−6.41	1.46	1.38
Sri Lanka	LMC	Late-dividend	−1.84	2.64	2.03
St. Lucia	UMC	Late-dividend	−0.91	3.65	1.82
St. Vincent and the Grenadines	UMC	Late-dividend	−1.32	3.10	1.90
Sudan	LMC	Pre-dividend	7.27	6.30	4.13
Suriname	UMC	Early-dividend	0.37	3.42	2.28

(Table continues next page)

TABLE C.3 Economies by World Bank Group classification and demographic typology (continued)

Name	World Bank Group income classification	Demographic type	Percent change in working-age population share, 2015–30	Total fertility rate, 1985–90	Total fertility rate, 2015–20
Swaziland	LMC	Early-dividend	5.15	6.13	3.06
Sweden	HIC	Post-dividend	−4.42	1.91	1.93
Switzerland	HIC	Post-dividend	−8.81	1.55	1.57
Syrian Arab Republic	LMC	Early-dividend	11.32	5.87	2.77
Tajikistan	LMC	Early-dividend	0.33	5.41	3.32
Tanzania	LIC	Pre-dividend	6.70	6.36	4.92
Thailand	UMC	Late-dividend	−7.29	2.30	1.46
Timor-Leste	LMC	Pre-dividend	7.27	5.21	5.33
Togo	LIC	Pre-dividend	7.63	6.62	4.35
Tonga	UMC	Early-dividend	7.86	4.74	3.58
Trinidad and Tobago	HIC	Late-dividend	−2.76	2.75	1.73
Tunisia	UMC	Late-dividend	−3.50	4.00	2.07
Turkey	UMC	Early-dividend	0.90	3.35	2.01
Turkmenistan	UMC	Early-dividend	1.49	4.55	2.22
Uganda	LIC	Pre-dividend	10.18	7.10	5.46
Ukraine	LMC	Post-dividend	−7.37	1.90	1.56
United Arab Emirates	HIC	Late-dividend	−4.19	4.83	1.73
United Kingdom	HIC	Post-dividend	−5.18	1.84	1.91
United States	HIC	Post-dividend	−7.77	1.91	1.90
Uruguay	HIC	Late-dividend	−0.61	2.53	1.98
Uzbekistan	LMC	Early-dividend	1.46	4.40	2.33
Vanuatu	LMC	Early-dividend	4.95	5.04	3.22
Venezuela, RB	HIC	Early-dividend	0.78	3.65	2.28
Vietnam	LMC	Late-dividend	−3.84	3.85	1.95
Virgin Islands (U.S.)	HIC	Late-dividend	−10.79	3.02	2.18
West Bank and Gaza	LMC	Early-dividend	6.24	6.76	3.95
Yemen, Rep.	LMC	Early-dividend	10.13	8.80	3.79
Zambia	LMC	Pre-dividend	7.43	6.68	5.14
Zimbabwe	LIC	Early-dividend	10.51	5.66	3.65

Source: UN World Population Prospects (2015) and World Bank 2015.
Note: This table uses the World Bank Group income classification of July 2015. LIC = low-income countries. LMC = lower-middle-income countries. UMC = is upper-middle-income countries. HIC = high-income countries.

References

Lee, R., and A. Mason. 2006. "What Is the Demographic Dividend?" *Finance and Development* 43 (3).

UN (United Nations). 2015. World Population Prospects: The 2015 Revision, New York: United Nations, Department of Economic and Social Affairs, Population Division.

World Bank. 2015. Country and Lending Groups (http://data.worldbank.org/about/country-and-lending-groups).

4. Data and econometric estimations

The basic association between demographic changes and growth is described by Bloom and Canning (2004) through an accounting identity:

$$\frac{Y}{N}=\frac{Y}{L}\cdot\frac{WAP}{N}\cdot\frac{L}{WAP} \qquad (1)$$

where Y is income, N is total population, WAP is the working-age population, and L is the number of workers. Equation (1) shows that income per capita (Y/N) equals output per worker (Y/L) times the share of the working-age population (WAP/N) times the participation rate (L/WAP). The equation suggests that, everything else constant, an increase of the output per worker (Y/L), or an increase in the share of working-age population (WAP/N), or in the participation rate (L/WAP) is associated with higher GDP per capita. Taking the log of the variables in (1) and presenting the relation in terms of growth leads to:

$$g_y = g_z + g_w + g_l \qquad (2)$$

where (g_y) is income per capita growth, (g_z) is productivity growth per worker, (g_w) is the growth of the share of working-age population, and (g_l) is the growth in labor force participation rate.

Assuming that productivity growth per worker is a function of X variables, such that $g_z = b\ f(X)$ and growth of labor force participation is constant, such that $g_l = a$, the following functional form is produced:

$$g_y = a + b\ f(X) + g_w + \varepsilon. \qquad (3)$$

where ε is the error term.

Equation (3) suggests that, keeping everything else constant, an increase in the share of working-age population leads to higher GDP per capita growth. The main issue behind this association is that, because (3) is derived from an accounting identity, a set of assumptions are necessary to suggest a causal relationship between changes in the share of working-age population and growth.

Over a short- to medium-term horizon, it is reasonable to assume that the working-age population is given in absolute terms, and that it is a function of past and current fertility, mortality, and migration rates. However, the current fertility rate also affects g_w, by changing the size of the total population (N). Increasing life expectancy and migration also affect N. An issue in the estimation of (3) is that unobservable factors (omitted variables) that affect per capita income growth can simultaneously affect the share of working-age population, leading to an endogeneity issue. In addition, it might be that changes in per capita income lead to demographic changes instead, a reverse causality problem.

Several studies attempt to analyze the effect of demographic change on economic growth (Bloom and Canning 2004; Eastwood and Lipton 2011; IMF 2004; Kelly and Schmidt 2005, 2007). Overall, their findings converge on a positive association between GDP per capita growth and the share of working-age population. These studies adopted different approaches to address the potential endogeneity issues previously described. One such approach is to use the lag of the change of the share of working-age population ($g_{w(t-1)}$) as an instrument for g_w. The intuition is that current income per capita growth does not affect the growth rate of the share of working-age population in the past. Although it can be argued that this approach deals with reverse causality, it does not necessarily address the omitted variable problem.

This report uses different approaches to deal with the problem of endogeneity. First, it shows the association between g_w and g_y by providing the results based on ordinary least squares estimation. Then, in order to deal with time-invariant unobservable factors that could simultaneously affect g_y and g_w, a panel fixed effects estimation is used. Finally, to deal

FIGURE C.4.1 Growth of the working-age share of the population can increase real GDP per capita

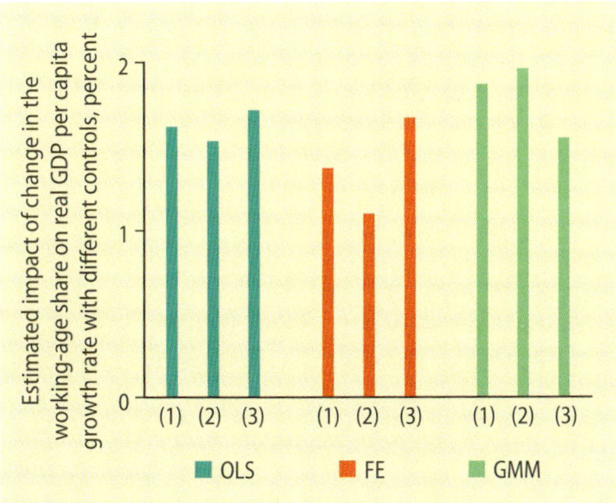

Source: World Bank calculations, based on data from Penn World Tables, UN 2015, World Development Indicators, Treisman 2007, and Barro and Lee 2010.
Note: All estimates, including Ordinary Least Squares (OLS), Panel with Fixed Effects (FE), and Generalized Method of Moments (GMM), are significant at the 5 percent level and include time fixed effect and regional fixed effect (World Bank regions). Data (unbalanced panel) cover 127 countries for 1950–2010, using five-year averages, and include 1,796 observations. Specifications (1), (2), and (3) differ according to the inclusion of specific covariates: (2) includes initial GDP per capita as a control to capture income convergence across countries; (3) includes initial per capita GDP, log of years of schooling, a set of geographical variables (such as latitude and a dummy identifying landlocked countries), and a set of institutional variables (such as dummy variables for countries that were not former colonies, former British colonies, and former French colonies). Additional covariates were tested (such as openness to trade) and results are robust. In the GMM specification (1), lags 2 to 8 of changes in the share of working-age population were used. In the GMM specifications (2) and (3), lags 2 to 8 of changes in the share of working-age population and the initial per capita GDP were used. Geographic and time variables were used as instruments. Results are also significant when reducing the number of instruments.

FIGURE C.4.2 Growth of the working-age share of the population can increase savings as a share of Gross National Income

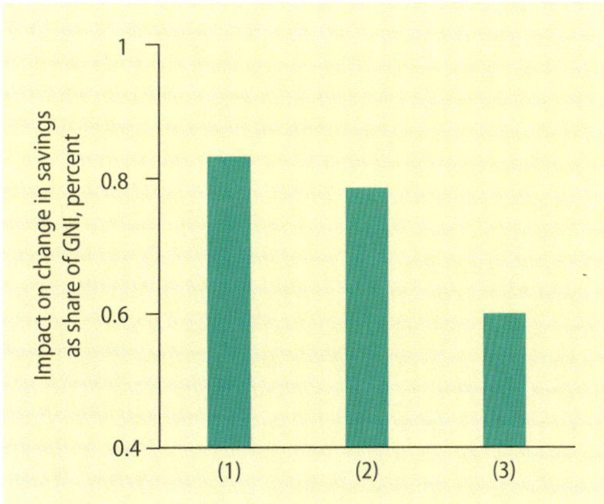

Source: World Bank calculations, based on data from Penn World Tables, UN 2015, World Development Indicators, and Treisman 2007.
Note: All estimates are significant at the 5 percent level and include time fixed effect and regional fixed effect (World Bank regions). Data (unbalanced panel) cover 173 countries for 1960–2010, using five-year averages, and include 1,107 observations. Specifications (1), (2), and (3) differ according to the inclusion of specific covariates: (2) includes initial per capita GDP as a control; (3) includes initial per capita GDP, a set of geographical variables (such as latitude and a dummy identifying landlocked countries), and a set of institutional variables (such as dummy variables for countries that were not former colonies, former British colonies, and former French colonies). Additional covariates were tested (such as openness to trade and years of schooling) and results are robust. In the GMM specification (1), lags 2 to 8 of the share of working-age population were used. In the GMM specifications (2) and (3), lags 2 to 8 of the share of working-age population and the initial per capita GDP was used. Geographic and time variables were used as instruments. Results are also significant when reducing the number of instruments.

with other potential endogeneity issues related to omitted variables that could simultaneously affect g_y and g_w, a procedure was adopted similar to that in Rajan and Subramanian (2008). That paper uses a system-GMM estimation to identify a causal relationship between international aid and growth. Similar approaches were adopted to estimate the effect of change in the share of the working-age population on growth and savings. The results under different specifications suggest that an increase in the share of working-age population has a positive effect on GDP per capita growth. An increase of 1 percentage point in the working-age population share is estimated to boost per capita GDP by 1.1 to 2.0 percentage points, on average (figure C.4.1). Also, an increase of 1 percentage point in the share of working-age population is associated with an increase of 0.6 to 0.8 percentage point on savings (figure C.4.2).[1]

Note

1. Because of potential endogeneity issues described in this appendix, the econometric results should be interpreted cautiously. The analysis using panel fixed effects and system-GMM estimators aims to address these issues.

References

Barro, R. and J.-W. Lee. 2010. "A New Data Set of Educational Attainment in the World, 1950–2010." *Journal of Development Economics* 104 (April): 184–98.

Bloom, D., and D. Canning. 2004. "Global Demographic Change: Dimensions and Economic Significance." In *Global Demographic Change: Economic Impacts and Policy Challenges,* proceedings of a symposium, sponsored by the Federal Reserve Bank of Kansas City, Jackson Hole, Wyoming, August 26–28, 9–56.

Eastwood, R., and M. Lipton. 2011. "Demographic Transition in Sub-Saharan Africa: How Big Will the Economic Dividend Be?" *Population Studies* 65(1): 9–35.

Kelley, A. C., and R. M. Schmidt. 2005. Evolution of recent economic-demographic modeling: A synthesis. *Journal of Population Economics, 18*(2), 275–300.

Kelley, A. C., & Schmidt, R. M. (2007). Evolution of recent economic-demographic modeling: A synthesis. *Population change, labor markets and sustainable growth: Towards a new economic paradigm,* 5–38.

IMF. 2004. World Economic Outlook: The Global Demographic Transition. Washington, DC: International Monetary Fund.

Rajan, R. G., and A. Subramanian. 2008. "Aid and Growth: What Does the Cross-Country Evidence Really Show?" *Review of Economics and Statistics* 90 (4): 643–65.

Treisman, D. 2007. "What Have We Learned about the Causes of Corruption from Ten Years of Cross-National Empirical Research?" *Annual Review of Political Science.*

UN (United Nations). 2015. *World Population Prospects: The 2015 Revision.* New York: United Nations, Department of Economic and Social Affairs, Population Division.

5. Economies of the world

TABLE C.5.1 World Bank Group classification of economies by region and income, fiscal year 2016

East Asia and Pacific		Latin America and the Caribbean		Sub-Saharan Africa		High-income OECD economies	Other high-income economies
American Samoa	UMC	Belize	UMC	Angola	UMC	Australia	Andorra
Cambodia	LIC	Bolivia	LMC	Benin	LIC	Austria	Antigua and Barbuda
China	UMC	Brazil	UMC	Botswana	UMC	Belgium	Argentina
Fiji	UMC	Colombia	UMC	Burkina Faso	LIC	Canada	Aruba
Indonesia	LMC	Costa Rica	UMC	Burundi	LIC	Chile	Bahamas, The
Kiribati	LMC	Cuba	UMC	Cabo Verde	LMC	Czech Republic	Bahrain
Korea, Dem. Rep.	LIC	Dominica	UMC	Cameroon	LMC	Denmark	Barbados
Lao PDR	LMC	Dominican Republic	UMC	Central African Republic	LIC	Estonia	Bermuda
Malaysia	UMC	Ecuador	UMC	Chad	LIC	Finland	Brunei Darussalam
Marshall Islands	UMC	El Salvador	LMC	Comoros	LIC	France	Cayman Islands
Micronesia, Fed. Sts.	LMC	Grenada	UMC	Congo, Dem. Rep.	LIC	Germany	Channel Islands
Mongolia	UMC	Guatemala	LMC	Congo, Rep.	LMC	Greece	Croatia
Myanmar	LMC	Guyana	LMC	Côte d'Ivoire	LMC	Hungary	Curaçao
Palau	UMC	Haiti	LIC	Eritrea	LIC	Iceland	Cyprus
Papua New Guinea	LMC	Honduras	LMC	Ethiopia	LIC	Ireland	Equatorial Guinea
Philippines	LMC	Jamaica	UMC	Gabon	UMC	Israel	Faeroe Islands
Samoa	LMC	Mexico	UMC	Gambia, The	LIC	Italy	French Polynesia
Solomon Islands	LMC	Nicaragua	LMC	Ghana	LMC	Japan	Greenland
Thailand	UMC	Panama	UMC	Guinea	LIC	Korea, Rep.	Guam
Timor-Leste	LMC	Paraguay	UMC	Guinea-Bissau	LIC	Luxembourg	Hong Kong SAR, China
Tonga	UMC	Peru	UMC	Kenya	LMC	Netherlands	Isle of Man
Tuvalu	UMC	St. Lucia	UMC	Lesotho	LMC	New Zealand	Kuwait
Vanuatu	LMC	St. Vincent and the		Liberia	LIC	Norway	Latvia
Vietnam	LMC	Grenadines	UMC	Madagascar	LIC	Poland	Liechtenstein
		Suriname	UMC	Malawi	LIC	Portugal	Lithuania
				Mali	LIC	Slovak Republic	Macao SAR, China
Europe and Central Asia		**Middle East and North Africa**		Mauritania	LMC	Slovenia	Malta
Albania	UMC	Algeria	UMC	Mozambique	LIC	Sweden	New Caledonia
Armenia	LMC	Djibouti	LMC	Namibia	UMC	Switzerland	Northern Mariana Islands
Azerbaijan	UMC	Egypt, Arab Rep.	LMC	Niger	LIC	United Kingdom	Oman
Belarus	UMC	Iran, Islamic Rep.	UMC	Nigeria	LMC	United States	Puerto Rico
Bosnia and Herzegovina	UMC	Iraq	UMC	Rwanda	LIC		Qatar
Bulgaria	UMC	Jordan	UMC	São Tomé and Príncipe	LMC		Russian Federation
Georgia	LMC	Lebanon	UMC	Senegal	LMC		San Marino
Kazakhstan	UMC	Libya	UMC	Sierra Leone	LIC		Saudi Arabia
Kosovo	LMC	Morocco	LMC	Somalia	LIC		Seychelles
Kyrgyz Republic	LMC	Syrian Arab Republic	LMC	South Africa	UMC		Singapore
Macedonia, FYR	UMC	Tunisia	UMC	South Sudan	LIC		Sint Maarten (Dutch part)
Moldova	LMC	West Bank and Gaza	LMC	Sudan	LMC		St. Kitts and Nevis
Montenegro	UMC	Yemen, Rep.	LMC	Swaziland	LMC		St. Martin (French part)
Romania	UMC			Tanzania	LIC		Taiwan, China
Serbia	UMC	**South Asia**		Togo	LIC		Trinidad and Tobago
Tajikistan	LMC	Afghanistan	LIC	Uganda	LIC		Turks and Caicos Islands
Turkey	UMC	Bangladesh	LMC	Zambia	LMC		United Arab Emirates
Turkmenistan	UMC	Bhutan	LMC	Zimbabwe	LIC		Uruguay
Ukraine	LMC	India	LMC				Venezuela, RB
Uzbekistan	LMC	Maldives	UMC				Virgin Islands (U.S.)
		Nepal	LIC				
		Pakistan	LMC				
		Sri Lanka	LMC				

Note: This table uses the World Bank Group income classification of July 2015. LIC = low-income countries. LMC = lower-middle-income countries. UMC = is upper-middle-income countries. HIC = high-income countries.

TABLE C.5.2 IMF member countries as classified in the *World Economic Outlook, 2015*

Advanced economy countries (35 countries)

Australia	France	Latvia	Singapore
Austria	Germany	Lithuania	Slovak Republic
Belgium	Greece	Luxembourg	Slovenia
Canada	Iceland	Malta	Spain
Cyprus	Ireland	Netherlands	Sweden
Czech Republic	Israel	New Zealand	Switzerland
Denmark	Italy	Norway	United Kingdom
Estonia	Japan	Portugal	United States
Finland	Korea, Republic of	San Marino	

Emerging market and developing countries (153 countries)[1]

Emerging and Developing Europe (12 countries)

Albania	FYR Macedonia
Bosnia and Herzegovina*	Montenegro**
Bulgaria	Poland
Croatia	Romania
Hungary	Serbia
Kosovo*	Turkey

Emerging and Developing Asia (29 countries)

Bangladesh	**Myanmar***
Bhutan**	**Nepal**
Brunei Darussalam[**,2]	Palau**
Cambodia	**Papua New Guinea**[2]
China	Philippines
Fiji**	Samoa**
India	**Solomon Islands**[*,**,2]
Indonesia	Sri Lanka
Kiribati[*,**]	Thailand
Lao People's Democratic Republic	Timor-Leste[*,**,2]
Malaysia	Tonga**
Maldives**	Tuvalu[*,**,2]
Marshall Islands[*,**]	Vanuatu**
Micronesia, Federated States of[*,**]	**Vietnam**
Mongolia	

Sub-Saharan Africa (45 countries)

Angola[2]	**Madagascar***
Benin	**Malawi**[2]
Botswana	**Mali**[*,2]
Burkina Faso[2]	Mauritius**
Burundi[*,2]	**Mozambique**[2]
Cameroon	Namibia
Cabo Verde**	**Niger**[2]
Central African Republic[*,2]	**Nigeria**[2]
Chad[*,2]	**Rwanda**
Comoros*,**	**São Tomé and Príncipe****
Congo, Dem. Rep. of[*,2]	**Senegal**
Congo, Rep. of[2]	Seychelles**
Côte d'Ivoire*	**Sierra Leone**[*,2]
Equatorial Guinea[**,2]	South Africa[2]
Eritrea[*,2]	**South Sudan**[*,2]
Ethiopia	Swaziland**
Gabon[2]	**Tanzania**
Gambia, The*	**Togo***
Ghana	**Uganda**
Guinea[2]	**Zambia**[2]
Guinea-Bissau[*,2]	**Zimbabwe**[*,2]
Kenya	
Lesotho	
Liberia*	

Middle East, North Africa, Afghanistan, and Pakistan (23 countries)	Commonwealth of Independent States (12 countries)
Afghanistan, Islamic Republic of[2]	Armenia
Algeria[2]	Azerbaijan[2]
Bahrain[**,2]	Belarus
Djibouti**	Georgia[3]
Egypt, Arab Rep.	Kazakhstan[2]
Iran, Islamic Republic of[2]	**Kyrgyz Republic**
Iraq[*,2]	**Moldova**
Jordan	Russian Federation[2]
Kuwait[2]	**Tajikistan**
Lebanon*	Turkmenistan[2]
Libya[*,2]	Ukraine
Mauritania[2]	**Uzbekistan**[2]
Morocco	
Oman[2]	
Pakistan	
Qatar[2]	
Saudi Arabia[2]	
Somalia*	
Sudan[*,2]	
Syrian Arab Republic*	
Tunisia	
United Arab Emirates[2]	
Yemen, Republic of[*,2]	

Latin America and the Caribbean (32 countries)

Antigua and Barbuda**	Paraguay[2]
Argentina	Peru
Bahamas, The**	St. Kitts and Nevis**
Barbados**	St. Lucia**
Belize**	St. Vincent and the Grenadines**
Bolivia[2]	Suriname[**,2]
Brazil	Trinidad and Tobago[**,2]
Chile[2]	Uruguay[2]
Colombia	Venezuela[2]
Costa Rica	
Dominica**	
Dominican Republic	
Ecuador[2]	
El Salvador	
Grenada**	
Guatemala	
Guyana[**,2]	
Haiti*	
Honduras	
Jamaica	
Mexico	
Nicaragua	
Panama	

Source: International Monetary Fund (IMF). 2015. *World Economic Outlook: Uneven Growth—Short and Long-term Factors.* April. Washington, D.C.

1. 60 countries in bold typeface are low-income developing countries (LIDC) and 94 countries in regular typeface are emerging market countries (EMC). The LIDCs are countries eligible for the IMF's concessional financial assistance with a per capita gross national income (measured according to the World Bank's Atlas method) in 2011 of below twice the IDA's effective operational cut-off level, and Zimbabwe. The EMCs are the non-LIDC emerging market and developing countries. 34 countries, with an asterisk, are included in the World Bank's list of countries in fragile situations, as of July 2015. 36 emerging market and developing countries, with two asterisks, are countries with a population of less than 1.5 millions in 2013. The two latter country groupings are denoted as fragile states and small states, respectively.
2. 56 emerging market and developing countries are fuel or primary commodity exporters.
3. Georgia, which is not a member of the Commonwealth of Independent States, is included in this group for reasons of geography and similarities in economic structure.

D

Methodology

LINKAGE: A dynamic global CGE model for policy analysis

LINKAGE is a dynamic, multiregion computable general equilibrium model (CGE), initially designed for trade policy but later extended to address a wider range of policy areas. The main features of LINKAGE are described here, while a full description is provided in van der Mensbrugghe (2011, 2013). The current version of LINKAGE relies on the GTAP version 9, a global database for 2011.[1] The data include social accounting matrices and bilateral trade flows for 140 regions (countries or country aggregates) and 57 sectors. The version employed in this study includes the following regions: Brazil, China, India, Japan, Nigeria, the Russian Federation, Sri Lanka, and the United States; the European Union and the European Free Trade Association; pre-dividend countries in Sub-Saharan Africa; early-dividend countries in Latin America and the Caribbean, Europe and Central Asia, East Asia and Pacific, Middle East and North Africa, South Asia, and Sub-Saharan Africa; late-dividend countries in Latin America and the Caribbean, Europe and Central Asia, East Asia and Pacific, and the Middle East and North Africa; post-dividend countries in Europe and Central Asia; and early-, late-, and post-dividend high-income countries. The sectors are disaggregated into agriculture, natural resources, low-skill manufacturing, low-skill services, high-skill manufacturing, and high-skill services.

The core specification of the model replicates a standard global dynamic CGE model.[2] Production is specified as a series of nested constant elasticity of substitution functions for the various inputs—unskilled and skilled labor, capital, land, natural resources (sector-specific), energy, and other material inputs. LINKAGE uses a vintage structure of production that allows for new vintages of capital to be more substitutable with other factors of production than old vintages. In the labor market, the unemployment rate is fixed and labor may migrate between rural and urban areas.

Demand by each domestic agent is specified at the so-called Armington level, that is, demand for a bundle of domestically produced and imported goods. Armington demand is aggregated across all agents and allocated at the national level between domestic production and imports by region of origin.

The standard scenario incorporates three closure rules. First, government expenditures are held constant as a share of GDP and direct taxes adjust to cover revenue changes needed to keep government savings (the fiscal balance) at an exogenous level. The second closure rule determines the investment-savings balance. Households save a portion of their incomes, with the average propensity to save influenced by elderly and youth dependency rates, as well as GDP per capita growth rates. The savings function specification follows Loayza, Schmidt-Hebbel, and Servén (2000) with different coefficients for developed and developing countries. For China and Russia, we impose projections of investment or savings rates up to 2030 from World Bank regional reports. The third savings component, foreign savings (or current account deficit), is exogenous. Given this, and the above-stated rules for household and government savings, investment is savings-driven. The last closure determines the external balance: the real exchange rate adjusts to maintain the fixed foreign savings. We first generate the long-term baseline, then run a number of counterfactual scenarios. By comparing the two, we can isolate the impacts of various policy changes.

The GTAP database is benchmarked to 2011. In model runs, key macroeconomic aggregates from the World Bank's *Global Economic Prospects* (World Bank 2015) report are replicated up to 2017.[3] Population growth is based on the medium fertility variant of the United Nation's 2012 population projections. Labor force growth follows the growth of the working-age population, defined here as the demographic cohort ages 15 to 64. The evolution of supply of skilled and unskilled workers is consistent with the constant educational trends scenario of the International Institute for Applied Systems Analysis, in which supply growth is faster for skilled workers than for unskilled workers. In each period, capital stocks are defined as the previous period's (depreciated) stocks plus investment. Up to 2017, productivity growth in the baseline is "calibrated" to achieve the growth rates for the baseline scenario (as in World Bank 2015); then we fix the productivity growth for 2018–30 at the 2017 rate. These productivity growth rates remain fixed in the counterfactual scenarios.

Demographic change affects the economy through two channels: the labor force and savings. In the baseline scenario, all new labor market entrants find productive employment. It is a neoclassical growth model; hence, increases in the labor force translate into higher output. Savings respond to changes in the demographic structure of the population, with declines in youth and elderly dependency rates increasing savings (and investment).

In the scenario that is designed to permit a lower-bound assessment of the impact of demographic change, we assume that benefits (losses) that are attributable to changes in the size of the labor force and savings (hence investment) do not materialize. More specifically, in this scenario, total population in each region changes at the same rate as in the baseline, but the share of the working-age population in total population remains fixed at the 2015 level over 2016–30. This scenario is beneficial to late- and post-dividend countries since their working-age populations increase at a faster rate than in the baseline, leading to more rapid labor-force growth and higher savings rates. It is detrimental to pre- and early-dividend countries since their working-age population growth rates are slower than in the baseline, leading to slower labor-force growth and lower savings rates. In short, in this scenario we reverse the benefits of demographic change in pre- and early-dividend countries, while we eliminate losses from the demographic change in late- and post-dividend countries. This approach permits us to isolate the impacts of demographic change on growth and poverty reduction, already embodied in the baseline scenario.

GIDD: A global microsimulation model of poverty and shared prosperity

The analysis on the effect of these different scenarios on poverty and income distribution is done using the Global Income Distribution Dynamics (GIDD) model. The GIDD combines a consistent set of price and volume changes from a global CGE model (in this case LINKAGE) with household surveys at the global level (Bussolo, de Hoyos, and Medvedev 2010). Developed by the World Bank's Development Prospects Group, the GIDD was inspired by previous efforts involving simulation exercises (Bourguignon and Bussolo 2012; Bourguignon and Pereira da Silva 2003; Davies 2009).

Counterfactual global and country-level income distributions are obtained by applying four changes to the initial distribution estimated from the household data. These include demographic changes (considering age structure and shifts in education); changes in sector of employment; changes in relative wages across skills and sectors; and growth in consumption per capita. Data on demographic changes are based on the population projections of the United Nations *World Population Prospect* and are consistent with those considered in LINKAGE. Data on the latter three pieces of information are based on the scenario analysis results from LINKAGE. Examples of earlier analyses using LINKAGE and GIDD include examinations of the effect of agriculture distortions in the global economy (Dessus, Herrera, and de Hoyos 2008), the effect of climate change on poverty and inequality (Bourguignon, Bussolo, and Pereira da Silva 2008), the effect of demographic change on Africa (Ahmed et al. 2014), and external and internal shocks in Africa (Devarajan et al. 2015).

For analyzing the impact of different demographic scenarios on poverty and income distribution, we employ a sample of 90 household surveys, covering approximately 90 percent of global population and global GDP. The GIDD model allows the analysis of macroeconomic shocks on poverty and sharing prosperity. Also, the richness of the microeconomic data can provide insights into regional and demographic characteristics of the most affected households, which can be useful for defining contingent policies.

In addition to incorporating the key changes in the variables derived from the CGE scenarios, the GIDD methodology updates the household survey data for the end year of our simulation, 2030. This update is done by reweighting the population characterized by the most recent available household survey in GIDD using nonparametric cross-entropy methods, but keeping it consistent with the UN population projections. For the skill-unskilled breakdown, the GIDD defines as skilled anyone with more than nine years of education.

MAMS: A country-level CGE model for policy analysis

The Maquette for Millennium Development Goal Simulations (MAMS) is an economic simulation model designed for analyzing medium- and long-run development policies. It is a country-level CGE model made up of a set of simultaneous linear and nonlinear equations. The model is economywide, providing a comprehensive and consistent view of the economy, including linkages between production and the income it generates, households, the government (its budget and fiscal policies), and the balance of payments. The model is solved dynamically into the future, providing a view of the economy in every year for a given scenario.

It thus considers interactions between four groups of agents: producers, households, governments, and the nation in its dealings with the outside world. In each period, the different agents are subject to budgets and their constraints. For each agent, receipts and spending, the latter including savings and net borrowing, are equal by construction. Producers maximize profits; households maximize utility. The government follows rules specified by the analyst. For the nation, adjustments in the real exchange rate ensure that its external accounts are in balance. Wages, rents, and prices play a crucial role by clearing markets for factors, goods, and services. For commodities that are traded internationally (exported and/or imported), domestic prices are influenced by international price developments. Unless the country has a large share of the global market, it assumed that international markets will demand and supply the exports and imports of the country at given world prices.

For MAMS analyses in this report, a new population module was developed. In this module, a detailed population scenario is generated on the basis of base-year population data by age (single-year-age-group) and gender, and projections for age- and gender-specific fertility, mortality, and migration rates. Over time, production growth is determined by growth in factor employment and changes in total factor productivity (TFP). Growth in capital stocks is endogenous while exogenous growth is imposed for labor and other factors. For capital, stock growth depends on investment and depreciation. For labor, stock growth is determined by the evolution of the population in labor-force age and an aggregate labor force participation rate which may change over time; the labor unemployment rate is endogenous, leading to a distinction between stock and employment levels. TFP growth is made up of two components: one that responds positively to growth in government capital stocks and one that is exogenous. MAMS includes a module in which poverty results are computed on the assumption that each household type in the model has a fixed log-normal consumption distribution (defined using the Gini coefficient).

In this report, MAMS is applied to Brazil, Ethiopia, Japan, and Niger. For this purpose, new databases were developed with base years between 2009 and 2013. Each database consists of a Social Accounting Matrix and various complementary data, primarily data on stocks (factors, debt, and population by single-year age group and gender), elasticities (in trade, production, and consumption), and projections for GDP, population, and other indicators. Given the interest of this report in forward-looking analysis, the analysis is based on simulation results starting from 2015. The end year for the simulations varies across the applications, ranging from 2030 to 2100. For more on MAMS, see Lofgren, Cicowiez, and Diaz-Bonilla (2013) and www.wordbank.org/mams.

Notes

1. The GTAP database was developed and is maintained by the Global Trade Analysis Program, based at Purdue University (www.gtap.org). The pre-release candidate 2 of version 9 database is used here.
2. Other well-known models in this class include the GTAP model (Hertel 1998) and CEPII's Mirage (Decreux and Valin 2007).
3. For China, we replicate the growth projections of World Bank (2014).

References

Ahmed, S. A., M. Cruz, D. S. Go, M. Maliszewska, and I. Osorio-Rodarte. 2014. "How Significant Is Africa's Demographic Dividend for its Future Growth." Policy Research Working Paper 7134, World Bank, Washington, DC.

Bourguignon, F., and M. Bussolo. 2012. "Income Distribution and Computable General Equilibrium Models." In *Handbook of Computable General Equilibrium Models*, edited by P. B. Dixon and D. Jorgenson. Amsterdam: North Holland.

Bourguignon, F., M. Bussolo, and L. Pereira da Silva, eds. 2008. *The Impact of Macroeconomic Policies on Poverty and Income Distribution—Macro-Micro Evaluation Techniques and Tools*. Washington, DC: World Bank and Palgrave Macmillan.

Bourguignon F., and L. Pereira da Silva, eds. 2003. *The Impact of Economic Policies on Poverty and Income Distribution: Evaluation Techniques and Tools*. Oxford, U.K.: World Bank and Oxford University Press.

Bussolo, M., R. de Hoyos, and D. Medvedev. 2010. "Economic Growth and Income Distribution: Linking Macro Economic Models with Household Survey Data at the Global Level." *International Journal of Microsimulation* 3 (1): 92–102.

Davies, J. 2009. "Combining Microsimulation with CGE and Macro Modelling for Distributional Analysis in Developing and Transition Countries." *International Journal of Microsimulation* 2 (1): 49–65.

Decreux, Y., and H. Valin. 2007. "MIRAGE, Updated Version of the Model for Trade Policy Analysis: Focus on Agriculture and Dynamics." CEPII Working Paper 15, Centre d'Etudes Prospectives et d'Informations Internationales, Paris.

Dessus S., S. Herrera, and R. de Hoyos. 2008. "The Impact of Food Inflation on Urban Poverty and Its Monetary Cost: Some Back-of-the-Envelope Calculations." Policy Research Working Paper 4666, World Bank, Washington, DC.

Devarajan S, D. Go, M. Maliszewska, I. Osorio-Rodarte, and H. Timmer. 2015. "Stress-Testing Africa's Recent Growth and Poverty Performance. *Journal of Policy Modeling* 37 (4): 521–47.

Hertel, T. W., ed. 1998. *Global Trade Analysis: Modeling and Applications.* New York: Cambridge University Press.

Loayza, N., K. Schmidt-Hebbel, and L. Servén. 2000. "What Drives Private Saving across the World?" *Review of Economics and Statistics* 82 (2): 165–81.

Lofgren, H., M. Cicowiez, and C. Diaz-Bonilla. 2013. "MAMS—A Computable General Equilibrium Model for Developing Country Strategy Analysis." In *Handbook of Computable General Equilibrium Modeling,* vol. 1A, edited by P. B. Dixon and D. W. Jorgenson. Amsterdam: North Holland.

van der Mensbrugghe, D. 2011. LINKAGE Technical Reference Document: Version 7.1. World Bank, Washington, DC.

———. 2013. "Modeling the Global Economy—Forward Looking Scenarios for Agriculture." In *Handbook of Computable General Equilibrium Modeling,* edited by P. B. Dixon and D. W. Jorgenson, 933–94. Amsterdam: North Holland.

World Bank. 2014. *Urban China: Toward Efficient, Inclusive, and Sustainable Urbanization.* World Bank and the Development Research Council of the State Council, The People's Republic of China.

———. 2015. *Global Economic Prospects.* Washington, DC: World Bank.

ECO-AUDIT

Environmental Benefits Statement

The World Bank Group is committed to reducing its environmental footprint. In support of this commitment, the Publishing and Knowledge Division leverages electronic publishing options and the print-on-demand technology that is located in regional hubs worldwide. Together, these initiatives enable print runs to be lowered and shipping distances decreased, resulting in reduced paper consumption, chemical use, greenhouse gas emissions, and waste.

The Publishing and Knowledge Division follows the recommended standards for paper use set by the Green Press Initiative. The majority of our books are printed on Forest Stewardship Council (FSC)–certified paper, with nearly all containing 50–100 percent recycled content. The recycled fiber in our book paper is either unbleached or bleached using totally chlorine-free (TCF), processed chlorine-free (PCF), or enhanced elemental chlorine-free (EECF) processes.

More information about the Bank's environmental philosophy can be found at http://crinfo.worldbank.org/wbcrinfo/node/4.

green press INITIATIVE